print&online

NAVIGATING THROUGH THE BOOK:

Chapter-concept and **formula-review tear-out cards**, found at the back of the text, provide you with a portable study tool for quick reference and revision.

Key concepts are summarised for each chapter on the **review cards** at the back of the book. A set of **concept questions** then gives you the opportunity to apply and reinforce these concepts.

✳ decision making
The process of identifying alternative courses of action and selecting an appropriate alternative in a given decision-making situation.

Key terms are highlighted throughout the text, with definitions located in the margins for easy reference. Key terms also appear on the **review cards** at the back of the book.

Exercises

1 Cost behaviour LO1

2 Calculation of total costs LO1

3 Cost behaviour analysis LO1

4 Cost behaviour analysis LO1

A set of **exercises**, **problems** and **cases** at the end of each chapter gives you the opportunity to apply and reinforce information covered in the chapter.

A Going Concern

Making It Real

Each year, The Ethisphere Institute identifies the world's most ethical companies by ranking the companies on seven key dimensions: corporate citizenship and responsibility; corporate governance; innovation that contributes to public wellbeing; industry leadership; executive leadership and tone from the top; legal, regulatory, and reputation track record; and internal systems and ethics/compliance program. Among the 99 winners in 2014 were 3M, Accenture, Adobe Systems inc., AECOM, CBRE, Capgemini, Cisco Systems, Dell, Inc., Ford Motor Company, Google Inc., and Colgate-Palmolive.

Making it Real boxes provide real-life Managerial Accounting scenarios to help you apply the chapter concepts to the real world.

Key formula 4.1: Overhead rate

$$\text{Overhead rate} = \frac{\text{Manufacturing overhead}}{\text{Cost Driver}}$$

Key formulas are highlighted and numbered for easy reference. These numbered formulas also appear on the **review cards** at the back of the book.

GUIDING YOU ONLINE:

apply this!

Apply this icons direct you to online quizzes, cases, interactive games, and other tools that will broaden your skills and knowledge.

CourseMate brings course concepts to life with interactive learning, study and exam preparation tools that support **ACCT Managerial**.

Login to CourseMate at http://login.cengagebrain.com to access a suite of resources to help you study, with:

- interactive quizzes
- animations
- animated activities
- glossary
- e-lectures
- videos
- flashcards and more!

 CourseMate

ACCT2 Managerial
2nd Edition
Prabhu Sivabalan
Roby Sawyers
Steve Jackson
Greg Jenkins

Publishing manager: Dorothy Chui
Publishing editor: Geoff Howard
Developmental editor: James Cole
Senior project editor: Nathan Katz
Cover designer: Ruth O'Connor
Text designer: Danielle Maccarone
Editor: Craig MacKenzie
Proofreader: James Anderson
Indexer: Russell Brooks
Permissions/Photo researcher: QBS Learning
Art direction: Olga Lavecchia
Cover: Getty Images
Typeset by QBS Learning and Pier Vido

Any URLs contained in this publication were checked for currency during the production process. Note, however, that the publisher cannot vouch for the ongoing currency of URLs.

Authorised adaptation of *ACCT Managerial* by Sawyers/Jackson/Jenkins, published by Cengage Learning.

First edition published in 2013
This second edition published in 2016

Cengage Learning would like to thank the following reviewers for their incisive and helpful feedback:
· Robyn Pilcher, Curtin Uni Tech
· Matt Dyki, University of Melbourne
· Ashfaq Khan, University of New England
· Tracey McDowall, Deakin University
· Amy Tung, Macquarie University

For product information and technology assistance,
in Australia call **1300 790 853**;
in New Zealand call **0800 449 725**

For permission to use material from this text or product, please email
aust.permissions@cengage.com

National Library of Australia Cataloguing-in-Publication Data
Creator: Sivabalan, Prabhu, author.
Title: ACCT2 managerial / Prabhu Sivabalan, Roby Sawyers, Steve Jackson, Greg Jenkins.
Edition: Second edition
ISBN: 9780170350358 (paperback)
Notes: Includes index.
Subjects: Managerial accounting. Managerial accounting--Problems, exercises, etc.
Other Creators/Contributors: Sawyers, Roby B, author. Jackson, Steve, author. Jenkins, Greg, author.
Dewey Number: 658.1511

Cengage Learning Australia
Level 7, 80 Dorcas Street
South Melbourne, Victoria Australia 3205

Cengage Learning New Zealand
Unit 4B Rosedale Office Park
331 Rosedale Road, Albany, North Shore 0632, NZ

For learning solutions, visit **cengage.com.au**

Printed in China by China Translation & Printing Services.
3 4 5 6 7 8 20 19 18 17

Brief contents

Contents

Source: Shutterstock.com/Ivancovlad

Source: Shutterstock.com/Matthew W Keefe

CHAPTER 14
Decentralisation and modern performance management systems – the balanced scorecard _____ 222

CHAPTER 13
Management accounting for cost control and performance evaluation – flexible budgets and variance analysis _____ 202

Learning objectives:

After studying the material in this chapter, you should be able to:

1   Describe the contemporary view of accounting information systems and describe and give examples of financial and non-financial accounting information.

2   Compare and contrast managerial accounting with financial accounting and distinguish between the information needs of external and internal users.

3   Recognise the role of relevant factors in decision making.

4   Understand sources of ethical issues in business and the importance of maintaining an ethical business environment.

INTRODUCTION TO MANAGERIAL ACCOUNTING

c 1

Accountants are at their core, numerical story-tellers. Further and ideally, these stories must represent high quality, ethical, honest, and meaningful explanations of the position, performance and general health of the organisations. No individual in an organisation is equipped with the skill of seeing a set of financial numbers relating to an organisation, and interpreting meaning (stories) to these numbers as much as an accountant. In Australia, the need for competent accountants who are able to not only prepare accounting numbers but also analyse and interpret (story-tell) the meaning of these numbers for decision making to senior executives is greater than ever before – because of the increasingly complex business models that have presented themselves globally, and the pressure for more efficient resource allocation in highly competitive and transparent markets caused by technology development.

Indeed, the Australian economy has undergone significant change in the past four decades. In the past, it was more reliant on the agricultural sector, but is now increasingly dominated by the mining and service sectors. With the expected slowdown of activity in the mining sector, and the announcements of the closures of Holden, Ford and Toyota automotive manufacturing in Australia, investors are being challenged to consider new value propositions for purposes of value creation. Two decades ago, the mainstream and global use of the Internet fundamentally altered how existing businesses functioned. It created a whole new area of business (electronic commerce, or e-business) and new industries. Managing these new business models and information channels requires a broader range of information than ever before. Downsizing, combined with a more mobile and service-driven skilled workforce, has placed a premium on retaining talented, knowledgeable employees. Customers demand specialised products and services and real-time information concerning product availability, order status and delivery times. Suppliers need information on their buyers' sales and inventory levels in order to tailor their production schedules and delivery times to meet the buyers' demands. Shareholders demand greater value

from their investments. Although these changes have provided opportunities for those companies that are able to adapt and take advantage of them, they have also resulted in challenges. Above all else, these changes require more effective management of knowledge within an organisation. In today's business environment, knowledge is power and must be managed for a company to remain competitive.

Although the terms are sometimes used interchangeably, knowledge should not be confused with data or information. Companies generate literally tonnes of **data** – financial statements, customer lists, inventory records, and the number and type of products and services sold. However, translating that data into an accessible and usable form is another matter. When data are organised, processed and summarised, they become **information**. When that information is shared and exploited so that it adds value to an organisation, it becomes **knowledge**. These pieces of knowledge are subsequently used to drive actions in organisations, which ultimately affects their performance.

✳ **data**
Reports such as financial statements, customer lists, and inventory records.

✳ **information**
Data that have been organised, processed, and summarised.

✳ **knowledge**
Information that is shared and exploited so that it adds value to an organisation.

© Alexander Silaev/Shutterstock

Turning data into knowledge is a key to business success.

All types of organisations, from large multinational manufacturing companies such as Ford Australia to small manufacturers of items such as custom furniture, need accounting information. Retailers, such as Woolworths, Coles, David Jones and Myer, hardware stores such as Bunnings, large service companies such as Australian Air Express and local certified public accounting (CPA) and chartered accounting (CA) firms, as well as law firms, and even non-profit organisations such as the Australian Red Cross and small local museums and homeless shelters, all need accounting information. This information is used by internal managers in their day-to-day decision making and also by external users, such as investors, creditors, donors and government bodies such as the Australian Taxation Office and the Australian Securities and Investments Commission (ASIC).

LEARNING OBJECTIVE 1 >>

apply this!

e-Lecture

Accounting information

Accounting information is usually provided by a company's **accounting information system (AIS)**. Traditionally, the AIS was simply a transaction-processing system that captured financial data resulting from accounting transactions. For example, the AIS might document a transaction to purchase materials by recording a journal entry showing the date of purchase, an increase to raw materials inventory and a corresponding increase to accounts payable or decrease in cash.

From this perspective of an AIS, accounting information simply represents financial information (sales, net income, total assets, costs of products and so on) expressed in terms of Australian dollars or other monetary units (for example, yen, euros, pesos). Other, non-financial information – such as the number of units of materials or inventory on hand, the number of budgeted labour hours to produce a product, the number of units necessary to break even and the time it takes to manufacture a product – were likely collected and processed outside the traditional AIS. The use of multiple information systems within a company causes a number of problems. It is costly to support multiple systems. Perhaps more important, it is difficult to integrate information coming from various

✳ **accounting information system (AIS)**

A transaction-processing system that captures financial data resulting from accounting transactions within a company.

systems and to make decisions for a company with multiple sources of information. In addition, other useful transaction information – such as the quality of the material purchased, the timeliness of its delivery or customer satisfaction with an order – may not be captured at all and therefore not evaluated by management.

Over the past few years, enterprise resource planning (ERP) systems have been developed in an attempt to address these shortcomings. ERP systems integrate the traditional AIS with other information systems to capture both quantitative and qualitative data to collect and organise into useful information. ERP systems also help transform that information into knowledge that can be communicated throughout an organisation.

Throughout our study of accounting information and its use in decision making, we emphasise the importance of considering both quantitative and qualitative information. To provide managers with the information they need to make effective business decisions, financial data must be linked to non-financial data, transformed into useful information and knowledge, and communicated throughout an organisation (see Exhibit 1.1). This is also important as non-financial data

Accounting information

Traditional financial accounting information → **Financial information**
- Assets
- Liabilities
- Revenues
- Gross margin
- Operating expenses

Non-financial information → **Other quantitative information**
- Percentage of defects
- Number of customer complaints
- Warranty claims
- Units in inventory
- Budgeted hours

Non-financial information → **Qualitative information**
- Customer satisfaction
- Employee satisfaction
- Product or service quality
- Reputation

EXHIBIT 1.1 A contemporary view of accounting information

usually represents leading indicators of future financial results. For example, if we purchase higher quality materials today (non-financial data), the resulting positive customer perception will likely drive customer loyalty and higher subsequent repeat customer acquisitions, causing sales revenues (financial data) to increase in the future.

LEARNING OBJECTIVE **2** >>

A comparison of financial and managerial accounting

Financial accounting is the area of accounting primarily concerned with the preparation of general-use financial statements for creditors, investors and other users outside the company (external users). On the other hand, **managerial accounting** is primarily concerned with generating financial and non-financial information for use by managers in their decision-making roles within a company (internal users). This information is not usually shared with those outside the company. Although both financial accounting information and managerial accounting information are generated from the same AIS, the information is used in different ways by the various stakeholders of the company. A stakeholder is any person or group that either affects or is affected by the company's actions and decisions. As such, stakeholders include both external and internal users of information.

Managerial accounting is primarily concerned with generating financial and non-financial information for use by managers in their decision-making roles within a company (internal users).

Source: racorn/Shutterstock

External users

Shareholders, potential investors, creditors, government bodies, regulators, suppliers and customers are all **external users**. What types of information do external users

need? Shareholders and potential investors might want information to help them analyse the current and future profitability of an organisation. Companies that have issued shares to the public (or those that plan to) provide this information in the form of annual reports, registration statements, prospectuses and other reports issued to shareholders, potential investors and the Australian Securities and Investments Commission (ASIC). The information required in these reports and the accounting methods used to prepare them are governed by the Australian Accounting Standards Board (AASB) and ASIC. Although this information is primarily financial (for example, sales and net profit), it also may include non-financial information, such as units shipped and market share. It also may include qualitative information typically described in the 'Management's Discussion and Analysis' section of annual reports.

What about smaller companies that are owned by just a few members of a family (called closely held) or non-profit organisations, such as the Salvation Army, Mission Australia or the Australian Red Cross? External users of financial information, such as banks or potential donors to non-profit organisations, still need accounting information to make the proper decision about lending or donating money. However, their needs may differ from those of shareholders and potential investors.

Creditors generally want to assess a company's overall financial health and may be particularly interested in a company's cash flow or ability to repay their loans. Potential contributors to non-profit organisations may have a need for both financial information, such as how much of the Australian Red Cross's budget is spent for charitable purposes, and non-financial information, such as how many women with children are served by the local homeless shelter of Mission Australia or the Salvation Army.

Government agencies (federal, state and local) have very specific information needs, including the measurement of income, payroll and assets for purposes of assessing taxes. This accounting information is typically provided on income tax returns, payroll reports and other forms designed specifically to meet the requirements of each agency.

Generally, accounting information provided to shareholders, creditors and government agencies is characterised by a lack of flexibility (its content is often dictated by the user), the reporting of past events using

* **financial accounting**
The area of accounting primarily concerned with the preparation and use of financial statements by creditors, investors, and other users outside the company.

* **managerial accounting**
The area of accounting primarily concerned with generating financial and non-financial information for use by managers in their decision-making roles within a company.

* **external users**
Shareholders, potential investors, creditors, government taxing agencies, regulators, suppliers, customers and others outside the company.

historical costs (financial statements for the previous three years) and an emphasis on the organisation as a whole.

Suppliers and customers are also external users. However, their accounting information needs are likely to be very different from those of other external users and may be more clearly aligned with the needs of internal users. For example, suppliers of car parts to GM Holden Australia need detailed information on inventory levels of specific parts in order to know when to manufacture and ship parts. They might be concerned that with the closure of GM manufacturing operations in Australia, the company is committed to its acquisitions from suppliers till that date – if earlier, then the financial ramifications of such a loss of a major customer must be communicated to suppliers.

Bank customers may want to check their account or loan balances before making a major purchase. Someone buying a new computer may want to check on the expected delivery date or whether a product is back-ordered before placing an order. This type of information needs to be much more detailed and timely than that provided to most other external users.

Internal users

Internal users of accounting information include individual employees as well as teams, departments, regions and top management of an organisation. For convenience, these internal users are often referred to as managers. Managers are involved in three primary activities commonly referred to as planning, operating and controlling.

Planning activities

Planning involves the development of both the short-term (operational) and long-term (strategic) objectives and goals of an organisation and the identification of the resources needed to achieve them. **Operational planning** involves the development of short-term objectives and goals (typically, those to be achieved in less than one year). Examples of operational planning for

Max Brenner Café (specialising in chocolate) include planning the raw material and production needs for each type of chocolate for the next annual period or determining their short-term cash needs. Operational planning for the Royal Prince Alfred Hospital in Sydney or the Epworth Hospital in Melbourne would include budgeting for the number of doctors, nurses and other staff needed for the upcoming month or determining the appropriate level of medical supplies to have in inventory. Operational planning also involves determining short-term performance goals and objectives, including meeting customer-service expectations, hospital bed quotas and time budgets.

Strategic planning addresses long-term questions of how an organisation positions and distinguishes itself from competitors. For example, the Max Brenner strategy for producing high-quality chocolate is very different from that used by a company producing a store brand of lower-priced chocolate. Long-term decisions about where to locate plants and other facilities, whether to invest in new, state-of-the-art production equipment and whether to introduce new products or services and enter new markets are strategic-planning decisions. Strategic planning also involves the determination of long-term performance and profitability measures, such as market share, sales growth and share price.

Operating activities

Operating activities encompass what managers must do to run the business on a day-to-day basis. Operating decisions for manufacturing companies include whether to accept special orders, how many parts or other raw materials to buy (or whether to make the parts internally), whether to sell a product or to process it further, whether to schedule overtime, which products to produce and what prices to charge. Other operating decisions affecting all organisations include assigning tasks to individual employees, choosing whether to advertise (and predicting the corresponding impact of advertising on sales and profits) and choosing whether to hire full-time employees or to outsource.

Controlling activities

Controlling activities involve the motivation and monitoring of employees and the evaluation of people and other resources used in the organisation's operations. The purpose of control is to make sure that the goals of the organisation are being attained. It includes using incentives and other rewards to motivate employees to accomplish an organisation's goals and using mechanisms to detect and correct deviations from those goals. Control often involves the comparison of actual outcomes (cost of products, sales and so on) with desired outcomes (as stated in the organisation's operating and strategic plans). Control decisions include questions of how to evaluate performance, what measures to use and what types of incentives to implement. For example, a company that emphasises high-quality products and excellent customer service may evaluate and reward production workers who have exceeded goals based on these virtues. (Such goals may involve specifying the percentage of allowable defective units or scrap, monitoring customer complaints or myriad other factors.)

The functional areas of management

Managers are found in all functional areas of an organisation, including operations and production, marketing, finance and human resources. Although managers rely on the same information provided to external users, they have other needs as well.

A management accountant is expected to meet the informational needs of a range of different arms in an organisation, be it a production department or any other.

The operations and production function

The **operations and production function** produces the products or services that an organisation sells to its customers. Operations and production managers are concerned with providing quality products and services that can compete in a global marketplace. They need accounting information to make planning decisions affecting how and when products are produced and services are provided. They need to know the costs of producing and storing products in order to decide how much inventory to keep on hand. They need to know the costs of labour when making decisions on whether to schedule overtime to complete a production run or when deciding

how many physicians are needed in an emergency room. These decisions are also influenced by information provided by the marketing managers, including the expected customer reaction if products are not available when orders are placed or if doctors are not available when patients need them.

The marketing function

The **marketing function** is involved with the process of developing, pricing, promoting and distributing goods and services sold to customers. Marketing managers need to know how much a product costs in order to help establish a reasonable selling price. They need to know how a given advertising campaign and its resulting impact on the number of units sold is expected to affect income. They need to know how enhancing a product's features or changing its packaging will influence its cost. Commissions paid to sales representatives may be based on a company's profits. All these marketing decisions require accounting information.

The finance function

The **finance function** is responsible for managing the financial resources of the organisation. Finance managers make decisions about how to raise capital as well as where and how to invest it. Finance managers need accounting information to answer such questions as whether money should be raised through borrowing (issuing bonds) or selling shares. Finance managers also make decisions concerning whether a new piece of manufacturing equipment should be purchased or leased and whether a plant expansion should be paid for in cash or by borrowing money from the bank.

The human resource function

Although all managers who supervise, motivate and evaluate other employees are human resource managers, the **human resource function** is concerned with the utilisation of human resources to help an organisation reach its goals. More specifically, human resource managers support other functions and managers by recruiting and staffing, designing compensation and benefit packages, ensuring the safety and overall health of personnel, and providing training and

* **operations and production function**
Produces the products or services that an organisation sells to its customers.

* **marketing function**
Involved with the process of developing, pricing, promoting and distributing goods and services sold to customers.

* **finance function**
Responsible for managing the financial resources of the organisation.

* **human resource function**
Concerned with the utilisation of human resources to help an organisation reach its goals.

development opportunities for employees. These decisions require input from all other functional areas. What kind of accounting information do human resource managers need? Human resource decisions, such as hiring new employees, are often made under budget constraints. Ensuring safe workplaces for employees may involve the redesign of manufacturing processes. Accountants can provide information regarding the cost of the redesign. The decision to train employees to use new equipment may require an analysis of the costs and benefits of the new program.

The information needs of internal and external users

As you can see, the information needs of internal users and external users differ in significant ways. Due to the varying needs of internal users, managerial accounting is more flexible than financial accounting. While financial accounting is geared toward the preparation of financial statements and other reports according to generally accepted accounting principles (GAAP) and other rules, managerial accounting can be customised to a specific company or segment of a company. While financial accounting is primarily concerned with reporting on the company as a whole, managerial accounting emphasises the various segments of a company such as divisions, departments, sales regions and product lines.

Because of the decision focus of internal managers, managerial accounting information must focus on the future rather than the past. Planning is an integral part of the manager's job, and in order to plan effectively, managers need up-to-date information. Although the timeliness of information is paramount, managerial accounting information frequently is less precise than financial accounting information and often includes the use of estimates.

Exhibit 1.2 summarises the external and internal users of accounting information, the type of information typically needed by these users and the source of the information.

The role of the managerial accountant

What is the role of the managerial accountant in providing information to this diverse group of internal users? Managerial accountants have traditionally been thought of as the bean counters or number crunchers in an organisation. However, advances in AIS and other changes in the past decade have resulted in the automation of traditional accounting functions involving data collection, data entry and data reporting, and

	Users	Type of accounting information needed	Source
External	Shareholders and creditors	Sales, gross profit, net income, cash flow, assets and liabilities, earnings per share, etc. Although this information is primarily financial, it may also include non-financial information (units in inventory). This information is often provided in summary form (for the company as a whole) and typically is historical in nature.	Annual reports, financial statements and other available documents
External	Government bodies	Varies by agency but includes taxable income, sales, assets, comparisons of actual expenditures to budgets, etc. This information is usually provided for the company as a whole and is historical in nature. It can include both financial and non-financial information.	Tax returns and other reports
External	Customers and suppliers	Order status, shipping dates, inventory levels, etc. This information must be very detailed and timely to be useful.	Limited-access databases available to specific customers and suppliers
Internal	Marketing, operations and production, finance and human resource managers	Timely and detailed information on sales and expenses, product costs, budget information and measures of performance. Often includes non-financial data (direct labour hours, units to break even, etc.). Accounting information is often needed for segments of an organisation and is more likely future oriented than historical.	Cost reports, budgets and other internal documents

EXHIBIT 1.2 External and internal users of accounting information

a corresponding shift of those functions from management accounting to clerical staff.

As a result, managerial accountants in many companies now focus on analysing information and creating knowledge from it rather than collecting data. Managerial accountants have become decision-support specialists who see their role as interpreting information, putting it into a useful format for other managers and facilitating management decision making. Put simply, the management accountant of the future must ask 'What can I do that a computer cannot?' Given the complexity of human interactions, customer behaviours and expanding markets, management accountants analyse accounting information to help managers plan, control and evaluate their future with consideration for the above factors. This has potential to add considerable value to organisations. In short, the management accountant is not only a finance professional in an organisation, but also a business partner (CIMA Global, 2012[1]).

Managerial accountants facilitate management decision making.

LEARNING OBJECTIVE 3

Relevant factors and decision making

Although the problems and questions facing marketing, production, finance and human resource managers of organisations differ, the decision-making process that they follow is remarkably uniform. In fact, it is the same decision-making model that you are likely to use when making non-business decisions. Do you remember the decision-making process you went through the last time you made a major decision? It could have been a decision to purchase or sell a car, a computer, or a stereo system. It could have been a decision to attend a particular university, accept a summer job, or perhaps even get married.

Decisions have many variables or factors that must be considered. If you were making a decision to purchase an iPhone, you might consider variables such as its cost, features, colour and phone-plan options. If you were making a decision about what university to attend, factors might include the cost, proximity to your home and academic reputation of the institution. Different decision makers might even consider different factors for the same decision situation. For example, the colour of an iPhone may be unimportant to one buyer but critical to another. The number and type of variables considered might differ for each individual and for each decision that individual makes.

Decisions may have to be made under time, budget, or other constraints. Your choice of an iPhone may be limited to those phone plans that cost under $55 per month. Your decision to accept a summer job may be limited to those that are within 30 kilometres of your home. Your decision to attend university may have to be made by a certain date. In addition, many decisions are made with missing information or at least with imperfect information. In deciding which car to buy, you might want to consider the cost of future repairs for various models. Although you might estimate these costs by reading information from sources such as the Drive or Carsales websites, you will not know the costs with certainty. Decisions may not be perfect, but they should be the best you can make given the information that is available to you at the time. The process you go through serves to gather all the information you can obtain in order to reduce the risk of an incorrect or less-than-optimal decision.

Finally, decisions often lead to other decisions. Once you have decided to buy a car or a stereo, you need to make other decisions, such as whether to pay cash or to finance the purchase or whether to buy an extended warranty. Life does seem like a never-ending string of decisions.

Decision making is the process of identifying different courses of action and selecting one appropriate to a given situation. The focus on the word 'appropriate' cannot be underestimated. With the information available at a point in time, the best decision is the decision that broadly encompasses all factors reasonably

❊ **decision making**
The process of identifying alternative courses of action and selecting an appropriate alternative in a given decision-making situation.

considered. The actual correctness of the decision is influenced by a range of factors and may not be fully realised until some time in the future. All decisions require judgement, and the quality of a decision often depends on the depth of that judgement. Judgement refers to the extent to which we take a logical, rational approach to making decisions rather than making decisions impulsively, on the spur of the moment.

Relevant costs

What should you consider in making a decision? An effective approach is to focus on factors that affect a particular decision. That is, relevant factors are those that differ among alternatives. For example, if you were deciding which car to purchase and each car you were considering had the same options at the same cost (air conditioning, CD player and so on), you would conclude that those options are not relevant to the decision because they do not differ among the various cars. Cost often is a key factor that must be considered in decisions. **Relevant costs** are those that differ among alternatives. Another way to view relevant costs is to identify those that are avoidable, or those that can be eliminated by choosing one alternative over another. In choosing among cars, if one car has air conditioning and

another does not, the cost of air conditioning is relevant because choosing one of the other cars could eliminate that cost.

Sunk costs

Sunk costs are costs that have already been incurred. Because sunk costs cannot be avoided, they are not relevant in a decision. In your decision to trade-in your old vehicle, the amount that you paid for it may appear to be important. However, that cost was paid in the past, many years ago; it is therefore a sunk cost and is not relevant, and should not be considered in your decision.

As another example, assume you've just spent $10 000 completing a course on welding and a company offers you two jobs. You must pick one. The first job is as a welder, earning $70 000 annually. The second is as a salesperson, earning $75 000. If you go with the welding job because you feel the need to justify your $10 000 spent on a welding course, you'd have considered a sunk cost that is irrelevant to your decision at this moment in time. Whatever choice you pick, you cannot get back the $10 000 spent on the welding course!

* **relevant costs**
Those costs that differ among alternatives.

* **sunk costs**
Costs that have already been incurred.

Toyota closes down operations in Australia from 2017

The Toyota Motor Corporation is shutting down their manufacturing operations in Australia in 2017, in a decision that will cause the loss of approximately 2500 Australian workers, and possibly many more through the loss of employment in related industries (suppliers of products and services to Toyota).

As explained below in an excerpt from an ABC news article:

> Toyota Australia president and chief executive officer Max Yasuda and Toyota Motor Corporation president and chief executive officer Akio Toyoda broke the news to employees at the company's Altona plant, in western Melbourne, this afternoon.
>
> 'To now have to break the news... to the many people who have supported our production for many years is most regretful for Toyota and for me personally, simply heartbreaking,' the Tokyo-based Mr Toyoda told a media conference.

Mr Yasuda added in a statement: 'This is devastating news for all of our employees who have dedicated their lives to the company during the past 50 years.'

He blamed the 'unfavourable Australian dollar', high costs of manufacturing and low economies of scale.

Mr Yasuda also cited increased competitiveness due to current and future free trade agreements as factors

that have made it 'not viable' to continue making cars.

'We did everything that we could to transform our business, but the reality is that there are too many factors beyond our control that make it unviable to build cars in Australia,' Mr Yasuda said. 'Although the company has made profits in the past, our manufacturing operations have continued to be loss making despite our best efforts.'

Making it real

Source: Emma Griffiths, 'Toyota to close: Thousands of jobs to go as carmaker closes Australian plants by 2017'. Reproduced by permission of the Australian Broadcasting Corporation and ABC Online. © 2015 ABC. All rights http://www.abc.net.au/news/2014-02-10/toyota-to-pull-out-of-australia-sources/5250114.

Car manufacturers in Australia have struggled in the face of fierce global competition, causing a raft of changes to the automotive industry.

If sunk costs are not relevant, what about costs that will be incurred in the future? Are all costs that are not sunk relevant? Again, the key is that relevant costs are avoidable costs. If future costs do not differ among alternatives, they are not avoidable (they will be incurred regardless of the alternative chosen) and therefore not relevant. In your choice among cars, if the cost of an option is the same, that cost is not relevant in your decision.

Opportunity costs

Opportunity costs are the benefits forgone by choosing one alternative over another and are relevant costs for decision-making purposes. For example, in choosing to go to university, you are forgoing the salary you could receive by working full time. In the Make It Real example concerning Toyota's decision to shut down operations in Australia, the decision to shift operations overseas involves making a choice – does the company keep making cars in Australia, or make them somewhere else in the world? Almost all alternatives have opportunity costs. In choosing to work instead of going to university, the opportunity cost is the higher salary that you might later earn if you choose to go to university. In choosing to produce cars in Australia and not overseas, Toyota might be missing out on savings in material supplier costs, economies of scale benefits (as explained by Toyota Motor Corporation CEO Akio Toyoda).

Opportunity costs might also be non-financial, instead being time or experientially driven, but no less important to decision making. For example, if you refuse lunch with Hugh Jackman or Cate Blanchett in order to attend your accounting lecture, one might say you've experienced a significant opportunity cost to attend your accounting lecture, though no obvious financial cost relates to that sacrifice! Opportunity costs are sometimes difficult to quantify but nevertheless are important to consider in making decisions (see Exhibit 1.3).

❋ **opportunity costs**
The benefits forgone by choosing one alternative over another.

Relevant costs	
Future costs that differ among alternatives	Opportunity costs – benefits forgone by choosing one alternative over another
Irrelevant costs	
Future costs that do not differ among alternatives	Sunk costs – costs that have already been incurred

EXHIBIT 1.3 Relevant and irrelevant costs

LEARNING OBJECTIVE 4

Ethics and decision making

apply this!

interactive quizzes

Business managers make ethical decisions every day. While some might argue that business decisions are simply a matter of economics, there are also ethical dimensions to most of these decisions. In today's business environment, companies have to be aware not only of the economic impact of their decisions, but also of their ethical impact.

Ethical problems arise in organisations for a variety of reasons. For example, undue pressure to achieve short-term productivity and profitability goals may lead to unethical behaviour, such as requiring employees to work long hours that exceed limits set by state and federal agencies, intentionally ignoring product safety concerns, or falsifying accounting records or other documentation. Such unethical behaviour often occurs in corporate environments in which employees feel they have no choice but to follow their superiors' orders and directives. Strictly adhering to an organisational hierarchy can be problematic if employees blindly follow orders.

Famed economist Milton Friedman once argued that the only social responsibility of corporations was to increase their profits. Further, he stated that business managers should not be expected to make socially responsible decisions because they are not trained to do so.[2] Given the world in which we now live, this perspective may no longer be valid. Managers simply cannot make business decisions without carefully considering their ethical dimensions. As you continue this study of managerial accounting, thoughtfully consider how managers can use information for both good and bad ends. Doing so will increase the likelihood that you will be prepared to make informed and ethical choices as a business manager.

Business ethics results from the interaction of personal morals and the processes and objectives of business. That is to say, business ethics is nothing more than our personal views of right and wrong applied in a business setting. For example, some business practices that are viewed as unethical include managers lying to employees, stealing from a company, divulging confidential information and taking credit for the work of others. Consider how these unethical business practices could occur in your personal life. For example, a child may lie to her mother, a roommate may steal money from you while you are in class, a friend may tell another person about a 'private' conversation that you and he had, and a group member may contribute nothing to a group project yet accept full credit for the project. Business ethics is, in many ways, an extension of our personal ethics. Of course, the stakes are often much higher, or at least very different. Consider the many billions of dollars that the tobacco industry paid in damages because its members lied to consumers and the government about the harmful effects of nicotine.

In addition, managers must consider various stakeholders when evaluating ethical dilemmas. A chief executive officer cannot simply make the decision that is best for her without considering the interests of other employees, shareholders, customers, suppliers, creditors and so forth.

Integrity is the cornerstone of ethical business practices. Failure to build a business on integrity carries costs. For example, deceptive business practices may harm a company's standing in the community, decrease employee productivity, reduce customer loyalty, build resentment among employees, increase the likelihood of further unethical behaviour by employees and cause scrutiny by government agencies. Although the costs of some of these consequences are difficult to quantify, there is no doubt that they can be substantial.

Ethics programs

Companies frequently create **ethics programs** to establish and help maintain an ethical business environment. Some of the most common elements of ethics programs include written codes of conduct, employee hotlines and ethics call centres, ethics training, processes to register anonymous complaints about wrongdoing and ethics offices.

✲ **ethics programs**
Company programs or policies created for the express purpose of establishing and maintaining an ethical business environment.

Corporate wrongdoing

Although companies establish ethics programs to encourage employees to act with integrity, some individuals engage in behaviours that are not only unethical, but also fraudulent. The case of Enron in the US and Clive Peeters in Australia are two examples where ethics programs within organisations were not effective. In late 2001, the once high-flying

Source: Kurt Drubbel/iStockphoto

An organisation can go out of business owing to the unethical actions of a single accountant.

company Enron filed for bankruptcy protection. Investigations into the company's failure revealed a series of questionable transactions designed by the company's top officials to enrich themselves. The company's former chief financial officer and two former chief executive officers were found guilty of the fraud. Though the actual cost of Enron's collapse will never be known, estimates are that shareholders and creditors lost more than $60 billion. In 2006, a senior accountant in Clive Peeters (a popular electrical goods retailer) transferred $20 million of the company's funds into her personal bank accounts, and bought 43 properties in Victoria, Queensland and Tasmania using the funds. In commenting on the fraud, the firm's forensic accountants conceded that her deception was complex and sophisticated.[3] Clearly, accountants are placed in positions of high financial trust in organisations. When they act unethically, grave consequences can result. In Clive Peeters, the accounting fraud is widely credited with causing the company's eventual liquidation.

Sarbanes-Oxley Act of 2002

The Sarbanes-Oxley Act is not mandatory in Australia, but may apply to Australian organisations that are subsidiaries of US parent companies. As a response to the rash of corporate scandals and frauds that began with the implosion of Enron in late 2001, the US Congress held hearings that eventually led to the passage of the Sarbanes-Oxley Act. Sarbanes-Oxley includes a number of significant provisions. For example, the law requires management to assess whether internal controls over financial reporting (ICFR) are effective. In addition, the company's external financial statement auditor is also required to audit ICFR and assess whether those controls are effective in preventing and detecting financial misstatements. These assessments become part of the so-called Section 404

report called for under the law. Because Congress wanted to include a significant deterrent, Sarbanes-Oxley also increases the criminal penalties associated with financial statement fraud to a maximum fine of $5 million and imprisonment for 20 years. Another provision of the law requires companies to establish procedures to allow employees to make complaints about accounting and auditing matters directly to members of the audit committee. Furthermore, companies must ensure that employees who make such complaints are not harassed or otherwise discriminated against by others within the organisation. In sum, the Sarbanes-Oxley Act has increased the level of scrutiny of public companies' financial statements. Many observers believe that the law significantly improved the quality of financial reporting in the US and has rebuilt the public's trust in the nation's financial markets.

Accounting Professional and Ethical Standards Board

The major professional accounting bodies in Australia jointly subscribe to the guidelines of the Accounting Professional and Ethical Standards Board (APESB). These standards broadly define the ethical obligations of accountants in practice. It is important that you appreciate that the title of 'professional' accorded to accountants is not one justified from technical competence, but a higher standard of behaviour. While in the workplace, professionals are expected to ethically conduct themselves at a standard higher than that expected of any other member of society. This has implications for you, should you wish to become a professional accountant (for example, a CPA or CA).

The APESs also make it very clear that an accountant's obligation is not only to the firm within which they are employed, but first and foremost, the public interest. The

Accounting information must always be furnished free of bias, and as objectively as possible.

'public interest' is defined by the APESB as the collective wellbeing of the community of people and institutions that an accountant serves. The accountancy profession's public consists of clients, credit providers, governments, employers, employees, investors, the business and financial community, and others who rely on the objectivity and integrity of accountants to maintain the orderly functioning of commerce.

So what is ethically expected of an accountant? There are five broad governing principles expected of professional accountants, as explained in the APESB guidelines.[4] These are:

1 *Integrity* – Being straightforward and honest, implying fair dealing and truthfulness.
2 *Objectivity* – Not compromising judgement owing to bias, conflict of interest or undue influence.
3 *Professional competence and due care* – Continuing awareness and understanding of relevant technical, professional and business developments.
4 *Confidentiality* – Disclosing information relating to the firm that is otherwise private (unless there is a legal obligation to disclose), or using private information for personal gain.
5 *Professional behaviour* – Complying with relevant laws and regulations and avoiding any action or omission that may bring discredit to the profession.

Finally, members that are found to have breached these standards of behaviour risk their professional membership being revoked and possible further legal action by disadvantaged internal or external stakeholders.

Exercises

1 Users of accounting information LO2

Accounting information is used by a variety of individuals and organisations for numerous purposes. Below is a small set of potential users of accounting information.
a Bank loan officer
b Employee labour union
c Production manager
d Current shareholder
e Sales manager
f Company chairman

Required
Identify the types of accounting information that may be of interest to each of these potential users. Be specific if possible.

2 Managerial vs financial accounting LO2

Financial and managerial accounting information serve different purposes. The following phrases are commonly used to describe either financial or managerial accounting.
- Must follow AASB
- Focused on past performance
- Timeliness is critical
- Emphasises reporting on the whole company
- Information is often less precise
- Future orientation
- Information is often 'old'
- Reports results by segments
- Highly customisable

Required
Indicate whether each of the preceding phrases describes financial accounting or managerial accounting.

3 Managerial vs financial accounting LO2

List a range of stakeholders who might be interested in Google Inc.'s financial accounting information, and do the same for management accounting information. How are these potential interested stakeholders different?

4 Types of business managers LO2

Business managers do not all have the same information needs. Some require detailed production data, while others require detailed data about sales and marketing performance. Read the following statements that describe business managers.
a These managers make decisions about how to raise capital as well as where and how it is invested.
b These managers need to know how much a product costs in order to help establish a reasonable selling price.
c These managers support other managers by recruiting and staffing, designing compensation and benefit packages, and providing training and development opportunities for employees.
d These managers make decisions about how and when products and services are produced or provided.

Required
Identify the type of business manager described in each of the preceding statements.

5 Types of business managers LO2

Consider the informational needs of a production manager in the Cadbury Chocolate Factory, versus the human resources manager in the same factory. How might their management accounting information needs differ?

6 Decision making and ethics LO4

Tall Grass Mowers (TGM) Pty Limited produces batteries for ride-on lawn mowers. The company provides the batteries to some of the largest manufacturers of ride-on lawn mowers in Australia. In the last few months, the company has received reports of batteries exploding as a result of high heat. The incidents have all been in northern states and have occurred with only one particular brand and model of lawn mower. In this model, the batteries are installed beneath the seats of the mower. In more than one case, the exploding batteries have resulted in serious injuries. TGM officials are aware of the potential danger, but have been unable to determine the cause of the problem. Some company officials think that the problem may be with the lawn mower and not with the batteries, and internal testing has been inconclusive.

Required
a In your opinion, what responsibility does the company bear for the potential dangers of the battery?

b Should company officials try to shift blame to the manufacturer of the lawn mower, as the problems are only with one particular brand of mower?

c Identify the stakeholders who are impacted by the issue and discuss ethical considerations faced by company officials in this situation.

Problems

7 Financial vs managerial accounting LO2

Imagine that you are home during a break from university and are talking to a friend about classes. You tell your friend, who is not a university student, that you are taking managerial accounting this semester. Your friend says that she remembers you took accounting last semester and wonders why you have to take another accounting course. You look a little perplexed and decide to give that question some thought.

Required

As you think about your friend's question, you decide to answer the following questions:

a What are the differences between financial and managerial accounting (explain concisely)?

b Why do the two types of accounting exist?

c Who are the users of financial accounting information? Who are the users of managerial accounting information?

8 Decision making and relevant factors LO3

You have an opportunity to choose a flight for your upcoming summer holiday break to Mexico, from Sydney. After a lot of thought and research, you have narrowed your options to four different flights. If there are no delays, each should get you to your destination on time. (It is important to arrive on time as you have to meet a bus at a particular time to take you and other students to your final destination.) If any of the flights are late, arranging for alternative transportation will be difficult. Basic information about each flight is presented in the following table:

	Flight 1	Flight 2	Flight 3	Flight 4
Base price	$1500	$1900	$2400	$3000
Flight time and connections	32 hours/3	26 hours/2	20 hours/1	15 hours/direct flight
First class upgrade	Not available	$250	$200	$300
Meals (airport and plane)	$30	$15	$10	Included in airfare
Wireless Internet access	Not available	$20	$25	Included in airfare
Beverages	$10	$10	$10	Included in airfare
Total price (all options)	$1540	$2185	$2645	$3300

Required

a Define the decision problem that you face in choosing a flight from among the options available to you.

b What are your objectives in choosing a flight? What is the most important objective to you? Why?

c What are the relevant factors affecting your choice of flight?

d If you were to choose from among the four flights, which would be the best choice? Why?

9 Decision making and ethics LO3, 4

Ken Martin is an engineer with a multinational aerospace firm that produces a jet engine that is widely used by aircraft manufacturers. Ken recently became aware of a potential defect in an engine part. As the lead engineer responsible for the component part, Ken directed that tests be performed to ascertain the conditions under which the part might fail. The results of the tests indicate that at low temperatures a critical seal may crack, possibly allowing fluids to leak into other portions of the engine. Although the risks of such a leak are very low, the consequences are potentially disastrous.

Required

a What are some of the objectives that Ken might identify when dealing with this dilemma?

b What options are available to Ken?

c Does the company have an ethical responsibility to fix the component part?

d Should the company consider the estimated cost of fixing the component part in its decision-making process? Why or why not?

10 Considering costs in organisation decision making LO3

Reflect on the Make It Real example concerning Toyota Corporation provided in the chapter.

Required

List a range of factors that you think contributed to Toyota's decision to stop making cars in Australia. Consider both financial and non-financial factors. On balance, do you think they made the right decision?

11 Ethics and the divide between financial and management accounting LO2, 04

Reflect on the fraud committed by the senior accountant in Clive Peeters, thinking about the nature of her actions that led to the fraud.

Required

To what extent was this fraud a financial accounting and/or management accounting problem? Please discuss by first explaining your understanding of financial accounting, and management accounting, then provide your analysis.

Cases

12 Considering costs in organisation decision making LO3

Please read the Daily Grind Café case study in Appendix 2.

Required

How do you think a management accountant might be able to contribute to the better running of this business? In crafting an answer, be clear in identifying how the information you suggest benefits the owners and managers of the Daily Grind Café.

13 Ethics and the divide between financial and management accounting
LO2, 04

Consider the brief excerpt below, regarding the BP Gulf of Mexico oil spill.

A court in the United States has found the oil giant BP 'grossly negligent' over the Gulf of Mexico oil spill in 2010.

The blowout at the Deepwater Horizon drilling rig killed 11 people and spilled 4.2 million barrels of oil into the Gulf, the worst offshore environmental disaster in US history.

The ruling could add nearly $US18 billion in fines to more than $US42 billion in charges the company has faced.

BP said it would 'immediately' appeal the decision to a higher court.

Federal court judge Carl Barbier said the disaster happened because BP's US subsidiaries, along with oil services company Halliburton and rig owner Transocean, did not take adequate care in drilling the highly risky well.

The disaster struck when a surge of methane gas known to rig hands as a 'kick' sparked an explosion aboard Deepwater Horizon as it was drilling the mile-deep Macondo 252 well off Louisiana.

Judge Barbier said BP knew the well, called by some working on it as the 'well from hell', was particularly dangerous because of the high risk of a blowout.

BP's decisions throughout the drilling process qualified as 'gross negligence' because they were 'an extreme departure from the care required under the circumstances or a failure to exercise even a slight care', the judge said.

Source: Extract from other news sites, as compiled by ABC, viewed at: http://www.abc.net.au/news/2014-09-05/bp-found-grossly-negligent-over-gulf-of-mexico-oil-spill/5721218

Required

How might a management accountant contribute to the better reporting of this disaster by the BP corporation? Is there a role for management accounting in communicating this high profile environmental breach to managers in the firm, or externally to the public in a more effective manner?

> I think this book is totally cutting-edge...it's making learning fun again.
> - Scotty Willamson, student.

LEARNING, YOUR WAY.

ACCT was designed for students just like you – busy people who want choices, flexibility, and multiple learning options.

ACCT delivers concise, focused information in a fresh and contemporary format. And … **ACCT** gives you a variety of online learning materials designed with you in mind.

At **http://login.cengagebrain.com/** you'll find electronic resources such as audio downloads and online flash cards for each chapter. These resources will help supplement your understanding of core organisational behaviour concepts in a format that fits your busy lifestyle.

Visit **http://login.cengagebrain.com/** to learn more about the multiple **ACCT** resources available to help you succeed!

Learning objectives:

After studying the material in this chapter, you should be able to:

1 Describe basic production processes used by manufacturing companies.

2 Identify the key characteristics and benefits of lean production and JIT manufacturing.

3 Distinguish manufacturing costs from non-manufacturing costs and classify manufacturing costs as direct materials, direct labour or overhead.

4 Diagram the flow of costs in manufacturing, merchandising and service companies and calculate the cost of manufacturing or selling goods and services.

5 Evaluate the impact of product costs and period costs on a company's income statement and balance sheet.

PRODUCT COSTING: MANUFACTURING PROCESSES, COST TERMINOLOGY AND COST FLOWS

c 2

Every company provides a product or a service to customers and clients. **Manufacturing companies** (such as General Motors Holden Australia and the Ford Motor Company) take raw materials and produce new products using them. Coca-Cola Amatil buys water, sugars, colouring, preservatives, additives and other materials, and combines them in a unique way to produce one of the world's most popular beverages, Coca-Cola.

Merchandising companies, on the other hand, sell products that someone else has manufactured. Woolworths or Coles are merchandisers. They buy the Coca-Cola bottles or cans from Coca-Cola Amatil, and sell them in their stores. Examples are large department stores, such as David Jones and Target, as well as music stores (HMV) or small to medium sized clothing stores (Country Road, Cue). Merchandising firms provide a product, but do not make the product – they simply provide convenience to customers seeking to access these products. Therefore, merchandisers justify their premium by making it easier for a customer to buy something made by a manufacturer.

In contrast to manufacturing and merchandising companies, **service companies** do not sell a tangible product as their primary business. Service providers include such diverse companies and industries as Qantas airlines, hospitals, brokerage firms, law firms and CPA (Certified Practising Accountant) or CA (Chartered Accountant) firms. The service sector accounts for approximately 70 per cent of our Australian economic activity (according to the Department of Foreign Affairs and Trade, Australia), employing the majority of our workforce. While it is growing at an industry level, not all service firms do it easily, even the larger more established ones. Qantas airlines is currently experiencing significant cost

❋ **manufacturing companies**
Companies that purchase raw materials from other companies and transform those raw materials into a finished product, usually with the assistance of labour and other supporting activities, technologies and infrastructure (overheads).

❋ **merchandising companies**
Companies that sell products that someone else has manufactured.

❋ **service companies**
Companies that do not sell a tangible product as their primary business.

Making it real

PMI points to decline

The decline in manufacturing activity in Australia is evidenced by the Australia Manufacturing Purchasing Managers Index (PMI) statistic. Any score below 50 in a period indicates a shrinking manufacturing sector, and vice versa. Consider the table below, highlighting the domination of activity scores below 50 in the last few years, whereas those that exceeded 50 only occurred twice in the two years ended December 2013:

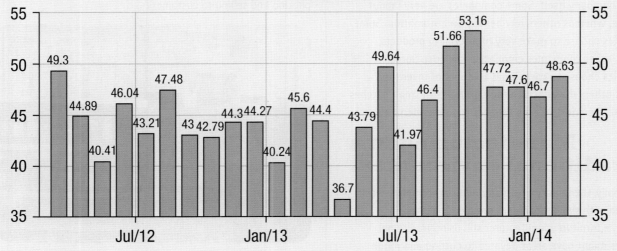

Australia manufacturing PMI

Source: Data from 'Australia Manufacturing PMI', published by Trading Economics, © 2014; http://www.tradingeconomics.com/australia/manufacturing-pmi

pressures, having announced a large loss for the half-year period ended 31 December 2013 of A$235 million. CEO Alan Joyce announced the difficult decision of cutting 5000 jobs as a result of this negative result.[1] Therefore, the need for accountants to manage and use resources in these sectors is important from the perspective of making difficult resource allocation decisions.

Regardless of the type of company involved, costs are associated with the products and services produced and sold. Although it might appear simple to determine the cost of a product or service, the process can be quite complicated, as you will see in the next few chapters. How should companies determine the costs of producing products and providing services?

What costs should be included? Before we can answer these questions, we should also ask why companies want to determine their product costs. For example, BHP Billiton might be preparing a set of financial statements for the National Australia Bank to use in determining whether to make a loan to the company or may be filing its income tax return to the Australian Taxation Office (ATO) for the year. The Australian Accounting Standards Board (AASB) and tax laws govern costing for financial statement purposes and for tax purposes, respectively. On the other hand, a company might want to determine the cost of a particular product in order to determine its sales price or to estimate a product's profitability.[2] Cost information is also helpful for budgeting and evaluation purposes.

LEARNING OBJECTIVE 1 >>

The production process

e-Lecture

Manufacturing companies purchase raw materials from other companies and transform them into a finished product. This transformation typically requires labour and the incurring of other costs, such as utilities, the depreciation of factory equipment and supplies. Manufacturing companies may produce a single product or many products. Likewise, companies may have only a few customers or many thousands. The process used to manufacture these products depends on the specific product or products made, the customers who buy the product(s) and the company itself. Some companies are very labour intensive, whereas others rely heavily on automation. Some companies choose to make very high-quality products, whereas other companies emphasise low cost. Some companies choose to carry large amounts of inventory, whereas others manufacture their products in small batches and make them just in time to meet customer demand.

Manufacturing in a traditional environment

Traditionally, the factory of a manufacturing company was organised with similar machines grouped together. For example, a furniture manufacturer still using traditional processes might have areas devoted to cutting and rough sanding, shaping the cut wood into furniture pieces (such as chair legs), using lathes and routers, drilling holes and

dovetailing joints, assembling the furniture pieces and finishing. As raw material (in this case, wood) is processed in each area, it is 'pushed' to the next area for further processing. Wood is brought into the factory from the warehouse and is cut and rough-sanded according to specifications for specific products. It is then moved to another area in the factory for shaping the rough wood into chair legs, bed posts and tabletops. Next, the wood might move to an area containing drill presses and machines to make dovetail joints. After drilling and jointing, it would be moved to still another area for assembly. In this area, workers glue or screw the various parts together and attach necessary hardware and glass. After assembly, the furniture is moved to an area where it is sanded again and varnish or paint finishes are applied. It would not be unusual for one or more of these areas to be in different buildings or sometimes in entirely different plants. After leaving the finishing department, the furniture is ready for packing and selling to customers.

Source: PAT SCALA/Faifax Photos

Businesses use sophisticated information systems to manage inventories so they can be responsive to consumer demands.

In this traditional system, it was normal (and perhaps even desirable) to accumulate **raw materials inventory** and **finished-goods inventory** to serve as buffers in case of unexpected demand for products or unexpected problems in production. It was also normal to accumulate inventories of partially completed products (called **work in process inventory, or WIP**). WIP might result, for example, when furniture pieces that have been drilled and jointed are pushed to the assembly area before the workers in that area are ready for them.

LEARNING OBJECTIVE **2** >>

Lean production and manufacturing in a JIT environment

One of the big changes affecting companies in the past 20 to 25 years has been the adoption of **lean production** systems and **just-in-time (JIT) manufacturing**. In an effort to reduce costs and increase efficiency, companies began to focus on the costs and problems associated with the traditional manufacturing facility and the practice of carrying large amounts of inventory.

Lean production is focused on eliminating waste associated with holding more inventory than required, making more product than is needed, over-processing a product (doing more than a customer values), moving products (and people) further than required and experiencing downtime caused by people waiting for work to do and products waiting in mid-assembly.

One of the key aspects of lean production is managing inventory so only that which is needed in the immediate future is carried. Carrying large amounts of inventory results in storage and insurance costs. Furthermore, traditional manufacturing systems may result in other, less obvious problems, including the production of lower-quality products with more defects. The buffers that seem so desirable may in fact lead workers to pay less attention to detail and work less efficiently. In addition, the organisation of factories in which similar machines are grouped together greatly increases the time necessary to manufacture products and makes it more difficult to meet special orders or unexpected increases in demand without having large amounts of inventory on hand.

In a just-in-time (JIT) system, materials are purchased and products are made 'just in time' to meet customer demand. Unlike traditional production, the process begins with a customer order, and products are 'pulled' through the manufacturing process. Under ideal conditions, companies operating in a JIT environment would reduce inventories of raw materials, work in process and finished goods to very low levels or even zero. For example, a dozen years ago, Dell Computer kept a 30-day supply of hard drives, Intel processors and other components on hand. Today, it holds only a few days' supply of parts.[3]

With only a small buffer of extra finished goods and raw materials, it is imperative that companies employing JIT be able to procure supplies and raw materials on a timely basis. This requires that companies work with suppliers that can deliver goods on time and free of defects. Typically, JIT companies rely on only a few suppliers that have proven to be highly reliable. In Dell's case, the company requires its suppliers to hold eight to 10 days of inventory and to deliver those parts to Dell within 90 minutes.[4]

Notwithstanding the benefits of lean processing, it is important to acknowledge the higher risks that might arise in satisfying customer demand when lower inventory stocks are held. The less you have on stock for customers to buy, the more you need your suppliers to guarantee availability and quick delivery (similar to Dell), should demand spikes occur.

❈ raw materials inventory
Inventory of materials needed in the production process but not yet moved to the production area. Usually sitting in a warehouse, awaiting transfer into the factory.

❈ finished-goods inventory
Inventory of finished product waiting for sale and shipment to customers.

❈ work in process (WIP) inventory
Inventory that is moved out of a warehouse and into a factory – they are in the process of being transformed (in other words, what is left in the factory at the end of the period).

❈ lean production
A system focused on eliminating waste associated with holding more inventory than required, making more product than is needed, over-processing a product, moving products (and people) further than required and waiting.

❈ just-in-time (JIT) manufacturing
The philosophy of having raw materials arrive just in time to be used in production and for finished goods inventory to be completed just in time to be shipped to customers.

Trico Australia

Making It Real

Trico Australia manufactures windscreen wiper systems for the Australian automotive industry. In the 1990s, the company acknowledged that it had '… inefficiencies in production operations, a high level of inventory, poor quality and overall an inflexible manufacturing system which was based on batch production' (Sohal, 1996).[5] In order to raise efficiency levels, Trico implemented a lean production system based on a Just In Time (JIT) philosophy, leading to product development times reducing by half and materials being supplied much more efficiently than previously. Trico in 2014 is much more profitable and in control of its costs than it was in the past, owing to lean accounting systems like JIT.

In order to successfully implement lean production and JIT manufacturing systems, companies must be able to manufacture products very quickly. This often entails restructuring the factory itself. In the traditional factory, similar machines are grouped together, resulting in raw materials and unfinished products being handled and moved a great deal from area to area. In the traditional factory, it is also more difficult and time consuming to switch production from one product to another (from tables to chairs, for example) because the same machines were used for both. In contrast, factories in a JIT environment are typically organised so that all the machinery and equipment needed to make a product is available in one area. These groupings of machines are called manufacturing cells. The use of cells minimises the handling and moving of products. It also reduces or eliminates setup time (the time needed to switch production from one product to another). Sometimes, workers are trained to operate all the machinery in a manufacturing cell, increasing speed and efficiency even more.

Source: Nataliya Hora/Shutterstock

The cost of materials to make a product, such as a car, is inversely related to the availability of the material.

Through the implementation of JIT and other process improvements, Dell has reduced the time and labour it takes to make a computer from two workers and 14 minutes to a single worker who takes 5 minutes. An order that comes into the factory at 9.00 in the morning typically is shipped out within 4 hours.[6] This ethos of continuous excellence in operations within Dell continues today, underpinned by management accounting systems that identify and maximise value-adding activities, while minimising non-value-adding activities.

While it is easy to think of lean production and JIT as inventory management tools only, successful implementation provides an array of benefits including:

1   reduced waste and scrap
2   improved product quality
3   lower overall production costs (although the costs of raw materials may increase in some cases)
4   lower labour costs
5   reduced inventory
6   reduced processing time, and
7   increased manufacturing flexibility.

These benefits often lead to increased customer satisfaction, increased motivation within the workforce and increased profits.

However, disruptions in supply can wreak havoc on companies that rely on just-in-time purchasing of parts and supplies. These disruptions may result from strikes by factory workers of the supplier, natural disasters or the unexpected closing of national borders (when suppliers are located in other countries).

For example, in the days following the terrorist attacks on the World Trade Center on 11 September 2001, delayed shipments of air freight and heightened security at border crossings slowed the delivery of parts, forcing several car manufacturers to temporarily shut down assembly lines. In 2010, Queensland floods impacted

the supply of bananas throughout the rest of Australia, pushing the retail price up from $1.50 per kg to $15 per kg within a few months. In a similar fashion, an 8.9 magnitude earthquake off the coast of Japan in 2011 caused a devastating tsunami on that country's Pacific coast. More recently, in mid 2014, the Coles and Woolworths grocery stores have charged up to $7.98 for a punnet of raspberries, owing to their scarcity when out of season. In the same period, these same fruits were selling for about A$3 in London, as they were in-season! We can also understand this principle in reverse – the heavy drop in the price of iron ore from late 2013 to late 2014 can be attributed to a drop in global demand for the mineral, owing to the construction slowdown in the Chinese economy over the same period. This significantly impacted the supply of food produce in the region. These effects must be carefully considered by management accountants when working with senior management to develop their organisation's strategy. For example, Woolworths and Coles often compete on the price of basic produce, in order to entice customers to frequent their respective stores. If the price of bananas increases tenfold, this strategy might have to be revisited, as fewer customers will choose to buy bananas. This causes management to re-align this strategy to other products, perhaps milk, bread or other vegetables.

LEARNING OBJECTIVE >>

Product costs in a manufacturing company

apply this!

Case

Regardless of the size of the company involved, the number of products made or the type of manufacturing system used, manufacturing

How much is enough when disaster strikes?

As hospitals focus on cutting costs, inventory management has gained importance. As a result, most hospitals carry no more than a 30-day supply of drugs. Although this is adequate in normal situations, hospitals and other health care organisations may not have enough medical supplies on hand to deal with a pandemic flu outbreak or other emergencies.

For example, as the world faced an outbreak of the Ebola virus in 2014, affluent countries such as Australia, Japan, Britain, and the United States might have had sufficient quantities of antibodies available as they are mass produced, as well as other antiviral medicines to treat a sizeable percentage of their citizens. However, poorer countries including the African nations that have been hardest hit by the virus are already complaining that they are not receiving sufficient quantities of the anti-virus. This is especially relevant in countries where the virus has mutated most rapidly, as highlighted in the ABC Science article referenced in the source line below.

Source: 'Ebola virus is rapidly mutating', by Julie Steenhuysen. Published by ABC News, ©2014. http://www.abc.net.au/science/articles/2014/08/29/4076805.htm?site=science/demonstrations&topic=latesti

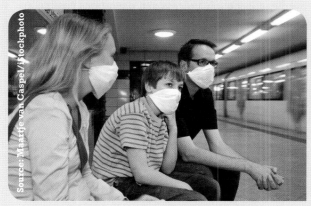

Source: Maartje van Caspel/iStockphoto

The cost of mitigating a disaster can be borne by advanced economies, but not all developing countries.

companies must know how much their products cost. It is useful to distinguish between direct and indirect costs. Direct costs are costs that are directly attached to the finished product and can be conveniently traced to that product. Indirect costs are costs that are attached to the product but cannot be conveniently traced to each separate product. It is also convenient to distinguish **manufacturing costs** (those incurred in the manufacture of a product) from non-manufacturing costs (those incurred elsewhere in the company). Manufacturing costs typically consist of three components: *direct materials, direct labour* and *manufacturing overhead* (see Exhibit 2.1).

❊ **manufacturing costs**

Costs incurred in the factory or plant to produce a product; typically consist of three elements: direct materials, direct labour and manufacturing overhead.

❊ **direct materials**

Materials that can easily and conveniently be traced to the final product.

Direct materials	Direct labour	Manufacturing overhead
Various materials that can be directly and conveniently traced to a product	Labour costs of assembly-line workers	Indirect materials such as welding material, glue, screws, etc.
		Indirect labour such as factory maintenance workers and factory cleaners
		Other factory costs

EXHIBIT 2.1 Manufacturing costs

Direct materials

Direct materials are defined as materials that can be directly and conveniently traced to a particular product or other cost object *and* that become an integral part of the finished product. At the Ford Motor Company plant in Victoria, Australia, sheet metal and tyres are direct materials. At the Pilkington Glass Manufacturing plant in Sydney, Australia, the minerals used to construct the glass products are direct materials.

Direct materials typically cause few problems in the costing of products. The amount of direct materials used in making products can usually be accurately measured by engineering studies, and the accounting systems of most companies are capable of tracing the materials used and the costs of those materials to specific products. However, questions do arise and judgement is often needed to correctly classify materials as direct or indirect. The key test differentiating a direct and indirect cost is – can the cost be economically feasibly linked to a cost object? If so, then it may be classed a direct cost. Otherwise, it is regarded as an indirect cost.

Direct labour

Direct labour is the labour cost (including fringe benefits) of all production employees who work directly on the product being made or service being provided. Sometimes, direct labour is called *touch labour* to reflect the hands-on relationship between the employee and the product or service. Assembly-line workers are the clearest example of

❊ **direct labour**

Labour that can easily and conveniently be traced to particular products.

direct labour. As with direct materials, identification of direct labour cost is usually straightforward and accurate. Time sheets may be used to keep track of the work employees perform on different products and the wages they are paid.

Manufacturing overhead

All costs incurred in the factory that are not feasibly classified as direct materials or direct labour are called **manufacturing overhead**. Manufacturing overhead includes both **indirect materials** and **indirect labour**. Materials that we know are used in the manufacture of products but cannot be measured with reasonable accuracy and easily and conveniently traced to a particular product are called indirect materials. For example, the rivets and welding materials used by Ford Manufacturing in their Melbourne plants, and the screws and glue used by a furniture manufacturer would probably be classified as indirect materials. Likewise, certain labour costs that are not directly associated with production are classified as indirect labour and included in manufacturing overhead. Examples include labour costs of janitorial/cleaning staff and maintenance workers in a factory and supervisors who do not directly work on a product.

Manufacturing overhead also includes utilities, depreciation of factory equipment and buildings, rent, repairs and maintenance, insurance and other factory costs. In a traditional manufacturing environment, the costs included in manufacturing overhead are most often indirect in nature and cannot be conveniently and accurately traced and assigned to a specific product. Remember, the machinery and equipment are typically used to make multiple products, making it difficult to trace the cost of a machine to a specific product. Although many overhead costs in a JIT environment will also be indirect in nature (rent and utilities, for example), more of the costs are likely to be direct in nature. For example, in a JIT environment, the cost of machinery in a manufacturing cell can be traced to a specific product (for example, tables) if it is used only to make that product.

Because of the indirect nature of most overhead costs and the inability of companies to directly measure the amount of overhead included in products or to trace manufacturing overhead to products, accountants have come up with various methods of allocating manufacturing overhead to products. Traditional methods of allocating overhead using job, process and operations costing are discussed in Chapters 4, 5 and 6. A more modern method, called activity-based costing, is discussed in Chapter 8.

Manufacturing costs are also called **product costs** or inventoriable costs because they attach to products as they go through the manufacturing process. Direct material, direct labour and overhead costs remain with the product until it is sold. Only when the product is sold are these costs expensed on the income statement as cost of goods sold.

Non-manufacturing costs

Non-manufacturing costs consist of those costs that are incurred outside the plant or factory and typically are categorised as selling and administrative costs. Although non-manufacturing costs are necessarily incurred in running a business, they are not directly incurred in the production of products. A general rule of thumb is to imagine the product not being produced. If a particular cost would still occur, it is generally a non-manufacturing cost. Common examples of non-manufacturing costs include advertising costs, commissions paid to salespersons, administrative and accounting salaries, and office supplies. Non-manufacturing costs also include rent, insurance, taxes, utilities and depreciation of equipment when used in selling and administrative activities. Non-manufacturing costs are called **period costs**. In contrast to manufacturing costs, non-manufacturing costs are expensed on the income statement in the period incurred. Exhibit 2.2 lists several examples of manufacturing and non-manufacturing costs. It is important to understand that a cost is not a production or non-production cost because of its type (for example, rent, electricity, depreciation, etc). Rather, it is the way the cost is used that determines whether it is a production or non-production cost – see Exhibit 2.2. Costs relating to 'factory' activities are production costs, while the same costs in relation to sales staff, office, human resources (HR) and administrative functions are treated as non-production costs.

❋ **manufacturing overhead**
Indirect materials and labour and any other expenses related to the production of products but not directly traceable to the specific product.

❋ **indirect materials**
Materials used in the production of products but not directly traceable to the specific product.

❋ **indirect labour**
Labour used in the production of products but not directly traceable to the specific product.

❋ **product costs**
Costs that attach to the products as they go through the manufacturing process; also called inventoriable costs. They appear as inventory in the balance sheet and only become expenses when products are sold (as Cost of Goods Sold – COGS).

❋ **non-manufacturing costs**
Costs that are not related to the production process are classed as selling and administrative costs. These costs cannot be classed as inventory and must be immediately expensed in the profit and loss statement.

❋ **period costs**
Costs that are expensed in the period incurred; attached to the period as opposed to the product.

Description	Manufacturing cost	Non-manufacturing cost
Depreciation of factory machinery	✓	
Depreciation of vehicles used by sales staff		✓
Lease expense on factory equipment	✓	
Lease expense on office computer		✓
Lubricants used for maintenance of factory machinery (indirect materials)	✓	
Supplies used in the human resources office		✓
Utilities used in the factory building	✓	
Utilities used in the administrative headquarters		✓
Salary of a supervisor in the factory (indirect labour)	✓	
Salary of a supervisor in the marketing department		✓

EXHIBIT 2.2 Manufacturing and non-manufacturing costs

LEARNING OBJECTIVE **4** >>

Cost flows in a manufacturing company – traditional environment with inventory

If companies simply used all the materials they purchased to make one product, finished making all the units of that product that they started and sold everything they finished in the same period, then calculating the income or loss from selling the product would be relatively easy. However, when multiple products are made or when materials are not all used, goods are not all finished, or products are not all sold, the process becomes more difficult.

To accurately determine the cost of manufactured products, a company must trace or allocate manufacturing costs to each individual product as it is being produced and then follow those costs through various inventory accounts as the product progresses toward eventual completion and sale. At the point of sale, the cost of producing the product (the cost of goods sold) must be matched with the sales price to compute a profit or loss on the sale (called gross margin, or gross profit). Subtracting non-manufacturing costs from the gross margin provides a measure of profitability for the company as a whole. When materials are

not all used in production, goods are not finished or finished goods are not all sold, costs must be accounted for in the appropriate raw materials, work in process or finished-goods inventory accounts.

Manufacturing costs include direct materials, direct labour and manufacturing overhead. These costs are also called product costs because they attach to the product as it goes through the production process. Picture a product moving down an assembly line. As labour, material and overhead costs are incurred, they attach to the product being produced and remain with that product (in an inventory account) until it is sold. Costs flow in the same way that products flow through a production facility (see Exhibit 2.3).

This basic cost-flow model is appropriate (with slight variations) for companies using either job costing, operations costing or process costing systems. The differences between the costing systems are discussed more fully in Chapter 4.

The cost-of-goods-sold model for a traditional manufacturing company with inventory

To illustrate the production process and some of the associated problems with costing products, we will use a fictional company called Northern Territory Lights Custom Cabinets. Northern Territory Lights Custom Cabinets manufactures and sells custom-ordered kitchen and bathroom cabinets. The company sells primarily to building contractors but occasionally deals directly with homeowners. Northern Territory

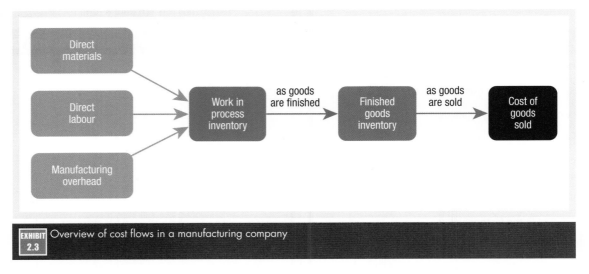

EXHIBIT 2.3 Overview of cost flows in a manufacturing company

Lights is located in Darwin, Australia, and has been in business only a few years, so management is still learning the business and how to properly determine the cost of each cabinet.

Northern Territory Lights has an engineering and design division, which is involved in all custom-cabinet jobs. Quality control dictates that the engineering and design division must design all cabinets. Northern Territory Lights strives to minimise the costs of production without sacrificing quality. Once the design phase of each cabinet job is complete, the material must be ordered. The material is stored in the raw materials warehouse until needed for the job and is then moved to the production area.

The production factory is separated into three distinct areas (see Exhibit 2.4): cutting, assembly and finishing. In the cutting area, all wood is cut into the required pieces, based on the plans from the engineering and design division. The pieces are all numbered and bundled for each particular section of the cabinet job. After cutting is completed, the bundles are moved to the assembly area, where the cabinets are constructed using glue and wood dowels. The assembled cabinets are then moved to the finishing area, where they are finished and stored for delivery to the home. This process can take up to one month to complete and is very labour intensive. Because each job is custom built, Northern Territory Lights also provides installation services for an extra charge.

Northern Territory Lights purchases raw materials and stores the materials in a warehouse that is separate from the production facility or factory. While these materials are in the warehouse, the costs of the raw materials are included in a raw materials inventory account. Northern Territory Lights began 2011 with raw materials costing $10 000 on hand and purchased an additional $40 000 of raw materials during the year. Therefore, the company had $50 000 of raw materials available for use during the year.

The purchase of raw materials

Description	Item	Amount
Raw materials on hand to start the period	Beginning inventory of raw materials	$10 000
Purchases of raw materials during the period	+ Cost of raw materials purchased	+ 40 000
The pool of raw materials available for use during the period	= Raw materials available for use	= $50 000

The journal entry to record the purchase of raw materials is:

Raw Materials Inventory	40 000	
Accounts Payable (or Cash)		40 000

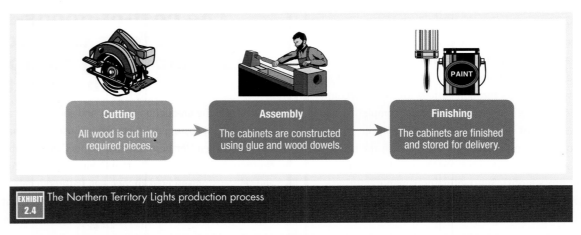

Cutting	Assembly	Finishing
All wood is cut into required pieces.	The cabinets are constructed using glue and wood dowels.	The cabinets are finished and stored for delivery.

EXHIBIT 2.4 The Northern Territory Lights production process

When the raw materials are moved to the factory, the raw material costs move with the material to a work in process (WIP) inventory account. Any raw materials not used during the year remain in the raw materials inventory account. As shown below, if Northern Territory Lights has $5000 of raw materials in ending inventory at the end of the year, the raw materials used in production is equal to $45000.

Transferring raw materials to work in process

Description	Item	Amount
Raw materials on hand to start the period	Beginning Inventory of raw materials	10 000
Purchases of raw materials during the period	+ Cost of raw materials purchased	+ 40 000
The pool of raw materials available for use during the period	= Raw materials available for use	= $50 000
Raw materials on hand at the end of the period	– Ending inventory of raw materials	– 5 000
The amount of raw materials used in production (and moved to work in process)	= Raw materials used in production	= $45 000

Raw materials		Work in process	
$10 000	=$45 000		
+ 40 000		$45 000	
–$ 5 000			

The journal entry to record the transfer of raw materials from raw materials inventory to WIP inventory is:

Work in Process Inventory	45 000	
Raw Materials Inventory		45 000

As direct labour costs of $65 000 are incurred (factory workers work on the cabinets), the cost of the workers is added to the raw material cost in the WIP inventory account. Likewise, as manufacturing overhead costs ($85 000 of machine costs, rent, depreciation, utilities, indirect materials and so forth) are incurred, they are added to the WIP account. As long as each set of cabinets remains in the factory, the costs associated with them are recorded in the WIP account.

The journal entry to record the incurrence of direct labour costs is:

Work in Process Inventory	65 000	
Salaries and Wages Payable (or Cash)		65 000

The journal entry to record the incurrence of manufacturing overhead costs is:

Work in Process Inventory	85 000	
Accounts Payable (or Cash)		85 000

Note that as the actual manufacturing overhead costs are incurred, they are entered directly into the WIP account with corresponding credits to accounts payable or cash. This system of product costing using the actual overhead costs incurred is called **actual costing**. For a number of reasons discussed in Chapter 4, most companies use a system of product costing called **normal costing**, in which estimated or predetermined overhead rates are used to apply overhead to the WIP account.

❋ actual costing
A product costing system in which actual overhead costs are entered directly into work in process.

❋ normal costing
A product costing system in which estimated or predetermined overhead rates are used to apply overhead to work in process.

If there is no beginning inventory of work in process and everything that is started in 2011 is finished (there is no ending inventory of WIP), the cost of goods manufactured is simply the sum of raw materials used, direct labour and manufacturing overhead. When beginning or ending inventories exist, the cost of goods manufactured must be adjusted accordingly. At the beginning of 2011, Northern Territory Lights had $15000 of unfinished cabinets (started in 2010) in the factory. These cabinets were completed in early 2011. However, the company got even further behind in 2011, resulting in $20000 of cabinets being partially finished at the end of the year. Therefore, the cost of goods (cabinets) manufactured in 2011 and transferred to finished goods was $190000.

The calculation of cost of goods manufactured

Description	Item	Amount
Work in process on hand at the beginning of the period	Beginning inventory of WIP	$ 15 000
The amount of raw materials used in production	+ Raw materials used	+ 45 000
The amount of direct labour cost incurred	+ Direct labour	+ 65 000
The amount of manufacturing overhead incurred	+ Manufacturing overhead	+ 85 000
Work in process at the end of the period	– Ending inventory of WIP	– 20 000
The cost of goods manufactured during the period	= Cost of goods manufactured	=$190 000

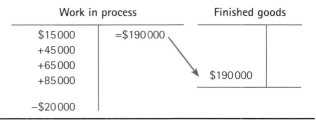

Work in process		Finished goods	
$15 000	=$190 000		
+45 000			
+65 000		$190 000	
+85 000			
–$20 000			

The journal entry to record the transfer of finished goods from WIP to finished goods inventory is:

Finished Goods Inventory	190 000	
Work in Process Inventory		190 000

When a cabinet is sold, the accumulated costs in the finished goods inventory account are moved to the cost of goods sold account. If there is no beginning inventory of finished goods, and all the goods finished in the current year are sold (there is no ending inventory), the cost of goods sold is equal to the cost of goods manufactured. However, when beginning and ending inventories exist, the cost of goods sold must be adjusted accordingly. Northern Territory Lights had one order (costing $30 000) that was not delivered to customers by the end of 2010. Likewise, at the end of 2011, the company had $5000 of cabinets that were finished but not sold. Therefore, the cost of goods (cabinets) sold during 2011 was $215 000.

The calculation of cost of goods sold

Description	Item	Amount
Finished goods on hand at the beginning of the period	Beginning inventory of finished goods	$ 30 000
The cost of goods manufactured during the period	+ Cost of goods manufactured	+ 190 000
Finished goods on hand at the end of the period	– Ending inventory of finished goods	–$ 5 000
The cost of goods sold during the period	= Cost of goods sold	=$215 000

Finished goods		Cost of goods sold	
$30 000	= $215 000		
+190 000		$215 000	
–$ 5 000			

The journal entry to record the cost of goods sold and the transfer of goods out of finished goods inventory as the product is sold is:

Cost of Goods Sold	215 000	
Finished Goods Inventory		215 000

In summary, the flow of costs from the raw materials storeroom to WIP inventory, from WIP inventory to finished goods inventory and from finished goods inventory to cost of goods sold is accounted for as shown in Exhibit 2.5.

A schedule of cost of goods manufactured and a schedule of cost of goods sold for Northern Territory Lights Custom Cabinets is presented in Exhibit 2.6.

Assuming that Northern Territory Lights had sales of $500 000 and selling and administrative expenses of $175 000, the company's 2011 income statement is presented in Exhibit 2.7.

Cost flows in a manufacturing company – JIT environment

How do cost flows differ in a manufacturing company utilising JIT? Remember, in a JIT environment, the physical flow of goods is streamlined by the use of manufacturing cells that largely eliminate inventories of raw materials, WIP and finished goods. Cost flows are streamlined as well. Direct materials, direct labour and overhead costs can

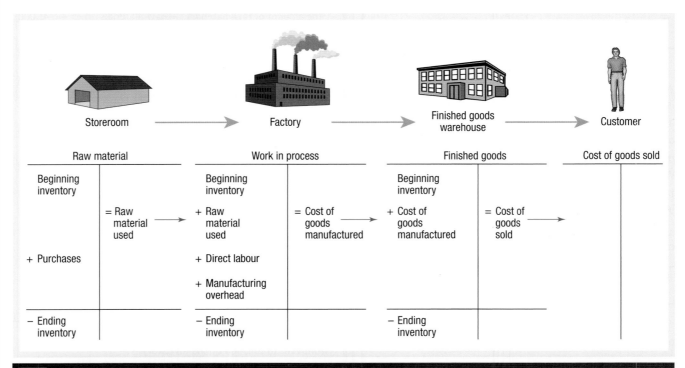

EXHIBIT 2.5 Cost flows in Northern Territory Lights Custom Cabinets

Northern Territory Lights Custom Cabinets schedule of cost of goods manufactured for the year ended 31 December 2011

Beginning raw materials	$10 000	
Add: Raw materials purchased	40 000	
Raw materials available	$50 000	
Deduct: Ending raw materials	5 000	
Raw materials used in production		$ 45 000
Add: Direct labour		65 000
Add: Manufacturing overhead		85 000
Total manufacturing costs		$195 000
Add: Beginning work in process		15 000
		$210 000
Deduct: Ending work in process		20 000
Cost of goods manufactured		$190 000

Northern Territory Lights Custom Cabinets schedule of cost of goods sold for the year ended 31 December 2011

Beginning finished goods inventory	$ 30 000
Add: Cost of goods manufactured	190 000
Goods available for sale	$220 000
Deduct: Ending finished goods inventory	5 000
Cost of goods sold	$215 000

EXHIBIT 2.6 Schedule of cost of goods manufactured and schedule of cost of goods sold for a manufacturing company

Northern Territory Lights Custom Cabinets income statement for the year ended 31 December 2011

Sales		$500 000
Cost of goods sold:		
Beginning finished goods inventory	$ 30 000	
Add: Cost of goods manufactured	190 000	
Goods available for sale	$220 000	
Deduct: Ending finished goods inventory	5 000	215 000
Gross margin		$285 000
Less: Selling and administrative expense		175 000
Net operating income		$110 000

EXHIBIT 2.7 Income statement for a manufacturing company

essentially be accumulated directly in a cost of goods sold account. Because raw materials are immediately put into production when purchased, there is no need to record their purchase in a separate raw materials inventory account. Likewise, because all goods are typically finished and shipped out immediately to customers, there is no reason to keep track of WIP or finished goods inventories.

The calculation of cost of goods sold – JIT environment

Description	Item	Amount
The amount of raw materials purchased and used in production	Raw materials purchased and used	$ 50 000
The amount of direct labour costs incurred	+ Direct labour	+ 65 000
The amount of overhead cost incurred	+ Manufacturing overhead	+ 85 000
The cost of goods sold during the period	= Cost of goods sold	=$200 000

Merchandising companies and the cost of products

Wholesalers and retailers purchase merchandise in finished form from other companies. With the exception of packaging and other minor changes, they simply offer the products for resale to other companies (wholesalers) or to the ultimate consumer (retailers). Therefore, the product cost of a wholesaler or retailer is simply the purchase price of the merchandise the wholesaler or retailer sells.

Because merchandising companies simply purchase goods for resale, the flow of costs in a retail or wholesale establishment is fairly simple. On the balance sheet, merchandising companies use a single account for inventory, called merchandise inventory. The costs incurred in inventory are simply the costs to purchase the inventory.

How are the costs incurred in purchasing inventory for resale expensed? You may recall from financial accounting that the principle of matching revenue from sales with the costs associated with that revenue means that the cost of purchasing merchandise is expensed as cost of goods sold as the merchandise is sold. However, the cost of goods sold is not necessarily equal to the cost of merchandise purchased during the period. If merchandise is purchased and not sold or if merchandise that was purchased in another period is sold in the current period, cost of goods sold must be adjusted accordingly.

In the following example, Cheryl's Bike Shop begins 2011 with a beginning inventory of bikes and parts of $15 000. During the year, the company purchases $63 000 of merchandise and has merchandise available for sale of $78 000. At the end of 2011, $18 000 of merchandise inventory remains on hand, resulting in $60 000 of cost of goods sold. The company's Schedule of Cost of Goods Sold is shown in Exhibit 2.8.

With sales of $175 000 and selling and administrative expenses totalling $40 000, the income statement is shown in Exhibit 2.9.

Cheryl's Bike Shop schedule of cost of goods sold for the year ended 31 December 2011

Beginning merchandise inventory	$15 000
Add: Purchases	63 000
Goods available for sale	$78 000
Deduct: Ending merchandise inventory	18 000
Cost of goods sold	$60 000

Source: Tatuasha/Shutterstock

The calculation of cost of goods sold for a merchandising company

Description	Item	Amount
Merchandise on hand to start the period	Beginning inventory	$15 000
Acquisitions of merchandise during the period	+ Cost of goods purchased	+ 63 000
The pool of merchandise available for sale during the period	= Cost of goods available for sale	= 78 000
Merchandise on hand at the end of the period	− Ending inventory	− 18 000
The expense recognised on the income statement	= Cost of goods sold	=$60 000

EXHIBIT 2.8 Schedule of cost of goods sold for a merchandising company

Cheryl's Bike Shop income statement for the year ended 31 December 2011

Sales		$175 000
Cost of goods sold:		
Beginning merchandise inventory	$15 000	
Add: Purchases	63 000	
Goods available for sale	$78 000	
Deduct: Ending merchandise inventory	18 000	60 000
Gross margin		$115 000
Less: Selling and administrative expense		40 000
Net operating income		$ 75 000

EXHIBIT 2.9 Income statement for a merchandising company

Service companies and the cost of services

Many similarities exist between the costing of products in a manufacturing company and the costing of services. Rather than costing products that are manufactured and sold, service providers must calculate the costs associated with the revenue earned by the company from selling its services. Income statements of service providers typically refer to the 'cost of services' as the 'cost of revenue'. Like product costs, the cost of services includes three components: direct materials, direct labour and overhead. However, the proportions of each may vary dramatically. Service companies typically have few material costs and large amounts of labour and overhead.

Although service companies have both direct and indirect costs, they generally have larger proportions of indirect costs. For example:

- In a movie studio, costumes and props are direct materials and the salaries of actors and directors are direct labour. Overhead would include the costs of the studio itself and all the recording and production equipment. Camera operators and other support people would more than likely be classified as indirect labour because they would likely work on more than one film at a time.
- In a CPA firm, material costs would likely be very small. Although paper and other materials are used in the preparation of tax returns, the materials would likely be considered an indirect cost and classified as overhead. On the other hand, direct labour costs for a CPA firm would be very large.
- In a hospital, although the costs of specific drugs and special tests or X-rays can be traced to a specific patient, the costs of operating rooms and equipment and the salaries of administrators, discharge personnel, orderlies and maintenance workers would all be indirect.

While service companies typically have little need for raw materials and finished goods inventory accounts, work in process (WIP) accounts are commonly used on projects that were incomplete at month end, such as audits by CPA firms, lengthy legal cases by law firms and consulting engagements that are long term.

Product costs and period costs

As previously discussed, manufacturing costs or product costs attach to products as they go through the manufacturing process. Until the sale of the product, the costs of manufacturing are included in one of three inventory accounts: raw materials, work in process and finished goods. These inventory accounts appear on the balance sheet along with other assets and liabilities. Only when a product is sold are manufacturing costs expensed as cost of goods sold on the income statement. On the other hand, non-manufacturing costs or period costs are expensed immediately on the income statement in the period in which they are incurred (see Exhibit 2.10).

For external financial reporting purposes, information on the cost of goods sold (frequently called the cost of sales) and the amount of inventory owned by a company is provided in financial statements and included in the company's annual report.

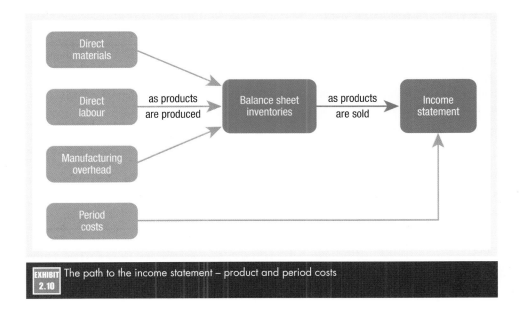

EXHIBIT 2.10 The path to the income statement – product and period costs

Exercises

1 JIT and lean production LO2

Just-in-time and lean production systems are widely viewed as improving the competitive position of companies. Complete the following sentences describing the effects of JIT and lean production using the words *increase(s)* or *decrease(s)*.

a Storage and other inventory carrying costs _____.
b The time required to make products typically _____.
c Customer satisfaction _____.
d The cost of raw materials may _____.
e Product quality improves because the number of defective units _____.
f Production flexibility _____ because employees are highly trained.
g The number of suppliers often _____ because companies must have highly reliable suppliers that can deliver raw materials whenever needed.

2 Features of lean production LO2

The following sentences describe key features of a lean production system. Indicate whether the statements are true or false.

a Lean production is focused on eliminating waste associated with holding more inventory than required.
b Lean production is focused on having extra inventory on hand in case customer demand rises unexpectedly.
c Lean production is focused on exceeding a customer's needs.
d Lean production is focused on minimising the amount of movement of products and people.
e Lean production is focused on reducing waiting time.

3 Product costs LO3

The Perfect Smile manufactures extra-whitening toothpaste. During the year the company had the following costs:

Direct materials used	$41000
Direct labour	28000
Factory rent	12000
Factory depreciation	9000
Office depreciation	4050
Selling expenses	3500
Administrative expenses	50000

The Perfect Smile produced 45000 units during the year.

Required
a Calculate the total manufacturing costs for the year.
b Calculate the product cost on a per-unit basis.

4 Product costs LO3

Berry Brothers is a new company that manufactures desks. In its first month of operation it began and completed 500 desks. The following production information has been provided:

Direct material cost per unit	$18
Indirect labour costs	400
Indirect material costs	220
Marketing expenses	750
Cost per direct labour hour	15
Factory rent	2000
Administrative expenses	1600
Direct labour per unit	4 hours

Required
a Calculate the cost of direct labour for one desk.
b Calculate the total overhead costs for the first month of production.
c Calculate the total manufacturing costs for the first month of production.

5 Types of manufacturing costs LO3

The following costs are manufacturing costs for a producer of personal computers.
a Wages of employees who conduct quality testing
b Purchase cost of processor chips included in the manufactured computers
c Wages paid to maintenance workers
d Property taxes paid for the manufacturing facility
e Salaries paid to a staff nurse who provides care for manufacturing employees
f Wages paid to assembly line employees
g Small screws and fasteners.

Required
Indicate whether each of the above costs is direct material (DM), direct labour (DL), indirect material (IM), indirect labour (IL) or another manufacturing overhead cost (MOH).

6 Cost flows: Raw materials used LO4

At the beginning of the month, AGN Manufacturing had the following information available for the month of September:

	Beginning	Ending
Raw materials inventory	$25000	$32000
Work in process inventory	60000	85000
Finished goods inventory	10000	2000

During the month of September, the company purchased $120000 of raw materials. How much raw material was used in September?

7 Cost flows: Raw materials used LO4

On 1 January 2014, AGN Manufacturing had the following information available for the upcoming month:

	Beginning	Ending
Raw materials inventory	$23000	$27000
Work in process inventory	65000	80000
Finished goods inventory	9000	3000

During January, the company used $80000 of raw materials. How much raw material was purchased in the month?

8 Cost of goods manufactured LO4

Candy's Chocolate Shoppe had the following information available for the month of September:

	Beginning	Ending
Raw materials inventory	$40000	$20000
Work in process inventory	25000	15000
Finished goods inventory	10000	20000
Raw materials purchased		75000
Direct labour (3000 hrs @ $10)		75000
Overhead		50000

Required
Calculate the cost of goods manufactured for the month.

9 Cost of goods sold LO4

Memories Inc., which produces specialty picture frames, had the following summary cost information:

Direct materials used	$24000
Direct labour	22000
Factory rent	6000
Equipment depreciation	7500
Marketing expense	15000
Administrative expense	13000
Shipping charges	5000
Number of units produced	25000

Required
Calculate the cost of goods sold if 24000 units are sold.

10 Calculation of net income LO5

You are the president of Our Bakery. Your new accountant, who recently graduated from a local university, presented you with the following income statement for the month of January:

Sales revenues	$660 000
Less: Total January expenses	595 000
Net income	$ 65 000

By talking to the production departments, you learn that 60 000 units were produced in January at a total cost of $420 000. The sales department notes that 55 000 units were sold for $11 each. Monthly administrative and marketing expenses totalled $75 000.

Required
Based on the above information, calculate the correct amount of net income for January.

11 Calculation of net income LO5

Classic Drinks manufactures portable stainless steel water bottles adorned with university logos, sold to students during graduations. During the first quarter of the year, the company had the following costs:

Direct materials used	$56 000
Direct labour	38 000
Factory rent	24 000
Factory equipment depreciation	10 000
Office equipment depreciation	1 400
Marketing expenses	5 500
Administrative expenses	12 000

The company began the year with no work in process and no finished goods inventory. Although 8000 units were started and finished during the quarter, just 5300 were sold, for an average price of $25 each.

12 Calculation of net income LO5

Break 'Em Plates manufactures plates for breaking in wedding celebrations. In the first month of the year, the following costs were incurred:

Direct materials used	$40 000
Direct labour	20 000
Factory rent	25 000
Factory equipment depreciation	10 000
Sales manager car depreciation	5 000
Marketing expenses	6 000
Administrative expenses	10 000

The company began the year with no work in process and no finished goods inventory. Although 9000 units were started and finished during the month, just 6000 were sold, for an average price of $30 each.

Required
Calculate Break' Em Plates' net income for the first quarter.

Problems

13 Cost of goods manufactured, cost of goods sold and impact on financial statements LO3, 4, 5

The accounting information system of Bosch Inc. reported the following cost and inventory data for the year.

Costs incurred		
Raw materials purchased	$125 000	
Direct labour		75 000
Indirect labour		40 000
Equipment maintenance	10 000	
Insurance on factory	12 000	
Rent on factory		30 000
Equipment depreciation	20 000	
Factory supplies		11 000
Advertising expenses	15 000	
Selling and administrative expenses	21 000	

Inventories	Beginning balance	Ending balance
Raw materials	$10 000	$17 000
Work in process	20 000	31 000
Finished goods	30 000	25 000

Required
a Calculate the cost of goods manufactured.
b Calculate the cost of goods sold.
c List the costs not included in the calculations of cost of goods manufactured and cost of goods sold, and discuss why you excluded them from those calculations.
d If raw materials and work in process inventories had decreased during the year, would the financial statements be different? How?

14 Direct vs indirect costs, impact on financial statements LO3, 4, 5

Madam Oak's Furniture manufactures wooden rocking chairs. Madam Oak's Furniture purchased the following materials in June:
- 1500 springs (part of the rocking mechanism) at a cost of $15 000; each chair uses 2 springs
- Glue at a cost of $1500 (enough to manufacture 500 chairs)
- Stain at a cost of $500 (enough to manufacture 500 chairs)
- Wood at a cost of $5000 (enough to build 1000 chair frames).
Madam Oak's Furniture produced 500 chairs during June and had no beginning balances in raw materials, work in process or finished goods inventories.

Required
a Which of Madam Oak's material costs would likely be

classified as direct materials? Which as indirect materials?

b If Madam Oak's Furniture completed only 400 of the 500 chairs on which production was started, what is the finished goods inventory account balance at the end of June?

c If 380 of the finished chairs were sold, what would be the cost of goods sold?

d What is the work in process inventory account balance at the end of June?

15 Basic cost flows, income statement
LO4, 5

Business managers frequently operate in a world where data are not readily available. Imagine a situation in which a company experiences a catastrophic event (for example, a hurricane, flood, or fire) and must reconstruct its accounting data. Consider the following independent situations in which selected data are missing:

	Company 1	Company 2
Direct materials used	$ 9000	$19000
Direct labour	4000	14000
Manufacturing overhead	11000	?
Total manufacturing costs	$?	35000
Beginning work in process	?	11000
Ending work in process	6000	13500
Cost of goods manufactured	$21000	$?
Sales	$35000	$50000
Beginning finished goods inventory	$ 7000	$?
Cost of goods manufactured	?	?
Goods available for sale	$?	$?
Ending finished goods inventory	10000	14000
Cost of goods sold	$?	$25000
Gross margin	$?	$?
Selling and administrative expenses	7000	?
Net income	$?	$15500

Required

a Supply the missing data for each independent situation.

b Prepare an income statement for each independent situation.

16 Basic Cost Flows LO4, 5

Home Cabinets manufactures and sells custom ordered kitchen and bathroom cabinets. The company sells primarily to building contractors but occasionally deals directly with homeowners. Following is a summary of inventory and cost information for the year:

	Beginning balance	Ending balance
Raw materials inventory	$10000	$15000
Work in process inventory	15000	12000
Finished-goods inventory	30000	32000

During the year, raw material purchases totalled $350000. Home Cabinets incurred $200000 in direct labour costs in the factory

and $175000 in manufacturing overhead for the year.

Required

a Calculate the amount of direct materials transferred to work in process during the year.

b Calculate total manufacturing costs for the year.

c Calculate the total cost of goods manufactured for the year.

d Calculate the cost of goods sold for the year.

Cases

17 Direct vs indirect costs, impact on financial statements LO3, 4, 5

Please read The Daily Grind café appendix at the back of this textbook and identify the materials, labour and overhead costs in this case. How might an understanding of these costs aid your management of the business?

18 Cost of goods manufactured, cost of goods sold and impact on financial statements LO3, 4, 5

Tyler Manufacturing provides you with the following information:

Opening Inventories as at 1 June 2014 for Work in Process Inventory was $9000, and Opening Finished Goods inventory was $11000.

During June, the following transactions occurred:

a Purchases of materials $17000

b Materials used:
   Direct $15000
   Indirect $5000 $20000

c Factory Payroll Incurred
   Direct labour – 6000 hours at $15 per hour $90000
   Indirect labour $5400

d Other factory overhead incurred during June amounted to $16200

e Overhead is applied to production at the rate of $5.00 per direct labour hour

f The closing balances of inventory accounts were as follows:
   Work in Process $13000
   Finished Goods $22000

g All goods are sold at a mark-up on cost of 60 per cent.

Required

Prepare a Manufacturing Statement, Cost of Goods Sold Statement and Income Statement for the month of June.

REVIEW

ACCT puts a multitude of study aids at your fingertips. After reading the chapters, check out these resources for further help:

- **Chapter Review cards,** found in the back of your book, include all learning outcomes, definitions and self-assessment activities for each chapter.

- **Online printable flash cards** give you additional ways to check your comprehension of key marketing concepts.

Other great ways to help you study include **games, podcasts, videos** and **online quizzes.**

You can find it all at: http://login.cengagebrain.com/

Learning objectives:

After studying the material in this chapter, you should be able to:

1. Describe the nature and behaviour of fixed and variable costs.
2. Define and analyse mixed costs using regression analysis and the high/low method.
3. Illustrate the impact of income taxes on costs and decision making.
4. Identify the difference between variable costing and absorption costing.
5. Identify the impact on the income statement of variable costing and absorption costing.
6. Recognise the benefits of using variable costing for decision making.

COST BEHAVIOUR

c **3**

How can costs 'behave'? The very term *cost behaviour* often invokes confusion, as the term *behaviour* derives its meaning from the actions of living entities, and not accounting terminology such as 'costs'! In investigating cost behaviour, we seek to explain how costs change (behave) as activity in organisations change. As production volume increases or decreases, some costs may increase or decrease while others might not. Generally, most costs behave in predictable ways, however complex the predictability might be to chart. This concept of predictable **cost behaviour** based on volume is very important to the effective use of accounting information for managerial decision making.

Source: Ulrich Baumgarten/Getty Images

Understanding how costs behave with changes in production is crucial for managers of an organisation.

LEARNING OBJECTIVE **1** >>

Fixed and variable costs

Fixed costs are costs that remain the same irrespective of production volume. Consequently, fixed cost per unit always decreases when production volume increases. Facility-level costs such as rent, depreciation of a factory building, the salary of a plant manager, insurance and property taxes are likely to be fixed costs.

Rent is an often-used example for fixed costs. If the cost to rent a factory building is $10 000 per year, the rent cost per unit of product will be $2.00 if 5000 units are produced ($10 000 ÷ 5000 units), and $4 per unit if 2500 units are produced ($10 000 ÷ 2500). If production volume increases to 7500 units, the cost per unit decreases to $1.33 ($10 000 ÷ 7500). Why does the cost per unit decrease as more units are produced? Because the total rent remains $10 000 per year (see Exhibit 3.1).

On the other hand, **variable costs** vary in *direct proportion* to changes in production volume. As a result, they are constant when expressed as per unit amounts. As production increases, variable costs increase in direct proportion to the change in volume; as production decreases, variable costs decrease in direct proportion to the change in

volume. Examples include direct material, direct labour (if paid per unit of output) and other unit-level costs, such as factory supplies, energy costs to run factory machinery and so on.

Consider the behaviour of direct material costs as production increases and decreases. If the production of a standard classroom desk requires $20 of direct materials (wood, hardware and so on), the total direct material costs incurred will increase or decrease proportionately with increases and decreases in production volume. If 5000 desks are produced, the total direct material cost will be $100 000 (5000 × $20). If production volume is increased to 7500 units (a 50 per cent increase), direct material costs will also increase 50 per cent to $150 000 (7500 × $20). The cost per unit is still $20. Likewise, if production volume decreases to 2500 desks, direct material costs decrease by 50 per cent to $50 000. Once again, the cost per unit remains $20 (see Exhibit 3.2).

A trend in manufacturing is to automate, to replace direct factory labour with robotics and other automated machinery and equipment. This trend has the effect of increasing fixed costs (depreciation) and decreasing variable costs (direct labour). Although there are many advantages to automation, the impact of automation on the employee workforce and on

* **cost behaviour**
How costs react to changes in production volume or other levels of activity.

* **fixed costs**
Costs that remain the same in total when production volume increases or decreases but vary per unit.

* **variable costs**
Costs that stay the same per unit but change in total as production volume increases or decreases.

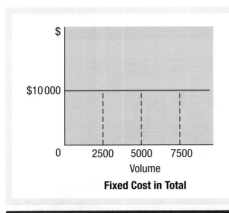
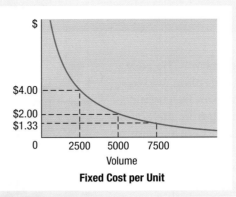

Fixed Cost in Total

Fixed Cost per Unit

EXHIBIT 3.1 The behaviour of fixed costs

Could we have made cars for less?

The exiting of the five major players in the Australian car manufacturing industry signals the possible lower competitiveness of manufacturing in Australia, relative to the global market. An argument often anecdotally put forward is the high cost of labour in advanced economies such as Australia, making cost control more difficult to enact and manage relative to competitors globally. Below is an excerpt from an article in www.macrobusiness.com.au, highlighting the high rate of growth in unit labour costs (ULC) in Australia, relative to other countries. This data might partially explain why manufacturing in Australia struggles to keep pace with that of other countries, and is consequently declining.

ULCs are a commonly used – albeit partial – measure of cost competitiveness. The OECD publishes these data for a number of member nations, calculated as the ratio of total labour costs to real output. These data show an increase in Australia's ULC measure (in domestic currency terms) relative to most of

Australia's OECD trading partners over the past decade or so. This has exacerbated the effect of the appreciation of Australia's nominal effective exchange rate on Australia's overall international competitiveness.

The decline in Australia's ULC-based measure of cost competitiveness has been even more pronounced for the manufacturing sector.

Source: 'Australia's huge manufacturing labour costs', by Leith van Onselen from Macro Business. Copyright © 2014 by Leith van Onselen. Used by permission. http://www.macrobusiness.com.au/2014/01/australias-huge-manufacturing-labour-costs/

The above excerpt highlights that among other factors, cost behaviour can explain why global players are exiting the Australian manufacturing environment. An understanding of the level and movements in these costs, and their implications for the cost per unit of a product or service, and its implications for pricing are key to helping organisations identify solutions to address this loss of competitiveness.

Making it real

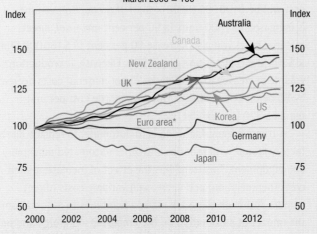

Unit Labour Costs
March 2000 = 100

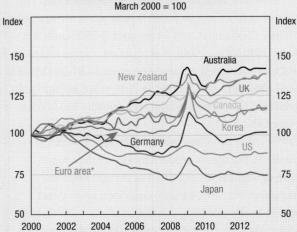

Manufacturing sector unit labour costs
March 2000 = 100

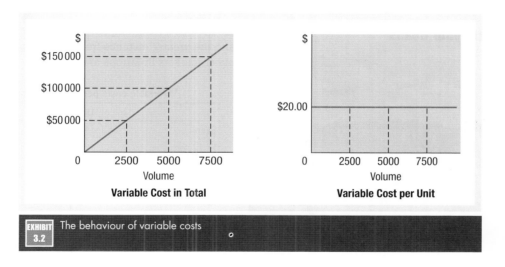

EXHIBIT 3.2 The behaviour of variable costs

day-to-day decisions made by managers must not be ignored.

When a cost varies in direct proportion to changes in volume, we say there is a linear (straight-line) relationship between cost and volume. However, in reality, costs may behave in a curvilinear fashion. Average costs or cost per unit may increase or decrease as production increases. For example, utility costs per kilowatt-hour may decrease at higher levels of electricity use (and production). Also, you might buy in bulk and save per unit. To use a simple example; you might pay $2 for 1 mango, or $5 for 3 mangoes ($1.67 per mango). Shops give you the incentive to buy greater quantities by reducing the cost per unit when greater quantities are bought. Managerial accountants typically get around this problem by assuming that the relationship between cost and volume is linear within a *relevant range* of production. In other words, the cost per unit is assumed to remain constant over the relevant range. The **relevant range** is the normal range of production that can be expected for a particular product and company. The relevant range can also be viewed as the volume of production for which the fixed cost stays the same, and the variable rate per unit remains unchanged. As you can see in Exhibit 3.3, within this narrower range of production, a curvilinear cost can be approximated by a linear relationship between the cost and volume.

Step costs

Classification of costs is not always a simple process. Some costs vary but only with relatively large changes in production volume. Batch-level costs related to transporting finished goods may vary with the number of batches of product produced but not with every unit of product. For example, at the conclusion of a production batch of 10 000 soft drink cans, we might place them in cartons and transport them to a warehouse for distribution. You only conduct an additional transporting activity when 10 000 cans are completed. This cost is therefore related to each 'batch' of 10 000 cans produced. Product-level costs associated with quality control inspections may also vary when new products are introduced. Costs like these are sometimes referred to as **step costs**. In practice, step costs may look like and be treated as either variable costs or fixed costs. Although step costs are technically not fixed costs, they may be treated as such if they remain constant within a relatively wide range of production. Consider the costs of cleaning services within a company. As long as production is below 7500 desks, the company will hire one cleaner with salary and fringe benefits totalling $25 000. The cost is fixed as long as production remains below 7500 units. But if desk production exceeds 7500, which increases the amount of waste and cleanup needed, it may be necessary to hire a second cleaner at a

* **relevant range**
The normal range of production that can be expected for a particular product and company.

* **step costs**
Costs that vary with activity in steps and may look like and be treated as either variable costs or fixed costs; step costs are technically not fixed costs but may be treated as such if they remain constant within a relevant range of production.

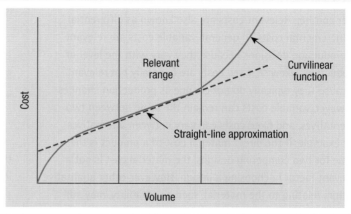

EXHIBIT 3.3 Curvilinear costs and the relevant range

It pays to count your beans

Source: Elena Elisseeva/Shutterstock

When the cost of raw materials increase, downstream products that use these materials inevitably become more expensive.

Due to the higher costs of fertiliser and chemicals, the variable costs of growing soybeans in Brazil are 68 per cent higher than the variable costs of growing soybeans in the US heartland. However, fixed costs in Brazil are 90 per cent lower than in the United States, primarily as a result of lower costs of leasing land and lower costs of and less reliance on machinery and equipment. While Brazil's soybean production now rivals that of the United States, much of the cost savings enjoyed by Brazil's soybean farmers is offset by the additional transportation and shipping costs

incurred as a result of poor roads and the greater distance from major markets in Europe and China.

Making it real

Variable costs per acre of soybeans	US Heartland	Brazil
Seed	$19.77	$ 11.23
Fertiliser	8.22	44.95
Chemicals	27.31	39.97
Machinery	20.19	18.22
Labour	1.29	5.58
Other	1.81	12.11
Total variable costs	$78.59	$132.06

Fixed costs per acre of soybeans		
Equipment depreciation	$ 47.99	$ 8.97
Land costs (lease costs)	87.96	5.84
Taxes and insurance	6.97	0.55
Farm overhead	13.40	0.00
Total fixed costs	$156.32	$15.36
Average yield per acre (in bushels)	46.00	41.65
Variable costs per bushel	$ 1.71	$ 3.17
Fixed costs per bushel	3.40	0.37
Total costs per bushel	$ 5.11	$ 3.54

Source: Kevin Diaz, 'Who feeds the world?', *The Raleigh News and Observer* (Raleigh, NC), 11 April 2004: 19A

---

cost of another $25 000. However, within a relevant range of production between 7501 and 15 000 units, the cost is essentially fixed ($50 000).

Relevant costs and cost behaviour

As mentioned in Chapter 1, relevant costs are those that are avoidable or can be eliminated by choosing one alternative over another. Relevant costs are also known as differential or incremental costs. In general, variable costs are relevant in production decisions because they vary with the level of production. Likewise, fixed costs are generally not relevant because they typically do not change as production changes. However, variable costs can remain the same between two alternatives, and fixed costs can vary between alternatives. For example, if the direct material cost of a product is the same for two competing designs, the material cost is not a relevant factor in choosing a design. However, other qualitative factors relating to the material, such as durability, may still be relevant. Likewise, fixed costs can be relevant if they vary between alternatives. Consider rent paid for a facility to store inventory. Although the rent is a fixed cost, it is relevant to

a decision to reduce inventory storage costs through just-in-time production techniques if the cost of the rent can be avoided (by subleasing the space, for example) by choosing one alternative over another. Additionally, some decisions may cause companies to produce outside their normal 'relevant range', causing fixed costs to change, which makes them relevant costs. The key when considering relevant costs is the idea of a *difference*. If a cost is different for multiple choices, it is a relevant cost for decision making, be it fixed or variable.

The cost equation

Expressing the link between costs and production volume as an algebraic equation is useful. The equation for a straight line is:

$$y = a + bx$$

The a in the equation is the point where the line intersects the vertical (y) axis and b is the slope of the line. In Exhibit 3.4, if y = total direct material costs and x = units produced, $y = \$0 + \$20x$. The y intercept is zero and the slope of the line is 20. For every one-unit increase (decrease) in production (x), direct material costs increase (decrease) by $20. You can see that direct material costs are variable because they stay

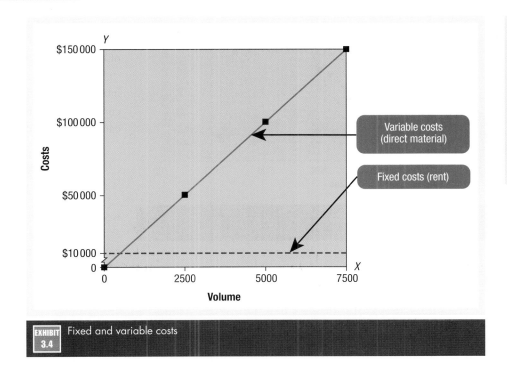

Exhibit shows a coordinate graph with Y-axis labeled "Costs" (values $10 000, $50 000, $100 000, $150 000) and X-axis labeled "Volume" (values 0, 2500, 5000, 7500). A rising line is labeled "Variable costs (direct material)" and a horizontal dashed line at $10 000 is labeled "Fixed costs (rent)".

EXHIBIT 3.4	Fixed and variable costs

the same on a per unit basis but increase in total as production increases. Likewise, we can express the fixed-cost line as an equation. If y = rent cost and x = units produced, y = $10 000 + 0x$. In this case, the y intercept is $10 000 and the slope is zero. In other words, fixed costs are $10 000 at any level of production within the relevant range.

LEARNING OBJECTIVE 2 >>

e-Lecture

apply this!

Mixed costs

Mixed costs exhibit characteristics of both fixed and variable costs. Mixed costs increase at a constant rate, characterising elements of variable costs, but do not vary in proportion with production volumes, and their costs per unit decrease as more units are produced, revealing characteristics of fixed costs. Consequently, it is difficult to predict the behaviour of a mixed cost (as production changes) unless the cost is first separated into its fixed and variable components. A good example of a mixed cost is the overhead costs of Adelaide Pizza Emporium (APE). APE's overhead typically has both a fixed and a variable component. For example, rent and insurance paid are fixed components of overhead, while utilities and supplies are more variable costs.

In the first seven weeks of operations, APE incurs the following overhead costs:

Week	Pizzas	Total overhead costs	Cost per unit
1 (Start-up)	0	$679	N/A
2	423	1842	$4.35
3	601	2350	3.91
4	347	1546	4.46
5	559	2250	4.03
6	398	1769	4.44
7	251	1288	5.13

Is the overhead cost a fixed, variable or mixed cost? Clearly, the cost is not fixed because it changes each week. However, is it a variable cost? Although the cost changes each week, it does not vary in direct proportion to changes in production. In addition, remember that variable costs remain constant when expressed per unit. In this case, the amount of overhead cost per pizza changes from week to week. A cost that changes in total and also changes per unit is a mixed cost. As you can see in Exhibit 3.5, a mixed cost looks somewhat like a variable cost. However, the cost does not vary in direct proportion to changes in the level of production (you can't draw a straight line through all the data points), and if a line were drawn through the data points back to the y-axis, we would still incur overhead cost at a production volume of zero. Like a fixed cost, a mixed cost has a component that is constant regardless of production volume. Even if no pizzas are produced, we must pay our fixed costs (rent, etc.).

Once we know that a cost is mixed, we are left with the task of separating the mixed cost into its fixed and variable components. How do we do this? We will now demonstrate the use of a statistical tool called regression analysis to

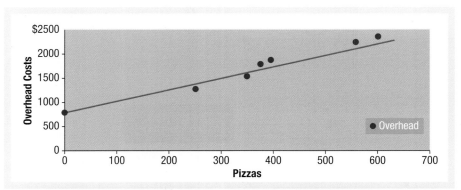

EXHIBIT
3.5   Mixed cost

Month	Pizzas	Overhead	Per pizza
1	2 100	$8 400	$4.00
2	2 600	10 100	3.88
3	2 300	8 800	3.83
4	2 450	9 250	3.78
5	2 100	8 050	3.83
6	2 175	8 200	3.77
7	1 450	6 950	4.79
8	1 200	6 750	5.63
9	1 350	7 250	5.37
10	1 750	7 300	4.17
11	1 550	7 250	4.68
12	2 050	7 950	3.88

EXHIBIT
3.6   Overhead costs per pizza

cost varies in total and on a per unit basis, it must be a mixed cost. A graph of the data is shown in Exhibit 3.7.

Mixed costs must be separated into fixed and variable cost components before their behaviour can be understood.

Regression analysis

A statistical technique used to estimate the fixed and variable components of a mixed cost is called least squares regression. **Regression analysis** uses statistical methods to fit a cost line (called a regression line) through a number of data points. Note that although the data points in our example do not lie along a straight line, regression analysis statistically finds the line that minimises the sum of the squared distances from each data point to the line (hence the name *least squares regression*). The line that is selected is therefore the line that's effectively closest to all the points identified, and therefore best represents the cost behaviour characterised by the data points. Remember that each dot (data point) is an expression of what really happened through the course of APE's operations, on a monthly basis. The line of best fit, therefore, is the line that best expresses cost behaviour based on what really happened in APE, over a period of 12 months.

✳ regression analysis
The procedure that uses statistical methods (least squares regression) to fit a cost line (called a regression line) through a number of data points.

estimate the fixed and variable components of a mixed cost.

A variety of tools can be used to estimate the fixed and variable components of a mixed cost. When we separate a mixed cost into its variable and fixed components, what we are really doing is generating the equation for a straight line, with the *y* intercept estimating the fixed cost and the slope estimating the variable cost per unit.

Continuing our example of Adelaide Pizza Emporium (APE), after the initial seven-week start-up period, the company's accountant compiles data regarding the total overhead cost and the number of pizzas produced in the next 12 months (see Exhibit 3.6). As you can see, because the overhead

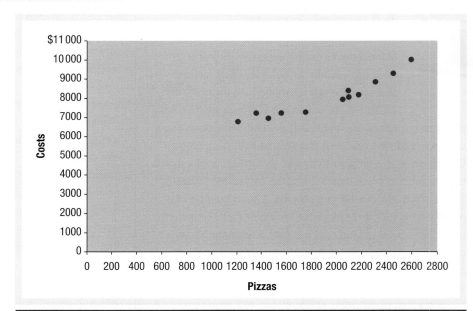

EXHIBIT
3.7   Overhead costs for Adelaide Pizza Emporium (APE)

Using a spreadsheet program to perform regression analysis

Using a spreadsheet program to estimate regression models is a relatively simple process. We are going to use Microsoft Excel in this example, but all spreadsheet programs are very similar. The first step is to enter the actual values for our mixed cost (called the **dependent variable** in regression analysis because the amount of cost is *dependent* on production) and the related volume of production (called the **independent variable** because it causes the cost of the dependent variable) into a spreadsheet using one column for each variable. Using data from Adelaide Pizza Emporium for overhead costs incurred and pizzas produced for the first 12 months of operations, we see the data shown in the Excel spreadsheet in Exhibit 3.8.

The next step in Excel (see Exhibit 3.9) is to click on the tools option from the toolbar and choose *data analysis* from the pull-down menu. From the data analysis screen, scroll down, highlight *regression* and either double-click or choose OK.

The regression screen will prompt you to choose a number of options. The first step is to input the *y* range. The *y* range will be used to identify the dependent variable (overhead costs) found in column C of your spreadsheet. You can either type in the range of cells or simply highlight the cells in the spreadsheet (be sure not to include the column heading), and click on the icon in the *y*-range box. The next step is to select the *x* range for the independent variable (volume of pizzas). Once again, you can enter the cells directly or highlight the cells in the second column of your spreadsheet.

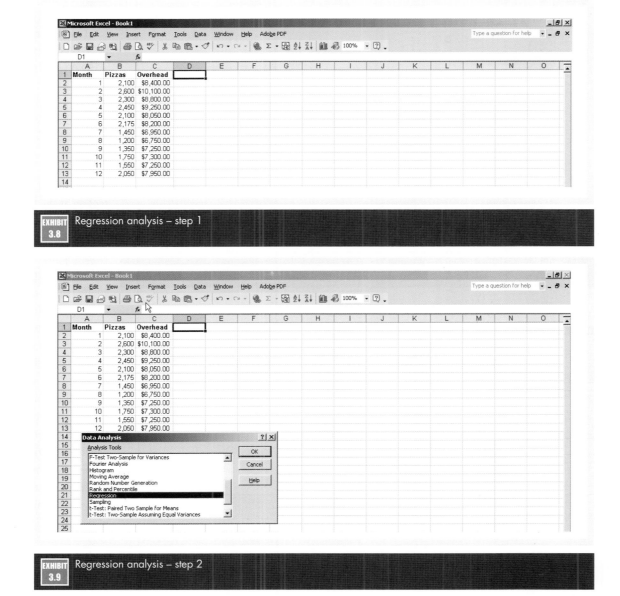

EXHIBIT 3.8 Regression analysis – step 1

EXHIBIT 3.9 Regression analysis – step 2

After inputting the appropriate *y* and *x* ranges, your Excel spreadsheet should look like the example shown in Exhibit 3.10. Click OK, and the regression model summary output appears as shown in Exhibit 3.11.

How is the summary output interpreted? First, note toward the bottom of Exhibit 3.11 that the estimated coefficient (value) of the intercept (the *y* intercept) is 3998.25 and the estimated coefficient (value) of the *x* variable (the slope) is 2.09. This means that the fixed-cost component of our mixed overhead cost is estimated to be $3998.25 and the variable-cost component is estimated to be $2.09 per pizza.

Using the least squares regression results, we can compute the regression line for overhead costs at Adelaide Pizza Emporium:

Total overhead cost	=	Fixed cost	+	(Variable cost per unit × Volume)
Total overhead cost	=	$3998.25	+	($2.09 × Volume)

Graphically, the line for the total overhead costs can be expressed as shown in the following illustration.

We can use this equation to help predict the total amount of overhead costs that will be incurred for any number of pizzas within the relevant range. The relevant range is that range of activity within which management expects to operate, or the range in which this equation is useful or meaningful. Our predictions should be limited to those activity levels within the relevant range. Based on last year's data, APE expects to produce between 1200 and 2600 pizzas each month. Next month, APE expects to produce 1750 pizzas. Based on the regression equation, APE estimates total overhead costs to be $7655.75 ($3998.25 + [$2.09 × 1750 pizzas]).

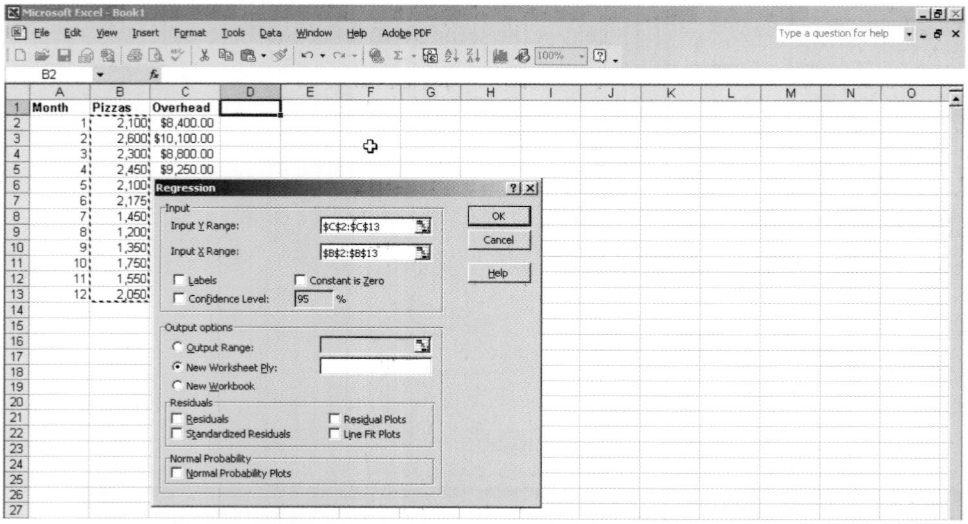

Regression statistics

The regression statistics section at the top of Exhibit 3.11 provides useful diagnostic tools. The multiple *R* (called the correlation coefficient) is a measure of the proximity of the data points to the regression line. In addition, the sign of the statistic (+ or −) tells us the direction of the correlation between the independent and dependent variables. In this case, there is a positive correlation between the number of pizzas produced and

EXHIBIT 3.10 Regression analysis – step 2 (continued)

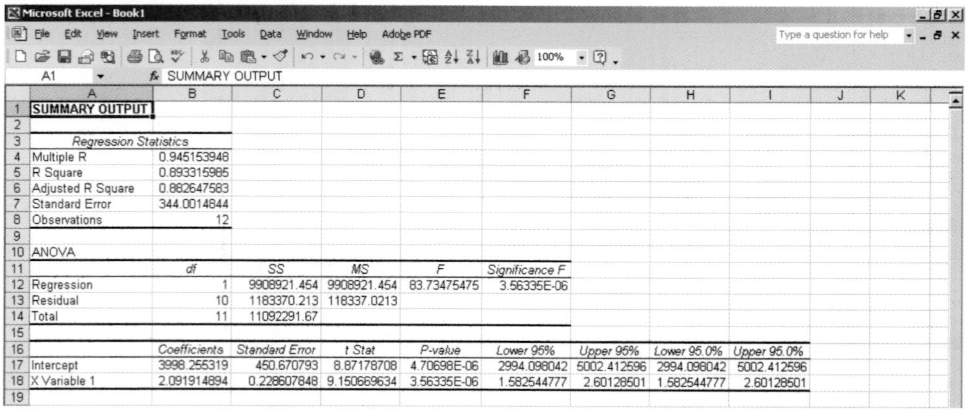

EXHIBIT 3.11 Regression analysis – summary output

the total overhead costs. The **R square** (often represented as R^2 and called the coefficient of determination) is a measure

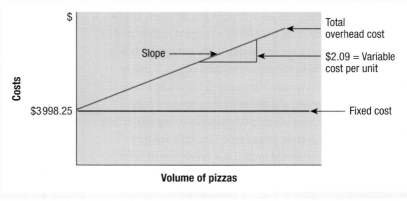

of goodness of fit (how well the regression line 'fits' the data). An R^2 of 1.0 indicates a perfect correlation between the independent and dependent variables in the regression equation; in other words, 100 per cent of the data points are on the regression line. R^2 can be interpreted as the proportion of dependent-variable variation that is explained by changes in the independent variable. In this case, the R^2 of 0.8933 indicates that over 89 per cent of the variation in overhead costs is explained by increasing or decreasing pizza production.

A low value of R^2 may indicate that the chosen independent variable is not a very reliable predictor of the dependent variable or that other independent variables may have an impact on the dependent variable. For example, outside temperature and other environmental factors might impact overhead costs incurred by APE.

The presence of outliers in the data may also result in low R^2 values. Outliers are simply extreme observations; that is, observations so far from the normal activity that they may not be representative of normal business levels (i.e. they are outside of the relevant range). Under the least squares method, a regression line may be pulled disproportionately toward the outlier and result in misleading estimates of fixed and variable costs and measures of goodness of fit.

Estimating regression results using the high/ low method

If we did not have access to a computer regression program or for some reason did not want to use this tool, we could estimate the regression equation using a simpler technique called the high/low method. The high/low method uses only two data points (related to the high and low levels of activity) and mathematically derives an equation for a straight line intersecting those two data points. Though technically inferior to regression analysis (which uses all the data points), from a practical perspective the high/low method can often provide a reasonable estimate of the regression equation.

In Exhibit 3.6, the high level of activity occurred in month 2, when 2600 pizzas were produced and $10 100 of overhead cost was incurred. The low level of activity occurred in month 8, when only 1200 pizzas were produced

and overhead costs totalled $6750. The slope of the line connecting those two points can be calculated by dividing the difference between the costs incurred at the high and low levels of activity by the difference in volume (number of pizzas at those levels). Remember, the slope of a line is calculated as the change in cost over the change in volume, in this case the difference in cost to produce pizzas over the difference in volume of pizzas made. As with the regression equation, the slope of the line is interpreted as the variable-cost component of the mixed cost:

> ### Key formula 3.1: Variable cost per unit
> $$\frac{\text{Change in cost}}{\text{Change in volume}} = \text{Variable cost per unit}$$

Inserting the data for Adelaide Pizza Emporium, the variable cost is $2.39 per unit ($10 100 − $6750) ÷ (2600 − 1200). This result compares with our regression estimate of $2.09. We then solve for the fixed-cost component by calculating the total variable cost incurred at either the high or the low level of activity and subtracting the variable costs from the total overhead cost incurred at that level. Mathematically, if

Total overhead costs =
Fixed costs + (Variable cost per unit × number of pizzas)

then

Total overhead costs − Variable costs = Fixed costs

At the high level of activity, total overhead costs are $10 100 and variable costs equal $6214 (2600 pizzas × $2.39 per pizza). Therefore, the fixed-cost component of overhead costs is estimated to be $3886 (total overhead costs of $10 100 less variable costs of $6214), and the total overhead cost is estimated to be $3886 + ($2.39 × number of pizzas produced).

Why is this equation different from the least squares regression equation? Regression is a statistical tool that fits the 'best' line through all 12 data points, whereas the high/low method mathematically derives a straight line between just two of the data points. By using the two points at the highest and lowest levels of activity, we are forcing a line between those points without regard to the remaining data points. If one or both of these points is unusual (an outlier), the result will be a cost line that is skewed and therefore may not be a good measure of the fixed and variable components of the mixed cost.

In the case of Adelaide Pizza Emporium, let's see how the high/low estimate would impact our prediction of total overhead costs next month when 1750 pizzas are produced. Using the high/low estimate of the cost equation, we would predict total overhead costs of $8068.50 ($3886 + [$2.39 × 1750 pizzas]). This result compares with our estimate of $7655.75 using the cost equation generated from the regression analysis.

Given the simplicity of generating regression equations using spreadsheet packages and handheld calculators, the need for using the high/low method for computing cost equations in practice is questionable. However, it remains an easy-to-use tool for estimating cost behaviour.

Source: Steve Mason/Getty Images

When making pizza, some costs increase as you make more (e.g. dough, meats, vegetables), while others remain the same, notwithstanding the number of pizzas produced (e.g. rent).

LEARNING OBJECTIVE **3** ->>

The impact of income taxes on costs and decision making

We always need to consider tax laws and the impact income and other taxes have on costs, revenues and decision making. Just as an individual should consider the impact of income taxes on a decision whether to hold or sell a share, managers must consider the impact of taxes for a variety of decisions. The first key to understanding the

impact of taxes on costs and revenues is the recognition that many costs of operating businesses are deductible for income tax purposes and that most business revenues are taxable. In Australia, the company tax rate is currently 30 per cent. This means that for every $1 of profit you earn, the Australian Taxation Office (ATO) collects 30 cents from you. To what extent does this significant cost affect our decision making?

After-tax costs and revenues

Consider an example in which your current taxable cash revenue is $100 and tax-deductible cash expenses equal $60. Assuming a 30 per cent tax rate, and as shown in Exhibit 3.13, taxable income equals $40. If the income tax rate is 30 per cent, $12 in income taxes will be paid, leaving you with $28 cash after tax. Now consider the impact of spending an additional $20 on tax-deductible expenditures. This reduces your taxable income to $20. With a 30 per cent income tax rate, $6 of income taxes will be paid instead of $12 (you saved $6 of income tax) and you will be left with $14 after tax. Even though you spent an additional $20, your cash flow decreased by only $14 ($28 less $14). Mathematically, the after-tax cost of a tax-deductible cash expenditure can be found by subtracting the income tax savings from the before-tax cost or by simply multiplying the before-tax amount by (1 − tax rate):

> **Key formula 3.2:** After-tax cost
>
> After-tax cost = Pretax cost × (1 − tax rate)

So, if the before-tax cost is $20 and the income tax rate is 30 per cent, the after-tax cost is $14 ($14 = $20 × [1 − 0.30]). In this case, the impact of income taxes is to reduce the 'real' cost of a tax-deductible expense to the business and to increase cash flow.

Income taxes also have an impact on cash revenues received by a business. Continuing our original example in Exhibit 3.13, if taxable cash revenue increases by $20, taxable

	Current	Increase spending by $20	Increase revenue by $20
Revenue	$100	$100	$120
Expense	−60	−80	−60
Taxable income	$ 40	$ 20	$ 60
Tax (rate = 30%)	−12	−6	−18
After-tax cash flow	$ 28	$ 14	$ 42

EXHIBIT 3.13 The impact of income taxes on cash

income will increase to $60 ($120 − $60). After payment of $18 of income taxes (30% of $60), you will be left with $42 cash. An increase in revenue of $20 increases your cash flow by only $14 ($42 − $28). Why? Because the $20 is taxable and results in the payment of an additional $6 of income tax ($20 × 0.30). Mathematically, the formula to find the after-tax benefit associated with a taxable cash revenue is analogous to the formula for after-tax cost. The after-tax benefit of a taxable cash receipt can be found by subtracting the additional income tax to be paid from the before-tax receipt or by simply multiplying the pretax receipt by (1 − tax rate):

Key formula 3.3: After-tax benefit

After-tax benefit = Pretax receipts × (1 − tax rate)

So, if the before-tax receipt is $20 and the tax rate is 30 per cent, the after-tax benefit is $14 ($14 = $20 × [1 − 0.30]). In this case, the impact of income taxes is to decrease cash flow to the business.

Before- and after-tax income

In a similar fashion, managers can calculate the impact of income taxes on income. If we have an income tax rate of 30 per cent and operating income of $1 000 000, we will have a tax liability of $300 000 (30 per cent of the $1 000 000) and be left with $700 000 of after-tax income. This is exactly the same thing that happens to our pay cheques as individuals. If an individual earns $1000 per week and faces a 30 per cent income tax rate, the individual's take-home pay (after considering income tax withholding) is only $700. Mathematically,

Key formula 3.4: After-tax benefit

After-tax income = Pretax income × (1 − tax rate)

Although tax laws are very complex and computing tax due is rarely as simple as applying one rate to income, estimating the impact of income tax and other taxes on cash receipts and disbursements is important in managerial decision making.

LEARNING OBJECTIVE **4** >>

A comparison of absorption costing and variable costing

Earlier in this chapter we introduced the concept of cost behaviour – that is, how costs behave in relation to production volume – and described the behaviour of fixed and variable costs.

Absorption costing

In Chapter 2, a system of product costing was introduced in which all manufacturing costs, fixed and variable, were treated as product costs. Product costs include direct materials, direct labour and all manufacturing overhead (both fixed and variable). You will recall that product costs attach to the product and are expensed only when the product is sold. Commonly called **absorption costing, or full costing**, this method is required for both external financial statements prepared under generally accepted accounting principles (GAAP), the Australian Accounting Standards Board (AASB) and for income tax reporting. Selling, general and administrative costs, also called period costs, are expensed immediately in the period in which they are incurred.

On the other hand, **variable costing, or direct costing**, treats only variable product costs (direct materials, direct labour and variable manufacturing overhead) as product costs and treats fixed manufacturing overhead as a period cost (along with selling, general and administrative costs). Variable costing is more consistent with the focus of cost-volume-profit analysis (discussed in Chapter 6) on differentiating fixed from variable costs and it provides useful information for internal decision making that is often not apparent when using absorption costing.

✳ **absorption (full) costing**
A method of costing in which product costs include direct materials, direct labour, and fixed and variable overhead; required for external financial statements and for income tax reporting.

✳ **variable (direct) costing**
A method of costing in which product costs include direct materials, direct labour and variable overhead; fixed overhead is treated as a period cost; consistent with a focus on cost behaviour.

Variable costing

Exhibit 3.14 provides a summary of the two costing methods. As you can see, *the only difference between absorption and variable costing is the treatment of fixed overhead*. Under absorption costing, fixed overhead is treated as a product cost, added to the cost of the product and expensed only when the product is sold. Under variable costing, fixed overhead is treated as a period cost and is expensed when incurred. The impact of this difference on reported income becomes evident when a company's production and sales are different (i.e. the number of units produced is greater than or less than the number of units sold).

Because absorption costing treats fixed overhead as a product cost, if units of production remain unsold at year-end, fixed overhead remains attached to those units and is included on the balance sheet as an asset as part of the cost of inventory. Using variable costing, all fixed overhead is

Absorption costing		Variable costing	
Product costs	Period costs	Product costs	Period costs
Direct materials		Direct materials	
Direct labour	Selling, general, and administrative costs	Direct labour	Selling, general, and administrative costs
Variable overhead		Variable overhead	
Fixed overhead			Fixed overhead

EXHIBIT 3.14 Absorption and variable costing

expensed each period, regardless of the level of production or sales. Consequently, when production is greater than sales and inventories increase, absorption costing will result in higher net income than variable costing.

LEARNING OBJECTIVE 5 >>

apply this!

Case

The impact of absorption and variable costing on the income statement

LuLu's Lockets is a custom jeweller manufacturing unique lockets. LuLu's CFO, Elise, is concerned about choosing the best costing method (variable vs absorption) to allow her to make the best decision regarding management compensation and to more easily understand the impact of production volume on the income statement. LuLu's Lockets produces 100 000 units each year with the following per unit costs: direct material of $0.30, direct labour of $0.35, variable overhead of $0.10 per unit and fixed manufacturing overhead costs of $30 000. The company also has variable selling and administrative costs of $0.05 per unit sold, and fixed selling and administrative costs of $10 000.

The selling price of each locket is $2. The cost of one unit of product under absorption and variable costing is calculated as follows:

Product costs

Absorption costing		Variable costing	
Direct material	$0.30	Direct material	$0.30
Direct labour	0.35	Direct labour	0.35
Variable overhead	0.10	Variable overhead	0.10
Fixed overhead	0.30	Variable selling and admin	0.05
Total per unit	$1.05	Total per unit	$0.80

The only difference between the two methods is $0.30 of fixed overhead ($30 000 ÷ 100 000 units), which is treated as a product cost under absorption costing and a period cost under variable costing.

Year 1 income comparison

In year 1, let's assume that all 100 000 units that are produced are sold. In this case, how much income would be reported under each method? To answer this question, remember that under absorption costing, fixed manufacturing overhead costs are expensed as part of cost of goods sold. Under variable costing, fixed manufacturing overhead costs are deducted as a fixed period cost. Regardless, when all units produced are sold, the net income reported under each method would be the same.

Year 1 comparison of absorption and variable costing
(100 000 units produced and sold)

Absorption costing		Variable costing	
Sales	$200 000	Sales	$200 000
Less: Cost of goods sold	105 000	Less: Variable costs	80 000
Gross profit	$ 95 000	Contribution margin	$120 000
Less: S&A costs	15 000	Less: Fixed costs	40 000
Net income	$ 80 000	Net income	$ 80 000

Year 2 income comparison

Let's suppose that in the next year, LuLu's Lockets produces 100 000 units (for the same costs), but due to a very slow Christmas season only sells 80 000 units. In this case, the variable costing method would expense the entire $30 000 of fixed manufacturing overhead as a period cost, whereas the absorption costing method would expense only $24 000 (80 000 units sold × $0.30 per unit). When production exceeds sales, absorption costing will report higher net income than variable costing. Part of the $30 000 of fixed overhead (20 000 unsold units × $0.30 per unit, or $6000) remains in inventory until those units are sold. The question for Elise is which method more closely represents what actually happened in the second year when production exceeded sales. Fixed overhead does not change with changes in sales volume, so variable costing seems to report a more accurate picture of the company's actual costs. Variable costing allows Elise to look at the contribution of each item sold to the company's overall profit, while absorption costing distorts that analysis by including fixed manufacturing overhead in the sales data when, in fact, that cost is incurred regardless of the sales volume.

Year 2 comparison of absorption and variable costing (100 000 units produced and 80 000 units sold)

Absorption costing		Variable costing	
Sales	$160 000	Sales	$160 000
Less: Cost of goods sold*	84 000	Less: Variable costs	64 000
Gross profit	$ 76 000	Contribution margin	$ 96 000
Less: S&A costs	14 000	Less: Fixed costs†	40 000
Net income	$ 62 000	Net income	$ 56 000

* Cost of goods sold includes $24 000 (80 000 × $0.30) of fixed manufacturing overhead.

† Fixed costs include $30 000 of fixed manufacturing overhead.

Year 3 income comparison

In Year 3, LuLu's Lockets holds production constant at 100 000 units, but increases sales to 120 000 units (the 20 000 units left over from Year 2 were sold in addition to all of the production for the third year). In this case, under variable costing, $30 000 of fixed manufacturing overhead would be expensed as a period cost. Under absorption costing, the $30 000 would be expensed along with an additional $6000 related to the

The reported production cost of a locket can vary greatly, if costed under an absorption versus variable costing system.

20 000 units produced in Year 2 and sold in Year 3 (20 000 units $0.30 per unit = $6000). When units sold exceed units produced, variable costing will report higher net income than will absorption costing. Remember from our previous discussion of cost behaviour that fixed costs remain constant from year to year regardless of sales volume. Absorption costing delays the expensing of a portion of the fixed cost incurred in Year 2 until all units are sold in Year 3. On the other hand, variable costing results in the expensing of fixed costs in the year in which they are incurred.

Year 3 comparison of absorption and variable costing (100 000 units produced and 120 000 units sold)

Absorption costing		Variable costing	
Sales	$240 000	Sales	$240 000
Less: Cost of goods sold*	126 000	Less: Variable costs	96 000
Gross profit	$ 114 000	Contribution margin	$144 000
Less: S&A costs	16 000	Less: Fixed costs†	40 000
Net income	$ 98 000	Net income	$104 000

* Cost of goods sold includes $36 000 (120 000 × $0.30) of fixed manufacturing overhead.

† Fixed costs include $30 000 of fixed manufacturing overhead.

Note that, over the three-year period, the total income is the same under each method. Why? Because when units produced are equal to units sold, the net income reported under each method is the same. While production was greater than sales in Year 2 and sales were greater than production in Year 3, over the three-year period the company produced and sold 300 000 units.

	Year 1	Year 2	Year 3	Total
Production	100 000	100 000	100 000	300 000
Sales	100 000	80 000	120 000	300 000
Absorption costing				
Sales	$200 000	$160 000	$240 000	$600 000
Less: Cost of goods sold	105 000	84 000	126 000	315 000
Gross margin	$95 000	$ 76 000	$ 114 000	$285 000
Less: S&A costs	15 000	14 000	16 000	45 000
Net income	$ 80 000	$ 62 000	$ 98 000	$240 000
Variable costing				
Sales	$200 000	$160 000	$240 000	$600 000
Less: Variable costs	80 000	64 000	96 000	240 000

Contribution margin	$120 000	$ 96 000	$144 000	$360 000
Less: Fixed costs	40 000	40 000	40 000	120 000
Net income	$ 80 000	$ 56 000	$104 000	$240 000

To summarise, in Year 1, when *units sold equalled units produced,* net income was the same under both costing methods. In Year 2, when *units produced exceeded units sold,* absorption costing reported higher net income than variable costing. In Year 3, when *units sold exceeded units produced,* variable costing reported higher net income than absorption costing.

Production, sales and income under absorption and variable costing

When Production = Sales	Absorption income = Variable income
When Production > Sales	Absorption income > Variable income
When Production < Sales	Absorption income < Variable income

LEARNING OBJECTIVE 6 >>

apply this!

Interactive quizzes

Variable costing and decision making

The use of absorption costing for internal decision making can result in less-than-optimal decisions. For example, consider the case of the unemployed executive who offered his services to a manufacturing company for only $1 per year in salary and a bonus equal to 50 per cent of any increase in net income generated for the year. Reviewing the absorption costing income statement for the previous year, he learned that although 10 000 units of product were produced and sold, the company had the capacity to produce 20 000 units. In addition, variable production costs were $40 per unit, variable selling and administrative (S&A) costs were $10 per unit sold, fixed manufacturing overhead costs were equal to $300 000 ($30 per unit produced), and fixed selling and administrative costs were equal to $100 000. As shown here, the previous year's net income was $100 000.

Absorption costing income (10 000 units produced)

Sales (10 000 units)	$1 000 000
Less: Cost of goods sold*	700 000
Gross profit	$ 300 000
Less: S&A costs	200 000
Net income	$ 100 000

* Includes $300 000 (10 000 units × $30) of fixed manufacturing overhead.

By increasing production to 20 000 units, the allocation of fixed manufacturing overhead is reduced to $15 per unit ($300 000 ÷ 20 000 units = $15). Remember that under absorption costing, fixed overhead is a product cost and is expensed only when the product is sold. Therefore, only $150 000 of fixed overhead costs will be expensed. The remaining $150 000 of fixed manufacturing overhead costs is included in inventory and is reported as an asset on the balance sheet. The cost of goods sold is reduced to $550 000, and net income is increased by $150 000, to $250 000. The manager is entitled to a bonus of $75 000, whereas the company is saddled with 10 000 units of unsold inventory and the attendant costs of storing and insuring it!

Absorption costing income (20 000 units produced)

Sales (10 000 units)	$1 000 000
Less: Cost of goods sold*	550 000
Gross profit	$ 450 000
Less: S&A costs	200 000
Net income	$ 250 000

* Includes $150 000 (10 000 units × $15) of fixed costs.

If income had been measured using a variable costing approach, net income would be the same each year and the manager would not have been able to pull off his scheme.

Variable costing income

(10 000 units produced)		(20 000 units produced)	
Sales (10 000 units)	$1 000 000	Sales (10 000 units)	$1 000 000
Variable costs	500 000	Variable costs	500 000
Contribution margin	$500 000	Contribution margin	$500 000
Fixed costs	400 000	Fixed costs	400 000
Net income	$100 000	Net income	$100 000

So, where are the costs that resulted from the increased production? Under variable costing, those production costs are attached to the inventory and are on the balance sheet as inventory. The fixed costs, under variable costing, are expensed each period in total regardless of the level of production.

Problems like these are less common in a just-in-time (JIT) environment, in which inventory levels are minimised and companies strive to produce only enough products to meet demand.

Choosing the best method for performance evaluation

For external reporting purposes, managers have no choice but to use absorption costing, as it is required by the AASB and GAAP. Managers are similarly required to use absorption costing for submitting company tax returns. However, for internal decision making, variable costing is often the best choice. If income is used to evaluate the performance of a manager of a division or segment of a company, it seems logical that the measure of income should reflect managerial effort and skill. If sales decrease from one period to another with no changes in production or other factors, it seems logical that income should decrease as it does under variable costing. On the other hand, increasing income by increasing production with no corresponding increase in sales (as is possible using absorption costing) is counterintuitive. All other things being equal, increases in sales should result in increases in income and decreases in sales should result in decreases in income.

So, using variable costing for internal decision making removes the impact of changing production levels on income. Accordingly, calculations of income are more likely to reflect managerial skill rather than simply an increase in production. If a manager's compensation package is based on net income, using absorption costing may motivate that manager to increase production simply to increase income. On the other hand, under variable costing, managers are more likely to make optimal production volume decisions.

Advantages of variable costing

Absorption costing is required by AASB and GAAP and must be used whenever a company provides financial statements to individuals outside the company. However, for internal management purposes, variable costing would seem to be a better choice. Variable costing has the following advantages:

- Changes in production and inventory levels do not impact the calculation of profits.
- Variable costing focuses attention on relevant product costs. That is, attention is focused on variable product costs, which can be avoided, rather than on fixed product costs, which are often unavoidable.
- Under variable costing, cost behaviour is emphasised and fixed costs are separated from variable costs on the income statement.
- Variable costing is consistent with the use of variance analysis, an important tool used to manage a business.
- Variable costing income is more closely aligned with a company's cash flows.

Exercises

1 Cost behaviour LO1

Baby Toys Co. produces fine porcelain dolls that are sold in exclusive gift shops. The controller and sales manager are discussing potential price increases and have started looking at various costs to consider their potential impact on price. The following are several of the costs they are discussing.

a Advertising
b Packaging (each doll is carefully packaged in a nicely designed collectible carton)
c Supervisors' salaries
d Fabric used in production (each doll is adorned in unique fabrics)
e Assembly labour
f Mortgage payment on the production facility
g Production facility utilities
h Quality assurance (each doll is carefully inspected).

Required
Assist the controller and sales manager by indicating whether each of the above costs is most likely a fixed cost (*FC*) or a variable cost (*VC*).

2 Calculation of total costs LO1

Doors and Keys, Inc., provides custom creation of door locks for expensive homes. The company has recently become concerned about its ability to plan and control costs. Howard Lockwood, the company's founder, believes that he can summarise the company's monthly cost with a simple formula that appears as 'Cost = $12 800 + $25.00 per labour hour'.

Required
If Doors and Keys' employees work 850 hours in a single month, calculate an estimate of the company's total costs.

3 Cost behaviour analysis LO1

Lock-up Locks produces a single type of high quality lock for commercial use in Melbourne. The company expects to produce and sell 5000 locks this year. Price is determined by marking up total production cost per unit by 60%. Total variable production costs are 40% of total fixed production costs, at the 5000 unit level of production. Rent, the only fixed production cost, is $50 000 this year.

Required:
Calculate the selling price of a single lock.
If rent is $60 000, what is the price of a single lock?

4 Cost behaviour analysis LO1

Sisters Erin Joyner and Teresa Hayes have started separate companies in the same city. Each company provides party planning services for weddings, birthday parties, holiday parties and other occasions. Erin and Teresa graduated from the University of Queensland and completed a managerial accounting course, so they both understand the importance of managing their company's costs. Erin has estimated her cost equation to be 'Total cost = $4000 + $40 per planning hour'. On the other hand, Teresa has estimated her cost equation to be 'Total cost = $250 + $60 per planning hour'.

Required
a What could explain such a difference in the cost equations?
b If each sister works a total of 135 planning hours, what total costs would each report?

5 Regression analysis: Calculation of total cost LO2

Valentine is a manufacturer of fine chocolates. Recently, the owner, Melinda Gross, asked her controller to perform a regression analysis on production costs. Melinda believes that pounds of chocolate produced drive all of the company's production costs. The controller generated the following regression output:

R Square	0.50688
Standard Error	1.43764

Analysis of variance

	DF	Sum of squares	Mean square
Regression	1	418.52992	481.52992
Residual	197	407.16375	2.06682

F = 202.49935   Signif. F = 0.0000

Variables in the equation

Variable	Coefficients	Standard error	t Stat	P-Value
Pounds	7.940	0.055794	14.230	0.0000
Intercept	204.070	0.261513	20.780	0.4361

Required
Calculate an estimated total cost assuming that Valentine manufactures 5000 pounds of chocolate.

6 Mixed costs using high/low method LO2

Gregory's Gems accumulated the following production and overhead cost data for the past five months.

	Production (units)	Overhead cost
January	10 600	$40 250
February	10 500	40 000
March	11 500	44 250
April	12 500	45 500
May	11 000	43 750

Required
a Use the high/low method to calculate the variable cost per unit and fixed costs for Gregory's Gems.
b What are estimated total costs for production of 12 000 units?

7 Mixed costs using high/low method LO2

Brisbane Boomerang manufactures souvenirs for distribution and sale in tourist stores. The company is concerned at the growth in its electricity costs and wishes to predict it better in future periods. Following are production and electricity cost data for the past six years.

	Production (units)	Overhead cost ($)
2008	10 000	$40 000
2009	12 000	49 000
2010	14 000	48 000
2011	12 500	45 000
2012	11 000	43 000
2013	9 000	41 000

Required
a Use the high/low method to calculate the variable cost per unit and fixed costs for electricity costs.
b If Brisbane Boomerangs expects to produce 13 500 souvenirs next year, what would be the predicted electricity cost?

8 Mixed costs using high/low method LO2

Captain Co. used the high/low method to derive the cost formula for electrical power cost. According to the cost formula, the variable cost per unit of activity is $3 per machine hour. Total electrical power cost at the high level of activity was $7600 and was $7300 at the low level of activity. The high level of activity was 1200 machine hours.

Required
Calculate the low level of activity.

9 Impact of income taxes LO3

Ben Rakusin is contemplating an expansion of his business. He believes he can increase revenues by $9000 each month if he leases 1500 additional square feet of showroom space. Rakusin has found the perfect showroom. It leases for $4000 per month. Ben's tax rate is 30 per cent.

Required
What estimated after-tax income will Rakusin earn from his expansion?

10 Impact of income taxes LO3

Most business transactions have tax consequences. Understanding the 'after-tax' effects of transactions is fundamentally important. Consider the following:

Before-tax revenue	Tax rate	After-tax revenue
$100 000	40%	?
200 000	20%	?
135 000	35%	?

Before-tax cost	Tax rate	After-tax cost
$25 000	40%	?
50 000	20%	?
35 000	35%	?

Required

Calculate the after-tax revenue or after-tax cost for each of the above transactions.

11 Absorption vs variable costing LO4, 5, 6

Munn Bicycle Company manufactures bicycles specifically for professionals cycling to work. They sell for $100 and are very sturdy, with built-in saddlebags on the rear designed to carry backpacks. Selected data for last year's operations are as follows:

Units in beginning inventory	0
Units produced	20 000
Units sold	18 000
Units in ending inventory	2 000

Variable costs per unit:	
Direct materials	$40
Direct labour	20
Variable manufacturing overhead	5
Variable selling and administrative	2

Fixed costs:	
Fixed manufacturing overhead	$250 000
Fixed S&A	$100 000

Required

a What is the cost per bicycle if the company uses absorption costing?

b What is the cost per bicycle if the company uses variable costing?

12 Absorption vs variable costing: Calculation of net income LO4, 5, 6

Refer to the data in Exercise 11.

Required

a Prepare income statements for each costing method.

b Explain the difference between the two income statements.

c If, in the next year of operation, sales exceed production by 1000 units, what would be the net income under each costing method? Explain the difference. (Assume that there is no change in the variable cost per unit or the fixed costs.)

13 Absorption vs variable costing: Calculation of net income LO4, 5, 6

Posey Manufacturing has the following cost information available for 2011:

Direct materials	$6.00 per unit
Direct labour	$4.00 per unit
Variable manufacturing overhead	$2.00 per unit
Variable S&A costs	$1.00 per unit
Fixed manufacturing overhead	$80 000
Fixed S&A costs	$25 000

During 2011, Posey produced 12 000 units, out of which 11 000 were sold for $60 each.

Required

a Produce an income statement using variable costing.

b Produce an income statement using absorption costing.

c If Posey needs to take one of these income statements to the bank to apply for a loan, which one should he use? Why?

d For internal decision making, which income statement would be more useful? Why?

Problems

14 Regression vs high/low method LO1, 2

Autodesk Corporation produces toolboxes used by construction professionals and homeowners. The company is concerned that it does not have an understanding of its utility consumption. The company's president, George, has asked the plant manager and cost accountant to work together to get information about utilities cost. The two of them accumulated the following data for the past 14 months (production volume is presented in units):

	Production	Utility cost
January	113 000	$1712
February	114 000	1716
March	90 000	1469
April	110 000	1600
May	112 000	1698
June	101 000	1691
July	104 000	1700
August	105 000	1721
September	115 000	1619
October	97 000	1452
November	98 000	1399
December	98 000	1403
January	112 000	1543
February	107 000	1608

Required

a Using the high/low method, what is the company's utility cost equation?

b What would be the expected utility cost of producing 120000 units? (The relevant range is 85000 to 125000 units of production.)

c Using the data shown and a spreadsheet program, perform a regression analysis. Discuss any differences in the results and the potential impact on decision making.

15 Regression analysis interpretation
LO1, 2

Global Office Services & Supplies sells various products and services in the greater Melbourne region. Duplicating is one of its most popular services for corporate customers and individuals alike. Selected data from the Duplicating Department for the previous six months are as follows:

	Number of copies made	Duplicating Department's costs
January	20000	$1700
February	25000	1950
March	27000	2100
April	22000	1800
May	24000	1900
June	30000	2400

Regression output based on the previous data is as follows:

Coefficient of intercept	280.79
R square	0.967696
Number of observations	6
X coefficient (independent variable)	0.0687

Required

a What is the variable cost per copy for Global Office Services & Supplies?

b What is the fixed cost for the Duplicating Department?

c Based on the limited regression output provided above, what cost formula should be used to compute an estimate of future total costs in the Duplicating Department?

d If 26000 copies are made next month, what total cost would be predicted?

e Based on the information given, how accurate will the cost formula developed in response to question C be at predicting total Duplicating Department cost each month?

16 Absorption vs variable costing: Benefits and calculation of net income
LO4, 5, 6

HD Inc. produces a variety of products for the computing industry. CD burners are among its most popular products. The company's controller, Katie Jergens, spoke to the company's president at a meeting last week and told her that the company

was doing well, but that the financial picture depended on how product costs and net income were calculated. The president did not realise that the company had options in regard to calculating these numbers, so she asked Katie to prepare some information and be ready to meet with her to talk more about this. In preparing for the meeting, Katie accumulated the following data:

Units produced	100000
Units sold	95000
Fixed manufacturing overhead	$300000
Direct materials per unit	$ 55.00
Direct labour per unit	$ 25.00
Variable manufacturing overhead per unit	$ 15.00

Required

a Compute the cost per unit using absorption costing.

b Compute the cost per unit using variable costing.

c Compute the difference in net income between the two methods. Which costing method results in the higher net income?

d Assume that production was 80000 units and sales were 100000 units. What would be the difference in net income between the two methods? Which costing method shows the greater net income?

e Assume that production was 100000 units and sales were 100000 units. What would be the difference in net income between the two methods?

f Which method is required by generally accepted accounting principles?

17 Absorption vs variable costing: Benefits and calculation of net income
LO4, 5, 6

Boots R Us produces a variety of products for the fashion industry. Leather boots are among its most popular products. The company's controller spoke to the company's president at a meeting last week and told her that the company was doing well, but that the financial picture depended on how product costs and net income were calculated. The president did not realise that the company had options with regard to calculating these numbers, so she asked the controller to prepare some information and be ready to meet with her to talk more about this. In preparing for the meeting, the controller accumulated the following data:

Beginning inventory	25000
Units produced	100000
Units sold	105000
Fixed manufacturing overhead	$400000
Direct materials per unit	$ 25.00
Direct labour per unit	$ 35.00
Variable manufacturing overhead per unit	$ 15.00

Required

a Compute the cost per unit using absorption costing.

b Compute the cost per unit using variable costing.

c Compute the difference in net income between the two methods. Which costing method results in the higher net income?

d Assume production was 80 000 units and sales were 70 000 units. What would be the difference in net income between the two methods? Which costing method shows the greater net income?

e Assume that production was 100 000 units and sales were 100 000 units. What would be the difference in net income between the two methods?

f Which method is required by generally accepted accounting principles?

18 Absorption vs variable costing: Benefits and calculation of net income
LO4, 5, 6

Leatherlicious produces world class leather jackets for high net worth individuals. The chief accountant of the company is considering the relative effects of the absorption and variable costing systems, and its effect on profit. Here is data on the company:

Beginning inventory	20 000
Closing inventory	35 000
Units sold	105 000
Fixed manufacturing overhead	$300 000
Direct materials per unit	$ 20.00
Direct labour per unit	$ 30.00
Variable manufacturing overhead per unit	$ 18.00

Required

a How many units were produced in the period?

b Compute the cost per unit using absorption costing, and variable costing separately.

c Compute the difference in net income between the two methods. Which costing method results in the higher net income?

d Assume production was 70 000 units and sales were 80 000 units. What would be the difference in net income between the two methods? Which costing method shows the greater net income?

Cases

19 Regression analysis interpretation
LO1, 2

Consider the Daily Grind Café appendix at the back of this textbook. Having read the case carefully, please answer questions 6, 7, and 8, relating to regression analysis and high-low calculations.

20 Mixed costs using high/low method
LO2

DB Pty Ltd manufactures a large range of processed food. The firm is concerned with the amount of wastage of material Z associated with the production of one of its products, Beta. Wastage is calculated as the difference between the actual raw material inputs used in production and the standard (expected) raw material content of output, in the units that are produced (currently estimated as 0.75 kg of material Z, per unit of Beta).

The following data is available:

	Jan	Feb	Mar	Apr	May	June
Sales Beta	150	230	184	191	129	240 (units)
Purchases Material Z	150	180	210	112	213	174 (kg)

Opening inventories:

Beta	40	30	20	16	25	40 (units)
Material Z	196	210	190	230	150	230 (kg)

Opening and closing stocks of work in process were zero throughout the period.
Closing inventories in June were 20 units of product Beta and 200 kilograms of Material Z.

Required

Using high-low analysis and based on the above data, calculate an estimate for wastage for July given projected sales of 300 units of Beta and a desired closing balance of finished goods equal to 20% of that month's projected sales.

(*Hint*: Wastage is your dependent variable, and units of Beta produced is your independent variable.)

Learning objectives:

After studying the material in this chapter, you should be able to:

1   Explain how job costing is used to accumulate, track and assign product costs.

2   Recognise issues related to the measurement of direct material and direct labour costs in job costing.

3   Recognise issues related to the allocation of manufacturing overhead costs to products in job costing.

4   Explain the need for using predetermined overhead rates and calculate overhead applied to production in job costing.

5   Determine whether overhead has been over- or underapplied and demonstrate the alternative treatments of the over- or underapplied amount in job costing.

JOB COSTING AND OVERHEAD COSTING SYSTEMS

c **4**

You may have been in a conversation with friends, where the topic of discussion turned to bottled water. Inevitably, one of you might raise the issue of the exorbitant cost of a bottle of water, and how a litre of water is costlier than a litre of petrol! How can this be?

One of the most important roles of managerial accountants is to help determine the true cost of a product being produced and sold by a company, beyond the materials that comprise the product. In order to make this bottle of water, we might need to *rent* a factory, buy machines that *depreciate*, pay for *electricity* and *other energy* costs, then packaging, distributing and selling the bottled water to retailers. Production staff salaries (supervisors, assembly line staff, machine operators), administrative staff salaries (CEO, CFO), security and cleaning costs … A whole range of costs need to be incurred so that the bottled water might be produced, for you to eventually purchase. There is no doubt that the selling price you pay is higher than the cost of doing all the above, but the cost itself is much more than just the cost of water! Management accountants specialise in determining the production cost of a product, which includes many (but not all) of the above costs, and some we have not mentioned in the above example.

The same might be said for services. Cost information is equally important for manufacturing and service businesses and is used by managers across the organisation. Pricing decisions made by marketing managers, manufacturing decisions made by production managers, and finance decisions made by finance managers are all influenced by the cost of products.

For example, marketing managers need to set a competitive price that will capture the needed market share and provide a fair profit. If the price of the product is set too low, a larger market share may be captured but the business may not earn a satisfactory profit. On the other hand, if the price of the product is too high, the business may not capture sufficient market share to remain competitive. These pricing decisions require product cost information in order for an optimal price to be set.

LEARNING OBJECTIVE **1** >>

Product costing systems

Job costing

Companies that manufacture customised products or provide customised services to clients use a costing system called **job costing**, which accumulates, tracks and assigns costs for each job. Jobs are simply the individual units of a product. For a builder of custom homes, each house is a job. For a CPA firm, a job might be an individual tax return, an audit engagement, or a consulting engagement for a particular client.

For a print shop, each order for wedding invitations, graduation announcements, or custom letterhead is a job. For a hospital, each patient is a job. In general, job costing is used in situations in which a customer initiates an order, which 'pulls' the product or service through the process.

✳ **job costing**
A costing system that accumulates, tracks and assigns costs for each job produced by a company.

Source: tobkatrina/Shutterstock

Aircraft manufacturers such as Boeing or Airbus likely use job costing to determine the cost of manufactured products.

Basic job costing for manufacturing and service companies

Canberra Custom Furniture (CCF) uses job costing to accumulate, track and assign costs to the cabinets it produces. CCF builds furniture based on customer orders so each piece is unique. The direct material, direct labour and overhead costs for a specific job are accumulated on a job cost report. This report may be prepared manually or be totally automated. Regardless, its role is to keep track of the material, labour and overhead costs that are incurred for a particular job. A job cost report for CCF is shown in Exhibit 4.1.

Broadly, job costing is argued to relate to organisations that undertake high value, low volume and heterogeneous production outputs. That is, separate and individual costing of each job (output) is necessary if:

1   an organisation makes a relatively small number of jobs (low volume)
2   each job is of high cost to deliver (high value)
3   no two jobs are the same, hence the need to individually cost each one (heterogeneity).

Measuring and tracking direct materials

Direct material costs include the costs of the primary materials used in production. In addition to the cost of the materials themselves, the cost of direct materials includes shipping costs (if paid by the purchaser), and any other costs incurred in delivering the materials to the factory.

Measuring direct material cost should be a relatively easy task for CCF. The company has to identify only the amount of material actually used in each job and attach the proper cost to it. CCF uses a variety of materials, including wood, fabric, glue, screws, dowels and stain in constructing a finished piece of furniture. Although some of the more common materials are stored in inventory, exotic and more expensive wood, fabric and hardware such as handles are typically purchased just in time for their use in a particular job. As they are needed for a particular job, raw materials are recorded on the job cost report.

In Exhibit 4.1, you can see that CCF used oak, maple, particleboard and glass in the manufacture of Job 101. These materials can all be traced directly to Job 101 and are treated as direct materials.

Clarendon Homes

Making it real

Homebuilders are one of the more traditional users of a job costing system. Take Clarendon Homes, for example – Clarendon is an Australian homebuilder. In a good year, Clarendon might make 500 homes in Sydney (low volume). In an output sense, 500 is low when compared to, let's say, thousands of Coke bottles produced a day in a Coca-Cola Amatil factory. However, each home built represents hundreds of thousands of dollars in expenditures (high value), and no two homes are exactly the same, as each homeowner requests individual alternatives that differentiate the costing and eventual pricing of the homes built. As such, Clarendon Homes adopts a job costing system, where each customer's home (job) is separately costed and priced.

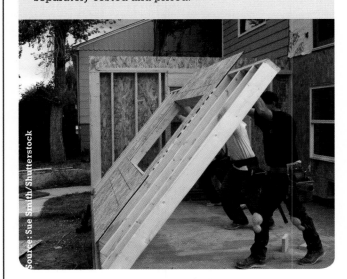

Source: Sue Smith/Shutterstock

CCF also uses a variety of wooden dowels, screws, glues and finishing nails in the construction of Job 101. However, you should note that these items are not listed as direct materials on the job cost report in Exhibit 4.1. Although it may be physically possible to track the specific screws, glue and nails to a particular job, the cost of doing so is great and the benefits are few, and so it is economically inefficient to do so. CCF has chosen to treat these materials as indirect materials that will be allocated to the job as part of overhead.

Companies that primarily provide services to clients or have minimal material costs may not treat any materials as direct. For example, a law firm that primarily prepares wills and other paper documents may choose to treat the costs of paper as an indirect material (part of overhead). Likewise, although CPA firms may use a lot of paper and other materials processing tax returns for clients, they may not track the paper to specific jobs on a job cost report as the cost of doing so probably outweighs the benefit of the slightly more accurate tracing of costs.

Canberra Custom Furniture

Job number: 101
Date started: 6 March
Description: TV cabinet

Customer: Robyn Gray
Date finished: 19 March

Direct materials		Direct labour			Manufacturing overhead		
Type	Cost	Employee	Hours	Amount	Hours	Rate	Amount
Oak	$ 875.00	Staley	12.6	$255.15	22.4	$12.50	$280.00
Maple	600.00	Chen	4.5	91.13			
Particle-board	78.00	Kent	5.3	107.33			
Glass	330.00						
	$1883.00		22.4	$453.61	22.4		$280.00

Cost summary

Direct materials		$1883.00
Direct labour		453.61
Manufacturing overhead		280.00
Total		$2616.61

 EXHIBIT 4.1 Job cost report

Sometimes, the benefits of better allocation, however small, are worthwhile. A hospital might choose to itemise every pill (even aspirin) and other medication given to a patient and every bandage used in an operation on a patient's job cost report (the patient's case file). Tracking the use of pills and other medications to a patient provides other valuable benefits to doctors and the hospital. Doctors need to know exactly what medications have been given and when. So, although it may also provide a way to more accurately charge patients for the cost of medications they consume during a hospital stay, the costing of the medications is not the primary motive. Rather, primary motive is the tracking of patient medication use.

Measuring and tracking direct labour

The costs of direct labour include the wages earned by production workers for the actual time spent working on a product. The measurement of direct labour cost also should be a relatively easy task. Direct labour cost refers to labour that is directly related to manufacturing a product or providing a service. Assembly-line workers in a manufacturing setting and CPAs working on tax returns are examples of direct labour. On the other hand, manufacturing supervisors, cleaning staff and maintenance personnel in a manufacturing company and secretarial staff in a CPA firm are considered indirect labour and are included in overhead. The costs of direct labour for a specific job may be accumulated on a job cost report, but most companies keep track of each employee's time by requiring the completion of time sheets. Time sheets may be prepared by hand or be totally automated and integrated with the company's accounting information system (AIS). Regardless of the form used, employees must keep track of how much time they spend on specific jobs. For assembly-line workers, management needs to know how much time is spent manufacturing a specific product. For CPAs and attorneys, the managing partner needs to know how many hours are spent serving a particular client.

Payroll Management Systems – Billing Tracker!

Making it real

In this era of technology, companies rarely account for labour time and costs in a professional services firm manually. Often, information technology systems are used to highlight how many hours staff have worked, allocated their hours to clients or general administration, their pay rates charged to clients and consequently, the amount in fees they generate for the professional services firm. Billing Tracker is one such piece of software. It claims to even track the time of staff, as they change from task to task on different clients. In this way, accounting information systems contain the potential to not only help organisations cost products, but also cost clients! We will investigate this in greater detail when studying services costing later in the textbook.

Source: Adapted from 'Time and Billing Software for CPA & Accounting Office'. Published by BillingTracker, www. billingtracker.com, © 2015.

The cost of direct labour is simply calculated by multiplying a wage rate for each employee by the number of hours that each employee works on each product.

Fringe benefits

In addition to the hourly cost of labour, wage rates must also include the cost of **fringe benefits**. Fringe benefits include the employer's costs for benefits employees receive as part of their employment not including their salary. These benefits can include such things as company cars for employees, free or subsidised accommodation, private health insurance for workers, low or no interest loans and the payment of workers' private expenses. The job cost report in Exhibit 4.1 shows that three employees of CCF worked 22.4 hours on Job 101 at a cost of $20.25 per hour. This cost includes a $15 hourly wage rate plus benefits of $5.25 per hour.

Idle time

As a result of a power outage, CCF incurred idle time while working on Job 101. Would CCF most likely treat this idle time as overhead or as an additional cost of direct labour assigned directly to Job 101? Not all the time that direct labour workers are paid for is spent productively. For example, if machinery and equipment break down or if materials are not available when needed, **idle time** results. Although idle time could be traced to a specific job (the job that is being worked on when the idle time occurs), most companies choose to treat idle time as an overhead cost rather than a cost of a specific job.

Overtime

Overtime premiums paid to direct labour workers cause similar classification problems. Overtime is typically paid at 150 per cent of the normal wage rate (sometimes called 'time and a half') for hours worked in excess of 38 per week. For example, let's hypothetically assume that the hourly pay for an assembly-line worker is $20. An overtime premium for this worker would be $10.00 per hour, increasing the total hourly wage to $30.00. Assuming fringe benefits at 35 per cent, the cost of labour rises to $40.50 per hour.

Overtime may be incurred for a number of reasons. Sometimes, production problems cause a company to get behind on a job. When this happens, the company may choose to incur overtime costs (work over the weekend) to finish up a job on time. In other situations, a company might accept an order, knowing that it will require the scheduling of overtime.

> **✳ fringe benefits**
> Payroll costs in addition to the basic hourly wage.
>
> **✳ idle time**
> Worker time that is not used in the production of the finished product.
>
> **✳ overtime premium**
> An additional amount added to the basic hourly wage owing to overtime worked by the workers.

In practice, the treatment of overtime costs depends on the perspective adopted by management for the incurrence of overtime. On the one hand, if overtime is incurred as a result of production problems, most companies treat the cost as overhead as the additional labour cost signals broader production or management inefficiencies. On the other hand, if the overtime results from the acceptance of a rush order, most companies would treat the overtime as a direct labour cost that would be assigned directly to the specific job (and would most likely be included in determining its price).

For example, on a Friday morning, the customer who had ordered Job 101 called CCF and said she needed the TV cabinet next Monday instead of next Wednesday. CCF craftspeople worked eight hours on Saturday, and the company incurred overtime premiums, in order to finish the job by the new due date. CCF likely would treat the overtime premium as a direct labour cost in this situation and explain to the customer that the cost of earlier completion (overtime hours) will be passed on to the customer, resulting in a higher price paid by the customer.

In highly automated manufacturing environments, the cost of direct labour has been reduced significantly as automated machinery and robotics have replaced direct labour workers. As discussed more thoroughly later in the chapter, this shift in product costs from labour to overhead has had important implications for product costing. Whereas the cost of direct labour is relatively easy to accumulate, trace and assign to products, automation related costs (depreciation, maintenance, electricity) are often more difficult to trace and hence regarded as overhead (indirect) costs.

LEARNING OBJECTIVE **3** >>

apply this!

Revise with Beat the Clock

Manufacturing overhead

Overhead is the most difficult product cost to accumulate, track and assign to products. Unlike direct materials and direct labour, overhead is made up of several seemingly unrelated costs – rent, depreciation, insurance, repairs and maintenance, utilities, indirect labour, indirect materials and so on. Some of these costs are likely to be fixed (rent, depreciation and insurance, for example), whereas other components of overhead are likely to be variable or mixed (such as repairs and utilities). As such, overhead cost can be thought of as a mixed cost that includes both a fixed and a variable component. In addition, overhead is indirect in nature. As a result, overhead cannot be directly tracked to products and services but must instead be allocated.

Allocation involves finding a logical method of assigning overhead costs to the products or services a company produces or provides. If a company produced only one product, the allocation would be simple. We could simply divide the total overhead cost by the total number of units produced. If our total overhead costs incurred during the year were $100 000 and we produced 20 000 identical tables during the year, it would be logical to assign $5 of overhead to each table ($100 000 ÷ 20 000 tables). However, what if we make 10 000 tables and 10 000 chairs? Does it still make sense to allocate overhead based on the number of units produced? Probably not. A more logical approach might be to allocate the overhead to the tables and chairs based on the number of direct labour hours or machine hours consumed in the manufacture of each. If chairs take twice as long to manufacture as tables, twice as much overhead would be allocated to them. The choice of an allocation base requires a thorough understanding of what causes overhead costs to be incurred.

Cost drivers and overhead rates

Understanding what causes overhead costs to be incurred is the key to allocating overhead. The choice of a logical base on which to allocate overhead depends on finding a cause-and-effect relationship between the base and the overhead. A good allocation base is one that drives the incurrence of the overhead cost. Therefore, allocation bases are often referred to as **cost drivers**.

A cost driver for overhead is an activity that causes overhead to be incurred. If we wanted to allocate the cost of utilities incurred to run machines in the factory to products, we would want to find a cost driver that causes the utility costs to be incurred. In this case, the time the machines were in use (machine hours) might be an appropriate allocation base. If it takes twice as many machine hours to make chairs as it does to make tables, chairs would correspondingly be allocated twice as much utility cost. In more labour intensive companies, the cost of utilities might be allocated using direct labour hours instead of machine hours as the cost driver. The choice of cost driver depends on the specific company and the processes it utilises in manufacturing products and providing services to customers.

Overhead consists of a variety of costs with potentially different drivers for each. For example, the salaries of cleaners and supervisors in the factory are overhead costs. The costs of rent and insurance for the factory building are overhead costs. The costs of indirect materials are overhead costs. Instead of identifying cost drivers for each component of overhead, companies have traditionally lumped overhead into similar **cost pools** to simplify the task. In the most extreme case, companies lump all overhead costs into one cost pool for the entire factory. Other companies have separate pools of overhead costs for each department. Still others use cost pools for each activity performed in making a product. Regardless of the number of cost pools and method of overhead allocation used, overhead rates are calculated using the same basic formula:

Key formula 4.1: Overhead rate

$$\text{Overhead rate} = \frac{\text{Manufacturing overhead}}{\text{Cost driver}}$$

Let's consider CCF's operations to explain this concept. Let's assume CCF incurs utility costs of $1000 during a month and starts and finishes 12 jobs. Each job requires machine time but the time varies greatly, depending on the materials used and the difficulty of the job. Job 101 required 22.4 labour hours whereas Job 104 required 60 hours. The total labour hours during that month totalled 500. If CCF allocates utility cost using labour hours as the cost driver, how much of the utility cost should be allocated to Job 101? How much to Job 104? The overhead rate for utility costs is $2 per direct labour hour ($1000 ÷ 500 direct labour hours). If Job 101 takes 22.4 labour hours, then $44.80 of utility costs (22.4 hours × $2 per hour) should be allocated to Job 101. Using the same logic, $120 of utility costs (60 hours × $2 per hour) should be allocated to Job 104.

Plantwide overhead rates

In labour-intensive manufacturing companies and service industries, direct labour hours or direct labour cost have often served as cost drivers. In automated manufacturing environments, machine hours historically have been used as the cost driver. Direct labour hours and machine hours are both volume-based cost drivers – that is, they are directly related to the volume or number of units produced. Allocating overhead based on direct labour hours or machine time works well when companies make only a few products, when they incur relatively small overhead costs compared to labour and material costs, and when that overhead is related to the volume of products produced.

For example, as demonstrated in Exhibit 4.2, a pizza restaurant might apply overhead by using a single predetermined overhead rate for the entire restaurant. The costs of pizza ovens, rent, utilities and other overhead costs would be lumped into one cost pool and allocated to products (pizzas), based on the amount of labour time (direct labour hours, or DLHs) it takes to make each pizza. In this case, the cost of overhead is relatively small and is likely to be related to the number of pizzas made.

In Exhibit 4.3, overhead costs total $8000 per month. If direct labour hours per month are 800, the overhead rate is equal to $10.00 per direct labour hour. If a thick crust pizza takes 10 minutes of direct labour time to produce, a thin crust pizza takes 6 minutes to produce, and a deep dish pizza takes 15 minutes to produce, the amount of overhead allocated to each is $1.66, $1.00 and $2.50, respectively.

LEARNING OBJECTIVE 4 >>

The use of estimates

It is not unusual for managers to want to estimate the cost of a product before it is actually produced or before the actual costs are known with certainty. Having timely cost information is useful for pricing decisions as well as for production decisions. However, because the actual amount of many overhead items will not be known until the end of a period (perhaps when an invoice is received), companies often estimate the amount of overhead that will be incurred in the coming period. For example, a manufacturer of computers that are custom-made to meet customer requirements needs to know the cost of producing each computer so it can establish a sales price. Customers place orders 24 hours a day and the company's policy is to ship computers to customers within 48 hours of the order. Although the company has records of each component and other materials used in the assembly of the computer and knows the exact amount of time workers spent putting the computer together (remember the job cost report discussed earlier), calculating the actual amount of overhead cost incurred is virtually impossible to do in a timely manner.

Why? Because the amount of most overhead items, such as utilities expense, maintenance expense, supplies and so forth, will not be known until after the computer is assembled and shipped. The only alternative, short of requiring the customer to wait until the end of the period to know the actual price of the computer, is to estimate the amount of overhead on each computer and to set the sales price accordingly. Using estimates has another advantage as well. It is not unusual for overhead to fluctuate during the year. For example, the utilities costs incurred by New Zealand Ice Cream to produce their ice

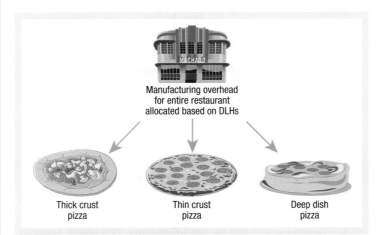

Manufacturing overhead for entire restaurant allocated based on DLHs

Thick crust pizza

Thin crust pizza

Deep dish pizza

EXHIBIT 4.2 Applying overhead using a plantwide rate

Overhead costs per month:

Depreciation on pizza ovens	$1 500
Rent	2 000
Utilities	1 000
Other	3 500
Total	$8 000
Direct labour hours (DLHs) per month	800 direct labour hours
Overhead per direct labour hour	($8 000 ÷ 800 DLHs) = $10.00 per DLH

Direct labour hours per pizza:

Thick crust	10 minutes
Thin crust	6 minutes
Deep dish	15 minutes

Allocation of overhead for each type of pizza:

Thick crust	$10.00 × ⅙ hour of labour	= $1.66
Thin crust	$10.00 × 1/10 hour of labour	= $1.00
Deep dish	$10.00 × ¼ hour of labour	= $2.50

EXHIBIT 4.3 Overhead allocation using direct labour hours as the cost driver

normal costing
A method of costing where predetermined overhead rates are calculated by dividing estimated overhead costs by a 'normal' level of production activity.

cream product during the winter are likely to be higher than those incurred in the summer. If they used actual overhead costs to cost products, the ice cream the company makes in May would cost more than the ice cream it makes in December. Using estimates smooths out, or normalises, seasonal and random fluctuations in overhead costs. Thus, this method of costing is often called **normal costing**. The 'normal' level of activity from which we cost is usually determined by considering the periodical level of output a company expects to continually generate over a medium to longer term. This 'normal' level of activity usually represents an average of production output levels. Often, it is also different from the actual level of operations, owing to the need to manage seasonal fluctuations or changes in markets within which companies operate.

Costing estimates help companies price; for example, when pricing smoothies, electricity costs for the month might be estimated by New Zealand Ice Cream in order to more accurately determine the true cost of a smoothie produced.

Predetermined overhead rates

Companies that estimate the amount of overhead cost incurred in costing products allocate overhead by using predetermined overhead rates. **Predetermined overhead rates** are calculated using a slight modification of the basic overhead rate formula:

Key formula 4.2: Predetermined overhead rate

$$\text{Predetermined overhead rate (for a cost pool)} = \frac{\text{Estimated overhead for the cost pool}}{\text{Estimated units of the cost driver}}$$

Predetermined overhead rates are typically calculated using annual estimates of overhead and cost drivers, although some companies do more frequent calculations.

The application of overhead to products

The allocation of overhead using predetermined overhead rates is called an application of overhead. The amount of overhead applied to a product is calculated by multiplying the predetermined overhead rate by the actual units of the cost driver incurred in producing the product or service.

The cost of a product or a service for a company utilising normal costing therefore includes an actual amount of direct material, an actual amount of direct labour and an applied amount of manufacturing overhead based on estimates.

Key formula 4.3: Applied overhead

$$\text{Applied overhead} = \text{Predetermined overhead rate} \times \text{Actual units of cost driver}$$

Calculating predetermined overhead rates is a three-step process:

- Step 1 involves the identification and estimation of the overhead costs included in the plantwide or departmental cost pool.
- Step 2 involves the identification and estimation of the appropriate allocation base (the cost driver).
- Step 3 is the actual computation of the predetermined overhead rate.

As an example, let's assume that CCF has chosen to lump all overhead into one cost pool for the entire factory (a plantwide cost pool). The company identifies overhead costs as including the cost of utilities, insurance and rent for the factory building; depreciation and repairs and maintenance of manufacturing equipment; supplies used in the factory; and the salaries of a production supervisor and cleaner in the factory. The company further estimates that these costs should total about $100 000 in the next year. As CCF is very labour intensive, it has chosen labour hours as the cost driver and estimates using 8000 labour hours during the next year. Dividing the estimated overhead of $100 000 by the estimated allocation base of 8000 labour hours results in a predetermined overhead rate of $12.50 per labour hour.

$$\frac{\$100\,000}{8000} = \$12.50 \text{ per labour hour}$$

In other words, for every labour hour worked on a product, the company should apply $12.50 in overhead cost. As shown in Exhibit 4.1, since Job 101 required 22.4 labour hours, it was allocated $280.00 of overhead.

predetermined overhead rates
Used to apply overhead to products; calculated by dividing the estimated overhead for a cost pool by the estimated units of the cost driver.

Source: New Zealand Natural Pty Ltd.

The problem of over- and underapplied overhead

Because overhead is applied to products using predetermined overhead rates estimated prior to the commencement of a period, it is likely that actual overhead costs (when they become known) will differ from those applied. If applied overhead is greater than actual overhead, the company **'overapplied' overhead**. If the applied overhead is less than actual overhead, the company **'underapplied' overhead**

❋ **overapplied overhead**
The amount of applied overhead in excess of actual overhead.

❋ **underapplied overhead**
The amount of actual overhead in excess of applied overhead.

in the period. Over- and underapplied overhead can occur for a couple of reasons – estimating the overhead incorrectly or estimating the cost driver incorrectly. Often, organisations experience both, as it is not easy to estimate either! As shown in Exhibit 4.4, CCF had a predetermined overhead rate of $12.50 per direct labour hour based on estimated overhead of $100 000 and estimated direct labour hours of 8000. If during the year, 8100 direct labour hours are actually incurred in making furniture, CCF's applied overhead will be $101 250.

Now, assume that the actual overhead costs for CCF total $102 000. Under a normal costing system, as actual overhead costs are incurred throughout the year, the manufacturing overhead account is increased (debited) for the amount of the actual costs. The journal entry to record the payment of overhead expenses and the transfer of those costs to manufacturing overhead is:

Manufacturing overhead	102 000	
Accounts payable or cash		102 000

Likewise, as individual jobs are completed throughout the year, overhead is applied to work in process using the predetermined overhead rate. As shown in Exhibit 4.5, CCF's applied overhead was $101 250. The journal entry to record the application of overhead to work in process requires a debit to work in process and a credit to manufacturing overhead.

Manufacturing overhead	
$102 000	$101 250
Actual overhead costs as incurred	Overhead applied to WIP using the predetermined overhead rate

EXHIBIT 4.5 The manufacturing overhead account

Work in process inventory	101 250	
Manufacturing overhead		101 250

By effectively debiting the manufacturing overhead account with actual overhead costs and crediting the same account with applied overhead costs, the balance of the manufacturing overhead account signals the extent of over- or underapplication of overhead during the period. The manufacturing overhead account therefore serves as a clearing account. At this point (see Exhibit 4.4), the manufacturing overhead account has a debit balance of $102 000 and a credit balance of $101 250.

CCF's actual overhead is greater than the applied overhead by $750. Debits to the account (actual overhead $102 000) exceed the credits (applied overhead $101 250) by $750. Consequently, CCF has not applied enough, relative to actual overhead for the period. They have *underapplied* overhead in the amount of $750. What impact does the underapplied overhead have on the cost of furniture produced by CCF?

Remember that applied overhead is accumulated in work in process (WIP), which subsequently transfers to finished goods as units are completed, and then transferred to cost of goods sold as units are sold. If everything made this period is sold, then adjusting for over- or underapplied overhead involves adjusting the balance of the cost of goods sold account. In practice (particularly in a just-in-time [JIT] manufacturing environment), this is likely to be the case. Jobs are typically completed and sold before any adjustment can be made to an inventory account. In our case, if CCF sells all the furniture it produces, its cost of goods sold will be understated by $750 and our adjustment will increase cost of goods sold by $750, to reflect that we undercosted WIP by $750 during the period, by only applying $101 250 and not $102 000. But what if some of the furniture is not sold or perhaps not even finished? Then, the $750 might be allocated in some fashion to WIP, finished goods and cost of goods sold to recognise that all three accounts are too low, in proportion to the amount of production this period that was incomplete

Estimated overhead	$100 000	
Estimated units of cost driver	8000 direct labour hours	
Predetermined overhead rate	$12.50 ($100 000 ÷ 8000 DLHs)	
Applied overhead = Predetermined overhead rate × actual direct labour hours		
Applied overhead	$101 250 ($12.50 per DLH × 8100 DLHs)	

EXHIBIT 4.4 The calculation of applied overhead

(WIP), completed but unsold (finished goods), or completed and sold (cost of goods sold). This allocation is based on the amount of overhead in each account. As an alternative, if the amount of the adjustment is immaterial, companies may choose to adjust only the cost of goods sold account.

For example, assume that the amount of overhead in WIP, finished goods and cost of goods sold is as follows:

Work in process	$ 20 250	(20% of total)
Finished goods	30 375	(30% of total)
Cost of goods sold	50 625	(50% of total)
Total	$101 250	

If the amount of underapplied overhead is considered immaterial, the cost of goods sold is adjusted by the entire $750. The balance after adjustment is $51 375.

Exotic and unique furniture designs often require quite differentiated material products and labour skills, and therefore require a job costing style of accounting method.

	Original balance	Underapplied overhead	Adjusted balance
Cost of goods sold	$50 625	+ $750	= $51 375*

* Note that the underapplied overhead increases the cost of goods sold amount. If overhead had been overapplied, the adjustment would have decreased the cost of goods sold balance.

The journal entry to record the adjustment to cost of goods sold is:

Cost of goods sold	750	
Manufacturing overhead		750

On the other hand, if the amount of underapplied overhead is considered material, the underapplied overhead might be allocated to WIP, finished goods and cost of goods sold according to the percentages shown on the previous page. For example, 20 per cent of the underapplied overhead, or $150, would be allocated to WIP ($750 × 20%), while 30 per cent of the underapplied amount, or $225, would be allocated to finished goods, and 50 per cent ($375) would be allocated to cost of goods sold. After adjustment, the amount of overhead in each inventory account is as follows:

	Original balance		Underapplied overhead		Adjusted balance
Work in process	$ 20 250	+	$150	=	$ 20 400
Finished goods	30 375	+	225	=	30 600
Cost of goods sold	50 625	+	375	=	51 000
Total	$101 250	+	$750	=	$102 000

The journal entry to allocate the underapplied overhead to the three accounts is:

Work in process	150	
Finished goods	225	
Cost of goods sold	375	
Manufacturing overhead		750

Exercises

1 Job costing LO2

Love's Pottery Barn had the following costs for June:

Direct labour	$400
Manufacturing overhead	375
Beginning work in process	0
Ending work in process	0
Costs of goods manufactured	1 050
Beginning finished goods	2 450
Ending finished goods	3 400

Required
How much direct material costs were incurred during June?

2 Job costing LO2

Airplane Manufacturers Inc. had the following costs in July:

Direct material	$7 500 000
Manufacturing overhead	3 750 000
Beginning work in process	0
Ending work in process	0
Costs of goods manufactured	6 000 000
Beginning finished goods	2 000 000
Ending finished goods	3 000 000

Required
How much in direct labour costs were incurred during June?

3 Job costing LO2, 3

Walter Meyer Productions had the following costs for March:

Purchases of direct materials	$30 000
Indirect labour	20 000
Ending direct materials inventory	10 000
Beginning direct materials inventory	0
Total manufacturing costs	115 000
Direct labour	25 000

Required

How much manufacturing overhead was incurred during March?

4 Job costing LO2, 3

Barry Salter Engineering purchased $15 000 in direct materials in May. There was $5000 in direct materials at the end of April, and $3000 in direct materials at the end of May. Additionally, indirect labour costs relating to engineering supervision tasks of $12 000 were incurred in May. Manufacturing costs are $125 000 and manufacturing overhead was 40 per cent of conversion costs.

Required

What is the direct labour cost for May?

5 Overhead costs, cost pools, cost drivers LO2, 3

The following statements describe various aspects of overhead costs and the roles of cost pools and cost drivers in the allocation of overhead:

a   Overhead costs cause cost drivers.

b   In traditional manufacturing environments, most overhead costs are directly related to production activities.

c   Overhead rates are calculated by dividing manufacturing overhead costs by the volume of cost pool activity.

d   Companies that are labour intensive are likely to allocate overhead costs such as utilities expense based on direct labour hours.

e   More overhead costs in a just-in-time environment are direct in nature as opposed to indirect.

f   A 'good' allocation base is one that drives the incurrence of overhead costs.

g   Companies generally allocate overhead equally to all products produced during a given period of time.

Required

Indicate whether each of the statements in exercise 5 is true or false.

6 Predetermined overhead rate and applied overhead LO3, 4

Rabbit Enterprises calculates predetermined overhead rates for each department. In the feeding department, total overhead costs were $19 240 in 2010, and they are expected to be $21 700 in 2011. The company maintained 515 rabbit pens in 2008 and plans to have 520 pens in 2011.

Required

a   If the number of rabbit pens is used as the cost driver, what is the company's 2011 predetermined overhead rate?

b   What amount of overhead was applied in 2011 if there were actually 530 pens?

7 Predetermined overhead rate and applied overhead LO2, 3

Ben Whitney manufactures holiday decorations. Overhead is applied to products based on direct labour hours. Last year, total overhead costs were expected to be $85 000. Actual overhead costs totalled $88 750 for 8400 actual hours. At the end of the year, overhead was underapplied by $4750.

Required

a   Calculate the predetermined overhead rate.

b   How much overhead should be applied to a job that was completed in three direct labour hours?

8 Predetermined overhead rate and applied overhead LO2, 3

Jacky Somers is an expert in furniture manufacturing. She applies overhead cost to furniture based on machine hours. Total overhead costs were expected to be $185 000 for this year. At the end of the year, it was observed that actual overhead costs totalled $198 450 for 7350 actual machine hours. This represented an overapplication of $4950 for the year.

Required

a   Calculate the overhead applied for the year.

b   How much overhead should be applied to a job that was completed in five machine hours?

c   A dining table consumed $125 in direct material costs and $75 in direct labour costs. Management expected it to take 7 machine hours to produce, but it actually took 9 machine hours. What is the total manufacturing cost of this table?

9 Predetermined overhead rate and applied overhead LO2, 3

Brent Wald produces residential water tanks for homes. He applies overhead to water tanks based on labour hours. Total labour hours were expected to be 1350, and the expected overhead costs were $41 850. At the end of the year, 1400 labour hours were actually used.

Required

a   Calculate the overhead applied for the year.

b   How much overhead should be applied to a water tank that took five labour hours and seven metres of materials?

c   A water tank consumed $400 in direct material costs and $100 in direct labour costs. Brent Wald expected it to take 15 labour hours to produce, but it actually took 10 labour hours. What is the total manufacturing cost of this tank?

Problems

10 Job costing: Supply the missing data
LO2, 3, 4

Grandma Whitney knits made-to-order blankets. The following is an incomplete job cost report for a Flower Petal blanket ordered by Anna Schotten. All employees are paid the same wage rate.

Direct materials			Direct labour		Overhead
Type of yarn	Total cost	Date	Knitting hours	Total cost	Total applied
Blue – 4 skeins	$14.00	23 January	5	$80.00	$4.50
Brown – 2 skeins	11.00	24 January	7	?	?
Green – 2 skeins	13.00	25 January	3	48.00	2.70

Required
a What is the direct labour cost per hour?
b What is the direct labour cost for 24 January?
c Based on this job cost report, how is overhead being assigned to each blanket? Do you believe that the chosen cost driver is appropriate in this instance? Why or why not?
d How much overhead should be applied on 24 January?
e What is the total manufacturing cost for this blanket?

11 Job costing: Supply the missing data
LO2, 3, 4

Furniture Joe makes customised furniture for clients who appreciate quality carvings in furniture. The following is an incomplete job cost report for Furniture Joe, ordered by Will Nguyen.

Direct materials			Direct labour		Overhead
Type of timber	Total cost	Build date	Total hours	Total cost	Applied
Oak – 5 sq m	$220.00	16 May	6	$168.00	$44.00
Pine – 3 sq m	72.00	19 May	2	56.00	14.40
Bamboo – 4 sq m	168.00	20 May	5	?	?

Required
a What is the direct labour cost per hour?
b What is the direct labour cost for 20 May?
c Based on this job cost report, how is overhead being assigned to each furniture? Do you believe that the chosen cost driver is appropriate in this instance? Why or why not?
d How much overhead should be applied on 20 May?
e What is the total manufacturing cost for this furniture?

12 Comprehensive job costing LO2, 3, 4, 5

Krall Kabinets produces custom cabinetry for homes, which is sold nationwide. The company adds overhead costs to cabinetry projects at the rate of $7.75 per direct labour hour. The company accumulates overhead costs in a separate manufacturing overhead account and uses normal costing to assign overhead. The following data provide details of the company's activity and balances during the last half of the year:

	1 July	31 December
Direct materials inventory	$60 250	$61 750
Work in process inventory	44 000	43 500
Finished goods inventory	24 150	23 000
Monthly production data:		
Direct materials purchased	$155 000	
Direct labour costs ($15/hr)	270 000	

Required
a Calculate the cost of direct materials used during the period.
b Calculate the cost of goods manufactured during the period.
c At the end of December, Krall found that it had actually incurred overhead costs of $145 000. If Krall adjusts over- or underapplied overhead to cost of goods sold at the end of the year, what is Krall's cost of goods sold after adjustment?

13 Comprehensive job costing LO2, 3, 4, 5

Maxim Builders applies overhead costs to projects at the rate of $9.00 per machine hour. The company accumulates overhead costs in a separate manufacturing overhead account and uses normal costing to apply overhead costs to projects. Following is information on the company's balances during the last half of the year:

	1 July	31 December
Direct materials inventory	$22 000	$24 900
Work in process inventory	52 000	54 500
Finished goods inventory	38 150	32 000
Other actual production data:		
Direct materials purchased	$170 000	
Direct labour costs ($36/hr)	288 000	
Machine hours = two times direct labour hours		

Required
a Calculate the cost of direct materials used during the period.
b Calculate the cost of goods manufactured during the period.
c At the end of December, Maxim Builders found that it had actually incurred overhead costs of $149 000. If Maxim Builders adjusts over- or underapplied overhead to cost of goods sold at the end of the year, what is Maxim's cost of goods sold after adjustment?

14 Comprehensive job costing LO2, 3, 4, 5

Car-rific makes custom spray paint solutions to motor vehicles for commercial purposes. The company applies overhead costs to projects at the rate of $20 per labour hour. The company accumulates overhead costs in a separate manufacturing overhead account and uses normal costing to apply overhead costs to separate car jobs. Following is information on the company's balances during the last financial year:

	1 July	30 June
Direct materials inventory	$10 000	$15 000
Work in process inventory	50 000	54 000
Finished goods inventory	40 000	35 000
Other actual production data:		
Direct materials purchased	$75 000	
Direct labour costs ($40/hr)	52 000	

Required

a Calculate the cost of direct materials used during the period.

b Calculate the cost of goods manufactured during the period.

c At the end of June, Car-rific calculated actual overhead costs to be $30 000. What is Car-rific's adjusted cost of goods sold?

Cases

15 Comprehensive job costing LO2, 3, 4, 5

Brad James, owner of James Manufacturing Inc. receives an Interim financial report on 29 June, 2014. The report covered all activities for the financial year from 1 July, 2013. Inventories of work in process and finished goods were $75 000 and $145 000 respectively as at 1 July 2013. All jobs on hand had been completed on 29 June 2014 except for one large job, No. 175. The job cost sheet for this job indicated to date direct labour of $12 000 and direct material of $10 000 had been used.

Records for the last day of the financial year showed that direct labour costs of $5000, direct material costs of $3000 and factory overhead costs of $2000 were incurred on that day. Job No. 175 was still incomplete.

Up to the close of business on 29 June 2014, the work in process account had been charged with $500 000 of direct material. Factory overhead is applied at 150% of direct labour costs. Factory overhead of $850 000 had been incurred up to the close of business on 29 June 2014.

Sales for the period were $3 300 000, representing a markup of 50% on factory cost. There were no sales recorded on the last day of the period. Closing balance of finished goods was $30 000.

Required

Incorporate records for the last day of the financial period and for the full financial period prepare:

a A cost of goods manufactured statement.

b A cost of goods sold statement.

c An income statement.

16 Predetermined overhead rate and applied overhead LO2, 3

Consider a home building company like Clarendon Homes, discussed in the chapter.

Required

List and explain a range of factors that might cause their overhead to be overapplied or underapplied in the period. How many of these reasons might be controllable by management?

TEST COMING UP?

NOW WHAT?

ACCT has it all, and you can too. Between the text and online offerings, you have everything at your fingertips to revise and prepare for your test. Make sure you check out all that **ACCT** has to offer:

- Printable flash cards
- Interactive games
- Videos

- Audio downloads
- Case studies
- Chapter review cards

- Online quizzing
- ...and more!

Visit **http://login.cengagebrain.com/** to find the resources you need today!

Learning objectives:

After studying the material in this chapter, you should be able to:

1 Explain how process costing systems are used to accumulate, track and assign product costs.

2 Describe basic process costing and the calculation of equivalent units of production.

3 Compare and contrast the weighted average and first-in, first-out (FIFO) methods of process costing and apply each step of the four-step process costing system under both methods.

4 Analyse the manner by which spoilage costs are considered in process costing.

5 Understand how varying resource types possess different equivalent units in order to better understand costing processes in modern organisations.

PROCESS COSTING SYSTEMS

c 5

Just as companies use different techniques to manufacture products or to provide services, companies also use various product costing systems to accumulate, track and assign the costs of production to the goods produced and services provided. In Chapter 4, we explained how job costing plays a role in helping companies accumulate costs in a production costing system. In this chapter, we explain how process costing is used by organisations. The process costing system is used by companies for which job costing does not align with, owing to their fundamentally different operations. We begin by explaining this difference below.

LEARNING OBJECTIVE **1** >>

Process costing systems

Companies that produce a homogeneous product on a continuous basis (oil refineries, breweries, paint and paper manufacturers, for example) use **process costing** to accumulate, track and assign costs to products. In general, process costing is used by companies that forecast demand and consequently 'push' a product through the manufacturing process. Rather than accumulating the costs for each unit produced and directly tracking and assigning costs to each unique unit, process costing accumulates and tracks costs for each process as products pass through the process and then assigns costs equally to the units that come out of each process. A process is simply the work that is performed on a product. For a paint manufacturer, blending and pouring are processes. For a bread baker, mixing, baking and slicing are processes.

A popularly understood example of a process costing operation is the Coca-Cola Amatil bottling operations in Australia and Indonesia. Millions of Coca-Cola bottles are made using an identical process that is subjected on all bottles. This allows accountants to make assumptions about the averaging of costs when trying to determine a manufacturing cost per bottle.

On the other hand, companies that manufacture customised products or provide customised services to clients use **job costing** (discussed in Chapter 4). Job costing accumulates, tracks and assigns costs for each job separately and individually. Jobs are simply the individual units of a product. For a builder of custom homes each house is a job. For a CPA firm a job might be an individual tax return, an audit engagement, or a consulting engagement for a particular client. For a print shop each order for wedding invitations, graduation announcements or custom letterhead is a job. For a hospital each patient is a job. In general, job costing is used in situations in which a customer initiates an order, which 'pulls' the product or service through the process. As previously explained, we will focus on process costing in this chapter.

Source: Ian Waldie/Bloomberg/Getty Images

Coca-Cola bottlers in Australia likely use process costing to determine the cost of a completed Coke bottle.

Printing those brochures – how much for a Coles brochure?

Making it real

Coles often engages in large-scale printing orders with commercial printers to produce tens of thousands of brochures for distribution to homes regularly. All these brochures are identical and usually printed within the same production run. In order to determine the cost of these brochures, a printing company might include direct materials (paper, ink, etc.), direct labour (staff working on the production run) and overhead costs (rent, electricity, machine depreciation, maintenance costs, indirect materials and indirect labour costs). The sum total of these costs make up the cost of a production run of brochures. By dividing this cost by the number of brochures printed, suppliers will determine the production cost per brochure. Having regard for the production cost, the supplier will then mark up on the cost of the brochure to determine a selling price that will be charged to Coles for the brochures. The process of averaging costs in order to determine a cost per brochure is a classic application of the process costing framework.

❉ **process costing**
A costing system that accumulates and tracks costs for each process performed and then assigns those costs equally to each unit produced.

❉ **job costing**
A costing system that accumulates, tracks and assigns costs for each job produced by a company.

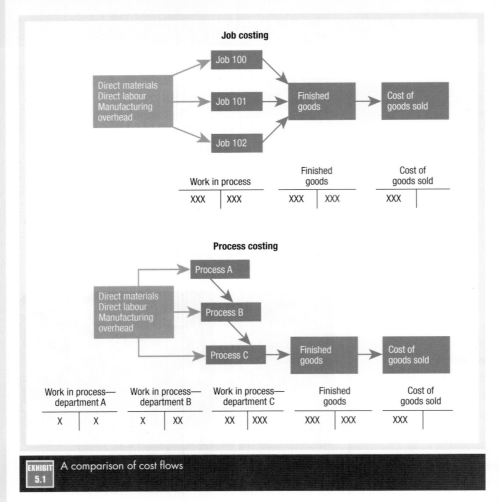

Job costing

Direct materials
Direct labour
Manufacturing overhead

Job 100
Job 101
Job 102

Finished goods

Cost of goods sold

Work in process		Finished goods		Cost of goods sold	
XXX	XXX	XXX	XXX	XXX	

Process costing

Direct materials
Direct labour
Manufacturing overhead

Process A
Process B
Process C

Finished goods

Cost of goods sold

Work in process—department A		Work in process—department B		Work in process—department C		Finished goods		Cost of goods sold	
X	X	X	XX	XX	XXX	XXX	XXX	XXX	

EXHIBIT 5.1 A comparison of cost flows

typically use process costing. As mentioned previously, instead of accumulating, tracking and assigning direct material and direct labour costs directly to each job, process costing systems accumulate and track direct material and direct labour costs by department and then assign the costs evenly to the products that pass through each department. Likewise, instead of applying overhead to each specific job, overhead is applied to each department and then assigned evenly to each product that passes through. Although the application to job or department differs, the amount of overhead applied is calculated in exactly the same way. After **predetermined overhead rates** are developed, overhead is applied by multiplying the predetermined overhead rate by the actual units of cost driver incurred in each department. A comparison of the cost flows in job costing and process costing is shown in Exhibit 5.1.

In companies with no beginning or ending inventories (all units are finished), the mechanics of process costing are very simple. Because all the units produced are identical, costs accumulated and tracked in each department can simply be averaged across all the units that are produced. If $30 000 of direct material costs and $70 000 of direct labour and overhead costs are incurred in the blending department of a paint manufacturer, and 10 000 litres of product are produced, the cost of blending each litre is $10 per litre and the 10 000 finished units cost $100 000 to produce.

However, problems quickly arise when companies have inventories. Let's assume that the blending department finishes blending only 8000 litres and that 2000 litres are left in ending WIP at the end of the year. These 2000 litres are 50 per cent complete and will require additional materials, labour and overhead during the next period before they are finished. Should each litre (finished or unfinished) still cost $10 in this case? That would mean that our 8000 finished units cost $80 000 and our 2000 unfinished units cost $20 000. Of course, that would not make sense because we would expect our finished units to cost more per litre than those that are only half finished!

A visual conceptualisation of the different approaches underlying job and process costing is presented in Exhibit 5.1. Job costing requires direct materials, direct labour and manufacturing overhead costs to be allocated to jobs, which are completed and sold. Process costing, on the other hand, costs products by identifying costs for processes, then dividing these process costs by the units that use the process to determine a process cost per unit. The sum total of costs required to complete each process is added and moved onto the next process, eventually culminating in the cost of a finished product that is finally sold (cost of goods sold). To identify the production cost per unit under a process costing system, the total production cost is divided by the number of units produced, for each process of all processes, depending on the type of cost information desired by a manager.

LEARNING OBJECTIVE 2 >>

Basic process costing

Companies that produce beverages or other products (paint, paper, oil and textiles) in a continuous-flow production process

※ equivalent units
The number of finished units that can be made from the materials, labour and overhead included in partially completed units.

To get around this problem, we need to calculate the number of **equivalent units** completed during the period. The equivalent units of a product is the whole number equivalent of units you completed, as tallied from all complete and incomplete production of goods in a period. If two units are uniformly 50 per cent finished at the end of a period, we have finished the equivalent of one complete unit. In the previous example, we partially finished 2000 units with each unit uniformly 50 per cent complete. How many finished units could we have completed using the same amount of direct materials, labour and overhead? The 2000 units that are 50 per cent finished are the equivalent of 1000 finished units. Therefore, our total equivalent units finished during the period equals 9000 – the 8000 units we actually finished plus another 1000 equivalent finished units in ending WIP.

Our cost per equivalent unit is therefore $11.11 ($100 000 ÷ 9000 equivalent units) and the 8000 finished units cost $88 880, whereas the 2000 units in ending inventory (1000 equivalent units) cost $11 120 ($100 000 – $88 880). Process costing and the calculation of equivalent units are substantially more complicated when companies have both beginning and ending inventories of WIP.

Expedia.com.au – no booking fees?

Expedia promotes itself as the world's largest online travel company. It also claims to charge customers 'no booking fees'. This claim is undoubtedly true, but you might wonder how the cost of booking is covered? To understand how, we must reflect on what comprises the booking 'process'. On the one hand, booking fees might include a per-booking approximation of the administrative costs required to acquire, develop and maintain systems that provide the online booking service. This cost usually covers a range of necessary operational and administrative costs, such as staff salaries, depreciation on computer systems, rent for the building space where Expedia staff work and so on. Expedia claims to have abolished its flight booking fees in September 2009, while competitors such as travel.com.au continue to charge booking fees. How then, does Expedia cover these costs? Expedia might raise the prices of their actual flight amounts quoted to cover this cost. This way, customers clearly see what they actually pay and are not unpleasantly surprised when struck with a booking fee at time of payment. Alternatively, Expedia might have structured an agreement with airline companies, receiving payments from airlines for each booking made – hence covering booking costs. However Expedia chooses to cover the booking cost, organisations all around the world adopt unique and varying systems to identify and associate costs to processes – in this instance, online flight bookings!

Making it real

As acquisition channels in the travel industry transform to more electronic ones, costing systems are similarly comprised less by human capital, and more on technological systems' related costs such as depreciation and maintenance expenses

Another difference between job costing and process costing is that process cost systems often require multiple WIP accounts – one for every process. As products are moved from one process to another, the costs of the previous process are simply transferred to the next process. For example, a paint manufacturer accumulates and tracks direct material, direct labour and overhead costs to a WIP account for each process (blending and pouring). The total costs for each process are then assigned to the paint by dividing by the number of litres of paint that come out of each process. The total cost of each litre is therefore the sum of the costs assigned from each process and an average of the costs incurred in each process.

Materials, labour and overhead cost journal entries

The use of multiple WIP accounts in process costing introduces some peculiarities in recording the flow of costs using journal entries. While the journal entries to record the flow of costs through a process costing system are similar to those in job costing, there are a few key differences.

Material costs

As materials are drawn from the raw materials inventory storeroom, the costs are traced to processing departments rather than individual jobs. The journal entry to record the materials used in processing department A is as follows:

Work in process inventory – Process A	xx	
Raw materials inventory		xx

It should be noted that materials can be added in any processing department. For example, if materials are also used in process B, a similar journal entry would record the materials used in that processing department:

Work in process inventory – Process B	xx	
Raw materials inventory		xx

Labour costs

Likewise, labour costs are traced directly to a processing department rather than to individual jobs. As labour costs are incurred in processing department A, the journal entry to record the labour costs is as follows:

Work in process inventory – Process A	xx	
Salaries and wages payable		xx

If labour costs are incurred in process B or process C, similar journal entries would be used to record the labour costs in those departments.

Overhead costs

Predetermined overhead rates are typically used in process costing to apply overhead. However, instead of applying overhead to a particular job, overhead is applied to units of product as they move through each processing department as follows:

Work in process inventory – Process A	xx	
Manufacturing overhead		xx

As with material and labour costs, as overhead costs are incurred in process B or C, similar journal entries would record the cost flows.

Transferring costs from process to process

As work is completed within a processing department, the accumulated costs of materials, labour and overhead must be transferred to the next processing department. For example, once processing is complete in process A, the accumulated costs in the WIP account would be transferred to the WIP account in process B as follows:

Work in process inventory – Process B	xx	
Work in process inventory – Process A		xx

Likewise, as work is completed in process B, the accumulated costs would be transferred to process C:

Work in process inventory – Process C	xx	
Work in process inventory – Process B		xx

Transferring costs to finished goods

As work is completed in process C, the product is ready to transfer to finished goods. The journal entry to transfer the costs of the completed units to finished goods inventory is as follows:

Finished goods inventory	xx	
Work in process inventory – Process C		xx

Recording the cost of goods sold

As the finished goods are sold, the cost of the goods is transferred out of finished goods inventory and recognised as the cost of goods sold:

Cost of goods sold	xx	
Finished goods inventory		xx

The manufacturing of high volume homogeneous products can occur for a variety of forms, including the production of staple products such as honey.

Process costing and weighted average and FIFO methods

When a company has both beginning and ending inventories of WIP, process costing becomes more complicated. In this situation, it is useful to view process costing in four steps.

In Step 1, the physical flow of units and their associated costs are analysed. In this step, it is essential to note the percentage of completion of both the beginning and ending inventories of WIP. For example, let's assume that the blending department of a paint manufacturer has 2000 litres of paint that is 80 per cent complete in its beginning inventory of WIP. These units were started last period but not completed by the end of the period and will be finished this period. In addition, let's assume that $1600 of direct material costs and $1000 of conversion costs (the cost of direct labour and overhead incurred to convert the direct materials to a finished product) have already been incurred in blending these 2000 litres of partially completed paint.

During the current period, another 12 000 litres of paint are started in the blending department, so 14 000 litres are now in process. The company incurs another $20 000 of direct material costs (DM) and $7370 of conversion costs (CC) working on these 14 000 litres. The total costs incurred in the blending department now include $21 600 for direct material ($1600 incurred last period and $20 000 incurred this period) and $8370 for conversion costs ($1000 incurred last period and $7370 incurred this period).

Of the 14 000 litres of paint now in process in the blending department, 13 000 litres are finished by the end of the period. Consequently, 1000 litres remain in ending inventory. Let's assume that these 1000 litres are 50 per cent complete (see Exhibit 5.2). Overall, the above discussion hints at a relationship between beginning units in WIP, units started, ending units and units completed. A formula depicting this relationship is given below:

> **Key formula 5.1:** Relationship between beginning units in WIP
>
> **Beginning Units + Current units started**
> **= Units completed + Ending units**

WIP – Blending Department

Total units accounted for

Beginning Inventory:	2000 litres (80% complete) $1600 DM $1000 CC	
Units started:	12 000 litres $20 000 DM $7370 CC	13 000 litres (units completed)
Ending inventory:	1000 litres (50% complete)	

EXHIBIT 5.2 Step 1 – the physical flow of units and their associated costs

The goal of a process costing system is to allocate the $29 970 of manufacturing costs that have been incurred in the blending department ($21 600 of DM and $8370 of CC) to the 13 000 litres of paint that are finished and transferred out (in this case to the next processing department) and to the 1000 litres of paint that remain in the blending department's ending inventory.

Equivalent units of production can be calculated in two different ways – the first-in, first-out (FIFO) method or the weighted average method. In the FIFO method, the equivalent units and unit costs for the current period relate only to the work done and the costs incurred in the current period. In contrast, in the weighted average method, the units and costs from the current period are combined with the units and costs from last period in the calculation of equivalent units and unit costs.

First-in, first-out (FIFO)

With the FIFO method, the 2000 litres in beginning WIP are assumed to be the first units finished. Consequently, of the 12 000 litres started this period, 11 000 are finished whereas 1000 litres are partially completed and remain in ending WIP (Exhibit 5.3).

In Step 2, equivalent units of production (EU) are calculated. With the FIFO method, the equivalent units in beginning WIP (the units considered already complete at the beginning of the period) are correctly excluded from the calculation of equivalent units of production for the current period. Basically, we want to know the number of equivalent units completed in *this* period.

In our example, the 2000 litres are 80 per cent complete at the beginning of the period. This is equivalent to 1600 EUs (2000 × 80 per cent). If 80 per cent of the work was completed last period, 20 per cent will be completed this period. Therefore, we will complete 400 equivalent units (2000 × 20 per cent) out of the beginning inventory *this* period.

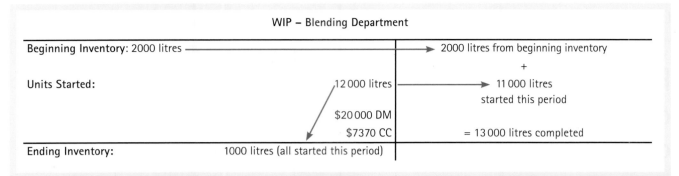

EXHIBIT 5.3 Step 1 – the physical flow of units with FIFO

What about the 12000 litres started new this period? According to Exhibit 5.4, 11000 of the 12000 litres are completely finished (11000 EUs), whereas another 1000 are 50 per cent finished (500 EUs). As shown in Exhibit 5.4, the total equivalent units are 11900 (400 from beginning inventory plus 11000 units started and completely finished plus 500 units in ending inventory).

Equivalent units of beginning WIP completed this period	2000 units × 20%* = 400 units
Equivalent units started and completed this period	11000 units
Equivalent units of ending WIP completed this period	1000 units × 50% = <u>500 units</u>
Total equivalent units	<u>11900 units</u>

* The beginning inventory was 80 per cent complete so 20 per cent is left to complete this period.

EXHIBIT 5.4 Step 2 – calculation of equivalent units with FIFO

If the completion percentage differs for direct materials and conversion costs, these calculations must be done separately. However, in our example, the completion percentage is uniform and the calculation of equivalent units for direct material and conversion costs is the same.

In Step 3, manufacturing costs per equivalent unit are calculated (see Exhibit 5.5). With the FIFO method, only the current period costs ($20000 of DM and $7370 of CC) are included in the calculation. Last period's costs of $2600 ($1600 of DM and $1000 of CC) are correctly segregated from the costs incurred this period. This allocation is consistent with including only the percentage of beginning inventory completed this period in the calculation of equivalent units.

Current period costs	$27370
Equivalent units of production	÷ 11900 EUs
Cost per equivalent unit	<u>$2.30 per EU</u>

EXHIBIT 5.5 Step 3 – calculation of cost per equivalent unit with FIFO

In Step 4, the $29970 of costs incurred ($2600 from last period associated with the beginning inventory and $27370 incurred this period) are allocated to the 13000 litres of completely finished paint and the 1000 litres of partially finished paint.

Because all 2000 units in beginning inventory are assumed to be completed this period, the $2600 of costs associated with those units will be allocated to the costs of the 13000 finished units. Of course, we incur additional costs this period to finish the 2000 units and to start and finish another 11000 units. How much are these additional costs? According to our calculation in Exhibit 5.5, it cost $2.30 per equivalent unit to blend paint in this period. As calculated in Exhibit 5.6, the 13000 litres of completely finished paint cost $28820.

Cost of the 2000 units from beginning inventory:	$ 2600
Cost incurred last period	
Cost to finish the units this period	920
DM and CC ($2.30 per EU × 400 EUs*)	
Cost of the 11000 units started and finished this period	25300
DM and CC ($2.30 per EU × 11000 EUs)	
Total cost	<u>$28820</u>

* The beginning inventory was 80 per cent complete so 20 per cent is left to complete this period (2000 units × 20 per cent = 400 EUs).

EXHIBIT 5.6 Step 4 – allocating costs to the finished units

Cost of the 1000 units in ending WIP

DM and CC ($2.30 per EU × 500 EUs) $1150

 Step 4 – allocating costs to the ending WIP

EXHIBIT 5.7

The 1000 units in ending work in process inventory are easier to cost. All are considered to come from the 12 000 units started this period and cost $2.30 per equivalent unit. As shown in Exhibit 5.7 the cost of the 1000 units (500 equivalent units) in ending WIP is $1150.

You should note that the total cost allocated to the 13 000 units of finished paint and the 1000 units of ending WIP must total $29 970. Consequently, if the finished units cost $28 820, the ending inventory must cost $1150 ($29 970 – $28 820).

The manufacturing cost of paint requires the summation of its component materials, labour costs as well as more aggregated overhead costs, apportioned to each unit (tin) of paint.

Weighted average method

In contrast to the FIFO method, the weighted average method treats the units in beginning inventory as if they were started in the current period. That is, we combine the units we know were partially completed last period with the units started this period. Consequently, the 13 000 litres of completed units and the 1000 litres of paint in ending WIP are both assumed to come from the 14 000 units we treat as having been started in the current period (Exhibit 5.8). This simplifies the calculation of equivalent units in Exhibit 5.9.

With the weighted average method, last period's costs are combined with the current period's costs in the calculation of cost per equivalent unit in Step 3 (see Exhibit 5.10). This is consistent with treating the units in beginning inventory as if they were started this period in the calculation of equivalent units.

WIP – Blending Department (Weighted Average)

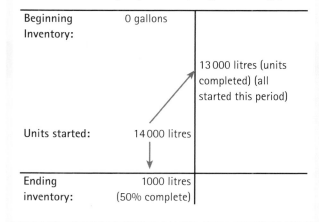

Beginning Inventory:	0 gallons	
		13 000 litres (units completed) (all started this period)
Units started:	14 000 litres	
Ending inventory:	1000 litres (50% complete)	

EXHIBIT 5.8 Step 1 – the physical flow of units with weighted average

Equivalent units started and completed this period:

Units completely finished		13 000 units
Equivalent units of ending WIP completed this period	1000 units × 50% =	500 units
Total equivalent units		13 500 units

EXHIBIT 5.9 Step 2 – calculation of equivalent units with weighted average

Total costs	$29 970
Equivalent units of production	÷ 13 500 EUs
Cost per equivalent unit	$2.22 per EU

EXHIBIT 5.10 Step 3 – calculation of cost per equivalent unit with weighted average

As with the FIFO method, in Step 4, the $29 970 of costs incurred are allocated to the 13 000 litres of completely finished paint and the 1000 litres of partially finished paint. As calculated in Exhibit 5.11, the 13 000 litres of completely finished paint cost $28 860.

The 1000 units in ending inventory must also have come from the 14 000 units assumed to be started this period.

Cost of the 13 000 units started and completely finished

DM and CC ($2.22 per EU × 13 000 EUs) $28 860

EXHIBIT 5.11 Step 4 – allocating costs to the finished units

Cost of the 1000 units in ending WIP	
DM and CC ($2.22 per EU × 500 EUs)	$1110

EXHIBIT 5.12 Step 4 – allocating costs to the ending WIP

Consequently, the cost of the 1000 units (500 equivalent units) in ending inventory is $1110 (see Exhibit 5.12).

Once again, note that regardless of whether FIFO or the weighted average method is used, the costs allocated to the finished units and ending WIP total $29 970.

Which method is preferable? Although the FIFO method is conceptually superior, the weighted average method will provide similar cost calculations when inventory levels are small (as in a JIT environment) or when costs are relatively stable from period to period.

LEARNING OBJECTIVE 4 >>

Process costing for spoilage in production

Defects during the production process often occur. The increasing complexity introduced by automation into manufacturing not only increases the speed and efficiency of production, but also the possibilities for error or spoilage during production runs. How do we account for this spoilage? That is, the resources wasted in production? Till now, we have only assumed two possibilities. First, that products are completed in WIP inventory and transferred to the next process, or to finished goods. Otherwise, and second, they are left incomplete at the end of a period in the WIP account. The possibility of material resources being wasted, considered as defective and therefore disposed of without being completed (spoilage) introduces a third possibility that management accounting systems must be able to measure.

In accounting for spoilage and defects, we follow the same four-step procedure characterising process costing. However, we consider spoilage as a third category of classification for units and costs, as will be explained below:

Let's assume the same information as explained above, for the paint production example, under the FIFO method. Again, as previously explained, there are 2000 litres that are 80 per cent complete at the beginning of the period and 12 000 litres are started this period. However, of the 14 000 litres undergoing blending, we discover that 1500 litres were not mixed correctly and had to be discarded. These litres were 40 per cent complete at the time of discovery of their defectiveness. Subsequently,

only 11 500 litres were actually completed. Also, and as per the previous example, 1000 litres remain incomplete at the end of the period. This scenario is explained below:

WIP – Blending Department (FIFO with spoilage)

Beginning Inventory:	2 000 litres (80% complete)	11 500 litres (units completed) 1 500 litres spoilage (40% complete when spoilage detected, all from units started this month)
Units started:	12 000 litres	
Ending inventory:	1 000 litres (50% complete)	

Equivalent units of beginning WIP			
Completed this period	2000 units × 20%* =	400 units	
Equivalent units of spoilage units	1500 units * 40% =	600 units	
Equivalent units started and completed this period	9500 units * 100% =	9 500 units	
(12 000 units – 1500 spoilage units – 1000 ending units)			
Equivalent units of ending WIP completed this period	1000 units × 50% =	500 units	
Total equivalent units		11 000 units	

* The beginning inventory was 80 per cent complete so 20 per cent is left to complete this period.

Having identified the physical units, we proceed to identify the total cost per equivalent units of production consumed this period, assuming 1500 spoilage units resulted from operations. Relative to Exhibit 5.4, we find that the equivalent units completed this period are 900 units less in Exhibit 5.14 when assuming spoilage. The 1500 spoilage units were not fully completed as previously assumed as per Exhibit 5.4, but rather 40 per cent completed then discarded. This 60 per cent reduction in production activity for the 1500 spoilage units equals the 900 equivalent unit reduction, resulting in 11 000 equivalent units calculated as shown in Exhibit 5.14. This 11 000 total equivalent units is a sum of:

1   20 per cent of the production required to complete the 2000 physical units in beginning WIP

2   40 per cent of the 1500 spoilage physical units as explained above

3   100 per cent of production for the 9500 physical units started and completed this period

4   50 per cent of the work completed on the 1000 units remaining in WIP at the end of the period.

As previously explained, the cost per equivalent unit under the FIFO method is determined by dividing the total costs incurred this period ($20 000 DM + $7370 CC) by the total equivalent units of work completed this period (11 000 litres). This gives a cost per equivalent unit of $2.4882 (Exhibit 5.15).

Current period costs ($20 000 DM + $7370 CC)	$27 370
Equivalent units of production	÷ 11 000 EUs
Cost per equivalent unit	$2.4882 per EU

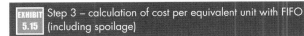
EXHIBIT 5.15 Step 3 – calculation of cost per equivalent unit with FIFO (including spoilage)

The final step involves the calculation of costs for the units completed, units still incomplete in WIP at the end of the period and the cost of spoilage units. These are determined by multiplying the equivalent units of the three items by the cost per EU ($2.4882), as shown in Exhibit 5.16.

Cost of the 2000 units from beginning inventory:	
Cost incurred last period ⟶	$2 600
Cost to finish the units this period	Total cost of completed
	Beg. WIP $3 595.28
DM and CC ($2.4882 per EU × 400 EUs*)	$995.28
Cost of the 9500 units started and finished this period	9500 units * $2.4882 = $23 637.90
Cost of ending WIP	500 * $2.4882 = $1 244.10
Cost of spoilage	600 * $2.4882 = $1 492.92
Total cost	$29 970**

* The beginning inventory was 80 per cent complete so 20 per cent is left to complete this period (2000 units × 20 per cent = 400 EUs).

** The sum of the four costs totals $29 970.20. This minor $0.20 difference owes to the rounding error resulting from limiting the $2.4882 EU rate to 4 decimal places.

EXHIBIT 5.16 Step 4 – allocating costs to the finished units with FIFO (including spoilage)

Note the cost of spoilage, which accumulates to almost $1492.92 of the $29 700 in costs this period. How is it treated? Clearly, spoilage can be excessive, but organisations often resign themselves to determining the cost of spoilage as being **normal** or **abnormal**. When spoilage costs are abnormal, they arise for reasons that do not relate to ordinary operations of a firm, and are treated as expenses disclosed in the profit and loss statement, usually classed as a 'Loss on abnormal spoilage' expense. The logic underpinning such an accounting treatment relates to the severity of abnormal spoilage. In being abnormal, such spoilage is often of a magnitude greater than expected, or caused by factors outside the spectrum of ordinary operations. In the interests of better informing management through our reporting systems, we separately disclose these costs as a line item in the expense section of our profit and loss statement.

In most instances, however, organisations experience spoilage as part of the natural production process. Such spoilage is considered unavoidable and in many cases independent of management control. For example, for every 10 000 Coca-Cola bottles produced, we might find that 2 bottles break or are damaged in some form due to uncontrollable reasons that relate to ordinary operations of automated equipment. Of course, this type of 'normal' spoilage is not desired, but nevertheless accepted owing to its common prevalence in most manufacturing processes. Normal spoilage is simply debited into the WIP costs of goods completed and not separately expensed (as is the case for abnormal spoilage). Why do we bother measuring normal spoilage costs if we intend to include it into our ordinary cost of goods completed in any case? Management still wants to understand the volume of this spoilage in order to possibly institute research and development efforts that might curb the level of such spoilage in the future, if it starts to become excessive.

✱ **normal spoilage**
Defective units discarded from the production process for reasons relating to the ordinary course of organisational operations. These costs are usually included as part of WIP inventory cost.

✱ **abnormal spoilage**
Defective units discarded from the production process for reasons outside the ordinary course of operations in companies. These costs are usually separately expensed in the profit-and-loss statement.

LEARNING OBJECTIVE 5 >>

Process costing for varying resource types

In the above examples, we implicitly assume that the direct materials and conversion costs (direct labour and overheads) are incurred uniformly and in parallel, throughout the production process. Therefore, if a product is 40 per cent complete, we implicitly assume it has had 40 per cent of its required direct materials put into the production process, and it has undergone only 40 per cent of its total conversion. This assumption may be true in some production processes, but many others do not exhibit similar behaviours. In many organisations, different resources are consumed at different stages of the production process. Consider the following hypothetical example from a typical beverage manufacturer, Coca-Cola Amatil. Coca-Cola Amatil might begin the production of Coke bottles by inserting some of their direct materials at the beginning of the process (water, colouring, sugars). Then, when the bottles are half converted, they may add other direct materials (flavouring, food preservatives). Finally, at the 95 per cent stage of conversion, the very final process might be the bottling of the Coke beverage. Therefore, the plastics direct materials are added at the 95 per cent stage of the production process. All the while, conversion costs (direct labour and overhead) might be added uniformly throughout the process, as described above. However, direct material costs often enter the production process sporadically, and at specific moments of part completion. This might be visually depicted below:

Consider a Coke bottle that is 70 per cent complete. What does this mean? The Coke bottle must have:

1   100 per cent of its required water, sugars and colouring (added at the start)

2   100 per cent of its required flavouring, food preservatives (added at 50 per cent stage)

3   0 per cent of its required plastics (not yet bottled, as it is only 70 per cent complete)

4   70 per cent of its conversion costs (70 per cent through its conversion to a Coke bottle).

While the physical units for all these products may remain the same, the equivalent units for direct materials must be split into three resource types. First is 'water, sugars and colouring' (WSC), second is 'flavouring and food preservatives' (FF) and third is 'plastics' (P). Additionally, conversion costs equivalent units must also be calculated. Based on the above information, let us hypothetically consider the following example:

Coca-Cola Amatil has 10 000 bottles that are 40 per cent complete at the beginning of August; 40 000 bottles are started in August; and 12 000 bottles are 50 per cent complete at the end of August. What is the equivalent units for August, for direct materials and conversion costs? Earlier in the chapter, we might have assumed the same equivalent units for all direct materials and conversion costs. Using the above information, however, all three categories of direct materials and conversion costs will show different levels of equivalent units, as in Exhibit 5.17 below.

In Exhibit 5.18, note that the 'Total to account for' that represents the sum of the 'Beginning' and 'Current period' units must add to give the same total, as the 'Total to account

| | 0% | | 50% | | 95% | 100% |
| Water, sugars, colouring | | | Flavouring, food preservatives | | | Plastics |

EXHIBIT 5.17 Stage of input to direct materials

	Physical units	Equiv. units (WSC) Added at beginning	Equiv. units (FF) Added at 50% stage	Equiv. units (P) Added at 95% stage	Equiv. units (CC) Added continuously
Beginning (50%)	10 000	10 000	10 000	0	5 000
Current period	40 000	40 000	28 000	38 000	36 000
Total to account for	50 000	50 000	38 000	38 000	41 000
Completed	38 000	38 000	38 000	38 000	38 000
Ending (25%)	12 000	12 000	0	0	3 000
Total to account for	50 000	50 000	38 000	38 000	41 000

EXHIBIT 5.18 Summary of physical and equivalent units

for' that represents the sum of the 'Completed' units and 'Ending' units. This is because whatever units are in production at the start of a period and which was started in the current period can only bear two destinies – they are either finished (and therefore completed and transferred out to the next department or to finished goods) or not finished and remain incomplete at the end of a period in the same WIP account (Ending). Therefore, (Beginning + Current period) units must equal (Completed + Ending) units.

Having identified the physical and equivalent units for the four resource categories, we proceed to divide their relevant costs by their respective equivalent units, to develop a cost per equivalent unit for each of the four resource types. We then multiply these costs per equivalent unit by their respective equivalent units completed and ending equivalent units, to derive the costs for each resource type, relating to completed and ending units. Finally, the sum total of the completed DM (WSC), DM (FF), DM (P) and CC costs represent the total cost of goods completed, and the sum total of the same four resource type costs for Ending represents the cost of Ending WIP for the period.

Exercises

1 Job vs process costing LO1

Product (service) costing systems are customised to provide accurate and timely cost data. A company should select a costing system that is appropriate for its production process. The following is a list of different organisations and selected products or services they provide.

a   Physical therapy clinic (mobility therapy)
b   Graphic design studio (logo design)
c   Auto repair shop (miscellaneous auto repairs)
d   Local bakery (wheat bread)
e   Dairy (whole milk)
f   Oil refinery (motor oil)
g   Construction contractor (custom-built homes).

Required
Indicate whether each of the above organisations would most likely choose *job costing* or *process costing*.

2 Process costing: FIFO method LO2, 3

O'Callahan Snack Company produces gourmet chips and other snack foods. One of the company's most popular snacks is a combination of several varieties of organic potatoes. The snack food goes through several processes including a potato peeling operation. Costs for operations during April are shown below. (Note: Production costs include direct materials and conversion costs for the department.)

	Number of bottles	Production costs
Beginning work in process		
(10% complete)	3 000	$10 000
Current period production	20 000	70 240
Ending work in process		
(85% complete)	5 000	

O'Callahan Snack Company uses the first-in, first-out method of computing equivalent units and assigning product costs.

Required
a   How many bags of the popular snack were completed during April?
b   Of the bags completed during April, how many bags were started and completed during the month?

3 Process costing: Weighted average method LO2, 3

For this exercise, use the information provided in question 2.

Required
If O'Callahan Snack Company uses the weighted average method of process costing, how would your answers to requirements A and B change?

4 Process costing: FIFO method LO2, 3

Chau Shoe Shine produces low value shoe shining kits by the tens of thousands. The shoe shining kit is subject to processes in two departments – Assembling and Packaging. Costs for the Assembling department during July are shown below. (Note: Production costs include direct materials and conversion costs for the department.)

	Number of bottles	Production costs
Beginning work in process		
(15% complete)	2 000	$15 000
Current period production	10 000	$65 000
Ending work in process		
(90% complete)	3 000	

Chau Shoe Shine uses the first-in, first-out method of computing equivalent units and assigning product costs.

Required

a How many shoe shining kits were completed during July?

b Of the shoe shining kits completed in July, how many were started and completed during the month?

c If beginning work in process was 10% complete (not 15%), how many kits were started and completed during the month?

5 Process costing: FIFO method LO2, 3

Juicee Drinks produces passionfruit drinks. These drinks are mixed, then bottled. Costs for the mixing operations during June are shown below. (Note: Production costs include direct materials and conversion costs for the department.)

	Number of bottles	Production costs
Beginning work in process (20% complete)	5 000	$7 000
Current period production	25 000	77 500
Units completed	20 000	

The incomplete drinks at the end of June were 60 per cent complete. Juicee Drinks uses the first-in, first-out method of computing equivalent units and assigning product costs.

Required

a How many drink bottles remained incomplete at the end of June?

b What is the cost per equivalent unit for production costs incurred in June?

c What is the cost of goods completed in June, and the ending WIP cost for June in the Mixing Department?

6 Process costing: Weighted average method LO2, 3

For this exercise, use the Juicee Drinks information provided in question 5.

Required

If Juicee Drinks uses the weighted average method of process costing, how would your answers to requirements A, B and C change?

7 Process costing: Spoilage LO2, 3, 4

For this exercise, use the Juicee Drinks information provided in question 5.

Required

How would your answers to C change if you were informed that 1000 units that were 30 per cent complete from this month's production had to be discarded as they were considered defective?

Problems

8 Comprehensive process costing: FIFO method LO2, 3

The Meekma Beverage Corporation manufactures flavoured bottled water and uses process costing to account for the cost of the products manufactured. Raw material and conversion costs are incurred at the same rate during the production process. Data for Meekma's mixing department for March are as follows:

	Units	Production costs
Work in process, 1 March (80% complete)	5 000	$60 000
Started during March	100 000	1 187 500
Work in process, 31 March (40% complete)	10 000	

Meekma uses the first-in, first-out method to calculate equivalent units.

Required

a How many units were completed in March?

b How many equivalent units were completed in March?

c What is the cost per equivalent unit?

d What is the cost of the ending WIP?

e What is the cost of the units transferred out of the mixing department? That is, what is the cost of goods manufactured during March?

9 Comprehensive process costing: Weighted Average Method LO2, 3

For this exercise, use the information provided in question 8.

Required

If Meekma Beverage Corporation uses the Weighted Average method of process costing, how would your answers to requirements A, B, C, D and E change?

10 Comprehensive process costing: Weighted average method LO2, 3

The Gibson & Zorich Bakery bakes breads for wholesale to restaurants. The company uses process costing to account for the cost of the breads and muffins that it produces. Raw material (for example, flour, sugar, flavouring, fruits) and conversion costs are incurred at the same rate during the production process. Data for Gibson & Zorich's blending department for December are as follows:

	Units	Production costs
Work in process, 1 December (80% complete)	5 000	$140 000
Started during December	100 000	1 060 000
Work in process, 31 December (50% complete)	10 000	

Gibson & Zorich Bakery uses the weighted average method to compute equivalent units.

Required

a How many units were completed in December?

b How many equivalent units were completed in December?

c What is the cost per equivalent unit?

d What is the cost of the ending WIP?

e What is the cost of the units transferred out of the blending department? That is, what is the cost of goods manufactured during December?

11 Process costing: FIFO method LO2, 3

For this exercise, use the information provided in question 10.

Required

If the Gibson and Zorich Bakery uses the FIFO method of process costing, how would your answers to requirements A, B, C, D and E change?

12 Comprehensive process costing: Multiple equivalent units LO2, 3, 5

How would your answers to question 10 change if you were informed that Gibson and Zorich Bakery added all their direct materials at the start of the baking process? You may assume that 40 per cent of all beginning costs and December costs are related to direct materials.

13 Comprehensive process costing: Spoilage LO2, 3, 4

What is the cost of bread completed and ending WIP for question 10, if you were informed that Gibson and Zorich Bakery found 3000 breads to be incorrectly blended, and discarded? The breads were 40 per cent completed when the defects were noticed and discarded.

14 Comprehensive process costing: FIFO method LO2, 3

The Fizz Drinks Corporation makes carbonated soft drinks and uses process costing to account for the cost of the products manufactured. Raw materials and conversion costs are incurred at the same rate during the production process. Fizz's bottling department costing information for September is given below:

	Units	Production costs
Work in process, 1 March		
(75% complete)	9 000	$63 000
Started during March	120 000	$1 800 000
Work in process, 31 March		
(50% complete)	10 000	

Fizz uses the first-in, first-out method to calculate equivalent units.

Required

a How many physical were completed in September?
b How many equivalent units were completed in September?
c What is the cost per equivalent unit?
d What is the cost of the ending WIP?
e What is the cost of the units transferred out of the bottling department? That is, what is the cost of goods manufactured during September?

15 Comprehensive process costing: Weighted Average Method LO2, 3

For this exercise, use the information provided in question 14.

Required

If Fizz uses the Weighted Average method of process costing, how would your answers to requirements A, B, C, D and E change?

Cases

16 Comprehensive process costing: FIFO Method LO2, O3

The Gunners Chemical Company makes a product type in a continuous process, in one department. Direct materials are all added at the beginning of the process, while direct labour costs and applied overhead costs are accumulated continuously throughout the process.

The information below relates to May operations:

Work In Process inventories 1 May:	2000 Litres 50% complete
Direct material costs	$4400
Direct labour	$2400
Applied factory overhead	$1800
Value of WIP 1 May	$8600

Details of May production are as follows:

Units Started	10 000 litres
Costs Incurred	
Direct material costs	$30 000
Direct labour	$25 000

Overhead is applied to production at the rate of 70% of direct labour cost. During May, the actual overhead amounted to $16 000.

At the end of the month (31 May), 1200 litres of product was in process, and these were 20% complete.

Required

a Determine the cost of finished Goods Transferred and the Closing Balance of Work In Process inventory, using the FIFO method.
b What is the unit cost of one finished litre of product in May?

17 Comprehensive process costing: Weighted Average Method LO2, O3

The George Company makes paint in 4 litre cans and uses a single production department. First various chemicals are added at the beginning of the process, and finally, the completed paint is canned. Canning occurs at the 99% stage of completion. The cans are then transferred to the Distribution Division to be readied for customer delivery. Labour and overhead costs are added continuously throughout the process. Factory Overhead is applied to production at the rate of 20% of direct labour cost.

The following data relates to the actual production results during February:

February costs

Work in Process Inventory 1 May	
Direct Materials – Chemicals	$48 000
Direct labour	$ 6 000
Factory Overhead	$ 2 000
Costs added during September	
Direct Materials – Chemicals	$230 000
Direct Materials – Cans	$ 8 000
Direct labour	$ 40 000
Factory Overhead Incurred	$ 10 000

Units of production for February

	Cans
Work in Process Inventory – September 1 (30% Complete)	5 000
Sent to Shipping Department during September	25 000
Work in Process Inventory – September 30 (70% Complete)	4 000

Required

Calculate the cost of goods transferred out and the cost of ending work in process inventory in February using the Weighted Average method.

GET ONLINE

HE DID

Discover your **ACCT** online experience at **http://login.cengagebrain.com/**

You'll find everything you need to succeed in class.

- Interactive quizzes
- Printable Flash Cards
- Podcasts
- Videos
- Animated Flash Games and Quizzes
- And more

http://login.cengagebrain.com/

Learning objectives:

After studying the material in this chapter, you should be able to:

1 Explain operations costing and how it is used to accumulate, track and assign product costs.

2 Identify a framework for categorising service firms in organisations.

3 Understand how service activities might contribute to profitability, using a service profit value chain.

4 Appreciate the link between the service organisation framework and job, process and hybrid costing models.

5 Recognise the relevance of services and service costs in the retail/merchandising sector.

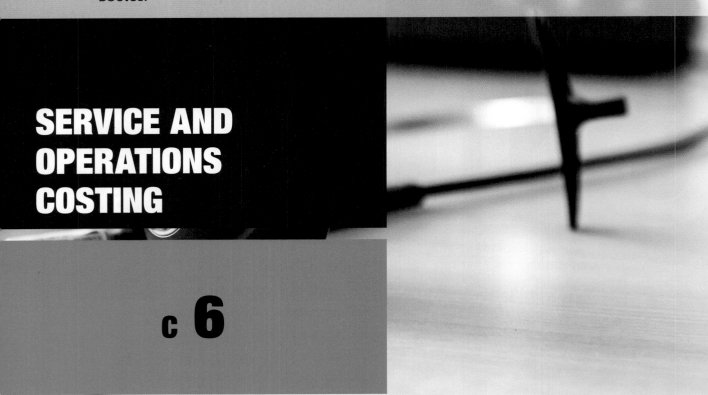

SERVICE AND OPERATIONS COSTING

c 6

The previous two chapters presented two costing approaches used by organisations to identify product costs: job costing and process costing. The use of either of these two approaches is dependent on the style of operations carried out by the organisation. However, there are two issues that require further clarification. First, is the idea that organisations may exhibit operational characteristics that require both job and process costing philosophies to be implemented. In such instances, *operations costing* more broadly presents an alternative costing approach, incorporating aspects of both cost systems. Second, the majority of contexts explained in the last two chapters covered product-based organisations – that is, organisations that provide a tangible product as a means of earning revenues. In Australia, the Australian Bureau of Statistics estimates that the service sector represents more than 70 per cent of our GDP. Service firms provide an intangible offering, usually manifesting as human skill, in order to derive revenues. How might the principles of job costing and process costing apply to service firms? By referring to the Silvestro (1999)[1] framework of service firms, we introduce a means for conceptualising how costing systems operate in service organisations, and present a service profit value chain to aid your understanding of how service organisations generate their value to customers. This allows for a better understanding of the role of cost measurement and management within service settings.

Source: Andrejs Zemdega/iStockphoto

The service sector accounts for more than 70 per cent of Australia's GDP and this proportion is expected to grow.

LEARNING OBJECTIVE **1** >>

Operations costing systems

Operations costing

Operations costing is a hybrid of job and process costing and is used by companies, such as clothing or automobile manufacturers, that make products in batches – large numbers of products that are standardised within a batch. Batch costing can be a peculiar style of costing to understand, as it exhibits attributes of job costing as well as process costing. We refer to it as operations costing. For example, a clothing manufacturer might make 5000 identical shirts in one batch. Each batch requires different grades of clothing material and ink/dye costs, and is therefore uniquely costed and different to all other batches (like a job in job costing). However, the cost of each shirt in the batch is determined by dividing the total cost for the batch by the number of shirts made in the batch. Though the batch is unique, the 5000 shirts in the batch are made identically, and their cost per unit can be deemed an average of the total costs of that particular batch (like a homogeneous product in process costing). Exhibit 6.1 summarises the types of products that would most likely be costed using job, operations and process costing.

As explained previously, organisations might also conduct operations by developing **hybrid costing** models such as operations costing that are costed in batches, with each batch being a job. The averaging of costs within a batch determines the

❖ **operations costing**
A hybrid of job and process costing; used by companies that make products in batches.

❖ **hybrid costing**
Methods of costing such as operations costing that involve more than one unique costing model.

	Job costing	Operations costing	Process costing
Type of product	Custom	Standardised within batches	Homogeneous
Examples	Construction, movie studios, hospitals, print shops, accounting and law firms	Automobile and clothing manufacturers	Beverages, oil refineries, paint, paper, rolled steel

EXHIBIT 6.1 Job, process and operations costing systems

cost per unit. These costing elements therefore also require a process costing approach. Following is a practical example to demonstrate how operations costing within an organisation might incorporate principles of job and process costing.

Hybrid costing systems – UltraTune car repairs

Making it real

UltraTune Repairs provides a mobile car repair and servicing operation Australia-wide. Its value proposition is customer convenience at a fair price. UltraTune mechanics come to the customer, performing automobile servicing at the customer's premises. The costing of each customer separately aligns to a job costing approach. However, the manner by which administrative costs within UltraTune are calculated – in order to determine an administrative cost per job that is impounded into the pricing of services to customers – reveals a process costing methodology. In this way, the UltraTune costing system must build into its architecture elements of job costing and process costing. UltraTune is not alone – many organisations face the same challenges in costing their products or services.

Source: Necip Yanmaz/iStockphoto

Ultratune offers a motoring service to consumers that requires a higher component of direct labour relative to direct materials and overheads, as is the case in service organisation business models.

Let's consider the example of a clothing manufacturer, who has been tasked with producing a batch of 5000 red shirts for Barrenjoey Pty Limited (BJY) and 4000 pairs of jeans for LegsBlue Pty Limited (LGB). The costs of the shirts are given below:

	BJY	LGB
Cloth (direct materials):	$25 000	$36 000
Salaries (direct labour):	$10 000	$13 000

In addition to the above direct costs, all overhead costs are general overheads relating to rent, maintenance, utilities and machine depreciation, and are uniformly applied at a rate of $60 per machine hour used in production. It takes 5 minutes to make a shirt and 6 minutes to make a pair of jeans. What is the total cost to the shirt manufacturer to produce a batch of BJY and a batch of LGB?

In order to solve the above questions, we must acknowledge the direct costs identified and individually link these to each batch uniquely, as enacted in a job costing methodology. We also observe, however, the application of a process costing approach with respect to overhead costs. Here, general overheads are going to be averaged into each batch, based on a preset overhead application rate that is similarly applied to all batches. If it takes 5 minutes to produce a shirt, then the overhead cost allocated to each shirt within a batch must be determined by calculating an overhead cost per minute, and multiplying it by 5. Factor in $60 per machine hour/60 minutes, which equals $1 per minute. Each shirt, taking 5 minutes of machine time, therefore receives an overhead allocation of $5. If 5000 shirts are produced in a batch, this represents an overhead cost of $25 000 for BJY.

Similarly, LGB's total overhead costs might be determined by multiplying the same rate of $1 overhead per minute as previously derived, by 6 minutes to obtain $6 overhead per pair of jeans. Therefore 4000 jeans receive an allocation of $24 000. Overall, the cost for a batch of production associated to BJY and LGB is as follows:

	BJY	LGB
Cloth (direct materials):	$25 000	$36 000
Salaries (direct labour):	$10 000	$13 000
Overheads applied ($60 per machine hour):	$25 000	$24 000
Total cost	$60 000	$73 000
Units	5000 shirts	4000 jeans
Cost per unit	$12 per shirt	$18.25 per pair of jeans

The operations costing example given above (as well as the job and process costing models previously discussed in Chapters 4 and 5) can be translated to service costing systems, though an appreciation of their application in non-production contexts requires careful clarification. We proceed to present a service costing framework identifying different types of service firms by two dimensions – the volume and variety of service (Silvestro, 1999).[2] Just as different types of product organisations exist in industry, there exists a myriad of service organisations. The service costing framework allows us to introduce three broad types of service firms – professional services, service shops and mass services.[3] Thereupon, job, hybrid and process costing systems are linked to these three types of service organisations. Examples are provided to illustrate how service costing might occur within each type, using these same costing principles covered in Chapters 4, 5 and the first half of this chapter.

LEARNING OBJECTIVE 2 >>

Interactive quizzes

Categorising service organisations

Services are incredibly varied, as evidenced by millions of service organisations around the world. A **service organisation** offers a non-physical, intangible and usually human sourced skill to customers in order to achieve its objectives. In order to engage in an effective discussion of service costing, we must first adopt a perspective for categorising service organisations.

❋ **service organisation**

An organisation that offers a non-physical, intangible and usually human-sourced skill in order to achieve its objectives.

Silvestro (1999) proposed a framework for positioning service organisations around a 'volume-variety' diagonal. This framework describes the range of service organisations existing in industry based on their volume of service outputs offered per day, and the variation in nature of service offered in providing

these services. Typically, service organisations that offer an extremely large volume of services would be expected to offer these services in a generic or standardised way. For example, Telstra offers the phone-calling service to millions of Australians daily, and the processes involved in offering the majority of these phone-call services are very similar. Such types of service organisations are termed 'mass service' organisations.

On the other end of the spectrum, Port Jackson Partners, a boutique and extremely reputable consulting firm, offers a highly diversified type of service to each one of its clients that number in the hundreds, and not millions, as is the case with Telstra. Furthermore, the nature of service offered to each client is unique and tailored to the clients' personal strategic challenges. These lower volume, highly tailored service offerings are described by Silvestro (1999) as being *'professional services'* type service organisations.

Finally, most service organisations do not cleanly represent the large scale standardised service offering of Telstra, nor the highly tailored, lower volume service style of Port Jackson Partners. Rather, they appear to exhibit shades of each. Some aspects of standardisation in services are offered, but there also exists a novelty in service offering that causes the offering of each service to differ from others. These service organisations are classed 'service shops'. An example of a service shop is H&R Block accountants. H&R Block offers standardised and generically costed services, such as the completing of a 'standard' income tax return covering income, interest and simple dividend payments. However, more complex tax returns are also offered, but these incur individually determined fees based on the nature of the work.

The volume-variety service organisation framework as discussed in Silvestro (1999) is presented below in Exhibit 6.2. This framework highlights the criterion upon which service organisations might be partitioned. Six criteria make up the definition. These include *contact time, customisation, discretion, people/equipment focus, front/back office orientation and process/product oriented*. Exhibit 6.2 also demonstrates how these criteria manifest to signal either of the 'professional services', 'service shops' and 'mass services' service organisation types.

The three service organisation types have different styles of operations, which cause quite different costing systems. We will consider each in detail, with calculative examples. Generally, the higher volume, more generic and standardised service organisations adopt a more process costing-type model, while the lower volume, higher value, unique and differentiated service organisations adopt a more individualistically determined job-costing model.

Mass services

Mass service organisations adopt a highly averaged form of costing, in accordance with the nature of their operations. While mass services conduct thousands of services daily, these services are generally supported with the aid of a large amount of equipment, whose ongoing operations ensure the delivery of a service. Given the scale of the effort, most large-scale operations tend to operate using highly automated processes. Consider the Telstra example discussed previously. How does Telstra determine the cost of a phone call? Telstra's network of cabling and satellites is coordinated by sophisticated equipment and complex systems. These networks of non-current assets must be costed and therefore associated costs of automation such as depreciation, maintenance and utility (electricity) costs must be considered in costing a phone call. Additionally, administrative costs and labour costs, mostly indirect, contribute to the cost of a phone call.

It is physically too cumbersome to individually trace each one of the above costs to a single phone call. Nor would an accountant wish to! The consumption of activities needed to generate a phone call is almost identical for all calls. Telstra therefore averages these costs into an estimated cost per call for domestic calls, and a cost per minute for international calls. The averaging of costs is not only mathematically easier, but better aligns to the reality of the way costs are incurred in Telstra.

A simple descriptive example illustrates the averaging nature of costing that might be conducted by Telstra, a mass services firm. For their 30 June 2011 financial statements, Telstra's operating expenses were $15.350 billion Australian dollars (AUD).[4] While there may be other forms of revenue generation in Telstra, a large proportion of these costs must be covered through Telstra's billing for phone calls by customers. Telstra's pricing system can only be enacted if we understand the nature of cost consumption that relates to the provision of these services. Let's simply assume that 40 per cent of these costs relate to the domestic phone network. Therefore, 40 per cent of $15.350 billion, or $6.14 billion in annual costs, can be related to domestic phone calls. If we estimate that Telstra facilitates 40 million phone calls a day, we annualise an estimate of 14.6 billion domestic phone calls a year (40 million calls a day × 365 days). Therefore, the cost per domestic phone call might be estimated as being ~$6.14 billion/14.6 billion calls, which is $0.4205 per call. You might reflect on the fact that Telstra charges as little as 30 cents (untimed) for a domestic call, meaning that it might be losing money on domestic phone calls. However, service organisations often subsidise some sources of revenues by making larger margins on other sources. In the case of Telstra, international calls might accrue larger margins and aid in covering the costs of domestic calls.

Overall, the low level of customisation and differentiation combined with the high volume of output required to enact their services allows mass services firms such as Telstra to use a highly automated and high-volume operation that inevitably aggregates and averages costs in order to determine unit costs (for example, cost per phone call). You might have also observed similarities in the way we cost for *mass services*, and the process costing method. We will refer to this later in the chapter.

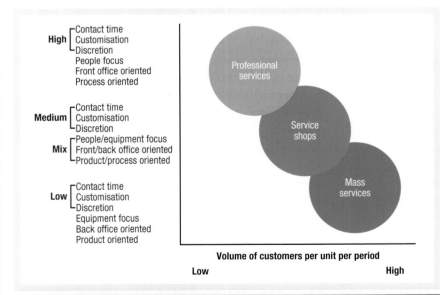

Volume of customers per unit per period
Low   High

EXHIBIT 6.2 Silvestro (1999) service organisation volume–variety framework

Source: 'Positioning services along the volume-variety diagonal: The contingencies of service design, control and improvement', by Rhian Silvestro from *International Journal of Operations & Production Management*, Vol. 19, Issue 4, pp. 399-421. Published by Emerald Group Publishing Limited, © 1999.

Professional services

As observed from Exhibit 6.2, **professional services** firms provide a highly customised service to individual customers. Within this type of firm, a high level of contact time is evidenced between customers and the professional services firm in order to enable the strong tailored services demanded by customers. Furthermore, employees within professional services firms are given strong discretion to perform services in ways that will satisfy the client, independent of rigid pre-established frameworks. Consequently, professional service costs are difficult to aggregate and average when costing for clients.

Professional Services – KPMG

KPMG is a well known and global leader in the provision of professional accounting, auditing and consulting services. The firm's motto is 'cutting through complexity', and doing so requires the tailoring of a unique service that addresses the unique needs of each client. Due to the firm's impeccable reputation, KPMG tends to employ highly qualified staff who possess at least degree level qualifications, and experienced hires can be costly. In costing their work for clients, KPMG therefore has a comprehensive system for estimating the costs of each job, and its consequent fee. Each fee is therefore unique and different for each client, dependent on the level of human capital required (a graduate might be less costly than a senior manager's time).

Making it real

Professional services firms rely heavily on the costing of labour when determining the prices for their services, as well as indirect costs such as rent and other service overheads.

Consider the boutique consulting firm, Port Jackson Partners (PJP), previously discussed in the chapter. Port Jackson Partners cannot tell a client that it costs them a standardised $25 000 per week to conduct a performance analysis. This value is based on the complexity of the client's business, the level of contact time allowed in the client business, the ability to measure the performance of the client business and other factors. As a result, Port Jackson Partners requires all employees to bill their clients a certain billing rate per hour. That billing rate includes an hourly rate for administration, overheads and direct labour consultant salaries, as hypothetically constructed in Exhibit 6.3. The desired profit per hour, hypothetically assumed to be 30 per cent, is added to the cost per hour to determine a billing rate per hour that employees will allocate to client accounts as work is completed. In this

❊ service shops
Service organisations that possess the underlying operations of both professional services organisations and mass services organisations.

	Hourly rate
Consultant salaries	$ 78
Administration	$ 26
Other overheads	$ 16
Total cost	$120
Margin (30% × $120)	$ 36
Total billing rate	$156

EXHIBIT 6.3 Billing rate estimation

way, more complex tasks undertaken for clients might require higher ability and more experienced staff who command higher billing rates to spend more hours on the client, further increasing the cost of the service.

The service cost per client is therefore individually determined and no two clients will consume the same costs in PJP. Consider the following example.

Client A and Client B both wish for PJP to conduct a performance analysis of their management operations. Client A exists as a monopoly in a low uncertainty industry, with very predictable competitor, supplier and customer behaviours. Client B operates in a dynamic, fast-paced, high-change environment where new competitors enter frequently as existing competitors exit. PJP has been separately asked to conduct each company's performance analysis. Exhibit 6.4 is a hypothetical service cost summary for each client in June 2011.

As observed from Exhibit 6.4, Client B's performance analysis was more complex, requiring the partner and senior manager to more actively involve themselves in the project, thus raising the amount billed as indicated in the billing worksheet. Note that the total hours worked remained the same by the same consulting team, but the nature of work caused Client B's bill to be higher.

Therefore, the need to separately cost each service and identify the nature of cost for each unique client necessitates a **professional services** costing system that is quite similar to a job costing system, as discussed in Chapter 4. We now proceed to consider the third costing system, the 'service shops' costing model.

Service shops

Service shop organisations reflect the underlying operations of professional services organisations and mass services organisations. These organisations offer sufficient

Client A	Title	Billing rate (hourly)	Hours worked	Total cost staff
J. Thomas	Partner	$700	5	$ 3 500
M. Clark	Senior manager	$550	9	$ 4 950
J. Evans	Manager	$390	18	$ 7 020
T. Lim	Senior Analyst	$250	23	$ 5 750
G. Singh	Analyst	$125	28	$ 3 500
Totals			83	$24 720
Client B				
J. Thomas	Partner	$700	12	$ 8 400
M. Clark	Senior manager	$550	18	$ 9 900
J. Evans	Manager	$390	20	$ 7 800
T. Lim	Senior Analyst	$250	15	$ 3 750
G. Singh	Analyst	$125	18	$ 2 250
Totals			83	$32 100

EXHIBIT 6.4 Client billing worksheet

volumes of a service in a way that is roughly similar, which allows them to average their cost per service for some cost elements as conducted in 'mass services' organisations. However, service shops also build into their service a level of unique customisation that necessitates the adoption of a unique and separate costing model for each service offered to customers, resulting in customers being billed uniquely. We proceed to explain this service shop model by referring to Questa Dolphin Tours, a hypothetical organisation that conducts dolphin watching tours in the Whitsundays off the coast of north Queensland. Questa offers a standard dolphin-watching package that costs $90 per person. Participants are taken by motorboat to areas where dolphins swim and may enjoy watching the dolphins from the boat. This is package 1,

the minimum package that all customers must take if they wish to go on a Questa tour. However, once on the boat, Questa offers a range of additional services. This includes an opportunity to swim with the dolphins ($45 per person for

Service costing applies to a wide variety of organisation – for example, a dolphin-watching cruise company.

half an hour), and for an additional cost feed giant manta rays ($20 per person for half an hour not including feed costs). Clients may choose to bring their own species of fish to feed the manta rays, or they may use the seafood provided by Questa at a further cost ($15 per person for 30 minutes of feeding).

As you can see the amount billed for each client is a minimum $90 for dolphin watching, covering the administration and operating costs relating to the boat, as well as yielding some profit. However, additional services are individually priced for each customer, depending on their personal preference. Therefore, a client that wishes to swim with the dolphins for 1 hour must pay the minimum fee of $90, as well as another $90 ($45 per half hour × 2) for 1 hour of dolphin swimming, bringing the total to $180. Another client who wishes to merely watch the dolphins will only pay $90. Finally, a client who wishes to swim with the dolphins for half an hour and feed manta rays using the food provided by Questa for 30 minutes will pay $90 (standard dolphin watching fee), $45 for 30 minutes of dolphin swimming, $20 for swimming and feeding the manta rays, as well as $15 for the food relating to the manta ray feeding. This totals a cost of $170.

As is observed from the above example, a standardised billing method per customer ($90 for standard dolphin watching) is used, but individualised and unique elements of billing are also included to cater to the needs of different customers. Such a system is therefore similar to the hybrid costing system described earlier in the chapter relating to the operations costing discussion.

LEARNING OBJECTIVE 3 >>

Managing a service organisation – a service profit value chain

Though not offering a physical product, service organisations clearly need to identify, develop and design services to cater to the needs of their customers. From this perspective, these organisations must engage in a reflection of their operations to better understand how their business model works in order to raise the cost awareness, and subsequent efficiency and productivity of their service offerings. As part of this analysis, Heskett et al. (2008)[5] identified a **service profit chain** (Exhibit 6.5) to enable a better understanding of how service organisations might reflect on their service offerings to customers, with the view to being more profitable. This chain is different to the more traditional value chain discussed in prior chapters, which relates to more traditional manufacturing firms. As you will observe from Exhibit 6.5, the service profit value chain has a strong customer focus and adopts a cause-and-effect model relating to attributes of service functions in organisations that ultimately lead to customer loyalty and profitability.

✳ **service profit chain**

A chain emphasising the cause-and-effect model relating attributes of service functions to customer loyalty and profitability.

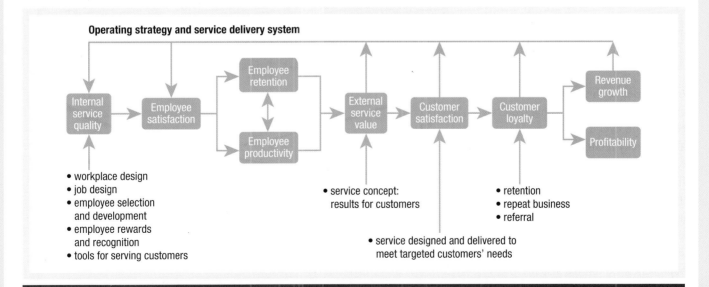

Operating strategy and service delivery system

- workplace design
- job design
- employee selection and development
- employee rewards and recognition
- tools for serving customers

- service concept: results for customers

- service designed and delivered to meet targeted customers' needs

- retention
- repeat business
- referral

EXHIBIT 6.5 Service-profit value chain (Heskett et al., 2008)[6]

Source: 'Putting the Service-Profit Chain to Work', by James L. Heskett, Thomas O. Jones, Gary W. Loveman, W. Earl Sasser, Jr., and Leonard A. Schlesinger from *Harvard Business Review*. Published by Harvard Business Publishing, © 2008.

The service profit chain identifies that internal service quality in the way a workplace is designed and employees are developed, evaluated, rewarded and empowered to serve customers, leading to satisfied employees. This reduces employee turnover and the greater tacit knowledge obtained by more experienced employees causes productivity improvements, which translates to greater value in service deliveries to customers. This should lead to customers being satisfied and referring the service to new customers or using the service repeatedly, thus raising retention and loyalty. Finally, greater customer loyalty ensures a longer term and more sustainable stream of revenues, contributing to profitability. In service organisations, the extent to which costs are invested in the attributes addressed in the service profit costing model aids an organisation's appreciation of the staff, process and customer-related investments required to ensure longer-term profitability. Of course, manufacturing and retail organisations may also adopt the service profit model as any aspect of their operations relating to the maintenance and retention of staff and customers can be relevantly managed by this model.

a mass services organisation aligns to a process costing model. The hybrid costing model, exhibiting aspects of job costing and process costing, might be aligned to the service shops organisation as it represents elements of both professional services and mass services organisations.

Three further criteria differentiating job and process costing in Chapters 4 and 5 might be linked to the three service organisations as shown in Exhibit 6.6. Professional services firms usually offer higher value services to a lower number of customers (volume) than mass services organisations. Furthermore, the nature of service offered by professional services firms is quite unique and differentiated when compared to mass services organisations. These attributes further justify the choice of aggregated and averaging process costing for mass services firms, as opposed to the unique, customised and individualised job-costing system adopted in professional services organisations. It is also important to acknowledge that costing is arguably most conceptually complex in service shop organisations because the hybrid form of costing must consider elements of both job and process costing.

LEARNING OBJECTIVE 4

>>

Linking service costing to job, process and hybrid costing

As discussed in this and previous chapters, the process costing, job costing and hybrid costing models are generally related to product-based costing systems. However, the costing approaches discussed in relation to mass services, professional services and service shops styles of service organisations strongly parallel these costing approaches. Exhibit 6.6 visually aligns the costing approaches to the three service organisation types. As observed below, professional service organisations' high customisation style suits a job costing model, while

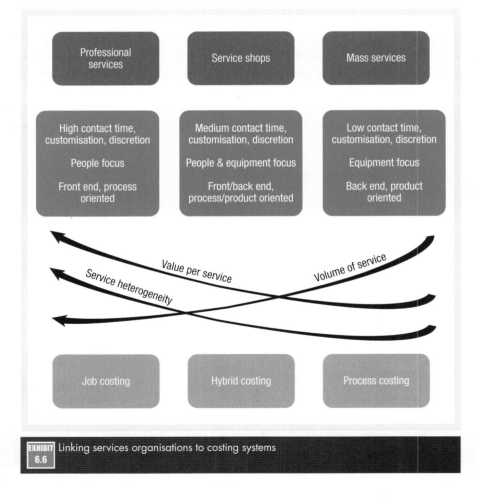

EXHIBIT 6.6 Linking services organisations to costing systems

Revise with
Beat the Clock

Service costing in the retail/ merchandising sector

Service activities are clearly most important and relevant to service organisations. However, many retail or merchandising organisations also exhibit a strong service component. Retail organisations acquire finished products and sell them to customers largely through a service function. For example, Athlete's Foot Australia specialises in providing expert advice to customers regarding their foot size, shape and running style, prior to recommending a shoe for sale. In this way, they offer both a product (shoes) and a service (staff expertise). Or, the Louis Vuitton store in Sydney emphasises a strong level of service quality in retailing the high-value Louis Vuitton accessories range to customers.

In separating industries into manufacturing, retail and service sectors, we sometimes overlook the overlap in service activities conducted in retail organisations and service organisations. The methods of service costing observed in this chapter that relate to professional services, mass services and service shops may be applied to the service components of retail organisations. These costing analyses can provide profound insights to companies regarding their investments in service quality. For example, the Louis Vuitton store might wonder about the amount of time that should be spent on a customer if other customers are waiting to be served. When might good customer service – spending 1–2 hours with a single customer – not prove beneficial?

Let's assume that the average spend of a Louis Vuitton customer is $600 in its Sydney store. If a staff member earns a salary of $35 per hour, then spending two hours with a customer prior to closing a sale effectively costs Louis Vuitton $70, or 11.6667 per cent of an average sale ($70/$600). Perhaps a quicker sale in another accessories store might have taken half an hour or $17.50 in staff salaries. Therefore, the costs of delivering a quality service might be estimated as $52.50 (the difference between $70 and $17.50, or two hours and half an hour of customer service time).

In this way, service organisations often reflect on the costs of their services and trade these off against the benefit of providing superior services.

Exercises

1 Mass services: Supply the missing data LO2, 3

Here is a selection of hypothetical costs relating to Telstra in June 2012. In May, 400 million calls were logged. Calls for June were 20 per cent lower than in May.

Costs (driver)	Drivers – states and territories ('000s)	Costs – states and territories ($'000s)	Cost per driver (costs/drivers)
Depreciation (machine hours)	25 875	?	$0.075
Electricity (machine hours)	25 875	$ 568	$0.022
Maintenance (maintenance hours)	720	?	$0.022
Administration (no. of admin staff hours)	3 890	$12 059	?
Labour (labour hours)	?	$26 503	$0.017

Required
Please fill in the blank cells, and calculate a cost per phone call in June.

2 Mass services: Supply the missing data LO2, 3

Refer to question 1 in answering this question. You may assume that administrative staff salaries make up the total administration cost and that all administrative staff are on the same salary.

Required
How many administrative staff must be let go if Telstra wishes to keep their costs under $0.14?

3 Professional services: Estimating a billing rate LO2, 3

James Coolay is starting an engineering services firm specialising in providing consulting advice to construction clients. He desires a profit of $180 000 from the business (ignore tax). He expects to work 1920 hours on clients in the year, if client work develops as expected. His business will incur costs, which include rent of $3000 per month, full-time secretarial assistance of $750 per week and utilities and other administration costs of $3000 per quarter.

Required
a How much should James bill per hour of client time?
b If the expected work on clients decreased to 1650 hours, what profit might James earn from his consultancy?

4 Professional services: Estimating a billing rate and costs LO2, 3, 5

Roger Gorman owns a law practice specialising in providing financial services legal advice to corporate clients. He desires a profit of $270 000 from the business (ignore tax). Roger expects to work 2100 hours on clients in the year if client work develops as expected. His business incurs the following costs:

Rent	$5000 per month
Personal assistant	$1000 per week
Meal and entertaining costs	$2000 per quarter (13 weeks)
Other administrative costs	$1000 per month

Required
a How much should Roger bill per hour of client time?
b If rent increased to $7000 per month and Roger agrees to a 10 per cent pay rise for his personal assistant, how many hours must Roger work in order to earn the same profit?

5 Operations costing/service shops LO1, 2, 3

Diane Lee manages a kite-flying business specialising in educating corporate clients on flying professional, high-value kites as team-building exercises. Diane has the following general costs:

Rent for premises:	$10 000 per month
Council permit to use park grounds:	$250 per group, per hour
Personal assistant	$3000 per month
Food, beverages	$20 per person
Kite depreciation	$400 per month

Groups may request one of two packages – the first is a half-day package, while the second is a full-day package. The half-day package is 4 hours long and the full-day package 8 hours. On average, Diane receives 7 people per package, and runs 2 half-day packages and 1 full-day package a week.

Required
a At a minimum, how much should Diane bill, per person, for a half-day package and a full-day package?
b If Diane desires a profit of $100 000 before tax per year, what should she charge for a half-day package and a full-day package?

6 Operations costing/service shops LO1, 2, 3

George Giles runs Happy Eaters Caterers and caters for small and medium-sized catering functions. Happy Eaters usually charge a minimum fee of $500 to cover administration costs and has three catering options for customers to choose:
Option 1: Peckish – for light eating catering assignments
Option 2: Ironman – for health-conscious catering assignments
Option 3: SuperSize – for high-consumption, full-meal catering packages.

On average, the size of a Happy Eaters' catering assignment is 100 customers. The Peckish option is priced at $15 per person, while the Ironman option is priced at $20 per person. The SuperSize option has just been introduced and George is not sure about its pricing. George expects to conduct 9 catering assignments this month and desires revenues of $25 000 per month. Four of the 9 catering assignments have requested the Peckish option, while another three have requested the Ironman option.

Required
At a minimum, how much per person should George charge for the SuperSize option this month?

7 Service profit value chain LO4

Please refer to question 6 in answering this question.

Required
How might George Giles use the service profit value chain to better manage Happy Eaters Caterers? What elements of the service profit value chain might be relevant to George Giles?

8 Operations costing/service shops LO1, 2, 3

Frances Fry owns Happy Children Party Planners. Happy Children organises games and entertainment for children in large community functions, such as large company Christmas party and Local Government Community Day celebrations. Frances offers three packages to entice the interest of her mainly corporate and governmental client base:
Option 1: Funkid – Face-painting only
Option 2: Funster – Face-painting and three fun activities for kids to play
Option 3: Funmax – Face painting, three fun activities for kids and individual costumes.

On average, a function contains 50 children. The Funkid is priced at $25 per child, while Funster is $35 per child. The Funmax option is $50 per child. Frances expects to conduct 10 functions this month and desires revenues of $8000 per month. Three of the 10 functions have requested the Funkid option, four have requested the Funster option and the remaining asked for the Funmax option. The average cost to Frances to offer a Funkid package is $10 per child. The cost of a Funster package is twice the Funkid package, and the cost of Funmax is $5 per child more than the Funster cost per child.

Required
Will Frances make her income target this month? Please explain with calculations.

9 Service profit value chain LO4

Please refer to question 8 in answering this question.

Required
How might Frances use the service profit value chain to better manage Happy Children Party Planners? What elements of the service profit value chain might be relevant to her?

Problems

10 Professional services: Supply the missing data LO2, 3

Lauren Chen is a partner in a successful accounting practice. The following is the running costs of one of her larger clients, Timbaa Wood Supplies (TWS). Lauren completes the accounts and tax returns for this client.

Timbaa is seeking to expand into an overseas market and wishes for additional work to be conducted by Lauren's accounting practice to assess the validity of this pursuit. Lauren thinks this will take an additional 2 hours of her time, as well as 3 hours of time for R. Matthews. However, the consultant is extremely interested in B. Borts providing consulting advice on this job, as Borts is an expert in international growth strategies. TWS is also aware that their bill for work this year has been high, and do not wish to spend more than $36 000 on fees to Lauren's firm.

TWS – staff billing list	Title	Billing rate (hourly)	Hours worked	Total cost staff
L. Chen	Partner	$850	5	$4750
R. Matthews	Manager	$600	9	$5400
B. Borts	Consultant	$400	12	$4800
T. Patel	Senior Analyst	$250	19	$4750
G. Rozinski	Analyst	$140	30	$4200

Required

a How many additional hours can B. Borts work on TWS without compromising the above constraints?

b If B. Borts has to work an additional 45 hours in order to properly consult for the client, what must his billing rate be for these 45 hours if the client can only spend a maximum of $38 000 in total fees to Lauren's accounting firm?

11 Service profit value chain LO4

Please refer to question 10 in answering this question.

Required

How might a professional services firm like Lauren's use the service profit value chain to better understand her costs? Discuss with examples of how she might use this value chain to communicate her costing structure and determine the elements of her business to focus on, reduce or discard.

12 Mass services: Calculating costs per unit LO2, 3

Quicktravel Rail operates frequent express train services from outlying areas of Sydney into the CBD. They generally experience a very high level of traffic most of the year as the fast growing Sydney population base over the last two decades has driven people to live further from the CBD. Quicktravel Rail is trying to estimate an average, single railway charge rate per kilometre for customers to justify their costing and subsequent pricing. Following are a series of cost estimates for an upcoming year.

Item	Rate
Staff salaries	$24 per labour hr
Infrastructure depreciation	$48 per machine hr
Rent	$25 per sq. metre
Overheads	$25 per machine hr

Quicktravel Rail expects to utilise 525 000 hours of labour effort, 1 046 500 hours in machine time and 14 000 square metres of rented space. Quicktravel Rail also expects 20 000 tickets to be sold this year and 4 million kilometres of rail travel to be conducted in servicing passengers.

Required

a What is the cost per kilometre for rail travel?

b If a passenger caught a train 45 km from the CBD, what is the daily return railway cost that relates to this passenger?

13 Service shops – calculating costs per unit LO2, 3

John Kim runs Smart Kids Tutoring, specialising in tutoring primary school children looking to gain entry into selective secondary (high) schools. John is trying to estimate the cost of running a class of students. Some of his costs are administrative costs incurred in running the business, while others are costs incurred specifically to facilitate the conduct of a tutoring class. John tries to conduct his classes by emphasising a balanced education philosophy, involving students learning through inspiration, and not merely memorisation and rote.

Following are examples of costs incurred by Smart Kids Tutoring:

Rent premises	$4000 per month
Tutor costs	$40 per hour of tutoring time
Stationery/equipment	$45 per class
Administration/office costs	$1500 per month

On average, John expects that 55 children will frequent his classes, twice a month. He expects to hold an average of 11 students per class.

Required

a What is the average cost per student based on the information above?

b How much must John charge per student in order to earn a profit of $12 000 per month (ignore taxes)?

c How would this profit change if John was to lose a class during the month?

14 Service profit value chain LO4

Explain how the service profit value chain might usefully aid an airline company to better understand how it might generate greater profitability. In your answer, please describe the various elements comprising the service profit value chain.

Cases

15 Service profit value chain LO4

Qantas Airlines has come under increasing scrutiny for its large losses incurred over the 2012 and 2013 financial years. Consider Qantas Airlines – how might you design a service profit value chain around the Qantas business model? What attributes might you focus on, and how might it allow you to consider areas of improvement that Qantas might target?

16 Service organisations and profitability

L03, L04

In recent years, Big Bucks Bank profits had been eroding. It became clear to managers that they required a better understanding of what their different loan products were costing. They had made decisions to offer a product which increased dollar balances without consideration of the cost to provide the service.

After some discussion, the bank hired you to compute the costs of three products: cheque accounts, personal loans and the gold VISA card. You've identified the following activities, costs, and activity drivers (annual data):

Activity	Activity Cost	Activity Driver	Activity Capacity
ATM service	$200 000	No. of transactions	400 000
Computer processing	2 000 000	No. of transactions	5 000 000
Providing statements	1 600 000	No. of statements	1 000 000
Customer inquiries	720 000	Phone minutes	1 200 000

The following annual information on the three products was also made available:

	Cheque Accounts	Personal Loans	VISA
Units of product	120 000	20 000	20 000
ATM transactions	360 000	0	40 000
Computer transactions	4 000 000	400 000	600 000
Number of statements	600 000	100 000	300 000
Telephone minutes	700 000	180 000	320 000

In light of the new information, Markus Modell, the bank president, wanted to know whether a decision made two years ago to modify the bank's cheque account product was sound or not. At that time the service charge was eliminated on accounts that had an average annual balance greater than $1000. Based on increases in the total dollars in cheque accounts, Larry felt good about the new product. The cheque account product is described as follows:

1. Cheque account balances greater than $500 earn interest of 2% per year, and
2. A service charge of $5 per month is charged for balances less than $1000.

The bank earns 4% on cheque account balances. Fifty per cent of the accounts are less than $500 and have an average balance of $400 per account. Ten per cent of the accounts are between $500 and $1000 and average $750 per account. Twenty-five per cent of the accounts are between $1000 and $2767; the average balance is $2000. The remaining accounts carry a balance greater than $2767. The average balance for these accounts is $5000. Research indicates that the $2000 category was by far the greatest contributor to the increase in dollar volume when the cheque account product was modified two years ago.

Required

a. Calculate cost rates for each of the four activities.
b. Use the rates computed in Requirement 1 to calculate the cost of each of the three products.
c. Compute the average annual profitability per account for the four categories of cheque accounts. What recommendations would you make to increase the profitability of the cheque account product?

REVIEW

ACCT puts a multitude of study aids at your fingertips. After reading the chapters, check out these resources for further help:

- **Chapter Review cards,** found in the back of your book, include all learning outcomes, definitions and self-assessment activities for each chapter.

- **Online printable flash cards** give you additional ways to check your comprehension of key marketing concepts.

Other great ways to help you study include **games, podcasts, videos** and **online quizzes.**

You can find it all at: http://login.cengagebrain.com/

Learning objectives:

After studying the material in this chapter, you should be able to:

1   Understand the importance of allocating aggregate costs to individual products/services.

2   Understand the difference between direct and indirect departmental overhead costs in assigning overhead costs to departments.

3   Appreciate the difference between service and production departments and the three methods for allocating service department overheads to production departments (direct, step-down and reciprocal).

4   Understand how production department overheads are allocated to products.

DEPARTMENTAL OVERHEAD COSTING

c 7

The allocation of production overheads in an organisation is no easy task. In large multinational organisations, there literally exist hundreds of very general and aggregated overhead costs that must be allocated down to individual units. This approach requires an accounting method that allows for the movement of overhead costs through multiple levels of an organisation, ultimately being linked to a single product.

Organisations wonder how indirect costs such as electricity and depreciation might relate to a single unit produced, such as a Coca-Cola bottle.

Source: LAKRUWAN WANNIARACHCHI/AFP/Getty Images

LEARNING OBJECTIVE **1** >>

Allocating aggregate costs to individual cost objects

Though he has now retired from Microsoft, think about the salary of Bill Gates in the time he was Microsoft's CEO. His salary represents an organisational cost, much like all other expenses incurred by Microsoft. In order to be sure of their profitability, Microsoft must be able to link costs to the products they sell, in order to be certain that they are selling their products at sufficiently high prices. To put it another way, the cost of a Windows 7 operating system package sold at stores around the world must to some small extent be slightly higher because Bill Gates' salary contributed to the cost of each package! However, by how much? Can we use accounting methods to inform this amount? In his time as Microsoft's global CEO, we know that Gates was responsible for the strategy and operations of Microsoft globally. Perhaps we might start by distributing his salary to Microsoft's regional centres. Let's hypothetically assume that these are structured by continents and that populations are used as the basis for determining the allocations – continents with greater populations receive a higher proportion of his salary. From the continents, we might further break the costs into individual nations within which Microsoft runs its operations. Each nation might then have regional centres. In Australia, it might be eight cities (let's hypothetically assume Sydney, Melbourne, Perth, Brisbane, Adelaide, Hobart, Canberra and Darwin). These cities will share

the Australian proportion of Gates' salary. Finally, the salary per city will be divided into the number of boxes sold in the city. This ultimately determines the extent to which the cost per Windows 7 package increases owing to Gates' salary. Of course, the above explanation is hypothetical, but not implausible, and broadly describes the challenge facing organisations in thinking up ways of allocating aggregated overhead costs to individual products. Whatever you do, you will always wonder whether you are right and you might also acknowledge other ways of splitting the costs that might provide different cost allocations. The departmental overhead costing framework that will be covered in this chapter will help you to reflect on all these different ways of allocating costs and choosing the right combination of costs, drivers and objects to cost, as will be explained.

As in previous chapters, we base our costing methods on the broad relationship between costs or cost pools, their cost drivers and the cost objects that we ultimately aim to allocate costs to. In the Microsoft example above, the cost was Bill Gates' salary. The driver used to allocate these costs at a continental level was demographic population. The cost object at the first level of allocation in the Microsoft example was the continents – we were trying to estimate the percentage of Gates' salary that might apply to the different continents, and so 'continents' were our object of costing. Of course, the ultimate cost object was a Windows 7 package, as we sought to estimate the amount by which each Windows 7 package might be more costly owing to Bill's salary.

Companies wonder about how overheads ultimately affect product costs for a number of reasons. These include product costing for inventory valuation purposes, product pricing in a marketplace and understanding product costs for purposes of making decisions within the organisation regarding product choices, market positioning or even budgeting departmental profitability targets.

❖ departmental overhead costing system

An overhead costing system that allows for aggregated overhead costs to be linked to individual products or services, by first allocating them to departments.

The **departmental overhead costing** method allows us to better tackle the above questions by including overhead costs into the cost of a final unit of product produced and sold. These costs are then added to the direct materials and direct labour costs of the same products to determine the production costs of the product. The logic of this type of costing can also be applied to period costs (non-production costs), such as selling and administration expenses, marketing and promotion expenses and so on. Indeed, many students might have assumed that in our example above, a large part of Bill Gates' salary in Microsoft relates to his marketing and administrative leadership of Microsoft, as opposed to production efforts that relate to overheads. If conducting departmental costing for purposes of identifying a selling price, we consider all indirect costs, both production and non-production related. However, if costing for purposes of identifying inventory costs, then only production overhead costs should be considered.

The departmental overhead costing system allows indirect overhead costs to be allocated to individual products by first allocating these costs to departments. From these departments, we allocate costs to products using cost drivers that explain the volume of resources consumed by a product in a department. In summary, there are four steps that must be considered to allocate departmental overhead costs to individual products or services.

1 Identify direct and indirect departmental overhead costs, and allocate indirect departmental overhead costs to all relevant departments.

2 Distinguish between service departments and production departments.

3 Allocate service department overheads to production departments using drivers that link service departments to production departments.

4 Allocate overheads from the production department to individual products or services using drivers that link the production department activities to individual products or services.

Direct and indirect departmental overhead cost allocations

As discussed previously, overhead costs must first be allocated to departments, prior to being allocated to individual level cost objects such as a product or service. In organisations, we argue that there exist two types of overheads at a departmental level. Direct departmental overheads are overhead costs that are easily traced to individual departments. These overhead costs naturally accumulate in individual departments ready for allocation into individual products. You may wonder how an overhead cost can be regarded as *direct*! Remember that the rules governing direct and indirect costs are relative to the cost and its cost object. If it's economically feasible for a cost to be linked to a cost object then that cost is termed a direct cost. Of course, all overhead costs are indirect, when the cost object being costed is an individual product or service. However, many overhead costs might yet

Westpac – Gail Kelly and a CEO's salary

Until recently Gail Kelly was the CEO of the Westpac Banking Corporation. As the highest ranking officer of one of Australia's big four banks, Ms Kelly commanded a significant salary – in 2013, her remuneration totalled $9.17 million.[1] Westpac's finance or accounting divisions might rightly wonder about how they link this sizeable salary to the products offered by Westpac. A departmental overhead costing system philosophy might aid Westpac in distributing Ms Kelly's remuneration to individual output units, which for Westpac might be an individual account, or a bank fee rate charged to accounts, or an administrative charge on a home loan account. In this way, large multinationals such as Westpac reflect on how costs might be absorbed, for purposes of pricing their services to customers.

GLENN HUNT/Fairfax Photos

be direct for larger, more aggregated cost objects such as departments. For example, the depreciation of machinery and equipment that are used in an assembly department in a factory clearly relates only to that department and no other department. Similarly, if each department occupies one floor of a large building, then the rent that relates to that one floor can be easily ascertained from the company's landlord. The rent cost for each floor directly relates to the department that occupies that floor. In this way, many departmental overhead costs are easily related to departments and therefore classed as **direct departmental overhead costs**.

However, there are other departmental overhead costs that are indirect at a departmental level. For example, insurance costs for a factory encompassing five departments may not be easily traced to a department. If the insurance relates to the equipment in the company, then equipment values might be used as the basis for apportioning these costs – but the link is not as clear as that discussed for direct departmental overhead costs. Other examples might be quality control costs, stock management costs or utility costs such as electricity and water consumption in a factory.

While direct departmental overhead costs can be easily traced to departments, indirect departmental overhead costs might have to be allocated to departments using cost drivers. **Indirect departmental overhead costs** are usually highly aggregated overhead costs that must be shared across departments by identifying cost drivers relating these costs to departments. Consider the following example for Sydney Mountain Cola (SMC) Pty Limited, which has four departments – maintenance, materials handling, assembly and mixing. As observed below, there are production costs that can be traced in an economically feasible fashion to departments. These include direct departmental overhead costs such as rent and depreciation for equipment in individual departments. However, there are two additional overhead costs that are indirect at a departmental level and therefore must be allocated to individual departments using cost drivers. These two costs are electricity costs and insurance costs. Electricity costs of $150 000 are driven by the consumption of kilowatt hours by each department, while insurance costs of $72 000 are driven by the value of equipment in each department. The table below provides a summary of this data, including kilowatt hours and equipment value information:

In order to allocate the electricity costs to the four departments we first divide the electricity cost by the total kilowatt hours ($150 000/50 000 kW hours). This gives us a rate of $3 per kW hour. Multiplying this rate per kW hour by the total kW hours of each department, we obtain the cost allocations below:

Materials handling:	5000 kW hrs × $3 =	$ 15 000
Maintenance:	8000 kW hrs × $3 =	$ 24 000
Assembly:	25 000 kW hrs × $3 =	$ 75 000
Mixing:	12 000 kW hrs × $3 =	$ 36 000
Total:		$150 000

To allocate the equipment insurance costs to the four departments, we divide the insurance cost by the total dollar value of equipment ($72 000/$3 600 000). This gives us a rate of $0.02 in insurance, per dollar of equipment. For every dollar of equipment a department owns, it bears responsibility for $0.02 in insurance costs. By multiplying this rate by the total dollar value of equipment in each department, we are able to allocate this cost to the four departments, as shown below:

Materials handling:	$ 100 000 × $0.02 =	$ 2000
Maintenance:	$ 200 000 × $0.02 =	$ 4000
Assembly:	$1 400 000 × $0.02 =	$28 000
Mixing:	$1 900 000 × $0.02 =	$38 000
Total:		$72 000

Having made the calculations for the above two indirect departmental overheads, we include them into the table along with the direct departmental overheads already known, as shown below:

Overhead costs	Departments			
	Materials handling	Maintenance	Assembly	Mixing
Rent*	$20 000	$10 000	$105 000	$ 70 000
Depreciation*	$23 000	$12 000	$ 92 000	$ 56 000
Electricity	$15 000	$24 000	$ 75 000	$ 36 000
Insurance	$ 2000	$ 4000	$ 28 000	$ 38 000
Total overheads	$60 000	$50 000	$300 000	$200 000

* Distributions already determined and provided in the table

In this way, organisations begin the departmental overhead costing process by allocating overhead costs or cost pools into departments. Having done this, we proceed to a consideration of departments as being service or production in nature – this has implications for how we actually move overhead costs to individual products or services.

Driver information	Departments				
	Materials handling	Maintenance	Assembly	Mixing	Total
Kilowatt hours	5000	8000	25 000	12 000	50 000 kWh
Equipment values	$100 000	$200 000	$1 400 000	$1 900 000	$3 600 000

Service departments and production departments

Many large organisations have both production departments and service departments. The production departments are involved in the direct manufacturing of the company's product or provision of a service to external customers. On the other hand, service departments provide various services to other departments within the organisation. These ideas will be expanded upon below.

Most manufacturing organisations are comprised of two types of departments. These are *production* departments and *service* departments. **Production departments** are the departments that actually work on a product and for which cost drivers can be strongly related to products. This is usually because physical work is actually done on the products in these departments and drivers relating to this work strongly link to cost consumption of the same products. For example, in making GM Holden vehicles in their manufacturing plants in Victoria, the painting and assembly departments might represent two *production* departments where car parts are spray painted (painting) and then put together (assembly) in readiness for sale. If all departments in manufacturing organisations were production departments, overhead costing to products might be extremely straightforward!

Many organisations, however, have **service departments**. These departments are very important in that they contribute to production and therefore possess overhead costs that should be allocated to products. However, *service* departments do not physically work on products. Consider a maintenance department in a GM factory in Victoria. The maintenance department plays an extremely important role by ensuring that the complex, high-value machines used on the assembly line are continuously functioning at optimal efficiency in order to minimise wastage in the production

✳ **production departments**
The departments that actually work on a product and for which cost drivers can be strongly related to products.

✳ **service departments**
Departments that are required in order for production to occur, but do not physically conduct production efforts to transform a product or offer a service.

run. Therefore, the costs incurred by the maintenance department can be related to the proper production of GM vehicles. However, the maintenance department does not actually work on any GM vehicle. GM vehicles do not pass through the maintenance department and therefore staff in the maintenance department do not physically work on GM Holden vehicles. So, while the maintenance department costs must certainly be linked to a GM vehicle, we are faced with a conundrum – how do we link them to products if there are no physical drivers directly linking the maintenance department costs to a vehicle? How do we then allocate these costs?

The departmental overhead costing system offers a method for tackling this challenge. One of the factors that make the allocation of indirect overhead costs to products more difficult than explained in previous chapters is that we first transfer overhead costs from service departments such as 'maintenance' to production departments such as 'assembly' and 'finishing'. While service departments do not physically work on products, they certainly play an important role in contributing to production departments. Hence, there are physical activities that might link service departments to production departments, and therefore justify the allocation of costs from service to production departments. For example, consider the maintenance department's costs. These costs might be transferred into assembly and finishing departments, using 'maintenance hours worked' as a cost driver (the basis for allocating these costs). Therefore, the more maintenance hours spent by maintenance department staff in the 'assembly' or 'finishing' departments, the greater the proportion of 'maintenance' department costs that will be allocated to 'assembly' and 'finishing' production departments respectively. Once these maintenance department costs have been transferred to the production (assembly and finishing) departments, they can be linked to products using the drivers that relate to the assembly department and finishing department.

A plethora of varied service departments exist in manufacturing organisations. As shown in Exhibit 7.1, examples include cafeterias, accounting departments and custodial services.

Allocation of service department costs to production departments that consume the services is one of the first steps in the overall product-costing process. Costs must be allocated using an allocation base or cost driver that is related to the particular costs incurred. For example, a cafeteria's costs would typically be allocated on the basis of the number of meals served to a production department. Other common cost drivers for various service departments are listed in the second column of Exhibit 7.1.

Service department	Common cost drivers
Cafeteria	Meals served
Accounting	Staff hours worked
Custodial services	Staff hours worked or square footage of space cleaned
Maintenance	Staff hours worked or service calls made
Materials handling	Work orders handled or volume of materials handled
Human resources	Number of employees served in production departments
Data processing	Computer time or operator hours

EXHIBIT 7.1 Service departments with common cost drivers

Companies allocate service department costs to production for various reasons, such as:

- *To provide more accurate product-cost information –* By allocating service department costs to production departments, we obtain a more accurate conceptualisation of product costs, consistent with the true resource consumption of a product in its manufacturing process. If the making of a GM Holden Commodore requires significant machine maintenance costs, these costs must rightly be allocated to the cost of a GM Holden Commodore.

- *To improve decisions concerning scarce resources –* when more accurate cost information is provided by an organisation's costing system, it is able to make key product decisions concerning the use of its limited resources to maximise profitability. If GM was not aware of the impact of maintenance costs on the GM Holden Commodore, it might have thought the Holden Commodore to be more profitable than it actually was! This might have caused GM to seek to market, promote and emphasise the Commodore over its other products, many of which might actually have been more profitable owing to their lower consumption of maintenance costs. The absence of more sophisticated costing systems such as departmental overhead costing might have profound ramifications for the strategic choices made by these organisations.

- *To hold service departments accountable for the costs they incur –* When service department costs are linked to products, management is more aware of their contribution to total product costs. Thus service department managers become more accountable for their own cost control within their departments. Senior management recognise the impact of these costs on the profitability of products and therefore place more pressure on service department

managers to rationalise their costs by increasing productivity or efficiency standards.

- *To hold production departments accountable for the services they consume –* Production departments can sometimes take service departments for granted. Consider the following example. Let's say that the production department continuously calls the IT department in to sort out even minor IT issues. This consumes significant IT department support time. If an organisation does not find a means for relating the IT support cost to each production department based on the 'number of support calls', there is no incentive for production department staff to actually think about what it is they're calling IT staff for and if they might solve the problem themselves. By pricing the IT service internally within an organisation, and internally 'charging' production departments for the use of the same service, management incentivises production departments to be more accountable regarding these services used. Management might also encourage staff within production departments to use their resources more judiciously, and carefully, in order to minimise the need to call in service departments. This might reduce the overall costs to organisations in the long run.

Service department costs can be allocated on the basis of actual or budgeted costs. In general, budgeted costs should be allocated to production departments because allocating actual costs allows the service department to pass cost inefficiencies in their departments to the production departments that consume their services. However, organisations will often allocate actual costs to production departments, purely for purposes relating to the proper costing of inventoriable product costs. There are three methods of allocating service department costs – the direct method, step-down method and the reciprocal method.

Waitering costs are a common and often significant service cost that is consumed by employees in production departments.

The direct method

❖ direct method
A method of allocating
service department
costs that allocates costs
directly to production
departments without
being allocated to other
service departments.

The **direct method** is the most widely used. It allocates each service department's costs directly to production departments and ignores the fact that service departments often provide services to other service departments. As an accounting method, the direct method is therefore most suited to organisations where service departments exist to only serve production departments and not other service departments. For example, we might reasonably assume that a company that has two service departments ('materials handling' and 'maintenance' as illustrated in Exhibit 7.2) might exist only to support its assembly and mixing production departments. The only materials handled by the materials handling department relate to those required to be delivered to the 'assembly' and 'mixing' departments, while the only servicing work conducted by the maintenance department relates to the servicing of assembly and mixing equipment used in the production process. The materials handling department and the maintenance department do not serve one another. In such a situation, the direct method for allocating service department overheads to production departments is best, as it reflects the underlying reality of organisational operations. Consider Exhibit 7.2 below, visually depicting this cost transfer.

Let's continue with the Sydney Mountain Cola (SMC) Pty Limited example, which has two service departments (maintenance department and materials handling department) and two production departments (assembly department and mixing department). As shown in the accompanying table, the materials handling department has $60 000 of total costs and the maintenance department has $50 000 of total costs. Prior to any allocation of service

department costs, the assembly department has costs of $300 000 and the mixing department has costs of $200 000. Materials handling costs are allocated on the basis of the number of handling hours used while the maintenance costs are allocated on the basis of maintenance hours used, as shown in Exhibit 7.3.

Exhibit 7.4 illustrates the direct method of allocating the costs in the two service departments to the assembly and mixing departments. The allocation of materials handling costs is based on the number of handling hours consumed in the two producing departments. Accordingly, 300/500 or 60 per cent of the $60 000 materials handling overhead costs are allocated to the assembly department ($36 000) and 200/500 or 40 per cent of the materials handling overhead costs are allocated to the mixing department ($24 000).

The allocation of maintenance costs is based on the maintenance hours in the two producing departments. Accordingly, 4000/6000 or two-thirds of the $50 000 maintenance overhead costs are allocated to the assembly department ($33 333) and 2000/6000 or one-third of the maintenance department costs are allocated to the mixing department ($16 667). Note that there is no attempt in the direct method to allocate maintenance or materials handling costs to one another, though Exhibit 7.3 reveals

	Service departments		Production departments	
	Materials handling	Maintenance	Assembly	Mixing
Departmental costs before allocation	$60 000	$50 000	$300 000	$200 000
Handling hours		100	300	200
Maintenance hours	300		4 000	2 000
Direct labour hours			20 000	10 000
Machine hours	150	200	5 000	40 000

EXHIBIT 7.3 Service department cost drivers

that materials handling used some maintenance hours and the maintenance department required some handling hours.

As previously explained, the direct method is simple, but ignores the possibility of consumption of services among service departments and thus might not be as accurate as other methods. Its widespread use arises from

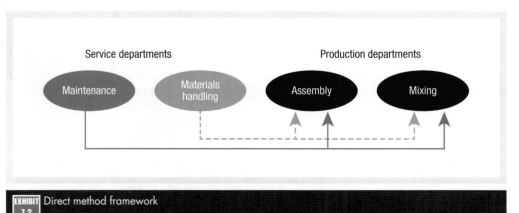

EXHIBIT 7.2 Direct method framework

	Service departments		Production departments	
	Materials handling	Maintenance	Assembly	Mixing
Departmental costs before allocation	$ 60 000	$ 50 000	$300 000	$200 000
Allocation:				
Materials handling costs	(60 000)		36 000	24 000
Allocation:				
Maintenance costs		(50 000)	33 333	16 667
Departmental costs after allocation	$ 0	$ 0	$369 333	$240 667
Handling hours (Exh. 7.3)		100	300	200
Maintenance hours (Exh. 7.3)	300		4 000	2 000

EXHIBIT 7.4 The direct method of service department cost allocation

its simplicity, which may also prove inaccurate when service departments use one another's services. Of course, if service departments in manufacturing organisations don't service one another, the direct method will prove to be the best method.

The step-down or sequential method

Revise with Beat the Clock

The **step-down** or **sequential method** recognises that service departments consume resources of other service departments and should therefore assume responsibility for these costs prior to transferring costs to production departments. Such costs are therefore allocated from service departments to other service departments and then to production departments in a sequential (one-way) fashion. This method is most relevant when service departments show a one-way dependence. That is, one service department uses another, but the other does not use the first. Consider the example above. Let's assume that though the maintenance department does not require any materials handling, maintenance does servicing work for the equipment in the materials handling

department as well as the equipment in the assembly and mixing departments. The overhead costs sourcing from the maintenance department must therefore be first allocated to all three departments (materials handling, assembly, mixing). Subsequently, and because materials handling does not support maintenance but only assembly and mixing, the total overhead in materials handling (including the amount that was allocated from maintenance) is allocated to assembly and mixing. Therefore, it does not require any share of materials handling overhead costs. Consider Exhibit 7.5 below.

The step-down method differs from the direct method in that the costs from one service department are allocated to other service departments and production departments sequentially, that is 'one-way' or uni-directionally. The allocation typically begins with the service department that provides the greatest percentage of service to other service departments or the service department with the highest costs. In this case, let's assume that the materials handling departmental costs are allocated first. As illustrated in Exhibit 7.5, its cost will be allocated to the maintenance department as well as the assembly and mixing departments. Following that allocation, the maintenance department's costs (which now include a portion of the assembly department costs recently allocated) will be allocated only to the assembly and mixing departments in a step-down fashion. Note that after the materials handling costs have been allocated, the costs of the maintenance service department is not allocated back to it, though the materials handling department uses some maintenance office hours. As per Exhibit 7.4, Exhibit 7.6 does not consider the 300 maintenance hours used in materials handling when determining its cost allocation. However, it is more accurate than the direct method owing to its consideration of the 100 handling hours used in the maintenance department.

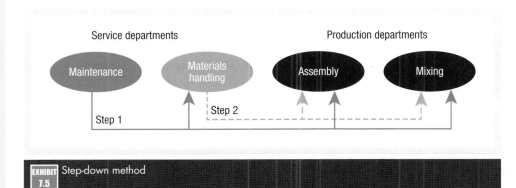

EXHIBIT 7.5 Step-down method

	Service departments		Production departments	
	Materials handling	Maintenance	Assembly	Mixing
Departmental costs before allocation	$60 000	$50 000	$300 000	$200 000
Allocation:				
Materials handling costs	(60 000)	10 000*	30 000*	20 000*
Allocation:				
Maintenance costs		(60 000)	40 000**	20 000**
Departmental costs after allocation	$ 0	$ 0	$370 000	$240 000
Handling hours (Exh. 7.3)		100	300	200
Maintenance hours (Exh. 7.3)	300		4 000	2 000

* Materials handling costs transferred to production departments

** Maintenance costs transferred to production departments.

EXHIBIT 7.6 The step-down method of service department cost allocation

The allocation of materials handling costs is based on the number of handling hours consumed in the maintenance department as well as the assembly and mixing production departments. Accordingly, 100/600 or 16.67 per cent of the $60 000 costs are allocated to the maintenance department ($10 000), 300/600 or 50 per cent of the $60 000 costs are allocated to the assembly department ($30 000) and 200/600 or 33.33 per cent of the $60 000 costs are allocated to the mixing department ($20 000).

The maintenance department cost to be allocated to the two production departments is now $60 000 owing to the additional $10 000 allocated from the materials handling department increasing its original amount from $50 000 to $60 000. The allocation of these maintenance department costs is based on the maintenance hours in the two production departments. As explained previously, in the step-down method the second service department does not allocate back to the first. Therefore, none of the maintenance department's overhead costs are allocated back to the materials handling department. Accordingly, 4000/6000 or two-thirds of the $60 000 costs are allocated to the assembly department ($40 000) and 20 000/60 000 or one-third of the $60 000 costs are allocated to the mixing department ($20 000).

The reciprocal method

The **reciprocal method** is similar to the step-down method in that it recognises that service departments consume resources of other service departments. However, the reciprocal method goes a step further than the step-down method, in assuming a two-way relationship between

service departments (see Exhibit 7.7). That is, both service departments use one another, as well as supporting the production departments. Advancing the example discussed above, let's now assume that the maintenance and materials handling service departments support one another in addition to supporting the two production departments (assembly and mixing). The maintenance department provides maintenance for the equipment in the materials handling department (as previously explained in the 'step-down' discussion), but the materials handling department also provides the handling for heavy servicing materials required by maintenance to perform their servicing function. Consequently, to mirror the nature of actual operations, there must first be a calculation to determine the bi-directional flow of costs between service departments prior to undertaking a cost transfer from service to production departments. The reciprocal method allocates costs back and forth among the service departments. Though it is rarely used in practice, we will discuss and explain it as the nature of relationships between service departments has increased in complexity as organisational operations become more automated. Let's visually depict this relationship:

The reciprocal method considers the possibility of a two-way relationship between the two service departments in determining cost allocations to production departments. First, simultaneous equations are used to determine the split of overheads between the two service departments. Subsequently the new overhead totals as determined in the two service departments are transferred to the production department using only production department cost drivers, somewhat similar to the direct method. What differentiates the reciprocal method is the initial step, whereby we reflect on the extent to which one service department is responsible for the overhead consumption of another service department, and vice versa.

Following from the previous two examples, we first establish equations that express the costs for which each service department is responsible. As shown in Exhibit 7.8, we note that the materials handling department has incurred $60 000. We also know that it is partially responsible for the

❋ reciprocal method
Recognises that service departments mutually consume one another's resources and therefore costs must be allocated between service departments prior to being allocated to production departments.

overhead costs in the maintenance department – but to what extent? We theorise that the materials handling department should be allocated a portion of the maintenance department's $60 000 overhead costs, as determined by the driver used to allocate maintenance department costs (maintenance hours). If the total maintenance hours used this period is the sum of the maintenance hours consumed by the assembly (4000 hours), mixing (2000 hours) and materials handling (300 hours) departments, then the maintenance hours must be 6300 hours. The materials handling department is responsible to the proportion of 300/6300, being its share of the total maintenance hours. This ratio may be reduced to an equivalent 3/63 fraction. Therefore the total overheads for which the materials handling department might be related to is its own $60 000 and a proportion equal to 3/63 of the maintenance department overheads. This statement may be expressed using the following equation:

$$MH = \$60\,000 + \frac{3}{63} \times MNT$$

where:

MH = the overheads for which materials handling is responsible

MNT = the overheads for which the maintenance department is responsible

We now apply the same approach to determine the overheads for which the maintenance department is responsible. The maintenance department has incurred $50 000. It is also partially responsible for the overhead costs in the materials handling. As explained previously, the maintenance department should be allocated a portion of the materials handling department's $50 000 overhead costs, as determined by the driver used to allocate the materials handling department costs (handling hours). If the total handling hours used this period is the sum of the handling hours consumed by the assembly (300), mixing (200) and materials handling (100) departments, then the handling hours is 600 hours. The maintenance department is responsible to the proportion of 100/600, being its share of the handling hours consumed this period. This ratio may be reduced to an equivalent 1/6 fraction. The total overheads which the maintenance department might be related to, is therefore its own $50 000 and a proportion equal to 1/6 of the materials handling department overheads. This statement may be expressed using the following equation:

$$MNT = \$50\,000 + \frac{1}{6} \times MH$$

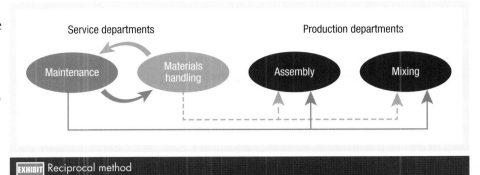

EXHIBIT 7.7 Reciprocal method

where:

MH = the overheads for which materials handling is responsible

MNT = the overheads for which the maintenance department is responsible

Combining both equations, we may construct the following simultaneous equations:

Equation 1: $\quad MH = \$60\,000 + \dfrac{1}{63} \times MNT$

Equation 2: $\quad MNT = \$50\,000 + \dfrac{1}{6} \times MH$

By process of substitution, we replace the 'MH' variable in Equation 2 with '60 000 + 3/63*MNT', as both are equivalent terms. This gives us the following equation (which we will call Equation 3):

Equation 3: $\quad MNT = \$50\,000 + \dfrac{1}{6} \times (\$60\,000 + \dfrac{3}{63} \times MNT)$

The purpose of substituting MH with its equivalent equation is to allow us to create a third equation that only has one unknown variable (in this instance, MNT). Solving this equation, we calculate MNT to be:

$$MNT = \$50\,000 + \$10\,000 + \frac{3}{378} \times MNT$$
$$\frac{375}{378}*MNT = \$60\,000$$
$$MNT = \$60\,480$$

Having determined MNT, we can now solve MH by substituting the MNT value into Equation 1:

$$MH = \$60\,000 + \frac{3}{63} \times (\$50\,000 + \frac{1}{6} \times MH)$$
$$MH = \$60\,000 + 2380.95238095 + \frac{3}{378} \times MH$$
$$\frac{375}{378} \times MH = 62\,380.95238095$$
$$MH = \$62\,880$$

Alternatively, you may simply apply MNT = $60 480 as calculated from Equation 3 and apply this value to the above equation:

$$MH = \$60\,000 + \frac{3}{63} \times \$60\,480$$
$$MH = \$62\,880$$

You may have observed that the original materials handling overhead was $60 000, while the maintenance overhead was $50 000. These add to give $110 000. However, the new totals for both departments as determined from the reciprocal method redistributions are $60 480 + $62 880, which add to give $123 360. Though this value is higher than the $110 000 originally in both, we will be including the driver hours for all three departments when allocating the two redistributed costs to the two production departments. Consequently, a proportionately lower allocation will be allotted to each producing department from these higher amounts than in the direct method, leading to a correction which ensures that the final overhead amounts allocated to the two production departments from maintenance and materials handling will tally to $110 000. Another way of conceptualising this difference is to consider the blue numbers in Exhibit 7.8. If we multiply $62 880 by 1/6, we get the maintenance department overhead share of the allocation, which is $10 480. Add $10 480 to the original $50 000, and we obtain the $60 480 determined from the reciprocal method redistribution for the maintenance department. Similarly, if we multiply $60 480 by 3/63, we calculate the materials handling department's overhead share of the maintenance department allocation, which is $2880. Add $2880 to the original materials handling overhead of $60 000, and we obtain $62 880, the materials handling reciprocal method amount redistributed using the simultaneous equations above.

As explained above, having derived through simultaneous equations that the materials handling department is responsible for $62 880 in overhead costs and that the maintenance department is responsible for $60 480 in overhead costs, we proceed to directly allocate these overheads to the production departments using their respective drivers. The allocation of materials handling costs is based on the number of handling hours consumed in all three departments: assembly, mixing and maintenance. Accordingly, 300/600 of the $62 880 materials handling overhead costs are allocated to the assembly department ($31 440) and 200/600 of the materials handling overhead costs are allocated to the mixing department ($20 960).

Similarly, the allocation of maintenance costs to the production departments is based on the maintenance hours in all three departments. Accordingly, 4000/6300 of the $60 480 maintenance overhead costs are allocated to the assembly department ($38 400) and 2000/6300 of the maintenance department costs are allocated to the mixing department ($19 200). These values are shown in Exhibit 7.8.

Note also that the sum total of all four allocations ($31 440 + $20 960 + $38 400 + $19 200) add to give $110 000, which is the original overhead amounts in materials handling and maintenance prior to the reciprocal method redistribution.

	Service departments		Production departments	
	Materials handling	Maintenance	Assembly	Mixing
Departmental costs before allocation	$60 000	$50 000	$300 000	$200 000
Allocation:				
Reciprocal method re-allocations				
Allocation:				
Materials handling costs	(62 880)	$ 10 480*	$ 31 440	$ 20 960
Allocation:				
Maintenance costs	$2 880**	$(60 480)	$ 38 400	$ 19 200
Departmental costs after allocation	$ 0	$ 0	$369 840	$240 160
Handling hours (Exh. 7.3)		100	300	200
Maintenance hours (Exh. 7.3)	300		4 000	2 000
Direct labour hours			20 000	10 000
Machine hours	150	200	5 000	40 000
Departmental overhead rate			$369 840/20 000 DL hours = $18.492	$240 160/40 000 machine hours = $6.004

* $10 480 = $62 880*100/600

** $2880 = $60 480*3/63

EXHIBIT 7.8 The reciprocal method of service department cost allocation

Contrasting the plantwide rate with the departmental overhead rate

The departmental overhead rates explained in this chapter are in many ways superior to the plantwide overhead rate calculation method previously discussed in Chapter 3. The plantwide rate requires organisations to identify one overhead rate, to apply all its overheads across all departments, to products or services. As such, the plantwide rate applies a highly aggregated and averaging style of costing to products. This can cause some products to be undercosted, while others are overcosted. For example, consider the Sydney Mountain Cola (SMC) example discussed in the previous section. If SMC calculates a plantwide rate, you might find this calculation relatively simple when compared to the departmental overhead costing rate calculation. The plantwide overhead rate is simply the total overhead cost divided by a single overhead driver applicable to all production departments. Let's assume management choose direct labour hours as their plantwide driver for overhead costs. This means that the single plantwide overhead rate applied to products is the total overhead cost ($610000) divided by the total number of direct labour hours (30000 hours). This gives us a single plantwide overhead rate of $20.33 per direct labour hour. Whatever the production department that a product is worked on, it receives $20.33 per direct labour hour it consumes of production time. The plantwide rate is easier to calculate, but generally considered less accurate as it uses only one rate to apply overhead in a wide range of production departments, all of which should probably be using different drivers owing to their varied operating styles.

Which method for costing departmental overhead rate is better?

It is tempting to think of the reciprocal method as being the most complex (and difficult!) to calculate, and therefore assume it to be a superior method to the step-down and direct methods. The mathematical ease of the direct method might cause you to consider it an over-simplified method, not reflective of the complex reality of organisational practice. Such assumptions equating complexity with accuracy can be incorrect. The complexity (or lack of) in a method simply reflects a mathematical approach. What is important is the 'fit' of the method to the organisational reality of your operations. If you think that your service departments only exist for the production departments, and not other service departments, then the direct method is the best method for your organisation, as its mathematical approach reflects what is actually going on in your organisation (no relationship between service departments)! If you believe that your service departments show a one-way dependence ('A' needs 'B',

'B' does not need 'A'), then the step-down or sequential method is the best. Finally, if you actually think that a two-way dependence between your service departments exists ('A' needs 'B', and 'B' needs 'A'), then the reciprocal method is the most appropriate.

LEARNING OBJECTIVE >>

Allocating production overheads to individual products/services

Once the allocation is complete using either the direct method, step-down method or reciprocal method, all of the service department costs will have been allocated to the production departments. The total costs of the production departments will now include all the overheads originally in the production departments as well as the amounts allocated from the service departments. These costs total $369840 in the assembly department and $240160 in the mixing department as per the Sydney Mountain Cola example. The total costs of the production departments can now be allocated to products, using cost drivers that link each production department to the units produced. Let's assume as per Exhibit 7.8 (and also highlighted in Exhibit 7.3) that assembly uses much more direct labour hours than machine hours. We will therefore consider it a labour-intensive production department, while the mixing department uses far more machine hours than direct labour hours and will therefore be considered a more automated department. For these reasons, we allocate the total overheads in the assembly department to products using direct labour hours, and total overheads in the mixing departments to products using machine hours. This gives us an assembly department rate of $18.492 per direct labour hour ($369840/20000) and a mixing department rate of $6.004 per machine hour ($240160/40000).

Source: Prisma Bildagentur AG/Alamy

One of the more challenging tasks of a management accountant is the construction of logical mathematical approaches for dividing indirect, overhead costs into products or services.

What does this mean? Quite simply, for every direct labour hour taken by a product in the assembly department, $18.492 will be added to its production cost. Similarly, for every machine hour taken by a product in the mixing department, $6.004 will be added to its production cost. In this way organisations are able to clearly cost products based on the actual resources they consume in production departments. It is also important for you to note that machine hours in assembly (5000) and direct labour hours in mixing (10 000) don't count! If a driver has quantities outside the department for which it is the driver, those outside quantities don't matter for purposes of cost allocation. We only consider the cost driver within the department for which it is used to allocate overhead costs.

Therefore, if Product A uses 2 direct labour (DL) hours in assembly and 1 direct labour hour in mixing, and also uses 3 machine hours (M. hours) in assembly and 10 machine hours in mixing, its allotted overhead costs are as follows:

From assembly:	2 DL hours × $18.492 per DL hour =	$ 36.984
From mixing:	10 M. hours × $6.004 per Mhr =	$ 60.04
	Total overhead cost allocated to product =	**$97.024**

To get the total product cost, we simply add the direct materials per unit and direct labour per unit of the product to the overhead cost per unit calculated above. Please also note that the overhead cost per unit calculated above was based on the reciprocal method redistributions. If the direct method or step-down method had been used, the final calculations would differ.

The departmental overhead costing system is often used as the basis for determining departmental overhead budget rates to apply to products. When budget numbers are used to determine cost allocations they are often done in order to estimate predetermined overhead rates that might be used to apply overhead costs to products in a forthcoming period.

Exercises

1 Departmental overhead cost allocation (indirect departmental overhead cost allocation) LO1, 2

Nettle Pen Makers Pty Limited produces high-quality pens that are distributed worldwide. The company has two service departments, cafeteria and maintenance, and two production departments, inking and assembly. The company requires you to allocate two overhead costs to the four departments. These are rent ($100 000) and electricity ($50 000). Rent should be allocated on the basis of floor space in square metres and electricity should be allocated on the basis of machine hours. The cafeteria department utilises 100 sq metres of space and 400 kW hours. The maintenance department takes 150 sq metres of space and 600 kW hours, while the inking department has double the space of the cafeteria, and twice the kW hours used by maintenance. The assembly department is the largest department in Nettle, using double the space and kW hours output of the inking department.

Required
a Please allocate the electricity costs and rent costs to the four departments.
b How would your answer change if the cafeteria department utilised 200 sq metres of space and 600 kW hours?

2 Service department cost allocation (direct method) LO2, 3

The Sawyer Company has two service departments and two production departments. The following data are available from last year.

The costs of service departments 1 and 2 are allocated on the basis of number of transactions and square metres occupied, respectively.

Required
Assuming that the Sawyer Company allocated service department costs by the direct method, how much overhead would be allocated from each service department to each producing department?

	Service 1	Service 2	Production 1	Production 2
Department costs	$63 000	$42 000	$200 000	$100 000
Number of transactions	10 000	12 000	14 000	16 000
Square metres occupied	2 000	1 000	3 000	2 000
Direct labour hours			3000	500
Machine hours			700	5 000

3 Service department cost allocation (step-down method) LO2, 3

Please refer to question 2. Assuming that the Sawyer Company allocated service department costs by the step-down method, starting with service department 1, how much overhead would be allocated from each service department to each producing department?

4 Service department cost allocation (reciprocal method) LO2, 3

Please refer to question 2. Assuming that the Sawyer Company allocated service department costs by the reciprocal method, how much overhead would be allocated from each service department to each production department?

5 Service department cost allocation (product cost allocation) LO2, 3

Please refer to question 2, and use the direct method allocations calculated in question 2.

Required
a If overhead is applied from production department 1 to products using direct labour hours and production department 2 to products using machine hours, what are the departmental overhead allocation rates for each department?
b If one unit of product takes 30 minutes in production department 1 and 90 minutes in production department 2 to manufacture, what is the overhead allocated to this product from both departments?

6 Service department cost allocation (direct method) LO2, 3

There are two service departments and two production departments in Richie Rich Razor, a company manufacturing high quality disposable shaving razors for tourists worldwide, sold to retailers in discount stores in packs of a hundred (one pack of a hundred is one 'unit'). Following is a summary of the costs associated to Richie's business. Maintenance and Quality Control are the service departments that support the Assembly and Packaging production departments.

The costs of Maintenance and Quality Control are allocated on the basis of number of transactions and square metres occupied, respectively.

	Maintenance	Quality Control	Assembling	Packaging
Department costs	$80 000	$40 000	$300 000	$100 000
Number of transactions	15 000	25 000	30 000	30 000
Square metres occupied	3 000	2 000	4 000	8 000
Direct Labour hours			4 000	1 000
Machine hours			1 000	4 000

Required

If Richie lets you know that he thinks the service departments do not support other service departments, but only production departments, how much overhead would be allocated from each service department to each producing department? (Hint: Think about the departmental allocation method that most fits this situation.)

7 Service department cost allocation (step-down method) LO2, 3

Please refer to question 6. If Richie allocates service department costs by the step-down method, starting with Maintenance, how much overhead would be allocated from each service department to each producing department?

8 Service department cost allocation (reciprocal method) LO2, 3

Please refer to question 6. If Richie allocates service department costs by the reciprocal method, how much overhead would be allocated from each service department to each production department?

9 Service department cost allocation (product cost allocation) LO2, 3

Please refer to question 6, and use the direct method allocations calculated in question 6.

Required

a   If overhead is applied from the Assembling Department to products using direct labour hours, and the Packaging Department to products using machine hours, what are the departmental overhead allocation rates for each department?

b   If one unit of product takes 60 minutes in Assembling and 30 minutes in Packaging to manufacture, what is the overhead allocated to this product from both departments?

Problems

10 Service department cost allocation (direct method and step method)
LO1, 2, 3, 4

Big Heavy Cement Limited manufactures cement mix used by large construction companies. It has three overhead costs that need to be allocated. These include rent ($200 000), electricity ($400 000) and insurance ($600 000) costs. These costs need to be allocated to four departments – quality control, maintenance, fabrications and mixing. While the first two departments are service departments, the latter two are production departments. Rent costs are to be allocated on the basis of floor space occupied, while electricity costs are allocated on the basis of machine hours. Finally, insurance costs are allocated on the basis of machine hours.

The quality control department allocates overheads to the other departments based on the number of inspections. The maintenance department allocates overheads to other departments based on machine hours. The fabrications department cost driver for product cost allocation is direct labour hours and management expects fabrications to use 7000 direct labour hours. The mixing department's cost driver for product cost allocations is machine hours.

Cost type	Quality control	Maintenance	Fabrications	Mixing
Number of Inspections	12	16	10	2
Floor space (sq. m)	450	550	1800	2200
Machine hours	300	400	1000	1300

Required

a   Use the direct method to allocate overheads from the service departments to production departments.

b   What is the overhead cost rate in the production departments respectively?

c   How much overhead is allocated to a product, if it uses 4 direct labour hours in fabrications and 2 direct labour hours in mixing, and if it uses 3 machine hours in fabrications and 2 machine hours in mixing?

11 Service department cost allocation (step method) LO 2, 3, 4

Please refer to question 10. Assume that Big Heavy Cement Limited allocated service department costs by the step-down method.

Required

a   Use the step-down method to allocate overheads from service departments to production departments.

b   What is the overhead cost rate in the production departments respectively?

c   How much overhead is allocated to a product, if it uses 4 direct labour hours in fabrications and 2 direct labour hours in mixing, and if it uses 3 machine hours in fabrications and 2 machine hours in mixing?

12 Service department cost allocation (reciprocal method) LO2, 3, 4

Please refer to question 10. Assume that Big Heavy Cement Limited allocated service department costs by the reciprocal method.

Required

a   Use the reciprocal method to allocate overheads from service departments to production departments.

b   What is the overhead cost rate in the production departments respectively?

c   How much overhead is allocated to a product, if it uses 3 direct labour hours in fabrications and 1 direct labour hour in mixing, and if it uses 5 machine hours in fabrications and 4 machine hours in mixing?

13 Service department cost allocation (direct method and step method) LO2, 3, 4

Sydney Central Bank is wondering about four overhead cost allocations for a particular month and the manner by which these costs might be allocated to an account. These include human resources costs ($3 million), rent ($450 000), utilities ($500 000) and insurance ($360 000). These costs need to be allocated to four departments – accounting, marketing, branch operation and investments. Accounting and marketing are perceived to be service departments, while branch operation and investments are regarded as core operational 'production' departments. Rent costs are to be allocated on the basis of floor space occupied, while utilities costs are allocated on the basis of machine hours. Finally, insurance costs will be allocated on the basis of the value of machines.

Cost type	Accounting	Marketing	Branch operations	Investments
Number of employees	20	30	300	400
Floor space (sq m)	750	450	2 600	3 200
Machine hours	200	900	5 000	1 900
Equipment values	3 500 000	2 500 000	10 000 000	4 000 000
Labour costs	$15 million	$22.5 million	$225 million	$300 million

The accounting department allocates overheads to the other departments based on labour hours. Employees work 150 hours a month each and the average salary earned in each department is $50 000 per employee. The marketing department allocates overheads to other departments based on machine hours. The branch operations cost driver for cost allocation to individual accounts is labour hours, while the investments driver for cost allocation to individual accounts is the dollar value of investments, which is currently $1 billion dollars ($1000 million).

Required

a   Use the direct method to allocate overheads from service departments to branch operations and investments departments.

b   What is the overhead cost rate in branch operations and investments departments respectively?

c   How much in costs is allocated to an individual account if it holds $3 000 000 and absorbs 2 hours of management time in branch operations and 3 hours of management time in investments?

14 Service department cost allocation (step method) LO2, 3, 4

Please refer to question 13. Assume that Sydney Central Bank allocated service department costs by the step method.

Required

a   Use the step-down method to allocate overheads from service departments to the branch operations and investments departments.

b   What is the overhead cost rate in the branch operations and investments departments respectively?

c   How much in costs is allocated to an individual account if it holds $25 000 000 and absorbs 7 hours of management time in branch operations and 10 hours of management time in investments?

15 Service department cost allocation (reciprocal method) LO2, 3, 4

Please refer to question 13. Assume that Sydney Central Bank allocated service department costs by the reciprocal method.

Required

a   Use the reciprocal method to allocate overheads from service departments to the branch operations and investments departments.

b   What is the overhead cost rate in the branch operations and investments departments respectively?

c   How much in costs is allocated to an individual account if it holds $50 000 000 and absorbs 11 hours of management time in branch operations and 20 hours of management time in investments?

Cases

16 Service department cost allocation (step method) LO2, 3, 4

Geoff Bridges runs a business that makes different products for tourism operators. Bridges has two producing departments and two service departments. Monthly budget estimates are as follows:

	Producing Departments		Service Departments	
	Machining	Assembly	Stores	Office
Dept. overhead	$ 80 000	$ 50 000	$ 10 000	$ 8 000
Direct material	$ 90 000		$ 18 000	
Indirect material	$ 5 000	$ 1 800	$ 1 200	
Number of employees	12	20	5	3
Direct labour hours	1 500	2 900		
Indirect labour hours	300	400	900	200
Floor area (sq m)	1 000	1 500	2 500	2 000
Labour charge rates:				
Direct (per hour)	$20.00	$15.00		
Indirect (per hour)	$15.00	$10.00	$12.00	$12.00

The company uses the *step method* to allocate service department overheads and has decided to use number of employees to allocate factory office overheads and to use the cost of materials issued to allocate the stores department overheads. In addition to the above budgeted department overhead costs the following general overhead costs are expected each month:

Overhead Cost		Allocation Basis
Insurance (buildings)	$ 2000	floor space
Electricity	$ 3000	number of employees
Transport/freight	$ 5000	prime cost
Canteen subsidy	$ 4000	labour hours

Overhead is applied to products on the basis of direct labour hours.

Required
a Calculate the overhead application rate for each producing department using the step method.
b How much overhead is applied to products during the period if there was 1600 DL hours expended in the machining department and 2900 DL hours in the assembly department?

c Calculate the respective overhead amounts applied in (b) if the company had allocated overhead on a plant-wide basis.

17 Service department cost allocation (direct method) LO2, 3, 4

Landon Manufacturing has two producing departments and two service departments. Following are a summary of its cost and operating estimates for an upcoming period:

	Producing Departments		Service Departments	
	Mixing	Finishing	Maintenance	Admin.
Indirect material	$5000	$1800	$1200	
Kilowatt hours	1000	2000	200	100
Direct labour hours	1500	2900		
Indirect labour hours	300	400	900	200
Floor area (sq m)	1000	1500	2500	2000
Labour charge rates:				
Direct (per hour)	$20.00	$15.00		
Indirect (per hour)	$15.00	$10.00	$12.00	$12.00

In addition to the above indirect material overhead costs the following general overhead costs are expected each month:

Overhead Cost		Allocation Basis
Insurance (buildings)	$ 10 000	floor space
Electricity	$ 5000	kilowatt hours

The company uses the *direct method* to allocate service department overheads and has decided to use indirect labour costs to allocate administration overheads and kilowatt hours to allocate the maintenance department overheads.

Overhead from production departments is applied to products using kilowatt hours.

Required
a Calculate the overhead application rate in each producing department using the direct method.
b How much overhead is applied to products during the period if the actual kilowatt hours in the production department was 10% more than budgeted?
c Calculate the respective overhead amounts applied in (b) if the company had allocated overhead on a plant-wide basis. How are the allocations different for the different methods?

Learning objectives:

After studying the material in this chapter, you should be able to:

1 Classify overhead costs as unit, batch, product or facility level.

2 Describe ABC and recognise typical activities and cost drivers in an ABC system.

3 Calculate the cost of a product using ABC and compare traditional volume-based costing to ABC.

4 Evaluate the benefits and limitations of ABC systems.

ACTIVITY-BASED COSTING

c 8

The previous chapter examined a number of problems associated with the application of overhead to products and services. Owing to the indirect nature of overhead and the fact that overhead consists of a variety of seemingly unrelated costs, it is often difficult to determine how much overhead should be included when costing specific products and services. To complicate matters further, overhead costs must often be estimated in order to provide timely cost information to managers.

In the past, overhead typically made up a smaller portion of the total cost of a product or service. The environment was one of 'labour-intensive' manufacturing. With labour as the dominant activity and therefore the cost driver, direct labour hours worked was a logical activity base to use to allocate overhead to products. Over time, the manufacturing environment has matured and as automation in production has increased, overhead cost has become a larger percentage of the total manufacturing cost. Costs such as depreciation for machinery, the maintenance costs of machinery and equipment, and electricity costs relating to the production of units in a factory are all common examples of overhead costs, and have arisen due to the proliferation of machinery. In heavily automated manufacturing environments, direct labour costs have shrunk to as little as 5 per cent of total production costs, whereas overhead costs have soared to 60 per cent or more of total product costs (see Exhibit 8.1). To be more specific,

consider a modern car-manufacturing plant. High-tech computers control robots that weld, paint and perform other jobs that used to be done by human labour. High-tech computer-operated robotics is very expensive and is treated as part of overhead cost. As overhead costs increase and make up a larger portion of the total costs of products, accuracy in overhead application has become much more important. At the same time, advances in information technology have allowed even the smallest businesses to take advantage of computers. These advances have provided more and more timely information to managers than ever before.

Source: iStockphoto/Fabio Filzi

Activity-based costing highlights the effects that common business activities have on costs.

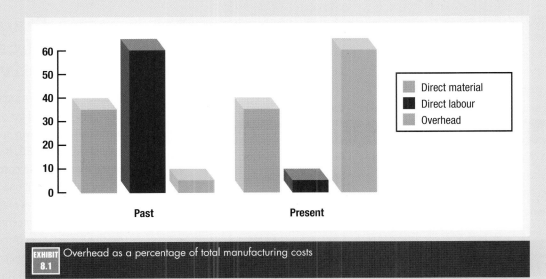

Unit-, batch-, product- and facility-level costs

❄ **unit-level costs**
Costs that are incurred each time a unit is produced.

❄ **batch-level costs**
Costs that are incurred each time a batch of goods is produced.

❄ **product-level costs**
Costs that are incurred as needed to support the production of each type of product.

❄ **facility-level costs**
Costs that are incurred to sustain the overall manufacturing process.

❄ **activity-based costing (ABC)**
A system of allocating overhead costs that assumes that activities, not volume of production, cause overhead costs to be incurred.

❄ **activities**
Procedures or processes that cause work to be accomplished.

Traditional overhead allocation methods, which use volume-based cost drivers to assign overhead costs to products, can provide misleading product-cost information in heavily automated manufacturing environments in which companies make a variety of diverse products. Traditional, volume-based allocation methods work best if the manufacturing environment includes mostly **unit-level costs** (costs that vary with every unit produced or the volume of production). Activity-based costing provides an alternative to traditional methods by allocating overhead costs on the basis of activities that lead to the overhead costs.

Costs incurred in setting up machinery to make different products, costs incurred in designing a new model and costs incurred in providing manufacturing facilities are not incurred every time an individual unit (for example, a table) is produced. Rather, **batch-level costs**, such as machine setups, are incurred only when a batch of products (100 tables) is produced.

Likewise, **product-level costs** (designing a new model) are incurred only when a new product is introduced. Finally, **facility-level costs,** such as the rent on the factory building, are incurred to sustain the overall manufacturing processes and do not vary with the number or type of products produced.[1]

It is worth noting that as we proceed from unit to batch, then product, and facility, we progress from narrower to broader areas of production. Put simply, many units make a batch, many batches add to make the total production of a product and many different products together make the total production of a facility (factory).

Examples of unit-, batch-, product-, and facility-level overhead costs are provided in Exhibit 8.2.

When costing is concentrated at the unit level, it makes sense that the number of units produced should be correlated with the amount of overhead costs allocated to each unit. However, as companies incur more and more batch-, product- and facility-level costs, the correlation between the volume of product produced and the allocation of overhead becomes very fuzzy.

Activity-based costing

Activity-based costing (ABC) provides an alternative to traditional costing methods by allocating overhead costs on the basis of activities that drive costs. **Activities** are procedures or processes that cause work to be accomplished. Activities consume resources, and products consume activities.

Overhead costs are assigned to products in an ABC system in two stages.

Unit-level costs	Product-level costs
Supplies for factory	Salaries of engineers
Depreciation of factory machinery	Depreciation of engineering equipment
Energy costs for factory machinery	Product development costs (testing)
Repairs and maintenance of factory machinery	Quality control costs
Batch-level costs	**Facility-level costs**
Salaries related to purchasing and receiving	Depreciation of factory building or rent
Salaries related to moving material	Salary of plant manager
Quality control costs	Insurance and taxes on factory building
Depreciation of setup equipment	Employee training

EXHIBIT 8.2 Overhead costs and Cooper's hierarchy

Stage 1 – identification of activities

In Stage 1, activities are identified. Examples of typical activities of a company are shown in the first column of Exhibit 8.3. It should be noted that overhead costs can be traced to more than one activity. For example, utilities may be related to purchasing, engineering and machining activities. An employee who provides maintenance services and runs machines in the factory might have his salary split between machining and maintenance activities. Likewise, whereas depreciation of factory equipment is related to machining, depreciation of other equipment might be related to maintenance or quality-control activities.

Stage 2 – identification of cost drivers

In Stage 2, cost drivers for activities are chosen. As discussed in Chapter 4, cost drivers should cause, or drive, the incurrence of costs. For example, the costs of purchasing might be driven by the number of purchase orders processed, whereas engineering costs might be driven by the number of parts used in a product. Typical cost drivers for the activities identified in the exhibit are provided in the third column of Exhibit 8.3. Please note that these are a representative guide, but should not be thought of as universal. In practice, different organisations identify subtly different activities for their cost drivers because of their different styles of operations. Also, the selection of cost drivers is often limited to what a firm is able to measure using the information systems implemented by management.

Unit-, batch- and product-level activities are assigned to products by using cost drivers that capture the underlying

Activity	Level	Typical cost drivers
Repair and maintenance	Unit	Machine hours, labour hours or number of units of factory equipment
Machining of products	Unit	Machine hours
Purchasing	Batch	Number of purchase orders or number of parts
Receiving	Batch	Amount of material or number of receipts
Setting up equipment	Batch	Number of setups
Product testing	Product	Number of change orders, number of tests or hours of testing time
Engineering	Product	Number of engineering hours or number of products
Product design	Product	Number of new or revised products
Quality control	Unit, batch	Number of inspections, hours of inspection or product number of defective units

 Activities and cost drivers

behaviour of the costs that are being assigned. Facility-level costs, however, are usually not allocated to products or are allocated to products in an arbitrary manner. For example, plant occupancy is a facility-level activity that would include such costs as plant managers' salaries, depreciation of the factory building, rent, taxes and insurance. Allocation of these costs would depend on the use of arbitrary cost drivers such as square footage, number of employees, labour hours or machine hours.

It should be recognised that because of different types of production processes and products, every business will have a different set of activities and cost drivers. In addition, the more complex the business or the production process, the more complex the ABC system is likely to be.

ABC systems in non-manufacturing environments

According to the Department of Foreign Affairs and Trade, Australia, the service sector comprises 70 per cent of the Australian economy. As service companies expand the scope and quality of services offered, the need for fast, accurate costing information becomes more important. Can ABC be used to cost services as well as products? Do the same principles that we learned for manufacturing companies apply to service businesses? The answer is an emphatic yes! In fact, ABC is every bit as important for service providers as it is for manufacturing companies. Although ABC was developed for use primarily by manufacturing companies, it has gained widespread acceptance in the service sector. For example, the Commonwealth Bank of Australia adopts activity-based costing principles to help determine the costs and benefits of allowing customers to pay with debit and credit cards, and identify fee structures for the use of their services such as bank fee charges per account. By reflecting on the activities required, and thinking about the cost drivers that relate to those activities, the Commonwealth Bank is able to identify costs per account for its transaction activities and justifiably explain its fee charge structures.

However, implementing ABC in service companies is not without its problems. One common problem is that the type of work done by service companies tends to be non-repetitive. Unlike highly automated manufacturing companies, analysing the activities of a service provider can be difficult when the activities differ greatly for each customer or service. In addition, service-oriented companies are likely to have proportionately more facility-level costs than do manufacturing companies. Remember from our earlier discussion that facility-level costs are allocated arbitrarily to goods and services (if at all).

Royal Flying Doctor Service

Making it real

The Royal Flying Doctor Service (RFDS) provides life-saving medical support to remote communities in Australia and is regarded very favourably within the Australian community. However, the RFDS requires continual funding from the government to aid its service delivery to rural communities. As part of this process, the Australian Government commissioned a budget estimate process to determine the level of funding required by the RFDS, moving into the future. By using an activity-based costing system as well as other financial models, a detailed estimate of the funding required by the RFDS was achieved. Given the very high infrastructure costs and ongoing maintenance and other indirect costs consumed in funding this operation, an activity-based costing system represented a key measurement system to help RFDS management understand their expected cost incurrence.

Source: Newspix/James Elsby

The principles of ABC can be applied to non-manufacturing activities as well. Instead of computing the manufacturing cost of a product or a service, the goal is to determine the total cost of a product or service. ABC can also be used to determine the cost of providing a particular non-manufacturing activity. For example, a company might use ABC to determine the cost of providing payroll services. This information can be used to help management determine whether to continue processing payroll in-house or to outsource.

LEARNING OBJECTIVE 3 >>

Traditional overhead allocation and ABC – an example

As an example, let's hypothetically consider DownUnder Construction, a modular home builder based in Perth. They have been asked to construct a new modular home called the 'Ayers Cottage'. These homes will be used in areas of the country impacted by floods to provide safe, temporary housing for families whose houses were destroyed or severely damaged by storms. DownUnder Construction usually builds about 300 units each year. On average it takes about two weeks to assemble the components for each model and then one to two days to assemble the units on-site. As in all manufactured products, the cost of a house consists of

three main components: direct materials, direct labour and overhead.

Many types of materials are used in the construction of a modular home. Raw materials needed in home construction include timber, roofing, insulation, wallboard and cladding. The costs for these types of raw materials can usually be accumulated, tracked and assigned to specific homes with relative ease, so these materials are classified as direct materials. Indirect materials include such items as nails, screws, fasteners, basic hardware, glue and other materials that are difficult to trace to a particular unit.

Direct labour is also fairly straightforward in the construction business. Like many home-building companies, DownUnder does not employ concrete contractors or bricklayers; rather, the company uses subcontractors to perform this work. Because subcontractor labour can be traced directly to each house, these costs are classified as direct labour. DownUnder has 140 full-time employees working in the factory. Most of these employees are carpenters who work in the assembly of modular homes, so their wages are classified as direct labour. The company also employs electricians and plumbers whose wages are also classified as direct labour. Some employees are construction supervisors whose primary job is to supervise and inspect the work done on each unit. DownUnder consequently classifies their salaries as indirect labour.

DownUnder also has a purchasing department that handles the ordering of raw materials and processing of purchase orders for the manufacturing operations of the company, as well as purchases of supplies and equipment for non-manufacturing operations. The company also has an administrative department that handles payroll, billing, accounts payable and other accounting and administrative tasks related to the business. A portion of the costs of both service departments is allocated to the manufacturing operations of DownUnder.

In addition to overhead costs associated with the service departments just described, DownUnder incurs other manufacturing overhead costs, including the cost of tools (saws and drills) and of trucks used for delivery of the completed modular homes. DownUnder estimates that its manufacturing overhead costs will total $3 830 000 in 2014. Exhibit 8.4 provides a breakdown of this estimate.

Source: iStockphoto.com/James Steidl

Overhead item	Estimated cost
Indirect materials	$1 800 000
Indirect labour:	
Construction supervisors	500 000
Part-time workers	200 000
Other overhead:	
Allocated service department costs	780 000
Tools	150 000
Trucks and other equipment	400 000
Total	$3 830 000

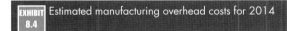

EXHIBIT 8.4 Estimated manufacturing overhead costs for 2014

If DownUnder produced only one type of modular home, the overhead allocation process would be very simple. As discussed in Chapter 4, all the company would have to do is divide the total overhead of $3 830 000 by the number of modular homes constructed. For example, if DownUnder constructed 300 identical modular homes in 2014, $12 767 of overhead costs would be allocated to each unit. This costing method is based on the assumption that all homes share overhead costs equally if they are all made using the same processes and consume the same resources. However, to meet the specific needs of its customers, DownUnder builds two basic models – a 1200-square-foot two-bedroom unit and a 1600-square-foot three-bedroom unit. These units are very similar except for size. Consequently, DownUnder applies overhead based on the square footage of each model. Based on an expected production of 150 two-bedroom units and 150 three-bedroom units in 2014, DownUnder estimates that it will manufacture units with total floor space of 420 000 square feet [(150 two-bedroom units × 1200 square feet) + (150 three-bedroom units × 1600 square feet) = 420 000]. The company's predetermined overhead rate for 2014 is $9.12 per square foot ($3 830 000 ÷ 420 000 square feet = $9.12). A two-bedroom model with 1200 square feet of floor space would be allocated $10 944 of overhead (1200 square feet ×

Construction firms engage in a variety of activities that incur different costs, and an activity-based costing system can therefore suit such firms well.

$9.12), whereas a three-bedroom unit with 1600 square feet of floor space would be allocated $14 592 of manufacturing overhead (1600 square feet × $9.12).

The Federal Government and emergency organisations expressed interest in emergency housing. This has caused DownUnder to design the new 500-square-foot Ayers Cottage, which can be constructed and shipped to a site within one week of receiving the order. The cottages are set on a concrete slab or a cement block foundation and can be used later as a guest cottage or storage building. The company expects to manufacture 1000 of these units in 2014.

According to the Federal Government, a cottage's total price may not exceed $37 500. In order to earn a sufficient profit, DownUnder estimates that its costs must not exceed $30 000. DownUnder will also offer these cottages for sale to others, just as they do with their regular models. The addition of the cottage to the company's product line will lead to more overhead and will require DownUnder to give more attention to the proper allocation of overhead costs to each house. The estimated manufacturing overhead is expected to increase to $6 720 000.

If DownUnder uses their traditional method of applying overhead based on square footage, the predetermined overhead rate would be $7.30 per square foot ($6 720 000 ÷ 920 000 total square feet [420 000 square feet from two- and three-bedroom units + 500 000 square feet from the Ayers cottages]). Accordingly, DownUnder would allocate $8760 of overhead to a two-bedroom unit (1200 square feet × $7.30), $11 680 of overhead to a three-bedroom unit (1600 square feet × $7.30), and $3650 of overhead to a cottage (500 square feet × $7.30).

As shown in Exhibit 8.5, when the company uses its traditional method of applying overhead based on the square footage of the unit, the $30 650 cost of the cottage exceeds the target cost by $650 per unit.

The company's chief financial officer (CFO) has some reservations about costing the new cottage using the traditional method of allocating overhead based on square footage. The cottage is expected to be simpler to build and does not need to be assembled on-site, thus requiring fewer resources than the current two-bedroom and three-bedroom modular units. Accordingly, she has recommended investigating the use of activity-based costing (ABC) because she has heard that this method will likely provide more accurate allocations of overhead.

	Two-bedroom unit	Three-bedroom unit	Cottage
Number of units	150	150	1 000
Direct material	$30 000	$40 000	$16 500
Direct labour	18 000	24 000	10 500
Overhead	8 760	11 680	3 650
Total cost per unit	$56 760	$75 680	$30 650

 Costs per unit using volume-based overhead allocation

DownUnder's stage 1: Identification of activities

The first step in DownUnder's implementation of an ABC system is the identification of activities and the tracing of overhead costs to each activity. Remember that activities are processes or procedures that cause work to be accomplished. DownUnder Construction has identified four primary activities that consume company resources:

1 Inspections
2 Purchasing
3 Supervision
4 Delivery and setup.

Exhibit 8.6 provides the overhead costs associated with each activity. Note that the total overhead is $6 720 000, regardless of whether it is allocated using volume-based cost drivers or ABC.

Activity	Estimated cost
Inspections	$900 000
Purchasing	500 000
Supervision	1 400 000
Delivery and setup	3 920 000
Total overhead	$6 720 000

 Estimated overhead costs for 2014 (with addition of Ayers Cottage)

DownUnder's stage 2: Identification of cost drivers and allocation of costs

Once the activities have been identified and overhead costs traced to each activity, cost drivers must be identified for each activity. The cost drivers are as follows:

Activity	Cost driver
Inspections	Number of inspections
Purchasing	Number of purchase orders
Supervision	Hours of supervisory time
Delivery and setup	Setup time (days)

Each of these cost drivers is directly associated with the related activity. Accordingly, the cost of inspections is driven by the number of inspections, the cost of purchasing is driven by the number of purchase orders processed, and so on. It simply makes more sense to allocate the cost of supervision based on the hours of supervisor time rather than on the amount of floor space in a unit.

The 1200-square-foot two-bedroom unit is estimated to require 25 inspections, whereas the larger 1600-square-foot three-bedroom unit is estimated to require 35 inspections. The cottage will only require 10 inspections. The cottage will also require the processing of fewer purchase orders (10) and less supervision (10 hours) than the other units. The two-bedroom unit requires the processing of 30 purchase orders and 72 hours of supervision, and the three-bedroom unit requires the processing of 40 purchase orders and 96 hours of supervision. Finally, whereas the two-bedroom unit requires four days to deliver and set up and the three-bedroom unit requires six days to deliver and set up, the cottage can generally be delivered and set up in only one day. Exhibit 8.7 summarises the total number of cost driver units for each activity.

In Exhibit 8.8, predetermined activity rates are calculated for each activity and cost driver, just as we did in Chapter 4 using a plantwide overhead rate with volume-based cost drivers.

Exhibit 8.9 illustrates the total cost of each unit built by DownUnder Construction using an activity-based costing system.

If we compare the two methods of allocating overhead cost to the three modular homes produced by DownUnder Construction, we can see why volume-based allocation and ABC result in different amounts of applied overhead. Under the traditional overhead allocation method based on square footage, the three-bedroom unit was allocated 320 per cent more overhead than the cottage ($11 680 compared to $3650) because it was 3.2 times larger (1600 square feet compared to 500 square feet).

Cost driver	Two-bedroom unit	Three-bedroom unit	Cottage	Total
Number of inspections	$(25 \times 150) = 3750$	$(35 \times 150) = 5250$	$(10 \times 1000) = 10000$	19 000
Number of purchase orders processed	$(30 \times 150) = 4500$	$(40 \times 150) = 6000$	$(10 \times 1000) = 10000$	20 500
Hours of supervisory time	$(72 \times 150) = 10800$	$(96 \times 150) = 14400$	$(10 \times 1000) = 10000$	35 200
Days of delivery and setup time	$(4 \times 150) = 600$	$(6 \times 150) = 900$	$(1 \times 1000) = 1000$	2 500

EXHIBIT 8.7 Estimated cost driver activity

Activity	Total estimated cost	Cost driver and estimated amount	Predetermined overhead rate
Inspections	$900 000	Number of inspections (19 000)	$47.37 per inspection
Purchasing	500 000	Number of purchase orders (20 500)	$24.39 per purchase order
Supervision	1 400 000	Hours of supervisory time (35 200)	$39.77 per supervisory hour
Delivery and setup	3 920 000	Setup time (days) (2500)	$1568.00 per day

EXHIBIT 8.8 The calculation of predetermined activity rates

Cost	Two-bedroom unit	Three-bedroom unit	Cottage
Direct materials	$30 000	$40 000	$16 500
Direct labour	18 000	24 000	10 500
Inspections	1 184	1 658	474
Purchases	732	976	244
Supervision	2 864	3 818	398
Delivery and setup	6 272	9 408	1 568
Total cost per unit	$59 052	$79 860	$29 684

EXHIBIT 8.9 Cost of units based on activity-based costing

Volume-based costing methods and ABC result in different allocations of overhead if products consume activities in different proportions. Allocating overhead costs using an ABC system results in greater allocations of overhead to the two- and three-bedroom units than under the traditional method of allocating overhead based on square footage. This is because the two- and three-bedroom units consume more of the inspection, purchasing, supervision, and delivery and setup activities (relative to the square footage of the units) than the cottage. For example, whereas the three-bedroom unit is just over three times as large as the cottage, it requires 350 per cent more inspections, 400 per cent more purchase orders, 960 per cent more supervision time and 600 per cent more delivery and setup time than the cottage.

In Exhibit 8.10, notice that compared to costing under ABC, using traditional costing methods resulted in overcosting the cottage and undercosting the two- and three-bedroom units.

In general, when there are batch- and product-level costs, ABC will typically shift costs from high-volume products produced in large batches to low-volume products produced in small batches. On a per-unit basis, this shift usually results in a greater impact on the low-volume products than on the high-volume products.

One important aspect of ABC systems is the elimination of cross subsidies between products. Cross subsidies occur when high-volume products, such as the cottage, are assigned more than their fair share of overhead costs. At the same time, more complicated low-volume products, such as the two- and three-bedroom units, are allocated too little overhead. This cross subsidy may make high-volume products appear unprofitable when they may not be, or it may make them appear to show less profit than they actually do. Activity-based costing systems eliminate the cross subsidy between high- and low-volume products.

	Two-bedroom unit	Three-bedroom unit	Cottage
Traditional costing	$56 760	$75 680	$30 650
Activity-based costing	$59 052	$79 860	$29 684
Difference in cost	$2292 higher using ABC	$4180 higher using ABC	$966 lower using ABC

EXHIBIT 8.10 Cost comparison between traditional and activity-based costing

	Two-bedroom unit	Three-bedroom unit	Cottage
Sales price based on traditional costing	$70 950	$94 600	$38 313
Sales price based on activity-based costing	$73 815	$99 825	$37 104
Difference in price	$2865 higher using ABC	$5225 higher using ABC	$1209 lower using ABC

EXHIBIT 8.11 Price comparison between traditional and activity-based costing

Different types of units incur different costs, and activity-based costing captures these costing differences.

Although the differences in cost may seem small, consider the impact on DownUnder's pricing policy (see Exhibit 8.11). DownUnder typically establishes a sales price equal to 125 per cent of total manufacturing costs. Under ABC, DownUnder would price the two-bedroom unit $2865 higher and the three-bedroom model $5225 higher than when using traditional costing. If these price increases can be made without affecting sales, total revenue for the two- and three-bedroom units will increase by $1 213 500 [(150 × $2865) + (150 × 5225)].

On the other hand, DownUnder's goal was to produce the new cottage for less than $30 000, which would allow the company to sell it to the Federal Government at a price of $37 500. Whereas traditional costing and overhead allocation based on square footage would have resulted in the company not being able to earn its desired profit, the revised ABC cost estimates indicate that the cottage can be manufactured for $29 684 and sold to the Federal Government for $37 104.

As this example illustrates, the allocation of costs using activity-based costing is more accurate and reflects the consumption of costs based on the activities that drive them rather than on one volume-based cost driver. In addition to providing management with more accurate cost information for pricing decisions, it also affects a variety of other decisions discussed in the remainder of this book.

LEARNING OBJECTIVE **4** >>

Benefits and limitations of ABC

apply this!

Case

Because of the increase in global competition, companies must strive to achieve and sustain a competitive advantage. This requires organisations to continually improve performance in all aspects of their business operations. By focusing on continuous improvement, organisations can minimise waste in the manufacturing process, reduce lead times for customer deliveries or vendor shipments, increase the quality of their products and services, control manufacturing and non-manufacturing costs, and increase customer satisfaction.

Activity-based costing systems provide more and more accurate cost information that focuses managers on opportunities for continuous improvement. Throughout their planning, operating and control activities, managers use the information provided by ABC systems. In Chapter 1, planning was defined as the development of short- and long-term objectives and goals of an organisation and the identification of the resources needed to achieve them. Using ABC in the budgeting process provides more accurate estimates of these resources.

One of the biggest advantages of ABC is the increased accuracy of cost information it provides for day-to-day decision making by managers (operating decisions). Managers use ABC information to make better decisions related to adding or dropping products, making or buying components used in the manufacturing process, marketing and pricing strategies, and so forth.

ABC also provides benefits related to the control function of managers. Costs that appear to be indirect using volume-based costing systems now are traced to specific activities using cost drivers. This method allows managers to better see what causes costs to be incurred, leading to better control.

However, ABC is not for everyone, and the benefits of increased accuracy do not come without costs. Accumulating, tracking and assigning costs to products and services using ABC requires the use of multiple activity pools and cost drivers. High measurement costs associated with ABC systems are a significant limitation. Companies may decide that the measurement costs associated with implementing ABC systems are greater than the expected benefit from having more accurate cost information. For example, if the market dictates prices, such as with commodity products, and companies have little control over pricing their products, highly reliable product costs may not be necessary for pricing. However, ABC may still prove valuable for planning and cost-reduction efforts.

In general, companies that have a high potential for cost distortions are more likely to benefit from ABC. Cost distortions are likely when companies make **diverse products** that consume resources differently. Products that vary a great deal in complexity are typically diverse, but minor differences such as a difference in colour

can cause differences in product costs consumed. For example, in making a gold shirt and a black shirt, the gold dye might be significantly more costly to source and use than a basic black dye. This might cause the cost of a gold shirt to be significantly more than a black shirt, though their production process is otherwise identical.

Companies that have a large proportion of non-unit-level costs are also likely to benefit from ABC. Remember, unit-level costs vary with the number of units produced and can be allocated with reasonable accuracy using volume-based cost systems and drivers such as direct labour hours and machine hours. For example, it is intuitively reasonable that in a highly automated manufacturing operation, products that require more machine hours to be manufactured probably take a higher percentage of depreciation costs for machines, power costs to run the same machines, maintenance costs relating to upkeep machines, and so on. However, the space required to make the product might not be proportional to machine hours – meaning costs such as rent should not be allocated based on machine hours. The same might be said for indirect material costs or indirect labour costs. Volume-based costing systems can therefore result in cost distortions to products when allocating batch-, product- and facility-level costs. Generally, cost that is

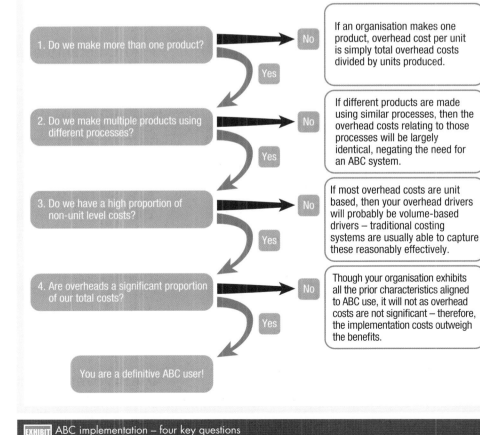

:: diverse products
Products that consume resources in different proportions.

EXHIBIT 8.12 ABC implementation – four key questions

incurred at a different level to the level for which the volume driver is sensitive to.

Companies that have relatively high proportions of overhead compared to direct materials and direct labour are likely to benefit from ABC as well. This situation is often the case with highly automated manufacturing companies or companies that have adopted JIT techniques. Note that service companies, such as law or CPA firms, may also have high overhead costs compared to direct materials and direct labour and likewise may benefit from the implementation of ABC.

Exhibit 8.12 summarises the extent to which organisations might consider ABC as being useful. There are four questions that are usually asked prior to embarking on an ABC implementation.

Finally, it is important to acknowledge that the extent to which you will use ABC lies on a continuum. That is, if you say yes to the first three, but not the fourth, you may still get benefits from implementing an ABC system, but for reasons relating to understanding your operations as opposed to increasing the mathematical accuracy of your costs per unit for products/services.

Exercises

1 Cost classifications LO1

Ballina Systems manufactures a variety of products for the fibre optic industry in its facility on the north coast of New South Wales. The following are examples of the activities performed by various personnel.

a   Purchase orders are generated for raw materials purchases from suppliers. Ballina orders raw materials as needed to fill customer orders and maintains a very small amount of raw materials inventory.
b   Engineers conduct research and development activities aimed at identifying new technologies for data transmission.
c   Ballina conducts continuous quality inspections during the production process. All cable is 100 per cent guaranteed to be free of defects.
d   Machine operators must calibrate production equipment whenever production is started on a new order.
e   Maintenance personnel regularly inspect the manufacturing facility's heating and cooling systems to ensure adequate conditions within the manufacturing environment.
f   Ballina recently hired several new engineers to begin work on development of a new product line.
g   Accounting personnel were billed for and paid property taxes for the manufacturing facility.
h   Ballina launched a website to auction excess cable to interested parties.
i   A new facility was built to house all design engineers in one central location. This new facility will be depreciated over 20 years.

Required
Classify each of the activities as a unit-level, batch-level, product-level or facility-level activity.

2 ABC activities and cost drivers LO2

Georgalis Chartered Accountants is a full-service accounting firm that provides accounting, tax and consulting services to its clients. The firm is considering changing to an activity-based costing system and has asked for your input regarding the design of the system. The firm has identified certain activities that are integral to the practice and would like your suggestions regarding potential cost drivers.

Activity	Cost driver
a Client interview	1 Professional staff hours
b Tax return preparation	2 Transactions
c Tax return review	3 Number of pages
d Data input	4 Number of employees
e Report assembly	5 Machine hours
f Research	6 Clerical staff hours
g Report writing	
h Site visits	

Required
Match each of the activities with a potential cost driver. Please note that you may not use all drivers and some may be used more than once.

3 ABC activities and cost drivers LO2

The University of Technology, Sydney has asked for your help with implementing an activity-based costing system for the admissions office. The following activities and cost drivers were identified by the chief admissions officer for the university.

Activity	Cost driver
a Receiving applications	1 Number of students
b Processing applications	2 Number of acceptances
c Receiving student inquiries	3 Number of applications
d Responding to student inquiries	4 Labour hours
e Accepting students	5 Number of inquiries
f Enrolling students	

Required
Match each of the activities with a potential cost driver. Please note that you may not use all drivers and some may be used more than once.

4 ABC overhead calculation LO3

Tip Top Company sells umbrellas suited for small and large picnic tables. Based on the advice of its accountant, Tip Top is considering whether to adopt an activity-based costing system. To evaluate the possible impact on cost, the company has accumulated the following data from last year:

Activity	Allocation base	Overhead cost
Purchasing	Number of purchase orders	$ 300 000
Receiving	Number of shipments received	150 000
Sales	Number of sales orders	150 000

The numbers of activities for small and large umbrellas were as follows:

	Small	Large
Purchase orders	10 000	5000
Shipments received	12 500	7500
Sales orders	8 500	6500

Required

a   Calculate the overhead rates for the following activities: purchasing, receiving and sales.

b   Calculate the dollar amount of overhead that should be assigned to small and large umbrellas for each of the three activities.

5 ABC overhead calculation LO3

Shoehorn Company sells two types of shoes – budget shoes and premium shoes. Though only recently introducing premium shoes, the company is astounded by the profit margin on that product. On the other hand, the returns on the budget shoes have declined since premium shoes started being made and sold. The expected production and sales are 1000 premium shoes and 20 000 budget shoes. Company management is concerned at the traditional overhead cost allocation system being used to cost overhead into the shoes and accumulated the following data from last year in order to conduct an activity-based costing overhead allocation:

Activity	Allocation base	Overhead cost
Purchasing	Number of purchase orders	$ 200 000
Stitching	Metres stitched	$ 100 000
Sales	Number of sales orders	$ 200 000

The numbers of activities for budget shoes and premium shoes are as follows:

	Budget	Premium
Purchase orders	7000	3000
Centimetres stitched	8000	2000
Sales orders	8000	2000

Required

a   Calculate the overhead rates for the following activities: purchasing, stitching and sales orders.

b   Calculate the dollar amount of overhead that should be assigned to a budget shoe and a premium shoe, under the ABC system.

6 Traditional costing vs ABC

LO2, 3, 4

Refer to Question 5. In addition to the information provided, you are now informed that the company currently calculates an overhead cost per shoe by using direct labour hours to allocate its overhead costs, and takes 30 minutes per premium shoe and 15 minutes per budget shoe in direct labour time. Direct material costs are $10 for a budget shoe, and $30 for a premium shoe. Direct labour costs are $5 for a budget shoe, and $15 for a premium shoe. A premium shoe currently sells for $160, and a budget shoe sells for $50.

Required:

a   Calculate the total cost per unit for one budget shoe using the traditional costing system, and for one premium shoe using the traditional costing system. How does this compare against the selling price?

b   Calculate the total cost per unit for one budget shoe using the ABC system, and for one premium shoe using the ABC system. How does this compare against the selling price?

c   What do we learn about the profitability of our budget and premium shoes from ABC, relative to traditional costing?

7 ABC overhead calculation LO3

The Bouncy Baby Crib Mattress Company sells firm and extra-firm mattresses. The company's president, Anna Greer, has become interested in the possibility of improving company performance by more closely monitoring overhead costs. She has decided to adopt an activity-based costing system for the current year. Last year, the company incurred $2 000 000 in overhead costs related to the following activities:

Activity	Allocation base	Overhead cost
Materials processing	Number of parts	$1 400 000
Firmness testing	Number of tests	$ 400 000
Customer calls	Number of customer calls	$ 200 000

During the year, 100 000 parts were handled (75 000 for firm mattresses and 25 000 for extra-firm mattresses), 20 000 firmness tests were conducted (12 500 for firm and 7500 for extra-firm) and 10 000 customer calls were answered (7500 for firm and 2500 for extra-firm).

Required

a   Based on an activity-based approach, determine the total amount of overhead that should be assigned to firm and extra-firm mattresses.

b   If a firm mattress requires five parts, two tests and one customer call, then what amount of overhead should be assigned to that mattress?

8 ABC overhead calculation: Traditional vs ABC LO3

The following overhead cost information is available for the Herbert Love Corporation for the prior year:

Activity	Allocation base	Overhead cost
Purchasing	Number of purchase orders	$ 400 000
Receiving	Number of shipments received	$ 100 000
Machine setups	Number of setups	$ 400 000
Quality control	Number of inspections	$ 150 000

During the year, 8000 purchase orders were issued; 25 000 shipments were received; 4000 machine setups occurred; and 7500 inspections were conducted. Employees worked a total of 10 000 hours on production. The corporate managers are trying to decide whether they should use a traditional overhead allocation method based on direct labour hours, or switch to an activity-based costing system. Assume that a batch of products has the following specifications.

Direct labour hours	7
Purchase orders	7
Shipments received	10
Machine setups	3
Inspections	3

Required

a Determine the overhead allocation for the batch under the traditional overhead allocation based on direct labour hours.

b Determine the overhead allocation for the batch under activity-based costing.

9 ABC overhead calculation LO2, 3, 4

Elise Entertainment is a progressive company that is considering the implementation of activity-based costing techniques to better understand and control costs associated with its human resources (HR) department. Currently, the department incurs annual costs of $750 000. Claire Elise, the company's president, believes there are four primary activities within the department: recruiting new employees, responding to employee questions about benefits, general employee administration and employee termination/separation. She asked the HR manager to identify possible drivers and costs associated with each of these activities. The manager provided the following data:

Activity	Allocation base	Overhead cost
Recruitment	Number of applicants	$250 000
Query response	Number of questions	$156 000
Administration	Number of employees	$294 000
Separation	Number of terminations/ separations	$ 50 000

The HR manager determined that in the most recent year there were 2000 applications received; 2400 benefits-related

questions from employees; an average monthly employment of 600 individuals; and 100 employees who were either terminated or otherwise left the company.

Required

a Estimate the overhead cost for each activity.

b Which activity is the most expensive and which is the least expensive?

Problems

10 ABC: Comparison to traditional costing LO2, 3, 4

Surfs Up manufactures surfboards. The company produces two models: the small board and the big board. Data regarding the two boards are as follows:

Product	Direct labour hours per unit	Annual production	Total direct labour hours
Big	1.5	10 000 boards	15 000
Small	1.0	35 000 boards	35 000

The big board requires $75 in direct materials per unit, whereas the small board requires $40. The company pays an average direct labour rate of $13 per hour. The company has historically used direct labour hours as the activity base for applying overhead to the boards. Manufacturing overhead is estimated to be $1 664 000 per year. The big board is more complex to manufacture than the small board because it requires more machine time.

Blake Moore, the company's controller, is considering the use of activity-based costing to apply overhead because the surfboards require such different amounts of machining. Blake has identified the following four separate activity centres.

Activity centre	Cost driver	Volume of annual activity		
		Traceable costs	Big board	Small board
Machine setup	Number of setups	$100 000	100	100
Special design	Design hours	$364 000	900	100
Production	Direct labour hours	$900 000	15 000	35 000
Machining	Machine hours	$300 000	9 000	1 000

Required

a Calculate the overhead rate based on traditional overhead allocation with direct labour hours as the base.

b Determine the total cost to produce one unit of each product. (Use the overhead rate calculated in question A.)

c Calculate the overhead rate for each activity centre based on activity-based costing techniques.

d Determine the total cost to produce one unit of each product. Use the overhead rates calculated in question C.

e Explain why overhead cost shifted from the high-volume product to the low-volume product under activity-based costing.

11 ABC: Comparison to traditional costing LO2, 3, 4

Bearhug Inc. manufactures two types of premium, high value teddy bears for children: the yellow teddy and the red teddy. The yellow teddy is a simple teddy bear with no costume and plain colour dye, while the red teddy includes costumes, uses a higher cost cover and contains premium, longer lasting, stain-free colour dye. Data regarding the two teddy types are as follows:

Product	Direct labour hours per unit	Annual production	Total direct labour hours
Red	2	5 000	10 000
Yellow	1	20 000	20 000

The red teddy requires $50 in direct materials per unit, whereas the yellow teddy requires $25. The average direct labour rate is $15 per hour. The company has historically used direct labour hours as the activity base for applying overhead products. Manufacturing overhead is estimated to be $2 000 000 per year.

The CFO is considering the use of activity-based costing to apply overhead because the two types of teddy bears require such different amounts of resources. She has split the $2 000 000 overheads into the following cost categories:

			Volume of annual activity	
Activity centre	Cost driver	Traceable costs	Yellow teddy drivers	Red teddy drivers
Machine setup	Number of setups	$ 200 000	100	100
Design	Design hours	$ 400 000	800	200
Assembling	Direct labour hours	$1 000 000	20 000	30 000
Finishing	Machine hours	$ 400 000	8 000	2 000

Required

a Calculate the overhead rate based on traditional overhead allocation with direct labour hours as the base.

b Determine the total cost to produce one unit of a yellow teddy and one unit of a red teddy. (Use the overhead rate calculated in question a.)

c Calculate the overhead rate for each activity centre based on activity-based costing techniques.

d Determine the total cost to produce one unit of each product. (Use the overhead rates calculated in question c.)

e Explain whether and how activity-based costing influenced your understanding of the costing allocation for the two products.

12 Traditional costing vs ABC LO2, 3, 4

Fairchild Pty Limited manufactures televisions that are designed for use in sports bars. The company has budgeted manufacturing overhead costs for the year as follows:

Type of cost	Cost pools
Electric power	$2 500 000
Inspection	$1 500 000

Under a traditional cost system, the company estimated the budgeted capacity for machine hours to be 40 000 hours. The company is considering changing to an activity-based cost system. As part of its consideration of the new costing system, the company developed the following estimates:

Type of cost	Activity-based cost drivers
Electric power	50 000 kilowatt hours (KWH)
Inspection	10 000 inspections (INSP)

The following information related to the production of 2000 units of Model #1003 was accumulated:

Direct materials cost	$50 000
Direct labour costs	$75 000
Machine hours	10 000
Direct labour hours	5 000
Electric power – kilowatt hours	20 000
Number of inspections	1 000

Based on the data, Fairchild's accounting department provided management with the following report:

Traditional costing system estimate:	
Overhead rate per machine hour	$100.00

Manufacturing costs for 2000 units:	
Direct materials	$ 50 000
Direct labour	75 000
Applied overhead	1 000 000
Total cost	$1 125 000
Cost per unit	$ 562.50

Activity-based costing system estimate:	
Electric power overhead rate (per KWH)	$ 50.00
Inspection cost overhead rate (per INSP)	$150.00

Manufacturing costs for 2000 units:	
Direct materials	$ 50 000
Direct labour	75 000
Applied overhead	1 150 000
Total cost	$1 275 000
Cost per unit	$ 637.50

Required

a Explain the difference between activity-based costing and traditional costing and describe how ABC might enhance the financial reporting of Fairchild.

b If Fairchild were setting a sales price based on a 20 per cent mark-up, how would profit be affected if the company did not change to an ABC system?

Cases

13 Traditional versus ABC LO1, 2, 3, 4

Duffy and Rowe is a full-service legal firm. During the year, corporate clients required 5000 hours of legal services whereas individuals required 3000 hours. In the past, the firm has assigned overhead to client engagements on the basis of direct labour hours. However, Duffy suspects that legal services to corporate clients drive firm overhead more than legal services to individuals and believes that adopting activity-based costing will allow a more accurate allocation of costs to various clients. The firm's revenues and costs for the year are as follows:

	Corporate	Individual	Total
Revenue	$ 150 000	$ 150 000	$ 300 000
Expenses			
Lawyers' salaries	100 000	50 000	150 000
Overhead			
Filing			$ 10 000
Quality control			5 000
Data entry			25 000
Total overhead			$ 40 000

Duffy and Rowe has kept records of the following data for use in the new activity-based costing system:

Overhead Cost	Cost Driver	Activity Level	
		Corporate	Individual
Filing	Number of clients	5	5
Quality control	Number of hours spent	75	25
Data entry	Number of pages entered	1000	1500

The accounting manager has prepared the following pro forma income statements:

Income Statement Using Traditional Costing

	Corporate	Individual	Total
Revenue	$ 150 000	$ 150 000	$ 300 000
Expenses			
Salaries	100 000	50 000	150 000
Overhead	25 000	15 000	40 000
Total expenses	$ 125 000	$ 65 000	$ 190 000
Operating profit	$ 25 000	$ 85 000	$ 110 000

Income Statement using Activity–Based Costing

	Corporate	Individual	Total
Revenue	$ 150 000	$ 150 000	$ 300 000
Expenses			
Salaries	100 000	50 000	150 000
Overhead			
Filing			
($1000 × 5)	5 000	5 000	10 000
Quality costs			
($50 × 75)	3 750		3 750
($50 × 25)		1 250	1 250
Data entry			
($10 × 1000)	10 000		10 000
($10 × 1500)		15 000	15 000
Total overhead	$ 18 750	$ 21 250	$ 40 000
Total expenses	$ 118 750	$ 71 250	$ 190 000
Operating profit	$ 31 250	$ 78 750	$ 110 000

Required

Calculate the overhead rate for individual and corporate clients for the traditional income statement. Compare those rates with the rates for the activity-based costing income statement. Discuss the best way to allocate costs in this example, and include the approximate difference in profits between corporate and individual clients. Why would activity-based costing be preferred as a cost allocation method?

TEST COMING UP?

NOW WHAT?

ACCT has it all, and you can too. Between the text and online offerings, you have everything at your fingertips to revise and prepare for your test. Make sure you check out all that **ACCT** has to offer:

- Printable flash cards
- Interactive games
- Videos

- Audio downloads
- Case studies
- Chapter review cards

- Online quizzing
- ...and more!

Visit **http://login.cengagebrain.com/** to find the resources you need today!

Learning objectives:

After studying the material in this chapter, you should be able to:

1. Use the contribution margin in its various forms to determine the impact of changes in sales on profit.

2. Analyse what-if decisions using CVP analysis.

3. Compute a company's break-even point in single- and multi-product environments.

4. Analyse target profit before and after the impact of income tax.

5. Compute a company's operating leverage and understand its relationship to cost structure.

COST-VOLUME-PROFIT ANALYSIS

c 9

Some of the more important decisions managers make involve analysing the relationships among the cost, volume and profitability of products produced and services provided by a company. **Cost-volume-profit (CVP) analysis** focuses on the relationships among the following five factors and the overall profitability of a company:

1 The prices of products or services
2 The volume of products or services produced and sold
3 The per-unit variable costs
4 The total fixed costs
5 The mix of products or services produced.
   CVP analysis requires projections of the future, and uses formulae that contain assumptions that must be reflected upon prior to its use. These assumptions are as follows:

1 The selling price is constant throughout the entire relevant range. In other words, we assume that the sales price of the product will not change as volume changes (that is, we sell more or sell less).
2 Costs are linear throughout the relevant range. As discussed in Chapter 3, although costs may behave in a curvilinear fashion, they can often be approximated by a linear relationship between cost and volume within the relevant range. This means variable cost rates remain the same, within a relevant range, and fixed costs remain unchanged.
3 The sales mix used to calculate the weighted-average contribution margin is constant.
4 The amount of inventory is constant. In other words, the number of units produced is equal to the number of units sold.
   Although some of these assumptions are often violated in real business settings, the violations are usually minor and have little or no impact on management decisions. CVP analysis is thus valid and considered useful for decision making. Additionally, the greater the extent to which an organisation satisfies the above assumptions, the more reliability it can place on the results of CVP calculations.

❋ cost–volume–profit (CVP) analysis
A tool that focuses on the relationship between a company's profits and (1) the selling prices of products or services, (2) the volume of products or services sold, (3) the per unit variable costs, (4) the total fixed costs and (5) the mix of products or services produced.

As Ultra HD curved LED monitors become more and more popular, the growth in demand allows companies to think about how they might spend more on marketing and promotion costs in order to yield higher sales and profits. Determining these trade-offs is a fundamental characteristic of CVP analysis.

The contribution margin and its uses

As mentioned in Chapters 2 and 3 the traditional profit and loss statement required for external financial reporting focuses on function (product costs versus period costs) in calculating the cost of goods sold and a company's gross profit. **Gross profit** is the difference between sales and cost of goods sold. However, because cost of goods sold includes both fixed costs (facility-level costs, such as rent) and variable costs (unit-level costs, such as direct materials), the behaviour of cost of goods sold and gross profit is difficult to predict when production increases or decreases.

In contrast, the contribution margin profit and loss statement is structured by behaviour rather than by function. In Exhibit 9.1, a traditional profit and loss statement and a contribution margin profit and loss statement are shown side by side so you can see the difference.

As you can see, although the net profit is the same for both statements, the traditional statement focuses on the function of the costs, whereas the contribution margin profit and loss statement focuses on the behaviour of the costs. In the traditional profit and loss statement, cost of goods sold and selling, general

and administrative (S, G & A) costs include both variable and fixed costs. In the contribution margin profit and loss statement, costs are separated by behaviour (variable versus fixed) rather than by function. Therefore, variable marketing expenses and fixed marketing expenses will be shown separately, whereas in a traditional profit and loss statement, both are shown within the one 'marketing expense' period cost item. This also means, however, that the contribution margin profit and loss statement combines product and period costs. Variable costs include both variable product costs (direct materials) and variable selling, general and administrative costs (commissions on sales). Fixed costs include both product and period costs.

What value does the 'contribution margin' term provide managers in organisations? We know the contribution margin equals sales revenues less variable costs. Managers find it extremely useful to understand how much they have 'left over' from sales revenues to cover fixed costs, once variable costs have been covered. In a sense, variable costs in their purest form present low risk to companies. If you don't make and sell a product, there is no variable cost. In the medium to longer term, no organisation will make a loss if it has a lean year, owing only to variable costs. If it makes and sells less, it also spends less on variable costs. The costs that managers worry about from a profitability point of view are often fixed costs. Fixed costs remain the same whether a company makes and sells more, or does not! When times are going well, business is 'booming' and sales are high, fixed costs are ideal in that they don't rise within the relevant range and profits from sales increases are maximised. However, the reverse occurs if a

Traditional			Contribution margin		
Sales		$1000	Sales		$1000
Less: Cost of goods sold:			Less: Variable costs:		
Variable costs	$350		Manufacturing costs	$350	
Fixed costs	150		S, G & A costs	50	
Total cost of goods sold		500	Total variable costs		400
Gross profit		$ 500	Contribution margin		$ 600
Less: S, G & A costs:			Less: Fixed costs:		
Variable costs	$ 50		Manufacturing costs	$150	
Fixed costs	250		S, G & A costs	250	
Total S, G & A costs		300	Total fixed costs		400
Net profit		$ 200	Net profit		$ 200

EXHIBIT 9.1 Comparison of profit and loss statements

company sells less than expected. Fixed costs, unlike variable costs, will not reduce and remain at their usual levels, which are now problematic as we have less revenues to cover the very same cost. Consequently, organisations will be left with relatively high fixed-cost bills relative to sales revenue and may even make a loss because of fixed costs. Fixed costs, therefore, concern managers more than variable costs, from a profitability control perspective. The CM therefore informs you of how much you have in revenues to cover the costs that you as a manager might worry about – fixed costs!

Contribution margin per unit

To illustrate the many uses of the contribution margin profit and loss statement in managerial decision making, let's look at the profit and loss statement of Happy Daze Games. Happy Daze, unlike large established firms such as Electronic Arts, is a start-up company and produces just one game but plans to increase its product line to include more games in the near future.

A contribution margin profit and loss statement for Happy Daze Game Company follows.

	Total	Per unit
Sales (8000 units)	$100 000	$12.50
Less: Variable costs	72 000	9.00
Contribution margin	$ 28 000	$ 3.50
Less: Fixed costs	35 000	
Net profit (loss)	$ (7 000)	

Note that in addition to the total sales, variable costs and contribution margin, per-unit cost information is also shown in the statement. Happy Daze sells each game for $12.50

and the variable cost of manufacturing each game is $9.00. As you can see, the **contribution margin per unit (CMU)** is $3.50 and can be found by subtracting the per-unit variable costs of $9.00 from the per-unit sales price of $12.50. The contribution margin per unit can also be calculated by dividing the contribution margin (in dollars) by the number of units sold:

※ **contribution margin per unit (CMU)**

The sales price per unit of product less all variable costs to produce and sell the unit of product; used to calculate the change in contribution margin resulting from a change in unit sales.

> **Key formula 9.1:** Contribution margin (per unit)
>
> $$\text{Contribution margin (per unit)} = \frac{\text{Contribution margin (in \$)}}{\text{Units sold}}$$
> $$= \frac{28\,000}{8\,000} = \$3.50$$

What exactly does this tell us? It tells us that every game that is sold adds $3.50 to the contribution margin. Assuming that fixed costs don't change, net profit increases by the same $3.50.

What happens if sales increase by 100 games? Since we know that the contribution margin is $3.50 per game, if sales increase by 100 games, net profit will increase by $350 ($3.50 × 100). In a similar fashion, if sales were to decrease by 200 games, then net profit would decrease by $700 ($3.50 × −200).

As summarised in Exhibit 9.2, the use of contribution margin per unit makes it very easy to predict how both increases and decreases in sales volume impact contribution margin and net profit.

	Decreased by 200 units	Original total	Increased by 100 units
	7800 units	8000 units	8100 units
Sales (sales price $12.50/unit)	$97 500	$100 000	$101 250
Less: Variable costs ($9/unit)	70 200	72 000	72 900
Contribution margin ($3.50/unit)	$27 300	$ 28 000	$ 28 350
Less: Fixed costs	35 000	35 000	35 000
Net profit (loss)	$(7 700)	$ (7 000)	$ (6 650)
Change in profit	Decreased by $700		Increased by $350
	(200 unit decrease × $3.50)		(100 unit increase × $3.50)

EXHIBIT 9.2 The impact of changes in sales on contribution margin and net profit

Contribution margin ratio

❖ **contribution margin ratio (CMR)**
The contribution margin divided by sales; used to calculate the change in contribution margin resulting from a dollar change in sales.

The contribution margin profit and loss statement can also be presented using percentages, as shown in the following profit and loss statement. The **contribution margin ratio (CMR)** is calculated by dividing the contribution margin in dollars by sales dollars:

Key formula 9.2: Contribution margin ratio

$$\text{Contribution margin ratio} = \frac{\text{Contribution margin (in \$)}}{\text{Sales (in \$)}}$$

The contribution margin ratio can be viewed as the amount of each sales dollar contributing to the payment of fixed costs and increasing net profit – in effect, it is a contribution margin per sales dollar, as opposed to a contribution margin per unit discussed previously. That is, 28 cents of each sales dollar earned in Happy Daze contributes to the payment of fixed costs or increases net profit. Like the contribution margin per unit, the contribution margin ratio will remain constant as long as sales vary in direct proportion to volume. In summary, a useful way of differentiating the CMU and CMR is by understanding that the CMR requires a denominator in sales *dollars*, while the CMU requires a denominator in sales *units*.

	Total	Percentage
Sales (8000 units)	$100 000	100
Less: Variable costs	72 000	72
Contribution margin	$ 28 000	28 ($28 000/$100 000)
Less: Fixed costs	35 000	
Net profit (loss)	$ (7 000)	

Like contribution margin per unit, the contribution margin ratio allows us to very quickly see the impact of a change in sales on contribution margin and net profit. As you saw in Exhibit 9.2, a $1250 increase in sales (100 units) will increase contribution margin by $350 ($1250 × 28%). Assuming that fixed costs don't change, this $350 increase in contribution margin increases net profit by the same amount. Likewise, in Exhibit 9.2, we decreased sales by 200 units ($2500), resulting in a decrease in contribution margin and net profit of $700 ($2500 × 28%).

LEARNING OBJECTIVE 2 >>

What-if decisions using CVP

Continuing with our example, Happy Daze had a net loss of $7000 when 8000 units were sold. At that level of sales, the total contribution margin of $28 000 is not sufficient to cover fixed costs of $35 000. The CEO of the company would like to consider options to increase net profit while maintaining the high quality of the company's products. After consultation with marketing, operations and accounting managers, the CEO identifies three options that she would like to consider in more depth:

1 Reducing the variable costs of manufacturing a product or offering a service
2 Increasing sales through a change in the sales incentive structure, or commissions (which would also increase variable costs)
3 Increasing sales through improved features and increased advertising.

Source: dpa picture alliance archive/Alamy

Computer gaming revenue streams are extremely difficult to predict. Consequently, CVP might allow for sensitivity analysis of alternative performance levels, helping management understand how potential unexpected outcomes affect company profits.

Option 1 – reduce variable costs

When variable costs are reduced, the contribution margin will increase. So the question becomes: What can be done to reduce the variable costs of manufacturing? Happy Daze could find a less expensive supplier of raw materials. The company could also investigate the possibility of reducing the amount of labour used in the production process or of using lower-wage employees in the production process.

In either case, qualitative factors must be considered. If Happy Daze finds a less expensive supplier of raw materials, the reliability of the supplier (shipments may be late, causing down time) and the quality of the material (paper products are not as good, adhesive is not bonding) must be considered. Reducing labour costs also has both quantitative and qualitative implications. If less labour is involved in the production process, more machine time may be needed. Although this option certainly lowers variable costs, it may also raise fixed costs. Using lower-skilled workers to save money could result in more defective products, owing to mistakes made by inexperienced workers. Another possible result of using fewer workers is that it can adversely affect employee morale. Being short-staffed can cause stress on workers owing to the likelihood that they will be overworked.

Happy Daze decides to decrease variable costs by reducing the costs of direct labour. The operations manager assures the CEO that the change can be made by outsourcing some of the current production activities. This change reduces variable costs by 10 per cent and, as shown in the following analysis, results in an overall increase in net profit of $7200.

Impact of reducing variable costs by 10 per cent

	Current	Option 1
Sales	$100 000	$100 000
Less: Variable costs	72 000	64 800
Contribution margin	$ 28 000	$ 35 200
Less: Fixed costs	35 000	35 000
Net profit (loss)	$ (7 000)	$ 200

Option 2 – increase sales incentives (commissions)

The CEO of Happy Daze would also like to consider providing additional sales incentives to motivate the sales staff in an effort to increase sales volume. The marketing manager estimates that if Happy Daze raises the sales commission by 10 per cent on all

sales above the present level, sales will increase by $40 000, or 3200 games. (The additional sales commission will be $4000.)

Happy Daze can increase net profit by $7200 by increasing the sales commission by 10 per cent on all sales of more than $100 000. The new variable costs are calculated by using a variable-cost percentage of 72 per cent on sales up to $100 000 and 82 per cent on all sales of more than $100 000. As you can see in the following profit and loss statement, if sales increase by $40 000, profit will increase by $7200 and Happy Daze will report net profit of $200.

Impact of increasing sales incentives (sales increase to $140 000)

	Current	Option 2
Sales	$100 000	$140 000
Less: Variable costs	72 000	104 800
Contribution margin	$ 28 000	$ 35 200
Less: Fixed costs	35 000	35 000
Net profit (loss)	$ (7 000)	$ 200

In Option 1 and Option 2, the ultimate change in net profit can be determined by focusing solely on the change in contribution margin. Fixed costs are not relevant in either analysis because they do not vary. However, as you will see in Option 3, that is not always the case.

Impact of changes to cost, price and volume

	Current (8000 units)	Option 3 (11 200 units)
Sales	$100 000 ($8000 × $12.50)	$148 400 (11 200 × $13.25)
Less: Variable costs	72 000 (8000 × $9.00)	103 600 (11 200 × $9.25)
Contribution margin	$ 28 000 (8000 × $3.50)	$ 44 800 (11 200 × $4.00)
Less: Fixed costs	35 000	40 000
Net profit (loss)	$ (7 000)	$ 4 800

How much does a Samsung Galaxy cost to make?

The cost of producing a Samsung Galaxy S4 might be as low as US$236, estimated by an *International Business Times* article in 2013. Upon closer inspection, however, the costing estimate focuses on the 'bill of materials', and possibly does not include indirect costs that can be largely fixed, such as rent overheads. When identifying cost estimates, it is important that we consider both variable and fixed costs. Variable costs are often easily included (such as direct materials), but direct labour and fixed costs can be missed by non-accountants in devising a total 'cost' for a product.

Source: 'Samsung Galaxy S4 Costs $236 To Build: Will Its Bill Of Materials Effect Its Retail Price?', by Fionna Agomuoh. Published by IBT Media, Inc., © 2013.

Making it real

How much does a Galaxy S4 really cost?

Source: STANCA SANDA/Alamy

Option 3 – change game features and increase advertising

Changes can be made to more than one variable at a time. In fact, changes in cost, price and volume are never made in a vacuum and almost always impact on one or both of the other variables. Happy Daze has decided to change some key features of its game. While this change will add $0.25 to the variable cost per game, the marketing manager estimates that with additional advertising of $5000, sales volume will increase by 40 per cent, or 3200 units. In order to offset some of these costs, the accounting manager proposes an increase in sales price of $0.75 per unit. As shown next, this option increases the contribution margin per unit to $4.00 per unit. The new sales price per unit is $13.25, and variable costs increase from $9.00 to $9.25 per unit. The increase in contribution margin of $16 800 is more than enough to offset the $5000 increase in fixed costs and results in an overall increase in net profit of $11 800.

How well does each option meet the stated objectives of increasing net profit while maintaining a high-quality product? The CEO of Happy Daze should analyse each alternative solution in the same manner and choose the best course of action based on both quantitative and qualitative factors.

From a quantitative perspective, Option 1 results in an increase in net profit of $7200, Option 2 increases net profit by the same $7200 and Option 3 increases net profit by $11 800. The CEO must also assess the risk inherent in each option, including the sensitivity of a decision to make changes in key assumptions. For example, while Option 1 appears to have little quantitative risk because the decrease in costs is known with certainty and no increase in sales is projected, Happy Daze should consider whether reducing labour costs in Option 1 will have a negative impact on the quality of its product. If the reduction in labour costs results from using lower-paid but inadequately skilled workers, quality may be adversely impacted.

LEARNING OBJECTIVE **3** >>

Case

Break-even analysis

❊ **break-even point**
The level of sales at which contribution margin just covers fixed costs and net profit is equal to zero.

In addition to what-if analysis, it is useful for managers to know the number of units sold or the dollar amount of sales that is necessary for a company to break even. The **break-even point** is the level of sales at which contribution margin just covers fixed costs and, consequently, net

profit is equal to zero. Break-even analysis is really just a variation of CVP analysis in which volume is increased or decreased in an effort to find the point at which net profit is equal to zero. Traditionally, it was seen as a critical figure for establishing the 'floor' level of any operations (that is, the minimum performance a company can attain without making a loss).

Break-even analysis is facilitated through the use of a mathematical equation derived directly from the contribution margin profit and loss statement. Another way to look at these relationships is to put the profit and loss statement into equation form:

$$\text{Sales} - \text{Variable Costs} - \text{Fixed Costs} = \text{Net Profit}$$
$$SP(x) - VC(x) - FC = NI$$

where

SP = Sales price per unit
VC = Variable costs per unit
FC = Total fixed costs
NI = Net profit
x = Number of units sold

At the break-even point, net profit is equal to zero, so:

$$SP(x) - VC(x) - FC = 0$$

Rearranging and dividing each side by the contribution margin ($SP - VC$), the number of units (x) that must be sold to reach the break-even point is found by dividing the total fixed costs by the contribution margin (CM) per unit:

$$(SP - VC)(x) = CF$$

and

$$x = \frac{FC}{CM}$$

By dividing the contribution margin of each product into the fixed cost, we are calculating the number of units that must be sold to cover the fixed costs. At that point, the total contribution margin will be equal to fixed costs, and net profit will be zero.

> **Key formula 9.3:** Break-even point. Break-even (units)
>
> $$\text{Break-even (units)} = \frac{\text{Fixed costs}}{\text{Contribution margin per unit}}$$

For example, if Happy Daze has fixed costs of $35 000 and the contribution margin per unit is $3.50, the break-even point is computed as follows:

$$\text{Break-even (units)} = \frac{\text{Fixed costs}}{\text{Contribution margin per unit}}$$
$$= \$35\,000 \div \$3.50$$
$$= 10\,000 \text{ units}$$

We can use a similar formula to compute the amount of sales dollars needed to break even:

> **Key formula 9.4:** Break-even point. Break-even ($)
>
> $$\text{Break-even (\$)} = \frac{\text{Fixed costs}}{\text{Contribution margin ratio}}$$

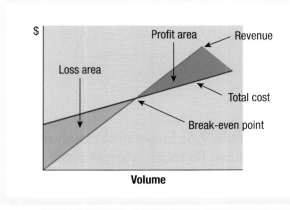

EXHIBIT 9.3 Break-even graph

Using the amounts from the previous example,

$$\text{Break-even (\$)} = \frac{\$35\,000}{28\% \text{ (see page 136)}}$$

$$= \$125\,000$$

Graphically, the break-even point can be found by comparing a company's total revenue with its total costs (both fixed and variable). As shown in Exhibit 9.3, the break-even point is the volume at which total revenue is equal to total cost.

Break-even calculations with multiple products

Break-even calculations become more difficult when more than one product is produced and sold. In a multiproduct environment, a manager calculating the break-even point is concerned not so much with the unit sales or the dollar sales of a single product but with the amount of total sales necessary to break even. This requires the calculation of an 'average' contribution margin for all the products produced and sold. This in turn requires an estimate of the sales mix – the relative percentage of total units or total sales dollars expected from each product.[1] However, customers (and sales volume) will not always behave in the manner that we predict. For example, although the expected sales product mix may be 600 units of Product A and 400 units of Product B, we can estimate our customers' buying habits only from past experience. If the sales product mix ends up being 700 units of A and 300 units of B, the break-even analysis will change accordingly.

Assume that Happy Daze adds another game to its product line. The company estimates that the new game will achieve sales of approximately 4500 units. The expected sales product mix (in units) is therefore 64 per cent (8000 ÷ 12 500) old game and 36 per cent (4500 ÷ 12 500) new game. The new game will be priced at $15 per unit and requires $11 of variable production, selling and administrative costs, so the contribution margin per unit is $4. The game will also require an investment of $15 000 in additional fixed costs. A summary of the price and cost of the old and new games follows.

	Happy Daze Game Company			
	Old game (8000 units)	Per unit	New game (4500 units)	Per unit
Sales	$100 000	$12.50	$67 500	$15.00
Less: Variable costs	72 000	9.00	49 500	11.00
Contribution margin	$28 000	$ 3.50	$18 000	$4.00
Less: Fixed costs	35 000		15 000	
Net profit (loss)	$ (7 000)		$ 3 000	

The average contribution margin can be found by weighting the contribution margin per unit for the old game and the new game by the relative sales mix and then summing the products.

$$\text{Old game} = 0.64 \times \$3.50 = \$2.24$$
$$\text{New game} = 0.36 \times \$4.00 = \$1.44$$

The weighted-average contribution margin for Happy Daze Game Company is therefore $3.68 per game ($2.24 + $1.44). The amount can also be calculated by dividing the total contribution margin earned by selling both games ($46 000) by the total number of units sold (12 500 games). ($46 000 ÷ 12 500 games = $3.68 per game). The break-even formula for a company with multiple products is as follows:

Key formula 9.5: Break-even point. Break-even (units)

$$\text{Break-even (units)} = \frac{\text{Fixed costs}}{\text{Weighted-average contribution margin per unit}}$$

Happy Daze's break-even point is therefore 13 587 units ($50 000 ÷ $3.68). How is this number interpreted? Remember that the weighted-average contribution margin is dependent on the sales mix. Likewise, the break-even point is dependent on the sales mix. Assuming a sales mix of 64 per cent old games and 36 per cent new games, Happy Daze must sell 8696 old games and 4891 new games to break even.

$$\text{Old game: } 13\,587 \times 0.64 = 8696$$
$$\text{New game: } 13\,587 \times 0.36 = 4891$$

If the sales mix changes to 50 per cent old games and 50 per cent new games, what will be the impact on the break-even point? What if the sales mix changes to 40 per cent old games and 60 per cent new games? With the sales mix at 50 per cent old and 50 per cent new, the weighted-average contribution margin becomes $3.75 [(0.50 × $3.50) + (0.50 × $4.00)]. When the mix changes to 40 per cent old and 60 per cent new, the weighted-average contribution margin changes to $3.80 [(0.40 × $3.50) + (0.60 × $4.00)]. Notice that when the volume shifts toward selling more of the product with the highest contribution margin, the weighted-average contribution margin increases. As the weighted-average contribution margin increases, the break-even point will decrease.

The break-even point calculated using a weighted-average contribution margin for multiple products is valid only for the sales mix used in the calculation. If the sales mix changes, the break-even point will also change. For example, if we sold the same total amount in units as the break-even units level, but the percentage of products sold was 80 per cent in new games and 20 per cent in old games (therefore, more new games than old games sold in comparison to what we expected), we will make a profit and not simply break even. This is because 80 per cent of our units sold actually earned a contribution margin per unit of $4 (new game), and 20 per cent earned $3.50 (old game) when we had previously only expected 36 per cent to earn $4 and 64 per cent to earn $3.50. Finally, the more products involved in the sales mix, the more sensitive the calculation becomes to changes in sales mix.

LEARNING OBJECTIVE **4** >>

Target profit analysis (before and after tax)

The goal of most businesses is not to break even but to earn a profit. Luckily, we can easily modify the break-even formula to compute the amount of sales needed to earn a target profit (before tax). Instead of solving for the sales necessary to earn a net profit of zero, we simply solve for the sales necessary to reach a target profit.

Sales − Variable Costs − Fixed Costs = Target Profit (before tax)

$$SP(x) - VC(x) - FC = TP$$

where

SP = Sales price per unit
VC = Variable costs per unit
FC = Total fixed costs
TP = Target profit (before tax)
x = Number of units sold

Rearranging and dividing each side by the contribution margin ($SP - VC$), the number of units (x) that must be sold to earn a before-tax target profit is found by dividing the sum of the fixed costs and the target profit by the contribution margin (CM) per unit:

$$x = \frac{[FC + TP(\text{before tax})]}{CM}$$

Consequently,

> **Key formula 9.6:** Target profit analysis. Sales volume (to reach a target profit before tax)
>
> $$\text{Sales volume (to reach a target profit before tax)} = \frac{\text{Fixed costs} + \text{Target profit (before tax)}}{\text{Contribution margin}}$$

Happy Daze has decided that it must earn a target profit of $100 000 on sales of the old game or the owners will not want to continue their investment in the business. The question is how many old games does the company have to sell to earn that amount of profit?

$$\text{Sales volume (to reach a target profit before tax)} = \frac{\$35\,000 + \$100\,000}{\$3.50}$$

$$= 38\,571 \text{ units (rounded)}$$

Although Happy Daze must sell only 10 000 old games to break even, the company must sell 38 571 old games to reach a before-tax target profit of $100 000. In fact, once we know that Happy Daze's break-even point is 10 000 units, we can directly calculate the sales necessary to reach a target profit of $100 000 using the CM per unit. Because each additional unit sold (above the break-even point) will contribute $3.50 toward net profit, Happy Daze must sell an additional 28 572 units ($100 000 ÷ $3.50) to earn a profit of $100 000.

The multiple-product break-even formula can be modified in a similar fashion to solve for the sales necessary to reach a target profit. In a multiple-product environment:

> **Key formula 9.7:** Target profit analysis. Sales volume (to reach target profit)
>
> $$\text{Sales volume (to reach a target profit)} = \frac{(\text{Fixed costs} + \text{Target profit})}{\text{Weighted-average contribution margin per unit}}$$

The impact of taxes

The payment of income taxes also needs to be considered in the target profit formula. If Happy Daze sells 38 572 games and earns the projected $100 000 in target profit, the company still won't have $100 000 in cash flow to distribute to the owners as dividends because it must pay income tax on the profit. If we assume that the income tax rate for Happy Daze is 35 per cent, the company will have to pay $35 000 in income tax ($100 000 × 35%) and will be left with after-tax profit of $65 000. The after-tax profit can be found by multiplying the before-tax profit by (1 − tax rate). Correspondingly, the before-tax profit equals the after-tax profit divided by (1 − tax rate):

Key formula 9.8: Before-tax profit

$$\text{Before-tax profit} = \frac{\text{After-tax profit}}{(1 - \text{tax rate})}$$

If Happy Daze desires to earn an after-tax profit of $100 000, the company must earn a before-tax profit of $153 846 (rounded).

$$\text{Before-tax profit} = \frac{\$100\,000}{(1 - 0.35)} = \$153\,846$$

Consequently, Happy Daze must sell 53 956 units of the old game in order to reach a before-tax profit of $153 846 and an after-tax profit of $100 000.

$$\text{Sales volume (to reach an after-tax target profit)} = \frac{(\$35\,000 + \$153\,846)}{\$3.50}$$

$$= 53\,956 \text{ units}$$

This is confirmed in the following profit and loss statement for Happy Daze:

Sales (53 956 units)	$674 450
Less: Variable costs	485 604
Contribution margin	$188 846
Less: Fixed costs	35 000
Profit before taxes	$153 846
Less: Profit tax @35%	53 846
Net profit after tax	$100 000

LEARNING OBJECTIVE 5 >>

Cost structure and operating leverage

As mentioned in Chapter 3, cost structure refers to the relative proportion of fixed and variable costs in a company. Highly automated manufacturing companies with large investments in property, plant and equipment are likely to have cost structures dominated by fixed costs. On the other hand, labour-intensive companies such as home builders are likely to have cost structures dominated by variable costs. Even companies in the same industry can have very different cost structures. A company's cost structure is important because it directly affects the sensitivity of that company's profits to changes in sales volume. Generally, the greater the proportion of fixed costs in your company, the more sensitivity of your company's profits to changes in sales volume. Consider, for example, two companies that make the same product (furniture), with the same sales and same net profit. Company A is highly automated and uses state-of-the-art machinery to design, cut and assemble its products. On the other hand, Company B is highly labour intensive and uses skilled craftspeople to cut and assemble its products. Contribution margin profit and loss statements for both companies are provided in Exhibit 9.4.

Which company would you prefer to run? Although you might opt for Company A, with its high level of automation and correspondingly higher contribution margin ratio relative to Company B, consider the impact of changes in sales volume on the net profit of each company. Although *increasing* sales will benefit Company A more than Company B, what happens when sales *decline*? If sales decline by 10 per cent ($20 000), the profit of Company A will decline by $16 000 ($20 000 × 80%), whereas the profit of Company B will decline by $12 000 ($20 000 × 60%).

Labour intensive companies often incur lower fixed costs and higher variable costs than automated or machine intensive organisations.

A company with a cost structure characterised by a large proportion of fixed costs relative to variable costs will experience wider fluctuations in net profit as sales increase and decrease than a company with more variable costs in its cost structure. This is because fixed costs don't decrease when sales volume reduces, or vice versa. This causes greater profit volatility, relative to companies with a greater proportion of variable costs.

	Company A	Company B
Sales	$200 000	$200 000
Less: Variable costs	$40 000	80 000
Contribution margin	$160 000	$120 000
Less: Fixed costs	80 000	40 000
Net profit	$ 80 000	$ 80 000
Contribution margin ratio	80%	60%
Operating leverage	2.0	1.5

EXHIBIT 9.4 Contribution margin ratio and operating leverage

Operating leverage

Operating leverage is a measure of the proportion of fixed costs in a company's cost structure and is used as an indicator of how sensitive profit is to changes in sales volume. A company with high fixed costs in relation to variable costs will have a high level of operating leverage. In this case, net profit will be very sensitive to changes in sales volume. In other words, a small percentage increase in sales dollars will result in a large percentage increase in net profit. On the other hand, a company with high variable costs in relation to fixed costs will have a low level of operating leverage, and profit will not be as sensitive to changes in sales volume. Operating leverage is computed using the following formula:

Key formula 9.9: Operating leverage

$$\text{Operating leverage} = \frac{\text{Contribution margin}}{\text{Net income}}$$

In Exhibit 9.4, Company A has an operating leverage of 2.0 ($160 000 ÷ $80 000), whereas Company B has an operating leverage of 1.5 ($120 000 ÷ $80 000). What does this mean? When sales increase (decrease) by a given percentage, the profit of Company A will increase (decrease) by 2 times that percentage increase (decrease), whereas the profit of Company B will increase (decrease) by 1.5 times the percentage change in sales. When sales increase by 10 per cent, the profit of Company A will increase by 20 per cent, or $16 000 ($80 000 × 20%). In other words, when sales of Company A increase to $220 000, profit will increase to $96 000. The profit of Company B will increase by 15 per cent, or $12 000 ($80 000 × 15%), to a new profit of $92 000. Likewise, when sales decrease by 10 per cent, the profit of Company A will decrease by 20 per cent, whereas the profit of Company B will decrease by 15 per cent.

	Operating leverage	
	High	Low
Per cent increase in profit with increase in sales	Large	Small
Per cent increase in loss with decrease in sales	Large	Small

EXHIBIT 9.5 Operating leverage and the impact on profit

As summarised in Exhibit 9.5, when operating leverage is high, a change in sales results in large changes in profit. On the other hand, when operating leverage is low, a change in sales results in small changes in profits.

Unlike measures of contribution margin, operating leverage changes as sales change (see Exhibit 9.6). At a sales level of 1000 units ($200 000), Company B's operating leverage is 1.5. A 10 per cent increase in sales increases net profit by 15 per cent. At a sales level of 500 units, operating leverage increases to 3.0 and a 10 per cent increase in sales will increase net profit by 30 per cent (3 × 10%). At a sales level of 2000 units, operating leverage is reduced to 1.2, and a 10 per cent increase in sales will increase profit by 12 per cent.

As a company gets closer and closer to the break-even point, operating leverage will continue to increase and profit will be very sensitive to changes in sales. For example, when Company B sells 334 units (see Exhibit 9.7), contribution margin is equal to $40 080, profit is equal to $80, and operating leverage is equal to 501 ($40 080 ÷ $80). A 10 per cent increase in sales at this point will increase net profit by a whopping 5010 per cent.

Understanding the concepts of contribution margin and operating leverage and how they are used in CVP analysis is very important in managerial decision making. Using these tools, managers can quickly estimate the impact on net profit of changes in cost, sales volume and price.

	500 Units	1000 Units	2000 Units
Sales	$100 000	$200 000	$400 000
Less: Variable costs	40 000	80 000	160 000
Contribution margin	$ 60 000	$120 000	$240 000
Less: Fixed costs	40 000	40 000	40 000
Net profit	$ 20 000	$ 80 000	$200 000
Operating leverage	$\frac{\$60\,000}{\$20\,000} = 3.0$	$\frac{\$120\,000}{\$80\,000} = 1.5$	$\frac{\$240\,000}{\$200\,000} = 1.2$

EXHIBIT 9.6 Company B – operating leverage at various levels of sales

Sales (334 units)	$66 800
Less: Variable costs	26 720
Contribution margin	$40 080
Less: Fixed costs	40 000
Net profit	$ 80
Operating leverage	$\frac{\$40\,080}{\$80} = 501$

EXHIBIT 9.7 Company B – operating near the break-even point

Exercises

1 Contribution margin LO1

Companies that wish to distribute their profit and loss statements to outside parties such as banks must prepare those statements using the traditional profit and loss statement format. These same companies may also prepare contribution margin profit and loss statements to more fully understand their costs. The following terms are commonly used in describing contribution margin profit and loss statements and related topics.

Gross profit	Decrease
Contribution margin	Fixed costs
Net profit	Contribution margin ratio
Variable costs	Increase

Required

Choose the term from the list above that most appropriately completes the following statements.

a Once a company has paid all of its fixed costs, net income increases in an amount equal to _____ for each unit sold to customers.

b When production and sales are equal, whether a company prepares a traditional profit and loss statement or a contribution margin profit and loss statement, two numbers do not change. One of these is sales, and the other is _____.

c _____, the difference between sales and cost of goods sold, is not reported on the contribution margin profit and loss statement.

d For every unit sold, contribution margin will _____ in total.

e The _____ is computed by dividing the contribution margin by sales dollars.

f Of these two cost categories, only _____ increases and decreases contribution margin.

g If a company is unable to increase sales or _____ variable costs, the company can increase net profit by reducing _____.

2 CVP: The impact on profit LO2

Eric Ziegler started a lawn-mowing service in high school. He currently prices his lawn-mowing service at $35 per yard. He estimates that variable expenses related to fuel, supplies and depreciation on his equipment total $21 per yard.

Required

If Eric wants to increase his price by 40 per cent, how many fewer yards can he mow before his net profit decreases?

3 CVP: What-if analysis LO2

Last year, Mayes Company had a contribution margin of 30 per cent. This year, fixed expenses are expected to remain at $120000 and sales are expected to be $550000, which is 10 per cent higher than last year.

Required

What must the contribution margin ratio be if the company wants to increase net profit by $15000 this year?

4 CVP: What-if analysis LO2

Gerald Corporation had a contribution margin per unit of $5 last year, and sold 10000 units. It earned a profit of $30000 last year. This year, fixed expenses are expected to double last year's fixed expense. The CM per unit this year will be three times what it was last year.

Required

What is profit this year, if the company sells 12000 units?

5 What-if decisions with changing fixed costs LO2

Walker Company has current sales of $600000 and variable costs of $360000. The company's fixed costs are equal to $200000. The marketing manager is considering a new advertising campaign, which will increase fixed costs by $10000. She anticipates that the campaign will cause sales to increase by 5 per cent as a result.

Required

Should the company implement the new advertising campaign? What will be the impact on Walker's profit?

6 Operating leverage LO2, 5

Burger Queen Restaurant had the following information available related to its operations from last year:

Sales (150000 units)	500000
Variable costs	200000
Contribution margin	$300000
Fixed costs	150000
Net profit	$150000

Required

a What is Burger Queen's operating leverage?

b If sales increased by 30 per cent, what would Burger Queen's net profit be?

7 Break-even analysis LO3

Katie and Holly founded Hokies Plumbing Company after graduating from TAFE. They wanted to be competitive, so they set their rate for house calls at a modest $100. After paying the company's petrol and other variable costs of $60, the women thought there would be enough profit. Because they were ready to live life a bit, they set their salaries at $100000 each. There were no other fixed costs at all.

Required

Calculate the number of house calls that Hokies Plumbing must make to break even.

8 Break-even analysis LO3

Stevie Rogers founded Captain Australia Carpenters after completing his apprenticeship. The company set their rate for house calls at $50, and expects 2000 house calls this year. Their fixed costs are $40000 per annum.

Required

a What is the highest variable costs per house call that they can incur while avoiding a loss?

b How would your answer change if their fixed costs increased $15 000, and their house call rate reduced to $40?

9 Break-even analysis LO3

Callahan's Calabash Seafood Restaurant is a family-owned business started by Marc Callahan over 10 years ago. Callahan's is only open Thursday to Saturday and only serves dinner. In recent months, Marc has seen a drop-off in business. Just last month the restaurant broke even. Marc looked over the records and saw that the restaurant served 1000 meals (variable cost is $10 per meal) and paid other bills totalling $25 000. He looked over the bills and realised that they all represented fixed costs. The restaurant currently breaks even at 1000 meals.

Required

Calculate Callahan's average selling price for a meal.

10 Break-even analysis LO3

Lincoln Company sells logs for an average of $18 per log. The company's president, Abraham, estimates the variable manufacturing and selling costs total $6 per log. Logging operations require substantial investments in equipment, so fixed costs are quite high and total $108 000 per month. Abraham is considering making an investment in a new piece of logging equipment that will increase monthly fixed costs by $12 000.

Required

Assist Abraham by calculating the number of additional logs that must be sold to break even after investing in the new equipment.

11 Break-even analysis: Multi product environment LO3

Kim Johnson's company produces two well-known products, Glide Magic and Slide Magic. Glide Magic accounts for 60 per cent of her sales, and Slide Magic accounts for the rest. Glide currently sells for $16 per tube and has variable manufacturing and selling costs of $8. Slide sells for just $12 and has variable costs of $9 per tube. Kim's company has total fixed costs of $36 000.

Required

Calculate the total number of tubes that must be sold for Kim's company to break even.

12 Break-even analysis: Multi product environment LO3

Donald Tweedt started a company to produce and distribute natural fertilisers. Donald's company sells two fertilisers that are wildly popular: green fertiliser and compost fertiliser. Green fertiliser, the most popular among environmentally minded consumers, commands the highest price and sells for $16 per 30-kilogram bag. Green fertiliser also requires additional processing and includes environmentally friendly ingredients that increase its variable costs to $10 per bag. Compost fertiliser sells for $12 and has easily acquired ingredients that require no special processing. It has variable costs of $8 per bag. Tweedt's total fixed costs are $35 000. After some aggressive marketing efforts, Tweedt has been able to drive consumer demand to be equal for each fertiliser.

Required

Calculate the number of bags of green fertiliser that will be sold at break-even.

13 Sales to reach after-tax profit LO4

Lockwood Company currently sells its deadbolt locks for $30 each. The locks have a variable cost of $10, and the company's annual fixed costs are $150 000. The company's tax rate is 40 per cent.

Required

Calculate the number of locks that must be sold to earn an after-tax profit of $24 000.

14 Target profit analysis LO4

Kingman Corp. has long been concerned with maintaining a solid annual profit. The company sells a line of fire extinguishers that are perfect for homeowners, for an average of $10 each. The company has perfected its production process and now produces extinguishers with a variable cost of $4 per extinguisher. Kingman's annual fixed costs are $92 000. Kingman's tax rate is 40 per cent.

Required

Calculate the number of extinguishers Kingman must sell to earn an after-tax profit of $60 000.

Problems

15 Multi product break-even analysis LO1, 3

Don Waller and Company sells canisters of three mosquito repellent products: Citronella, DEET and Mean Green. The company has annual fixed costs of $260 000. Last year, the company sold 5000 canisters of its mosquito repellent in the ratio of 1:2:2. Waller's accounting department has compiled the following data related to the three mosquito repellents:

	Citronella	DEET	Mean Green
Price per canister	$11.00	$15.00	$17.00
Variable costs per canister	6.00	12.00	16.00

Required

a Calculate the total number of canisters that must be sold for the company to break even.

b Calculate the number of canisters of Citronella, DEET and Mean Green that must be sold to break even.

c How might Don Waller and Company reduce its break-even point?

16 Multi product break-even analysis
LO1, 3

Aussie Plastics sells three types of plastic cups, A, B and C. The company has annual fixed costs of $1 500 000. Last year, the company sold 1 800 000 cups in the ratio of 5:4:1 (A:B:C). Waller's accounting department has compiled the following data related to the cups:

	Cup A	Cup B	Cup C
Price per cup	$2.00	$1.50	$1.00
Variable costs per cup	0.70	0.90	0.60

Required
a   Calculate the cups that must be sold for the company to break even, assuming the same ratio.
b   If the company sells the required number of total cups to break-even (as per question a) why might they still not? Please explain with calculations.

17 CVP: What-if analysis LO1, 2, 3

Hacker Aggregates mines and distributes various types of rocks. Most of the company's rock is sold to contractors who use the product in highway construction projects. Treva Hacker, company CEO, believes that the company needs to advertise to increase sales. She has proposed a plan to the other managers that Hacker Aggregates spend $100 000 on a targeted advertising campaign. The company currently sells 25 000 tonnes of aggregate for total revenue of $5 000 000. Other data related to the company's production and operational costs follow:

Direct labour	$1 500 000
Variable production overhead	200 000
Fixed production overhead	350 000
Selling and administrative expenses:	
Variable	50 000
Fixed	300 000

Required
a   Compute the break-even point in units (i.e. tonnes) for Hacker Aggregates.
b   Compute the contribution margin ratio for Hacker Aggregates.
c   If Treva decides to spend $100 000 on advertising and the company expects the advertising to increase sales by $200 000, should the company increase the advertising? Why or why not?

18 CVP and break-even analysis LO1, 2, 3

Lauren Tarson and Michele Progransky opened Top Drawer Optical seven years ago with the goal of producing fashionable and affordable eyewear. Tarson and Progransky have been very pleased with their revenue growth. One particular design, available in plastic and metal, has become one of the company's best sellers. The following data relate to this design:

	Plastic frames	Metal frames
Sales price	$60.00	$80.00
Direct materials	20.00	18.00
Direct labour	13.50	13.50
Variable overhead	6.50	8.50
Budgeted unit sales	10 000	30 000

Currently, the company produces exactly as many frames as it can sell. Therefore, it has no opportunity to substitute a more expensive frame for a less expensive one. Top Drawer Optical's annual fixed costs are currently $1.225 million.

Required
Each of the following questions relates to an independent situation.
a   Calculate the total number of frames that Top Drawer Optical needs to produce and sell to break even.
b   Calculate the total number of frames that Top Drawer Optical needs to produce and sell to break even if budgeted direct material costs for plastic frames decrease by $10 and annual fixed costs increase by $12 500 for depreciation of a new production machine.
c   Tarson and Progransky have been able to reduce the company's fixed costs by eliminating certain unnecessary expenditures and downsizing supervisory personnel. Now, the company's fixed costs are $1 122 000. Calculate the number of frames that Top Drawer Optical needs to produce and sell to break even if the company sales mix changes to 35 per cent plastic frames and 65 per cent metal frames.

19 Break-even and target profit LO1, 2, 3

Matthew Hagen started his company, The Sign of Things to Come, three years ago after graduating from the Australian National University (ANU). While earning his engineering degree, Matthew became intrigued by all of the neon signs he saw at bars and taverns around the university. Few of his friends were surprised to see him start a neon sign company after leaving university. Matthew is currently considering the introduction of a new custom neon signage product that he believes will sell like hotcakes. In fact, he is estimating that the company will sell 7000 of the signs. The signs are expected to sell for $75 and require variable costs of $25. The Sign of Things to Come has annual fixed costs of $300 000.

Required
a   How many signs must be sold to break even?
b   How many signs must be sold to earn a profit of $15 000?
c   If 7000 signs are sold, how much profit will The Sign of Things to Come earn?
d   What would be the break-even point if the sales price decreased by 20 per cent? Round your answer to the next-highest number.
e   What would be the break-even point if variable costs per sign decreased by 40 per cent?
f   What would be the break-even point if fixed costs increased by $50 000?

Cases

20 CVP analysis: Target profit with constraints LO1, 2, 4

Moore, Inc., invented a secret process to double the growth rate of hatchery trout. The company manufactures a variety of products related to this process. Each product is independent of the others and is treated as a separate division.

The Morey Division sells an additive that is added to pond water. Morey has had a new manager in each of the three previous years because each manager failed to reach Moore's target profit. Bryan Endreson has just been promoted to manager and is studying ways to meet the current target profit for Morey.

The target profit for Morey for the coming year is $800 000 (20 per cent return on the investment in the annual fixed costs of the division). Other constraints on division operations are that production cannot exceed sales, because Moore's corporate advertising stresses completely new additives each year, even though the 'newness' of the models may be only cosmetic. The Morey selling price may not vary above the current selling price of $200 per gallon, but it may vary as much as 10 per cent below $200 (i.e., $180).

Endreson is now examining data gathered by his staff to determine whether Morey can achieve its target profit of $800 000. The data are as follows:

- Last year's sales were 30 000 units at $200 per gallon. The present capacity of Morey's manufacturing facility is 40 000 gallons per year, but capacity can be increased to 80 000 gallons per year with an additional investment of $1 million per year in fixed costs.

- Present variable costs amount to $80 per unit, but if commitments are made for more than 60 000 gallons, Morey's vendors are willing to offer raw material discounts amounting to $20 per gallon, beginning with gallon 60 001.

Endreson believes that these projections are reliable, and he is now trying to determine what Morey must do to meet the profit objectives assigned by Moore's board of directors.

Required

a Calculate the dollar value of Morey's current annual fixed costs.

b Determine the number of gallons that Morey must sell at $200 per gallon to achieve the profit objective. Be sure to consider any relevant constraints. What if the selling price is $180?

c Without prejudice to your previous answers, assume that Bryan Endreson decides to sell 40 000 gallons at $200 per gallon and 24 000 gallons at $180 per gallon. Prepare a pro forma income statement for Morey, showing whether Endreson's decision will achieve Morey's profit objectives.

21 CVP and break-even analysis LO1, 2, 3

Consider The Daily Grind café appendix at the back of the textbook and answer questions 1, 2, 3, 4, 5, 9, 10, 11 and 12.

> I think this book is totally cutting-edge...it's making learning fun again.
> – Scotty Willamson, student.

LEARNING, YOUR WAY.

ACCT was designed for students just like you – busy people who want choices, flexibility, and multiple learning options.

ACCT delivers concise, focussed information in a fresh and contemporary format. And... **ACCT** gives you a variety of online learning materials designed with you in mind.

At **http://login.cengagebrain.com/** you'll find electronic resources such as audio downloads and online flash cards for each chapter. These resources will help supplement your understanding of core organisational behaviour concepts in a format that fits your busy lifestyle.

Visit **http://login.cengagebrain.com/** to learn more about the multiple **ACCT** resources available to help you succeed!

Learning objectives:

After studying the material in this chapter, you should be able to:

1. Analyse the pricing of a special order.
2. Analyse a decision involving the outsourcing of labour or making or buying a component.
3. Analyse a decision dealing with adding or dropping a product, product line or service.
4. Analyse a decision dealing with scarce or limited resources.
5. Describe the theory of constraints and explain the importance of identifying bottlenecks in the production process.
6. Analyse a decision dealing with selling a product or processing it further.

RELEVANT COSTS AND PRODUCT PLANNING DECISIONS

c 10

As we discussed in Chapter 1, operating activities include a wide range of decisions that managers make on a day-to-day basis. The manager of a company that makes T-shirts must determine the price for a special onetime order. The manager of a restaurant must continually assess the status of its menu items, just as managers of a large manufacturer of stereo components must consider whether to add new products or drop unprofitable ones. Managers of a company that makes bicycles must decide whether to buy tyres from another manufacturer or make them internally. Colleges and universities must decide whether to provide cleaning services in dorms and provide food service (cafeterias and so on) to students using their own employees or to outsource those services to someone else. The manager of a hardware store must determine which products to put on the shelves, and a book publisher must determine which books to publish. All these decisions require relevant, timely accounting information to aid in the decision-making process. As discussed earlier in the book, relevant costs are costs that differ among alternatives – that is, costs that are avoidable or can be eliminated by choosing one alternative over another. Because sunk costs have already been incurred and cannot be avoided, they are not relevant in decisions. Likewise, future

Source: Brendon Thorne/Bloomberg/Getty Images

In the face of strong international competition, Qantas has partnered with Emirates Airlines to raise its ability to serve its customers through Asia and Europe. Many of the costs of flying an airline are fixed and don't vary with the number of passengers on the plane, and so flights with free seats can often turn into revenue sources, when 'lent' to passengers from other airlines. Understanding cost behaviour is therefore critical for companies making everyday decisions such as those discussed in this chapter.

costs that do not differ among alternatives are not relevant because they cannot be eliminated by choosing one alternative over another. On the other hand, opportunity costs are relevant in decision making. In this chapter, we discuss the tools that managers use to make these short-term tactical decisions.

LEARNING OBJECTIVE **1** >>

Special orders

Deciding whether to accept a special order is really just a pricing decision. However, **special-order decisions** are short-run decisions. Management must decide what sales price is appropriate when customers place orders that are different from those placed in the regular course of business (onetime sale to a foreign customer, etc.).[1] These decisions are affected by whether the company has excess production capacity and can produce additional units with existing machinery, labour and facilities. A special order would almost never be accepted if a company does not have excess capacity. If a company does not have excess capacity, it will have to turn away current customers in order to fill a special order. These current customers may very well turn to other companies to fill their

needs. Filling a special order under these circumstances may permanently damage the relationship with these customers. Even if a special order is profitable from a quantitative perspective, the impact on customer relations should be considered before deciding whether to accept or reject the order. If customers find other suppliers due to delivery delays, the overall profit of the company might decrease.

However, it is important to recognise that if there is no capacity but a selling price offered from a prospective customer is attractive enough, companies may well ignore all the risks mentioned above and take sales away from existing customers, selling to the new customer in pursuit of higher short-term profits. The qualitative risks of this approach cannot be emphasised strongly enough, as explained above.

:: **special-order decisions**
Short-run pricing decisions in which management must decide which sales price is appropriate when customers place orders that are different from those placed in the regular course of business (onetime sale to a foreign customer, etc.).

Even when a company has excess capacity, qualitative factors must be considered before deciding to accept a special order, particularly if the special-order price is below the price offered to regular customers. In these situations, care must be taken so that regular customers do not feel they have been treated unfairly.

Consider Qantas Airlines, a major Australian airline. Let's assume BHP Billiton asked Qantas to provide 150 seats for a Melbourne to Brisbane return flight for corporate executives attending a convention. BHP Billiton offers $125 per ticket, although the normal fare for this route is $275. The tickets can be used on only one day, but the executives need to be able to fly on one of five flights offered that day. Let's also assume that the aircraft that Qantas Airlines flies on this route carries 180 passengers, so the five scheduled flights provide a capacity of 900 seats. The normal passenger load on the day requested is between 77 per cent and 78 per cent of available capacity (700 passengers), so Qantas should have plenty of excess capacity (40 seats per plane, or 200 seats total). However, should Qantas accept the special order at the discounted price of $125 per ticket? That depends on the company's objective.

The objective of Qantas Airlines is to maximise profit in the short run without reducing profit in the long run. The options in this case include selling the tickets for $125 (accepting the special order), letting the marketplace determine the level of sales at a predetermined price of $275 or selling the tickets at another price. An analysis of the options requires that the relevant costs and other factors be identified. Let's suppose that the accounting department of Qantas Airlines has provided the following information:

	Per passenger	Per round trip
Cost of meals and drinks	$ 6.50	$ 1170
Cost of fuel	88.89	16000
Cost of cabin crew (four flight attendants)	6.11	1100
Cost of flight crew	11.11	2000
Depreciation of aircraft	16.67	3000
Aircraft maintenance	8.33	1500
Total	$137.61	$24770

This decision appears to be an easy one, as the special-order price of $125 is less than the total cost per passenger of $137.61. Based on the full cost reported by the accounting department, Qantas Airlines would be losing $12.61 on each passenger purchasing a ticket for $125. But would it? To analyse the options in this decision problem correctly, only the relevant costs should be considered. In this decision, the only costs that are relevant are those that will differ depending on whether the special order is accepted. Another way to look at the problem is by determining which costs can be avoided by choosing one alternative over the other.

In this case, almost all the costs are fixed with respect to the number of passengers on the plane. In fact, owing to the unique nature of the airline business, most operating costs are fixed. For example, the aircraft will require the same maintenance and flight crew costs regardless of how many passengers are on board. Although the costs of the cabin crew may vary, let us assume that in this situation, regulations require four flight attendants for any flight with more than 125 passengers. In this case, four flight attendants are required regardless of whether the plane carries 125 passengers or 180 passengers, so acceptance of the special order will not change the cost of the cabin crew. In essence, the costs of the maintenance, flight crew and cabin crew are fixed. Likewise, depreciation is a fixed cost. Even fuel costs would not be expected to vary much with the addition of 30 to 40 passengers. In fact, the only cost that would likely vary with the number of passengers on the plane is the small additional cost of meals and drinks. Because Qantas Airlines appears to have plenty of excess capacity (empty seats), any sales price above the variable costs of providing the seats will increase the profit of the company. If the cost of meals and drinks is the only variable cost, Qantas should be willing to accept the special order at any price over $6.50. In situations in which excess capacity exists, the general rule is that in order to maximise profit, the special-order price must simply be higher than the additional variable costs incurred in accepting the special order.

What if Qantas does not have any excess capacity? If the airline expects to sell all its tickets at the regular price of $275, accepting the special order involves an opportunity cost. The risk in this situation is that the airline will have to turn away full-fare passengers if it accepts the special order. Remember from Chapter 2 that an opportunity cost is the benefit forgone by choosing one alternative over another. If Qantas Airlines accepts the special order, it will forgo the receipt of $268.50 of contribution margin on each ticket ($275 selling price less the $6.50 variable cost of meals and drinks). Therefore, it would not be willing to accept a special order for any price below the $275 market price. The relevant costs in this case are the variable costs of $6.50 and the opportunity cost of $268.50. As demonstrated in Exhibit 10.1, when Qantas Airlines has excess capacity, accepting the special order will result in a profit of $118.50 for each ticket sold. However, when there is not sufficient capacity, Qantas Airlines can only meet the special order by turning away full-paying customers and incurring an opportunity cost. As a result, the company would lose $150.00 for each ticket sold.

Fixed costs can be relevant to a special-order decision when they change depending on the option chosen. For example, let's consider the case of flight attendants again. Instead of requiring four flight attendants for any flight with more than 125 passengers, let's assume that regulations require one flight attendant for every 35 passengers. Whereas four attendants are sufficient for a flight of 140 passengers,

	Excess capacity	No excess capacity
Relevant costs:		
Meals	$ 6.50	$ 6.50
Opportunity costs from lost ticket revenue (Contribution margin lost)	0	$ 268.50
Total relevant costs	$ 6.50	$ 275.00
Special-order ticket price	125.00	125.00
Profit (loss) from accepting special order	$118.50	$(150.00)

EXHIBIT 10.1 The special-order decision

adding 30 additional passengers will require the addition of an extra flight attendant at a cost of $275, or $9.17 per additional passenger. Assuming that excess capacity exists, the special-order price would need to exceed $15.67 to be acceptable to Qantas Airlines.

Instead of 150 extra passengers flying on the five regularly scheduled flights, assume that Qantas Airlines has an additional plane that is currently idle but can be chartered for the flight. In this case, fuel costs, salaries of the flight and cabin crews, and maintenance are likely to be relevant, but depreciation is still not relevant. It is important to note that determining what is relevant and what is not depends on the specific situation.

A number of qualitative factors must also be considered in special-order decisions. First, if it accepts the special order on the basis of expected excess capacity but its passenger-load predictions are wrong, Qantas Airlines may have to turn away passengers who would otherwise pay the full fare. If that happens and these passengers turn to competing airlines, Qantas Airlines faces the potential of losing long-term customers and consequent market share. Second, the impact of selling seats at a discount on those customers paying regular fares must be considered.

LEARNING OBJECTIVE **2** >>

Outsourcing and other make-or-buy decisions

The decision to outsource labour or to purchase components used in manufacturing from another company rather than to provide the services or to produce the components internally affects a wide range of manufacturing, merchandising and service organisations. For example, a university can contract with an outside company to provide cleaning and repair services for on-campus dormitories, or it can provide those services by using university employees. A local florist can provide payroll processing internally, or it can hire a CPA or CA to provide those services. Heinz Australia can make packaging for its products internally, or buy them from an outside supplier.

Strategic aspects of outsourcing and make-or-buy decisions

Animation

An analysis of outsourcing and **make-or-buy decisions** requires an in-depth analysis of relevant quantitative and qualitative factors and a consideration of the costs and benefits of outsourcing and vertical integration. For example, Qantas Airlines might consider outsourcing the maintenance function on their planes to an outside organisation. Suppose that Qantas Airlines now pays all maintenance personnel $20 per hour plus 30 per cent for fringe benefits. Total labour costs are $26 per hour. An outside agency offers to perform the maintenance for $22 per hour plus the cost of parts and supplies. From a quantitative perspective this is a money-saving move. Let's assume that Qantas Airlines has 100 maintenance personnel who all work 40 hours per week. The savings from outsourcing would be $16 000 per week or $832 000 per year. However, Qantas Airlines needs to consider a number of qualitative factors before making this decision. Is the quality of work the same? What are the risks associated with outsourcing maintenance if poor-quality work results in an aircraft accident? How will outsourcing maintenance impact other employees of the airline, including ticket agents and ground service personnel? Other employees may become demoralised and worry about losing their own jobs. They may be less motivated to do the best job possible, leading to quality problems, operational slowdowns and even employee strikes. They may very well leave the company if and when a better opportunity presents itself.

Vertical integration is accomplished when a company is involved in multiple steps of the value chain. In an extreme example, the same company might own a gold mine, a manufacturing facility to produce gold jewellery and a retail jewellery store. Most companies operate with some form of vertical integration (they market the products they produce, or they develop the products they manufacture), but the extent of integration varies greatly from company to company and indeed from product to product

❉ **make-or-buy decisions**
Short-term decisions to outsource labour or to purchase components used in manufacturing from another company rather than to provide services or produce components internally.

❉ **vertical integration**
Accomplished when a company is involved in multiple steps of the value chain.

within a company. All elements of the value chain – from initial research and development through design, manufacture, marketing, distribution and customer service – must be considered for decisions about making or buying components needed for production of the final product.

There are advantages to making components internally instead of buying them from an outside supplier. Vertically integrated companies are not dependent on suppliers for timely delivery of services or components needed in the production process or for the quality of those services and components. However, vertically integrated companies have disadvantages as well.

There are disadvantages to making parts internally. The supplier may be able to provide a higher-quality part for less cost. For this reason, computer manufacturers do not produce their own computer chips. The producers of those chips produce in such large quantities that they can provide the chips more cheaply than the companies could produce them internally. Chip manufacturers also spend billions of dollars on research and development to ensure high-quality and high-performance chips.

The make-or-buy decision

Birdie Maker Golf Company produces custom sets of golf clubs that are advertised to be far superior to other golf clubs on the market. These golf clubs sell for $1000 per set, and Birdie currently sells about 1000 sets each year. Birdie Maker currently manufactures all the golf clubs in the set but is considering acquiring the putter from Ace Putters, Inc., a manufacturer of custom putters. The purchased putter would be customised for Birdie and matched to the other clubs, so customers should not be able to distinguish it from the rest of the clubs in the set. The costs incurred in the manufacture of the putter are as follows:

	Total (1000 putters)	Per unit
Direct materials	$ 5 000	$ 5.00
Direct labour	9 000	9.00
Variable manufacturing overhead	3 000	3.00
Fixed manufacturing overhead	9 500	9.50
Total cost	$26 500	$26.50

The expected production for the year is 1000 putters, so the full cost of each putter is $26.50 ($26 500 ÷ 1000). Ace Putters is offering to sell the putters to Birdie Maker for $25 per putter. Although this decision seems to be a very easy one ($25 is less than $26.50), the decision is more complex than it appears.

Although Birdie Maker would like to maximise profit by producing or buying the putter at the lowest possible cost, the company is also very concerned about the quality of the putter and the potential impact of the putter on sales of other clubs.

As we discussed in Chapter 1, relevant costs are those that can be avoided by choosing one alternative over another. The

Relevant costing can play a key role in shaping perceptions of the cost of high value products, such as golf clubs.

key, then, is to analyse the costs of manufacturing the putter with an eye toward identifying those costs that can be *avoided* or eliminated if the putter is purchased from Ace Putters. If Birdie Maker continues to manufacture the putter internally, it will incur costs of $26 500. If Birdie Maker decides to purchase the putters from Ace Putters, it will incur costs of $25 000 ($25 × 1000 putters) *plus* any manufacturing costs that are not avoidable. Although the costs related to direct material, direct labour and variable manufacturing overhead are variable (and thus avoidable), fixed manufacturing overhead is not.

So, although it appears on the surface that Birdie Maker can save $1500 ($26 500 – $25 000) by buying the putters from Ace Putters, as you can see in Exhibit 10.2, it will in reality cost Birdie an additional $8 per club, or $8000. Note that the fixed overhead of $9.50 per unit is incurred regardless of the decision to make or buy. We could have come to the same conclusion by comparing the $17 variable costs of making putters

	Cost to make (per unit)	Cost to buy (per unit)
Direct materials	$ 5.00	
Direct labour	9.00	
Variable manufacturing overhead	3.00	
Fixed manufacturing overhead	9.50	$ 9.50
Purchase price from Ace Putters		25.00
	$26.50	$34.50

 The make-or-buy decision

($5.00 of direct materials + $9.00 of direct labour + $3.00 of variable overhead) to the outside purchase price of $25. What is the best solution? From a purely quantitative perspective, Birdie Maker would maximise its profit by choosing to continue making putters. However, before making this decision, the company must be convinced that it can manufacture a putter of acceptable quality and that it will be able to keep up with any technological changes affecting the manufacture of the putter in the future.

Sometimes, fixed costs are relevant to the analysis. For example, assume that $5500 of the fixed manufacturing cost is for specialised machinery that is currently being leased under a month-to-month contract. If the putters are purchased from Ace Putters, the equipment will be returned to the lessor. That means that $5.50 of the fixed manufacturing costs ($5500 ÷ 1000 putters) is avoidable if the putter is bought from Ace Putters and that only $4.00 of fixed overhead will be incurred if the putter is purchased. The resulting analysis is shown in Exhibit 10.3.

Although it still remains preferable to make the putters internally, the cost difference shrinks to $2.50 per putter instead of $8.00. In this situation, Birdie Maker must carefully consider the qualitative factors relevant to the decision, including the quality of the putters, the importance of keeping up with changing technology and the dependability of the supplier.

Another way to look at this analysis is to compare the total avoidable costs to the purchase price. In this case, if the putter is purchased, the avoidable costs include direct materials ($5.00), direct labour ($9.00), variable manufacturing overhead ($3.00) and $5.50 per putter for fixed manufacturing overhead. The $22.50 of total avoidable costs should then be compared to the $25.00 purchase price. Regardless of how you choose to look at the problem, Birdie Maker is better off by $2.50 per putter if it continues making the putter.

Opportunity costs should also be considered in make-or-buy decisions. Using the same facts as in Exhibit 10.2, consider the impact of renting out for $10 000 the factory space that is now used to manufacture putters.

	Cost to make (per unit)	Cost to buy (per unit)
Direct materials	$ 5.00	
Direct labour	9.00	
Variable manufacturing overhead	3.00	
Fixed manufacturing overhead	9.50	$ 4.00
Purchase price from Ace Putters		25.00
	$26.50	$29.00

	Cost to make (per unit)	Cost to buy (per unit)
Direct materials	$ 5.00	
Direct labour	9.00	
Variable manufacturing overhead	3.00	
Fixed manufacturing overhead	9.50	$ 9.50
Purchase price from Ace Putters		25.00
Rental of unused factory space		(10.00)
	$26.50	$ 24.50

By effectively reducing the cost to purchase the putters by $10 000, or $10 per putter, Exhibit 10.4 shows that the effective cost to purchase the putter is reduced to $24.50, so Birdie Maker would be better off by $2.00 per putter by purchasing the putters.

Once again, as an alternative, we could treat the $10 opportunity cost as a relevant cost of making the putter internally. In that case, the total relevant costs of making the putter increase to $36.50, compared to the purchase price of $34.50. In addition to quality and reliability considerations, other factors to consider in this case include the long-term potential for renting out the unused space, potential other uses of the space, and so on.

LEARNING OBJECTIVE **3** >>

The decision to drop a product or a service

The decision to drop a product or a service is among the most difficult that a manager can make. Like other decisions discussed in this chapter, deciding whether to drop an old product or product line hinges on an analysis of the relevant costs and qualitative factors affecting the decision. Qualitative factors are sometimes more important than focusing solely on profit.

Clayton Herring Tyre Company is considering dropping one of the 10 models of tyres that it manufactures and sells. Sales of a special mud and snow tyre have been disappointing and based on the latest financial information (shown in the following table), the tyres appear to be losing money.

	Mud and snow	All other tyres	Total
Sales	$25 500	$150 000	$175 500
Less: Direct materials	12 000	50 600	62 600
Direct labour	5 000	30 000	35 000
Variable overhead	2 000	12 000	14 000
Contribution margin	$ 6 500	$ 57 400	$ 63 900
Less: Fixed overhead	7 000	21 000	28 000
Net profit	$ (500)	$36 400	$ 35 900

Chris (the CEO of Clayton Herring Tyre) asked Karen (the controller) why the mud and snow tyres were losing money. Karen explained that the tyres required more machine time than other tyres. Consequently, they were allocated a greater portion of fixed overhead. Chris then asked Karen whether she would recommend that production of the mud and snow tyres be discontinued. Karen explained that although it appears that net profit for the company would increase to $36 400 if the mud and snow tyres were dropped from the product line, further analysis had revealed that a large portion of the fixed overhead allocated to the tyres resulted from the rental of machines used to make the tyres. On further inspection, Karen determined that these machines were used to make several models of tyres and could not be disposed of if the mud and snow tyres were dropped. Consequently, $5000 of the fixed costs allocated to mud and snow tyres would have to be reallocated to other product lines. These costs would remain even if the mud and snow tyres were discontinued. Based on this new information, Karen prepared another report for Chris, showing the effect of dropping the mud and snow tyres (see Exhibit 10.5).

Why would the net profit for the company decrease by $4500 (from $35 900 to $31 400) if the mud and snow tyres were dropped, even though they appear to be losing money? The answer is that contribution margin decreases by $6500, whereas fixed costs decrease by only $2000 if the tyres are dropped. Only $2000 of the fixed costs are avoidable and relevant to this decision. The other $5000 of fixed costs originally allocated to the mud and snow tyres would simply be reallocated to one or more of the other models of tyres. A simple way to analyse this problem is to compare the contribution margin lost if the product line is dropped to the fixed costs that are avoided. In this case, Clayton Herring Tyre Company loses $6500

of contribution margin while saving (avoiding) only $2000 of fixed overhead (see Exhibit 10.5).

If the machine used to produce the tyres were used only for making these tyres and could be disposed of, resulting in savings of $5000, how much would profit increase (decrease) if the mud and snow tyres were discontinued? (Assume that the other $2000 of fixed overhead could still be avoided.) Although contribution margin would still be reduced by $6500, the entire $7000 of fixed costs would be avoided, resulting in an overall increase in net profit of $500.

But what about qualitative factors in this decision? As we discussed earlier, qualitative factors are sometimes more important than quantitative factors in these decisions. For example, what impact will discontinuing the sale of mud and snow tyres have on sales of the remaining product lines? Tyre retailers are likely to prefer purchasing tyres from a company offering a full line of tyres. Retailers that cannot offer mud and snow tyres may have difficulty selling tyres to individuals in the winter.

Manufacturers have to take great care when eliminating non-profitable products as they may impact the profitability of other more profitable products in the company, which they may complement.

	With mud and snow tyres	Without mud and snow tyres	Difference
Tyre sales	$175 500	$150 000	
Less: Direct materials	62 600	50 600	
Direct labour	35 000	30 000	
Variable overhead	14 000	12 000	
Contribution margin	$ 63 900	$ 57 400	$(6500)
Less: Fixed overhead	28 000	26 000	2000
Net profit	$ 35 900	$ 31 400	$(4500)

EXHIBIT 10.5 The decision to drop a product

LEARNING OBJECTIVE **4** >>

apply this!

Case

Resource utilisation decisions

A company faces a **constraint** when the capacity to manufacture a product or to provide a service is limited in some manner. A **resource utilisation decision** requires an analysis of how best to use a resource that is available in limited supply. The limited resource may be a rare material or component used in manufacturing a product, but more likely is related to the time required to make a product or provide a service or to the space required to store a product. For example, building custom furniture requires skilled craftspeople, who may be in short supply. Deciding how best to utilise the limited labour time available is a resource utilisation decision. The manufacture of golf clubs requires special machinery. If a company has only one machine that can be used to manufacture shafts for putters and other clubs, machine time may be a limited resource.

What is likely to be a limited resource in a grocery store? Grocery stores and other retail stores have limited shelf space. The resource utilisation decision involves an analysis of how best to use this limited resource. Which products should be carried? How many? Although it may seem easy to conclude that stores should carry those products that are most profitable, decisions like this are complicated by the fact that the multitudes of products carried in large stores require different amounts of shelf space. Multipacks of paper towels take up several times the shelf space required for a box of macaroni and cheese. Although the multipack of paper towels may be more profitable per unit, this information has to be balanced with the requirement of more shelf space. A decision concerning how much of each product to have on hand must also consider the impact of qualitative factors, such as customer reaction if a product is not carried, the impact on sales of other products and so on.

Resource utilisation decisions are typically short-term decisions. In the short run, such resources as machine time, labour hours and shelf space are fixed and cannot be increased. However, in the long run, new machines can be purchased, additional skilled labourers can be hired and stores can be expanded.

✻ constraint

A restriction that occurs when the capacity to manufacture a product or to provide a service is limited in some manner.

✻ resource utilisation decision

A decision requiring an analysis of how best to use a resource that is available in limited supply.

When faced with short-run constraints, managers must focus on the contribution margin provided by each product per unit of limited resource rather than on the profitability of each product.[2]

Birdie Maker produces two types of golf balls: the pro model and the tour model. The balls are sold to retailers in cartons containing 360 balls (30 boxes containing 4 sleeves per box, with each sleeve holding 3 balls). Both models are made using the same machines. The constraint, or limited resource, is the number of hours that the machines can run. The pro model golf ball takes 30 minutes of machine time to produce 360 balls, whereas the tour ball takes 45 minutes to produce the same number. The difference in production time results mainly from the different materials used in construction. Although weekend golfers purchase both models, professionals on the PGA Tour use the tour model. The relevant data concerning the two models follow:

	Pro model	Tour model
Sales price (per carton)	$450	$540
Less: Direct materials	200	265
Direct labour	50	50
Variable overhead	50	75
Contribution margin	$150	$150

In this case, the contribution margin per carton is the same for both the pro model and the tour model. Other things being equal, each model is equally profitable. However, if we compute contribution margin per unit of the constrained or limited resource, we see that each carton of pro model balls has a contribution margin of $300 per hour of machine time, whereas each carton of tour model balls has a contribution margin of $200 per hour of machine time (see Exhibit 10.6).

	Pro model	Tour model
Sales price (per carton)	$ 450	$ 540
Less: Direct materials	200	265
Direct labour	50	50
Variable overhead	50	75
Contribution margin	$ 150	$ 150
Required machine time (in hours)	÷ 0.50	÷ 0.75
Contribution margin per machine hour	$ 300	$ 200

EXHIBIT 10.6 The resource utilisation decision

If demand is not a factor and qualitative considerations are not important, Birdie Maker will maximise profit by producing and selling only pro model golf balls. However, if demand for either product is limited, the company must decide on the optimal product mix. For example, if machine time is limited to 300 hours per month the demand for the pro model is 400 cartons per month, and the demand for the tour model is 150 cartons, how much of each product should Birdie Maker produce? Although Birdie Maker has the capacity to produce 600 cartons (300 hours ÷ 0.5 hour) of pro model balls, it can sell only 400 cartons. Producing 400 cartons requires 200 machine hours, leaving 100 additional machine hours per month for the production of tour balls. Birdie Maker can maximise profit by producing 400 cartons of pro balls and 133 cartons of tour balls each month.

Qualitative factors, including the impact of discontinuing the sale of the tour ball, must also be considered. Visibility of the tour ball on the professional tour may be a valuable source of advertising, contributing to sales of the pro model.

Other options include adding machines to increase the amount of available machine hours or reducing the machine time needed to produce a carton of balls. Maximising profits by focusing on the constraint itself in order to loosen the constraint is the focus of the theory of constraints.

LEARNING OBJECTIVE 5 >>

The theory of constraints

❊ theory of constraints

A management tool for dealing with constraints; identifies and focuses on bottlenecks in the production process.

❊ bottlenecks

Production-process steps that limit throughput or the number of finished products that go through the production process.

The **theory of constraints** is a management tool for dealing with constraints. The theory of constraints identifies **bottlenecks** in the production process. Bottlenecks limit throughput, which can be thought of as the amount of finished goods that result from the production process. In the previous example, machine time is a bottleneck that limits the amount of throughput. In the airline industry, certain tasks performed while the aircraft is on the ground may delay departure and increase the turnaround time for the plane.

The key to the theory of constraints is identifying and managing bottlenecks. Once a bottleneck is identified, management must focus its time and resources on relieving the bottleneck. Utilising resources to increase the efficiency of a non-bottleneck operation will rarely increase throughput. For example, increasing the efficiency of machines with excess capacity in a factory or reducing flight time for an airline will result in very limited increases in throughput (if any) until bottlenecks are relieved.

In Exhibit 10.7, Birdie Maker has discovered that delays in delivery of golf clubs to customers result from the extra time it takes to order and receive putters from Ace Putters. Options for relieving this bottleneck include requiring Ace Putters to reduce its delivery time. If Ace cannot speed up delivery, Birdie Maker might consider using another supplier or perhaps making the putters in-house instead of outsourcing. Reducing the time spent manufacturing irons or woods will not reduce overall delivery time until the bottleneck with the putters is relieved.

LEARNING OBJECTIVE 6 >>

Decisions to sell or process further

The decision whether to sell a product as is or to process it further to generate additional revenue is another common management decision. For example, furniture manufacturers may sell furniture unassembled and unfinished, assembled and unfinished, or assembled and finished (see Exhibit 10.8). The key in deciding whether to sell or process further is that all costs that are incurred up to the point where the decision is made are sunk costs and therefore not relevant.

The relevant costs are the incremental or additional processing costs. Managers should compare the additional sales revenue that can be earned from processing the product further to the additional processing costs. If the additional revenue is greater than the additional costs, the product should be processed further. If the additional costs exceed the revenues, the product should be sold as is.

For example, assume that unassembled and unfinished tables cost $100 to produce and can be sold for $150. The company is considering selling assembled and finished tables for $225 each. Additional assembly and finishing costs of $45 per table would be required.

As shown in the previous table, the additional (incremental) revenue from selling assembled and finished furniture is $75 per unit. As long as the additional (incremental) costs of assembly and finishing are less than $75, the company will maximise profits by further processing of the tables. Assuming that it has sufficient demand for the assembled and finished tables, the company

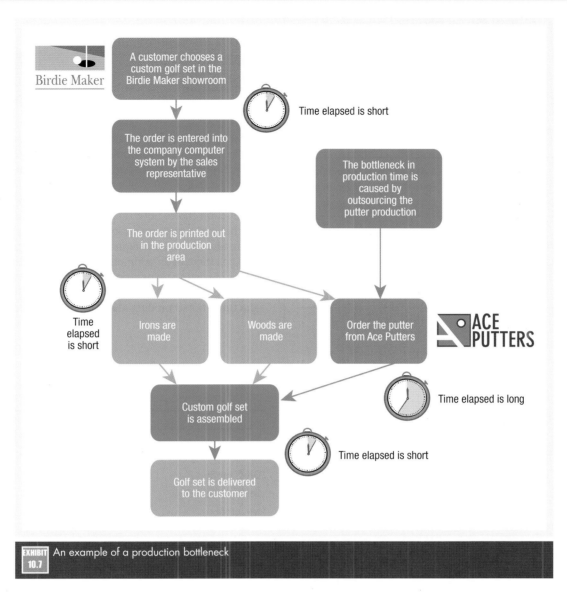

Birdie Maker

A customer chooses a custom golf set in the Birdie Maker showroom

Time elapsed is short

The order is entered into the company computer system by the sales representative

The bottleneck in production time is caused by outsourcing the putter production

The order is printed out in the production area

Time elapsed is short

Irons are made

Woods are made

Order the putter from Ace Putters

ACE PUTTERS

Time elapsed is long

Custom golf set is assembled

Time elapsed is short

Golf set is delivered to the customer

EXHIBIT 10.7 An example of a production bottleneck

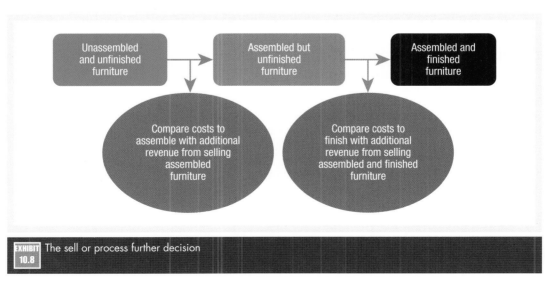

Unassembled and unfinished furniture

Assembled but unfinished furniture

Assembled and finished furniture

Compare costs to assemble with additional revenue from selling assembled furniture

Compare costs to finish with additional revenue from selling assembled and finished furniture

EXHIBIT 10.8 The sell or process further decision

will make an additional $30 per table ($75 incremental revenue less $45 incremental costs) by selling assembled, finished tables. Note that the $100 cost of producing the unassembled and unfinished table is not relevant in the analysis because it is a sunk cost. It is incurred regardless of the decision whether to sell unassembled and unfinished tables or to process further.

	Unassembled and unfinished tables	Assembled and finished tables	Incremental revenue and cost
Sales price	$150	$225	$75
Cost to produce	100	145	45
Increase in profit from further processing			$30

Exercises

1 Special order pricing decision LO1

Bob Johnson, Inc., sells a lounge chair for $25 per unit. It incurs the following costs for the product: direct materials, $11; direct labour, $7; variable overhead, $2; and fixed overhead, $1. The company has received a special order for 50 chairs. The order would require rental of a special tool that rents for $300. Bob Johnson, Inc., has sufficient idle capacity to produce the chairs for this order.

Required
Calculate the minimum price per chair that the company could charge for this special order if management requires a $500 minimum profit on any special order.

2 Special order pricing decision LO1

Jane Doe, Inc., sells a teddy bear for $15 per unit. It incurs the following costs for the product: direct materials, $5; direct labour, $3; variable overhead, $2; and fixed overhead, $3. The company has received a special order for 100 teddy bears. The order would require rental of a special tool that rents for $300.

Required
If the special order customer insists on paying no more than $14 for this order, should Jane Doe accept it?

3 Special order decision: Relevant costs LO1

Footy Sports manufactures footballs. The forecasted profit and loss statement for the year before any special orders is as follows:

	Total	Per unit
Sales	$4 000 000	$10.00
Manufacturing cost of goods sold	3 200 000	8.00
Gross profit	$ 800 000	$ 2.00
Selling expenses	300 000	0.75
Net profit	$ 500 000	$ 1.25

Fixed costs included in the preceding forecasted profit and loss statement are $1 200 000 in manufacturing cost of goods sold and $100 000 in selling expenses. Footy Sports received a special order for 50 000 footballs at $7.50 each. Assume that Footy Sports has sufficient capacity to manufacture 50 000 more footballs.

Required
Calculate the relevant unit cost that Footy Sports should consider in evaluating this special order.

4 Make or buy: Effect on profit LO2

Engstrom, Inc., uses 10 000 kilograms of a specific component in the production of life preservers each year. Presently, the component is purchased from an outside supplier for $11 per kilogram. For some time now, the factory has had idle capacity that could be utilised to make the component. Engstrom's costs associated with manufacturing the component are as follows:

Direct materials per kg.	$3
Direct labour per kg.	3
Variable overhead per kg.	2
Fixed overhead per unit (based on annual production of 10 000 kg)	2

In addition, if the component is manufactured by Engstrom, the company will hire a new factory supervisor at an annual cost of $32 000.

Required

If Engstrom chooses to make the component instead of buying it from the outside supplier, what would be the change, if any, in the company's profit?

5 Make or buy decision LO2

Switzer Corporation makes motorcycle engines. The company's records show the following unit costs to manufacture part #61645:

Direct materials	$12
Direct labour	15
Variable overhead	20
Fixed overhead	10

Another manufacturer has offered to supply Switzer Corporation with part #61645 for a cost of $50 per unit. Switzer uses 1000 units annually.

Required

If Switzer accepts the offer, what will be the short-run impact on profit? Consider and describe both qualitative and quantitative reasons for your decision.

6 Impact of dropping a product line LO3

Langer Company has three products (A, B and C) that use common facilities. The relevant data concerning these three products follow.

	A	B	C	Total
Sales	$10 000	$30 000	$ 40 000	$ 80 000
Variable costs	5 000	20 000	25 000	50 000
Contribution margin	$ 5 000	$10 000	$ 15 000	$ 30 000
Fixed costs	5 000	15 000	30 000	50 000
Operating loss	$ 0	$ (5 000)	$(15 000)	$(20 000)

Required

If fixed costs allocated to product line C are not avoidable and if product line C is dropped, what will be the impact on profit?

7 Impact of dropping a product line LO3

Woodruff Ltd. sells three rocking chairs (Unfinished, Stained and Painted) that use common facilities. The relevant data concerning these three products follow.

	Unfinished	Stained	Painted	Total
Sales	$10 000	$30 000	$ 40 000	$ 80 000
Variable costs	5 000	20 000	25 000	50 000
Contribution margin	$ 5 000	$10 000	$ 15 000	$ 30 000
Fixed costs	5 000	15 000	30 000	50 000
Operating loss	$ 0	$ (5 000)	$(15 000)	$(20 000)

Required

If $15 000 of the fixed costs allocated to the Painted rocking chairs are avoidable and the company drops Painted rockers from its product line, what will be the impact on profit?

8 Limited resource decision LO4

Kerrie Velinsky Productions produces music videos in two lengths on separate compact discs. The company can sell its entire production of either product. The relevant data for these two products follow.

	Compact Disc 1	Compact Disc 2
Machine time per CD (hours)	2	5
Selling price per CD	$10	$20
Variable costs per CD	$ 2	$ 4

Total fixed overhead is $240 000. The company has only 100 000 machine hours available for production. Because of the constraint on the maximum number of machine hours, Kerrie must decide which CD to produce to maximise the company's profit.

Required

Which product should the company select to maximise operating profits?

9 Maximising contribution margin given a limited resource LO4

Soft Mattress Inc. produces both a queen- and a king-size soft mattress. Selected data related to each product follow:

	Queen	King
Sales price	$525.00	$635.00
Direct materials	$350.00	$365.00
Direct labour	$ 75.00	$ 85.00
Variable overhead	$ 25.00	$ 35.00
Stuffing hours per mattress	1	3

Only two employees are trained to stuff the secret soft ingredient into the mattresses. They have a maximum of 4000 total stuffing hours per year.

Required

a What is the contribution margin per limited resource for each type of bed?

b Assuming that demand is not a constraint, how many queen- and king-size mattresses should be produced by Soft Mattress Inc.?

10 Sell or process further decision LO6

Ryan Miller Toys manufactured 500 stuffed lobsters that were defective. The manufacturing costs of the lobsters were:

Direct materials	$30
Direct labour	24
Variable overhead	10
Fixed overhead	12

The lobsters normally sell for $100. The company can rework the lobsters, which will cost $20 for direct materials, $20 for direct labour and $2 for variable overhead. In addition, fixed overhead will be applied at the rate of 75 per cent of direct labour cost. Alternatively, the company could sell the lobsters 'as is' for a selling price of $70.

Required

What should management do to maximise profits?

11 Sell or process further decision LO6

Brent Sitten manufactured 300 chairs for last season sales, that were not purchased by customers. The manufacturing costs of the chairs were:

Direct materials	$300
Direct labour	230
Variable overhead	110
Fixed overhead	120

The chairs normally sell for $1000. The company can rework them, which will cost $50 for direct materials, $140 for direct labour and $60 for variable overhead. In addition, fixed overhead will be applied at the rate of 80 per cent of direct labour cost. By doing so, the chairs will be sold for $800. Alternatively, the company could sell the chairs 'as is' for a selling price of $560.

Required

What should management do to maximise profits?

12 Sell or process further decision LO6

DePaulis Furniture Manufacturers makes unfinished furniture for sale to customers from its own stores. Recently, the company has been considering taking production one additional step and finishing some of the furniture to sell as finished furniture. To analyse the problem, DePaulis is going to look at only one product, a very popular dining room chair. The chair can be produced now for $65 and sells for $85 unfinished. If DePaulis were to finish the chair, the cost would increase to $90, but the company could sell the finished chairs for $125.

Required

Should DePaulis finish the chairs or continue to sell them unfinished? Show computations to support your decision.

Problems

13 Special order decision: Qualitative factors LO1

Lindsey Smith, Inc. has a maximum production capacity of 25 000 units, and exhibits the following cost structure for the upcoming year:

Sales (20 000 units @ $25)	$500 000
Manufacturing costs:	
Variable	$10 per unit
Fixed	$180 000
Marketing and administrative costs:	
Variable	$5 per unit
Fixed	$20 000

Required

a What is the expected level of profit based on the above information?

b Should the company accept a special order for 1000 units at a selling price of $20 if variable marketing expenses associated with the special order are $2 per unit? What will be the incremental profit if the order is accepted?

c Suppose that the company received a special order for 3000 units at a selling price of $19, with no variable marketing expenses. What would be the impact on profit?

d Assume that if the special order were accepted, all the regular customers would be aware of the price paid for the special order. Would that influence your decision? Why?

14 Make or buy decision: Relevant costs and qualitative factors LO2

Jain Simmons Company needs 10 000 units of a certain part to be used in production. If Jain Simmons buys the part from Sullivan Company instead of making it themselves, Jain Simmons could not use the present facilities for another manufacturing activity. Sixty per cent of the fixed overhead applied will continue regardless of what decision is made. The following quantitative information is available regarding the situation presented:

Cost to make the part:	
Direct materials	$ 6
Direct labour	24
Variable overhead	12
Fixed overhead applied	15
	$57
Cost to buy the part:	$53

Required

a In deciding whether to make or buy the part, what are Jain Simmons's total relevant costs to make the part?

b Which alternative (make or buy) is more desirable for Jain Simmons and by what amount?

c Suppose that Jain Simmons Company is in an area of the country with high unemployment and that it is unlikely that displaced employees will find other employment. How might that impact your decision?

15 Temporary suspension of operations: Qualitative factors LO3

Smoluk Mining Company currently is operating at less than 50 per cent of capacity. The management of the company expects sales to drop below the present level of 10 000 tonnes of ore per month very soon. The sales price per tonne is $3 and the variable cost per tonne is $2. Fixed costs per month total $10 000.

Management is concerned that a further drop in sales volume will generate a loss and, accordingly, is considering the temporary suspension of operations until demand in the metals markets rebounds and prices once again rise. Over the past year, management has implemented a cost-reduction program that has been successful in reducing costs to the point that suspending operations appears to be the only viable alternative. Management estimates that suspending operations would reduce fixed costs by $6000 per month.

Required

a Why does management estimate that the fixed costs will persist at $4000 even though the mine is temporarily closed?

b At what sales volume will the loss be greater or less than the shutdown cost of $4000 per month?

c List any qualitative factors that you think management should consider in this decision and discuss the potential impact of each factor on the decision.

16 Limited resource decision LO4, 5

Trailblazers produces two types of hiking boots: the men's boot and the women's boot. The two types of boots are similar except that the women's boots are more stylish. Both types are made using the same machines. It takes 15 minutes of machine time to produce one pair of men's boots, whereas it takes 30 minutes of machine time to produce one pair of women's boots. The difference in production time results mainly from the different materials used in construction. The relevant data concerning the two types are as follows:

	Men's	Women's
Sales price (per pair)	$35	$40
Less: Direct materials	10	13
Direct labour	4	4
Variable overhead	8	10
Contribution margin	$13	$13
Required machine time	¼ hour	½ hour

Required

a If the amount of machine time available to Trailblazers is limited, which boot should be produced first?

b If the total machine time available is 640 hours per month and the demand for each type of boot is 1000 pairs per month, how many of each type should be produced to maximise profit? (Round your answer to the nearest pair.)

c What other factors should be considered in this decision, and how would they impact the decision?

17 Sell or process further decision LO6

DeBaca's Fish House buys fish from local fishermen and sells the fish to the public from its booth at the public market. Lately, the fish house has had a number of requests for smoked salmon and has decided to investigate whether that would be a profitable item. The salmon DeBaca's buys now costs the company $6 per kg. DeBaca's would have to take the new

salmon to a smokehouse to have it smoked, which would increase the total cost to $9.75 for each kg of salmon. The salmon currently sells for $16.50 per kg but would sell for $19.50 per kg if it were smoked.

Required

a Based on the facts given, would it be profitable to smoke the salmon? Why or why not?

b If the cost of the smoking process could be reduced by $1.50 per kg, would it be profitable to smoke the salmon?

c What qualitative factors should be considered before making a final decision?

Cases

18 Comprehensive make-or-buy decision
LO1, LO2, LO4

Foggy Mountain Company manufactures several styles of banjos. Management estimates that during the second quarter of the current year, the company will be operating at 80 per cent of normal capacity. Because Foggy Mountain wants to increase utilisation of the plant, the company has decided to consider special orders for its products.

Foggy Mountain has just received inquiries from a number of companies concerning the possibility of a special order and has narrowed the decision to two companies. The first inquiry is from CCR Company, which would like to market a banjo very similar to one of Foggy Mountain's. The CCR banjo would be marketed under CCR's own label. CCR has offered Foggy Mountain $57.50 per banjo for 20 000 banjos to be shipped by 1 June. The cost data for the Foggy Mountain banjo are as follows:

Regular selling price per banjo	$90.00
Costs per unit:	
Raw material	$25.00
Direct labour (5 hours @ $6)	30.00
Overhead (2.5 machine hours @ $4)	10.00
Total costs	$65.00

According to the specifications provided by CCR, the banjo that the company wants requires less expensive raw material. Consequently, the raw material would cost only $22 per banjo. Foggy Mountain has estimated that all remaining costs would not change.

The second special order was submitted by Seager and Buffet Company for 7500 banjos at $75 per banjo. These banjos would be marketed under the Seager and Buffet label and also would be shipped by 1 June. However, the Seager and Buffet model is different from any banjo in the Foggy Mountain product line. The estimated per-unit costs are as follows:

Raw material	$32.50
Direct labour (5 hours @ $6)	30.00
Overhead (5 machine hours @ $4)	20.00
Total costs	$82.50

In addition, Foggy Mountain would incur $15 000 in additional setup costs and would have to purchase a $22 500 special machine to manufacture these banjos; this machine would be discarded once the special order has been completed.

The Foggy Mountain manufacturing capabilities are limited in the total machine hours available. The plant capacity under normal operations is 900 000 machine hours per year, or 75 000 machine hours per month. The budgeted fixed overhead for the year is $2 160 000. All manufacturing overhead costs are applied to production on the basis of machine hours at $4 per hour.

Foggy Mountain will have the entire second quarter to work on the special orders. Management does not expect any repeat sales to be generated from either special order. Company practice precludes Foggy Mountain from subcontracting any portion of an order when special orders are not expected to generate repeat sales.

Required

a What is the excess capacity of machine hours available in the second quarter?

b What is the variable overhead rate per machine hour?

c On the basis of the preceding information and your analysis, would you accept CCR's offer?

d What is the unit contribution margin per banjo for the Seager and Buffet order?

e What is the actual gain (loss) incurred by accepting Seager and Buffet's offer?

19 Decision focus: Comprehensive make or buy LO1, LO2, LO4

Avery, Inc., is a wholesale distributor supplying a wide range of moderately priced sporting equipment to large chain stores. About 60 per cent of Avery's products are purchased from other companies, and the remainder of the products are manufactured by Avery. The company has a plastics department that is currently manufacturing moulded fishing tackle boxes. Avery is able to manufacture and sell 8000 tackle boxes annually, making full use of its direct labour capacity at available workstations. The following table presents the selling price and costs associated with Avery's tackle boxes:

Selling price		$86.00
Costs per box:		
Moulded plastic	$ 8.00	
Hinges, latches, handle	9.00	
Direct labour ($ 15/hour)	18.75	
Manufacturing overhead	12.50	
Selling and administrative cost	17.00*	65.25
Profit per box		$ 20.75

*Includes $ 6 per unit of fixed distribution costs.

Because Avery believes that it could sell 12 000 tackle boxes, the company has looked into the possibility of purchasing the tackle boxes from another manufacturer. Craig Products, a supplier of quality products, could provide up to 9000 tackle boxes per year at a per unit price of $68. Variable selling and administrative costs of $4 per unit will be incurred if the tackle boxes are purchased from Craig Products.

Bart Johnson, Avery's product manager, has suggested that the company could make better use of its plastics department by purchasing the tackle boxes and manufacturing skateboards. To support his position, Johnson has a market study that indicates an expanding market for skateboards and a need for additional suppliers. Johnson believes that Avery could expect to sell 17 500 skateboards annually at a price of $45.00 per skateboard. Johnson's estimate of the costs to manufacture the skateboards is as follows:

Selling price per skateboard		$ 45.00
Costs per skateboard:		
Moulded plastic	$ 5.50	
Wheels, plastic	7.00	
Direct labour ($ 15/hour)	7.50	
Manufacturing overhead	5.00	
Selling and administrative cost	9.00*	34.00
Profit per skateboard		$ 11.00

*Includes $ 6 per unit of fixed distribution costs.

In the plastics department, Avery uses direct labour hours as the base for applying manufacturing overhead. Included in the manufacturing overhead for the current year is $50 000 factorywide, fixed manufacturing overhead that has been allocated to the plastics department.

Required

a Define the problem faced by Avery on the basis of the facts as presented.

b What options are available to Avery in solving the problem?

c Rank the options in order of preference on the basis of quantitative factors.

d What qualitative factors should Avery consider in the decision?

e Should Avery consider the potential liability that comes with selling skateboards? It has been shown that skateboards are responsible for 25 deaths per year and more than 500 serious accidents. Would that change your decision to make skateboards?

REVIEW

ACCT puts a multitude of study aids at your fingertips. After reading the chapters, check out these resources for further help:

- **Chapter Review cards,** found in the back of your book, include all learning outcomes, definitions and self-assessment activities for each chapter.

- **Online printable flash cards** give you additional ways to check your comprehension of key marketing concepts.

Other great ways to help you study include **games, podcasts, videos** and **online quizzes.**

You can find it all at: http://login.cengagebrain.com/

Learning objectives:

After studying the material in this chapter, you should be able to:

1   Evaluate capital investment decisions using the NPV method.

2   Evaluate capital investment decisions using the IRR method.

3   Distinguish between screening and preference decisions and use the profitability index to evaluate preference decisions.

4   Evaluate the impact of taxes on capital investment decisions.

5   Evaluate capital investment decisions using the payback method and discuss the limitations of the method.

LONG-TERM (CAPITAL INVESTMENT) DECISIONS

c 11

Capital investment decisions are made by all types and sizes of organisations and involve the purchase (or lease) of new machinery and equipment and the acquisition or expansion of facilities used in a business. A decision by a local florist to purchase or lease a new delivery van is a capital investment decision, as is the decision to upgrade the computer system at a law firm. A decision by Woolworths to build and open a new store and a decision by Ford Australia to invest in new automated production equipment are capital investment decisions. Of course, capital investments may also include intangible asset-related acquisitions, such as buying a brand-name (for example, SAB Miller acquiring Foster's in order to leverage their brand name and control a larger slice of the alcoholic beverages market), or the decision by a company to sponsor a sporting stadium (for example, Qantas Credit Union obtaining the naming rights for the Sydney Entertainment Centre – now the Qantas Credit Union Arena). Long-term decisions such as these often involve large sums of money and considerable risk because they commit companies to a chosen course of action for many years.

One of the key factors to be considered in a long-term purchasing decision is the return of the investment and also the return on the investment – in other words, whether the benefits of the investment exceed its cost. The costs and benefits include both qualitative and quantitative factors. Qualitative costs and benefits include employee, customer and community reaction to changes in location, the impact of automation on displaced employees, quality improvements that result from new equipment and so forth. Quantitative costs and benefits include large initial outlays of cash, the need for future repairs and maintenance, the potential for increased sales, and reductions in production and other costs.

Because capital investments involve large sums of money and last for many years, a quantitative analysis of the costs and benefits of capital investment decisions must consider the **time value of money.** The focus of the time value of money is on cash flow, not accounting net income. Accounting net income and cash flow are often not the same. Accounting net income is calculated based on the accrual of income and expenses rather than on the receipt and payment of cash. Whereas measurements of both income and cash flow are useful to managers, investors and creditors, time-value-of-money calculations are based on the concept that a dollar received today is worth more than a dollar received in the future and thus focus on the cash flow of an organisation.

Typical cash outflows include the original investment in the project, any additional working capital needed during the life of the investment, repairs and maintenance needed for machinery and equipment, and additional operating costs that may be incurred. Typical cash inflows include projected incremental revenues from the project, cost reductions in operating expenses, the salvage value (if any) of the investment at the end of its useful life and the release of working capital at the end of a project's useful life.

With the exception of the initial cash outflow associated with the investment, other cash inflows and outflows are likely to be estimates. The extended time period involved in long-term purchasing decisions makes the projection of these cash inflows and outflows difficult at best. The impact of uncertainty on capital investment decisions and the use of sensitivity analysis are discussed in more detail later in the chapter.

Companies routinely evaluate the benefits and costs of investing in new equipment using techniques that take into account the time value of money.

※ **capital investment decisions**
Long-term decisions involving the purchase (or lease) of new machinery and equipment and the acquisition or expansion of facilities used in a business.

※ **time value of money**
The concept that a dollar received today is worth more than a dollar received in the future.

Net present value

The **net present value (NPV)** method requires the choice of a discount rate to be used in the analysis. Many companies choose to use the **cost of capital**. The cost of capital represents what the firm would have to pay to borrow (issue bonds) or to raise funds through equity (issue stock) in the financial marketplace. In NPV analysis, the **discount rate** serves as a minimum required rate of return, or a hurdle rate – the return that the company feels must be earned in order for any potential investment to be profitable. For purposes of this chapter, we will refer to this discount rate as the minimum required rate of return rather than the hurdle rate although, in practice, it is commonplace to use both terms. The discount rate is often adjusted to reflect the risk and the uncertainty of cash flows expected to occur many years in the future.

Computing net present value requires comparing the present value of all cash inflows associated with a project with the present value of all cash outflows. If the present value of the inflows is greater than or equal to the present value of the outflows (the NPV is greater than or equal to zero), the investment provides a return at least equal to the discount rate (the minimum required rate of return), and the investment is acceptable. If the present value of the outflows is greater than the present value of the inflows, the NPV will be negative and the investment will not be acceptable because it provides a return less than the discount rate.

To illustrate NPV decisions, let's discuss Bud and Rose's Flower Shop, which is considering the purchase of a new refrigerated delivery van that will cost $50 000. This will allow the company to accept large flower orders for weddings, receptions and so on and is expected to increase cash income from sales (net of increased expenses) by $14 000 per year for six years. The van is not expected to have any salvage value at the end of

✳ net present value (NPV)

A technique for considering the time value of money whereby the present value of all cash inflows associated with a project is compared with the present value of all cash outflows.

✳ cost of capital

What the firm would have to pay to borrow (issue bonds) or raise funds through equity (issue stock) in the financial marketplace.

✳ discount rate

Used as a hurdle rate, or minimum rate of return, in calculations of the time value of money; adjusted to reflect risk and uncertainty.

the six years. Bud and Rose have a minimum required rate of return of 12 per cent and use that as their discount rate.

The only cash outflow in this case is the initial purchase price of $50 000. The annual cash inflow of $14 000 can most easily be viewed as an ordinary annuity for purposes of calculating present value. NPV calculations using present value factors are as follows:[1]

Transaction	Cash flow	Year	Amount	12% factor	Present value
Purchase of refrigerated van	Initial investment	Now	$(50 000)	1.0000	$(50 000.00)
Sales of flowers	Annual cash income (net of increased expenses)	1–6	14 000	4.1114	57 559.60
	Net present value				$ 7 559.60

The built-in function in Microsoft Excel, =PV(12%,6,–14000), returns a present value for the cash inflows equal to $57 559.70 (see Exhibit 11.1). The $0.10 difference results from rounding.

Because the NPV is positive, the delivery van should be purchased. Although the positive NPV tells us that the return on the investment is at least 12 per cent, it does not tell us exactly what the return is. Is it 14 per cent, 16 per cent or an even higher number? We could find the actual return by trial and error. Remember, an NPV of zero means that an investment is earning exactly the discount rate used in the analysis. Increasing the discount rate to 14 per cent reduces the NPV to $4442. Going up to 16 per cent reduces the NPV to $1586, but going up to 18 per cent results in a negative NPV of $1034. The true yield of the investment must be somewhere between 16 per cent and 18 per cent and would be close to 17 per cent. The present value of an annuity table can also be used to find the true rate of return for the delivery van.

As discussed in the appendix at the end of the text, the present value of an annuity (PVA) can be found using the following formula:

Key formula 11.1: Present value of annuity

$$PVA = R(DFA_{n,r})$$

In this case, we know the PVA, the annual cash inflow (R) and the number of periods (n) and can solve indirectly for the interest rate (r).

$$PVA_{6,??} = \$14\,000(DFA_{6,??})$$
$$\$50\,000 = \$14\,000(DFA_{6,??})$$
$$DFA_{6,??} = 3.5714$$

Using the present value of annuity table in the (online) Time Value of Money appendix and looking at the row for an *n* of 6, we see that a *DFA* of 3.5714 is about halfway between an *r* of 16 per cent and an *r* of 18 per cent.

LEARNING OBJECTIVE **2** >>

Internal rate of return

The **internal rate of return (IRR)** is the actual yield, or return, earned by an investment. We can find the yield of an investment in a number of ways. One way of looking at the IRR is as the discount rate that equates the present value of all cash inflows to the present value of all cash outflows. In other words, IRR is the discount rate that makes the NPV = 0.

Although a present value table *can* be used to calculate IRR, it is inconvenient in this case because the true yield lies between the rates provided in the table. However, IRR can easily be calculated using a financial calculator or Microsoft Excel (see appendix at the end of the text). In Excel, =RATE(6,–14000,50000,0,0) generates an annual yield of 17.191 per cent (see Exhibit 11.2).

✳ **internal rate of return (IRR)**
The actual yield, or return, earned by an investment.

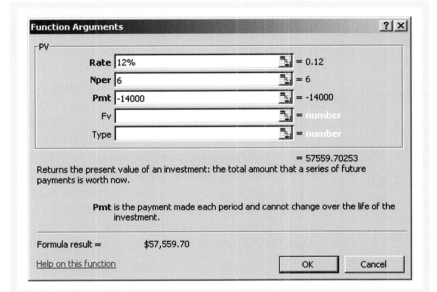

EXHIBIT 11.1 Finding the present value using the PV function in Excel

EXHIBIT 11.2 Finding the internal rate of return using the rate function in Excel

The problem of uneven cash flows

Calculations of net present value and internal rate of return get significantly more difficult when cash inflows and outflows are more numerous and when the cash flows are uneven. Consider a hypothetical example in which the Royal Prince Alfred (RPA) Hospital in Sydney is considering the purchase of a new X-ray machine for cardiac care patients. Let's hypothetically assume that RPA wishes to earn a minimum rate of return of 10 per cent on its investments. In addition, one of the hospital's objectives is to improve the quality of care provided to cardiac patients in the area. Currently, patients have to travel as far as 200 kilometres to a hospital equipped with this type of X-ray machine. The machine will cost $1 200 000 plus installation costs of another $50 000 and will have a useful life of approximately six years. Owing to frequent changes in technology, the machine would have little salvage value at the end of its useful life; RPA expects that it can sell the machine to a hospital in a developing country for $20 000. The machine is expected to increase revenues by $400 000 per year but will require the hiring of two new technicians at $40 000 per year for each technician, and it will require maintenance and repairs averaging $20 000 per year, which results in a net annual cash flow of $300 000 ($400 000 – $80 000 – $20 000). In addition, it is expected to require the installation of a new X-ray tube at the end of years 3 and 5 at a cost of $50 000 each. The detailed NPV analysis follows.

Transaction	Cash flow	Year	Amount	10% factor	Present value
Purchase of new machine	Initial investment	Now	$(1 250 000)	1.0000	$(1 250 000)
Increased patient revenue less related expenses	Net annual cash inflows	1–6	300 000	4.3553	1 306 590
Repairs and maintenance	Cash outflow	3	(50 000)	0.7513	(37 565)
Repairs and maintenance	Cash outflow	5	(50 000)	0.6209	(31 045)
Sale of machine	Cash inflow	6	20 000	0.5645	11 290
	Net present value				$ (730)

In this case, the NPV is negative, indicating that this investment would earn RPA less than its minimum required rate of return of 10 per cent. Using Microsoft Excel's IRR function, the internal rate of return of the X-ray machine is calculated as 9.9796 per cent (see Exhibit 11.3).

Although the quantitative analysis indicates that the investment is not acceptable, RPA should also consider qualitative factors in its decision. In this case, because improving the quality of patient care is very important to RPA, it may very well approve the investment even though its IRR is slightly below the normal acceptable level. RPA must also consider the impact of uncertainty on the decision. In this case, the only cash flow known with certainty is likely to be the initial purchase price. Changes in assumptions about future revenue and costs are likely to affect the decision.

The time value of money is considered in capital investment decisions by using one of two techniques: the net present value (NPV) method or the internal rate of return (IRR) method.[2]

Key assumptions of discounted cash flow analysis

In both the net present value and internal rate of return, two simplifying assumptions are made when discounting cash flows to their present value. The first is that all cash flows are assumed to occur at the end of each period (typically at the end of a year). Although most cost reductions and cash inflows resulting from increased sales actually occur uniformly throughout the year, this assumption greatly simplifies present value calculations. The second assumption is that all cash inflows are immediately reinvested in another project or investment. This assumption is analogous to the immediate reinvesting of dividends in a stock investment. The rate of return assumed to be earned on the reinvested amounts

depends on whether the NPV or the IRR method is used. Under the NPV method, cash inflows are assumed to be reinvested at the discount rate used in the analysis. Under the IRR method, cash inflows are assumed to be reinvested at the internal rate of return of the original investment.

The importance of qualitative factors

Investments in automated and computerised design and manufacturing equipment and robotics tend to be very large, although many of the benefits may be indirect and intangible or at the very least difficult to quantify (for example, increased quality resulting in fewer warranty expenses). These types of investments may be difficult to evaluate using purely quantitative data. For this reason, it is critically important to consider the impact of qualitative factors in these decisions.

Automating a process in a manufacturing environment is much more extensive and expensive than just purchasing a piece of equipment. The total cost of automating a process can be as much as 30 or 40 times that of installing a single machine, owing to additional software needs, additional training of personnel and the development of new processes. The benefits of automating production processes include the following:

1 Decreased labour costs
2 An increase in the quality of the finished product or a reduction in defects, resulting in fewer inspections, less waste in the production process, less rework of defective goods and less warranty work on defective goods
3 Increased speed of the production process
4 Increased reliability of the finished product
5 An overall reduction in the amount of inventory.

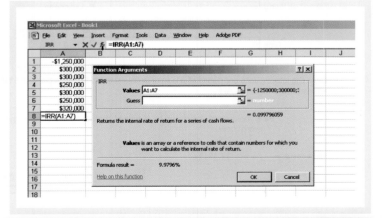

EXHIBIT 11.3 Finding the internal rate of return using the IRR function in Excel

These improvements will not only save costs but may also allow the company to increase market share. When the competition has automated production systems, companies must often follow suit or risk loss of business. Although some of the preceding benefits are difficult to measure, they must nevertheless be considered when making capital investment decisions in the new manufacturing environment.

LEARNING OBJECTIVE **3** >>

Screening and preference decisions

Capital investment decisions typically fall into one of two categories: screening decisions or preference decisions. **Screening decisions** involve deciding whether an investment meets a predetermined company standard, that is, whether it is acceptable, whereas **preference decisions** involve choosing among alternatives.

Typical problems addressed in capital investment decisions are as follows:

1   Should old equipment be replaced with new equipment that promises to be more cost efficient?
2   Should a new delivery vehicle be purchased or leased?
3   Should a manufacturing plant be expanded?
4   Should a new retail store be opened?

Once the problem is defined, the next step is to identify objectives. Objectives include both quantitative factors (increase production, increase sales, reduce costs) and qualitative factors (make a higher-quality product, provide better customer service). Analysing the options involves both a quantitative analysis of the options, using tools that recognise the time value of money, and a qualitative analysis. Once the potential investments are screened and analysed, the best option is chosen.

✻ screening decisions
Decisions about whether an investment meets a predetermined company standard.

✻ preference decisions
Decisions that involve choosing between alternatives.

✻ profitability index (PI)
Calculated by dividing the present value of cash inflows by the initial investment.

Both NPV and IRR can be used as screening tools. They allow a manager to identify and eliminate undesirable projects. Although the methods accomplish the same objective, it is important to remember that they are used in different ways. With net present value, the cost of capital is typically used as the discount rate to compute the net present value of each proposed investment. Any project that has a negative net present value should be rejected unless qualitative reasons exist for considering the project further.

With the internal rate of return, the cost of capital or other measure of a company's minimum required rate of return is compared to the computed internal rate of return. If the internal rate of return is equal to or greater than the minimum required rate of return, the investment is acceptable unless qualitative reasons exist for rejecting the project (see Exhibit 11.4).

The NPV method does have some advantages over the IRR method for making screening decisions. Adjusting the discount rate to take into account the increased risk and the uncertainty of cash flows expected to occur many years in the future is possible using NPV. When using the IRR method, users have to modify cash flows directly to adjust for risk.

However, NPV (without adjustment) cannot be used to compare investments (make preference decisions) unless the competing investments are of similar magnitude. Consider, for example, two competing investments, each with a five-year useful life. The first requires an investment of $10000 and generates cash savings with a present value of $12000 (cash inflows of $3165.56 per year for five years discounted at 10 per cent). Its NPV is therefore $2000. The second requires an initial investment of $20000 and generates cash inflows with a present value of $22000 (cash inflows of $5803.52 per year for five years). As you can see, both investments have the same NPV of $2000.

	Investment 1	Investment 2
Initial investment	$(10000)	$(20000)
Present value of cash inflows	12000	22000
Net present value	$ 2000	$ 2000

Which is preferred? Intuitively, the $10000 investment should be preferred to the $20000 investment. Think of it this way. You could invest in two $10000 projects and generate cash inflows of $6331.12 ($3165.56 × 2) per year instead of the $5803.52 generated from one $20000 investment.

Profitability index

The NPV analysis can be modified slightly through the calculation of a profitability index to better allow the comparison of investments of different size. The **profitability index (PI)** is calculated by dividing the present value of the cash inflows (netted with the present value of any cash outflows occurring after the project starts) by the initial investment (netted with any other cash flows occurring on the project start date). A PI greater than 1.0 means that the NPV is positive (the PV of the inflows is greater than the initial investment), and the project is acceptable. When comparing the PI of competing projects, the project with the highest PI

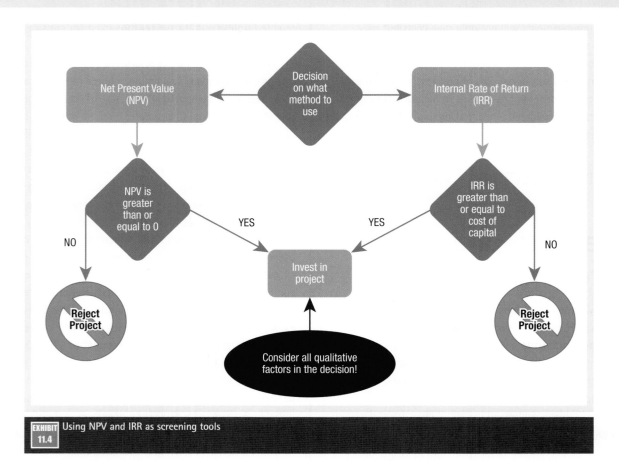

EXHIBIT 11.4 Using NPV and IRR as screening tools

is preferred. The PI of investments 1 and 2 is calculated as follows:

	Investment 1	Investment 2
Present value of cash inflows	$12 000	+$22 000
Initial investment	÷$10 000	÷$20 000
Profitability index	1.20	1.10

The $10 000 investment has a higher PI of 1.20 and is preferred over the $20 000 investment with a PI of 1.10. We can confirm this by calculating the IRR of both investments.

Using Microsoft Excel's RATE function, the IRR of investment 1 is 17.55 per cent (=RATE(5,3165.56,−10000,0,0) = 17.55%), whereas the IRR of investment 2 is only 13.84 per cent (=RATE(5,5803.52,−20000,0,0) = 13.84%).

In cases like this, in which the investment lives are equal and the cash flows follow similar patterns (annual cash flows for five years), IRR can be used to make preference decisions. However, when asset lives are unequal and cash flows follow different patterns, the use of IRR can result in incorrect decisions even when the initial investment is the same.

Consider the following example in which two $20 000 projects are being considered. Project A reduces cash operating costs (increases cash flow) by $12 500 per year for the next two years, whereas project B reduces operating costs by $5000 per

year for six years. Assuming a discount rate of 10 per cent, the NPV, PI and IRR of each investment are calculated as follows:

	Project A	Project B
Initial investment	$(20 000.00)	$(20 000.00)
PV of cash inflows	21 693.75	21 776.50
NPV	$ 1693.75	$ 1776.50
PI	1.085	1.089
IRR	16.26%	12.98%

Although IRR would indicate that project A is preferable to project B, NPV and PI indicate that project B is better. Which is right? Well, it depends. As we discussed earlier in the chapter, the IRR method assumes that cash inflows are immediately reinvested at the IRR earned on the original investment – in this case, over 16 per cent. In contrast, the NPV method assumes that cash inflows are reinvested at the cost of capital or other discount rate used in the analysis – 10 per cent in our analysis. If you can reinvest the large cash inflows received in project A at the end of years 1 and 2 at a high rate of return, project A would indeed be preferred. If not, project B, offering a return of almost 13 per cent for six years, would be preferred. The use of IRR generally favours short-term investments with high yields, whereas NPV favours longer-term investments even if the return is lower.

apply this!

Case

The impact of taxes on capital investment decisions

Organisations such as charitable institutions do not pay income taxes and do not need to consider the impact of income taxes on capital investment decisions (or other decisions, for that matter).[3] However, most profit-making companies must pay income taxes on any taxable income earned (just as individuals must) and must therefore consider the impact of income taxes on capital investment and other management decisions. With the company income tax rates in Australia currently being 30 per cent of taxable income, taxes are a major source of cash outflows for many companies and must be taken into consideration for any long-term investment decision.

As demonstrated in Chapter 2, the after-tax benefit or cost of a taxable cash inflow or a tax-deductible cash outflow is found by multiplying the before-tax cash inflow or before-tax cash outflow by (1 − tax rate). Hypothetically, if a company must pay a tax rate of 40 per cent, a taxable cash inflow of $100 000 results in a $60 000 after-tax cash inflow [$100 000 × (1 − 0.40)]. Likewise, a $20 000 tax-deductible cash outflow for repairs results in an after-tax outflow of only $12 000.

The disposal of assets may also have tax consequences. When an asset is sold or otherwise disposed of, the gain or loss is calculated on the excess of sales price over book value (usually original cost less accumulated depreciation), and vice versa for a loss on sale. The after-tax cash flow associated with the sale of an asset at a gain on sale is therefore found by multiplying the difference between selling price and salvage value by (1 − tax rate).[4] For simplicity, we will assume that a gain on disposal of an asset is taxed at the same rate as the operating income of a company. In practice, the tax calculation on the sale of depreciable assets can be quite complicated.

The depreciation tax shield

Not all tax-deductible expenses involve cash outflows. Depreciation is a tax-deductible expense that does not involve a direct payment of cash.

Although depreciation does not result in a direct cash outflow, it does result in an indirect cash *inflow* owing to the impact of depreciation on income taxes paid. Depreciation expense reduces a company's taxable income and thus its income tax, resulting in an increase in cash flow.

For example, in Exhibit 11.5, the revenue and expenses of Company A and Company B are identical except for $10 000 of depreciation expense incurred by Company B. This depreciation reduces Company B's taxable income by $10 000 and reduces its income tax by $4000. As a result, Company B's cash flow *increases* by $4000. (Remember that the depreciation expense itself does not result in a cash outflow.)

> ✳ **depreciation tax shield**
> The tax savings from depreciation.

The tax savings from depreciation (called the **depreciation tax shield**) can easily be found by multiplying the depreciation expense by the tax rate. In this case, Company B's $10 000 of depreciation expense multiplied by the 40 per cent tax rate results in $4000 of tax savings.

As an example, consider a company contemplating the purchase of a new piece of manufacturing equipment. The equipment will cost $50 000 and will generate cost savings of $13 000 per year for six years. The company has a cost of capital of 10 per cent.

Let's assume that the equipment will be depreciated using the straight-line method over six years for income tax purposes.[5] Depreciation expense is equal to $5000 for years 1 and 6 and $10 000 for years 2 to 5. Assuming an income tax rate of 40 per cent, the depreciation deduction results in tax savings of $2000 for years 1 and 6 ($5000 × 40%) and $4000 for years 2 to 5 ($10 000 × 40%), as shown in the table overleaf. A tax saving is therefore classed as a cash inflow, as it represents the avoidance of a payment.

	Company A		Company B	
	Income	Cash flow	Income	Cash flow
Cash revenue	$100 000	$100 000	$100 000	$100 000
Cash expense	60 000	60 000	60 000	60 000
Depreciation	0	0	10 000	0
Income (before tax)	$ 40 000		$ 30 000	
Income tax (40% rate)	16 000	16 000	12 000	12 000
Net income	$ 24 000		$ 18 000	
Cash flow		$ 24 000		$28 000

EXHIBIT 11.5 Tax savings from depreciation

The impact of depreciation on cash flow

Year	Depreciation expense calculation		Tax savings from depreciation	
	Non-cash depreciation expense		Depreciation expense × tax rate	Cash inflow
1	$50 000 ÷ 5 × 1/2	$5 000	$5000 × 0.40	$2000
2	$50 000 ÷ 5	10 000	10 000 × 0.40	4000
3	$50 000 ÷ 5	10 000	10 000 × 0.40	4000
4	$50 000 ÷ 5	10 000	10 000 × 0.40	4000
5	$50 000 ÷ 5	10 000	10 000 × 0.40	4000
6	$50 000 ÷ 5 × 1/2	5 000	5 000 × 0.40	2000

Now let's calculate the after-tax NPV. In the following table, the annual cash inflow of $13 000 has been adjusted to the equivalent after-tax amount ($13 000 × 0.6 = $7800). In addition, the discount rate has been changed to its equivalent after-tax rate (10% × 0.6 = 6%).

Cash flow	Year	After-tax amount	6% factor	Present value
Initial investment	Now	($50 000)	1.0000	($50 000.00)
Annual cash income	1–6	7 800	4.9173	38 354.94
Tax savings from depreciation	1	2 000	0.9434	1 866.80
	2	4 000	0.8900	3 560.00
	3	4 000	0.8396	3 358.40
	4	4 000	0.7921	3 168.40
	5	4 000	0.7473	2 989.20
	6	2 000	0.7050	1 410.00
Net present value				$4 707.74

The investment in technology has long-term financial ramifications for a company and presents an important but difficult evaluation exercise from a capital-budgeting perspective.

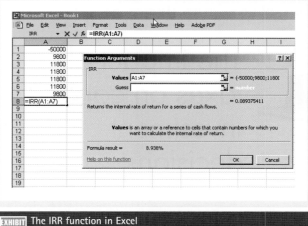

The IRR function in Excel

The NPV of the new equipment is positive, indicating that it will provide a return greater than the company's 6 per cent after-tax cost of capital. Using Excel's IRR function, the after-tax return of the investment is 8.938 per cent (see Exhibit 11.6).

LEARNING OBJECTIVE 5 >>

apply this!

Interactive quizzes

The payback method

Capital investment tools that recognise the time value of money and use discounted cash-flow techniques are preferred by most decision makers when dealing with capital-investment decisions. In practice, however, some managers still use non-discounting methods. Although these methods are declining in popularity, the payback method can still be useful in some cases as a fast, easy approximation of the more complicated, discounted cash-flow methods. We also find that small- and medium-sized businesses prefer the payback method as they conceptualise their own investments similarly (i.e. they wonder how quickly they will earn money to pay their loan off). This is effectively the payback period.

The **payback period** is the length of time needed for a long-term project to recapture, or *pay back*, the initial investment. In other words, how long does it take for a project to pay for itself? Obviously, the quicker the payback, the more desirable the investment. The formula used to compute the payback period is as follows:

❉ **payback period**
The length of time needed for a long-term project to recapture, or pay back, the initial investment.

Key formula 11.2: Payback period

$$\text{Payback period} = \frac{\text{Original investment}}{\text{Net annual cash inflows}}$$

For example, using our earlier example of Bud and Rose's purchase of a delivery van (see page 166), the delivery van's payback period would be 3.57 years.

$$\frac{\$50\,000 \text{ original investment}}{\$14\,000 \text{ net annual cash inflow}} = 3.57 \text{ years}$$

Because the payback method ignores the time value of money, it must be used with caution. Consider our earlier example in which we consider investing in either project A or project B, each requiring an initial investment of $20 000. Project A promises cash inflows of $12 500 per year for two years, whereas project B promises cash inflows of $5000 per year for six years.

	Project A	Project B
Initial investment	$(20 000.00)	$ (20 000.00)
Annual cash inflows	12 500.00	5000.00
PV of cash inflows	21 693.75	21 776.50
NPV	$ 1693.75	$ 1 776.50
PI	1.085	1.089
Payback	1.6 years ($20 000 ÷ $12 500)	4 years ($20 000 ÷ $5000)

Although a manager using the payback method would prefer project A, the method ignores the time value of money and ignores any cash flow received after the initial investment is paid for. While NPV and PI signal that project B should be chosen, project A has the shorter payback period.

The payback method can be useful as a quick approximation of the discounted cash flow methods when the cash flows follow similar patterns. It can also be useful in screening decisions if cash flow is a serious concern and management wants to eliminate projects that would have adverse cash flow consequences. For example, smaller businesses, such as Bud and Rose's Flower Shop, may be very concerned about cash flow in the short run even if the long-term profitability of a project is higher than with alternative projects. In these situations, the amount of time needed to recover cash outlays may be a very important criterion when evaluating capital investment decisions.

What method is used in practice? According to one recent survey of chief financial officers (CFOs), most CFOs use the NPV or IRR techniques to evaluate long-term investment options. On the other hand, only about half use the payback method. Additionally, older CFOs and CFOs of smaller companies tend to use the payback method more frequently than younger CFOs or those working for larger companies.[6]

East-West toll tripled!

Long term forecasting is never perfect – even the experts mis-estimate! Victoria's highly publicised East-West link, which seems set to be scrapped by the Daniel Andrews State government, appears to be significantly under-priced according to experts. Tolls would have had to be around $10.50 per motorist for the controversial project to be regarded as viable. This represents a tripling of forecasted toll rates. In long-term projects, even the best accountants make incorrect estimates. Owing to the future being inherently uncertain, or government regulation reducing the pricing power of private providers, these mega-projects stand to accrue less profits than usually attributed to them.

Source: 'Warning on high tunnel toll', by Adam Carey from *The Age*. Published by Fairfax Media Pty Ltd., © 2013.

Source: Trevor Pinder/Newspix

Estimating the future cash flows and therefore viability of large-scale infrastructure projects is a complex and challenging activity.

Exercises

1 NPV: No salvage value or taxes LO1

Kim Johnson purchased an asset for $80 000. Annual operating cash inflows are expected to be $30 000 each year for four years. At the end of the asset life, Kim will not be able to sell the asset because it will have no salvage value.

Required

What is the net present value if the cost of capital is 12 per cent (ignore income taxes)?

2 NPV and IRR assumptions LO1, 2

Discounted cash flow analysis techniques are used by managers to understand the impact of investment decisions in terms of 'today's dollars'. Two common techniques that use discounted cash flows are net present value (NPV) and internal rate of return (IRR). Like most analysis techniques, each of these methods requires us to make certain assumptions.

Required

Describe the assumptions underlying NPV and IRR.

3 IRR with uneven cash flows LO2

Powers, Inc., has a project that requires an initial investment of $43 000 and has the following expected stream of cash flows:

Year 1	$20 000
Year 2	30 000

Required

Use Excel to calculate the project's internal rate of return.

4 IRR: Even cash flows LO2

Williams and Park Accounting Practice is considering investing in a new computer system that costs $9000 and would reduce processing costs by $2000 a year for the next six years.

Required

Calculate the internal rate of return using the time value of money charts located at the end of the Review Cards.

5 IRR: Tax effects LO2, 4

The Pearce Club, Inc., is considering investing in an exercise machine that costs $5000 and would increase revenues by $1500 a year for five years. The machine would be depreciated using the straight-line method over its useful life and have no salvage value.

Required

Use Excel to calculate the equipment's internal rate of return. Assume that the tax rate is 30 per cent. Round your answer to two decimals.

6 Profitability index LO3

An investment manager is currently evaluating a project that requires an initial investment of $10 000 and will provide future cash flows that have a present value of $17 000.

Required

Calculate the project's profitability index and explain what the number means.

7 Profitability index LO3

Kuntz Company has a project that requires an initial investment of $35 000 and has the following expected stream of cash flows:

Year 1	$25 000
Year 2	20 000
Year 3	10 000

Required

Assuming the company's cost of capital is 12 per cent, what is the profitability index for the project?

8 Depreciation tax shield LO4

Harris Corp. recently purchased a manufacturing facility for $2.5 million. The company will depreciate the facility by recording $125 000 of depreciation expense each year for 20 years. Harris Corp. expects that its tax rate will be 35 per cent in the coming year.

Required

What is the tax savings (i.e. the depreciation tax shield) associated with the new facility in the coming year?

9 After-tax NPV LO4

Gemini LLC invested $1 million in a state-of-the-art information system that promises to reduce processing costs for its purchasing activities by $120 000 per year. The company will scrap its old information system and will receive no money as a consequence. The new system will be depreciated over 10 years at a rate of $100 000 per year. Gemini's tax rate is 30 per cent and it has a 7 per cent after-tax cost of capital.

Required

What is the after-tax net present value of Gemini's new information system?

10 Payback method with uneven cash flows LO5

A particular project requires an initial investment of $10 000 and is expected to generate future cash flows of $4000 for Year 1 and $3000 for years 2 through 5.

Required

Calculate the project's payback period in years.

11 Payback method LO5

The Happy Day Care Centre is considering an investment that will require an initial cash outlay of $300 000 to purchase non-depreciable assets that have a 10-year life. The organisation requires a minimum four-year payback.

Required

Assuming the investment generates equivalent annual cash flows, what minimum amount of annual cash flows must be generated by the project for the company to make the investment?

Problems

12 Preference decisions: NPV vs IRR vs profitability index LO1, 2, 3

Stephens Industries is contemplating four projects: Project P, Project Q, Project R and Project S. The capital costs and estimated after-tax net cash flows of each mutually exclusive project are shown in the table below. Stephens' after-tax cost of capital is 12 per cent, and the company has a capital budget of $450 000 for the year. Excess funds cannot be reinvested at greater than 12 per cent.

	Project P	Project Q	Project R	Project S
Initial cost	$200 000	$235 000	$190 000	$210 000
Annual cash flows:				
Year 1	93 000	90 000	45 000	40 000
Year 2	93 000	85 000	55 000	50 000
Year 3	93 000	75 000	65 000	60 000
Year 4	0	55 000	70 000	65 000
Year 5	0	50 000	75 000	75 000
Net present value	$23 370	$29 827	$27 233	$(7 854)
Internal rate of return	18.7%	17.6%	17.2%	10.6%
Profitability index	1.12	1.13	1.14	0.95

Required
a Which projects will the company choose? Why?
b If only one project can be accepted, which one should the company choose?

13 NPV vs payback method: Impact of varying cash flow assumptions LO1, 2, 5

Winona Miller, president of CLJ Products, is considering the purchase of a computer-aided manufacturing system that requires an initial investment of $4 000 000 and is estimated to have a useful life of 10 years. CLJ Products' cost of capital is currently 12 per cent. The annual after-tax cash benefits/savings associated with the system are as follows:

Decrease in defective products	$100 000
Revenue increase due to improved quality	150 000
Decrease in operating costs	300 000

Required
a Calculate the payback period for the system. Assume that the company has a policy of accepting only projects with a payback of five years or less. Should the system be purchased?

b Calculate the NPV and the IRR (use Excel to calculate the IRR) for the project. Should the system be purchased? What if the system purchase does not meet the payback criterion?

c The project manager reviewed the projected cash flows and pointed out that two items had been missed. First, the system would have a salvage value, net of any tax effects, of $500 000 at the end of 10 years. Second, the increased quality would allow the company to increase its market share by 30 per cent, leading to an additional annual after-tax benefit of $180 000. Given this new information, recalculate the payback period, NPV and IRR. Would your recommendation change? Why or why not?

14 After-tax NPV LO1, 4

Greer Law Associates is evaluating a capital investment proposal for new office equipment for the current year. The initial investment would require the firm to spend $50 000. The equipment would be depreciated on a straight-line basis over five years with no salvage value. The firm's accountant has estimated the before-tax annual cash inflow from the investment to be $15 000. The income tax rate is 40 per cent and all taxes are paid in the year that the related cash flows occur. The desired after-tax rate of return is 15 per cent. All cash flows occur at year-end.

Required
What is the net present value of the capital investment proposal? Should the proposal be accepted? Why or why not?

15 NPV vs payback method vs profitability index LO1, 3, 5

Alfred Stein is about to invest $1000. Alfred is a very cautious man and would like to have some expert advice on which of two projects is best for him. He has not told you of his exact cost of capital because he likes to keep such information private, but he has told you to consider 8 per cent, 10 per cent, and 12 per cent in your calculations. He has also told you that the salesperson from whom he expects to purchase his equipment has given him the following expected cost savings patterns:

Year	Project 1	Project 2
1	$600	$300
2	600	600
3	600	800
4	600	700

Required
a Calculate the present value of each project at each of Alfred's potential costs of capital and indicate which project is acceptable at each.
b Calculate the payback period for each project. Does your recommendation to Alfred change?
c Calculate the profitability index for each project, using a cost of capital of 10 per cent. Which project would you recommend Alfred pursue?

Required
Calculate the project's profitability index and explain what the number means.

Cases

16 Decision focus: Make-or-buy decision with NPV analysis LO1, LO4

Armstrong Company manufactures three models of paper shredders, including the waste container, which serves as the base. Whereas the shredder heads are different for all three models, the waste container is the same. The estimated numbers of waste containers that Armstrong will need during the next five years are as follows:

Year	Number of Containers
1	50 000
2	50 000
3	52 000
4	55 000
5	55 000

The equipment used to manufacture the waste container must be replaced because it is broken and cannot be repaired. The new equipment has a purchase price of $945 000 and is expected to have a salvage value of $12 000 at the end of its economic life in 5 years. The new equipment would be more efficient than the old equipment, resulting in a 25 per cent reduction in direct materials.

The old equipment is fully depreciated and is not included in the fixed overhead. The old equipment can be sold for a salvage amount of $1500. Armstrong has no alternative use for the manufacturing space at this time. Rather than replace the equipment, one of Armstrong's production managers has suggested that the waste containers be purchased. One supplier has quoted a price of $27 per container. This price is $8 less than the current manufacturing cost, which is composed of the following costs:

Direct materials	$ 10.00	
Direct labour	8.00	
Variable overhead	6.00	$24.00
Fixed overhead:		
Supervision	$ 2.00	
Facilities	5.00	
General	4.00	11.00
Total manufacturing cost per unit		$35.00

Armstrong employs a plant-wide fixed overhead rate in its operations. If the waste containers are purchased outside, the salary and benefits of one supervisor, included in the fixed overhead at $45 000, will be eliminated. There will be no other changes in the other cash and non-cash items included in fixed overhead.

Armstrong is subject to a 40 per cent income tax rate. Management assumes that all annual cash flows and tax payments occur at the end of the year and uses a 12 per cent after-tax discount rate.

Required

a Calculate the net present value of the estimated after-tax cash flows for each option you identify.

b What is your recommendation? Support your recommendation by explaining the logic behind it.

17 Comprehensive NPV LO1, 4

Rob Thorton is a member of the planning and analysis staff of Thurston, Inc., an established manufacturer of frozen foods. Rick Ungerman, chief financial officer of Thurston, Inc., has asked Thorton to prepare an analysis of net present value for a proposed capital equipment expenditure that should improve the profitability of the Southwestern plant.

The Southwestern plant's production manager submitted a proposal for the acquisition of an automated materials-movement system. The plan calls for the replacement of a number of forklift trucks and operators with a computer-controlled conveyor belt system that feeds directly into the refrigeration units. Ungerman has given this proposal to Thorton and instructed him to use the information in the subsequent table to prepare his analysis. The forklift trucks have been fully depreciated and have a zero net book value. If the conveyor belt system is purchased now, these trucks will be sold for $100 000. Thurston has a 40 per cent effective tax rate, has chosen the straight-line depreciation method, and uses a 12 per cent after-tax discount rate. For the purpose of analysis, all tax effects and cash flows from the acquisition and disposal of equipment are considered to occur at the time of the transactions, whereas those from operations are considered to occur at the end of each year.

Projected useful life	10 years
Purchase/installation of equipment	$ 4 500 000
Increased working capital needed*	1 000 000
Increased annual operating costs (exclusive of depreciation)	200 000
Equipment repairs to maintain production efficiency (end of year 5)	800 000
Increase in annual sales revenue	700 000
Reduction in annual manufacturing costs	500 000
Reduction in annual maintenance costs	300 000
Estimated salvage value of conveyor belt system	850 000

* The working capital will be released at the end of the 10-year useful life of the conveyor belt system.

Required

a Prepare an analysis of the net present value of the purchase and installation of the materials-movement system. Be sure to present supporting calculations.

b What is the best alternative from a quantitative analysis?

c What other qualitative factors should be considered and why?

Learning objectives:

After studying the material in this chapter, you should be able to:

1 Describe the budget development process, behavioural implications of budgeting, advantages of budgeting and the master budget.

2 Explain how managers develop a sales forecast and demonstrate the preparation of a sales budget.

3 Prepare a production budget and recognise how it relates to the material purchases, direct labour and manufacturing overhead budgets.

4 Prepare budgets for material purchases, direct labour, manufacturing overhead, and selling and administrative expenses.

5 Explain the importance of budgeting for cash and prepare a cash receipts budget, a cash disbursements budget and a summary cash budget.

6 Prepare budgeted income statements and balance sheets and evaluate the importance of budgeted financial statements for decision making.

7 Contrast budgeting in a manufacturing company with budgeting in a merchandising company and a service company.

8 Differentiate static budgets from flexible budgets.

9 Explain and understand the concept of rolling budgets in modern organisations.

FIXED AND ROLLING BUDGETS FOR PLANNING AND DECISION MAKING

c 12

Budgets are the financial quantification of plans dealing with the acquisition and use of resources over a specified time period. Everyone budgets, from a university student to large multinational corporations. Although budgets are often thought of in terms of dollars (monetary or financial budgets), they may be used for other purposes. For example, a university student carrying 15 credit hours, working 20 hours a week in a part-time job and volunteering 10 hours per week at the local hospital might need to prepare a time budget to plan his or her use of time throughout the week. The focus of this chapter, however, will largely be on monetary budgets.

Creating a monetary budget for a university student can be as simple as jotting down expected cash inflows from loans, parents and maybe a part-time job and expected outflows for school and living expenses. At the other end of the budgeting spectrum, multinational companies often have very sophisticated budgets used to plan for the acquisition and use of thousands of different materials and the manufacture and sale of hundreds of products.

Managers use budgeting as they go about their **planning**, **operating** and **control** activities (see Exhibit 12.1). Planning is the cornerstone of good management and requires the development of objectives and goals for the organisation as well as the actual preparation of budgets. Operating activities entail day-to-day decision making by managers, which is facilitated by budgets. Control activities include ensuring that the objectives and goals developed by the organisation are attained. Control often involves a comparison of budgets to actual performance and the use of budgets for performance-evaluation purposes. The use of budgets for cost control and performance evaluation is discussed in more depth in Chapter 13.

In this chapter, we emphasise the use of budgets in planning and operating activities, including decisions concerning how much of a product to produce, how much material to buy, how much labour to hire and how much cash to borrow and invest. The concept of budgeting for cash is tied back to the operating cycle. The operating cycle focuses on cash flow, beginning with the investment of cash in inventory or the use of cash to manufacture products, continuing with the sale of those products to customers and ending with the collection of cash from those customers (see Exhibit 12.2).

One of the main reasons why small businesses fail is the lack of adequate planning for cash needs. A small business that views budgeting for cash as too time-consuming or expensive risks failure. With the availability and affordability of information systems in today's business environment, even the smallest business can very easily perform the analysis necessary to successfully plan and budget for the future.

* budgets
Plans dealing with the acquisition and use of resources over a specified time period.

* planning
The cornerstone of good management; involves developing objectives and goals for the organisation, as well as the actual preparation of budgets.

* operating
Involves day-to-day decision making by managers, which is often facilitated by budgeting.

* control
Involves ensuring that the objectives and goals developed by the organisation are being attained; often involves a comparison of budgets to actual performance and the use of budgets for performance-evaluation purposes.

Budgeting is a critical element in building and sustaining a successful business.

Source: Pressmaster/Shutterstock

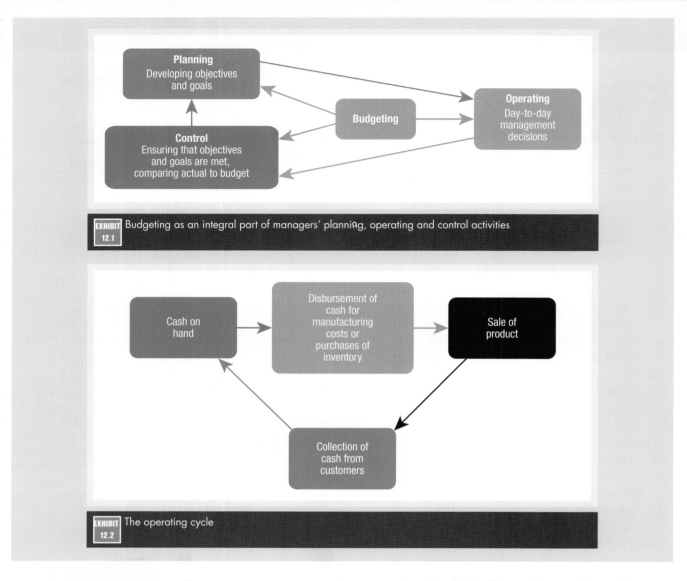

EXHIBIT 12.1 Budgeting as an integral part of managers' planning, operating and control activities

EXHIBIT 12.2 The operating cycle

LEARNING OBJECTIVE **1** >>

The budget development process

One of the misconceptions about budgeting is that the budgeting process is just a mechanical number-crunching task for bookkeepers. In reality, budgeting is a management task, not a bookkeeping task, and it requires a great deal of planning and thoughtful input from a broad range of managers in a company. Although budgeting is time-consuming (it often takes as long as 60 to 90 days to prepare an annual budget), the use of spreadsheets, such as Microsoft Excel, makes the process much simpler. A survey by *CFO Magazine* found that 78 per cent of companies with annual revenues less than $100 million utilise spreadsheets for budgeting and planning.[1] However, more and more companies are using enterprise resource planning (ERP) systems as a key budgeting tool. ERP systems link data from across all areas of a business, ensuring that the same assumptions are used throughout the different budgets and speeding up the budgeting process.

Some companies start their budget process based on last year's numbers, whereas others employ **zero-based budgeting**. Zero-based budgets require managers to build budgets from the ground up each year rather than just add a percentage increase to last year's numbers. Consequently, managers must justify all items in the budget, not just changes from last year's budget. Although zero-based budgeting is a good idea in theory, it can be very time-consuming when done on an annual basis. In some cases, companies may require zero-based budgets only every few years or rotate among departments the requirement that budgets be justified in full.

Although we typically think of budgets as being prepared annually, companies frequently use monthly budgets and

❋ zero-based budgeting

Requires managers to build budgets from the ground up each year.

rolling 12-month budgets to provide a mechanism for adjusting items in response to unforeseen circumstances. Many State governments prepare budgets biennially (every two years). This can cause major problems if unexpected costs are incurred because of a natural disaster or if tax revenue falls because of an unexpected downturn in the economy.

Though the focus of the chapter will be on monthly or annual budgets as single documents, we will introduce the concept of rolling budgets at the end of the chapter to explain how budgets may be updated over shorter periods in order to maintain their relevance for planning and control.

Participation in the budget development process

Traditionally, budgeting is a bottom-up process dependent on departmental managers providing a detailed plan for the upcoming month, quarter or year. Many companies use a system of **participatory budgeting**, which starts with departmental managers and then flows up through middle management and ultimately to top management. At each level, budget estimates are prepared and then submitted to the next level of management, which has responsibility for reviewing the budget and negotiating any changes that need to be made.

Regardless of the specific process used, budget development must be guided by a strategic plan that focuses attention on the company as a whole and integrates individual budgets. A budgeting process that is clearly guided and focused by a strategic plan makes managers more focused on important aspects of the budget and less worried about irrelevant details.[2] In addition, in order to motivate managers and other employees to meet the objectives and goals provided in budgets, companies should structure bonuses, merit pay, and other tangible and intangible rewards in ways that link these rewards to measurable goals outlined in the budgets.

Behavioural implications of budgeting

When budgets are used for both planning and control purposes, conflicts invariably arise. If managers are evaluated and compensated according to whether they 'meet the budget', they may have incentives to pad the budget, thus making the targets easier to reach. This style of behaviour is often described as budget 'gaming'. For example, if a manager knows that she will receive a bonus if sales in her department exceed the budget, she may attempt to set the sales budget at an unrealistically low level. Likewise, if a manager is to receive a bonus if costs are held below budget, he may attempt to pad the budget by estimating that the costs will be higher than he really expects them to be. While these forms of gaming refer to managers attempting to manipulate the budget numbers, gaming can have more 'real' effects. For example, if a manager is $1000 behind their sales target on the last day of this period, and they expect a sale at the start of the next period (the very next day), they might record this sale in their accounts today in order to show that they reached their budgetary sales target this period. This action directly affects the profit and loss statement, as the revenue should have been recorded in the profit and loss statement of the next period, not this. This has the effect of overstating this period's profit and understating next year's profit. Therefore, budget-related gaming can have strong negative effects on the quality of financial reporting. This type of behaviour is unethical and clearly not beneficial for the company as a whole.

Tying compensation to meeting targeted budgets can also cause managers to manipulate expenses, and not only revenues – managers are incentivised to inequitably shift expenses from one period to another in order to make certain that the budget is met. Companies can reduce incentives for this type of behaviour by holding managers accountable and punishing unethical behaviour with strong sanctions. However, they can also reduce its likelihood by taking more positive steps, such as assuring managers that performance evaluation will be done in a fair and equitable manner and will include other factors such as customer-satisfaction surveys, the quality of goods and services provided and similar metrics.

Advantages of budgeting

Budgeting has many advantages, including:
1 The budgeting process compels communication to occur throughout the organisation.
2 The budgeting process forces management to focus on the future and not be distracted by daily crises in the organisation.
3 The budgeting process can help management identify and deal with potential bottlenecks or constraints before they become major problems.
4 The budgeting process can increase the coordination of organisational activities and help facilitate goal congruence. Implementing goal congruence means making sure that the personal goals of the managers are closely aligned with the goals of the organisation.
5 The budgeting process can define specific goals and objectives that become benchmarks, or standards of performance, for evaluating future performance.

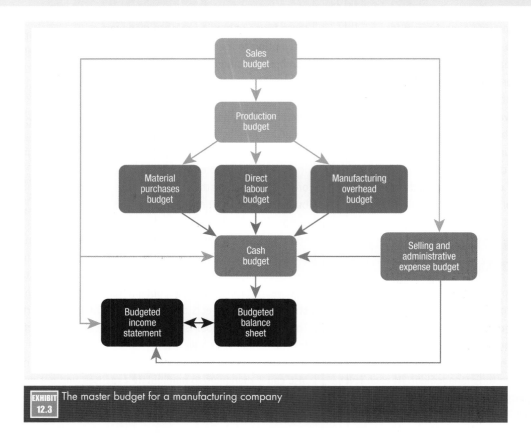

EXHIBIT 12.3 The master budget for a manufacturing company

The master budget

The **master budget** consists of an interrelated set of budgets prepared by a business. A master budget for a manufacturing company is shown in Exhibit 12.3 with a corresponding master budget for a merchandising company shown in Exhibit 12.4. The starting point in both is forecasting sales and preparing a sales budget.

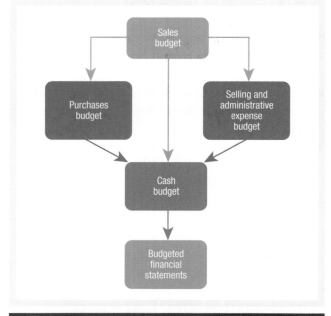

EXHIBIT 12.4 The master budget for a merchandising company

LEARNING OBJECTIVE **2** >>

The sales budget

All organisations require the forecasting of future sales volume and the preparation of a sales budget. A professional rugby team needs to forecast the number of fans who will attend home games each season. Airlines need to forecast the number of passengers who will fly on each route and hotels need to forecast occupancy rates for various days and months. Retail stores, such as David Jones and Woolworths, must forecast retail sales of many different products at many different locations. Manufacturing firms such as Ford, Toyota and General Motors must forecast consumer demand for each model of car or truck that they sell.

The **sales forecast** and **sales budget** are the starting points in the preparation of production budgets for manufacturing companies and purchases budgets for merchandising companies. The sales budget is a key component used in the overall strategic planning process and is also used in planning the cash needs of businesses.

There are many different ways to forecast sales. Most forecasting will combine information from many different sources either informally or through the use of computer programs. Regardless of the size of the company or the sophistication of the forecasting methods used, the usual starting point in sales forecasting is last year's level of sales. Other factors and information sources typically used in sales forecasting are as follows:

1 Historical data, such as sales trends for the company, competitors and the industry (if available)
2 General economic trends or factors, such as inflation rates, interest rates, population growth and personal spending
3 Regional and local factors expected to affect sales
4 Anticipated price changes in both purchasing costs and sales prices
5 Anticipated marketing or advertising plans
6 The impact of new products or changes in product mix on the entire product line
7 Technology or process changes in an industry (for example, the change from DVDs to Blu-Ray DVDs)
8 Other factors such as political and legal events.

Every organisation will have unique factors that it needs to consider and each organisation will also attach a different level of importance to each factor. For example, forecasting sales revenue (and the number of skiers) for a Thredbo ski resort requires not only the consideration of general economic conditions, the impact of new resorts and the potential impact of advertising, but also a consideration of the weather. While snow-making equipment has reduced the dependence of resorts on natural snow, weather can sometimes affect these businesses in ways that cannot be easily predicted. If the Snowy Mountains had plenty of snow, but surrounding areas are warmer than expected, fewer individuals might frequent the Thredbo ski slopes. The skiers might stay away from the slopes because of the warm weather and lack of snow in the surrounding areas.

The size and complexity of the organisation will often determine the complexity of the sales forecasting system. In large companies, preparation of the sales forecast is usually accomplished by the marketing department and requires significant effort in the area of market research to arrive at an accurate forecast of expected sales. In smaller companies, the sales forecast may be made by an individual or a small group of managers. Some companies will use elaborate econometric planning models and regression analysis to forecast sales volume. Others may use very informal models and rely heavily on the intuition and opinions of managers. Regardless of the level of sophistication used in forecasting models, it is important to remember that sales forecasting is still just that – a forecast.

As you will see in the rest of this chapter, all the remaining budgets and the decisions that are made on the basis of their forecasts are dependent on this estimate of sales. For that reason, it is important to estimate sales with as much accuracy as possible. A small error in a sales forecast can cause larger

The starting point in most budgetary processes is the estimate of volume of sales, and their expected prices.

errors in other budgets that depend on the sales forecast.

Operating budgets are used by companies to plan for the short term – usually one year or less. As an example of the budgeting process, let's hypothetically consider the case of Bob's Bewdiful Juices, an orange juice bottler. Bob's produces bottled orange juice from fruit concentrate purchased from suppliers in Victoria and South Australia. The only ingredients in the juice are water and concentrate. The juice is blended, pasteurised and bottled for sale in 1-litre plastic bottles. The process is heavily automated and is centred on five machines that control the mixing and bottling of the juice. Each machine is run by one employee and can process 10 bottles of juice per minute, or 600 bottles per hour.

The juice is sold by a number of grocery stores under their store brand name and in smaller restaurants, delis and bagel shops under the name of Bob's Bewdiful Juices. Bob's has been in business for several years and uses a sophisticated sales forecasting model based on prior sales, expected changes in demand and economic factors affecting the industry. Sales of juice are highly seasonal, peaking in the first quarter of the year. Forecasted sales for the first quarter of the year are as follows:

✳ **operating budgets**
Used to plan for the short term (typically one year or less).

Sales forecast	
January	250 000 bottles
February	325 000 bottles
March	450 000 bottles

Bob's sells the juice for $1.05 per litre bottle, in cartons of 50 bottles. A sales budget is the projected volume of product to be sold times the expected sales price per unit (see Exhibit 12.5).

	A	B	C	D	E	F	G	H
1				Bob's Bewdiful Juices				
2				Sales Budget				
3				January	February	March	1st Quarter	
4	Budgeted sales in bottles			250,000	325,000	450,000	1,025,000	
5	Selling price per bottle			$1.05	$1.05	$1.05	$1.05	
6	Total budgeted sales			$262,500	$341,250	$472,500	$1,076,250	
7								

EXHIBIT 12.5 Sales budget

LEARNING OBJECTIVE 3 >>

Animation

Production budget

For manufacturing companies, the next step in the budgeting process is to complete the **production budget**. Once the sales volume has been projected, companies must forecast how many units of product to produce in order to meet the sales projections. Although this might seem to be an easy task – just manufacture what you plan to sell – traditional manufacturing companies, as you will recall from Chapter 2, often choose to hold an established minimum level of finished-goods inventory (as well as direct materials inventory) to serve as buffers in case of unexpected demand for products or unexpected problems in production.

In this case, the sales forecast must be adjusted to account for any expected increase or decrease in finished goods inventory. The formula for a basic production budget is as follows:

✳ **production budget**
Used to forecast how many units of product to produce in order to meet the sales projections.

Key formula 12.1: Required production

Sales forecast (in units)
+ Desired ending inventory of finished goods

= Total budgeted production needs
– Beginning inventory of finished goods

= Required production

Bob's Bewdiful Juices tries to maintain at least 10 per cent of the next month's sales forecast in inventory at the end of each month. Because sales have been projected to increase very rapidly, the company does not want to run the risk of running out of juice to ship to customers, so Bob's Bewdiful

Juices keeps a minimum amount on hand at all times. Other problems, such as shipping delays or weather, could also affect the amount of desired ending inventory. Based on these requirements, Bob's would want to have 32 500 bottles of juice on hand at the end of January (10 per cent of February's forecasted sales of 325 000). A production budget for Bob's Bewdiful Juices is shown in Exhibit 12.6.

As shown in Exhibit 12.6, the arrows demonstrate that the projected ending inventory of finished goods for one month is the projected beginning inventory for the following month. The projected ending inventory for the quarter is the ending inventory on the last day of the quarter, in this case 31 March, and the projected beginning inventory for the quarter is the beginning inventory on the first day of the quarter, or 1 January.

You should note that to complete the production budget for the first quarter we need to have some additional information. We need to know the forecasted sales for April in order to determine the projected ending inventory for the end of March. If management expects April sales to be 500 000 units, the projected ending inventory in March is 50 000 units. The beginning inventory for January is 25 000 bottles. (This amount is also the ending inventory for December.) Closer examination of the production budget model will show that required production needs are just the budgeted sales plus or minus any projected change in finished goods inventory during the month.

Key formula 12.2: Required production

Required production = Budgeted sales + (–) Increase (Decrease) in finished goods inventory

---

In January, the budgeted sales are 250 000 units and inventories are projected to increase by 7500 units (from 25 000 to 32 500). If we add the projected inventory increase to the sales projection, we have a required production level of 257 500 (250 000 + 7500). Applying the same logic to February and March, we obtain the production levels of 337 500 units and 455 000 units respectively.

Material, labour, overhead, and selling and administrative expense budgets

Material purchases budget

Once the production budget is completed, the next budget to be prepared is the **material purchases budget**. Once again, because many traditional companies desire to keep materials on hand at all times in order to plan for unforeseen changes in demand, the desired ending inventory for materials must be added to the projected production needs for materials to arrive at the total expected needs for materials. Then an adjustment is made for any raw materials inventory on hand at the beginning of the month.

Bob's Bewdiful Juices needs to prepare two purchases budgets – one for the concentrate used in its orange juice and one for the bottles that are purchased from an outside supplier. Bob's has determined that it takes one litre of orange concentrate for every 32 bottles of finished product. Each litre of concentrate costs $4.80. Bob's also requires 20 per cent of next month's direct material needs to be on hand at the end of this budget period. Note that the starting point for this budget is the production budget (Exhibit 12.6).

The first step in the preparation of the direct material purchases budget is to compute the raw materials needed based on the projected production from Exhibit 12.6. In this case, we take the number of bottles to be produced and divide by 32. This represents the number of bottles that can be produced with one litre of concentrate. The ending inventory needs are then added to that figure to arrive at the projected direct materials needed to fulfil the production requirements and ending inventory needs. Beginning inventory is then subtracted from the projected needs to arrive at the projected purchases in litres. Why subtract the beginning inventory? Simply because any quantity already in stock at the start of

	A	B	C	D	E	F	G	H	I	J	K
1					Bob's Bewdiful Juices						
2					Production Budget						
3						January	February	March	1st Quarter		
4	Budgeted sales (Exh. 12-6)					250,000	325,000	450,000	1,025,000		
5	Add: Desired ending inventory of finished goods					32,500	45,000	50,000	50,000 *		
6	Total budgeted production needs					282,500	370,000	500,000	1,075,000		
7	Less: Beginning inventory of finished goods					-25,000	-32,500	-45,000	-25,000 **		
8	Required production					257,500	337,500	455,000	1,050,000		
9											
10	* March ending inventory is calculated as follows: April sales are projected to be 500,000 units of finished goods										
11	(500,000 *0.10 = 50,000 units of finished goods)										
12											
13											
14	** January beginning inventroy of 25,000 units of finished goods is given										

EXHIBIT 12.6 Production budget

	A	B	C	D	E	F	G	H	I	J
1					Bob's Bewdiful Juices					
2				Material Purchases Budget - orange concentrate						
3						January	February	March	1st Quarter	
4	Required production (Exhibit 12-6)					257,500	337,500	455,000	1,050,000	
5	Orange concentrate needed (litres)*					8,047	10,547	14,219	32,813	
6	Add: Desired ending inventory of orange		**			2,109	2,844	3,063	3,063	
7	Total budgeted needs of orange					10,156	13,391	17,282	35,876	
8	Less: Beginning inventory of orange					1,609	2,109	2,844	1,609	
9	Orange to be purchased					8,547	11,282	14,438	34,267	
10	Cost per litre of orange					$4.80	$4.80	$4.80	$4.80	
11	Cost of orange concentrate to be purchased					$41,026	$54,154	$69,302	$164,482	
12										
13										
14	* Required litres/ 32 bottles per litre (rounded to the nearest litre)									
15	** Twenty percent of next month's materials needed									
16	*** January beginning inventory of 1,609 units is given.									

EXHIBIT 12.7 Material purchases budget – orange concentrate

❊ **material purchases budget**
Used to project the dollar amount of raw materials purchased for production.

the month that is able to be used for production, reduces the quantity that has to be purchased – it's already in stock, so no need to buy it! The last step is to convert that amount to dollars by multiplying the number of litres by the price per litre.

To calculate the projected ending inventory in March, Bob's must estimate sales for May. (April sales were already estimated to be 500 000 bottles.) If May sales are estimated at 400 000 bottles, April ending inventory will be estimated to be 40 000 bottles (0.10 × 400 000) and April production will be 490 000 bottles (April sales of 500 000 bottles + ending inventory of 40 000 bottles – beginning inventory of 50 000 bottles). The production of 490 000 bottles in April requires 15 313 litres of concentrate (490 000 bottles ÷ 32 bottles per litre). Accordingly, Bob's will plan on holding 3063 litres of concentrate in inventory at the end of March (20 per cent of the materials usage for April). The material purchases budget for orange concentrate is shown in Exhibit 12.7.

Bob's will prepare a similar budget for bottles. The bottles are purchased from an outside supplier for $0.10 per bottle. The supplier provides labels and caps for the bottles as part of the purchase price. Bob's has the same inventory policy for bottles and orange concentrate. A material purchases budget for bottles is shown in Exhibit 12.8.

Direct labour budget

As with the material purchases budget, the **direct labour budget** starts with the production budget. However, since labour cannot be accumulated like raw materials, no adjustments need to be made for beginning and ending inventory.

The direct labour budget is prepared by multiplying the units to be produced by the number of direct labour hours required to produce each unit. As was discussed earlier, the production process utilises a worker assigned to each of the five mixing and bottling machines. Each machine (and thus each worker) can process 600 bottles of orange juice per hour. At Bob's Bewdiful Juices, factory workers are paid an average of $15 per hour, including fringe benefits. If the production schedule doesn't allow for full utilisation of the workers and machines, one or more workers are temporarily moved to another department. Dividing the labour rate of $15 by the time required per bottle shows that the amount of direct labour is $0.025 per bottle of juice ($15 ÷ 600 bottles). A direct labour budget for the first quarter is shown in Exhibit 12.9.

❋ direct labour budget

Used to project the dollar amount of direct labour cost needed for production.

	A	B	C	D	E	F	G	H	I	J
1						Bob's Bewdiful Juices				
2						Materials Purchases Budget - bottles				
3						January	February	March	1st Quarter	
4	Required production (Exhibit 12-6)					257,500	337,500	455,000	1,050,000	
5	Add: Desired ending inventory of bottles*					67,500	91,000	98,000	98,000	
6	Total budgeted needs of bottles					325,000	428,500	553,000	1,148,000	
7	Less: Beginning inventory of bottles**					-51,500	-67,500	-91,000	-51,500	
8	Bottles to be purchased					273,500	361,000	462,000	1,096,500	
9	Cost per bottle					$0.10	$0.10	$0.10	$0.10	
10	Cost of bottles to be purchased					$ 27,350	$ 36,100	$ 46,200	$ 109,650	
11										
12										
13	* March ending inventory is 20% of April forecasted production, and									
14	forecasted April production is 490,000 bottles. 20% of $=490,000 bottles is 98,000 bottles.									
15	** January beginning inventory of 51,500 bottles is given.									
16										

EXHIBIT 12.8 Material purchases budget – bottles

	A	B	C	D	E	F	G	H	I	J
1						Bob's Bewdiful Juices				
2						Direct Labour Budget				
3						January	February	March	1st Quarter	
4	Required production (Exhibit 12-6)					257,500	337,500	455,000	1,050,000	
5	Direct Labour hours per bottle					1/600	1/600	1/600	1/600	
6	Total direct labour hours needed for production					429.17	562.50	758.33	1750.00	
7	Direct labour cost per hour					$15.00	$15.00	$15.00	$15.00	
8	Total direct labour cost					$6,438	$8,438	$11,375	$26,250	
9										

EXHIBIT 12.9 Direct labour budget

Manufacturing overhead budget

Preparation of the **manufacturing overhead budget** involves estimating overhead costs. As was discussed in detail earlier in this book, estimating overhead can be accomplished in a number of ways, by using plantwide or departmental predetermined overhead rates or activity-based costing. At Bob's Bewdiful Juices, most of the production process is automated, the juice is mixed by machine and machines do the bottling and packaging. Overhead costs are incurred almost entirely in the mixing and bottling process. Consequently, Bob's has chosen to use a plantwide cost driver (machine hours) to apply manufacturing overhead to products.

However, as you will recall from Chapter 3, not all overhead is expected to behave in the same fashion, as production increases and decreases each month. Although variable overhead costs will vary in direct proportion to the number of bottles of juice produced, fixed overhead costs will remain constant regardless of production. For budgeting purposes, Bob's separates variable overhead from fixed overhead and calculates a predetermined overhead rate for variable manufacturing overhead costs.

Bob's Bewdiful Juices has estimated that variable overhead will total $438 000 for the year and that the machines will run approximately 8000 hours at the projected production volume for the year (4 775 000 bottles). The estimated machine hours are 80 per cent of capacity for the five machines. Therefore, Bob's predetermined overhead rate for variable overhead is $54.75 per machine hour ($438 000 ÷ 8000 machine hours). Bob's has also estimated fixed overhead to be $1 480 000 per year ($123 333 per month), of which $1 240 000 per year ($103 333 per month) is depreciation on existing property, plant and equipment.

The manufacturing overhead budget is presented in Exhibit 12.10. Note that variable overhead is budgeted on the basis of the predetermined overhead rate and varies with production each month, whereas fixed manufacturing overhead is budgeted at a constant $123 333 per month.

The material purchases budget, the direct labour budget and the manufacturing overhead budget are summarised in a total manufacturing cost budget (see Exhibit 12.11). This budget provides Bob's Bewdiful Juices with an estimate of the total manufacturing costs expected to be incurred in the first quarter of the year.

> ❄ **manufacturing overhead budget**
>
> Used to project the dollar amount of manufacturing overhead needed for production.

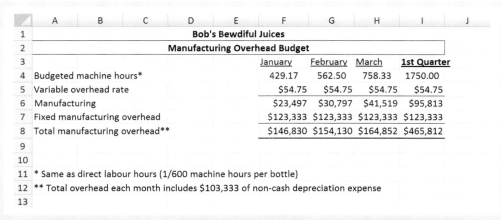

	Bob's Bewdiful Juices			
	Manufacturing Overhead Budget			
	January	February	March	1st Quarter
Budgeted machine hours*	429.17	562.50	758.33	1750.00
Variable overhead rate	$54.75	$54.75	$54.75	$54.75
Manufacturing	$23,497	$30,797	$41,519	$95,813
Fixed manufacturing overhead	$123,333	$123,333	$123,333	$123,333
Total manufacturing overhead**	$146,830	$154,130	$164,852	$465,812

* Same as direct labour hours (1/600 machine hours per bottle)

** Total overhead each month includes $103,333 of non-cash depreciation expense

EXHIBIT 12.10 Manufacturing overhead budget

	Bob's Bewdiful Juices			
	Total Manufacturing Cost Budget			
	January	February	March	1st Quarter
Budget material cost - orange (Exhibit 12-7)	$ 41,026	$ 54,154	$ 69,302	$ 164,482
Budget material cost - bottles (Exhibit 12-8)	$ 27,350	$ 36,100	$ 46,200	$ 109,650
Budget direct labour cost (Exhibit 12-9)	$ 6,438	$ 8,438	$ 11,375	$ 26,250
Budget manufacturing overhead cost (Exhibit 12-10)	$ 146,830	$ 154,130	$ 164,852	$ 465,812
Total budgeted manufacturing cost (Exhibit 12-11)	$ 221,643	$ 252,821	$ 291,729	$ 766,193

EXHIBIT 12.11 Total manufacturing cost budget

Selling and administrative expense budget

A selling and administrative expense budget for Bob's includes variable expenses such as commissions, shipping costs and supplies, as well as fixed costs such as rent, insurance, salaries and advertising. Bob's commissions are a function of projected sales and are calculated as 10 per cent of projected sales. Bob's selling and administrative expense budget is shown in Exhibit 12.12.

LEARNING OBJECTIVE **5** >>

Case

apply this!

Cash budgets
Why focus on cash?

Many managers consider managing cash flow to be the single most important consideration in running a successful business. After all, cash, *not* income, pays the bills. Whereas income (earnings per share) is often important to external investors, cash flow often takes centre stage for managers.

The timing of cash inflows and outflows is critical to the overall planning process. When cash inflows are delayed because of the extension of credit to buyers, there may not be sufficient cash to pay suppliers, creditors and employee wages. Timely payment is necessary to maintain good business relationships with suppliers (and to keep employees happy) and to take the maximum discounts that may be available on purchases. Cash budgeting forces managers to focus on cash

flow and to plan for the purchase of materials, the payment of creditors and the payment of salaries. Sufficient cash must be available to pay dividends to shareholders and to acquire new fixed assets. As can be seen in the example in the next section, cash budgets also point out the need for borrowing cash or when excess cash can be invested or used to repay debt.

The cash receipts budget

The first cash budget that must be prepared is the **cash receipts budget**. The cash receipts budget shows cash receipts that are generated from operating activities – cash sales of inventory or services and customer payments on account. Other cash receipts (from the sale of property, investment income and so on) are included in the summary cash budget.

All the sales of Bob's Bewdiful Juices are on account. Based on experience in previous years, Bob's estimates that 50 per cent of the sales each month will be paid for in the month of sale. Bob's also estimates that 35 per cent of each month's sales will be collected in the month following sale and that 15 per cent of each month's sales will be collected in the second month following sale.[3] As you will recall from the sales budget (Exhibit 12.5), sales for January, February and March were projected to be $262 500, $341 250 and $472 500, respectively. Because collections lag sales by up to two months (some of November's sales will not be collected until January, and some of December's sales will not be collected until February), completing the cash receipts budget also requires that we include sales for November and December. November's sales were $200 000 and December's sales were $250 000.

The preparation of the cash receipts budget is straightforward once the payment scheme is set. In each

> ✳ **cash receipts budget**
> Used to project the amount of cash expected to be received from sales and cash collections from customers.

	A	B	C	D	E	F	G	H	I	J
1	Bob's Bewdiful Juices									
2	Selling and Administrative Expenses Budget									
3						January	February	March	1st Quarter	
4	**Variable selling and administrative expenses**									
5	Commissions					$26,250	$34,125	$47,250	$107,625	
6	Shipping costs					$10,500	$13,650	$18,900	$43,050	
7	Supplies					$2,100	$2,750	$3,780	$8,630	
8	**Fixed selling and administrative expenses**									
9	Rent					$20,000	$20,000	$20,000	$60,000	
10	Insurance					$5,000	$5,000	$5,000	$15,000	
11	Salaries					$15,000	$15,000	$15,000	$45,000	
12	Advertising					$8,000	$8,000	$8,000	$24,000	
13	**Total selling and administrative expenses**					$86,850	$98,525	$117,930	$303,305	
14										
15	* Commission are based on 10% of projected sales (Exhibit 12-5)									
16										

EXHIBIT 12.12 Selling and administrative expense budget

month, we collect 50 per cent of that month's sales (50 per cent of January's sales are collected in January), 35 per cent of the previous month's sales (35 per cent of December's sales are collected in January) and 15 per cent of the second previous month's sales (15 per cent of November's sales are collected in January). Then the payment scheme is repeated for the remainder of the months in the budget. A cash receipts budget for cash received from operating activities is presented in Exhibit 12.13.

A closer look at the cash receipts budget shows that budgeted cash receipts are significantly different from budgeted sales revenue. In February and March, cash receipts are expected to be less than sales revenue. When sales are increasing and there is a lag between sales and the collection of cash, this is usually the case. It seems ironic, but businesses that are growing rapidly will often be short of cash.

The cash disbursements budget

The next component in the cash budgeting process is the **cash disbursements budget**. The cash disbursements budget includes cash outflows resulting from operating activities – payments to suppliers for materials, cash outflows for salaries and other labour costs, and cash outflows for overhead expenditures. Cash disbursements for selling and administrative costs are also included, although other cash outflows (for equipment purchases, payment of dividends, etc.) are usually not included. These non-operating disbursements will be included in the summary cash budget but not in the cash disbursements budget for operating activities.

Budgeting for the cash disbursements related to materials, labour and overhead is not as easy as just looking at the materials, labour and overhead budgets. Purchases of materials are often made on account, resulting in lags between the date items are purchased and the date cash actually changes hands. The manufacturing overhead budget often includes non-cash items such as depreciation, that must be adjusted as well.

A cash disbursements budget for Bob's Bewdiful Juices is shown in Exhibit 12.14. Bob's has a policy of paying 50 per cent of the direct material purchases in the month of purchase and the balance in the month after purchase. This policy offsets to a certain extent the lag in cash receipts from sales. Purchases of direct materials are taken directly off the material purchases budgets (Exhibits 12.7 and 12.8) and then cash payments are adjusted for the payment lag. For example, in January, Bob's budgeted purchases of orange concentrate total $41 026 (see Exhibit 12.7). As shown in row 6 of the cash disbursements budget (Exhibit 12.14), 50 per cent of this amount, or $20 513, will be paid in January, with the other 50 per cent paid in February. Similar calculations are made for purchases of orange concentrate in February and March.

Likewise, in January, Bob's budgeted purchases of bottles total $27 350 (see Exhibit 12.8). As with purchases of orange concentrate, half of this amount, or $13 675, will be paid in January and the other half in February (see row 11 of Exhibit 12.14). Similar calculations are made for purchases of bottles in February and March.

All direct labour costs are paid in the month incurred and come directly from the direct labour budget (see Exhibit 12.9).

Like materials, manufacturing overhead costs are paid on a lag, with 50 per cent paid for in the month incurred and 50 per cent in the following month. However, the manufacturing overhead budget (Exhibit 12.10) must be adjusted for depreciation of property, plant and equipment, which does not have a direct impact on cash flow.[4] Although total budgeted manufacturing overhead for January is estimated to be $146 830, $103 333 of this amount pertains to non-cash depreciation and will not be included in the cash disbursements budget. Of the $43 497 of cash overhead expected in January ($146 830 – $103 333), 50 per cent, or $21 748, will be paid in January, with the remaining $21 749 paid in February (see row 20 of Exhibit 12.14). Similar calculations are made for payments of manufacturing overhead expenses in February and March.

Cash disbursements for selling and administrative costs are taken directly from Exhibit 12.12.

※ **cash disbursements budget**
Used to project the amount of cash to be disbursed during the budget period.

	A	B	C	D	E	F	G	H	I	J	K
1					Bob's Bewdiful Juices						
2					Cash Receipts Budget - Operating Activities						
3		Sales			January		February		March		1st Quarter
4	November	$200,000			$30,000	15%					$30,000
5	December	$250,000			$87,500	35%	$37,500	15%			$125,000
6	January	$262,500	Exhibit 12-5		$131,250	50%	$91,875	35%	$39,375	15%	$262,500
7	February	$341,250	Exhibit 12-5				$170,625	50%	$119,438	35%	$290,063
8	March	$472,500	Exhibit 12-5						$236,250	50%	$236,250
9	Total cash receipts from sales				$248,750		$300,000		$395,063		$943,813
10											

EXHIBIT 12.13 Cash receipts budget – operating activities

	A	B	C	D	E	F	G	H	I	J
1					**Bob's Bewdiful Juices**					
2					**Cash Disbursements Budget - Operating Activities**					
3						January	February	March	**1st Quarter**	
4	Purchases of orange (Exhibit 12-7)									
5	December (given)					$17,279			$17,279	
6	January					$20,513	$20,513		$41,026	
7	February						$27,077	$27,077	$54,154	
8	March							$34,651	$34,651	
9	Purchases of bottles (Exhibit 12-8)									
10	December (given)					$12,146			$12,146	
11	January					$13,675	$13,675		$27,350	
12	February						$18,050	$18,050	$36,100	
13	March							$23,100	$23,100	
14	**Total disbursements for material**					$63,613	$79,315	$102,878	$245,806	
15										
16	**Disbursements for direct labour (Exhibit 12-9)**					$6,438	$8,437	$11,375	$26,250	
17										
18	Manufacturing overhead (Exhibit 12-10)									
19	December (given)					$20,917			$20,917	
20	January					$21,748	$21,749		$43,497	
21	February						$25,398	$25,399	$50,797	
22	March							$30,759	$30,759	
23	**Total disbursements for manufacturing overhead**					$42,665	$47,147	$56,158	$145,970	
24										
25	**Disbursements - selling admin exp's (Exhibit 12-12)**					$86,850	$98,525	$117,930	$303,305	
26	**Total cash disbursements**					$199,566	$233,424	$288,341	$721,331	
27										

EXHIBIT 12.14 Cash disbursements budget – operating activities

Summary cash budget

A **summary cash budget** consists of three sections: (1) cash flows from operating activities, (2) cash flows from investing activities and (3) cash flows from financing activities. These three sections are the same as those used in the cash flow statement prepared under generally accepted accounting principles (GAAP).

Cash flows from operating activities have already been discussed. Cash flows from investing activities include purchases and sales of property, plant, equipment and other investments, and interest and dividends earned on investment assets. Cash flows from financing activities include payments for the retirement of any debt issued by the company, sales or repurchases of stock, payment of dividends and any borrowing or repayments of other long-term liabilities.

Summary cash budgets can be fairly straightforward or very complex, depending on the size and complexity of the company. Bob's summary cash budget is shown in Exhibit 12.15.

Cash receipts and disbursements from operating activities have already been summarised in the cash receipts and disbursements budgets. Bob's plans to buy some new machinery in February at a cost of $75 000 (see Exhibit 12.15, row 10). The company also plans on paying a dividend of $50 000 in January (see Exhibit 12.15, row 12). Bob's also desires to keep a cash balance of at least $50 000 on hand at the end of any month. If the projected cash balance is less than that, a line of credit at Bob's local bank will be used to make up the shortage.

If Bob's draws on the line of credit, the company is charged an interest rate of 10 per cent annually. If the line of credit is used, money is borrowed at the beginning of the month. Repayments are made at the end of months in which there is sufficient excess cash (over $50 000) to pay back the entire line of credit. Last, but not least, Bob's pays estimated income taxes on a quarterly basis (in March, June, September and December) on the income earned during the respective quarter. Bob's estimates that its tax liability is 30 per cent of taxable income.

> ❋ **summary cash budget**
> Consists of three sections: (1) cash flows from operating activities, (2) cash flows from investing activities, and (3) cash flows from financing activities; these three sections are the same as those used in the cash flow statement prepared under generally accepted accounting principles (GAAP).

	A	B	C	D	E	F	G	H	I	J
1						Bob's Bewdiful Juices				
2						Summary Cash Budget				
3						January	February	March	1st Quarter	
4	Beginning cash balance					$ 50,000	$ 50,000	$ 50,000	$ 50,000	
5	Cash Flows from operating activities									
6	Cash receipts	Exhibit 12-13				$ 248,750	$ 300,000	$ 395,063	$ 943,813	
7	Cash disbursements	Exhibit 12-14				-$ 199,566	-$ 233,424	-$ 288,341	-$ 721,331	
8	Income taxes	Exhibit 12-18						-$ 1,849	-$ 1,849	
9	Cash Flows from investing activities									
10	Equipment purchases (given)						-$ 75,000		-$ 75,000	
11	Cash flows from financing activities									
12	Payment of Dividends					-$ 50,000			-$ 50,000	
13	Interest on Long Term debt *							-$ 30,000	-$ 30,000	
14	Borrowing from line of credit **					$ 1,757	$ 8,394		$ 10,151	
15	Repayments of line of credit							-$ 10,151	-$ 10,151	
16	Interest on line of credit ***							-$ 184	-$ 184	
17	Ending cash balance					$ 50,941	$ 49,970	$ 114,538	$ 115,449	
18										
19	* Long term debt is $1,500,000, and interest is paid									
20	quarterly at an annual rate of 8%, so $1,500,000 * 8% * 3/12 = $30,000									
21										
22	** The minimum cash balance at the end of each month is $50,000									
23										
24	*** The line of credit with interest is repaid at the end of March.									
25	The interest is $1,757 * 10% * 3/12 + $8,394*10%*2/12									
26										

EXHIBIT 12.15 Summary cash budget

LEARNING OBJECTIVE 6 >>

Budgeted financial statements

Companies may also prepare budgeted financial statements. These are used both for internal planning purposes and to provide information to external users. For example, a bank might want to examine a budgeted income statement and balance sheet before lending money to a company. The budgeted financial statements are often called **pro forma financial statements**.

Budgeted schedules of cost of goods manufactured and cost of goods sold are shown in Exhibits 12.16 and 12.17, respectively.

Note that the cost of goods manufactured and the cost of goods sold are calculated using absorption costing. Likewise,

✳ **pro forma financial statements**

Budgeted financial statements that are sometimes used for internal planning purposes but more often are used by external users.

	A	B	C	D	E	F	G	H
1				Bob's Bewdiful Juices				
2			Budget Cost of Goods Manufactured (Absorption Costing)					
3								
4	Beginning inventory of raw material*						$12,873	
5	Add: Purchases of raw material (Exhibit 12-7 & 12-8)						$274,132	
6	Raw materials available for sale						$287,005	
7	Less: Ending inventory of raw material **						-$24,502	
8	Raw materials used in production							$262,503
9	Add: Direct Labour		(Exhibit 12-9)					$26,250
10	Add: Manufacturing Overhead	(Exhibit 12-10)						$465,812
11	Total manufacturing costs							$754,565
12	Add: Beginning inventory of WIP							0
13	Less: Ending inventory of WIP							$0
14	**Cost of Goods Manufactured**							**$754,565**
15								
16	* Cost of beginning inventory is given							
17	** 3,063 litres * $4.80 per litre + 98,000 bottles * $0.10 per bottle							

EXHIBIT 12.16 Budgeted cost of goods manufactured (absorption)

the budgeted income statement in Exhibit 12.18 is prepared using the traditional format. The budgeted balance sheet is shown in Exhibit 12.19.

As you can see, the set of operating budgets and budgeted financial statements form an interrelated set of planning tools that are vital for managers' decisions affecting the number of units to produce, the amount of materials to purchase, how many employees to schedule for a particular time period (and when to schedule training, for example), the timing of major acquisitions and sales of equipment, and the overall management of cash.

	A	B	C	D	E	F	G	H
1				Bob's Bewdiful Juices				
2				Budget Cost of Goods Sold (Absorption Costing)				
3								
4	Beginning inventory of finished goods *							$17,986
5	+ Cost of goods manufactured (Exhibit 12-16)							$754,565
6	= Cost of goods available for sale							$772,531
7	- Ending inventory of finished goods**							-$35,932
8	Cost of Goods Sold							$736,599
9								
10	* Beginning inventory of finished goods is given							
11	** The cost of each of the 50,000 litres is $0.71863 per litre							
12	($754,565 cost of goods manufactured/ 1,050,000 bottles produced)							
13								

EXHIBIT 12.17 Budgeted cost of goods sold (absorption)

	A	B	C	D	E	F	G	H	I
1				Bob's Bewdiful Juices					
2				Budgeted Income Statement (Traditional)					
3	Sales					Exhibit 12-5		$1,076,250	
4	Less: Cost of Goods Sold					Exhibit 12-17		$736,599	
5	Gross Margin							$339,651	
6	Less: Selling and administrative expenses					Exhibit 12-12		-$303,305	
7	Net operating income							$36,346	
8	Less: Interest expense					Exhibit 12-15		-$30,184	
9	Income (before taxes)							$6,162	
10	Less income taxes (tax rate 30%)							-$1,849	
11	Net income							$4,313	
12									

EXHIBIT 12.18 Budgeted income statement (traditional)

Budgets for merchandising companies and service companies

The budgeting process for merchandising and service companies is similar to that of manufacturing companies, with a few important differences. It can also be every bit as complex. For example, consider the difficulty of budgeting for a professional cricket body such as Cricket Australia. It can be a challenge to predict revenue from ticket sales because revenue is dependent on attendance and attendance is dependent on performance (winning). Other revenue, such as from parking, concessions and souvenir sales, is also dependent on attendance. Of course, a large slice of Cricket Australia's revenues arises from television rights, and this amount is negotiated approximately every four to five years, sometimes longer. On the cost side, the administration costs associated in running the game such as the number of security people hired for an international cricket game and the share of stadium takings given to stadium management around Australia, depends on attendance. Accordingly, the budgeting process must be very adaptable. In sporting contexts, sometimes budgets are even changed daily to take into account attendance fluctuations![5]

Although service companies do not manufacture products, they may still prepare modified 'production' budgets. For example, a CPA firm may budget not only for total revenues, but also for the amount of revenue expected to be generated by each type of engagement (tax, audit and so forth), the number of those engagements expected (how many tax returns will be prepared) and the number of labour hours expected to

	A	B	C	D	E	F	G	H	I	J
1					Bob's Bewdiful Juices					
2					Budgeted Balance Sheet (Traditional)					
3	Current Assets									
4	Cash				$115,449	Exhibit 12-15				
5	Accounts Receivable				$287,437	($341,250 x 0.15 + $472,500 x 0.50)				
6	Inventory: Direct Materials				$24,502	Exhibit 12-16				
7	Inventory: Finished Goods				$35,932	Exhibit 12-17				
8	Inventory: WIP				$0					
9	Total Current Assets				$463,320					
10						$5 million (beg. Balance given)				
11	Fixed Assets				$5,075,000	+ $75,000 (Exhibit 12-15)				
12	Total Assets				$5,538,320					
13	Liabilities and Equity									
14	Current Liabilities:									
15	Accounts Payable				$88,511	($69,302x0.5 + $46,200x0.5 + $61,519 x 0.5)				
16	Line of Credit				0					
17	Income Tax				$1,849					
18	Total Current Liabilities				$90,360					
19	Long Term Liabilities				$1,500,000					
20	Total Liabilities				$1,590,360					
21	Shareholder's Equity									
22	Share capital				$3,500,000	Beginning balance of $493,626 (given)				
23						+ income of $4,334 (Exhibit 12-18)				
24						- dividends paid of $50,000 (Exhibit 12-15)				
25	Retained Profits				447960					
26	Total Liabilities and Shareholder's Equity				$5,538,320					
27										

EXHIBIT 12.19 Budgeted balance sheet

be incurred in each. As a result, the main focus of budgeting for service companies will often be the labour budget. (The use of time budgets by service companies is discussed in more detail in the next section on non-financial budgets.) Overhead is another important area of concern for service companies. A detailed budget of expected overhead expenditures (rent, utilities, insurance and so on) is extremely useful in planning for cash outflows.

Merchandising companies are not involved in manufacturing the goods they sell. A merchandising company buys finished goods from manufacturing companies and sells them to other companies for resale (wholesalers) or to final

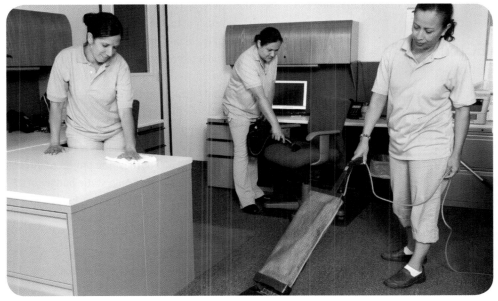

Labour costs and volumes in hours are key estimates in the development of budgets.

Budgeting and uncertainty – even governments worry!

When faced with the difficult task of predicting the financial future of the Australian economy, unexpected events can make budgetary predictions almost impossible. In September 2014, the *Sydney Morning Herald* reported that the Australian Treasurer, Joe Hockey, announced a $48.5 billion deficit, $30 billion more than expected. As stated in the paper, 'Mr Hockey said that 60 per cent of the $30 billion deterioration in the bottom line was from the write-down of receipts, particularly tax receipts'.

Clearly, budgetary management concerns are not only held at the individual and organisational levels of an economy, but by the very governments that develop policy to run the economies that organisations and individuals exist within.

Source: 'Joe Hockey says $30b overestimation has left 2013-14 in deficit by $48.5b', by Lisa Cox from *The Sydney Morning Herald*. Published by Fairfax Media Pty Ltd, ©2014.

Forecasting revenues and expenditures for the economy of nations is arguably even harder than that for a single organisation.

---

customers (retailers). Although merchandising companies will prepare a sales budget, they will not prepare budgets for production, direct material purchases, direct labour or manufacturing overhead. However, merchandising companies will prepare a purchases budget (for goods to be sold to customers) based on the projections in the sales budget. In addition, many merchandising companies hold some level of merchandise inventory and will need to estimate desired inventory balances and adjust sales projections accordingly. The preparation of selling and administrative expense budgets, cash budgets and budgeted financial statements in merchandising companies is similar to that in manufacturing companies.

LEARNING OBJECTIVE 8 >>

Interactive quizzes

apply this!

Static versus flexible budgets

Static budgets are budgets that are established at the beginning of the period for one set level of activity and remain constant throughout the budget period. The budgets that are presented for Bob's Bewdiful Juices are static budgets. Although static budgets are useful for planning and operating purposes, they can be problematic when used for control. As we discussed in Chapter 1, control involves motivating and monitoring employees and evaluating people

and other resources used in the operations of an organisation. The purpose of control is to make sure that the goals of the organisation are being attained. Control requires the comparison of actual outcomes (cost of products, sales and so on) with desired outcomes as stated in the organisation's operating and strategic plans (including budgets). The idea is to compare budgeted amounts to actual results and then to analyse any differences for likely causes. However, when static budgets are used and actual sales are different from budgeted sales, such a comparison is like comparing apples to oranges. If actual sales differ from projected sales, differences in production, material purchases, labour costs and variable overhead should be expected. If actual sales are lower than budgeted sales, actual costs of materials, labour and variable overhead *should* be lower than budgeted costs. The fact that a company's actual costs are lower than those budgeted under static conditions does not necessarily mean that the company (or its employees) spent less or was more efficient than budgeted.

For example, assume that Bob's Bewdiful Juices produces 250 000 bottles of juice in January instead of the budgeted amount of 257 500 bottles. The projected direct labour cost (see Exhibit 12.9) based on a static budget of 257 500 bottles was $6438. At the end of January, Bob's had actual direct labour costs of $6300. So Bob's spent $138 *less* than provided for in the static budget.

However, the comparison of actual labour costs to make 250 000 bottles with the budgeted labour costs to

❉ **static budgets**
Budgets that are set at the beginning of the period and remain constant throughout the budget period.

✻ flexible budgets
Budgets that take differences in spending owing to volume differences out of the analysis by budgeting for labour (and other costs) based on the actual number of units produced.

produce 257 500 bottles really does not make sense. Bob's ought to spend less for labour because fewer bottles were produced. The question becomes: How much less? What we would really like to know is how much the labour costs should have been had we known that production was going to be 250 000 bottles instead of 257 500.

Flexible budgets do just that. Flexible budgets take differences in cost owing to volume differences out of the analysis by budgeting for labour (and other costs) based on the *actual number* of units produced.

A flexible direct labour budget for Bob's Bewdiful Juices would budget labour costs based on the actual January production of 250 000 bottles. Based on the labour time needed to produce 600 bottles and the direct labour rate per hour of $15, Bob's projected labour costs would be $6250 (250 000 bottles ÷ 600 bottles per hour = 416.666 hours; 416.666 × $15 per hour = $6250), instead of $6438. If we now compare the actual direct labour cost of $6300 to the flexible budget amount of $6250, we see that Bob's actually spent $50 *more* than expected instead of $138 *less* than expected.

	Flexible budget	Actual	Difference
Production (bottles)	250 000	250 000	
Direct labour time per 600 bottles	1 hour		
Direct labour hours needed for production (250 000/600)	416.67		
Direct labour rate per hour	× $15		
Direct labour cost	$6 250	$6 300	$(50)

What explains the turnaround? By using flexible budgeting, Bob's removes any differences in cost caused by differences in volume of production and focuses only on differences arising from other factors.

What are those other factors? Perhaps Bob's paid more than $15 per hour for labour. However, another explanation is that Bob's used more than 417 labour hours or even some combination of the two. Without further analysis, we simply don't know. In Chapter 13, the use of flexible budgets is expanded to allow managers to break down these differences into variances resulting from either spending too much (or too little) or using too much (or too little). This process is called variance analysis.

LEARNING OBJECTIVE 9 >>

Explain and understand the concept of rolling budgets in modern organisations

When organisations operate in high uncertainty environments, the traditional annual budget can be less relevant. The annual budget is prepared for the full year ahead, and often strategic or operational events happen during that year that are unexpected (high uncertainty), causing the budget to become redundant. Examples of such events might be a new competitor entering a market, the introduction of complementary or substitute products by other organisations that cause sales in your organisation to increase or decrease substantially, or employees going on strike and demanding a significant pay rise, which disrupts production and sales, as well as increases labour costs significantly and unexpectedly. All these examples change the rules that we assumed applied when preparing the annual budget prior to the start of the period.

When faced with such uncertainty, many organisations implement the rolling budget. Rolling budgets are a series of short-term budgets that are updated periodically. For example, if we construct six quarterly (three-month) rolling budgets, in January 2012, we commit to budget from January 2012 to June 2013 – that is, 18 months into the future (three months per period multiplied by six periods). At the end of the first quarter (31 March 2012), we update the remaining five quarters based on a consideration of any change in circumstances that might impact them, and also construct a new sixth quarter, for 1 July 2013–30 September 2013. Every three months, we look forward another 18 months and rethink how we might change the budget numbers. Other than this different methodological approach to preparing budgets, calculations within rolling budgets are prepared in exactly the same manner as has been explained in this chapter for traditional annual budgets. It is only the frequency of preparation and modification that increases substantially, relative to the annual budget.

Please see the table below for further clarification:

		Rolling budget periods							
		Jan–Mar 12	Apr–Jun 12	Jul–Sep 12	Oct–Dec 12	Jan–Mar 13	Apr–Jun 13	Jul–Sep 13	Oct–Dec 13
Date prepared	31 Dec 11	Period 1	Period 2	Period 3	Period 4	Period 5	Period 6		
	31 Mar 12		Period 1	Period 2	Period 3	Period 4	Period 5	New Period 6	
	30 Jun 12			Period 1	Period 2	Period 3	Period 4	Period 5	New Period 6

To what extent are rolling budgets used in organisations? A survey of 331 medium and large Australian organisations found that rolling budgets were used by 65 per cent of respondents.[6] This broadly indicates that rolling budgets are strongly used by business managers in corporate Australia. This level of usage will only increase, as in fast-paced, dynamic and strategically changing competitive environments, rolling budgets are a very effective control device for managing uncertainty.

We do acknowledge, however, that rolling budgets are less suitable for the performance evaluation of individuals. This is because rolling budgets continually 'shift the goalposts' – that is, employees struggle to understand what is expected of them, as they constantly find their budget numbers changing. For this reason, most Australian organisations continue to prepare the annual budget and rolling budget simultaneously. The annual budget is used for evaluating annual performance, while the rolling budget helps managers plan shorter-term future activities through their provision of more relevant and accurate budget numbers. Finally, the three-month, six-period rolling budget example given above represents one of many ways of constructing rolling budgets. Organisations might conduct four quarterly budgets (budgets look forward 12 months and updated every three months), or nine one-month budget periods (budgets look forward 9 months and updated every month). Generally, the greater the uncertainty facing an organisation, the more an organisation prepares rolling budgets for shorter periods, and a shorter number of periods – this is because business reality is so much harder to predict as environments become increasingly uncertain.

Exercises

1 Advantages of budgeting LO1

Review the following incomplete statements regarding the advantages of budgeting.

a The budgeting process forces management to focus on the _____ and not be distracted by daily crises in the organisation.

b The budgeting process can define specific _____ and objectives that can become _____, or standards of performance, for evaluating future performance.

c The budgeting process forces _____ throughout the organisation.

d The budgeting process can increase the coordination of organisational activities and help facilitate goal _____.

e The budgeting process can help management identify and deal with potential _____ or constraints before they become major problems.

Required
Complete each of the above incomplete statements with the correct term or terms from the following list: *bottlenecks, communication, future, goals, congruence, benchmarks.*

2 Sales budget LO2

Tim's Temple Tools sells small eyeglass repair tools for $1.25 each. Tim's marketing department prepared the following first-quarter sales forecast (in units):

January	125 000
February	135 000
March	170 000
Total	430 000

Required
Prepare Tim's sales budget for each month of the quarter.

3 Production budget LO3

Mountain High makes and sells specialty mountain bikes. On 30 June, the company had 50 bikes in finished goods inventory. The company's policy is to maintain a bike inventory of 5 per cent of the next month's sales. The company expects the following sales activity for the third quarter of the year:

July	1200 bikes
August	1000 bikes
September	900 bikes

Required
What is the projected production for August?

4 Purchases budget LO4

Lazy Day Donuts makes powdered donuts that are sold by the dozen. Each box of a dozen donuts requires ½ kilogram of flour. The company began the year with 20 000 kilograms of flour on hand, but would like to have just 10 000 kilograms of flour on hand at the end of the current year. Lazy Day expects to produce 200 000 boxes of donuts during the year.

Required
How many kilograms of flour must be purchased during the year to have enough for production needs and the desired ending inventory?

5 Purchases budget for a merchandising company LO4

Loud Sounds sells specialty car stereo systems. On 31 March, the company had 60 systems in inventory. The company's policy is to maintain inventory equal to 5 per cent of next month's projected sales. The company expects the following sales activity for the second quarter of the year:

April	140 stereos
May	100 stereos
June	120 stereos

Required
Prepare a purchases budget for the month of May.

6 Direct labour budget LO4

Hammonds Hammocks produces and sells top-of-the-line Brazilian-style hammocks. The company prepared a production budget for the second quarter of the year that revealed that required production is 15000 hammocks for April, 12500 for May and 12500 for June. Each hammock requires 3 hours of direct labour at an average cost of $12 per hour (including all benefits and taxes).

Required
Prepare Hammonds Hammocks' direct labour budget for the second quarter.

7 Selling and administrative budget LO4

Will's Wheel Shop sells high-end bicycles. Although business has been good, Will is concerned that some of the company's selling and administrative expenses are getting too high. He has asked you to help prepare a selling and administrative expense budget for him to review for the coming month. Another employee has accumulated information for you to use, but you should be careful because the employee does not know a lot about preparing this type of budget, so some items may not belong on the budget.

Direct labour	$2500
Store rental	1200
Store supplies	450
Sales commission	925
Cost of bicycles	5600
Advertising in the local paper	150
Insurance on bicycles in the store	100
Shipping costs for bicycle parts Will ordered	135

Required
Prepare a selling and administrative expense budget with separate sections for variable and fixed expenses.

8 Cash receipts budget LO5

Thirst Quencher sells plastic water bottles to outdoor enthusiasts for $1.25 each. The company's marketing manager prepared the following sales forecast (in units) for the first half of 2009:

January	150000
February	125000
March	180000
April	165000
May	165000
June	155000
Total	940000

Historically, the cash collection of sales has been as follows: 55 per cent of sales collected in month of sale, 35 per cent of sales collected in month following sale and 9 per cent of sales collected in second month following sale. The remaining 1 per cent is never collected because customers do not pay.

Required
Prepare a cash receipts budget for each month of the second quarter (April, May and June).

9 Cash receipts budget LO5

Cookies and Cream begins business on 1 January of the current year and sells delicious chocolate chip cookies for $2.50 per box.

The company's founder and lead marketing guru estimates first-quarter sales (in boxes) as follows:

January	1500
February	1200
March	1600
Total	4300

Cookies and Cream expects cash to be collected in the following manner:
- 55 per cent of sales collected in month of sale
- 35 per cent of sales collected in month following sale
- 10 per cent of sales collected in second month following sale.

Required
Prepare a cash receipts budget for the first quarter. How much will customers owe the company at the end of March if sales are exactly as estimated?

10 Cash disbursements budget LO5

Robyn's Rocket Shop sells various types of sparklers and novelty candles. The following data were taken from Robyn's detailed budgeted income statement for the month of June. Although the labour costs and rent will be paid during June, the advertising expense and inventory purchases will be paid for in July. Half of the selling expense is paid in June while the other half is not due until July.

Labour expenses	$10000
Advertising expenses	1400
Rent on store	5000
Inventory purchases	3800
Selling expenses	6750

Required
Prepare a cash disbursements budget for Robyn's Rocket Shop for the month of June.

11 Budgeted income statement LO6

Robyn's Rocket Shop is in the midst of negotiating a loan from National Australia Bank. The bank has asked Robyn to prepare a budgeted income statement for the third quarter of the year (July through September). Robyn has accumulated the following data from various budgets for this purpose:

Sales forecast	$185000
Interest expense	2400
Selling and administrative expenses	74450
Cost of goods sold	56800

Required
Prepare a budgeted income statement for Robyn's Rocket Shop for the third quarter for presentation to National Australia Bank. Assume the company's income tax rate is 30 per cent.

12 Budgeting in a JIT environment LO7

Many companies now employ just-in-time (JIT) techniques to reduce inventory and costs and to streamline their business processes. A company that uses JIT will need to modify its budget process to accommodate the change in operations.

Required

Briefly describe the budgeting process that might be employed by a company that uses JIT.

13 Flexible budget LO8

Coffs Harbour Pineapple Corp. produces pineapple sweets. The company currently uses a static budget process. The company's controller prepared the following budget for April's production:

Estimated production	24 000 boxes
Direct labour per box	4 minutes
Direct labour required for estimated production	1 600 hours
Average direct labour rate per hour	$12.50
Estimated direct labour cost	$20 000

Actual production during April was 26 400 boxes and actual direct labour cost was $22 850.

Required

Prepare a flexible budget for Coffs Harbour Pineapple Corp that shows the projected direct labour cost and any difference between the budget and actual labour cost.

Problems

14 The sales budget and CVP analysis LO1, 2

CNX Motors is preparing a sales budget for the current year for the service department that is based on last year's actual amounts. Management is interested in understanding what might happen if the service department has an increase in sales volume (i.e. the number of mechanic hours) or an increase in the average revenue per mechanic hour. They believe it is unlikely that both would increase, due to economic conditions in the local market. Last year's sales amounts were as follows:

	Mechanic hours	Total revenues
January	1 174	$11 681
February	1 057	10 538
March	1 125	11 261
April	1 516	15 008
May	1 724	16 981
June	2 515	25 014
July	2 746	27 185
August	3 107	30 604
September	2 421	23 823
October	2 211	22 154
November	1 709	17 090
December	1 524	15 125

Required

a   Compute the average revenue per mechanic hour for the current year based on last year's actual data. You should round the average hourly rate to the nearest cent.
b   Prepare a monthly sales budget for the current year, assuming that monthly sales volume (i.e. mechanic hours) will be 10 per

cent greater than in the same month last year. Assume that the average revenue per mechanic hour is the same as you computed in question A. You should round budgeted hours to one decimal and budgeted revenues to the nearest dollar.
c   Prepare a monthly sales budget for the current year assuming that the average revenue per mechanic hour computed in question A increased by 5 per cent. Assume that the number of mechanic hours stays the same as in the prior year. That is, there is no increase or decrease in the monthly sales volume. You should round the rate per mechanic hour to two decimals and budgeted revenues to the nearest dollar.
d   For the current year in total, is it more advantageous to increase sales volume by 10 per cent or average revenue per hour by 5 per cent? Remember the impact of variable and fixed costs on these projections.

15 Sales, production and material purchases budgets LO2, 3, 4

Curiosity Corner sells books and various other reading-related products. One of the store's most popular products is a book pillow for hard cover and soft cover books. The pillows each sell for $8.00. Originally the pillows were handmade by a local artisan. The store's owner has been impressed with the demand for the pillow and has recently begun a small manufacturing company to produce and distribute the pillows to other stores. Estimated sales for the fourth quarter (in units) are as follows:

October	6 500
November	7 200
December	9 600
Total	23 300

Each pillow requires ½ a metre of fabric that costs, on average, $6 per metre.

Required

a   Prepare a sales budget for the fourth quarter based on the above information.
b   Prepare a production budget for the pillow manufacturing company. The company did not have any inventory of pillows at the end of September, but the company does want to maintain a 10 per cent inventory at the end of each month based on the next month's estimated sales. January's sales are expected to be low, given the post-holiday trends, and are estimated to be 4800 units.
c   Prepare a fabric purchases budget. The company did not have any inventory of fabric at the end of September, but the company does want to maintain a fabric inventory equal to 20 per cent of the next month's material needs. January's projected production is expected to be 4820 units.

16 Direct labour and manufacturing overhead budgets LO4

KenCor Pizza Emporium produces frozen pizzas for sale to grocery stores. The company has built a strong reputation for high-quality pizzas and has been profitable for a number of years. Because of increasing costs they are trying to control costs in the future. The CEO has asked the accounting and marketing departments to provide data related to labour costs and manufacturing overhead. Production budgets for the period ending 31 December 2009, are as follows:

Month	Pizzas	Month	Pizzas
January	2100	July	1450
February	2600	August	1200
March	2300	September	1350
April	2450	October	1750
May	2100	November	1550
June	2175	December	2050

Each pizza requires a ½ hour of direct labour to produce. The company currently applies manufacturing overhead to production at the rate of $2.50 per direct labour hour.

Required

a Prepare a direct labour budget for the year. Direct labour averages $12 per hour.

b Prepare a manufacturing overhead budget for the same period.

17 Cash receipts, disbursements and summary budgets LO5

Hailey's Hats manufactures and distributes hats for every imaginable occasion. Henrietta Hailey started the company in her house three years ago and has been surprised at her success. She is considering an expansion of her business and needs to prepare cash budgeting information for presentation to Second National Bank to secure a loan. Henrietta is not an accountant, so she has asked you to help her with preparing the necessary reports.

Hailey's Hats began the month with a bank balance of $10000. The budgeted sales for March to June are as follows:

	March	April	May	June
Cash sales	$14000	$16500	$15500	$17500
Sales on account	29000	30000	40000	50000
Total sales	$43000	$46500	$55500	$67500

Henrietta has found that she generally collects payment for credit sales over a two-month period. Typically, 70 per cent is collected in the month of sale and the remainder is collected in the next month. Her policy is to purchase inventory each month equivalent to 60 per cent of that month's budgeted sales. She thinks this provides her sufficient inventory levels to manage unanticipated changes in demand. Hailey's Hats pays for inventory purchases in the month following purchase. Selling and administrative expenses are budgeted to be 30 per cent of each month's sales. One-half of the selling and administrative expenses is accounted for by depreciation on Henrietta's manufacturing equipment. The company purchased additional manufacturing equipment in April at a cost of $24000. Henrietta does not receive a salary, but she does pay herself dividends as company performance allows. The first quarter of the year was very profitable, so Henrietta paid herself a dividend of $12500 in April. Henrietta wants to maintain a minimum cash balance of $10000 and has established a line of credit so she can borrow enough money to make up any shortfall. If the company has excess cash on hand at the end of a month (in excess of $10000), the line of credit will be paid back. Interest on the line of credit will not be paid until the end of the year. (Ignore any interest payments that the company would make on their borrowings.)

Required

a Prepare a cash receipts budget for April, May and June.

b Prepare a cash disbursements budget for April, May and June.

c Prepare a summary cash budget for April, May and June.

18 Budgeted income statement and balance sheet LO6

The Cold Mountain Heater Company is a retail store with locations across eastern Australia. The company's income statement for its first year of operations, ended 31 December 2011, and its balance sheet as of 31 December 2011, are shown here:

Income statement	
Sales	$4000000
Less cost of sales	2300000
Gross margin	$1700000
Less selling, general and administrative costs	800000
Income before taxes	$ 900000
Less income taxes	360000
Net income	$ 540000

Balance sheet	
Cash	$ 300000
Accounts receivable	150000
Inventory	400000
Property, plant and equipment (net of accumulated depreciation)	200000
Total assets	$1050000
Accounts payable	$ 110000
Retained earnings	540000
Common stock	400000
Total liabilities and owner's equity	$1050000

Additional information for 2012 is as follows:

- Sales budget (budgeted sales) for 2012

First quarter	$1050000
Second quarter	1100000
Third quarter	1150000
Fourth quarter	1100000

- Sales are collected in two portions, consisting of 85 per cent in the quarter of the sale and 15 per cent in the quarter following the sale. All of the accounts receivable as of 31 December 2011, relate to sales in the fourth quarter of 2011.
- The cost of sales is expected to increase to 60 per cent of sales in 2012. Inventory is purchased in the quarter of expected sale. Eighty per cent of inventory purchases are paid for in the quarter of purchase and 20 per cent are paid for in the quarter following purchase.
- The accounts payable balance as of 31 December 2011, relates to inventory purchases made in the fourth quarter of 2011.
- Selling, general and administrative costs are expected to increase to $225000 per quarter in 2012. Of this quarterly amount, $10000 is depreciation expense of the property, plant and equipment.
- The inventory balance at the end of 2012 is $400000.
- The company's tax rate is expected to be 40 per cent.

Required

a Prepare a budgeted income statement for 2012.

b Prepare a budgeted balance sheet as of 31 December 2012.

19 Static vs flexible budgets LO8

The static budget for the University Book Division of Chasse and Joos Publishers estimated sales revenue of $10 000 000 on sales of 165 000 units. The variable production costs (cost of goods sold) were estimated at $4 125 000, or $25 per unit sold. Actual results for the company exceeded expectations, with revenue of over $11 000 000 on sales of 180 000 units. However, the production manager was disappointed to see that the actual variable production costs of $4 400 000 exceeded the costs in the static budget by $275 000. The production manager did not understand why his costs were so much higher than the budgeted amount. If anything, he thought that his division had been very efficient and that costs should have been lower than reflected in the budget.

Required

Explain why the production manager's actual costs exceeded the amount estimated in the static budget. Should the production division be disappointed with the results?

Cases

20 Comprehensive budget problem LO2, 3, 4, 5, 6

Tina's Fine Juices is a bottler of orange juice located in the Northeast. The company produces bottled orange juice from fruit concentrate purchased from suppliers in Florida, Arizona, and California. The only ingredients in the juice are water and concentrate. The juice is blended, pasteurised, and bottled for sale in 350-ml plastic bottles. The process is heavily automated and is centred on five machines that control the mixing and bottling of the juice. The amount of labour required is very small per bottle of juice. The average worker can process 10 bottles of juice per minute, or 600 bottles per hour. The juice is sold by a number of grocery stores under their store brand name and in smaller restaurants, delis, and cafés under the name of Tina's Fine Juices. Tina's has been in business for several years and uses a sophisticated sales forecasting model based on previous sales, expected changes in demand, and economic factors affecting the industry. Sales of juice are highly seasonal, peaking in the first quarter of the calendar year.

Forecasted sales for the last two months of 2012 and all of 2013 are as follows:

2012	Bottles	2013	Bottles
November	375 000	May	375 000
December	370 000	June	350 000
2013		July	375 000
January	350 000	August	385 000
February	425 000	September	395 000
March	400 000	October	405 000
April	395 000	November	400 000
May	375 000	December	365 000

Following is some other information that relates to Tina's Fine Juices:

- Juice is sold for $1.05 per 350-ml bottle, in cartons that hold 50 bottles each.
- Tina's Fine Juices tries to maintain at least 10 per cent of the next month's estimated sales in inventory at the end of each month.
- The company needs to prepare two purchases budgets: one for the concentrate used in its orange juice and one for the bottles that are purchased from an outside supplier. Tina's has determined that it takes 1 litre of orange concentrate for every 32 bottles of finished product. Each litre of concentrate costs $4.80. Tina's also requires 20 per cent of next month's direct material needs to be on hand at the end of the budget period. Bottles can be purchased from an outside supplier for $0.10 each.
- Factory workers are paid an average of $15 per hour, including fringe benefits and payroll taxes. If the production schedule doesn't allow for full utilisation of the workers and machines, one or more workers are temporarily moved to another department.
- Most of the production process is automated, the juice is mixed by machine, and machines do the bottling and packaging. Overhead costs are incurred almost entirely in the mixing and bottling process. Consequently, Tina's has chosen to use a plantwide cost driver (machine hours) to apply manufacturing overhead to products.
- Variable overhead costs will be in direct proportion to the number of bottles of juice produced, but fixed overhead costs will remain constant, regardless of production. For budgeting purposes, Tina's separates variable overhead from fixed overhead and calculates a predetermined overhead rate for variable manufacturing overhead costs.
- Variable overhead is estimated to be $438 000 for the year, and the production machines will run approximately 8000 hours at the projected production volume for the year (4 775 000 bottles). Therefore, Tina's predetermined rate for variable overhead is $54.75 per machine hour ($438 000 ÷ 8000 machine hours). Tina's has also estimated fixed overhead to be $1 480 000 per year ($123 333 per month), of which $1 240 000 per year ($103 333 per month) is depreciation on existing property, plant, and equipment.
- All of the company's sales are on account. On the basis of the company's experience in previous years, the company estimates that 50 per cent of the sales each month will be paid for in the month of sale. The company also estimates that 35 per cent of the month's sales will be collected in the month following sale and that 15 per cent of each month's sales will be collected in the second month following sale.
- Tina's has a policy of paying 50 per cent of the direct material purchases in the month of purchase and the balance in the month after purchase. Overhead costs are also paid 50 per cent in the month they are incurred and 50 per cent in the next month.
- Selling and administrative expenses are $100 000 per month and are paid in cash as they are incurred.

Required

a Prepare a sales budget for the first quarter of 2013.

b Prepare a production budget for the first quarter of 2013.

c Prepare a purchases budget for the first quarter of 2013.

d Prepare a direct labour budget for the first quarter of 2013.

e Prepare an overhead budget for the first quarter of 2013.

f Prepare cash receipts and disbursements budgets for the first quarter of 2013.

I think this book is totally cutting-edge...it's making learning fun again.
- Scotty Willamson, student.

LEARNING, YOUR WAY.

ACCT was designed for students just like you – busy people who want choices, flexibility, and multiple learning options.

ACCT delivers concise, focussed information in a fresh and contemporary format. And... **ACCT** gives you a variety of online learning materials designed with you in mind.

At **http://login.cengagebrain.com/** you'll find electronic resources such as audio downloads and online flash cards for each chapter. These resources will help supplement your understanding of core organisational behaviour concepts in a format that fits your busy lifestyle.

Visit **http://login.cengagebrain.com/** to learn more about the multiple **ACCT** resources available to help you succeed!

Learning objectives:

After studying the material in this chapter, you should be able to:

1. Describe methods of determining standard costs and discuss the use of ideal versus practical standards.

2. Prepare a flexible budget using standard costs and contrast a flexible budget with a static budget.

3. Calculate a flexible budget variance and break it down into its components.

4. Break down the variable manufacturing cost variance into direct material, direct labour and variable overhead variances.

5. Compute and interpret price and usage variances for direct materials.

6. Compute and interpret rate and efficiency variances for direct labour.

7. Compute and interpret spending and efficiency variances for variable overhead.

8. Compute and interpret spending and volume variances for fixed overhead.

9. Analyse important considerations in using and interpreting variances, including the concept of management by exception.

MANAGEMENT ACCOUNTING FOR COST CONTROL AND PERFORMANCE EVALUATION – FLEXIBLE BUDGETS AND VARIANCE ANALYSIS

c 13

As discussed in the previous chapter, budgeting is a tool that managers use to plan and to make decisions. In this chapter, we expand our discussion of budgeting to include its use as a control tool.

Control involves the motivation and monitoring of employees and the evaluation of people and other resources used in the operations of the organisation. The purpose of control is to make sure that the goals of the organisation are being attained. It includes the use of incentives and other rewards to motivate employees to accomplish an organisation's goals as well as mechanisms to detect and correct deviations from those goals.

A control mechanism is a little like a thermostat in your house. If you desire to keep your house at 20 degrees (the budgeted temperature), the thermostat continually measures the actual temperature in the room and compares the actual temperature to the budgeted temperature. If the actual temperature deviates from 20 degrees, the thermostat will signal the heating system to come on (if the actual temperature is less than 20 degrees) or will turn on the air conditioning (if the temperature is above 20 degrees). Managers need a similar type of control system to control budgetary differences.

In business, control often involves the comparison of actual outcomes (cost of products, units sold, sales prices and so on) with desired outcomes as stated in an organisation's operating and strategic plans. Control decisions include questions of how to evaluate performance, what measures to use and what types of incentives to use. At the end of an accounting period (month, quarter, year), managers can use the budget as a control tool by comparing budgeted sales, budgeted production and budgeted manufacturing costs with actual sales, production and manufacturing costs. These comparisons are typically made through a process called **variance analysis**. Variance analysis allows managers to see whether sales, production and manufacturing costs are higher or lower than planned and, more importantly, *why* actual sales, production and costs differ from those budgeted.

The key to effective variance analysis is **management by exception**. Management by exception is the process of taking action only when actual results deviate significantly from planned. The key term in this definition is *significantly*. Managers typically do not have the time to investigate every deviation from budget (nor would such investigations likely add value to the organisation), so they should focus on material, or significant, differences. This allows managers to focus their energy where it is needed and where it is likely to make a difference. The concept of materiality and its use in variance analysis is discussed in more depth later in the chapter.

✳ **control**
Involves the motivation and monitoring of employees and the evaluation of people and other resources used in the operations of the organisation.

✳ **variance analysis**
Allows managers to see whether sales, production and manufacturing costs are higher or lower than planned and, more importantly, why actual sales, production and costs differ from budget.

✳ **management by exception**
The process of taking action only when actual results deviate significantly from planned results.

Variance analysis helps companies such as Corinne's Country Rocking Chairs control costs and evaluate performance.

Standard costing

To facilitate the use of flexible budgeting for control purposes, it is useful to examine the budget at a micro level rather than a macro level – that is, to develop a budget for a single unit of a product or a service rather than for the company as a whole. A budget for a single unit of a product or a service is known as its **standard cost**. Just as the cost of a product consists of three components – direct materials, direct labour and manufacturing overhead – a standard cost will be developed for each component. In addition, each component consists of two separate standards – a standard quantity and a standard price. The **standard quantity** tells us the budgeted *amount* of materials, labour and overhead in a product, whereas the **standard price** tells us the budgeted *price* of the materials, labour or overhead for each unit (litre, hour and so on). Standard costs are extremely important, as standards are the building blocks of performance measurement and evaluation. A 'standard' represents an expectation. When an organisation identifies a direct material or direct labour standard price, or rate, they are implicitly affirming that a manager will only have performed well if she is able to buy materials to pay for labour at a level equal to or better than the standard. Standards can be determined in a couple of ways. Management can analyse historical cost and production data to determine how much materials and labour were used in each unit of product and how much the materials and labour costs. Likewise, management can look at historical data to determine the amount of overhead costs incurred in producing a certain number of units. For companies with a long history of producing the same product, historical data can be very useful in forecasting future prices and quantities. However, historical data must be used with caution and adjusted when necessary. For example, changes in product design or manufacturing processes can dramatically change both the amounts and the prices of materials, labour and overhead.

❖ **standard cost**
A budget for a single unit of product or service.

❖ **standard quantity**
The budgeted amount of materials, labour or overhead for each product.

❖ **standard price**
The budgeted price of the materials, labour or overhead for each unit.

❖ **task analysis**
A method of setting standards that also examines the production process in detail to determine what it should cost to produce a product.

❖ **ideal standard**
A standard that is attained only when near-perfect conditions are present.

❖ **practical standard**
A standard that should be attained under normal, efficient operating conditions.

Another method of setting standards is called **task analysis**. Task analysis examines the production process in detail, with an emphasis on determining what it *should* cost to produce a product, not what it cost last year. Task analysis typically involves the use of engineers who perform time-and-motion studies to determine how much material should be used in a product, how long it takes to perform certain labour tasks in manufacturing the product, how much electricity is consumed and so on. Typically, some combination of task analysis and historical cost analysis will be used in determining standard costs.

Ideal versus practical standards

Because standard costs are used to evaluate performance, human behaviour can influence how the standards are determined. Should standards be set so they are easy to attain or set so they can rarely be attained? An **ideal standard** (sometimes called a theoretical standard) is one that is attained only when near-perfect conditions are present. An ideal standard assumes that every aspect of the production process, from purchasing through shipment, is at peak efficiency. Some managers like ideal standards because they believe that employees will be motivated to achieve more when the goals are set very high. Others argue that employees are discouraged by unattainable standards. Employees may be motivated to cut corners, use less-than-optimum material or skimp on labour to achieve the standards. This type of behaviour can lead to poor quality and an increase in defective units produced, which may cost the company more in the long run.

A **practical standard** should be attainable under normal, efficient operating conditions. It is sometimes referred to as the 'normal' standard. Practical standards take into consideration that machines break down occasionally, that employees are not always perfect, that waste in materials does occur. Most managers would agree that practical standards encourage employees to be more positive and productive.

Use of standards by retailing and service organisations

The use of standard costing applies to merchandising and service organisations as well. Just as Panasonic needs to determine how much it should cost to make a telephone, an automobile dealership needs to know how much it should cost to sell a car, the city council of Sydney needs to know how much it should cost to provide garbage pickup to a residence

When a drop in profits increases share price!

Standards condition our satisfaction with our actual performance, more so than it affects the actual level of performance itself. When Cochlear, the Bionic ear maker, announced a fall in profits its share price surprisingly surged higher owing to a strong increase in sales from the previous year impressing the share market – exceeding the market's expectations. A standard of performance is very important, as key stakeholders find it desirable that organisations perform at least to standard, or better. The actual result is surprisingly irrelevant when affecting our *perception* of our performance, next to our standards.

Source: 'Cochlear profit falls but sales, shares surge', by Stephen Letts. Published by ABC News, © 2014.

Source: ELizabethHoffmann/iStockphoto

Profits do not always cause a company's market value to increase.

and universities need to determine how much it should cost to provide an education to an incoming student. CPA firms have standards for the amount of time needed to prepare certain types of tax forms or returns, car repair shops have standards for the time needed to make each repair and airlines have standards for on-time departures. The use of standards is very common in all types of businesses. For example, the DHL courier company identifies standards for how long it should take to handle a customer's package. Managed health-care companies have developed standard times for doctors seeing patients for particular ailments. An initial office visit might have a standard time of 20 minutes, whereas a full physical for a patient might have a standard time of 45 minutes.

LEARNING OBJECTIVE 2 >>

Flexible budgeting with standard costs

In Chapter 12, we introduced the concept of flexible budgeting, based on the actual volume of production rather than on the planned level of production. Flexible budgets based on standard costs are the centrepiece of effective variance analysis.

To illustrate the concept of flexible budgets, consider the case of Corinne's Country Rocking Chairs. Corinne's builds a high-quality rocking chair with a reputation for lasting a lifetime and also uses a unique (and patented) rocking mechanism. The rocking chairs are sold directly by Corinne's through mail order and the Internet and have a retail price of $250 each. Corinne's produces each rocking chair to order and has the capacity to produce 1600 rocking chairs per quarter. The standard quantity, standard price and standard cost of direct materials, direct labour and variable overhead in each chair is summarised in Exhibit 13.1. Estimated variable selling and administrative costs (per unit) and total fixed overhead and fixed selling and administrative costs are also provided.

A static budget based on estimated production and sale of 1500 chairs is provided in Exhibit 13.2. In addition, a flexible budget based on the actual production and sale of 1600 rocking chairs is provided.

As you can see, the actual operating income for Corinne's is somewhere in the middle of that predicted by the static budget and the flexible budget. What does that mean? Unfortunately, not much! It means that Corinne's earned more than budgeted at the beginning of the year. But remember, the static budget was based on expected production and sales of 1500 units. Corinne's ended up producing and selling 1600 units. Comparing the static budget to the actual results is like comparing apples with oranges. It just does not make sense!

	Standard quantity	Standard price	Standard cost
Direct materials	20 linear metres of oak	$ 2 per metre	$ 40
Direct labour	5 labour hours	12 per hour	60
Variable overhead	5 labour hours	3 per hour	15
Total variable production costs			$ 115
Variable selling and administrative costs			25
Total variable costs			$ 140
Fixed overhead ($5000 per month, or $15 000 per quarter)			$15 000
Fixed selling and administrative costs ($6000 per month, or $18 000 per quarter)			18 000
Total fixed costs			$33 000

EXHIBIT 13.1 Standard costs for Corinne's Country Rocking Chairs

	Static budget	Flexible budget	Actual results
Units produced and sold	1 500	1 600	1 600
Sales revenue	$375 000	$400 000	$396 800
Variable manufacturing costs	−172 500	−184 000	−189 200
Variable selling and administrative costs	− 37 500	− 40 000	− 40 800
Contribution margin	$165 000	$176 000	$166 800
Fixed manufacturing costs	− 15 000	− 15 000	− 16 000
Fixed selling and administrative costs	− 18 000	− 18 000	− 16 000
Operating income	$132 000	$143 000	$134 800

EXHIBIT 13.2 Static budget, flexible budget and actual results for Corinne's Country Rocking Chairs

LEARNING OBJECTIVE **3** >>

Flexible budget variance

Comparing the flexible budget amounts with the actual results in Exhibit 13.3 is more meaningful. Remember that the flexible budget was calculated on the basis of the actual production and sales of 1600 units. It represents the amount of revenue and cost that Corinne's expected to incur during the first quarter for the actual number of units produced and sold. The difference between the flexible budget operating income and actual operating income is called the **flexible budget variance**. As shown in Exhibit 13.3, the flexible budget variance for Corinne's is $8200. Because actual income is less than budgeted income, the variance is considered unfavourable.

However, we still do not have much information concerning exactly *why* operating income is $8200 below budget. As shown in Exhibit 13.4, the unfavourable (U) flexible budget variance of $8200 is caused by a combination of factors – a $3200 unfavourable sales price variance, a $5200 unfavourable variable manufacturing cost variance, a $1000 unfavourable fixed manufacturing overhead spending variance, an $800 unfavourable variable selling and administrative cost variance, and a $2000 favourable (F) fixed selling and administrative cost variance. These variances are discussed more fully in the following pages.

Sales price variance

The flexible budgeting process removes any differences or variances due to variations in production and sales volume. Therefore, any differences in sales revenue between the flexible budget and actual results must be caused by differences in the sales price.

The **sales price variance** is computed by comparing the actual sales price to the flexible budget sales price and multiplying that amount by the actual sales volume.

Key formula 13.1: Sales price variance

Sales price variance =
(Actual − Expected sales price) × Actual volume

Plugging in the numbers for Corinne's, the sales price variance is as follows:

($248 − $250) × 1600 = $3200 (unfavourable)

	Flexible budget	Flexible budget variance	Actual results
Units produced and sold	1600		1600
Average sales price per unit	× $250		× $248
Sales revenue	$400 000	$3200 unfavourable	$396 800
Variable manufacturing costs	184 000	5200 unfavourable	189 200
Variable selling and administrative costs	40 000	800 unfavourable	40 800
Contribution margin	$176 000	9200 unfavourable	$166 800
Fixed manufacturing costs	15 000	1000 unfavourable	16 000
Fixed selling and administrative costs	18 000	2000 favourable	16 000
Operating income	$143 000	$8200 unfavourable	$134 800

EXHIBIT 13.3 The flexible budget variance for Corinne's Country Rocking Chairs

The sales price variance can direct management's attention to a potential problem area. However, at this point, it is difficult to tell whether this unfavourable variance is the result of reducing the sales price of all rocking chairs by $2 or perhaps the result of accepting a special order of 100 rocking chairs at a price of $218 per chair. The variance simply points out that the actual sales price is different from the budgeted sales price. Management should investigate it further to determine its cause.

Selling and administrative expense variance

As shown in the flexible budget variance calculation in Exhibit 13.3, Corinne's had an $800 unfavourable variance for variable selling and administrative costs and a $2000 favourable variance for fixed selling and administrative costs. Variable selling and administrative costs include such things as commissions on sales, advertising brochures that are sent out with each chair purchased, administrative time to process each sale and so on. Fixed selling and administrative costs include the salaries of the sales manager and personnel manager and such facility costs as rent and insurance. Like overhead variances, selling and administrative variances are difficult to analyse and interpret. However, companies utilising ABC systems may have sufficient information to analyse portions of this variance in more detail. For example, Corinne's is interested in reducing the costs associated with processing telephone sales and has established a quantity standard for the time spent to process each call (6 minutes). Likewise, it has established a pricing standard for this activity, consisting of the salary costs incurred by sales representatives handling the call ($1 per call based on a salary of $10 per hour) plus the direct costs of the toll-free line ($0.60 at $0.10 per minute). The actual costs incurred in handling sales calls can then be compared to the flexible budget amount, and price and usage variances can be calculated.

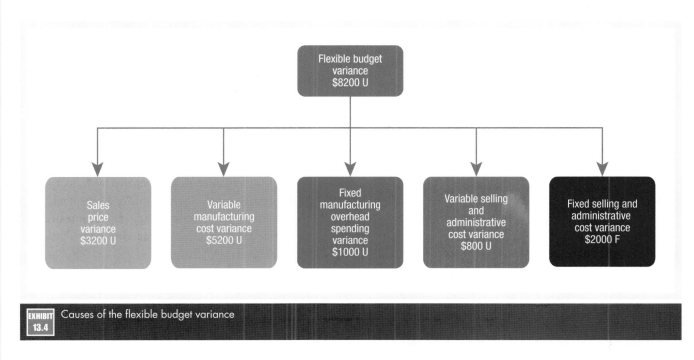

EXHIBIT 13.4 Causes of the flexible budget variance

Variable manufacturing cost variances

Revise with Beat the Clock

The flexible budget variance (see Exhibit 13.3) shows us that actual variable manufacturing costs were $5200 higher than budgeted, but determining the true cause of that variance is a little more difficult. Did Corinne's spend too much on materials or use too much? Did the company incur more labour costs than usual, owing to paying a higher wage, or did it spend more time making each chair than budgeted? Did Corinne's spend more than budgeted on electricity, supplies and other variable overhead or use more than budgeted? We simply do not know. In fact, the real reason may be a combination of any or all of the preceding.

To analyse the variable cost variances based on a flexible budget, we must step back and examine the flexible budget in more detail. Based on the standard cost information provided in Exhibit 13.1, the flexible budget for variable manufacturing costs is as shown in Exhibit 13.5. More detail concerning the actual variable manufacturing costs of $189 200 is also provided.

The total variance for variable manufacturing costs is $5200. Note that this is the same as the flexible budget variance for variable manufacturing costs shown in Exhibit 13.3. Because actual costs are greater than budgeted, this variance is called 'unfavourable' (indicated by the 'U' following the amount in the last column of the table). Even though Corinne's actual expenditures for total variable production costs were greater than budgeted, Corinne's spent slightly less than the amount budgeted for direct materials and variable overhead but much more for direct labour.

Because actual costs for direct materials are less than the flexible budget amount, the $160 difference is 'favourable'. Although it is useful to know that we spent less than budgeted for direct materials, this type of analysis still does not tell us *why* Corinne's spent less. Did the company use less wood than budgeted or pay less for each metre? To fully utilise the available information, we need to break down the total direct material variance presented earlier into its components and calculate both price and usage (quantity) variances.

We can examine the direct labour variance in the same way. Because actual labour costs are greater than the flexible budget amount, the variance is unfavourable. However, once again we do not really know *why* Corinne's spent more than budgeted. It could be because the company used more labour hours than budgeted or paid more for each hour of labour or some combination of the two. Further analysis is necessary to break down the total labour variance into its price and usage components and to fully understand the cause of the variances.

Analysing variable overhead is much like analysing direct materials and direct labour. Of course, direct materials and direct labour are also variable costs. Although we know that Corinne's spent less on variable overhead than budgeted (the variance is favourable), we do not know whether the price paid for electricity, supplies and other variable overhead was less than budgeted or whether Corinne's used less.

As you will recall, rather than budget each individual overhead item, we prepared the flexible budget in Chapter 12 by combining all variable overhead costs and budgeting these separately from fixed overhead costs. The flexible budget for variable overhead for Corinne's was prepared by multiplying the predetermined overhead rate of $3 per direct labour hour by the number of direct labour hours expected to be incurred in producing 1600 units (8000 hours).

Although traditional variance analysis of variable overhead can help provide answers to questions about whether a company spent more or less or used more or less in total, it does not provide us with information concerning the components of overhead.

	Flexible budget	Actual costs	Flexible budget variance
Direct materials	$ 64 000[1]	$ 63 840[4]	$ 160 F
Direct labour	96 000[2]	101 640[5]	5640 U
Variable overhead	24 000[3]	23 720[6]	280 F
Total variable manufacturing costs	$184 000	$189 200	$5200 U

[1] Flexible budget for direct materials = (20 metres per unit × 1600 units) × $2 per unit = $64 000.

[2] Flexible budget for direct labour = (5 hours per unit × 1600 units) × $12 per hour = $96 000.

[3] Flexible budget for variable overhead = (5 hours per unit × 1600 units) × $3 per hour = $24 000.

[4] 33 600 metres × $1.90 per metre = $63 840.

[5] 8400 hours × $12.10 per hour = $101 640.

[6] Actual variable overhead costs consist of the variable portion of utilities ($16 390), shop supplies and indirect materials ($4140), and repairs and maintenance ($3190).

EXHIBIT 13.5 Variable manufacturing costs for Corinne's Country Rocking Chairs

In other words, traditional analysis does not tell us whether we spent more than budgeted on electricity or supplies, just that the overall amount of spending was higher than budgeted. Companies adopting activity-based costing to allocate overhead to products can extend variance analysis to look at the overhead costs associated with each activity and its associated cost driver. This analysis provides much more detailed information than provided by traditional variance analysis.

The variance analysis model

The next step in variance analysis is to break down the direct material, direct labour and variable overhead variances into their components (a price variance and a usage or quantity variance), using the basic variance analysis model shown in Exhibit 13.6.

> **Key formula 13.2:** Price variance
>
> Price variance = Actual quantity (AQ) × [Actual price (AP) – Standard price (SP)]

> **Key formula 13.3:** Usage variance
>
> Usage variance = Standard price (SP) × [Actual quantity (AQ) – Standard quantity (SQ)]

Whereas AQ, AP and SP are self-explanatory, the calculation of SQ (standard quantity) needs to be explained a little. In Chapter 9, the flexible budget was prepared based on the cost that should have been incurred to manufacture the actual number of units produced. SQ is a similar concept. It is the standard (budgeted) quantity of material or number of hours that should be incurred for the actual level of production.

Price variance

As you can see, the material **price variance** is the difference between the actual quantity multiplied by the actual price (AQ × AP) and the actual quantity multiplied by the standard price (AQ × SP). Simplifying, (AQ × AP) – (AQ × SP) = AQ (AP – SP). The price variance is simply the difference in price multiplied by the actual quantity.

Usage variance

Likewise, the **usage variance** is the difference between the actual quantity multiplied by the standard price (AQ × SP) and the standard quantity multiplied by the standard price (SQ × SP). Simplifying, (AQ × SP) – (SQ × SP) = SP (AQ – SQ). The usage variance is simply the difference in quantity multiplied by the standard price. The variance model separates the overall flexible budget variance (AQ × AP) – (SQ × SP) into two components – one the result of paying more or less than budgeted and the other the result of using more or less than budgeted.

LEARNING OBJECTIVE **5** >>

Direct material variances

Using the standard cost data for Corinne's Country Rocking Chairs provided in Exhibit 13.1 and the breakdown of actual direct material costs shown in Exhibit 13.5, direct material variances are calculated as shown in Exhibit 13.7.

❊ **price variance**
The difference between the actual price and the standard price times the actual volume purchased.

❊ **usage variance**
The difference between the actual quantity and the standard quantity times the standard price.

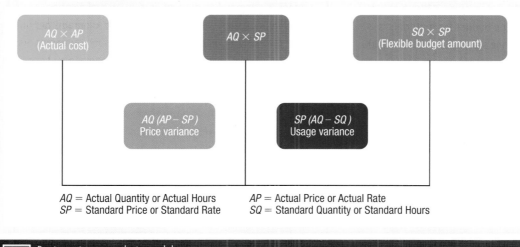

AQ = Actual Quantity or Actual Hours   AP = Actual Price or Actual Rate
SP = Standard Price or Standard Rate   SQ = Standard Quantity or Standard Hours

EXHIBIT 13.6 Basic variance analysis model

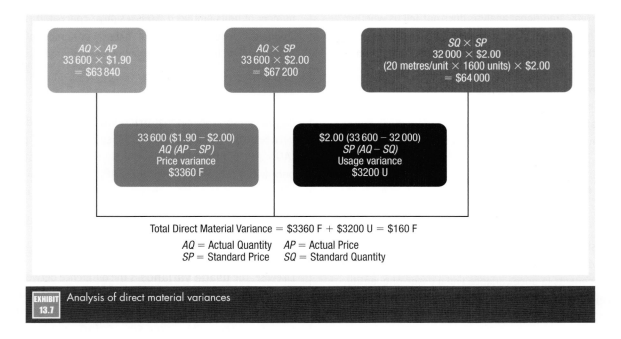

Total Direct Material Variance = $3360 F + $3200 U = $160 F

AQ = Actual Quantity   AP = Actual Price
SP = Standard Price   SQ = Standard Quantity

EXHIBIT 13.7 Analysis of direct material variances

Direct material price variance

The price variance is calculated by multiplying the actual amount of material purchased (33 600 metres) by the difference in the actual price paid per metre ($1.90) and the standard, or budgeted, price per metre ($2.00). This variance of $3360 is considered favourable because the actual price was less than the budgeted price.

Direct material usage variance

The usage variance for direct materials is found by multiplying the standard price by the difference in the actual quantity used and standard quantity allowed. Remember that the standard quantity allowed is the amount of direct material that *should* have been used to produce the actual output (the flexible budget amount). In this case, the budget for materials is 20 metres of wood per chair. Corinne's actually produced 1600 chairs during the quarter and should have used 32 000 metres of wood (1600 chairs × 20 metres per chair = 32 000 metres). The variance of $3200 is considered unfavourable because the actual quantity of material used (33 600 metres) was greater than the flexible budget amount (32 000 metres).

The total favourable variance of $160 for direct materials can now be examined in more detail. It is the sum of a favourable price variance of $3360 and an unfavourable usage variance of $3200. Although the overall direct material variance was quite small, you can see that both the price variance and the usage variance are quite large and just happen to offset each other. Possible reasons for a favourable price variance include taking advantage of unexpected quantity discounts or negotiating reduced prices with suppliers. However, favourable direct material price variances can also result from the purchase of low-quality materials. Unfavourable material usage variances can likewise be caused by a number of reasons – poorly trained workers, machine breakdowns or perhaps even the use of low-quality materials if they result in more defective units, machine downtime, rework and so on.

What are some possible reasons for an unfavourable direct material price variance and a favourable material usage variance? Unfavourable material price variances might result from rush orders (requiring faster delivery and higher prices), purchasing in small lot sizes (and not taking advantage of quantity discounts) and purchasing higher-quality materials than budgeted. Favourable material usage variances are likely a result of highly efficient workers and well-maintained machinery and equipment. From the perspective of direct material variances, it is also important to appreciate that unfavourable variances are merely a consequence of an organisation spending more per kilogram, or using more kilograms per unit. There may be very reasonable reasons for such outcomes. As previously explained, the material price variance may have been unfavourable as managers consciously planned to buy higher quality materials after standards were set, in order to respond to increased competition. Conversely, a favourable material price variance could result from managers buying cheaper, lower quality materials than expected, in order to reduce their costs. These might result in wastage in the production cycle, leading to unfavourable material usage variances. For these reasons and many others, the evaluation of variances must be conducted after speaking with managers in order to understand the underlying rationale for variances in organisations being favourable or unfavourable. We will expand on these arguments in discussing the final objective of this chapter.

Direct material variances when amount purchased differs from amount used

If the amount of material purchased is not the same as the amount of material used in production, the variance model for materials must be slightly modified (see Exhibit 13.8). To isolate the variances as soon as possible, the price variance should be calculated using the total amount of material purchased, whereas the usage variance should be calculated based on the amount of material actually used in production. For example, if Corinne's purchases 35 000 metres of wood but uses only 33 600 metres, the price variance would be calculated as follows:

$$AQ_{purchased}(AP - SP)$$

$$35\,000(\$1.90 - \$2.00) = \$3500\ F$$

The usage variance is calculated as before, that is,

$$SP(AQ_{used} - SQ)$$

$$\$2.00(33\,600 - 32\,000) = \$3200\ U$$

You should note that when the amount of material purchased is not equal to the amount of material used, the price and usage variances should not be added together to calculate the total direct material variance.

LEARNING OBJECTIVE **6** >>

Case

Direct labour variances

Direct labour variances are calculated using the same basic variance model used to calculate direct material variances. Because we are talking about labour instead of materials, we substitute rates for price (*AR* and *SR* instead of *AP* and *SP*) and hours for quantity (*AH* and *SH* instead of *AQ* and *SQ*). In addition, the direct labour usage variance is often referred to as an efficiency variance. Using the standard cost data for Corinne's Country Rocking Chairs provided in Exhibit 13.1 and the breakdown of actual direct labour costs in Exhibit 13.5, direct labour variances are calculated as shown in Exhibit 13.9.

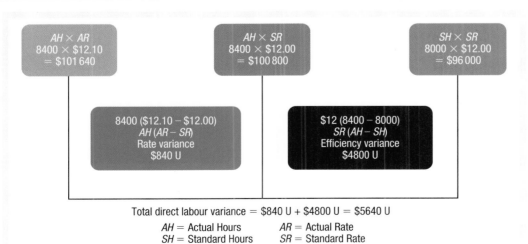

$AQ_{purchased} \times AP$	$AQ_{purchased} \times SP$	$AQ_{used} \times SP$	$SQ \times SP$
35 000 × \$1.90 = \$66 500	35 000 × \$2.00 = \$70 000	33 600 × \$2.00 = \$67 200	32 000 × \$2.00 = \$64 000

35 000 (\$1.90 − \$2.00)
$AQ_{purchased}(AP - SP)$
Price variance
\$3500 F

\$2.00 (33 600 − 32 000)
$SP(AQ_{used} - SQ)$
Usage variance
\$3200 U

$AQ_{purchased}$ = Actual Quantity Purchased
SP = Standard Price
AQ_{used} = Actual Quantity Used

AP = Actual Price
SQ = Standard Quantity

EXHIBIT 13.8 Analysis of direct material variances when quantity purchased differs from quantity used

$AH \times AR$	$AH \times SR$	$SH \times SR$
8400 × \$12.10 = \$101 640	8400 × \$12.00 = \$100 800	8000 × \$12.00 = \$96 000

8400 (\$12.10 − \$12.00)
$AH(AR - SR)$
Rate variance
\$840 U

\$12 (8400 − 8000)
$SR(AH - SH)$
Efficiency variance
\$4800 U

Total direct labour variance = \$840 U + \$4800 U = \$5640 U

AH = Actual Hours AR = Actual Rate
SH = Standard Hours SR = Standard Rate

EXHIBIT 13.9 Direct labour variances

If we evaluate the two components of the direct labour variance, we see that most of the variance results from inefficiencies in the use of labour. Potential causes of an unfavourable direct labour efficiency variance include poorly trained workers, machine breakdowns, the use of poor-quality raw materials (resulting in more time spent in production), or just general employee inefficiencies resulting from poor supervision. In this case, the unfavourable direct labour rate variance is small but still may be important. Potential causes of unfavourable direct labour rate variances include the use of higher-paid workers than budgeted, unexpected increases in wages owing to union negotiations and so on.

What are some possible reasons for favourable direct labour rate and efficiency variances? Hiring workers at a lower wage rate is one obvious reason for a favourable direct labour rate variance. However, that may be problematic if the workers are less skilled than required. On the other hand, favourable labour efficiency variances most often result from using highly skilled workers. Obviously, there are trade-offs here. Paying higher wage rates than expected can result in unfavourable labour rate variances, yet motivated staff work more efficiently, leading to favourable labour efficiency variances, whereas paying lower wage rates can result in favourable labour rate variances, but demoralised staff lose their zest for work, which adversely impacts their efficiency, causing an unfavourable labour efficiency variance.

LEARNING OBJECTIVE **7** >>

Variable overhead variances

With slight modifications, we can calculate variable overhead variances using the same variance model as for direct material and direct labour variances. As with direct material and direct labour, $(AQ \times AP)$ is simply the actual cost incurred – in this case, the actual variable overhead costs. SR is the variable predetermined overhead rate (sometimes called SVR). Because variable overhead was estimated using direct labour as the

Source: Blend Images/Shutterstock

Printing and general office stationery costs often fall into the variable overhead category, as greater levels of production activity causes these costs to increase.

cost driver, AH is simply the actual number of labour hours incurred. Likewise, SH is the standard number of labour hours allowed for actual production. Consequently, $SH \times SVR$ is the amount of applied variable overhead.[1] The price variance is often called a variable overhead spending variance and, like the labour usage variance, the usage variance for variable overhead is called an efficiency variance.

The variable overhead spending and efficiency variances are calculated as shown in Exhibit 13.10. What do these variances tell us? Whereas the price variance for materials and the rate variance for labour tell us whether the price of materials and the rate for labour are more or less than budgeted, the interpretation of the variable overhead spending

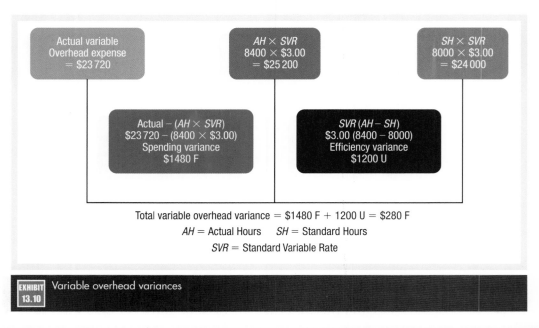

| Actual variable Overhead expense = \$23 720 | $AH \times SVR$ 8400 × \$3.00 = \$25 200 | $SH \times SVR$ 8000 × \$3.00 = \$24 000 |

| Actual − $(AH \times SVR)$ \$23 720 − (8400 × \$3.00) Spending variance \$1480 F | $SVR (AH − SH)$ \$3.00 (8400 − 8000) Efficiency variance \$1200 U |

Total variable overhead variance = \$1480 F + 1200 U = \$280 F

AH = Actual Hours SH = Standard Hours

SVR = Standard Variable Rate

EXHIBIT 13.10 Variable overhead variances

variance is a little different. Whereas a spending variance for variable overhead indicates that the actual price of variable overhead items, such as supplies, utilities, repairs and maintenance, was more or less than the flexible budget amount, it is also affected by excessive *usage* of overhead caused by inefficient operations or waste. For example, although the rates for electricity usage (charged by the utility) might be exactly as budgeted, excessive usage might result from poorly maintained equipment. Likewise, even if the price of supplies was lower than budgeted, excessive use of the supplies owing to waste could still result in an unfavourable variable overhead spending variance.

The variable overhead efficiency variance is also interpreted differently from the direct material and direct labour usage variances. It does not measure the efficient use of overhead at all but rather the efficient use of the cost driver, or overhead allocation base, used in the flexible budget. The efficiency variance has nothing to do with the efficient use of utilities, maintenance and supplies. The efficiency variance shows only how efficiently the organisation used the base chosen to apply overhead to the cost of product produced.

In the case of Corinne's Country Rocking Chairs, the favourable variable overhead spending variance tells us that Corinne's spent less than budgeted on the items included in the variable overhead portion of its flexible budget. Although this might have resulted from paying less per kilowatt hour for electricity, it might also have resulted from using less electricity than expected. A detailed analysis of each line item would provide more information. The unfavourable variable overhead efficiency variance tells us simply that more *direct labour hours* were used than budgeted. It does not tell us anything about the efficient use of electricity, supplies, or repairs and maintenance.

The interpretation of variable overhead spending and efficiency variances is made difficult by the use of a single cost driver to apply variable overhead to products and services.

In summary, the total variable manufacturing cost variance of $5200 that we saw in Exhibits 13.3 and 13.4 has now been broken down into six separate variances – two for direct materials, two for direct labour, and two for variable overhead (see Exhibit 13.11).

LEARNING OBJECTIVE **8** >>

Fixed overhead variances

Corinne's fixed manufacturing overhead variance (see Exhibit 13.3) is $1000 over budget ($16000 actual costs compared to the flexible budget amount of $15000). Unlike variable overhead, fixed overhead (and other fixed costs) should not be affected when production increases or decreases. Consequently, the variance model used in analysing variable costs (direct material, direct labour, and variable overhead) is not appropriate for analysing the fixed overhead variance.

Fixed overhead variances consist of a budget variance and a volume variance. The **budget variance** (or spending variance) is simply the difference between the amount of fixed overhead actually incurred and the flexible budget amount. Because fixed overhead does not depend on production volume, no activity levels are used in its calculation.

✳ **budget variance**
The difference between the amount of fixed overhead actually incurred and the flexible budget amount; also known as the spending variance.

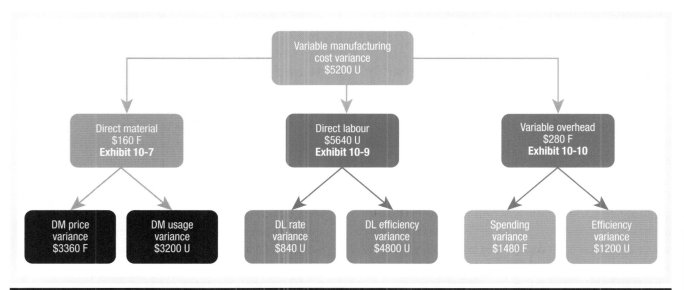

EXHIBIT 13.11 Summary of variable manufacturing cost variances

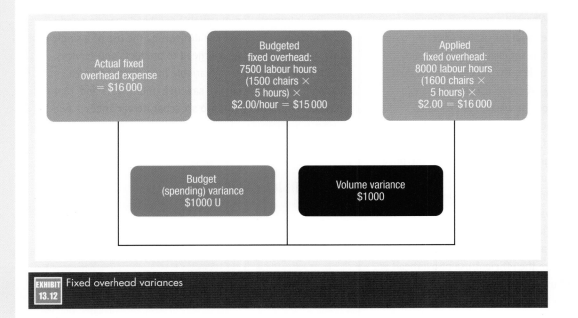

| Actual fixed overhead expense = $16 000 | Budgeted fixed overhead: 7500 labour hours (1500 chairs × 5 hours) × $2.00/hour = $15 000 | Applied fixed overhead: 8000 labour hours (1600 chairs × 5 hours) × $2.00 = $16 000 |

Budget (spending) variance $1000 U

Volume variance $1000

EXHIBIT 13.12 Fixed overhead variances

✻ volume variance
The difference between the flexible budget amount and the fixed overhead applied to products.

The **volume variance** is the difference between the flexible budget amount and the amount of fixed overhead *applied* to products. Overhead is applied by multiplying the predetermined overhead rate (for fixed overhead) by the standard hours (or budgeted hours) allowed to complete the actual units produced.

Key formula 13.4: Fixed overhead budget

Fixed overhead budget (spending) variance =
Actual fixed overhead – Budgeted fixed overhead

Key formula 13.5: Fixed overhead volume variance

Fixed overhead volume variance =
Budgeted fixed overhead – Applied fixed overhead

A company using variable (direct) costing rather than absorption (full) costing treats fixed overhead as a period cost and expenses it immediately (see Chapter 3). In these companies, there will not be a fixed overhead volume variance, because fixed overhead is not 'applied' to products. It is simply expensed in the period incurred.

Fixed overhead variances for Corinne's Country Rocking Chairs are calculated in Exhibit 13.12. The predetermined fixed overhead rate is $2 per labour hour ($15 000 budgeted fixed overhead divided by 7500 budgeted labour hours [1500 budgeted units × 5 hours per unit]). Applied fixed overhead is $16 000 ($2 predetermined overhead rate × 8000 hours [1600 actual units × 5 hours per unit]).

The spending variance is unfavourable because Corinne's spent more on fixed overhead items than the company had

budgeted. As you can see, the volume variance is simply a result of Corinne's manufacturing more chairs than budgeted (1600 instead of 1500). Everything else in the comparison of budgeted and applied overhead is the same. The fixed overhead volume variance is calculated primarily as a method of reconciling the amount of overhead applied to products under an absorption costing system with the amount of overhead actually incurred – and, consequently, the over- or underapplied overhead. The total amount of the variable overhead spending variance, variable overhead efficiency variance, fixed overhead spending variance, and fixed overhead volume variance will equal the company's over- or underapplied overhead for a period.

For Corinne's, manufacturing overhead was overapplied by $280 for the quarter. Actual overhead cost was $39 720 and consisted of variable overhead of $23 720 (Exhibit 13.10) and fixed overhead of $16 000 (Exhibit 13.12). Applied overhead was $40 000 and consisted of variable overhead of $24 000 (Exhibit 13.10) and fixed overhead of $16 000 (Exhibit 13.12). The $280 difference is the sum of Corinne's $1480 favourable variable overhead spending variance, $1200 unfavourable variable overhead efficiency variance, $1000 unfavourable fixed overhead spending variance, and $1000 fixed overhead volume variance.

The fixed overhead volume variance generally should not be interpreted as favourable or unfavourable and should not be interpreted as a measure of over- or underutilisation of facilities. This misinterpretation can be particularly problematic when the applied overhead is smaller than the budgeted amount (when a company produces fewer products than budgeted). Companies may reduce production for a number of reasons, including reduced demand for products, temporary material or labour shortages, and so on.

A summary table of the variances discussed in this chapter with references and formulas is shown in Exhibit 13.13.

Variance	Reference	Formula
Flexible budget variance	Exhibit 13.3; page 207	Flexible Budget – Actual Results
Sales price variance	Exhibit 13.4; page 207	(Actual – Expected Sales Price) × Actual Volume
Direct material price variance	Exhibit 13.7; page 210	Actual Quantity × (Actual Price – Standard Price)
Direct material usage variance	Exhibit 13.7; page 210	Standard Price × (Actual Quantity – Standard Quantity)
Direct labour rate variance	Exhibit 13.9; page 211	Actual Hours × (Actual Rate – Standard Rate)
Direct labour efficiency variance	Exhibit 13.9; page 211	Standard Rate × (Actual Hours – Standard Hours)
Variable overhead spending variance	Exhibit 13.10; page 212	Actual Overhead – (Actual Hours × Standard Variable Rate)
Variable overhead efficiency variance	Exhibit 13.10; page 212	Standard Variable Rate × (Actual Hours – Standard Hours)
Fixed overhead spending variance	Exhibit 13.12; page 214	Actual Fixed Overhead – Budgeted Fixed Overhead
Fixed overhead volume variance	Exhibit 13.12; page 214	Budgeted Fixed Overhead – Applied Overhead

 EXHIBIT 13.13 Summary of variances

LEARNING OBJECTIVE 9 >>

Interpreting and using variance analysis

Although standard costs and variance analysis can be useful to managers attempting to diagnose organisational performance, they are most effective in stable companies with mature production environments characterised by a heavy reliance on direct labour. On the other hand, they may not be much help in rapidly changing companies, companies with flexible manufacturing systems (in which more than one product is manufactured on an assembly line), companies with heavily automated manufacturing processes, or companies that emphasise continuous improvement and reducing non-value-added activities in the production process. Although variance analysis may still be of value as a summary report for top management, it has a number of drawbacks when used in many modern manufacturing environments:

1   The information from variance analysis is likely to be too aggregated for operating managers to use. To be useful, material variances may need to be broken down into detail by specific product lines and even batches of product, and labour variances may need to be calculated for specific manufacturing cells.

2   The information from variance analysis is not timely enough to be useful to managers. As product life cycles are reduced, timely reporting is even more critical than in the past.

3   Traditional variance analysis of variable and fixed overhead provides little useful information for managers.

4   Traditional variance analysis focuses on cost control instead of product quality, customer service, delivery time,

and other non-financial measures of performance. These measures are discussed in more detail in Chapter 14.

Even in traditional and stable manufacturing environments, the effective use of variance analysis for control and performance purposes requires the proper application of 'management by exception' and careful interpretation of variances (including understanding their causes).

Management by exception

The proper application of 'management by exception' requires an understanding that it is neither necessary nor desirable to investigate all variances. If you think about it, it is likely that actual costs will always deviate from budgeted costs to some extent. Utility prices are affected by the weather, and prices of raw materials can change suddenly owing to shortages, surpluses, or new sources of competing products. Unexpected machine breakdowns affect the amount of time workers spend manufacturing products. Even fixed costs can differ from budgeted costs when rent is unexpectedly increased, new equipment is purchased, or insurance rates go up. Because of these random fluctuations, managers should generally investigate variances (favourable or unfavourable) that are material in amount and outside a normal acceptable range. Traditionally, materiality thresholds were often based on absolute size (investigate everything over $1000) or relative size (investigate everything over 10 per cent of the budgeted amount) or some combination of the two. Today, companies are more likely to use statistical techniques and to investigate variances that fall outside a 'normal' range of fluctuations. For example, companies may investigate variances that are more than two standard deviations from the mean. Regardless of materiality, trends in variances might also warrant investigation. For example, continually occurring and increasing material price variances might be vitally important to a restaurant regardless of their absolute size.

Interpreting favourable and unfavourable variances

Although we have referred to variances as favourable or unfavourable, these designations should not necessarily be interpreted as good or bad. In order to interpret variances, the underlying cause must be determined.

For example, consider a manager who is investigating an unfavourable direct labour efficiency variance. Although, on the surface, the unfavourable variance would seem to indicate a problem in worker efficiency, the real problem may be the combination of a workforce that is fixed in the short run and a lack of sufficient orders to keep workers busy. Companies may be reluctant to lay off workers for short periods of time when demand is unexpectedly reduced or other production problems make it difficult to keep them fully employed. It may be costly to rehire workers or they may find other jobs. As discussed elsewhere, this often makes direct labour a fixed cost in the short run.

Likewise, an unfavourable direct material usage variance generally points to a problem in production. However, further analysis might reveal that usage was high because of an unusual number of defective parts and that the large number of defective parts was a result of the purchasing manager buying materials of inferior quality. This problem becomes one of the purchasing manager buying inferior materials, not the production manager using excessive amounts of material. Note that in this case, even though the purchasing manager's action led to the unfavourable direct material usage variance, the material price variance itself would likely be favourable.

Identifying management's objectives is vitally important in deciding how to use and interpret variances. If the problem is one of insufficient orders and management is truly concerned about controlling costs, management must be careful not to use the direct labour efficiency variance for purposes of motivating and controlling the production supervisor. Although this conclusion may seem counterintuitive, put yourself in the shoes of the production supervisor. The production supervisor really has two options – either continue producing products to keep workers busy or have an unfavourable labour efficiency variance. But keeping workers busy has definite drawbacks. For example, building inventory levels is costly. Holding high levels of inventory results in additional costs of storage and insurance and can result in increased waste from theft and obsolescence.

In other situations, understanding whether the primary objective of management is cost control or producing a high-quality product is important. If cost control is paramount, an unfavourable direct material price variance might well be considered 'bad'; however, if management's objective is to provide a high-quality product, an unfavourable material price variance might be acceptable if the higher price is necessary to obtain high-quality materials.

Once managers are sure of the root cause(s) of a variance and have considered their own objectives in utilising variance analysis, they can intelligently consider options available to deal with the problem. For example, if management finds that an unfavourable direct labour efficiency variance is caused by a lack of customer orders and a workforce that is fixed in the short run, options may include accepting special orders, utilising the workers in other areas, utilising the time to train workers or to repair machinery and so on.

Behavioural considerations

As you have seen throughout this chapter, the use of standard costs and variance analysis, although useful for control and performance evaluation, can also cause dysfunctional behaviour among employees and management. The use of ideal standards can cause resentment among managers continually faced with 'unfavourable' variances. Some companies tie compensation to performance that is at least partly measured by variances. Even though this is likely to make managers aware of costs, it may have undesirable side effects. Too much emphasis on the direct material usage variance can cause production managers to increase production so as to appear efficient, causing inventories to rise above acceptable levels. By focusing on variances, a purchasing manager may be encouraged to purchase inferior products to make his or her performance appear better, even though the manager knows that the poor-quality material will cause problems in the production area. It is important to understand the root causes of variances and to assign responsibility accordingly. It is also important to remember that variance analysis provides just one measure of performance. The uses of other financial and non-financial measures of performance are discussed in Chapter 14.

Exercises

1 Standard costing LO1

Review the following incomplete statements about standard costing and related issues.

a   A(n) _____ standard allows for normal and efficient operations and takes into consideration typical production problems.

b   A budget for a single unit of a product is referred to as a(n) _____.

c   Managers must compare actual and budgeted results to control operations. This comparison process is generally called _____.

d   The _____ indicates how much a company should generally pay for the materials, labour, or overhead for a single unit of product.

e   _____ is often the key to effective variance analysis.

Required

Complete the above incomplete statements with the correct term from the list of terms provided (note that not all terms will be used): *variance analysis, ideal standard, practical standard, standard cost, standard price, management by exception, task analysis.*

2 Flexible budget preparation LO2

Garcia and Buffet, a local CPA firm, has budgeted $100 000 in fixed expenses per month for the tax department. It has also budgeted variable costs of $5 per tax return prepared for supplies, $35 per return for labour, and $10 per return for computer time. The firm expects revenue from tax return preparation to be $300 000, based on 2000 tax returns at $150 each. During the current month, 1850 tax returns were actually prepared, at an average fee of $147 each. Actual variable costs were $9100 for supplies, $65 000 for labour, and $18 000 for computer time. Actual fixed costs were $100 000.

Required

Prepare a flexible budget for the tax department of Garcia and Buffet for the current month.

3 Flexible budget variance LO3

Refer to the information in question 2 above.

Required

Compute the flexible budget variance for Garcia and Buffet.

4 Flexible budget preparation LO2

Pitt and Jolie Inc., an architectural firm, has budgeted $100 000 in fixed expenses. It has also budgeted variable costs of $25 per architectural drawing sheet (there are two sheets per drawing assignment), $90 per drawing assignment for staff architect costs, and $40 per drawing assignment for technological equipment depreciation. The firm expects revenues from drawings to be $600 000, based on 1500 drawing assignments at $400 each. During the current month, 1600 drawing assignments were actually prepared, at an average fee of $385 each. Actual variable costs were $85 000 for drawing sheets, $150 000 for labour, and $55 000 for technology depreciation. Actual fixed costs were $105 000.

Required

Prepare a flexible budget for Pitt and Jolie Inc., for the current month.

5 Flexible budget variance LO3

Refer to the information in question 4 above.

Required

Compute the flexible budget variance for Pitt and Jolie, Inc.

6 Sales price variance LO3

The Quick Brick Shop had an unfavourable sales price variance of $150. The budgeted selling price was $10 per unit and 50 bricks were sold.

Required

What was the actual selling price of Quick Brick's bricks?

7 Direct materials price and usage variances LO5

Wheeler Corporation produces and sells special eyeglass straps for sporting enthusiasts. In 2011, the company budgeted for production and sales of 1200 straps. However, the company produced and sold just 1100 straps. Each strap has a standard requiring one metre of material at a budgeted cost of $1.50 per metre and two hours of assembly time at a cost of $12 per hour. Actual costs for the production of 1100 items were $1435.50 for materials (990 metres at $1.45 per metre) and $29 161 for labour (2420 hours at $12.05 per hour).

Required

a   Calculate the direct material price variance.

b   Calculate the direct material usage variance.

8 Labour rate and efficiency variances LO6

Refer to the information in question 5 above.

Required

a   Calculate the direct labour rate variance.

b   Calculate the direct labour efficiency variance.

9 Variable overhead spending and efficiency variances LO7

Hennings Travel Company specialises in the production of travel items (for example, clocks, personal care kits). The following data were prepared so that a variance analysis could be performed.

Forecast data (expected capacity)	
Direct labour hours	40 000
Estimated overhead:	
Fixed	$16 000
Variable	$30 000

Actual results	
Direct labour hours	37 200
Overhead:	
Fixed	$16 120
Variable	$28 060

The number of standard hours allowed for actual production was 37 000 hours.

Required

a Calculate the variable overhead spending variance.
b Calculate the variable overhead efficiency variance.

10 Fixed overhead volume and spending variances LO8

Refer to the information in question 9 above.

Required

a Calculate the fixed overhead volume variance.
b Calculate the fixed overhead spending variance.

11 Drawbacks of variance analysis LO9

Variance analysis allows managers to compare budgeted and actual performance so that necessary corrective steps can be taken. Frequently, the analysis helps managers identify operational inefficiencies and other areas that can be improved. Nonetheless, variance analysis does have several potential drawbacks.

Required

Describe the various drawbacks of variance analysis.

Problems

12 Standard costing LO1

Petty Petroleum, Inc., uses various chemicals to manufacture its products. Variance data for last month for the three primary chemicals used in production are shown below (F indicates a favourable variance; U indicates an unfavourable variance):

	X42	AY8	9BZ
Material price variance	$84 000 F	$50 000 F	$42 000 U
Material usage variance	80 000 U	60 000 U	96 000 U
Total materials variance (net)	$4 000 F	$10 000 U	$138 000 U
Products requiring this chemical	200 000	220 000	250 000

The standard required 1 kg of chemical for each product requiring the specific chemical. Because of falling prices in the chemical industry, Petty Petroleum generally paid less for chemicals last month than in previous months. Specifically, the average price paid was $0.40 per kg less than standard for chemical X42; it was $0.20 less for chemical AY8; and it was $0.14 greater for chemical 9BZ. All of the chemicals purchased last month were also used during the month.

Required

a For chemical X42, calculate the number of kilograms of material purchased, the standard cost per kilogram of material, and the total standard material cost.

b For chemical AY8, calculate the number of kilograms of material purchased, the standard cost per kilogram of material, and the total standard material cost.

c For chemical 9BZ, calculate the number of kilograms of material purchased, the standard cost per kilogram of material, and the total standard material cost.

13 Comprehensive variance analysis LO2, 3

Byrd Company is a manufacturer affiliated with the furniture industry. The company produces a wide variety of 'hardware' component parts. Product examples include drawer slides, hinges, door pulls and handles, springs and locks. Dent Tripoli is the company's new chief financial officer. Dent is very concerned with providing the company's president and board of directors with accurate financial reports. He is concerned that the company's use of static budgeting does not convey a fair presentation of the company's performance. The following contribution margin format income statement reports the results of Byrd Company's operations for the last quarter of 2011.

Sales revenues (400 000 units)		$2 440 000
Variable costs		
Manufacturing	$1 060 000	
Marketing and administrative	748 000	1 808 000
Contribution margin		$ 632 000
Fixed costs		
Manufacturing	$ 400 000	
Marketing and administrative	200 000	600 000
Operating profit		$ 32 000

Byrd's 2011 budgets were based on production and sales of 375 000 units at an average selling price of $6. At that volume, variable manufacturing costs were budgeted to be $2.50 per unit, and variable marketing and administrative costs were budgeted to be $2.00 each. Had the company's actual performance equalled the budgeted performance, Byrd would have reported operating profit of $62 500.

Required

a Based on the information provided in the problem, recreate Byrd's 2011 static budget. Be sure to include a comparison between the static budget and the actual results for the year.

b Based on the information provided in the problem, prepare a flexible budget for Byrd for 2011. Be sure to include a comparison between the flexible budget and the actual results that report the flexible budget variance.

c Calculate Byrd's sales price variance for 2011. Is the variance favourable or unfavourable?

14 Comprehensive variance analysis LO3, 4, 5, 6

Timmer Bachman founded the Bachman Corporation over 25 years ago. The company's genesis was the unique climbing apparatus developed by Timmer, an avid mountain climber. Bachman Corporation has continued to produce that first product, but it has now diversified into other outdoor activity equipment as well. In fact, the vast majority of the company's revenues are now accounted for by non-climbing product sales. Timmer is considering whether his company should continue producing and selling some of its oldest products, all of which relate to mountain climbing.

To begin his decision-making process, Timmer has asked the company's controller, Marin Hennesy, to accumulate data on the original locking karabiner that set the company on its way. Accordingly, Marin accumulates the following data for last year:

- Budgeted production and sales: 5000 karabiners
- Actual production and sales: 6000 karabiners
- The standard for a karabiner requires 1.5 kg of material at a budgeted cost of $1.52 per kg and two hours of assembly and testing time at a cost of $12.50 per hour
- The karabiner sells for $32 each
- Actual production costs for the 6000 karabiners totalled $12 900 for 8600 kg of materials and $161 700 for 13 200 labour hours.

Required

a What was the budgeted contribution margin per karabiner?
b What was the actual contribution margin per karabiner?
c What was Bachman's flexible budget variance?
d What was Bachman's direct material price variance?
e What was Bachman's direct material usage variance?
f What was Bachman's direct labour rate variance?
g What was Bachman's direct labour efficiency variance?
h What would the sales price variance be if each karabiner sold for $33?
i Based on the available information, should Bachman continue making the karabiner?

15 Variable and fixed overhead variances
LO7, 8

Surfs Up manufactures surf boards on Bondi Beach. The company's founder Danny Johnson has an accounting degree from the University of New South Wales. He understands the importance of standards for production control and planning. The following standard costing data are available for the current period:

Actual fixed overhead	$10 500
Actual variable overhead	66 810
Budgeted fixed overhead	11 000
Variable overhead rate per labour hour	5.00
Fixed overhead rate per labour hour	0.80
Standard hours allowed for actual production	13 100
Actual labour hours used	13 000

Required

a Calculate the variable overhead spending variance.
b Calculate the variable overhead efficiency variance.
c Calculate the fixed overhead spending variance.
d Calculate the fixed overhead volume variance.

16 Variable and fixed overhead variances
LO7, 8

Brilliant Lipsticks manufactures a range of exotic lipsticks for high end consumers. The company's founder Brynne Lipman identifies a set of standards surrounding overhead costs that she'd like the company to adhere to. The standard cost data is given below:

Budgeted fixed overhead	10 000
Budgeted variable overhead rate per labour hour	6.00
Budgeted fixed overhead rate per labour hour	1.00
Standard hours allowed for actual production	10 000
Actual labour hours used in production	10 200

At the conclusion of the period, Brynne noted that the actual variable overhead for the period was $65 000 and the actual fixed overhead cost for the period was $15 000.

Required
Calculate all relevant overhead variances based on the above information.

Case

17 Comprehensive variance analysis with behavioural issues LO1, 5, 6, 7, 8, 9

Jan Dan, Inc. (JDI), is a specialty frozen-food processor located in the southeastern United States. Since its founding in 1992, JDI has enjoyed a loyal local clientele that is willing to pay premium prices for the high-quality frozen foods it prepares from specialised recipes. In the past two years, the company experienced rapid sales growth in its operating region and had many inquiries about supplying its products on a national basis. To meet this growth, JDI expanded its processing capabilities, resulting in increased production and distribution costs. Moving onto the national scene also caused JDI to encounter pricing pressure from competitors outside its region.

Because JDI wants to continue expanding, Nick Guice, the company's chief executive officer, engaged a consulting firm to assist in determining JDI's best course of action. The consulting firm concluded that premium pricing is sustainable in some areas, but if sales growth is to be achieved, JDI must make price concessions in other areas. Also, to maintain profit margins, costs must be reduced and more tightly controlled. The consulting firm recommended the implementation of a standard cost system that would facilitate a flexible budgeting system to better accommodate the changes in demand that can be expected when serving an expanding market area.

Janie Morgan, purchasing manager, advised the management team that expanded production would necessitate obtaining basic food supplies from companies other than JDI's traditional sources. This in turn would entail increased raw material and shipping costs and might result in lower quality supplies. Consequently, these increased costs will need to be counter-balanced by reduced costs in the processing department if current cost levels are to be maintained or reduced.

Dan Walters, processing manager, suggested that the need to accelerate processing cycles to increase production, coupled with the possibility of receiving lower grade supplies, could be expected to result in poorer quality and a greater product rejection rate. Under these circumstances, per-unit labour utilisation cannot be maintained or increased and forecasting future unit labour content becomes very difficult. Corinne Kelly, production engineer, advised that if the equipment is not properly maintained and thoroughly cleaned at prescribed daily intervals, it can be anticipated that the quality and unique taste of the frozen-food product will be affected. Kent Jackson, vice-president of sales, stated that if quality cannot be maintained, JDI cannot expect to increase sales to the levels projected.

When Guice was apprised of the problems enumerated by his management team, he advised the team members that if agreement could not be reached on appropriate standards, he would arrange to have the standards set by the consulting firm and everyone would have to live with the results.

Required

a Identify those who should participate in setting standards, and describe the benefits of their participation in the standard-setting process.

b Explain the general features and characteristics associated with the introduction and operation of a standard cost system that make it an effective tool for cost control.

c What could be the consequences if Nick Guice has the standards set by the consulting firm?

d Explain overhead variances in the context of this case. Include a discussion of variable and fixed overhead variances.

> I think this book is totally cutting-edge...it's making learning fun again.
> - Scotty Willamson, student.

LEARNING, YOUR WAY.

ACCT was designed for students just like you – busy people who want choices, flexibility, and multiple learning options.

ACCT delivers concise, focussed information in a fresh and contemporary format. And... **ACCT** gives you a variety of online learning materials designed with you in mind.

At **http://login.cengagebrain.com/** you'll find electronic resources such as audio downloads and online flash cards for each chapter. These resources will help supplement your understanding of core organisational behaviour concepts in a format that fits your busy lifestyle.

Visit **http://login.cengagebrain.com/** to learn more about the multiple **ACCT** resources available to help you succeed!

Learning objectives:

After studying the material in this chapter, you should be able to:

1   Describe the structure and management of decentralised organisations and evaluate the benefits and drawbacks of decentralisation.

2   Evaluate how responsibility accounting is used to help manage a decentralised organisation.

3   Define cost, revenue, profit and investment centres and explain why managers of each must be evaluated differently.

4   Compute and interpret segment margin in an organisation.

5   Compute, interpret and compare return on investment (ROI) and residual income.

6   Describe the balanced scorecard and its key dimensions.

7   Define quality costs and explain the trade-offs among prevention costs, appraisal costs, internal failure costs and external failure costs.

8   Recognise the importance of using incentives to motivate managers and discuss the advantages and disadvantages of using cash-based, stock-based and other forms of managerial compensation.

DECENTRALISATION AND MODERN PERFORMANCE MANAGEMENT SYSTEMS – THE BALANCED SCORECARD

c **14**

Source: iStockphoto/Aeya

As the CEO of a chain of local retail shoe stores, you would be responsible for all aspects of your company's performance – from purchasing shoes to setting prices to investing in new fixtures or even to expanding operations by opening new stores. Consequently, your performance should be evaluated on the basis of all these factors – the costs incurred, the revenue generated and the investment made in the company. Contrast the responsibilities of the CEO of the company to the responsibilities of a manager of a specific store. As the store manager, you are likely to have some authority over setting prices of shoes, but purchasing decisions are made for the entire chain. Likewise, although you are likely to have some responsibility for making improvements to your store, major renovations and expansions can be made only with the approval of the CEO. Obviously, it would not be fair to the store manager to evaluate his or her performance based on the profit earned by the entire chain. In addition, it would probably not be appropriate to evaluate the store manager's performance based on the profit of his or her store, as a major component of the costs (the costs of shoes sold) is out of the store manager's control. In general, managers should be held responsible for only those things over which they have control. The challenge for companies is to find tools that allow the evaluation of managers at all levels in the organisation – from a plant manager in a factory to the manager of a retail store to the regional sales manager to the CEO.

LEARNING OBJECTIVE **1** >>

Management of decentralised organisations

In the late 1990s, in an effort to react more quickly to changing market conditions, Ford Motor Company reorganised its senior management by shifting authority to its regional operations. Under the new structure, Ford's regional and brand executives were given more authority in deciding what types of cars and trucks to manufacture and how to market them. In essence, Ford decentralised its operations.

A **decentralised organisation** is one in which decision-making authority is spread throughout the organisation as opposed to being confined to top-level management. When a few individuals at the top of an organisation retain decision-making authority, the organisation is referred to as centralised. In a decentralised environment, managers at various levels throughout the organisation make key decisions about operations relating to their specific areas of responsibility. These areas are called segments. Segments can be branches, divisions, departments or individual products. Any activity or part of the business for which a manager needs

Evaluating performance of a retail store requires a consideration of responsibility accounting.

cost, revenue or profit data can be considered a segment. Reporting financial and other information by segments is called segment reporting. This chapter discusses segment reporting and cost control and performance evaluation issues in segments of decentralised organisations.

Decentralisation varies from organisation to organisation. Most organisations are decentralised to some degree. At one end of the spectrum, managers are given complete authority to make decisions at their level of operations. At the other extreme, managers have little, if any, authority to make decisions. Most firms will fall somewhere in the middle. However, the tendency is to move toward more, rather than less, decentralisation.

❖ **decentralised organisation**

An organisation in which decision-making authority is spread throughout the organisation.

Benefits of decentralisation

There are several benefits to decentralisation:

- Generally, those closest to a problem are most familiar with the problem and its root causes. By pushing decision-making authority down to lower levels, managers most familiar with a problem have the opportunity to solve it.
- Top management has more time to devote to long-range strategic planning, as decentralisation removes the responsibility for much of the day-to-day decision making.
- Studies have shown that managers allowed to make decisions in a decentralised environment have higher job satisfaction than do managers in centralised organisations.
- Managers who are given increased responsibility for decision making early in their careers generally become better managers because of the on-the-job training they receive. In other words, experience is the best teacher.
- Decisions are often made in a more timely fashion.

Drawbacks of decentralisation

However, there can be drawbacks as well:

- When decision-making authority is spread among too many managers, a lack of company focus can occur. Managers may become so concerned with their own areas of responsibility that they lose sight of the big picture. Because of this lack of focus on the company as a whole, managers may tend to make decisions benefiting their own segments, which may not always be in the best interest of the company.
- Managers may not be adequately trained in decision making at the early stages of their careers. The costs of training managers can be high, and the potential costs of bad decisions while new managers are being trained should be considered.
- There may be a lack of coordination and communication between segments.
- Decentralisation may make it difficult to share unique and innovative ideas.
- Decentralisation may result in duplicative efforts and duplicative costs.

Decentralised organisations require well-developed and well-integrated information systems. The flow of information and open communication between divisions and upper and lower management is critical. This can be a problem for companies whose systems do not provide the kind of quantitative and qualitative information needed at the segment level. For this reason, the use of enterprise resource planning (ERP) systems has been particularly helpful in decentralised organisations.

LEARNING OBJECTIVE **2** >>

Responsibility accounting and segment reporting

The key to effective decision making in a decentralised organisation is **responsibility accounting** – holding managers responsible for only those things under their control. In reality, the amount of control a manager has can vary greatly from situation to situation. For example, 75 per cent of the shoes offered for sale at the shoe department of a store may be purchased by a regional purchasing manager in order to obtain quantity-purchase discounts from suppliers. Only 25 per cent are purchased at the discretion of the individual store managers. In this case, since a local manager does not control the quantity or style of most of the shoes in his or her store or how much was paid for them, that manager should not be held responsible for the cost of shoes purchased and the profit earned on shoe sales in the store.

In the previous chapter, variance analysis was used to help evaluate the performance of managers by focusing on who had responsibility for a variance. Usage variances were typically the responsibility of production managers and price variances were typically the responsibility of purchasing managers. However, as you will recall, general rules like this must be used with caution. For example, the purchasing manager might be responsible for a usage variance if low-quality materials contributed to excessive waste.

In decentralised organisations, detailed information is needed to evaluate the effectiveness of managerial decision making. Companywide budgets, cost standards, profit and loss statements and so on are not sufficient to evaluate the performance of each of a company's segments. For example, overall financial statements generated for external reporting purposes would be of limited use in evaluating the performance of the numerous managers at Ford Australia's car manufacturing plant in Victoria. The manager of the Ford Falcon car division should be evaluated just on the results of that division, while the manager of the Ford Territory division should be evaluated just on the results of that division. Going down a step further, a production manager dealing only with the manufacture of the Ford Territory Ghia and a production manager who works only with the Ford Territory base model should be evaluated using different information. Even within a product line, managers

> ❋ **responsibility accounting**
> An accounting system that assigns responsibility to a manager for those areas that are under that manager's control.

should be held responsible only for those things under their control. A manager on an engine assembly line should not be evaluated and held responsible for a production problem dealing with the vehicle body. Plant managers should be evaluated based on activities in their plant, regional sales managers should be held responsible for sales in their region and so on.

LEARNING OBJECTIVE **3** >>

Cost, revenue, profit and investment centres

To enhance the use of responsibility accounting for decision making, organisations typically identify the different segments, or levels of responsibility, as cost, revenue, profit or investment centres and attach different levels of responsibility to each segment (see Exhibit 14.1).

Cost centres

A **cost centre** manager has control over costs but not over revenue or capital investment (long-term purchasing) decisions. The purchasing manager of a store, the production manager for a particular type of DVD player, the maintenance manager in a hotel and the human resources manager of a CPA firm would likely be considered managers of cost centres. The manager of a cost centre should be evaluated on how well he or she controls costs in the respective segment. Consequently, performance reports typically focus on differences between budgeted and actual costs using variance analysis. A **performance report** provides key financial and non-financial measures of performance appropriate for a particular segment.

Revenue centres

A **revenue centre** manager has control over the generation of revenue but not costs. Examples include the sales manager of a retail store, the sales department of a production facility and the reservations department of an airline. Performance reports of a revenue centre often focus on sales price variances (discussed in Chapter 13).

Profit centres

A **profit centre** manager has control over both cost and revenue but not capital investment decisions. While the purchasing manager of a retail store is a cost centre manager, the overall manager of the store will probably be a profit centre manager. Likewise, the manager of an entire product line in a factory, the manager of a particular location of a hotel chain and the partner in charge of the tax department at a CPA firm would be considered profit centre managers. It is important to understand that profit centre managers still do not have control over decisions to invest in and purchase new property, plant and equipment. For example, the profit centre managers described here could not make decisions to remodel a store, buy new manufacturing equipment, add a swimming pool to a hotel or open a new office.

The manager of a profit centre should be evaluated on both revenue generation and cost control. Consequently, performance reports typically focus on profit measures, such as the overall flexible budget variance (discussed in Chapter 13). The flexible budget variance is the difference between the actual and budgeted operating profit. However, this can be a problem when uncontrollable fixed costs are included in the analysis. Segment managers should be held responsible for only those costs under their control. Consequently, other measures of profit centre performance, such as segment margin (discussed on page 228), are also commonly used.

***

❉ cost centre
An organisational segment, or division, in which the manager has control over costs but not over revenue or investment decisions.

❉ performance report
Provides key financial and non-financial measures of performance for a particular segment.

❉ revenue centre
An organisational segment, or division, in which the manager has control over revenue but not costs or investment decisions.

❉ profit centre
An organisational segment, or division, in which the manager has control over both costs and revenue but not investment decisions.

***

Cost centre	Revenue centre	Profit centre	Investment centre
Responsible for costs only	Responsible for revenue only	Responsible for costs and revenues	Responsible for profit and investments in property, plant and equipment

EXHIBIT 14.1 Responsibility levels at cost, revenue, profit and investment centres

Investment centres

In addition to being responsible for a segment's revenue and expenses, an **investment centre** manager is responsible for the amount of cash and other assets invested in generating its profit. An investment centre is in essence a separate business with its own value chain. Consequently, investment centres are frequently referred to as **strategic business units (SBUs)**. An investment centre manager is involved in decisions ranging from research and development to production to marketing and sales and customer service. Large international companies may have several core businesses operating as investment centres or SBUs.

Although the manager of an investment centre can be evaluated using some of the same tools as profit centres, the amount of assets or investment under the manager's control must also be considered. Measures of performance for investment centres are discussed later in the chapter.

Large firms with complex practices particularly benefit from modern cost allocation techniques.

Source: Agencja Fotograficzna Caro/Alamy

LEARNING OBJECTIVE 4 >>

Profit centre performance and segmented profit and loss statements

Segmented profit and loss statements calculate profit for each major segment of an organisation in addition to the company as a whole. Although it is usually easy to keep records of sales by segment, tracing costs to a particular segment and deciding how to treat costs that benefit more than one segment can be very difficult.

Variable costs are generally traced directly to a segment. Remember, variable costs vary in direct proportion to sales volume. Therefore, they can be allocated to a segment based on sales volume.

Deciding which fixed costs to assign, or allocate, to a segment requires an analysis of the overall company and the individual areas of responsibility (segments) within an organisation. **Segment costs** should include *all* costs

attributable to that segment but *only* those costs that are actually caused by the segment. Fixed costs that can be easily and conveniently traced to a segment should obviously be assigned to that segment. The problem is that many fixed costs are indirect in nature. Should indirect fixed costs be allocated to segments? A good test for deciding whether to allocate indirect fixed costs is to determine whether the cost would be reduced or eliminated if the segment were eliminated. If the cost cannot be reduced or eliminated, it is referred to as a common cost. **Common costs** are indirect costs that are incurred to benefit more than one segment and cannot be directly traced to a particular segment or allocated in a reasonable manner based on what causes the cost to be incurred. In general, common costs should not be allocated to segments for purposes of performance evaluation.

For example, ANZ Bank (headquartered in Melbourne, Victoria) has at least four branches within a 2-km radius in the Melbourne CBD. One of those branches is located in William Street. Let's hypothetically assume that the William Street branch incurs a fixed lease expense to rent the building in which the bank is located. Obviously, this lease expense is directly traceable to the individual branch (a segment) and should be allocated to that segment. However, if there is a lease expense for the corporate headquarters building in Collins Street, you might consider some part of that cost might have to be indirectly absorbed by the William Street branch. However, it is doubtful that the lease expense for the headquarters building would be reduced or eliminated if the William Street branch were eliminated. Therefore, from a performance management perspective, it is probably best treated as a common cost and not allocated to the segment. In practice, companies sometimes allocate common costs from headquarters to segments without using them for evaluation purposes. This practice has the advantage of making the segment manager aware that the cost is being incurred and that the cost must ultimately be paid for by revenue generated by the segment.

Other indirect costs can be allocated to segments if there is a sufficient causal relationship between the cost and the segment. For example, all loan processing for ANZ Bank might be done in the headquarters building in Collins Street. Although these costs (for credit checks, loan processing, staff salaries and so on) may be difficult to directly trace to the William Street branch, they can be allocated in a manner that reflects the cause of the costs (the number of loans processed, the dollar amount of loans processed and so on). In addition, it is reasonable to assume that at least some of the loan processing costs would be reduced or eliminated if the branch were closed, as there would arguably be fewer loans to process if there was one less branch in the Melbourne CBD.

To allocate indirect costs, there should be a causal relationship between the allocation base and a segment's use of the common cost. Allocating costs using an arbitrary allocation base is inappropriate. Although ANZ Bank could allocate the lease cost of the headquarters building to its branches based on an allocation base, such as square metreage or total deposits, such a base would be completely arbitrary. There is no causal relationship between the square metreage or total deposits in a branch and the lease expense in the headquarters building. Arbitrary allocations like this may result in a profitable segment appearing unprofitable and may lead to less-than-optimal decisions concerning that segment.

Divisions

Smith and Chang is a full-service local CPA firm offering services in three departments: tax, audit and consulting. The tax department is further broken down into individual and business divisions. Smith and Chang has annual client billings of $1 million, with 50 per cent generated from the tax department, 40 per cent from the audit department and the remaining 10 per cent from the consulting department. The accompanying table shows a segmented profit and loss statement broken down into three segments based on the three practice departments.

The $100000 of fixed costs traceable to the tax department include advertising specifically geared to the tax department, the salary of the tax manager, the costs of research material used in the tax library and computer software used for tax preparation. Common fixed costs (for the firm as a whole) include salaries of

Segmented profit and loss statement				
		(Segments defined as departments)		
	Total firm	Tax department	Audit department	Consulting department
Client billings	$1 000 000	$500 000	$400 000	$100 000
Less: Variable expenses	400 000	200 000	160 000	40 000
Contribution margin	$ 600 000	$300 000	$240 000	$ 60 000
Less: Traceable fixed expenses	200 000	100 000	75 000	25 000
Segment margin	$ 400 000	$200 000	$165 000	$ 35 000
Less: Common fixed expenses	200 000			
Net profit	$ 200 000			

the managing partner of the firm, human resources manager and receptionist, and the depreciation of the office building.

In the following table, Smith and Chang goes a step further and provides a segmented profit and loss statement for the two divisions within the tax department. Note that the statements are based on the contribution margin format introduced in Chapter 9. The primary differences are the separation of fixed costs into traceable fixed costs and common fixed costs and the interim calculation of segment margin.

Segmented profit and loss statement			
	(Segments defined as divisions)		
	Tax department	Individual tax division	Business tax division
Client billings	$500 000	$100 000	$400 000
Less: Variable expenses	200 000	80 000	120 000
Contribution margin	$300 000	$ 20 000	$280 000
Less: Traceable fixed expenses	80 000	30 000	50 000
Divisional segment margin	$220 000	$(10 000)	$230 000
Less: Common fixed expenses	20 000		
Departmental segment margin	$200 000		

Note that although $100000 of fixed costs were traced to the tax department in the first table (when segments were defined as departments), only $80000 are subsequently traced to the individual and business divisions; $20000 of traceable costs have become common costs. In this case, the advertising costs for the tax division and the cost of research materials in the tax library cannot be traced directly to either the individual or the business division.

As discussed in Chapter 9, contribution margin is primarily a measure of short-run profitability, as it ignores fixed costs. It is used extensively in short-run decisions, such as CVP analysis and evaluation of special orders. On the other hand, **segment margin** is a measure of long-term profitability and is more appropriate in addressing long-term decisions, such as whether to drop product lines.

In the case of Smith and Chang, the segment margin of the tax department is positive, but the segment margin of the individual tax division is negative. In the long run, the individual tax division is not profitable. However, before the firm decides to eliminate the individual tax division, it should consider other factors (both quantitative and qualitative), including the impact on its highly profitable business tax division.

For example, it may be important for the firm to be perceived as a full-service firm where owners of small businesses can come for help with all their tax and business problems. In addition, planning for a small business must often be integrated with planning for the individual owner of the business. For these reasons, the firm may decide to retain the division even if it has not been profitable. Instead of eliminating the division, Smith and Chang may decide to focus on ways to make the division profitable through expanding the array of services offered to clients. For example, the firm may begin offering personal financial planning services to its clients to help them meet their overall financial goals.

LEARNING OBJECTIVE **5** >>

Investment centres and measures of performance

Case

In addition to being responsible for a segment's revenue and expenses, an investment centre manager is responsible for the amount of capital invested in generating its profit. Investment centre managers can make capital purchasing decisions, including decisions to remodel facilities, purchase new equipment, expand facilities or add new locations. Investment centres are typically major divisions or branch operations of a company involved in all aspects of the value chain. In addition to using the approaches discussed earlier for cost and profit centres, evaluating investment centres requires focusing on the level of investment needed to generate a segment's profit. For this reason, performance reports focus on measures specifically developed for this purpose – return on investment and residual income.

Managers of investment centres are given complete control over all activities in their respective segments. Managers want to be associated with well-run, profitable divisions. Competition between investment centre managers within an organisation is sometimes intense. Because of compensation issues, such as year-end bonuses based on performance, managers of investment centres must also be evaluated. Although all the financial measures of performance used in evaluating the managers of cost, revenue and profit centres apply to investment centre managers, they are not sufficient.

To some extent, controlling costs and generating revenue is a function of the amount of assets under a manager's control. For example, if a manager had unlimited assets and resources, production costs could be reduced by buying the most efficient manufacturing equipment available. Likewise, sales might be maximised by additional spending on advertising. Very large companies typically have higher revenue and higher profit than very small companies. However, the manager of an investment centre should not be evaluated with respect to the amount of costs, revenue, and profit generated without reference to the size of the investment centre being managed and the assets under the manager's control.

❋ **segment margin**
The profit margin of a particular segment of an organisation, typically the best measure of long-term profitability.

❋ **return on investment (ROI)**
Measures the rate of return generated by an investment centre's assets.

Return on investment

The DuPont Corporation was one of the first major organisations in the world to recognise that the performance of an investment centre must consider the level of investment along with the profit generated from that investment. **Return on investment (ROI)** measures the rate of return generated by an investment centre's assets.

ROI can be a very simple concept. For example, if you invest $1000 in a bank certificate of deposit for one year and receive $50 at the end of the year, your return on that investment is 5 per cent ($50 ÷ $1000). However, the calculation of return gets a little more complicated when the profit is reinvested in another certificate, the amount of assets change and costs are incurred to manage the money.

Margin and turnover

In business, the calculation of ROI is generally broken down into two components – a measure of operating performance (called margin) and a measure of how effectively assets are used during a period (called asset turnover). **Margin** is found by dividing an investment centre's net operating profit by its sales. As such, it can be viewed as the profit that is earned on each dollar of sales. A margin of 10 per cent indicates that 10 cents of every sales dollar is profit. **Asset turnover** is calculated by dividing an investment centre's sales by its average operating assets during a period. It measures the sales that are generated for a given level of assets.

The formula for return on investment (ROI) is as follows:

The elements comprising ROI are shown in graphical form in Exhibit 14.2.

Although various investment centres (including companies) may have similar ROIs, their margin and turnover may be very different. For example, a grocery store and a furniture store both have an ROI of 20 per cent. However, the grocery store's ROI may be made up of a profit margin of $0.02 per dollar of product sold and a turnover of 10, whereas the furniture store may have a margin of $0.10 per dollar of product sold and a turnover of 2. In this case, the grocery store does not make much from each dollar of sales but generates a lot of sales for the amount of its assets. On the other hand, the furniture store makes more from each sale but does not generate as many sales for the amount of assets under its control.

Net operating profit is most frequently used as the measure of profit in the ROI formula. **Net operating profit** is a measure of operating performance and is defined as profit before interest and taxes. Interest and taxes are typically omitted from the measure of profit in the ROI calculation because they may not be controllable by the manager of the segment being evaluated.

Likewise, the most common measure of investment is average operating assets. **Operating assets** typically include cash, accounts receivable, inventory and the property, plant and equipment needed to operate a business. Land and other assets held for resale or assets that are idle (a plant that is not being used) are typically not included in operating assets. Because profit is measured over time, assets are also generally measured as an average of beginning- and end-of-period numbers. By focusing on operating profit and average operating assets, ROI attempts to isolate the financial performance of a company's core operations.

Whereas cash, accounts receivable and inventory are generally easy to measure, the measurement of depreciable property, plant and equipment for purposes of determining

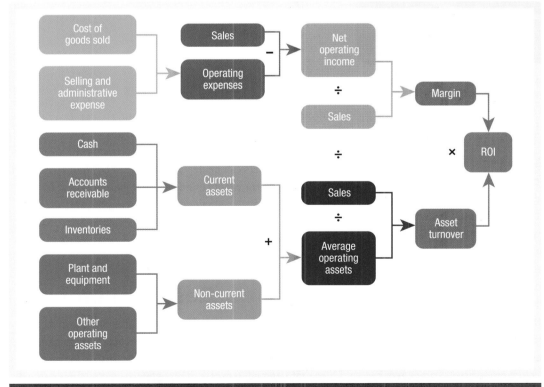

margin
For each sales dollar, the percentage that is recognised as net profit.

asset turnover
The measure of activity used in the ROI calculation; it measures the sales that are generated for a given level of assets.

net operating profit
Net profit from operations before interest and taxes.

operating assets
Typically include cash, accounts receivable, inventory and the property, plant and equipment needed to operate a business.

EXHIBIT 14.2 Elements of return on investment (ROI)

ROI poses some interesting questions. The use of net book value (the cost of the assets less accumulated depreciation) is consistent with the calculation of operating profit (which includes depreciation expense) but can have some undesirable consequences. For example, as an asset ages, the net book value of the asset decreases. Using net book value can cause ROI to increase over time simply because of the reduction in book value of assets used in the calculation. Choice of depreciation method can also affect ROI calculations. By choosing an accelerated method over straight-line, the book value of the asset decreases more rapidly, increasing ROI. Both of these factors may discourage managers from replacing old assets, such as manufacturing equipment. If managers are evaluated based on ROI, they may be very reluctant to replace ageing machinery with a very low book value with an expensive but more efficient piece of equipment.

The use of gross book value to measure operating assets eliminates age of an asset as a factor in the ROI calculation and any distortions that can be caused by the depreciation method chosen.

Source: Hal_P/Shutterstock

Depreciation methods can impact the perceived profitability of fixed assets replaced by newer assets.

Example

To illustrate the use of ROI, consider the financial results for Big Al's Pizza Emporium (see Exhibit 14.3). Last year, Big Al's had average operating assets of $100 000, consisting of cash, accounts receivable, inventory, and furniture and equipment at book value. Big Al's sales for the year were $350 000 (consisting of $275 000 for 23 000 pizzas and $75 000 for drinks and other side orders). The ROI for Big Al's, using the net book value method, would be 17.5 per cent, consisting of margin of 0.05 ($17 500 ÷ $350 000) and asset turnover of 3.5 ($350 000 ÷ $100 000).

If Al would like to increase ROI, what are his options? In general, sales can be increased, operating expenses can be reduced or the investment in operating assets can be reduced. The first two alternatives increase operating profit and the last option decreases net operating assets.

Increase sales volume or sales price

Sales revenue can be raised by either increasing sales volume without changing the sales price or by increasing the sales price without affecting volume. Remember that when sales volume increases, variable costs increase by the same proportional amount because variable costs stay the same per unit but increase in total as more units are sold. In addition, fixed costs remain the same. Thus, if sales volume increases by 5 per cent (resulting in sales revenue of $367 500), profit will increase by $5000, to $22 500. As shown in Exhibit 14.4, ROI will correspondingly increase to 22.5 per cent.

If Al just changes the price of his products, the analysis is a little different. Increasing sales prices (without a corresponding change in volume) does not affect variable costs or fixed costs. Thus, if revenue were increased by $17 500 because of a 5 per cent increase in sales price, profit would increase by the same $17 500. ROI would increase to 35 per cent ($35 000 ÷ $100 000).

Decrease operating costs

ROI can also be increased by decreasing operating costs. The decrease in costs can be concentrated in variable or fixed costs or both. The key is that any decrease in operating costs will increase operating profit and have a positive impact on ROI. In Exhibit 14.5, variable costs are reduced to $241 250 by using a different supplier for direct materials. Profit increases by $8750, resulting in an ROI of 26.25 per cent.

Decrease the amount of operating assets

The third way to increase ROI is to decrease the amount invested in operating assets. Although this may be difficult to do in the short run with property, plant and equipment, average operating assets can be decreased through better management of inventory. For example, let's assume that Big Al's reduces operating assets by 10 per cent by reducing the amount of materials kept in inventory. As shown in Exhibit 14.6, reducing average operating assets to $90 000 will increase ROI to 19.44 per cent.

✻ residual income
The amount of profit earned in excess of a predetermined minimum rate of return on assets.

Residual income

As an alternative to ROI, the manager of an investment centre can be evaluated on the basis of the residual income generated by the investment centre. **Residual income** is the amount of profit earned in excess of a predetermined minimum rate of return on assets. All other things being equal, the higher the residual income of an investment centre, the better.

Key formula 14.2: Residual income

Residual Income = Net operating profit − (Average operating assets × Minimum required rate of return)

Referring back to the original scenario in Exhibit 14.3 (average operating assets of $100 000 and net operating profit of $17 500), and assuming that Big Al's has a minimum required rate of return of 15 per cent, the residual income would be calculated as follows:

$$\$17\,500 - (\$100\,000 \times 15\%) = \$2500$$

If Big Al's increases sales to $367 500, net operating profit increases to $22 500 and ROI increases to 22.5 per cent (see Exhibit 14.4). Likewise, residual income will increase to $7500:

$$\$22\,500 - (\$100\,000 \times 15\%) = \$7500$$

If Big Al's decreases variable costs to $241 250, net operating profit increases to $26 250 and ROI increases to 26.25 per cent (see Exhibit 14.5). Under the new scenario, residual income would be $11 250:

$$\$26\,250 - (\$100\,000 \times 15\%) = \$11\,250$$

ROI vs residual income

In some cases, evaluating the performance of an investment centre and its manager using ROI can cause problems. For example, Al recently opened a second location and hired a new manager to run the business at the original location. Because the new location is substantially larger than the original location, he wants to devote his full attention to the successful start-up of the new location.

Currently, ROI at the original location is 25 per cent ($25 000 net operating profit and average operating assets of $100 000). Big Al's goal and minimum acceptable return for both locations is to maintain an ROI of 15 per cent. However, if the new manager is evaluated on the basis of the location's ROI, he may reject potential projects or investments that would be profitable (and earn a return greater than 15 per cent) but would lower the location's overall ROI.

As an example, the new manager is considering purchasing a new automated pizza oven that will reduce the time it takes to make a pizza and the electricity consumed. The equipment costs $15 000 and is expected to result in increased profit of $3200. Although the return on investment for this particular piece of equipment is over 21 per cent ($3200 ÷ $15 000), the manager is likely to reject the purchase because it will reduce his overall ROI from 25 per cent ($25 000 ÷ $100 000) to 24.5 per cent ($28 200 ÷ $115 000).

Note that using residual income avoids this problem. If the new manager has the opportunity to purchase a new pizza oven at a cost of $15 000 and expects that profits will increase by $3200, evaluating the new manager using

Sales revenue	$350 000
Variable costs	250 000
Contribution margin	$100 000
Fixed costs	82 500
Net operating profit	$ 17 500
Average operating assets	$100 000
ROI	$17 500 ÷ $100 000 = 17.5%

EXHIBIT 14.3 ROI with operating assets of $100 000 and sales of $350 000

Sales revenue	$367 500
Variable costs	262 500
Contribution margin	$105 000
Fixed costs	82 500
Net operating profit	$ 22 500
Average operating assets	$100 000
ROI	$22 500 ÷ $100 000 = 22.5%

EXHIBIT 14.4 ROI when sales increase to $367 500

Sales revenue	$350 000
Variable costs	241 250
Contribution margin	$108 750
Fixed costs	82 500
Net operating profit	$ 26 250
Average operating assets	$100 000
ROI	$26 250 ÷ $100 000 = 26.25%

EXHIBIT 14.5 ROI when variable costs are reduced to $241 250

Sales revenue	$350 000
Variable costs	250 000
Contribution margin	$100 000
Fixed costs	82 500
Net operating profit	$ 17 500
Average operating assets	$ 90 000
ROI	$17 500 ÷ $90 000 = 19.44%

EXHIBIT 14.6 ROI when operating assets are reduced to $90 000

residual income will encourage the manager to purchase the new oven. The residual income of the existing location will increase from $10 000 [$25 000 − ($100 000 × 15%)] to $10 950 [$28 200 − ($115 000 × 15%)].

In small business, the adoption of residual income methods can cause the streamlining of operations, catapulting growth in the business.

However, residual income is not without its own problems. Since it is an absolute measure, it should not be used to compare the performance of investment centres of different sizes. For example, Big Al's new location is considerably larger than the existing location. As shown in Exhibit 14.7, average operating assets in the new location total $300 000, compared to $100 000 in the existing location.

As demonstrated in Exhibit 14.7, the residual income of the new location (run by Al) is higher than the residual income of the existing location (run by the new manager). However, Al is not necessarily managing the new location better; it's just bigger. As you can see, the ROI of the new location is actually lower than the ROI of the existing location. Which measure is better? Both are useful but often for different purposes. Residual income is more useful as a performance measure for a single investment centre. On the other hand, since ROI is independent of size, it is better suited as a comparative measure.

Decentralisation and performance evaluation in a multinational company

Segments or divisions in a multinational company are often created along geographic lines. Frequently, Australian companies have subsidiaries that operate in other countries in the Asia Pacific region. Sometimes these subsidiaries are involved in manufacturing, but in other cases they may be responsible for marketing or distributing products and services in foreign countries. These foreign divisions may operate as cost, profit, revenue or investment centres.

	Existing location	New location
Average operating assets	$100 000	$300 000
Minimum required return	15%	15%
Net operating profit	$ 25 000	$ 70 000
Residual income	$ 10 000	$ 25 000
ROI	25%	23.3%

EXHIBIT 14.7 Return on investment and residual income

When responsibility centres are located in more than one country, the management style and decision-making structures used by the companies and the methods of performance evaluation employed by the companies must take into account differences in economic, legal and political, educational and cultural factors in the business environment of each country.

Economic factors include such things as the stability of the economy, whether a country is experiencing high inflation, the strength of underlying capital markets and the strength of the local currency. Legal and political factors include the degree of governmental control and regulation of business and the political stability of each country. Educational factors include the availability of an educated, adequately trained work force. Cultural factors may include such things as attitudes toward authority, work ethic, and loyalty and commitment to employers by employees and to employees by employers. Due to the unique challenges facing multinational companies as a result of these factors, there are often clear advantages to decentralising operations in a multinational company, including improving the quality and timeliness of decision making when done at the local level, and the minimisation of social, cultural, political and language barriers.

LEARNING OBJECTIVE **6** >>

Performance evaluation using the balanced scorecard

Traditional accounting measures of performance that rely on historical financial data are of little use in making decisions concerning customer satisfaction, quality issues, productivity, efficiency and employee satisfaction. Managers also need timely information concerning the success or failure of new products or marketing campaigns and the success of programs designed to enhance customer value. The **balanced**

✽ **balanced scorecard**

An approach to performance measurement that uses a set of financial and non-financial measures that relate to the overall strategy of the organisation.

scorecard approach to performance measurement uses a set of financial and non-financial measures that relate to the overall strategy of the organisation. By integrating financial and non-financial performance measures, the balanced scorecard helps to keep management focused on all of a company's critical success factors, not just its financial ones. The balanced scorecard also helps to keep short-term operating performance in line with long-term strategy.

As shown in Exhibit 14.8, utilising a balanced scorecard approach requires looking at performance from four different but related perspectives: financial, customer, internal business, and learning and growth.

Financial perspective

The primary goal of every profit-making enterprise is to show a profit. Profit allows the enterprise to provide a return on investment (ROI) to investors, to repay creditors and to adequately compensate management and employees. Critical success factors under this perspective include sales, costs, measures of profit such as operating profit and segment margin, and measures of investment centre performance such as ROI and residual income. However, under the balanced scorecard approach, financial performance is seen in the larger context of the company's overall goals and objectives relating to its customers and suppliers, internal processes and employees.

Customer perspective

Many successful businesses have found that focusing on customers and meeting or exceeding their needs is more important in the long run than simply focusing on financial measures of performance. After all, it is the customer who ultimately incurs the costs of producing products and contributes to a company's profits. Considering the customer perspective is therefore critical in attaining the financial goals of a company. Critical success factors under this perspective are likely to include increasing the quality of products and services, reducing delivery time and increasing customer satisfaction. Measures of performance appropriate under this perspective include the number of warranty claims and returned products (for quality), customer response time and the percentage of on-time deliveries (for reducing delivery time), and customer complaints and repeat business (for customer satisfaction).

A second dimension of the customer perspective focuses on the critical success factors of increasing market share and penetrating new markets. Measures of performance appropriate for this dimension include market share, market saturation, customer loyalty and new products introduced into the marketplace. Focusing on the customer perspective can result in impressive financial returns. For example, at Ford, a one percentage point increase in customer loyalty results in significant increases in sales and profits.

Internal business perspective

The internal business process perspective deals with objectives across the company's entire value chain: from research and development to post-sale customer service. It is linked to the financial perspective through its emphasis on improving the efficiency of manufacturing processes and to the customer perspective through its focus on improving processes and products to better meet customer needs. Every company will approach this perspective differently, as the processes that add value to products and services are likely to differ by company. However, critical success factors include productivity, manufacturing cycle time, throughput and manufacturing cycle efficiency (MCE).

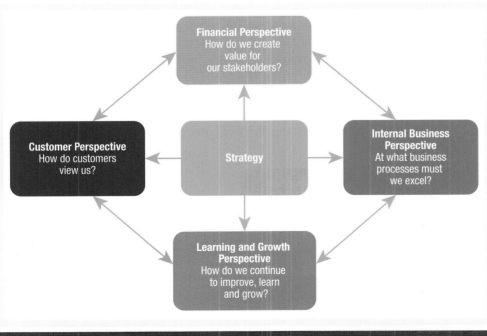

EXHIBIT 14.8 The balanced scorecard approach to performance measurement

Productivity

Productivity is a measure of the relationship between outputs and inputs. How many cars are produced per labour hour, how many loaves of bread are baked per bag of flour, how many calculators are produced per machine hour, how many customers are serviced per shift and how many sales dollars are generated per full-time sales clerk are all measures of productivity.

Manufacturing cycle time and throughput

✳ **productivity**
A measure of the relationship between outputs and inputs.

✳ **manufacturing cycle time**
The total time a product is in production, which includes process time, inspection time, wait time and move time; cycle time will include both value-added and non-value-added time.

✳ **throughput**
The amount of product produced in a given amount of time, such as a day, week or month.

✳ **manufacturing cycle efficiency (MCE)**
The value-added time in the production process divided by the throughput, or cycle time.

Manufacturing cycle time is the amount of time it takes to produce a defect-free unit of product from the time raw material is received until the product is ready to deliver to customers. In addition to actual processing time, cycle time includes time spent moving materials and products from one place to the next, time spent waiting for machine availability and time spent inspecting materials and finished goods. The concept of manufacturing cycle time is directly related to velocity, or throughput. Whereas manufacturing cycle time is the time required to produce a unit of product, **throughput** refers to the number of defect-free units that can be made in a given period of time. The shorter the manufacturing cycle time, the greater the throughput. Because manufacturing cycle time and throughput focus on the production of defect-free units, they are directly influenced by quality (see Exhibit 14.9). As such, you can view throughput and manufacturing cycle time as directly related to quality and productivity measures.

Manufacturing cycle efficiency (MCE)

MCE is the value-added time in the production process divided by the total manufacturing cycle time:

> **Key formula 14.3:** Manufacturing cycle efficiency (MCE)
>
> $$MCE = \frac{\text{Value-added time}}{\text{Manufacturing cycle time}}$$

Value-added time includes time spent in the actual manufacturing of a product (machining, assembly, painting and so on). Non-value-added time includes the time a product is waiting to move to the next step in the production process or time spent moving the product to the next step. Manufacturing cycle efficiency is a key measure of performance directly related to the customer service perspective as well as to the internal business perspective. By increasing MCE, customer response time is reduced, and non-value-added activities are reduced.

Learning and growth perspective

The learning and growth perspective links the critical success factors in the other perspectives and ensures an environment that supports and allows the objectives of the other three perspectives to be achieved. If learning improves, internal business processes will improve, leading to increased customer value and satisfaction and ultimately to better financial performance. Critical success factors centre on three areas. The first is the efficient and effective use of employees (employee empowerment). Measures include improving employee morale, increasing skill development, increasing employee satisfaction, reducing employee turnover and increasing the participation of employees in the decision process. The second critical success factor is increasing information systems capabilities through improving the availability and timeliness of information. The third critical success factor involves measures of product innovation, such as increasing the number of new products, new patents and so on. Exhibit 14.10 provides a summary of critical success factors within each of these perspectives.

EXHIBIT 14-9 High quality leads to low cycle time and high throughput

Perspectives of the balanced scorecard				
	Financial	Customer	Internal business	Learning and growth
Critical success factors	X			
Sales, costs, measures of profit (operating profit, segment margin, etc.), ROI, residual income				
Quality		X	X	
Delivery time (customer response time)		X		
Customer satisfaction		X		
Market share		X		
New markets		X		
Productivity			X	
Manufacturing cycle time and throughput			X	
Manufacturing cycle efficiency (MCE)		X	X	
Employee empowerment				X
Information systems capabilities				X
Product innovation		X		X

EXHIBIT 14.10 Critical success factors related to the four perspectives of the balanced scorecard

LEARNING OBJECTIVE 7 >>

Measuring and controlling quality costs

Interactive quizzes

Over the past 25 years or so, the demand by customers for quality products and services at affordable prices has drastically changed the way companies do business. As a result, one of the critical success factors under the customer perspective of the balanced scorecard is increasing the quality of products and services. Quality is no longer just a buzzword, but a way of life. Managers have come to realise that improving quality increases sales through higher customer satisfaction and demand, reduces costs and increases the long-term profitability of companies.

However, before we go any further, just what is meant by quality? Although you may 'know it when you see it', most businesses describe **quality** as 'meeting or exceeding customers' expectations'. Of course, this requires that a product perform as it is intended but also requires that a product be reliable and durable and that these features be provided at a competitive price.

Companies have focused on improving the quality of the products or services they sell through a variety of initiatives, such as total quality management (TQM), market-driven quality and strategic quality management. Although the details of these methods may differ, all focus on meeting or exceeding customer expectations, continuous improvement and employee empowerment. Continuous improvement, an idea pioneered by Toyota in Japan, refers to a system of improvement based on a series of gradual and often small improvements rather than major changes requiring very large investments. Called **kaizen** in Japan, continuous improvement requires active participation by all of a company's employees – from the CEO to the worker on the assembly line. Everyone is responsible for continuous improvement.[1] Employee empowerment refers to companies' providing appropriate opportunities for training, skill development and advancement so that employees can become active participants and active decision makers in an organisation. As discussed earlier, empowering employees is a key dimension of the learning and growth perspective of the balanced scorecard.

While Toyota strives for kaizen, or continuous improvement, in its manufacturing processes, it also strives for **hejunka**, or standardisation. How does standardisation increase quality? In a stable manufacturing environment, the sudden disruption caused by a malfunctioning machine, low-quality materials or other problems stands out to such an extent that it is easy for managers to identify and fix.[2]

Improving the quality of products and services is an important component of both the customer perspective and the internal business perspective of the balanced scorecard. From a customer perspective, one of the most important measures of quality is customer satisfaction and the number of customer complaints. If the number of meals returned to the kitchen is increasing, management should probably infer that customers are unhappy with the quality of the food. The number of warranty

✳ quality
Usually defined as meeting or exceeding customers' expectations.

✳ kaizen
A system of improvement based on a series of gradual and often small improvements.

✳ hejunka
A system of standardising manufacturing processes to improve efficiency.

claims can also serve as a measure of quality. An increase in warranty work performed on a certain model of automobile indicates a potential problem with the production process and the quality of the car produced. However, poor quality is not the only explanation for increasing customer complaints or warranty claims. In addition, these measures are not perfect in that customers do not always complain or return products when quality problems are evident. For example, restaurant patrons may not complain about subpar meals, and customers may simply discard defective merchandise instead of returning it. Therefore, management must be careful to provide a mechanism to make it easy for customers to complain, easy for them to return defective products and so on.

From the internal business perspective, quality measures centre on improving output yields, reducing defects in raw materials and finished products, and reducing downtime owing to quality problems. Ideally, defects are detected before they leave the factory and the manufacturing process adapted accordingly. The amount of scrap can also indicate potential quality problems in the production process. Although a certain amount of scrap is acceptable and even necessary in most manufacturing environments, an excessive amount should raise a red flag because it indicates possible problems causing an increase in the number of defective units in the process.

The costs of quality

Improving quality can be costly. On average, companies in the US spend 20 to 30 per cent of every sales dollar on quality costs.[3] The results of a study published in *Business Week* found that companies that had received quality awards enjoyed higher growth in sales, assets and operating profit compared with a control group and that the stock price of the quality award winners showed higher appreciation than the stock price of other companies.[4]

In evaluating managers based on quality concerns, it is useful to have a framework for comparing the benefits of providing a high-quality product or service with the costs that result from poor quality. To facilitate this comparison, quality costs are typically classified into four general categories: (1) prevention costs, (2) appraisal costs, (3) internal failure costs and (4) external failure costs. Examples of specific types of prevention, appraisal, internal failure and external failure costs are shown in Exhibit 14.11.

Prevention costs are incurred to prevent product failure from occurring. These costs are typically incurred early in the value chain and include design and engineering costs as well as training, supervision and the costs of quality improvement projects. If parts are purchased from an outside supplier, prevention costs may include providing training and technical support to the supplier in order to increase the quality of purchased materials. Prevention costs are incurred to eliminate quality problems before they occur. Most companies find that incurring prevention costs up front is less expensive in the long run than product failure costs.

Appraisal (detection) costs are incurred in inspecting, identifying and isolating defective products and services before they reach the customer. These include the costs of inspecting raw materials, testing goods throughout the manufacturing process, and final product testing and inspection. In practice, it is very difficult to ensure quality through inspection. It is time consuming and costly to inspect every unit of product. Therefore, sampling is usually used to identify the problems with the production process. However, sampling is certainly not foolproof and is not

❋ **prevention costs**
Costs incurred to prevent product failures from occurring, typically related to design and engineering.

❋ **appraisal (detection) costs**
Costs incurred to inspect finished products or products in the process of production.

Prevention costs	Appraisal (detection) costs	Internal failure costs	External failure costs
Design and engineering costs	Inspecting raw materials	Material, labour and other manufacturing costs incurred in rework	Cost of repairs made under warranty
Quality training	Testing goods during the production process	Cost of scrap	Replacement of defective parts
Supervision	Final product testing and inspection	Cost of spoilage	Cost of product recalls
Quality improvement projects		Cost of downtime	Liability costs from defective products
Training and technical support provided to suppliers		Cost of design changes	Lost sales
		Cost of reinspections	
		Disposal of defective products	

EXHIBIT 14.11 Quality costs

❖ internal failure costs

Costs incurred once the product is produced and then determined to be defective.

❖ external failure costs

Costs incurred when a defective product is delivered to a customer.

likely to catch all quality problems. In general, it is more effective to design quality into a product through prevention activities rather than to inspect quality into a product using appraisal activities.

If a product or a service is defective in any way or does not meet customer expectations, failure costs are incurred. **Internal failure costs** are incurred once the product is produced and then determined to be defective (through the appraisal process) but before it is sold to customers. Internal failure costs include the material, labour and other manufacturing costs incurred in reworking defective products and the costs of scrap and spoilage. Internal failure costs also include downtime caused by quality problems, design changes and the costs of reinspections and retesting. If no defects exist, internal failure costs will be zero. On the other hand, a high level of internal failure costs should be an indication to management that more attention needs to be paid to preventing quality problems to eliminate or reduce the number of defective products during the production process.

External failure costs are incurred after a defective product is delivered to a customer. External failure costs include the cost of repairs made under warranty or the replacement of defective parts, product recalls (such as in the automobile industry), liability costs arising from legal actions against the seller and eventually lost sales. Although the cost of potential lawsuits and lost sales may be difficult to measure, the cost of external failures is likely to exceed other quality costs. Failure costs, both internal and external, are like bandages – they only address symptoms rather than fixing the underlying problem. When unhappy customers decide not to purchase products from a company because of quality problems, the domino effect can be devastating – particularly when safety is a concern.

Minimising quality costs

Although quality costs in many US companies may reach 20 to 30 per cent of sales, experts suggest that the total costs of quality should not exceed 2 to 4 per cent of sales. The problem faced by management is to reduce the costs of quality while maintaining a high-quality product or service. The goal, of course, is to minimise all

the quality costs. However, it may be prudent to increase expenditures in one or more areas in order to decrease other costs. For example, as you have seen, external failure costs are serious and potentially devastating to companies. Both external and internal failure costs can be reduced (theoretically to zero) by paying more attention to quality issues early in the value chain. Products can be designed to emphasise quality and durability, suppliers can be certified, employees can be trained and the manufacturing process can be improved to increase quality throughout the value chain. Increasing expenditures related to prevention and appraisal can result in significant overall cost savings in the long run. As you can see in Exhibit 14.12, the traditional view of managing total quality costs suggests that increasing prevention and appraisal costs will reduce defective units (and failure costs) but that there are trade-offs in doing so. The traditional view suggests that total quality costs are minimised at a level of product quality below 100 per cent.

Exhibit 14.12 implies that total quality costs are minimised at a point less than that associated with zero defects. However, additional prevention and appraisal activities are likely to reduce defects even further. Should companies continue to incur prevention and appraisal costs beyond this point?

A more contemporary view of quality costs recognises that a number of failure costs are difficult to measure. For example, poor quality can lead to lost sales. This outcome tends to increase the costs of external failures as the percentage of defective units increases. In addition, rather than continually

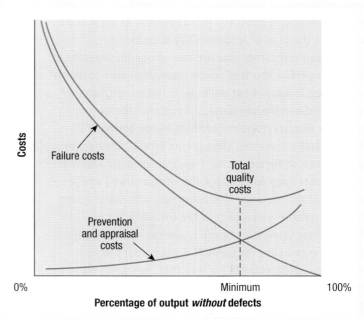

EXHIBIT 14.12 Traditional view of the costs of quality

increasing as quality improves (as in Exhibit 14.12), prevention and appraisal costs may actually decrease as a company nears a level of zero defects. As you can see in Exhibit 14.13, this implies that total quality costs are minimised at a level of zero defects.

LEARNING OBJECTIVE **8** >>

Performance and management compensation decisions

Measuring the performance of a segment is not always the same as measuring the performance of the manager of that segment. For example, certain types of advertising might be specifically traced to a segment representing a geographic sales district (such as Queensland or Tasmania) or for a particular product. However, if advertising decisions and the advertising budget are controlled at the national level instead of by the segment manager, the cost of advertising should not be included in evaluating the performance of the segment manager. Likewise, while the segment manager's own salary or the property taxes paid by a segment are traceable to the segment, they are either controllable by others or not controllable at all. Measuring the performance of a manager should be based on variables that the manager controls. This approach, as mentioned earlier, is the goal of responsibility accounting.

In small companies that are owned and managed by the same person, motivating the owner/manager to do his or her best is usually not an issue. If the owner/manager works hard and the company is successful, the owner/manager directly reaps the benefits of the company's success and is rewarded through the receipt of salary or other forms of compensation from the company. Likewise, if the owner does not manage the company well and the company fails, the owner/manager runs the risk of losing his or her entire investment in the company.

However, in most companies, owners hire managers to run the company for them. It is the owner's job to motivate managers in such a way that the managers make decisions and work to improve the performance of the company as a whole and hence maximise the owner's wealth, not just the individual manager's salary or other compensation. As such, management compensation plans typically include incentives tied to company performance.

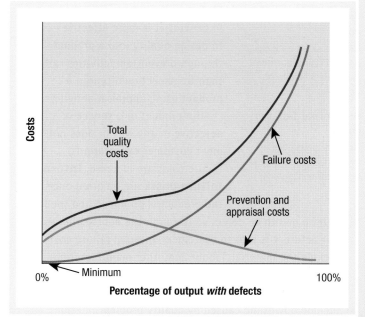

Source: RiverNorthPhotography/iStockphoto

EXHIBIT 14.13 Contemporary view of the costs of quality

Toyota troubles!

Making it real

A good example of external failure costs in Australia involves the safety recall in 2014 of 19 600 Toyota vehicles over an airbag defect that could cause a fire. As explained in an ABC news report, though no injuries or accidents resulted in Australia from this failing, Toyota did not take any risks and recalled all potentially affected cars. There is little doubt that a more comprehensive quality control process during the manufacturing phase might have prevented such problems from occurring, and this recall could affect Toyota's brand reputation in Australia, possibly adversely impacting future sales.

Source: 'Toyota recalls 2.27 million cars globally over airbag defect that could cause fires'. Published by ABC News/AFP, © 2014.

The cost of fixing a defect in a car can go far beyond the financial cost of doing so – the impact on reputation, customer loyalty and retention can be greater and for a longer term.

The objective is to encourage goal congruence between the individual manager and the company and its owners.

The choice of a specific incentive structure is very important for both parties involved and can include cash compensation in the form of salary and bonuses, stock-based compensation in the form of stock options and restricted stock, and other non-cash benefits and perquisites (often called perks).

Cash compensation

Cash compensation can be paid in the form of salary or end-of-period bonuses. Many companies use a combination of the two in which a base salary is paid without regard to meeting individual or company performance criteria and bonuses are paid if managers meet or exceed established goals. For example, a manager may earn a base annual salary of $150 000 and a yearly bonus of $30 000 if the individual (or company) meets certain pre-established goals. Goals vary from company to company but might include individual measures such as meeting individual sales quotas, success in attracting and retaining key employees, attracting new customers and so on. Bonuses may also be tied to companywide measures of performance such as ROI, residual income, increasing sales or increasing net profit by a certain dollar amount or percentage.

Tying bonuses to single measures of performance such as profit can be problematic. For example, a manager may increase profit by putting off needed repairs and maintenance or may postpone the acquisition of new equipment (in order to keep depreciation low). As discussed in Chapter 2, if a company uses absorption costing to cost products, a manager may be able to increase profit (at least in the short run) by increasing production.

Stock-based compensation

To encourage managers to take a longer-term view, many companies provide compensation to top managers and executives in the form of stock-based compensation. The inclusion of stock in the management compensation package is designed to encourage goal congruence between the owners and management by making managers owners. One frequently used method of stock-based compensation is the granting of stock options to key employees.

A **stock option** is the right to buy a share of stock at a set price (called the option price or strike price) at some point in the future. For example, a company may give a manager an option to buy 1000 shares of stock at a strike price of $15 per share. If the stock is currently selling for $10, the options are worthless. (A rational person would not pay $15 to exercise the option when the stock can be bought outright for $10.) However, if the stock price increases to $25 per share, the manager has the right to exercise the option and purchase 1000 shares for $15 per share. The value of the options increases as the stock price increases. This policy should encourage management to work hard to enhance the value of the stock over the long run. However, the use of stock options as compensation can result in short-term dysfunctional behaviour if managers focus on increasing the share price in the short term rather than focus on the longer-term success of the business. Stock options may have other disadvantages as well. From an individual manager's perspective, the stock price can vary due to other factors not subject to his or her control. As such, a manager may not be rewarded even if his or her individual performance is very good.

A related method of stock-based compensation involves the use of **restricted stock**. With restricted stock compensation plans, a company makes outright transfers of company stock instead of stock options. However, the shares of stock come with restrictions. Frequently, in order to ultimately receive the stock, the manager has to stay with the company for a set period of time or meet established performance measures.

Non-cash benefits and perks

Most management compensation plans include a variety of non-cash benefits and perquisites. These may include club memberships, company cars, a corner office and so on, depending on the desires of the particular manager. Benefits and perks such as these can be used to motivate managers to strive to attain the goals of the organisation.

Measuring and rewarding performance in a multinational environment

Like all organisations, companies that do business in more than one country must develop and use performance measures that provide incentives for managers to work toward the goals of the overall organisation. However, what works as an incentive in one country may not work in another. Cultural differences may impact the desires

* **stock option**
The right to buy a share of stock at a set price (called the option price or strike price) at some point in the future.

* **restricted stock**
A form of management compensation in which employees receive shares of stock with restrictions such as requirements to stay with the company for a set period of time or requirements to meet established performance measures.

and needs of managers in different countries. Attitudes toward work and leisure time vary in different countries. For example, German and French workers typically enjoy shorter work weeks than their American counterparts in addition to having more leave time and more holidays. The average worker in France gets 30 days of paid leave. In Germany, the average worker gets 24 days off. In contrast, workers in Japan average 18 days and workers in Australia average 20 days per year. In some global markets leave is tied to notions of work ethic, which encourages and rewards hard work and risk taking.

As another example, in Japan, employees are often evaluated as part of teams. Because many management control systems in Australia are designed around individual responsibility centres, developing and implementing measures evaluating team performance may be difficult for Australian companies with operations in Japan (or vice versa).

Exercises

1 Performance measures and centres
LO2, 3

Organisations use a variety of performance measures to evaluate managers. Central to the idea of responsibility accounting is that performance measures are reflective of activities under a manager's influence and control. Organisations often identify different levels of responsibility and refer to these levels as segments. The following performance measures and reports are used to evaluate managers of various segments:

a   Return on investment
b   Cost budgets
c   Labour usage variance
d   Sales budget
e   Segment margin
f   Sales volume variance
g   Residual income
h   Overall flexible budget variance
i   Sales price variance.

Required
For each performance measure and report listed above, indicate which segment (cost centre, revenue centre, profit centre, investment centre) they would most likely be used to evaluate.

2 Segmented profit and loss statement
LO4

BTO, Inc., produces and sells two products – the X 100 and X 200. Revenue and cost information for the two products are as follows:

	X 100	X 200
Selling price per unit	$ 10.00	$ 27.00
Variable expenses per unit	4.30	19.00
Traceable fixed expenses per year	$142 000	$54 000

BTO's common fixed expenses total $125 000 per year. Last year, the company produced and sold 42 500 units of X 100 and 19 000 units of X 200.

Required
Prepare a segmented profit and loss statement using the contribution format for BTO.

3 Segmented profit and loss statement
LO4

Carlton, Inc., produces and sells the A300 and B400 product lines. Revenue and cost information for the two products are as follows:

	A 300	B 400
Selling price per unit	$ 12.00	$ 27.00
Variable expenses per unit	$ 4.50	$ 19.00
Traceable fixed expenses per year	$ 120 000	$ 54 000

B400's selling price is twice that of A300, and its variable expenses per unit are quadruple that of the A300's variable expenses per unit. BTO's common fixed expenses total $160 000 per year. Last year, the company produced and sold 50 000 units of A300 and 25 000 units of B400.

Required
Prepare a segmented profit and loss statement using the contribution format for Carlton, Inc.

4 ROI with margin and turnover and residual income LO5

Advanced Electronics has two separate but related divisions: digital video and analogue video. The digital video division has sales of $800 000, net operating profit of $80 000 and average operating assets of $1 million.

Required
a   What is the digital division's margin and turnover?
b   What is the ROI for the digital division?

5 ROI and residual income LO5

You are trying to determine which of two retail clothing stores would be a more beneficial investment to you. You have a minimum required rate of return of 7 per cent and have collected the following information about the two retail clothing stores:

	Company A	Company B
Sales	$800 000	$900 000
Net operating profit	50 000	70 000
Average operating assets	500 000	800 000

Required

Calculate the ROI and residual income for each store. Explain the meaning of your calculations.

6 Dimensions of the balanced scorecard
LO6

The balanced scorecard integrates financial and non-financial measures that relate to four perspectives: financial, customer, internal business, and learning and growth. This view of a company places emphasis on both financial and non-financial measures as each contributes to the understanding of a company's performance.

Required

List two possible performance measures for each of the four perspectives included in the balanced scorecard.

7 Quality costs LO7

The following are partially completed statements that relate to quality and the costs of quality. Read each of the statements carefully.

a _____ include(s) the cost of repairs made under warranty or the replacement of defective parts.

b Costs incurred in reworking defective products and the costs of scrap and spoilage are referred to as _____.

c Costs of inspecting, identifying and isolating defective products before they reach the customer are called _____.

d _____ is/are incurred to prevent product failures from occurring.

e The _____ developed ISO 9000 as a set of guidelines for quality management.

f Kaizen, also called _____, refers to a system of improvement based on a series of gradual and often small improvements.

Required

Complete each of the above partially completed statements by using one of the following terms: appraisal costs, prevention costs, external failure costs, International Standards Organisation, continuous improvement, internal failure costs.

8 Quality costs LO7

Tiffany Lamp Company produces stained glass lamps appropriate for home and office use. The company expects sales to total approximately $50 million for the current year. Tiffany's management team has become increasingly concerned about a perception among some customers that quality is not particularly important to the company. Consequently, management recently implemented a quality improvement program and after several months accumulated the following data:

Warranty claims	$60 000
Rework costs	200 000
Quality training	305 000
Inspection of incoming materials	900 000
Statistical process control	400 000
Scrap costs	100 000
Product quality audits	250 000

Required

a What are total prevention costs?

b What are total appraisal costs?

c What are total internal failure costs?

d What are total external failure costs?

e Based on your calculations, is there a basis for the perception that quality is not important to Tiffany Lamp Company?

9 Stock options and restricted stock LO8

You recently spoke to a former classmate of yours who has worked for a start-up company since graduating from business school more than 10 years ago. She told you that she expects to receive some type of stock-based compensation in the near future. She has heard that she might receive stock options or a grant of restricted stock, but she is unsure of the difference.

Required

Explain to your friend the differences between stock options and grants of restricted stock.

Problems

10 Segment margin and contribution margin LO4

Simon Hinson Company operates two divisions: Gordon and Ronin. A segmented profit and loss statement for the company's most recent year is as follows:

	Total company	Gordon division	Ronin division
Sales	$850 000	$250 000	$600 000
Less variable expenses	505 000	145 000	360 000
Contribution margin	$345 000	$105 000	$240 000
Less traceable fixed costs	145 000	45 000	100 000
Division segment margin	$200 000	$ 60 000	$140 000
Less common fixed costs	130 000		
Net profit	$ 70 000		

Required

a If the Gordon Division increased its sales by $85 000 per year, how much would the company's net profit change? Assume that all cost behaviour patterns remained constant.

b Assume that the Ronin Division increased sales by $100 000, the Gordon Division sales remained the same, and there was no change in fixed costs.

  (i) Calculate the net profit amounts for each division and the total company.

  (ii) Calculate the segment margin ratios before and after these changes and comment on the results. Explain the changes.

c How do the sales increases and decreases impact divisional contribution margin ratio and segment margin ratio?

11 ROI vs residual income using different asset measures LO5

Top management is trying to determine a consistent but fair valuation system to use to evaluate each of its four divisions. This year's performance data are summarised as follows:

	Division			
	1	2	3	4
Operating profit	$1000	$1200	$1600	$1600
Operating assets	4000	6000	15000	8000
Current liabilities	400	2000	2400	200

Required

a Which division would earn a bonus if top management used ROI based on operating assets?

b Which division would earn a bonus if top management used ROI based on operating assets minus current liabilities?

c Which division would earn a bonus if top management calculated residual income based on operating assets with a minimum return of 12 per cent?

d Which division would earn a bonus if top management calculated residual income based on operating assets minus current liabilities with a minimum return of 12 per cent?

12 ROI: Decision focus LO5

You are the manager of a franchise operating division of the Kwik-Copies Company. Your company evaluates your division using ROI, computed with end-of-year gross asset balances, and calculates manager bonuses based on the percentage increase in ROI over the prior year. Your division has $9 million in assets. Your budgeted profit and loss statement for the fiscal year is as follows:

Sales	$16 500 000
Variable expenses	3 000 000
Contribution margin	$13 500 000
Fixed expenses	7 750 000
Depreciation expense	2 375 000
Division profit	$ 3 375 000

During the year, you consider buying a new copy machine for $4 million, which will enable you to expand the output of your division and reduce operating costs. The copy machine would have no salvage value and would be depreciated over five years using straight-line depreciation. It will increase output by 10 per cent while reducing fixed costs by $4 million. If you decide to purchase the copy machine, it will be installed in late December but will not be ready for use until the following year. As a result, no depreciation will be taken on it this year.

If you do buy the copy machine, you will have to dispose of the copy machine you are now using, which you just purchased during the current year. The old copy machine cost you $4 million but has no salvage value. Of the depreciation in the profit and loss statement, $1 million is for this machine. In the ROI calculations, the company includes any gains or losses from copy equipment disposal as part of the company's operating profit.

Required

a What is your division's ROI this year if you do not acquire the new machine?

b What is your division's ROI this year if you do acquire the new copy machine?

c What is your division's expected ROI for next year if the copy machine is acquired and meets expectations? Assume that unit costs and prices do not change.

d As the manager, what action will you take and why?

13 Quality costing LO7

Rebecca's Pottery Loft makes a variety of handmade pottery items. She has asked for your advice on one of the items manufactured – a clay pelican. The following information is provided:

Number of defective pelicans	1 100
Number of pelicans returned	150
Number of pelicans reworked	200
Profit per defect-free pelican	$10.00
Processing cost of a returned pelican	$20.00
Profit per defective pelican	$ 5.00
Cost to rework defective pelican	$ 4.00
Total appraisal costs	$ 3400
Total prevention costs	$ 6000

Required

a Calculate the total profits lost because Rebecca sold defective pelicans.

b Calculate the rework cost.

c Calculate the cost of processing customer returns.

d Calculate total failure cost.

e Calculate total quality cost.

14 Quality costing LO7

Milton makes high quality, handmade cooking appliances. He has asked for your advice on one of the items manufactured – a steel frying pan. Cost information is as follows:

Number of defective frying pans	2000
Number of frying pans returned	250
Number of frying pans reworked	300
Profit per defect-free frying pan	$ 15.00
Processing cost of a returned frying pan	$ 8.00
Profit per defective frying pan	$ 7.00
Cost to rework defective frying pan	$ 6.00
Total appraisal costs	$ 5000
Total prevention costs	$ 4000

Required

a Calculate the total profits lost because Milton sold defective pans.

b Calculate the rework cost.

c Calculate total failure cost.

d Calculate total quality cost.

15 Forms of management compensation
LO8

Watson Water Heaters (WWH) opened for business 30 years ago with fewer than 10 employees and sales in the first year of business of just $500 000. Today, the company has more than 1000 employees and annual revenues of $450 million. The company's growth has caused management to begin considering how best to compensate employees. Historically, WWH has used a strictly cash-based compensation system. The company's chief executive officer, Will Harrell, and chief financial officer, Claire Greer, now believe that such a system is no longer feasible, primarily because they worry that it does not adequately motivate employees to think of the company's long-term interests. Will and Claire recently met with a compensation consultant to discuss new ways of compensating employees that may better link compensation and performance.

Required

a   Excluding cash compensation, what are the possible types of compensation that WWH may use?

b   What are the advantages and disadvantages of each type of compensation identified by you in question A?

c   Do you have a recommendation as to the types of compensation that would be most appropriate for WWH? What is the basis for your recommendation?

Cases

16 Comprehensive responsibility accounting, segment margin, and management compensation LO2, 4, 8

Gantry Manufacturing is a medium-sized organisation with manufacturing facilities in seven locations around the southwestern United States. Of these facilities, Galveston and Amarillo are treated as profit centres, with local management exercising authority over manufacturing costs, certain non-manufacturing costs (e.g., advertising at local minor league baseball stadiums, sponsoring local charity events), and sales revenue. The segment income statements that follow were prepared by facility-level accountants and were provided to the corporate office in Denver, Colorado, shortly after the end of this year's second quarter. Note that the statements are shown in parallel for convenience and are not intended to be combined for analysis purposes.

Segmented Income Statements
Galveston and Amarillo Facilities
For the Quarter Ending 30 June 2012

	Galveston	Amarillo
Sales	$ 22 500 000	$ 18 450 000
Variable expenses	19 850 000	17 640 000
Contribution margin	$ 2 650 000	$ 810 000
Divisional fixed expenses	1 400 000	1 030 000
Segment margin	$ 1 250 000	$ (220 000)

The managers of these two facilities are former classmates at the University of Texas at Austin and routinely stay in touch with each other. Shortly after receiving the quarterly results from his accountant, the Amarillo manager, Jim Lowell, called his friend in Galveston to talk about the surprising loss shown on his facility's income statement. After a short conversation with the Galveston manager, Jim met with his accountant. He learned the following:

A recent memo sent from the corporate controller to all facility controllers indicated that new manufacturing overhead rates should be used beginning 1 May, 2012. The old rate was $2.80 per direct labour hour and the new rate is $3.25 per direct labour hour. The memo had a new policy statement attached to it asserting that individual manufacturing facilities could no longer establish individual overhead rates.

An average of 210 employees worked 40 hours per week during the quarter. There were 13 weeks in the second quarter.

Each division was required to record a onetime expense associated with ethics training for all new and current employees. The Amarillo facility received an expense allocation of $58 000. Sixty-five per cent of the allocation is related to manufacturing employees, and the remainder is related to administrative employees.

The corporate office also implemented a new policy related to certain divisional employees' retirement, insurance, and other benefits. In past years, all benefits were paid by the corporate office and were not allocated to local facilities. However, the company's new president believes that those costs are more properly reflected in the expenses of the individual facilities because they are incurred by local employees. In total, additional retirement and insurance expenses of $46 500 were incurred for each month during the quarter ended 30 June, 2012. Thirty per cent of the monthly expenses are related to manufacturing employees, and the remainder is related to administrative employees.

Jim was immediately frustrated by all that he learned from the accountant. Because his and other managers' bonuses depend on quarterly financial performance, he feels that the corporate memos unfairly reduce his division's profits. He asked his controller to prepare a revised income statement without the changes implemented by the corporate office during the quarter. Amarillo's revised income statement appeared as follows:

Segmented Income Statements Amarillo Facility
For the Quarter Ending 30 June 2012 (Revised)

Sales	$ 18 450 000
Variable expenses	17 511 310
Contribution margin	$ 938 690
Divisional fixed expenses	912 050
Segment margin	$ 26 640

Jim is not particularly pleased with the financial performance of his facility, preferring to report a small profit as opposed to a more significant loss. He now must decide how to communicate with the corporate office about this revised income statement. You should bear in mind that the corporate office only provides administrative services and does not manufacture goods; however, sales activities for five of the company's facilities are handled in the corporate office.

Required

a   Assist Jim by identifying reasons that support his desire that the Amarillo facility not be required to implement the changes made by the corporate office.

b   What are the implications of having the corporate office issue memos requiring the facilities to record certain expenses, given the company's bonus structure?

c How will the corporate office's new policy affect the facility management's motivation?

d What are some of the possible bases that Gantry Manufacturing could use to allocate fixed expenses?

17 Comprehensive ROI: Decision focus
LO5, 8

Elaine Shumate has been working for GSM, a pharmaceutical research company, for more than seven years. It is her first job since finishing her graduate work in molecular biology, and her performance evaluations have been exemplary. She has received increasing responsibility as opportunities have become available at GSM. Unfortunately, her knowledge and experience have not prepared her for the situation she currently faces. GSM has invested heavily in a molecular identification process (MIP) that the company's top management believes holds tremendous promise for the future. If all goes well, the company plans to patent the process and license it to large pharmaceutical companies for use in medication production. Elaine is the lead manager on MIP, and she is worried that the latest research results do not look as promising as earlier results. The vice president of research, Blake Walton, has asked Elaine to meet with him to discuss the results. After a brief discussion in the hallway, Blake suggests that Elaine take another look at the latest results. He doesn't believe that her interpretation of the data is correct.

In preparing for their meeting, she looks over the company's earlier cost estimates and operating income projections for the project. Records indicate that the estimated research-and-development costs are $140 million, and annual operating income is expected to be approximately $25 million. Given the latest results, MIP may have fewer applications in the pharmaceutical industry than originally believed.

Elaine speaks with Richard Lawrence, vice president of sales, to get an updated estimate of the potential market value for MIP. Richard suggests that MIP would likely generate operating income of just $17.5 million per year if the recent results hold up after further testing. Elaine knows that Blake is not going to be happy with this news. Blake is scheduled to meet with the company's board of directors next week to discuss the need for additional investment capital from venture capitalists in the next year and the company's plans for a public stock offering in the next several years. Elaine stands to benefit substantially from stock options if the company goes public. GSM's future may ride on the outcome of that meeting.

Required

a What is the ROI for MIP, given the original estimates? What is the ROI if Richard Lawrence's new revenue projections are used?

b Elaine feels pressure to deliver 'good news' to Blake. What advice would you give to her? Given the possible personal financial rewards that Elaine may enjoy if GSM goes public, would your advice change?

c What responsibilities does Elaine have to other GSM employees, the board of directors, and the venture capitalists?

REVIEW

HE DID

ACCT Managerial puts a multitude of study aids at your fingertips. After reading the chapters, check out these resources for further help:

- **Chapter review cards,** found in the back of your book, include all learning outcomes, definitions and self-assessment activities for each chapter.

- **Online printable flash cards** give you additional ways to check your comprehension of key marketing concepts.

Other great ways to help you study include **interactive games**, **flashcards**, **e-lectures** and **quizzes**.

You can find it all at: http://login.cengagebrain.com/

Learning objectives:

After studying the material in this chapter, you should be able to:

1 Understand the role of management accounting in documenting sustainability practices.

2 Understand externalised costs for which organisations are responsible.

3 Appreciate the role of sustainability value chains and its link to management accounting.

4 Consider triple bottom line reporting and sustainability-related KPIs.

5 Identify and understand environmental costs in organisations.

ACCOUNTING FOR SUSTAINABILITY – SOCIAL AND ENVIRONMENTAL REPORTING AND MANAGEMENT ACCOUNTING

c 15

Management accounting is predominantly concerned with the provision of decision-relevant information relating to an organisation's internal operations and strategy, which ultimately aids management decision making. Increasingly, corporate and broader society is beginning to acknowledge the importance of valuing the physical environment within which we exist, to better appreciate the true cost of our actions at both a corporate and individual level. To this end, companies have started thinking more deeply about how they might use accounting to identify and measure their environmental costs and broadly conceptualise the **sustainability** of their pursuits. By 'sustainability' we mean the pursuit of endeavours which prolongs the use of, reduces or eliminates resources being consumed in performing transactions to achieve an individual or organisational objective. For example, Qantas recently implemented a financial system that estimates the carbon emissions cost per passenger travelling on their planes. Based on the distance travelled, Qantas offers its passengers the opportunity to offset their carbon emissions and many customers pay as they wish to account for their share. The money paid contributes to initiatives that seek to minimise the environmental degradation caused by these emissions. This system is a classic example of organisations using accounting to put a value to a previously nebulous idea – carbon emissions. By valuing the cost of carbon emissions, Qantas is able to motivate passengers who are passionate about reducing emissions to pay their fair portion to contribute to its reduction. Accounting allows for interested stakeholders to better understand the consequences of their actions and act accordingly.

To what extent can we framework and identify systems for thinking about sustainability issues such as environmental and social issues through the lens of accounting? In this chapter, we attempt to provide frameworks and examples that encourage management accountants to more actively contribute to the environmental accounting debate. Through accounting systems you are able to tell a story about the impact of organisations on the environment – these stories are regarded as extremely valuable by interested stakeholders!

LEARNING OBJECTIVE **1** >>

Management accounting and sustainability practices

... recently, the developed world has struggled to expand the original concept of sustainable development – meeting environmental concerns whilst maintaining economic development – to a more holistic concept where environmental, social and economic considerations are identified and can be considered concurrently in decision making.[1]

We define **sustainability practices** as any pursuit that prolongs the use of, reduces or eliminates resources being consumed in performing transactions to achieve an individual or organisational objective. Sustainability is broadly seen as a necessary focus in a large portion of broader society, owing to two factors – concerns over the stability of the environment and the underlying economic challenge faced by governmental, scientific and corporate world leaders in devising strategies to support an increasingly populous human species in a finite planet Earth.

To this end, the 'sustainability' proposition lies at the centre of much debate and discussion in organisations around the world owing to its importance to a range of stakeholders – government, customers in society and so on. For example, Aston Martin, usually a maker of premium, quality, highly aesthetic sports cars, launched the Cygnet, a small-engine, low-powered vehicle that is a clear departure from the nature of its existing models. When questioned about this change, management cited quite rational reasons. These

✳ sustainability
The pursuit of endeavours which prolongs the use of or reduces or eliminates resources being consumed in performing transactions to achieve an individual or organisational objective.

✳ sustainability practices
Activities conducted to prolong the use of, reduce or eliminate resource consumption.

included the need to capture a larger percentage of the population than currently reached and the importance of having a low fuel consumption vehicle that minimised costs for city-based driving, relative to its other vehicles.[2] Another reason cited by industry experts was the need for the Aston Martin brand to lower the average fuel consumption rate of the vehicles in its brand so as to avoid financial penalties from the European Union. This cross-government automobile industry policy was introduced to incentivise lower fuel consumption in vehicles in order to reduce harm to the environment.[3] To what extent did this decision impact Aston Martin's thinking? It's highly likely that at the very least it was an issue raised to Aston Martin senior management in making the case for the Cygnet's introduction. Is the cost of the above equal to or less than the benefit obtained from these reductions in fines and access to larger customer markets? The financial quantification of estimates in order to help Aston Martin senior management make this decision represents a management accounting problem.

We can see from the above example that sustainability practices have the twin effect of lowering consumption for environmental preservation reasons and also lowering costs. By using less, companies pay less. To this end, sustainability practices are relevant to all organisations, independent of their views concerning the impact of human behaviours on the environment. A minority of scientists in the world, along with a minority of the global population, do not believe in human-driven climate change. However, most of these individuals probably consider using fewer resources through efficiencies, productivities or technology advances as important, owing to its cost-reduction focus and impacts on improving the prospects for managing human population growth in a finite world.

Organisations, therefore, need management accountants to investigate their sustainability-related investments and reflect on the short- and long-term costs and benefits of these investments. By identifying these and producing accounting analyses that allow for organisations to better save costs while reducing resource consumption and maximising firm profitability, it is conceivable that a management accounting analysis of sustainability issues might allow us to develop win–win scenarios for organisations, governments and the populations they represent.

Sustainability issues are also cited as driving down economic productivity as they reduce consumption. However, let's not forget the very positive impact of sustainability-motivated creativity and innovation in introducing whole new industries such as the electric motor industry and the alternative-energy innovation industries. These industries spur new employment, redistribute labour resources into new employment areas and allow organisations to reflect on the importance of the balance between resource consumption and environmental degradation/population growth concerns. Overall, sustainability can plausibly co-exist with organisational performance, as noted by Epstein and Roy (2001).[4] These authors identify the drivers of long-term financial performance that arise from a sustainability ethos in organisations, as shown in Exhibit 15.1.

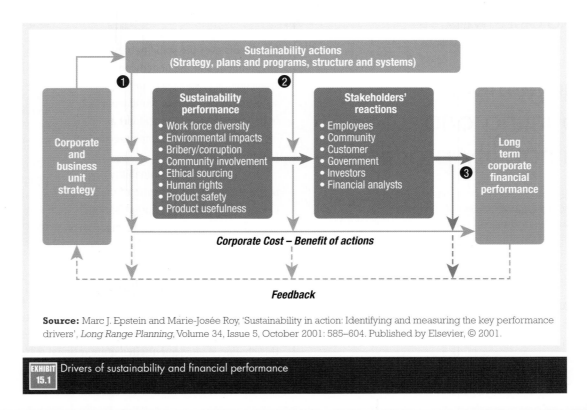

Source: Marc J. Epstein and Marie-Josée Roy, 'Sustainability in action: Identifying and measuring the key performance drivers', *Long Range Planning*, Volume 34, Issue 5, October 2001: 585–604. Published by Elsevier, © 2001.

EXHIBIT 15.1 Drivers of sustainability and financial performance

The broad thrust of Exhibit 15.1 lies in organisation strategy driving sustainable business practices. This ensures positive stakeholder reactions – when stakeholders are satisfied they ultimately shape and ensure the longer term financial performance of an organisation. By focusing on broad sustainability issues such as work-force diversity, environmental impacts, human rights, safety issues and ethical sourcing, organisations impress customers to a degree that customers feel inclined to buy their products. Furthermore, greater goodwill in the community causes a steady supply of prospective employees expressing an interest in employment, leading to a higher quality pool of labour capital. Also, positive consumer perceptions tend to translate to greater acquiescence from government, creditors and regulators, and a generally more positive outlook from investors owing to broad stakeholder goodwill. These factors combine to ensure the longer term financial health of the organisation. Of course, investments in sustainability come at a short-term cost and these costs must be measured against the longer-term benefits. The information presented in Exhibit 15.1 serves as a reminder that sustainable practices have significant positive second- and third-order effects for organisations.

The identification of a link between sustainability and financial performance first requires a cost-benefit analysis. Clearly, some organisations simply cannot afford to undertake the investment necessary to produce long-term sustainable outcomes due to a lack of resources to cover the short-term

costs of implementing such changes. Therefore, organisations must carefully weigh their cost constraints and balance these against their pursuit of longer-term sustainability outcomes. It is here that management accounting practices can provide numbers and indicators that shape such decision-making trade-offs. Exhibit 15.2 highlights the relationship between organisational profitability and sustainability practices.

Similar to Exhibit 15.1, Exhibit 15.2 highlights the nature by which sustainability practices activate five value creation levers. These levers are the means by which value creation occurs in organisations, as discussed in Exhibit 15.1. They include: an organisation's pricing power and ability to engender longer-term cost savings through innovation, its identification of a quality labour market, a more loyal and established market share and greater ability to enter new markets. The sum total of these levers is an overall reduction in an organisation's risk premium; that is, the organisation maintains similar returns at lower risk premiums (perhaps even generating higher returns!).

The remainder of the chapter looks at the role of accounting systems in informing sustainability. We continue with a discussion of external costs and explain a framework for conceptualising environmental costs for the purposes of costs management. We then describe how the accounting, social and environmental performance of a company might be simultaneously presented in annual reports, using the *triple bottom line* reporting method.

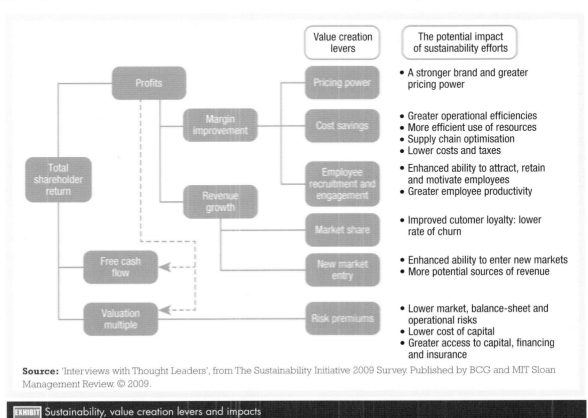

Source: 'Interviews with Thought Leaders', from The Sustainability Initiative 2009 Survey. Published by BCG and MIT Sloan Management Review. © 2009.

EXHIBIT 15.2 Sustainability, value creation levers and impacts

Conceptualising external costs

The **sustainability value chain** framework allows organisations to conceptualise the full spectrum of effects relating to organisational practices, including cost elements not shown in traditional value chains. Consider the value chain previously shown in this textbook (Chapter 6). While appropriate for most organisations seeking to streamline and improve their operations, this framework does not consider the effects caused by organisational business practices for which the same companies are not accountable. This is usually because there is only an indirect causal relationship between the company's activities and the ultimate cost resulting.

For example, the Apple Corporation received criticism from many sections of the community for sourcing materials from a supplier in Asia that used low-pay labour and required unreasonably long daily work hours from its employees, who had to accept the job owing to a lack of employment opportunities. In fairness to Apple, management argued that it had conducted the requisite checks with suppliers and regarded the issue of labour exploitation very seriously. The supplier was soon dismissed and an internal review is ongoing.

This form of exploitation by suppliers in increasing production to meet the voracious worldwide demand for Apple goods has strong ramifications for these employees and broader society. Many of these effects cause high social costs that are difficult to measure. These costs might be directly attributable to the health and safety costs relating to the unreasonable work demands the employees have been subjected to, as well as broader social stability issues and the effect on future generations, who may have grown up in less socially stable settings because of this worker exploitation. These social costs can raise crime rates, unemployment, productivity in economies and so on. Clearly we are discussing a wide range of effects, but they are all plausible and they all relate to the need (however indirectly) of the Apple corporation to source cheap production for its iPhones or iPads. To what extent must Apple bear responsibility for these costs? The extent to which organisations knowingly or unknowingly cause the incurrence of costs owing to the second- and third-order effects of their actions is an **external cost**. These costs are typically not recognised in an accounting system. Apple is not required to estimate the possible social costs relating to production activities conducted by *another supplier*. The entity concept within the accounting framework requires Apple only to denote the cost incurrences relating to its own activities.

External costs provide a more complete conceptualisation of the costs for which an organisation is responsible. These are usually greater than what the organisation is legally accountable for as required by accounting standards such as the Australian Accounting Standards Board (AASB). Let's now discuss a practical application of external cost valuation in an organisation. By extending the logic underlying cost pools, cost drivers and cost objects beyond an individual organisation boundary, we more closely identify the true cost-benefit responsibility of an organisation.

Let's consider a hypothetical example of Ezicloth, an Australian company manufacturing clothing garments in a plant in Thailand. These clothes are subsequently exported to Australia and other parts of the world for sale. Ezicloth has the following production and full costs per garment:

Direct materials per garment (average):	$ 4.50
Direct labour per garment (average):	$ 2.30
Overheads per garment (average):	$ 1.50
Total production cost per garment	$ 8.30
Selling and admin. expenses per garment	$ 2.50
Full cost per garment	$10.80

Management is wondering about the impact of its practices on the wellbeing of the communities around which Ezicloth's plants operate and whose villagers are employed in the plant. They conduct a social analysis of these communities and obtain the following data relating to changes in relevant societal characteristics:

- Theft has increased 20 per cent from $10 million to $12 million per year.
- School attendance rates have dropped 12 per cent owing to less parental supervision. Economists estimate that social welfare payments will increase from $15 million to $18 million a year.
- Strong fumes can be detected in the rivers surrounding the plant, reducing the suitability of the river as a source of clean water. Environmental engineers estimate that the extraction of the chemicals causing the fumes in the river system will cost $9 million dollars a year if spillage is maintained at present rates.

✳ sustainability value chain
A visual depiction identifying key broad categories of activity defining an organisation's activities conducted to deliver value that allows it to attain its objectives.

✳ external costs
Costs that organisations are indirectly responsible for, but which are not captured in their financial statements owing to the entity concept.

- Key local fauna have vacated the immediate areas surrounding the plant due to noise. This has affected tourism-related industries to the tune of $1 million in lost sales for the year.

If Ezicloth expects to sell 2 million garments in the coming year, what are the approximate external costs for producing these garments?

The key external cost estimates include:

Crime rate increase	$2 million
Welfare payment increase	$3 million
Chemical removal from river system	$9 million
Lost tourism	$1 million
Total external cost estimate	$15 million
Total number of garments	$2 million
Average external cost per garment	$7.50 per garment.
Total cost per garment including full cost and external costs	$18.30

Reflect on the above scenario – when incorporating a full cost measure that includes external costs, the total costs for which Ezicloth operations are responsible, not only in their own organisation but across broader society, almost doubles when compared to the previously calculated full cost of $10.80. In this way, Ezicloth can reflect on how it might go about reducing its external cost burden. As explained in the previous section, the acknowledgement of this cost might be regarded as a potentially cathartic moment for Ezicloth management.

Sustainability value chains and management accounting

Given that organisations might be responsible for external costs that are not acknowledged within traditional financial reporting methods prescribed by accounting standards, a more traditional value chain (such as that discussed in Chapter 6) might not sufficiently explain the true costs incurred and value contributed by organisations. Consider how Unilever Hindustan has modified its value chain in producing a sustainability value chain to describe its food production, as shown in Exhibit 15.3 below.

The value chain tells us a story of how Unilever Hindustan has sought to make its food production more sustainable. First, Unilever has only sourced tea from Rainforest Alliance certified tea farmers. These farmers grow tea leaves and pick them in a manner that ensures employees are treated humanely and operate in reasonable working conditions. Having acquired the tea leaves, Unilever Hindustan has sought to reduce its CO_2 emissions and water use in its production cycle, and the value chain shows the significant reduction in these amounts relative to their consumption in 2004. Similar examples are cited for the use of infrastructure assets that reduce emissions and electricity or gas use in the distribution and consumer use stages, and Unilever Hindustan also is attempting to reduce

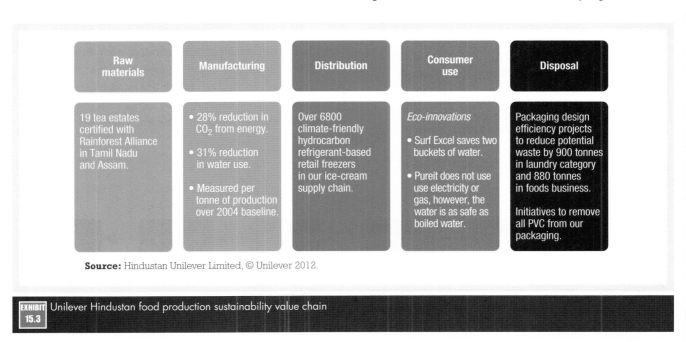

Raw materials	Manufacturing	Distribution	Consumer use	Disposal
19 tea estates certified with Rainforest Alliance in Tamil Nadu and Assam.	• 28% reduction in CO_2 from energy. • 31% reduction in water use. • Measured per tonne of production over 2004 baseline.	Over 6800 climate-friendly hydrocarbon refrigerant-based retail freezers in our ice-cream supply chain.	*Eco-innovations* • Surf Excel saves two buckets of water. • Pureit does not use use electricity or gas, however, the water is as safe as boiled water.	Packaging design efficiency projects to reduce potential waste by 900 tonnes in laundry category and 880 tonnes in foods business. Initiatives to remove all PVC from our packaging.

Source: Hindustan Unilever Limited, © Unilever 2012.

EXHIBIT 15.3 Unilever Hindustan food production sustainability value chain

its packaging and the PVC content in the packaging (PVC is a substance that does not break down easily and is considered harmful to the environment).

While the first three stages in the Unilever chain can be aligned to traditional value chains, the last two are quite unique to a sustainability value chain. The style of consumer use and subsequent disposal of Unilever products might traditionally not have been considered, as they represented actions that were outside the company's purview. While Unilever would concede that there is always more it can do, the value chain in Exhibit 15.3 provides a starting point to aid our understanding of a broader chain of activities that consider the social and environmental consequences of our operations incorporating external cost factors.

Broadly speaking, an organisational value chain must consider the wastage and re-use of resources relating to its primary and secondary activities. To this end, we want to think about how organisations might be more efficient or productive in how they use their resources (materials, labour and others) or re-use/recycle the resources consumed or wasted in their operating process.

Let's consider the example of BHP Billiton, one of Australia's largest corporations and a world-leading minerals extraction and processing corporation. How might BHP Billiton apply sustainability practices into its operations from a management accounting perspective? If we were to characterise a value chain for BHP Billiton's operations, we might structure it as shown in Exhibit 15.4.

The sustainability practices BHP Billiton might consider in relation to the above can be linked to its broader focus on community and environmental sustainability as a key value driver of the corporation. This can be seen in its 2014 sustainability report, which shows that BHP Billiton takes the issue of sustainability very seriously, as explained by CEO Andrew Mackenzie:

> I have had the pleasure of working with teams across the Company as our people continue our commitment to sustainably supply the energy and resources that support development and growth. We believe there is great opportunity and sustainable competitive advantage in simplifying what we do and doing more with what we have, and this is now delivering significant productivity gains across our business. Yet it is how we have achieved these gains which we are most proud of. We have maintained our focus on the health and safety of our people, continued our commitment to support our host communities and protect the environment, while enhancing the performance of our operations.[5]

In the next section we consider how companies might use management accounting principles in constructing sustainability performance indicators, in order to better understand the longer term viability and alignment of their operations to social and environmental systems.

LEARNING OBJECTIVE 4 >>

apply this!

Revise with
Beat the Clock

Sustainability performance indicators and triple bottom line reporting

Performance indicators are usually quantitative summary numbers that signal the performance of an organisation. These indicators are usually expressed as a ratio, but can also be a stand-alone number or qualitative estimate. By identifying target levels of performance and relating them to performance indicators, organisations form perceptions of their actual performance. Senior management ensures the importance of reaching these indicators is impressed upon all staff and communicates the desirable behaviours necessary to achieve them. In this way, accounting numbers drive desirable behaviours among employees and increase the likelihood that organisational outcomes are achieved.

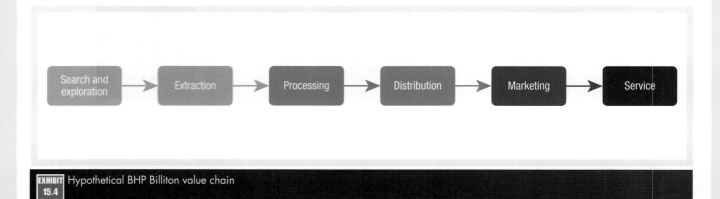

EXHIBIT 15.4 Hypothetical BHP Billiton value chain

Search and exploration → Extraction → Processing → Distribution → Marketing → Service

Coca-Cola and multiple perspectives to performance

Following is an excerpt from triplepundit.com, a website focusing on a more sustainable approach to individual and organisational practices. The excerpt focuses on Coca-Cola's initiative in 2004 to make its operations more sustainable.

> In 2004, the CEO at the time, Neville Isdell, recognized that something needed to change. And fast. He wanted to 'put the ugly baby on the table', according to Jeff Seabright, Coca-Cola's Director of Environment & Water Resources. Isdell wanted to expose all that was working wrong for the company and 'reconnect' with the ethos of the company: Coke is a provider of refreshment (and he was referring to more than just selling cold sodas). Isdell created the Manifesto for Growth, which included what the company's leaders termed the 5Ps. They are guiding light principles for thinking about business, given that amongst other things, Coca-Cola's relationships with its customers, the environment, and local communities are integral to the company's success. The 5Ps are:
>
> 1 People
> 2 Portfolio
> 3 Profit
> 4 Partnership
> 5 Planet
>
> Very similar to triple bottom line thinking, all are immutable and interconnected. Leadership and improvement in terms of one *P* will bring about leadership and improvement with the others. Aligning business practices with these new principles meant, however, redefining the company's operations across the board, from working with its bottlers to where and how it sources water to how it gets its products to you, the customer. As Seabright reiterated many times in a recent interview, 'Coca-Cola is not just the four walls of the plant.'

Source: Adapted from 'Coca-Cola: How a Large, Multinational Corporation Goes Green', by Ashwin Seshagiri. Published by Triple Pundit, © 2009.

That decision in 2004 paved the way for Coca-Cola to become a leading presence in the sustainability reporting space. What is interesting here, and a multifaceted, complex question to pose for you to reflect on, is whether one of the world's largest soft drinks manufacturers can comfortably seek to measure and report the entirety of its products' impact on society, openly and transparently without compromising its core business model?

How might sustainability indicators be developed and operationalised (made to work)? We propose a seven-step checklist – the first four steps help us create sustainability indicators, while the last three steps aid in their working in organisations.

1 *Identify a company's strategic imperative(s)* – An organisation's strategy defines how it pursues the attainment of its objectives. Therefore, whatever indicators we devise must be consistent with an organisation's strategy.

2 *Identify broad operational categories that relate to these strategic imperative(s)* – In order to achieve an organisation's strategy, management usually focuses on broad areas relating to that strategic imperative. For example, an organisation that seeks to maximise profits might focus on customers to raise revenues, as well as processes to reduce costs by minimising non-value-adding activities.

3 *Select financial and operating information that helps us chart the categories* – Within each of these categories we select key pieces of information. It might be revenues, number of customers, overall production costs, wastage costs, staff hours lost through employee injury, etc. Any financial or operating number that we think contributes to telling a story about our performance in these categories is included in this list.

4 *Assess relationships between the information selected to create performance indicators for categories* – By combining different information pieces to create ratios, or by simply using individual information as raw numbers, we populate each category with a series of indicators that paint a picture of our performance in that category.

The first four steps lead us to establishing sustainability performance indicators. However, how do we make them work in organisations? This requires the next three steps, as usually applied in conducting performance management for any indicator in organisations.

5 *Identify levels of performance for indicators* – Having determined a raw number or ratio as being an indicator, what levels do you believe necessarily define 'good' performance? The setting of a sufficient level is extremely important as good measures can be rendered irrelevant by target levels being too difficult or easy to attain.

6 *Define adequate rewards for their attainment* – If employees attain these indicators, how are you going to reward them? Reward systems usually motivate employees

to better perform their actions, as the reward represents a 'carrot' for which they will strive.

7   *Identify feedback systems to manage success/failure in attaining indicators* – At the end of a period, what do we do when a target is or isn't met? It is as important to reflect on the extent to which we might improve targets that have been met, as it is to consider how we might change our practices to ensure the future attainment of targets that have not been met.

To show you how indicators might develop in practice, we proceed to consider a selection of sustainability indicators and discuss the 'story(ies)' they communicate. We will consider the sustainability performance of BHP Billiton, whose focus on sustainability has been evidenced earlier in the chapter. The information presented below relates to BHP Billiton's 2014 Sustainability Report.

The overall regard by BHP Billiton for sustainability appears evident through communication channels such as the company website. Sustainability is communicated as the first value. This therefore represents an important strategic imperative of BHP Billiton. In order to operate sustainably and satisfy this strategic imperative, management has identified five categories that define the company's sustainability performance and these are shown in Exhibit 15.5.

These five categories are identified as being key to the company's attainment of its sustainability value. They are *Safety, Health, Environment* and *Community*. Having identified the broad categories, the firm proceeds to identify values or ratios that might relate to them. This can only be done after a set of key financial and operating numbers are identified and tell a story about the company's sustainability performance.

■ Not achieved   ▶ On track   ◀ Behind schedule   ◆ No change   ▲ Improvement   ▼ Deterioration

Target*	Performance			Target date
Zero Harm	Result	Trend**	Commentary	
Zero fatalities	■	▲	Two fatalities at our controlled operations	Annual
Zero significant environmental incidents and zero significant community incidents	▶	▲	No significant environmental or community incidents reported	Annual
Health				
All operating sites to finalise baseline health exposure assessments on occupational exposure hazards for physical exposures	▶	◆	Finalised FY2010, target met	30 June 2010
15% reduction in potential employee exposures (but for the use of personal protective equipment) over the occupational exposure limit	◀	▲	Total employees† exposed 21 464 (reduction of 7.8% on FY2007 base year)	30 June 2012
30% reduction in the incidence of occupational disease	▶	▲	We are on track to meet the public target with 68 fewer cases than reported in FY2007 (39% reduction)	30 June 2012
Safety				
50% reduction in total recordable injury frequency (TRIF) at sites	◀	▲	The TRIF for FY2011 was 5.0 (32% reduction since FY2007 base year)	30 June 2012
Environment				
Aggregate Group target of 6% reduction in greenhouse gas emissions per unit of production	▶	▲	GHG emissions intensity is 18% lower than FY2006 base year	30 June 2012
Aggregate Group target of a 13% reduction in carbon-based energy per unit of production	▶	▲	Energy intensity is 17% lower than FY2006 base year	30 June 2012
Aggregate Group target of a 10% improvement in the ratio of water recycled/reused to high-quality water consumed	▶	▲	Our water use index is currently tracking at 8% improvement on our FY2007 base year	30 June 2012
Aggregate Group target of a 10% improvement in the land rehabilitation index	◀	◆	There has been a 1% improvement on the FY2007 base year rehabilitation index	30 June 2012
Community				
1% of pre-tax profits to be invested in community programs, including cash, in-kind support and administration, calculated on the average of the previous three years' pre-tax profit	▶	◆	US$195.5 million invested in community programs, including US$30 million deposited into BHP Billiton Sustainable Communities, our UK-based charitable company	Annual

*   The baseline year for the target is 1 July 2006 – 30 June 2007, except for Energy Use and Greenhouse Gas Emissions, where it is 1 July 2005 – 30 June 2006.

** Trend compared with previous year.

†   Operational assets are the only ones to provide occupational exposure data.

Source: BHP Billiton Sustainability Report 2014. http://www.bhpbilliton.com/home/society/reports/Documents/2014/BHPBillitonSustainability Report2014_interactive.pdf, p. 1

EXHIBIT 15.5 BHP sustainability performance indicators

Having developed the performance indicators, BHP Billiton proceeds to set targets for these indicators, targets that employees will strive towards. For the year 2014, these targets are presented on the far left column. Finally, the performance of the firm with respect to the values is provided to the right of the results column. Interested stakeholders can affirm whether BHP Billiton is 'on-track', 'behind schedule' or 'not achieved' in its sustainability indicator targets. To better understand how these indicators might paint a picture of sustainability performance, we will discuss how they fared in BHP Billiton for the 2014 year.

Safety represents the pursuit of zero fatalities, environmental incidents or community incidents. Organisations, including BHP Billiton, do their best to avoid the destabilisation of communities around which they conduct their operations. The absence of environmental or social incidents as well as zero employee fatalities signals that, at a minimum, the operations conducted are not harming these local stakeholders. You might note that the risk of harm is not adequately represented by the absence of fatalities (deaths). Unsafe workplaces can cause high levels of injury to employees and leave zero fatalities. It is therefore important that organisations acknowledge, measure and monitor the extent to which injuries might be caused by unsafe practices. To this end, BHP Billiton measures the extent to which zero fatalities, total recordable injury frequency (TRIF) and alignment to broader safety policies are met. BHP Billiton targeted and achieved zero fatalities, an improvement in its TRIF and the implementation of plans to manage the Security and Human Rights of its related stakeholders.

From a Health perspective, BHP Billiton targets the reduction in employee exposure to carcinogens by 10%, a target they met as the percentage reduction was 22% (Exhibit 15.5).

Though not the case in this section, where metrics are behind schedule (yellow arrow), they signal the need for more vigorous efforts by management to improve sustainability performance in these areas. Metrics that are on track (green arrows) will still be monitored, but with less urgency.

The safety and wellbeing of employees as shown by Safety and Health is clearly important in any organisation. However, achieving sustainability objectives is not limited to employee wellbeing, as is the case with the first three measures. It more broadly requires a balancing of economic, environmental and social levers in any given situation. To this extent, BHP Billiton also regards its *Environment* and *Community* (social) categories as being key to defining its sustainability performance.

The *Environment* category relates to greenhouse gas emissions, carbon-based energy consumption, the use of recycled water and land rehabilitation in previously used sites. Management targeted no significant environmental incidents

and a lower level of greenhouse gas emissions than its 2006 base year and operations are currently 18 per cent lower. A 13 per cent reduction in carbon-based energy consumption per unit was also targeted, based on 2006 levels, a level being achieved. BHP Billiton also sought to implement land and biodiversity plans in all of its operations, a target it achieved (land rehabilitation is the process of returning a site that has been damaged by the activities conducted by the company, to a degree mirroring its previous condition). It also sought to reduce its impact on water resources.

The final category is the *Community* category. BHP Billiton affirms that it will contribute 1 per cent of its pre-tax profits to community programs for societies within which it conducts its operations. The company has argued that it remains 'on-track' to deliver on this indicator as evidenced by the $241.7 million investment in community programs, an increase from the $195.5 million invested in such programs in 2011. However, it is also in this category alone that BHP Billiton failed to reach a target. They intended for no significant community incidents to result from their operations, but one significant community incident involving a local community protest occurred.

The identification of the above indicators relating to 'Safety', 'Health', 'Environment' and 'Community' categories allows BHP Billiton to track its performance from a sustainability perspective. While clearly being an economically profitable organisation, BHP Billiton is coming under increasing pressure from regulators and communities worldwide to run its operations with greater regard for the environments and societies impacted by its business conduct. Overall, it is noteworthy that BHP Billiton has transparently identified and communicated its sustainability performance to the broader market, and seeks to improve it as evidenced by the comments of former CEO Marius Kloppers.[6]

However, remember that the above operational ratios relating to sustainability practices might not be as informative as they appear. We must be careful when judging any performance indicator. BHP Billiton sets its own targets and regards its performance as being 'good' when targets are attained or surpassed. To this extent, if targets are easily achieved, BHP Billiton's sustainability performance might yet hold further improvement, though management may not wish to risk its attainment as they may fear setting more challenging targets and not meeting them. Also, it's important for us to appreciate that targets are revealing not only in what they tell us, but *what they don't*. Consider greenhouse gas emissions target level in the *environment* category. The target is expressed as requiring to be less than the 2006 baseline. The assumption here is that if the level is lower than almost a decade ago, they've done well. There is no discussion of the actual current level, and the extent to which that level could be better, or whether it represented an improvement from the previous year, and the year before. Much is not revealed, though the ratio reads positively. We are not implying that BHP Billiton has not performed well from a sustainability perspective, rather that we do not have sufficient information to definitively evidence that they have! We simply don't know what the actual water re-use percentage is and so it's difficult to gauge the actual physical improvement in water re-use as a percentage of the total of high-quality water consumed. Similarly, some might regard the contribution of only 1 per cent of profits to community programs as not being sufficient. Ultimately, as a private corporation, BHP Billiton is accountable to its shareholders. However, as environmental and social concerns permeate its stakeholders, including shareholders, governments and communities, BHP Billiton will only increasingly experience pressure to improve on its sustainability performance. To this extent, the above performance indicators represent an attempt by the firm to allay the concerns of stakeholders.

Source: 'Balancing Act: A Triple Bottom Line Analysis of the Australian Economy, Volume 1', by Barney Foran, Manfred Lenzen and Christopher Dey. Published by The University of Sydney, © 2005 by Commonwealth of Australia.

EXHIBIT 15.6 Triple bottom line elements

❊ **triple bottom line reporting**

A form of reporting performance that considers the economic, social and environmental performance of an organisation.

❊ **economic outcomes**

The predominantly financial outcomes as captured by accounting values in organisations, affected through the conduct of their operations.

❊ **social outcomes**

Outcomes relating to the broader society within which an organisation exists, which it has impacted through its operations.

❊ **environmental outcomes**

Outcomes relating to the broader environment within which an organisation exists, which it has impacted through its operations.

Triple bottom line reporting

Triple bottom line reporting is a reporting system that simultaneously considers the economic, social and environmental performance of an organisation. This reporting system has been in place for almost two decades, and readily provides a framework for organisations seeking to communicate more than accounting/economic information in their annual reporting. The TBL system believes that in order to better understand an organisation's performance, a consideration of its financial performance must be judged against its social and environmental impacts (positive and negative), in order to more completely appreciate its impact on broader societies.

- **Economic outcomes**: Broadly relates to the financial performance of an organisation, incorporating its profit and loss statement, and other economic indicators such as market share price.
- **Social outcomes**: The degree to which societies within physical, financial and influential proximity of an organisation have been impacted by its operations.
- **Environmental outcomes**: The degree to which natural environments have been impacted by an organisation's operations.

Consider Exhibit 15.6, extracted from a 2005 CSIRO and University of Sydney report, summarising the organisational level factors that affect these three areas.

By reporting on all the above indicators, organisations develop a better understanding of the second- and third-order effects of their operations. This contributes to their better conceptualisation of external costs, as well as sustainability value chains and indicators that define their performance.

LEARNING OBJECTIVE **5** >>

apply this!

interactive quizzes

Environmental costs – prevention, appraisal, internal and external failure costs

Originally sourcing from the Total Quality Management literature, a framework comprising *prevention*, *appraisal*, *internal failure* and *external failure* costs allows us to better measure how environmental costs are expended in organisations. We proceed to describe these costs, defining them with respect to environmental contexts:

1. **Prevention costs** – Organisations might expend resources to reduce or eliminate the likelihood that environmental problems will arise in the future. For example, an organisation that implements a filtration system to eliminate chemical spillage into river streams is undertaking a preventative measure that eliminates the possibility of future environmental pollution impacting the eco-system around which it conducts its operations. The focus on prevention costs pre-empts future problems from arising, and is generally seen as being a longer term, increasingly sustainable and more engaging style of environmental investment.

2. **Appraisal costs** – Independent of the presence or absence of preventative measures, organisations might invest in technologies to monitor their environmental exposures. For example, Qantas might invest a few hundred thousand dollars to implement electronic monitoring systems that measure the fuel emissions of its aircraft as they age. When older planes with more dated engines start to show higher fuel emissions, Qantas might consider retiring them from service. Monitoring systems therefore don't prevent problems from arising. However, if an environmental problem was to eventuate, monitoring systems allow for their prompt detection and subsequent management.

3. **Internal failure costs** – If an environmental breach occurs for which a company is responsible, internal failure costs are the expenditures incurred to address problems that arise within the company, as affecting any company resource (people, materials, processes, etc.). For example, in November 2011, Orica's Kooragang Chemical plant experienced an ammonia leak. If employees had to be hospitalised owing to the leak, internal failure costs are the costs incurred by Orica to rehabilitate and cover the medical expenses of these employees.

4. **External failure costs** – Because organisations and broader communities share the environment collectively, the environmental problems caused by an organisation often have broader societal impacts. Any costs incurred to alleviate these broader societal and environmental impacts are external failure costs. For example, the approximately US $40 billion clean-up bill incurred by BP for the Gulf of Mexico oil spill (for which the US Government deemed it responsible), represents a significant external failure cost.

Generally speaking, more sophisticated environmental management programs in organisations exhibit a higher percentage of prevention and appraisal costs, relative to internal and external failure costs. Ideally, organisations should be spending money on systems that stop or monitor the likelihood of environmental problems arising, as opposed to paying for injury, government fines or compensation to broader society after problems arise.

※ **prevention costs**
Costs incurred by an organisation to ensure that environmental problems do not arise, or their likelihood of arising is minimised.

※ **appraisal costs**
The costs of monitoring the effects of our operations, in this chapter with respect to our environmental performance.

※ **internal failure costs**
Environmental costs incurred by organisations to address problems that have arisen within an organisation – they include costs to fix technologies, or care for employees owing to environmental incidents that may have occurred.

※ **external failure costs**
Environmental costs incurred by organisations to cover the costs or incur fines relating to environmental breaches that have impacted stakeholders outside itself.

Exercises

1 Sustainability value chains and performance indicators LO3, LO4

Consider the BHP Billiton sustainability indicators put forward in Exhibit 15.5. How would you describe BHP Billiton's performance? What do you believe they're doing well, and how could they be doing better? Can you think of any other sustainability indicators you might suggest to improve BHP Billiton's performance?

2 Sustainability value chains LO3

Considering Exhibit 15.5, suggest a brief sustainability value chain for a mining corporation like BHP Billiton. How might this style of value chain inform BHP Billiton beyond that provided by a traditional value chain?

3 Environmental costs analysis LO3, LO4

Consider the environmental costs expended by the three organisations below:

	Prevention	Appraisal	Internal failure	External failure
Dextra	$ 45 000	$67 000	$120 000	$240 000
Flexis	$ 20 000	$25 000	$ 5 000	$ 10 000
Creata	$100 000	$25 000	$ 0	$ 0

Required

a Write one paragraph for each company, explaining their environmental performance.

b In your opinion, which company is best managing its environmental performance?

c Reflect on Creata's environmental costs – are there any grounds for criticising their environmental cost expenditures?

4 Sustainability value chains and environmental costs LO3, LO5

The Sydney Opera House hosts high-profile events and corporate functions as part of its revenue-earning activities. How might the inclusion of recycling cause Opera House management to restructure their operations? Provide three sustainability performance indicators around recycling and re-use that might relate to operations in the Sydney Opera House.

5 Externalised costs LO2

Following is an excerpt from an article from the *Newcastle Herald* regarding a chemical spill involving Orica, a large chemicals manufacturer:

Orica ammonia leak sends two to hospital
MATTHEW KELLY
10 Nov. 2011 04:37 AM

THE Greens have called for Orica's Kooragang Island chemical plant to be closed and its operating licence revoked after two people were taken to hospital following an ammonia leak from the plant yesterday.

A NSW Ambulance spokeswoman said officers treated two people in Selwyn Street, Mayfield East, at 3pm after they suffered breathing difficulties.

The patients were taken to Calvary-Mater Hospital in a stable condition.

NSW Fire and Rescue crews identified the gas as ammonia and traced its source to the Kooragang Island Orica plant, about five kilometres away.

Source: 'Orica ammonia leak sends two to hospital', by Mathew Kelly. Published by *Newcastle Herald*, © 2011.

Required
If the Environmental Protection Authority is considering imposing a fine on Orica to cover the costs for this ammonia leak, what external cost types should they be considering? Please list as many cost types you think are relevant.

6 Externalised costs and environmental costs LO2, LO5

Refer to the discussion of external costs conducted in the chapter. Which of the following costs might be external costs, and what prevention or appraisal costs might help alleviate them?
1 Direct materials for the production of a Coca-Cola can
2 Employee illness owing to additional work hours, covered by an employer
3 Increasing crime rates owing to juvenile youth crime, arising from the absence of parental supervision. This is strongly attributed to the introduction of a production plant 10 years ago in the immediate area

4 Landslides impacting village communities arising from mining activities on the other side of a mountain range
5 Rent for a factory premises
6 Workers' compensation arising from employee injuries.

7 Sustainability value chain and triple bottom line reporting LO3, LO4

Create a sustainability value chain for Coca-Cola Amatil, the world-leading beverage maker, using Exhibit 15.4 as a guide. What key activities do you think Coca-Cola Amatil might focus on in trying to become a more sustainable organisation?

Problems

8 Triple bottom line analysis and performance indicators LO4

Information on the Gulf of Mexico oil spill is briefly provided below.

Eleven men were killed in the 20 April 2010 blowout on the Deepwater Horizon. By the time BP regained control of its well 87 days later, the Gulf was fouled by some 4.9m barrels of crude, destroying shrimp and oyster harvests and the tourist season. It was America's worst oil spill and the civil trial of BP and the other companies involved on the Deepwater Horizon had been expected to be one of the biggest and most complex legal proceedings in modern history. Hundreds of lawyers for all parties were involved in preparing for the trial – and in parallel negotiations to try to get a settlement. There were 340 lawyers from 90 different firms working on the plaintiffs' side alone. The deal between BP and more than 120 000 victims of the spill – from shrimp boat captains to sales teams at time-share condos, restaurateurs and wedding planners – settles what is arguably the most complicated part of the legal proceedings. But it will not be universally welcomed in the Gulf, where there is a strong undercurrent of opinion that wants to see BP held to account in court in addition to offering financial compensation.[7]

Required
Identify the four social, environmental and economic indicators (12 in total) that BP might consider in estimating and negotiating its compensation bill for this oil spill.

9 Environmental costs analysis LO3, LO4

Tulloch Ltd is a multinational construction company with subsidiary organisations all around the world. Following are five of their subsidiaries. Tulloch management is reflecting on the environmental costs expended by the five subsidiaries – this information is provided here:

	Prevention	Appraisal	Internal failure	External failure
Braydon Inc.	$ 30 000	$ 100 000	$200 000	$ 0
Thompson Inc.	$ 60 000	$ 20 000	$ 50 000	$ 90 000
Braxis Pty Ltd	$ 200 000	$ 300 000	$ 90 000	$100 000
Trawson Ltd.	$1 million	$2 million	$ 25 000	$ 10 000
Ghent Pty Ltd.	$ 45 000	$ 20 000	$ 40 000	$ 80 000

Required

a In your opinion, which subsidiary is the best performing, and why?

b Which is the worst performing subsidiary, and why?

c Overall, what criteria did you use to differentiate between the subsidiaries? Could you have developed alternative rationales that might have changed your answers to A and B?

10 Sustainability value chain and performance indicators LO3, LO4, LO5

Consider the Unilever Hindustan value chain, previously shown in the chapter as Exhibit 15.3 and displayed below.

The table below has been hypothetically supplemented with information regarding the prevention, appraisal, internal failure and external failure costs for the value chain:

	Raw materials	Manufacturing	Distribution	Consumer use	Disposal
Prevention	$20 000	$100 000	$60 000	$ 80 000	$100 000
Appraisal	$30 000	$ 30 000	$30 000	$ 40 000	$ 20 000
Int. failure	$50 000	$ 20 000	$10 000	$ 30 000	$ 50 000
Ext. failure	$10 000	$ 50 000	$ 0	$100 000	$200 000

Required

How would you analyse the environmental performance of Unilever Hindustan, based on the information provided?

11 Triple bottom line analysis and performance indicators LO4

Consider the following excerpt from a *Sydney Morning Herald* article, summarising an investigation by Oxfam and Profundo, a European research and economics firm:

Australia's major banks are funding large-scale illegal 'land grabs' in the developing world and enabling illegal logging, child labour or other human rights abuses. ANZ, National Australia Bank, Commonwealth Bank and Westpac have funded overseas companies investigated for illegally or improperly acquiring large tracts of land from local communities in developing countries, according to an investigation by NGO Oxfam Australia and European research and economics firm Profundo. Responding to the investigation, the four banks have pledged to work with Oxfam to deal with the claims. It is believed that ANZ and Westpac are considering severing their ties with the companies accused of impropriety.

Source: 'Banks face land grab claims in developing world', by Nick Mckenzie and Richard Baker from *The Sydney Morning Herald*. Copyright © 2014 by Fairfax Media. Used by permission.
This work has been licensed by Copyright Agency Limited (CAL). Except as permitted by the CopyrightAct, you must not re-use this work without the permission of the copyright owner or CAL.

Required

Reflect and discuss the economic, social and environmental factors that possibly relate to these phenomena, as viewed by

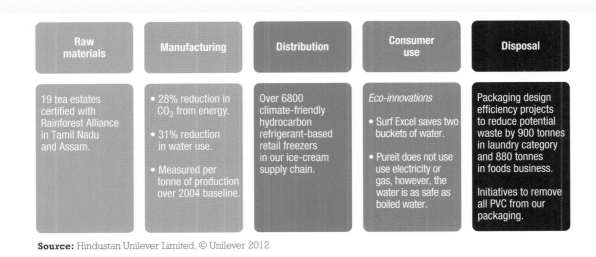

Raw materials	Manufacturing	Distribution	Consumer use	Disposal
19 tea estates certified with Rainforest Alliance in Tamil Nadu and Assam.	• 28% reduction in CO_2 from energy. • 31% reduction in water use. • Measured per tonne of production over 2004 baseline.	Over 6800 climate-friendly hydrocarbon refrigerant-based retail freezers in our ice-cream supply chain.	*Eco-innovations* • Surf Excel saves two buckets of water. • Pureit does not use use electricity or gas, however, the water is as safe as boiled water.	Packaging design efficiency projects to reduce potential waste by 900 tonnes in laundry category and 880 tonnes in foods business. Initiatives to remove all PVC from our packaging.

Source: Hindustan Unilever Limited, © Unilever 2012.

Unilever Hindustan food production sustainability value chain

managers of a large bank implicated. What triple bottom line factors do you think are key to this situation?

12 Externalised costs and environmental costs LO2, LO5

Read the paragraph below, extracted from a 2010 news article. It refers to fines charged to three central Queensland mines for water-release breaches.

The three central Queensland mines were fined for discharging into the Fitzroy River in breach of their environmental licence conditions. Moranbah North coal mine has been fined $4000 for exceeding its water release limits and for releasing water from an unauthorised discharge point. Rolleston and Callide coal mines were each fined $2000 for exceeding their water release limits. 'These fines are a clear message to mine operators that breaches will not be tolerated,' said Kate Jones, Queensland Minister for Climate Change and Sustainability.[8]

Required
a How would the three mines classify the above environmental fines in terms of our environmental costing framework?
b To what extent do you believe these fines might capture the external costs of these breaches?

Cases

13 External costs and environmental cost estimation LO2, LO5

Consider the following excerpt relating to pollution of the Queanbeyan River in 2007 caused by the Queanbeyan City Council.

Queanbeyan City Council has been ordered to pay almost $425 000 in fines and legal costs, for polluting the Queanbeyan River in 2007.

About 1 million litres of untreated sewage was released into the Queanbeyan and Molonglo Rivers causing significant contamination downstream.

Lake Burley Griffin was closed to swimming and water activities because of the health risks.

The sewage was released when the old Morisset Street Pumping Station malfunctioned.

Queanbeyan Council was convicted in the Land and Environment Court on Tuesday, after legal proceedings by the New South Wales Environment Protection Agency.

The Council says ratepayers will not be impacted by the legal costs and the penalty will be paid from a $23 million sewer fund.

Source: Adapted from 'Queanbeyan Council fined for polluting river'. Reproduced by permission of the Australian Broadcasting Corporation and ABC Online. © 2015 ABC. All rights reserved

Required
Identify the elements that you think the NSW Environment Protection Agency took into consideration, when imposing this fine? How might the cost and resulting fine have been estimated?

14 Sustainability value chains LO3

Please read the following excerpt from an article regarding sweat shop-based low-cost labour production occurring in Bangladesh:

Impoverished Bangladeshi workers claim they have been physically abused and threatened while working in sweatshops used by some of Australia's best-known retailers.

In one case, they were beaten and their representatives were told they would be killed if they protested against working conditions.

The ABC's Four Corners program has travelled to the country's capital Dhaka, where a number of workers revealed big Australian brands including Rivers, Coles, Target and Kmart ordered clothes from factories in Bangladesh that did not meet international standards.

The revelations come just months after international outcry over the tragic building collapse in Rana Plaza, which killed more than 1000 people and highlighted the plight of the nation's garment workers.[9]

Required
Explain how a sustainability value chain might cause a large manufacturer to revisit the way in which they use an overseas low-cost clothing manufacturing function. In discussing the value chain, consider opportunities and concerns raised by a sustainability value chain analysis.

TEST COMING UP?

NOW WHAT?

Learning objectives

1 Defining ethics and understanding the 'grey' in the ethical view of accounting.
2 Defining and describing the principles of ethical conduct.
3 Defining and describing the threats to ethical conduct.
4 Identifying safeguards to the practice of ethics in organisations.
5 Understanding an ethical framework for decision making.

ETHICS AND MANAGEMENT ACCOUNTING

c 16

Ethics and accounting must go together, but sometimes don't. Accountants, being in positions of significant financial responsibility in organisations, often act in ways that might be considered unethical, in the interests of objectives that might represent ideal economic practice. In the name of maximising firm profits, improving a division's bargaining position or keeping costs down, we might engage in behaviours that appear rational, but might present ethical conundrums. A *Financial Review* article published in February 2013, showed that accounting fraud above 41 million was on the rise, as per a biannual survey of fraud in Australia and NZ by KPMG.[1] How can we pursue the profit motive, while treating all firm stakeholders ethically?

In this chapter, we present ethical concepts as they relate to the practices of a management accountant discharging the role of accounting in their work settings. Ethics are a deeply personal and an individually unique phenomenon. No two persons regard ethics identically. Yet, we must start from a common point of understanding and we will therefore define ethics in order to more clearly discuss and impart its implications for management accounting.

LEARNING OBJECTIVE **1** >>

Defining ethics and appreciating the 'grey' in accounting ethics

Ethics is defined by the Chartered Institute of Management Accountants (CIMA), the premier professional management accounting body in the world, as being 'taking decisions for the right moral reasons, taking into account the wider needs of all stakeholders'.[2] CIMA subsequently explains business ethics as being the application of this ethics definition to business behaviour.

Ethics can be black and white, in that it might be clear that one should not engage in a conduct. A lot of the time, unethical conduct will be illegal as well ('Dimension 1' in Exhibit 16.1). For example, it's clear that accountants should not be stealing from the companies they are employed by! Similarly, it is worth affirming that most accountants act legally and these legal acts have a strong ethical basis ('Dimension 4', Exhibit 16.1). However, ethics can also be 'grey', in that the decisions taken by individuals might be personally construed as being acceptable and certainly legal within the law of the economy they operate within, but not ethical ('Dimension 3', Exhibit 16.1) when reflected against a stringent ethical code. Many individuals rationalise their practices in organisations as acceptable, in so far as they contribute to a company's performance – that is, the role of the employee to improve the firm's performance. Consequently, actions that achieve this purpose are construed as acceptable for the same reason. However, there are behaviours

relating to the preservation of profitability that might be unacceptable though positive for an organisation's financial performance. In such instances, ethics can become ambiguous in its application in practice. Picking an accelerated depreciation method that maximises tax savings in the short run is certainly legal practice, but if an asset is used evenly throughout its life, a straight line method of depreciation more accurately depicts the spread of the asset's cost, consistent with its usage (as is the intent of the depreciation concept), and this logic is what drives accounting standard setters' reasoning in providing alternative depreciation choices. An accountant who knows this basic idea, but nevertheless adopts a depreciation method that saves taxes in the short run, is arguably acting unethically (though entirely legally), in that stakeholders inside and outside the firm will now view the company asset position differently when it might have been more accurately depicted. Finally, an individual might engage in illegal behaviour that is ethical ('Dimension 2', Exhibit 16.1)! An accountant providing a staff discount to a non-staff, low-income customer in a hotel might be acting in a manner that breaches their allowed behaviour as per their work contract, and subject to legal action (however minor). However,

DIMENSION 1 Behaviour that is illegal and unethical	**DIMENSION 2** Behaviour that is illegal yet ethical
DIMENSION 3 Behaviour that is legal yet unethical	**DIMENSION 4** Behaviour that is both legal and ethical

EXHIBIT 16.1 Four dimensions of ethical behaviour

such actions were done in order to benefit an individual who is 'doing it tough'. They were not done for any personal benefit and are underpinned by a decidedly philanthropic ideal. These 'Robin Hood' circumstances, where we perform an illegal act to benefit someone less fortunate and not ourselves, make the issue of ethics much more perplexing in organisations.

In order to provide more direction to accountants, the Accounting Professional and Ethical Standards Board developed a range of professional and ethical principles that binds the conduct of accountants. Although these standards do not require it, they have been endorsed by the Chartered Accountants Australia and New Zealand, Certified Practising Accountants in Australia and the Institute of Public Accountants in Australia. The CIMA body also has a more limited but relevant list of ethical principles that can be compared to some of the APESB standards. These standards therefore bind the actions of the vast majority of practising accountants in Australian organisations.

Following is a discussion of the five APESB ethical principles, followed by the five threats that make it less likely that the five principles will be followed by accountants. From this perspective, the APESB standards are unique – they not only emphasise how accountants should behave (principles), but what circumstances they should avoid (threats) in order to more easily engage in ethical behaviours. Subsequently, we engage in an explanation of a list of safeguards that reduce the likelihood of unethical behaviours within the work environment or as imposed by external regulations and conclude the chapter by providing an ethical conflict resolution framework as recommended by the APESB, should an ethical conflict manifest itself. Throughout the chapter, definitions for the principles, threats, safeguards and ethical conflict resolution framework are sourced from the APESB standards, consistent with the expectations imposed on the vast majority of professional accountants in Australia.

In discussing the concepts described overleaf, it is important to commence by acknowledging that the

Clive Peeters and Specialty Fashions accounting fraud

Consider the examples below. Clive Peeters and Specialty Fashions were stung by accounting fraud totalling nearly $40 million each. Note that the practices stem from obvious deceit on the party of the accountants/perpetrators, but also arose due to the absence of key supervision or control systems, as claimed by some of the forensic accounting experts interviewed at the time.

In 2007, senior accountant Sonya Causer stole $20 million from electrical appliance retailers Clive Peeters. Mrs Causer was employed at the electrical retailer from March 2006. She started transferring company money into her own bank accounts in July 2007, using the funds to buy 43 properties in Victoria, Queensland and Tasmania, and a car in a charity auction.

According to Equity Trustees' Shaun Manuell this was almost the entire annual profit for the company. The firm's forensic accountant at the time said Mrs Causer's deception was highly sophisticated, but Manuell suggested that Clive Peeters' senior management should accept responsibility for the incident, because such a significant theft should have been detected due to the relative size of the business at the time. Clive Peeters (who later went into receivership) took civil action to recover the property and recovered just over $16 million. Causer was jailed for the theft in 2010.

Specialty Fashion Group, owning several chains, including Katies and Millers Retail was another Australian company grappling with a multimillion dollar fraud. In May 2009, the group revealed $16 million was falsely charged over four or five years. Specialty Fashion's former head of property Simon Feldman was

charged with the theft and was sentenced to six years in prison. Only approximately $50 000 of Specialty Fashion Group's losses were recovered.

Forensic accountant Darryl Swindells indicated that deceptions like these are uncovered by chance and could have been prevented. Swindells indicated that most frauds are not sophisticated, and are often a matter of someone falsifying an invoice. He also suggested that most organisations know that you should have controls over such things as how you make a payment and that they must closely scrutinise costs and ask questions if expenses seem to be going up by more than what is reasonable.

Source Wikimedia Commons/Wags05 (talk)

Did a lack of accounting controls lead to the downfall of electrical retailer Clive Peeters?

Sources: 'Jail term looms for executive's $16.6m fraud' & 'He tried to be a hero, and then it all unravelled', by Vanda Carson. Published by *The Sydney Morning Herald*, © 2011; 'Mother jailed for $20m Clive Peeters theft', by Andrea Petrie. Published by *The Age*, © 2010; 'Clive Peeters, Specialty Fashion $20m-fraud victims', by Neal Woolrich. Publsihed by ABC News, © 2009.

public interest

The public interest includes the totality of all stakeholders outside an organisation that are affected by, or can possibly be perceived to be affected by, the actions of the organisation.

APESB considers it key that accountants act, in organisations, in the **public interest.** The duty of an accountant, first and foremost, is to the public interest. If an action conducted by an accountant in an organisation endangers the public interest, it is likely that the accountant's actions will transgress one of the five ethical principles. Indeed, APES 110 paragraph 100.1 specifically states '…a Member's responsibility is not exclusively to satisfy the needs of an individual client or employer'.

Finally, when our understanding of an accountant's ethical obligations are made clear it will become evident that much about ethics in accounting that you might have thought as being uncertain or 'grey', is actually not so, In ethical speak, what an 'average' person might get away with in society is quite clearly not ethical for accountants. Why the higher standard? Simply, accounting is a profession of repute that has potential to significantly impact corporate and broader society through its members' ethical choices. It is therefore essential that accountants engage in ethical behaviours, and the 'bar' on ethical conduct is consequently set far higher for accountants than many other individuals or groups in society.

LEARNING OBJECTIVE **2** >>

Five ethical principles
Integrity

The principle of integrity requires that accountants are 'straightforward and honest in all professional and business relationships' (APES 110 paragraph 100.5 a).[3] This meaning is quite simple, but also wide ranging in its meaning. In dealing with other accountants or non-accountants, an accountant must communicate information surrounding the effect of accounting concepts in a way that does not intentionally mislead or drives behaviours in affected individuals that otherwise would not have occurred.

This principle covers the possibility of misrepresentation through **sleight of meaning** – using terminology to confuse, or influence other stakeholders in ways that benefit an organisation or individual, at the expense of another, without their knowing.

Here is a 'grey' ethics example to get you talking, perhaps even challenging or disagreeing with (that is the point – it's grey!). A management accountant in Firm Z promises Supplier A that his

sleight of meaning

Using terminology to confuse, or influence other stakeholders in ways that benefit an organisation or individual, at the expense of another, without their knowing.

company will acquire their product, causing Supplier A to hold the inventory, and not sell it to others. The accountant then shops around and finds a cheaper product from Supplier B, and purchases the product from Supplier B instead. It is unquestionable that the accountant has acted extremely prudently in an economic sense, lowering costs for his firm. Some might even say that Supplier A should know better, was naïve and should have made the accountant from Firm Z pay a deposit to secure the purchase. All these arguments are correct, but are operating or financial arguments for how the supplier could have 'locked in' the customer. It does not change the fact that the accountant told Supplier A he was going to purchase from them, all the while knowing he was shopping around, and was going to take any price that was better. Functionally, the supplier was misled (naively), and held the inventory for the accountant thinking it was a 'done' deal, missing sales opportunities to other customers. This almost certainly means the accountant acted unethically, though economically prudently.

Managers in organisations may also receive financial or non-financial perks or kickbacks from their clients for facilitating transactions between their firm and those of a client. If their decision to do so was based on a genuine belief that it represents the interests of their organisation, there is no issue. However, if they select a client because they received two tickets to an international rugby, football or cricket match from the client, and were 'wined and dined', and this contributed to their decision to transact with the client, that is another matter altogether, and represents unethical conduct.

Objectivity

The principle of objectivity refers to accountants avoiding 'bias, conflict of interest or the undue influence of others to override professional or business judgements' (APES 110 paragraph 110.5 b).[4] There are three components to this principle. **Bias** refers to the inclination to disproportionately favour one entity over another. **Conflict of interest** exists when an individual is burdened by competing interests that oppose, but which are under the control of the same individual. **Undue influence** refers to entities impacting our judgement owing to the presence of a material dependence that impairs our reasoning of their actions. All these three signal a similar issue – that an accountant might lose sight of their objectivity owing to the above three phenomena. Perhaps we might be dined by a senior manager

bias

The inclination to disproportionately favour one entity over another.

conflict of interest

When an individual is burdened by competing interests that oppose, but which are under the control of the same individual.

undue influence

Entities impacting our judgement owing to the presence of a material dependence that impairs our reasoning of their actions.

that wishes us to apply a management accounting technique that provides the manager an easier budget target in an upcoming period. Or, we might be advised by the CEO that if we engage in a questionable practice, the CEO 'will not forget what you did for the firm'. These 'temptations' do not detract from the unethical nature of our actions, should we yield to these influences.

Would a free dinner have an impact on your objectivity?

For example, a CFO supervising the budget allocation process for different departments might be partial to a department that she used to work in before being promoted, and therefore implicitly more amenable when negotiating numbers with the head of that particular department, relative to the other heads of department. This mode of behaviour is unethical, as it is not based on the quality of arguments but rather on personal affinity that is independent of the budgeting task at hand. As with the Firm Z example above, there are wonderful social reasons for why the CFO is biased, and some might even say 'that's just the way the world works, it's connections and networks' – all these arguments are most certainly valid, but not from an ethical perspective. It doesn't change the fact that going easier on a department because you like them is an unfair practice (and therefore unethical), which disadvantages other departments.

Professional competence and due care

This principle is unique in that it reminds an accountant that the lack of knowledge and proper discharging of their work as accountants is not simply symptomatic of the absence of knowledge, but actually representative of unethical conduct. APES 110 paragraph 100.5 c identifies that accountants must maintain a level of professional knowledge that allows the delivery of a quality service to clients, and engages in the requisite training and development to do so. Is it fair that the lack of knowledge in an accountant allows us to call that accountant unethical? Yes, if that accountant advises clients, deals with non-accountants in an organisation and influences employee behaviours, all the while being aware that his/her knowledge of the accounting concepts being espoused is lacking.

Confidentiality

The confidentiality principle balances the duty of an accountant to ethically maintain the secrets of an organisation, while at the same time acting in the public interest should the need arise. APES 110 paragraph 110.5 d explains that accountants must '... respect the confidentiality of information acquired as a result of professional and business relationships and, therefore, not disclose any such information to third parties without proper and specific authority, unless there is a legal or professional right or duty to disclose, nor use the information for the personal advantage of the Member or third parties.'[5] Therein lies the balance – keep company secrets and do not disclose them, nor use them for personal benefit, unless one is legally expected to do so, or professionally considers that it must be done for the accountant to maintain her professional integrity. **Whistleblowing** is a controversial practice that some laud and others despise.

> Australia lags a long way behind other G20 countries when it comes to whistleblower protection laws, a new report claims. Melbourne and Griffith University researchers compared the safeguards offered by each of the world's leading economic powers to those who try to expose wrong-doing. They concluded that Australia has significant room for improvement, particularly in the private sector. The G20 has identified fighting corruption as a major part of its agenda, saying it results in losses of around $1 trillion in revenue every year. It made commitments in 2010 and 2012 to protect whistleblowers. One of the report authors, Suelette Dreyfus, said Australia ranked around the middle of the G20 nations – behind similar countries like the US and the UK. 'I don't think that average is good enough, really,' she said.[6]

The whistleblower observes practices that are not correct in organisations, then reports it to the broader public in order that an awareness of the organisation's conduct might be placed in the spotlight, causing organisations

✳ **whistleblowing**
The decision by an employee to reveal perceived unethical or illegal conduct occurring within an entity, to the general public or interested outside stakeholders who are adversely affected by the conduct.

to change their practices. Whistleblowing clearly breaches the confidentiality criteria, as an individual reveals internal private information to the broader public, presumably against the wishes of the organisation. However, if a whistleblower genuinely acts in the public interest, wanting to stamp out corrupt practices or undesirable behaviours that continue in organisations, he/she is implicitly constructing an ethical basis for conducting the same action. Management accountants who inform auditors of accounting malpractice in a company might lose their jobs and 'martyr' their careers, in the quest to improve the ethics of an organisation's practice. We do not make direct recommendations regarding the nature of whistleblowing behaviours, owing to their highly individualised circumstances, but we can assert that the space within which 'whistleblowing' operates can be ambiguous from an ethical perspective and certainly divide opinions among different stakeholders of the organisation concerned.

Professional behaviour

The fifth principle requires that accountants '...comply with relevant laws and regulations and avoid any action that discredits the profession' (APES 110 paragraph 100.5 e).[7] This principle broadly requires accountants to engage in behaviours that are not only ethical from the perspective of other stakeholders relating to a company (customers, suppliers, employees, etc.), but also more generally behave in a way that will not bring the accounting profession into disrepute. This principle naturally controls for changing norms and expectations over time, or different cultures in business globally. Whatever the context, if an accountant is acting in a way that might bring his profession into disrepute, the accountant will be considered as being in breach of the 'Professional Behaviour' principle. The standard goes on to describe that accountants cannot speak negatively of other accountants' practices in spruiking their own (unless materially evidenced), thus indirectly upholding the high reputational standard of the profession. For example, if a management accountant says in an interview 'I am better at

Whistleblowing – Lehman Brothers making it real

Consider the following article, outlining the whistleblowing example of Matthew Lee, a senior vice-president in Lehman Brothers, the US bank that collapsed in 2008:

> A worried accounting executive at Lehman Brothers, who raised the alarm about what he saw as dubious number-crunching at the doomed Wall Street bank, lost his job barely a month after alerting the auditor Ernst & Young, his lawyer claimed yesterday, in a case prompting calls for tighter protection for corporate whistleblowers.
>
> Matthew Lee, a senior vice-president in Lehman's finance division, outlined six allegations of unethical accounting in a memo sent on 16 May 2008 to Lehman's senior managers, who asked Ernst & Young to investigate. In discussions with partners at Ernst & Young, he highlighted controversial 'repo 105' transactions that artificially boosted Lehman's balance sheet by $50bn (£33bn).
>
> But the London-based accounting firm took 'virtually no action', according to an official report into Lehman's demise and Lee's lawyer, Erwin Shustak, said his client lost his job in late June 2008, officially as part of a broader downsizing. Shustak told the Wall Street Journal: 'It was just easier to shut him up and let him go.'

Lee acted in a manner that clearly did not please his employer, however many herald him as having attempted to do the right thing, in informing his auditor of what he believed were suspect accounting

practices by his employer. In this instance, if we are to believe Lee's assertions, he has been fired for engaging in ethical conduct that broke his employment contract requiring confidentiality, but met his professional ethical standards for not wanting to be party to practices he felt were not acceptable.

Source: Copyright Guardian News & Media Ltd 2010. http://www.theguardian.com/business/2010/mar/16/lehman-whistleblower-auditors-matthew-lee

Whistleblowers construct an ethical basis for breaching an organisation's confidentiality. This practice is controversial and often highly publicised.

constructing performance management systems than all the useless accountants in your company' – that might be construed as a breach of the 'professional behaviour' principle. Why? The accountant is putting their fellow professional members down, in order to advance their own career. However, if the accountant won the 'Management accountant – performance management excellence' award at an industry body awards night, they could use that as the basis to assert their superiority over other accountants. In a nutshell, if one is going to claim superiority or criticise another, it must be evidenced.

Having considered the five principles, we now consider the five threats that drive accountant behaviours to act unethically, knowingly or unknowingly.

LEARNING OBJECTIVE 3>>

Ethical threats

Why do some accountants act unethically, that is, behave in a manner that transgresses the above principles? Indeed, 99.99% of accountants walk into an organisation without the intention to engage in fraud! Nevertheless, a minority of these individuals will at some time, act unethically. The APESB identifies situations accountants must be wary of, in order to minimise the likelihood of breaching the ethical principles. These threats are

multifaceted, and should not be thought of in isolation. APES 110 paragraph 100.12 explains that 'When a relationship or circumstance creates a threat, such a threat could compromise, or could be perceived to compromise, a Member's compliance with the fundamental principles. A circumstance or relationship may create more than one threat, and a threat may affect compliance with more than one fundamental principle.'[8]

Following are the five threats to the principles, explained below.

Self interest

The self interest threat is somewhat self explanatory. Generally, accountants that place their personal gain at the expense of the broader organisational objectives put themselves in positions where they might act unethically. APES 110 paragraph 110.12 a defines self interest as '…the threat that a financial or other interest will inappropriately influence the Member's judgment or behaviour'.[9] Management accountants who are tasked with determining departmental budgets in their own departments might be tempted to request more costs and underquote the volume of revenues being targeted, as it makes it easier for their department to achieve their financial indicators, possibly meaning a promotion or bonus salary payment for the accountant. In this way, it is in the interest of the departmental accountant to make her budget easier than otherwise might be the case.

EPAC Salary Solutions accountant fraud

Following is an excerpt from an ABC article, outlining how an accountant in charge of reconciling motor charge card payments siphoned more than a million dollars into his personal accounts, thus relating to self interest. The individual concerned intended to personally and financially benefit, at the expense of the corporation. While his lawyers argued that he felt stressed and undervalued in the workplace, the judge disagreed, arguing that an accountant with financial acumen should have known better:

> Demetres Kyriacos Zacharoudes, 31, pleaded guilty to five charges of deception. The Adelaide District Court was told he diverted money to personal bank accounts from his employer EPAC Salary Solutions between November 2011 and April 2012.
>
> The court heard Zacharoudes had the job of reconciling payments made on motor charge cards to determine reimbursement. He falsified reports and made payments into his personal account and

another in the name of his parents, who acted as trustees. A total of $1,024,144.76 was siphoned off.

The court heard some of that money was then withdrawn in small amounts at various locations and no large purchases were ever made. The offending was uncovered when the National Australia Bank noticed Zacharoudes redirecting the money. Zacharoudes originally faced 27 charges of deception, but pleaded on five.

Judge David Smith said the crimes were devious, cunning and gravely serious and could not be considered as sudden or isolated acts. The defence argued the theft was not motivated by greed but an inordinate amount of stress in the workplace, with Zacharoudes sometimes working up to 50 hours per week.

Source: 'Accountant jailed for $1 million fraud', by Matthew Doran. Reproduced by permission of the Australian Broadcasting Corporation and ABC Online. © 2015 ABC. All rights reserved.

Making it real

More generally, parallels might be drawn between self interest and the breaching of many of the principles. Indeed, it might be argued that self interest is a root cause for much unethical conduct in society, more broadly, beyond accounting!

Self review

The self review threat exists when there is 'the threat that a Member will not appropriately evaluate the results of a previous judgement made or service performed by the Member, or by another individual within the Member's Firm or employing organisation, on which the Member will rely when forming a judgement as part of providing a current service' (APES 110 paragraph 100.12 b).[10] It is natural that if evaluating our own work, or making judgements surrounding aspects of a decision that relates to our prior contribution, we might be inclined to evaluate more loosely, without being as stringent as we ordinarily might.

For example, the American Insurance Group (AIG) conducted accounting fraud approximating US$3.9 billion, and incurred penalties and settlement fees for this fraud for approximately US$2.6 billion. Interestingly, executives in AIG posted the largest quarterly corporate loss in history at the time (2008), but rewarded themselves with US$165 million in bonuses. No doubt, these actions were legal within the framework of the corporate governance standards and regulation. If the bonuses are deserving, then these actions are ethical. However, many might argue that the receipt of bonuses in a year where record quarterly loss was announced is less than ethical, notwithstanding the legal agreements and remuneration contracts in existence for executives.

Advocacy

The fourth threat, advocacy, is defined in APES 110 paragraph 100.12 c as being 'the threat that a Member will promote a client's or employer's position to the point that the Member's objectivity is compromised'.[11] This threat has relations to the self-interest threat, in that an accountant might be tempted to push the agenda of a related entity, as it furthers the positive perception of the same accountant. Consider a management accountant in a firm being asked about the accuracy of the company's forecast for the upcoming period. Even if the accountant thought the forecasts were optimistic, he might not say as much, or 'dance' around the issue with a vague answer. Does the accountant want to mislead the individual asking? Probably not, but the accountant seeks to 'talk up' the firm, so that the positive external perception of the firm by outside stakeholders might improve its market value, thus positively affecting the salary of the accountant. Another area where the 'advocacy' ethical threat often arises is in the provision of expert witnesses by one organisation over a long period of time. If an accountant is paid a large sum in fees to provide expert witness evidence on behalf of a firm repeatedly, it is possible that the accountant might become partial to the views of the firm over time, not wanting to lose a significant revenue stream from the 'expert witness' activity.

Familiarity

The familiarity threat is when an accountant acts in a way that benefits another individual or institution that is familiar to the accountant. This threat strongly relates to the objectivity principle, in that the presence of familiarity in our dealings with another party can compromise our ability to act impartially, hence causing us to compromise our ethical choices. APES 110 paragraph 100.12 d defines this threat as 'the threat that due to a long or close relationship with a client or employer, a Member will be too sympathetic to their interests or too accepting of their work'.[12] By way of example, consider the accountant that has a long-time friend working as a marketing executive in the same company. This might cause the accountant to create softer targets for the marketing department, so that her acquaintance in marketing might benefit. Making accounting judgements in favour of other known individuals are consequently examples of unethical behaviours brought about by the 'familiarity' threat.

Intimidation

The final threat is intimidation. This threat is concerning, in that it might manifest as an unsafe or undesirable work environment for an accountant. Senior management might pressure an accountant to act unethically, such that the company benefits at the expense of the broader public interest. An accountant knows the behaviour is unethical, but is pressured to do so by intimidation. APES 110 paragraph 100.12 e defines intimidation as 'the threat that a Member will be deterred from acting objectively because of actual or perceived pressures, including attempts to exercise undue influence over the Member'.[13]

Having considered the APES principles and threats, we now discuss safeguards that might be employed by accountants in organisations to ensure that threats are less likely to manifest, or influence the practising of ethical principles. That brings us to an important point. The ethical standards do not guarantee the avoidance of a threat situation, merely an awareness of its existence. The belief here is that the understanding and awareness that accrues from knowing the threat exists prevents its effect on accountant behaviours. For example, if accountants acknowledge the presence of the 'self review' threat, they might make a more concerted effort to be judicious and diligent in evaluating work that involves their own prior effort. Ideally, they should not be engaging in self review at all. However, in the absence of any other choice, it is pragmatically acceptable that they engage in self review but are aware of the risks, and compensate accordingly. The same can be said for any of the other threats.

LEARNING OBJECTIVE **4**>>

Safeguards to counter threats

Safeguards are measures that can be put in place to counter the threats, assuming the accountant considers that the threats will not compromise the member's adherence to any of the five principles. As outlined in APES 110 paragraph 100.2 c: *'Safeguards are necessary when the Member determines that the threats are not at a level at which a reasonable and informed third party would be likely to conclude, weighing all the specific facts and circumstances available to the Member at that time, that compliance with the fundamental principles is not compromised.'*[14]

Safeguards fall into two broad categories. First are safeguards created by the profession, legislation or regulation (as per APES 110 paragraph 100.14). These include:

1   Educational, training and experience requirements, whereby accountants undertake training in university, then professionally through a professional accounting body, and concurrently work in an accounting capacity while doing so. These exposures to accounting thought and practice educate accountants on the acceptable norms that relate to the role of an accountant.

2   Continuing professional development (CPD) requirements, refers to the ongoing annual training that accountants must undertake in order to maintain their professional certification as a CA, CPA, etc. To the extent that accountants attend training sessions that educate them on the ethical norms of practice, reminding them of acceptable modes of conduct, CPD training assists accountants to be informed of relevant ethical standards.

3   Corporate governance regulations identify norms surrounding the proper management and direction with which senior officers are expected to discharge their duties when managing organisations. This implicitly constrains the behaviour of senior accountants that perform a managerial/governance function in their firms.

4   Professional standards, professional or regulatory monitoring and disciplinary procedures act as deterrents to accountants, further minimising the likelihood that unethical behaviours might be actioned.

5   Finally, if all the above fails, organisations can execute an external review by a legally empowered third party who independently judges the actions of an accountant or firm, making a determination on the ethical nature (or otherwise) of conduct by accountants.[15]

Continuous development training is designed to educate accountants about the most current ethical safeguards.

The second category of safeguards refers to safeguards in a work environment, and are adapted from APES 110 paragraph 300.14. These are internal systems, practices, perspectives or structures within organisations that cause it to reduce the likelihood of threats (independent of external regulations). These safeguards remind managers and executives that ethical behaviours can be directed from within a firm – that well-designed internal control practices can incentivise ethical behaviours, or at the very least, make it more difficult for unethical behaviours to arise.

1   An organisation's systems of oversight within – organisations often create their own monitoring systems, attempting to drive out unethical or undesirable employee behaviours through the implementation of management systems that documents or critiques their work practices.

2   Organisational ethics and conduct programs act as clear barriers to the occurrence of unethical conduct.

3   Recruitment procedures – high calibre competent staff. Generally, the recruiting of high quality staff aligns strongly to ethical conduct. Such staff are less likely to rely on 'foul play' in order to achieve their objectives.

4   Strong internal controls – internal controls are planning, controlling or evaluation systems that ensure employees act in a manner consistent with the organisation achieving its objectives.

5   Appropriate disciplinary processes – when aware of the possible threat of severe disciplinary action, employees often gravitate toward behaving conservatively and in line with organisational expectations.

6   Leadership – when the leaders of an organisation set an example by conducting themselves ethically, junior employees or managers tend to follow suit, as unethical conduct is implicitly signalled as undesirable – succinctly, if the leader isn't doing it, how can I?

7 Monitor the quality of employee performance – it is sometimes necessary for companies to not only observe employee adherence to performance, but the manner by which the performance has been met. Were compromises made to achieve targets? Are stakeholders outside the organisation adversely affected by the actions of an accountant?

8 Timely communication of an organisation's policies and procedures, and appropriate training and education on the same. By communicating an organisation's behavioural expectations through its policies, employees are clearly made aware that any unethical behaviours lie outside the boundary of acceptable behaviours, thus acting as a deterrent.

9 Senior management willing to hear employee descriptions of ethical grievances without experiencing a fear of reprisal. Employees must feel like their detection and reporting of ethical breaches does not cause them to be penalised.

10 Consultation with another appropriate Member – this safeguard simply reinforces that at times, a realistic approach when reflecting on an accountant's possible unethical conduct is to communicate their conduct to another accountant, gauging their practice leaning view, and acting as a second opinion.[16]

LEARNING OBJECTIVE 5 >>

Ethical conflict resolution framework

The APESB has developed an ethical conflict resolution framework to help its member managers resolve accounting ethical problems (indeed, the framework applies to most ethical issues). To resolve ethical conflict, we need to identify an ethical conflict resolution process:

a Relevant facts – what do we know of the matters concerning the problem at hand? The first step of the process requires managers to understand the factual content of the events that transpired, relating to the ethical conduct. Consider the ING accounting fraud, described in the 'Making It Real' example above. The events as explained in the article might serve as a summary of the relevant facts relating to the case (to the extent that the public is aware of the issues, through the media).

b Ethical issues involved – the ethical matters that relate to the relevant facts are then extracted from the 'story' encapsulating the problem at hand. In the ING case, we might argue that the ethical issues relate to the intentional pilfering of cash out of an organisation, without management consent.

c Fundamental principles related to the matter in question – the five principles as communicated in Learning Objective 1 are assessed next to the matter being investigated. For example, the relevant principles affected by the ING case might be 'Integrity', as the accountant acted in her personal interest, and not in a straightforward or honest way; and 'Professional Behaviour', as her conduct was not becoming of an accountant, and placed her profession in disrepute. Her actions were arguably less related to the 'Objectivity', 'Professional Competence and Due Care' or 'Confidentiality' principles.

d Established internal procedures – what went wrong in the case concerned, and how might we mitigate the likelihood of its occurrence? By identifying internal procedures that make it harder for such fraud to occur, we improve controls in our organisation. In the ING case, ING might step up its monitoring of all accounting staff, and more concertedly segregate duties relating to acquisitions or disbursements in the firm. Further, managers might be trained on methods for more actively monitoring employees.

e Alternative courses of action – the final step relates to the other actions that can be mobilised. As opposed to allowing the accountant to do what is currently being done, can we change the way we do things so that this problem never happens again, whoever the accountant. For example, ING might institute more electronic or automated payment systems to reduce the possibility of individuals manipulating manual payment processes, paying falsified invoices, etc.

Overall, the above conflict resolution seeks to identify the problem, and provide solutions to allow an organisation to move forward from the incidences of fraud. Also, a firm might not necessarily feel the need to apply all five steps, or may indeed use additional steps in the conflict resolution process outside of those suggested (as discussed in APES 110 paragraph 100.18).

Exercises

1 Understanding ethical principles – integrity LO 1, 2

Identify the principle of integrity, and give one example of conduct with Integrity that a management accountant might engage in during the course of her work.

2 Understanding ethical principles – confidentiality LO 1, 2

Can an accountant pursue the principle of Confidentiality and act unethically in the process? Please explain with an example.

3 Understanding ethical principles – objectivity LO 2, 4

What is the difference between 'conflict of interest', and 'bias', as discussed within the Objectivity principle? Give an example of each, from an accounting perspective, and discuss how we might safeguard against these two elements.

4 Understanding ethical principles – professional competence and due care LO 2

Is an accountant who has not kept up with her training being unethical? Discuss with reference to the 'Professional competence and due care' ethical principle.

5 Ethical professional obligations LO 2, 3

To what extent is an accountant expected to act in the interests of the profession, from an ethical perspective? Reflect on the accounting principles and threats in justifying your answer.

6 Understanding ethical principles LO 2, 3

What principles and threats become relevant if an accountant criticises another accountant, in order to further his own career? Please explain with specific reference to any of the ethical principles.

Problems

7 Legality, ethics and APES principles LO 1, 2, 3

Consider the following statement:
> I am a very ethical accountant. I have never, ever broken the law, or any accounting standard – there is no way I could possibly transgress any accounting professional and ethical standard.

Required
Can an individual making the above statement transgress the APES principles? Please explain with examples, and with reference to the APES principles/threats if relevant.

8 Threats to ethical practice LO 2, 3

Jenny Edwards, CFO of Mining Inc. is good friends with Jay Grosse, the HR manager. Jenny explains to the CEO that she implicitly trusts Jay's budget estimates, as Jay is a person of high integrity, in her opinion. She is unsure about the other divisional managers, and is considering being tougher on their budget requests.

Required
As the CEO, and with your knowledge of the APESB principles/threats, how might you respond?

9 Threats to ethical practice LO 3, 4

Rosie Johnson runs Johnson Motors, a company making high quality motor parts. Rosie is considering having Julie Macklin, her payables manager, also run the cash payments division. Rosie trusts Julie implicitly, and would rather she govern the whole process than leave someone else running the payments function.

Required
What ethical threats might come into play, if this change in responsibility structure were to occur? What safeguards might Rosie employ to mitigate these?

10 Applying an ethical framework LO 4, 5

Consider the Clive Peeters 'Making It Real' example in the chapter and answer the following:

Required
Identify a conflict resolution framework that might relate to this scenario, based on your reading of this 'Making It Real' example.

11 Ethical issues analysis LO 2, 3

You are in charge of a departmental budget, and your CEO tells you to increase the requested costs in the budget to be submitted to the US parent company, as it will allow her to better resource staff. She wants to you to throw the additional budget costs into the 'projects' budget line, as these are rarely questioned by the US parent firm. The CEO explains that she does not want the money for her own personal benefit, but simply to look after staff better and provide them with a more enjoyable work environment.

Required
To what extent are you acting consistently with the APES, if you request more funds in the budget using the method described by the CEO? Is this even an unethical conduct? Please explain your answer with reference to the APESB principles and threats.

12 Ethics in context LO 3

Consider the EPAC Salary Solutions accounting fraud provided as a 'Making It Real' example earlier in the chapter.

Required
Recommend three safeguards that could be implemented to prevent this occurrence in the future, explaining the relevance of each.

Cases

13 Ethics and fraud LO3, LO4

Consider the following excerpt from a report by CPA Australia on fraud:

> Fraud is behaviour that is deceptive, dishonest, corrupt or unethical. For fraud to exist there needs to be an offender, a victim and an absence of control or safeguards.
>
> Fraud is generally described in three categories:
> 1 asset misappropriation
> 2 fraudulent accounting and financial reporting
> 3 corruption.
>
> Conversely, fraudulent activity is usually motivated by one or more of three main factors:
> 1 pressures
> 2 opportunity
> 3 rationalisation.
>
> **Source:** 'Employee Fraud: A guide to reducing the risk of employee fraud and what to do after a fraud is detected'. Copyright © 2011 by CPA Australia Ltd. Used by permission.

Required:

Reflect on the ethics content of this chapter, and identify how three 'work environment' safeguards discussed might reduce the existence of fraud occurrences in organisations. Then, consider your suggestions just made, and reflect on any new ethical risks you introduce to the firm as a result of the suggestions made. (Hint: No system is perfect and the introduction of any new measure potentially hinders another aspect of ethical conduct, or raises its likelihood.)

14 Ethical principles and threats LO1, LO2, LO3, LO4

The following extract outlines how a long-time ING employee, trusted and respected in her firm, conducted large scale fraud to the value of approximately A$30 million. The employee claimed that the fraud was made possible by a lax supervisor, and the author of the article below questioned the controls in ING. ING responded by arguing that it was satisfied with its security measures. Consider the article below:

> The multinational insurance and finance company ING suffered a $30 million net loss from the massive fraud committed by its senior accountant, Rajina Subramaniam, court documents reveal. Files released after Subramaniam was sentenced to at least seven years' jail last week, show the company has recovered only a third of the $45.3 million the 42-year-old stole over five years. While most of the incredible haul of luxury goods and property purchased with the money – including $16 million worth of Paspaley Pearls jewellery and eight waterfront apartments – has been recovered and resold by the company, it has taken a substantial hit. 'There is no realistic possibility that the full cost of those items can be fully recovered,' documents tendered by the prosecution state.
>
> This is due, in part, to the fact that Subramaniam paid well above market rates for the properties she purchased. The court documents also paint a less-than-flattering picture of internal security at the section of ING where Subramaniam worked, ING Australia Holdings. During her interview with police shortly after being arrested, Subramaniam said: 'My manager is so slack, he didn't care, so I was sort of doing it to see when I would get caught [but] you know, he just left it open for me.' She said the manager – who cannot be named – would come in at 10am, and appeared not to be interested in the job.
>
> It is understood Subramaniam did not have any formal accounting qualifications, but had worked her way up from the position of assistant accountant. As a senior accountant she made 200 illegal transfers into her personal accounts or directly to shops and real estate agents. She then used the computer log-ins of former staff to delete the records or alter them so the transactions appeared legitimate.
>
> **Source:** 'ING takes a $30m hit in accountancy fraud case', by Paul Bibby from *The Sydney Morning Herald*. Copyright © 2014 by Fairfax Media. This work has been licensed by Copyright Agency Limited (CAL). Except as permitted by the CopyrightAct, you must not re-use this work without the permission of the copyright owner or CAL.

Required

a In your opinion, what could ING have done better in this situation?

b What principles or threats did the staff member breach?

c What safeguards can ING put in place in the future, to minimise the possibility of this occurrence again?

TIME VALUE
OF MONEY

APPENDIX A

When decisions are affected by cash flows that are paid or received in different time periods, it is necessary to adjust those cash flows for the time value of money (TVM). Because of our ability to earn interest on money invested, we would prefer to receive $1 today rather than a year from now. Likewise, we would prefer to pay $1 a year from now rather than today. A common technique used to adjust cash flows received or paid in different time periods is to discount those cash flows by finding their present value. **Present value (PV)** of cash flows is the amount of future cash flows discounted to their equivalent worth today. To fully understand the calculations involved in finding the present value of future cash flows, it is necessary to step back and examine the nature of interest and the calculation of interest received and paid. Interest is simply a payment made to use someone else's money. When you invest money in a bank account, the bank pays you interest for the use of your money for a period of time. If you invest $100 and the bank pays you $106 at the end of the year, it is clear that you earned $6 of interest on your money (and 6 per cent interest for the year).

Future value

Mathematically, the relationship between your initial investment (present value), the amount in the bank at the end of the year (future value) and the interest rate (r) is as follows:

$$FV_{(Year\ 1)} = PV(1 + r)$$

In our example, $FV_{(Year\ 1)} = 100(1 + 0.06) = \$106$. If you leave your money in the bank for a second year, what happens? Will you earn an additional $6 of interest? It depends on whether the bank pays you simple interest or compound interest. **Simple interest** is interest on the invested amount only, whereas **compound interest** is interest on the invested amount plus interest on previous interest earned but not withdrawn. Simple interest is sometimes computed on short-term investments and debts (that is, those that are shorter than six months to a year). Compound interest is typically computed for financial arrangements longer than one year. We will assume that interest is compounded in all examples in this book. Extending the future-value formula to find the amount we have in the bank in two years gives us the following formula:

$$FV_{(Year\ 2)} = PV(1 + r)(1 + r)$$

or

$$FV_{(Year\ 2)} = PV(1 + r)^2$$

In our example, $FV_{(Year\ 2)} = 100(1 + 0.06)^2$, or $112.36. We earned $6.36 of interest in Year 2 – $6 on our original $100 investment and $0.36 on the $6 of interest earned but not withdrawn in Year 1 ($6 × 0.06).

In this example, we have assumed that compounding is on an annual basis. Compounding can also be calculated semiannually, quarterly, monthly, daily or even continually. Go back to our original $100 investment in the bank. If the bank pays 6 per cent interest compounded semiannually instead of annually, we would have $106.09 after one year. Note that the interest rate is typically expressed as a percentage rate per year. We are really earning 3 per cent for each semiannual period, not 6 per cent. It is usually easier to visualise the concept of interest rate compounding graphically with the help of time lines. Exhibit A.1 graphically demonstrates the impact of annual, semiannual and monthly compounding of the 6 per cent annual rate on our original $100 investment.

Mathematically, our formula for future value can once again be modified slightly to account for interest rates compounded at different intervals. $FV_{(n\ periods\ in\ the\ future)} = PV(1 + r)n$, where n is the number of compounding periods per year multiplied by the number of years, and r is the annual interest rate divided by the number of compounding periods per year. Before the advent of handheld calculators and computers, tables were developed to simplify the calculation of FV by providing values for $(1 + r)n$ for several combinations of n and r. These tables are still commonly used, and an example is provided in Exhibit A.2. The factors in Exhibit A.2 are commonly referred to as cumulative factors (CF) and are simply calculations of $(1 + r)n$ for various values of n and r.

* **present value (PV)**

The amount of future cash flows discounted to their equivalent worth today.

* **simple interest**

Interest on the invested amount only.

* **compound interest**

Interest on the invested amount plus interest on previous interest earned but not withdrawn.

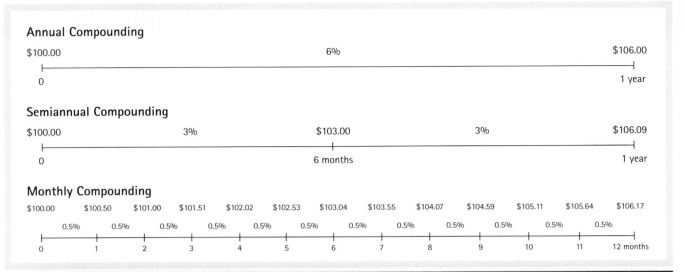

Annual Compounding

$100.00   6% $106.00

0   1 year

Semiannual Compounding

$100.00   3% $103.00   3% $106.09

0   6 months   1 year

Monthly Compounding

$100.00 | $100.50 | $101.00 | $101.51 | $102.02 | $102.53 | $103.04 | $103.55 | $104.07 | $104.59 | $105.11 | $105.64 | $106.17

0.5% across each period

0 1 2 3 4 5 6 7 8 9 10 11 12 months

EXHIBIT A.1 The impact of more frequent compounding on the future value of $100

n/r	0.5%	1%	2%	3%	4%	5%	6%	7%	8%	10%	12%
1	1.0050	1.0100	1.0200	1.0300	1.0400	1.0500	1.0600	1.0700	1.0800	1.1000	1.1200
2	1.0100	1.0201	1.0404	1.0609	1.0816	1.1025	1.1236	1.1449	1.1664	1.2100	1.2544
3	1.0151	1.0303	1.0612	1.0927	1.1249	1.1576	1.1910	1.2250	1.2597	1.3310	1.4049
4	1.0202	1.0406	1.0824	1.1255	1.1699	1.2155	1.2625	1.3108	1.3605	1.4641	1.5735
5	1.0253	1.0510	1.1041	1.1593	1.2167	1.2763	1.3382	1.4026	1.4693	1.6105	1.7623
6	1.0304	1.0615	1.1262	1.1941	1.2653	1.3401	1.4185	1.5007	1.5869	1.7716	1.9738
7	1.0355	1.0721	1.1487	1.2299	1.3159	1.4071	1.5036	1.6058	1.7138	1.9487	2.2107
8	1.0407	1.0829	1.1717	1.2668	1.3686	1.4775	1.5938	1.7182	1.8509	2.1436	2.4760
9	1.0459	1.0937	1.1951	1.3048	1.4233	1.5513	1.6895	1.8385	1.9990	2.3579	2.7731
10	1.0511	1.1046	1.2190	1.3439	1.4802	1.6289	1.7908	1.9672	2.1589	2.5937	3.1058
11	1.0564	1.1157	1.2434	1.3842	1.5395	1.7103	1.8983	2.1049	2.3316	2.8531	3.4785
12	1.0617	1.1268	1.2682	1.4258	1.6010	1.7959	2.0122	2.2522	2.5182	3.1384	3.8960
24	1.1272	1.2697	1.6084	2.0328	2.5633	3.2251	4.0489	5.0724	6.3412	9.8497	15.1786
36	1.1967	1.4308	2.0399	2.8983	4.1039	5.7918	8.1473	11.4239	15.9682	30.9127	59.1356
48	1.2705	1.6122	2.5871	4.1323	6.5705	10.4013	16.3939	25.7289	40.2106	97.0172	230.3908

EXHIBIT A.2 Future Value of $1

Using this new terminology, the future value formula is simply

$$FV_{(n \text{ periods in the future})} = PV(CF_{n,r})$$

With 6 per cent annual compounding, our $100 investment grows to

$$\$100(CF_{1,6\%}) = \$100(1.060) = \$106.00$$

With 6 per cent semiannual compounding,

$$\$100(CF_{2,3\%}) = \$100(1.0609) = \$106.09$$

With 6 per cent monthly compounding,

$$\$100(CF_{12,.5\%}) = \$100(1.0617) = \$106.17$$

Most financial calculators will compute future value after the user inputs data for present value, the annual interest rate, the number of compounding periods per year and the number of years. For example, using a business calculator to compute the future value of $100.00 with 6 per cent annual compounding requires the following steps:

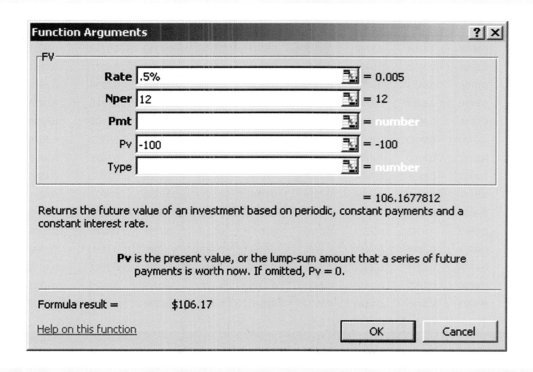

Keys	Display	Description
1 [P/YR]	1.00	Sets compounding periods per year to 1 because interest is compounded annually
100 [±] [PV]	−100.00	Stores the present value as a negative number
6.0 [I/YR]	6.0	Stores the annual interest rate
1 [N]	1	Sets the number of years or compounding periods to 1
[FV]	106.00	Calculates the future value

Calculating the future value of $100 with 6 per cent monthly compounding simply requires changing both the compounding periods per year (*P/YR*) and number of compounding periods (*N*) to 12.

Keys	Display	Description
12 [P/YR]	12	Sets compounding periods per year to 12
12 [N]	12	Sets the number of compounding periods to 12
[FV]	106.17	Calculates the future value

Likewise, many spreadsheet programs have built-in functions (formulas) that calculate future value. The Excel function called FV simply requires input of an interest rate (Rate), number of compounding periods (Nper) and present value (Pv) in the following format: =FV(Rate, Nper, Pmt, Pv, Type).[1] Entries for Pmt and Type are not applicable to simple future-value problems. To calculate the future value of $100 in one year at 6 per cent interest compounded monthly, enter =FV(.5%,12,−100). Excel returns a value of $106.17 (see Exhibit A.3).

Present value

A present value formula can be derived directly from the future value formula. If

$$FV_{(n \text{ periods in the future})} = PV(1 + r)^n$$

then

$$PV = \frac{FV}{(1+r)^n} \text{ or } PV = FV\frac{1}{(1+r)^n}$$

Just as a cumulative factor table was developed to calculate $(1 + r)n$, present value tables calculate $1 \div (1 + r)n$ for various combinations of n and r. These factors are called discount factors, or DFs. An example of a DF table is provided in Exhibit A.4. Our PV formula can now be rewritten as follows:

$$PV = FV(DF_{n,r})$$

n/r	0.5%	1%	2%	3%	4%	5%	6%	7%	8%	10%	12%
1	0.9950	0.9901	0.9804	0.9709	0.9615	0.9524	0.9434	0.9346	0.9259	0.9091	0.8929
2	0.9901	0.9803	0.9612	0.9426	0.9246	0.9070	0.8900	0.8734	0.8573	0.8264	0.7972
3	0.9851	0.9706	0.9423	0.9151	0.8890	0.8638	0.8396	0.8163	0.7938	0.7513	0.7118
4	0.9802	0.9610	0.9238	0.8885	0.8548	0.8227	0.7921	0.7629	0.7350	0.6830	0.6355
5	0.9754	0.9515	0.9057	0.8626	0.8219	0.7835	0.7473	0.7130	0.6806	0.6209	0.5674
6	0.9705	0.9420	0.8880	0.8375	0.7903	0.7462	0.7050	0.6663	0.6302	0.5645	0.5066
7	0.9657	0.9327	0.8706	0.8131	0.7599	0.7107	0.6651	0.6227	0.5835	0.5132	0.4523
8	0.9609	0.9235	0.8535	0.7894	0.7307	0.6768	0.6274	0.5820	0.5403	0.4665	0.4039
9	0.9561	0.9143	0.8368	0.7664	0.7026	0.6446	0.5919	0.5439	0.5002	0.4241	0.3606
10	0.9513	0.9053	0.8203	0.7441	0.6756	0.6139	0.5584	0.5083	0.4632	0.3855	0.3220
11	0.9466	0.8963	0.8043	0.7224	0.6496	0.5847	0.5268	0.4751	0.4289	0.3505	0.2875
12	0.9419	0.8874	0.7885	0.7014	0.6246	0.5568	0.4970	0.4440	0.3971	0.3186	0.2567
24	0.8872	0.7876	0.6217	0.4919	0.3901	0.3101	0.2470	0.1971	0.1577	0.1015	0.0659
36	0.8356	0.6989	0.4902	0.3450	0.2437	0.1727	0.1227	0.0875	0.0626	0.0323	0.0169
48	0.7871	0.6203	0.3865	0.2420	0.1522	0.0961	0.0610	0.0389	0.0249	0.0103	0.0043

EXHIBIT A.4 Present value of $1

Now we are ready to calculate the present value of a future cash flow. For example, how much must be invested today at 8 per cent compounded annually to have $1000 in two years? Mathematically,

$$PV = \$1000 \frac{1}{(1 \times 0.08)^2} = \$857.34$$

or using the DF table,

$$PV = \$1000(DF_{2,.08}) = \$1000(0.8573) = \$857.30 \text{ (rounded)}$$

Once again, the frequency of compounding affects our calculation. Just as more frequent compounding *increases* future values, increasing the frequency of compounding decreases present values. This is demonstrated in Exhibit A.5 for annual, semiannual and quarterly compounding.

Using a business calculator to compute present value is similar to computing future value. For example, the present value of $1000 received or paid in two years at 8 per cent compounded quarterly requires the following steps:

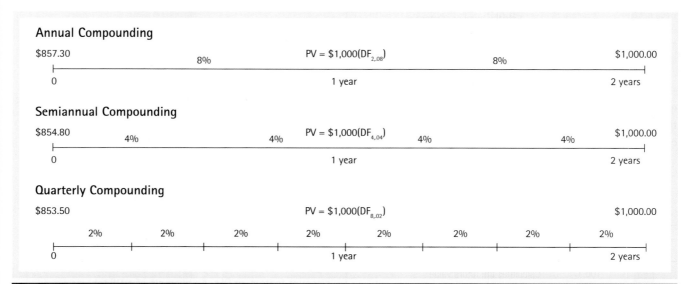

EXHIBIT A.5 The impact of more frequent compounding on the present value of $1000

Keys	Display	Description
4 [PYR]	4.00	Sets the compounding periods per year to 4
1,000 [FV]	1000.00	Stores the future value as a positive number
8.0 [I/YR]	8.0	Stores the annual interest rate
8 [N]	8.0	Sets the number of compounding periods to 8
[PV]	−853.49	Calculates the present value

In Microsoft Excel, the built-in function is called PV and requires input of the applicable interest rate (Rate), number of compounding periods (Nper) and future value (Fv) in the following format: =PV(Rate, Nper, Pmt, Fv, Type). In the previous example, entering =PV(2%,8,−1000) returns a value of $853.49. Note once again that Pmt and Type are left blank in simple present-value problems, as they were in future-value calculations (see Exhibit A.6).

When *FV* and *PV* are known, either formula can be used to calculate one of the other variables in the equations (*n* or *r*). For example, if you know that your $100 bank deposit is worth $200 in six years, what rate of interest compounded annually did you earn? Using the mathematical present-value formula,

$$PV = FV\left(\frac{1}{(1+r)^n}\right) \text{ or } \$100 = \$200\left(\frac{1}{(1+r)^6}\right)$$

Simplifying by dividing each side by $100, $1 = 2 \div (1 + r)^6$, and multiplying each side by $(1 + r)^6$, the equation is simplified to $(1 + r)^6 = 2$. The value of *r* can be calculated by using a financial calculator or mathematically by using logarithmic functions.[2] When using a business calculator, the following steps are typical:

Keys	Display	Description
1 [PYR]	1.00	Sets compounding periods per year to 1
200 [FV]	200	Stores the future value
100 [±][PV]	−100	Stores the present value as a negative number
2 [N]	2.0	Sets the number of compounding periods to 2
[I/YR]	0.122462	Calculates the annual interest rate

The tables can also be used to solve for *n* and *r*. Using our table formula, $PV = FV(DFn,r)$, if $PV = 100$ and $FV = 200$, *DF* must be equal to 0.5. If we know that *n* is equal to 6, we can simply move across the table until we find a factor close to 0.5. The factor at 12 per cent is 0.5066. If we examine the factors at both 10 per cent (0.5645) and 14 per cent (0.456), we can infer that the actual interest rate will be slightly higher than 12 per cent. Our logarithmic calculation is 12.2462 per cent. In

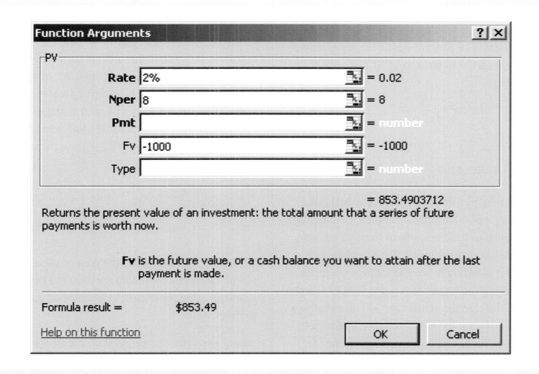

Function Arguments

PV

Rate: 2% = 0.02
Nper: 8 = 8
Pmt: = number
Fv: -1000 = -1000
Type: = number

= 853.4903712

Returns the present value of an investment: the total amount that a series of future payments is worth now.

Fv is the future value, or a cash balance you want to attain after the last payment is made.

Formula result = $853.49

Help on this function   OK   Cancel

EXHIBIT A.6 Finding the present value using the PV function in Excel

Function Arguments

RATE

Nper	6	= 6
Pmt		= number
Pv	-100	= -100
Fv	200	= 200
Type		= number

= 0.122462048

Returns the interest rate per period of a loan or an investment. For example, use 6%/4 for quarterly payments at 6% APR.

Fv is the future value, or a cash balance you want to attain after the last payment is made. If omitted, uses Fv = 0.

Formula result =   12.2462%

Help on this function   OK   Cancel

EXHIBIT A.7 Finding the interest rate using the RATE function in Excel

Microsoft Excel, the RATE function requires input of Nper, Pv, and Fv in the following format: =RATE(Nper, Pmt, Pv, Fv, Type, Guess). Because Excel uses an iterative trial-and-error method to calculate the interest rate, Guess provides a starting point. It is generally not necessary but may be required in complicated problems. Entering = RATE(6,–100,200) returns an interest rate of 12.2462 per cent (see Exhibit A.7).

The calculation of n is done in a similar fashion. If we know that our investment earns 12 per cent but do not know how long it will take for our $100 to grow to $200, mathematically, we have the following:

$$PV = FV \frac{1}{(1+r)^n}$$

or

$$\$100 = \$200 \frac{1}{(1+0.12)^n}$$

Solving the equation by using logarithms or a financial calculator gives us an n of 6.116 years.[3] Using the DF formula, DF must again be equal to 0.5. If r is known to be 12 per cent, we simply move down the 12 per cent column until we find a DF close to 0.5. Not surprisingly, we find a factor of 0.5066 for an n of 6. Examining the factors for an n of 5 (0.5674) and 7 (0.4523), we can infer that the actual time will be something slightly greater than 6 years. The NPER function in Microsoft Excel requires input of Rate, Pmt, Pv, Fv and Type in the following format: =NPER(12%,–100,200), and returns a value of 6.116 years. Note that Pv is entered as a negative amount and that Pmt and Type are not necessary, as this is essentially a present-value problem (see Exhibit A.8).

Annuities

An **annuity** is a series of cash flows of equal amount paid or received at regular intervals.[4] Common examples include mortgage and loan payments. The present value of an ordinary annuity (PVA) is the amount invested or borrowed today that will provide for a series of withdrawals or payments of equal amount for a set number of periods. Conceptually, the present value of an annuity is simply the sum of the present values of each withdrawal or payment. For example, the present value of an annuity of $100 paid at the end of each of the next four years at an interest rate of 10 per cent looks like this:

❋ **annuity**
A series of cash flows of equal amount paid or received at regular intervals.

Although cumbersome, the present value of an annuity can be calculated by finding the present value of each $100 payment, using the present value table on page 278 (see Exhibit A.4).

$$PVA = \$100(DF_{1,.10}) + \$100(DF_{2,.10}) + \$100(DF_{3,.10}) + \$100(DF_{4,.10})$$

$$= \$100(0.9091) + \$100(0.8264) + \$100(0.7513) + \$100(0.6830)$$

$$= \$316.98$$

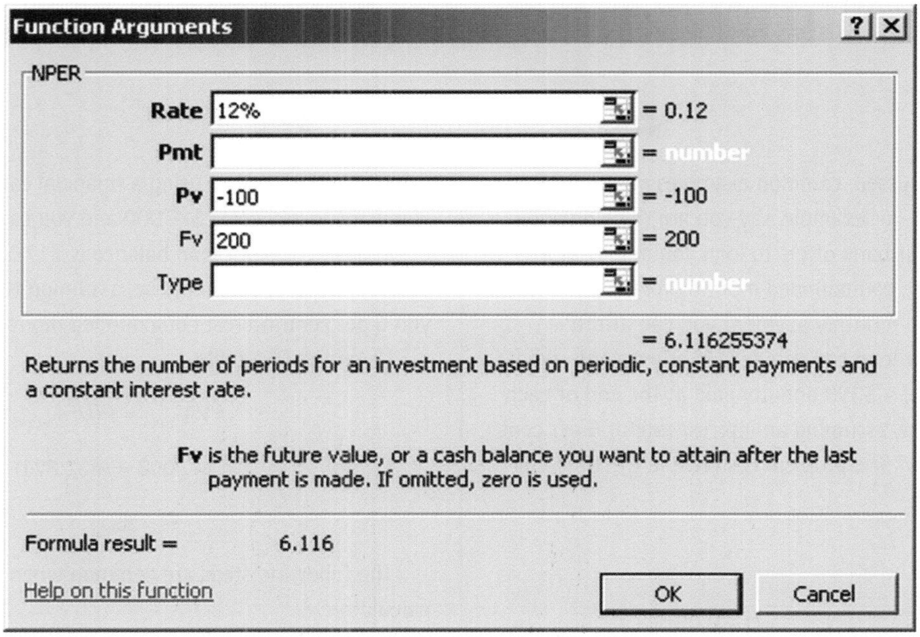

Function Arguments [?] [X]

NPER

Rate	12%		= 0.12
Pmt			= number
Pv	-100		= -100
Fv	200		= 200
Type			= number

= 6.116255374

Returns the number of periods for an investment based on periodic, constant payments and a constant interest rate.

Fv is the future value, or a cash balance you want to attain after the last payment is made. If omitted, zero is used.

Formula result =   6.116

Help on this function   [OK]   [Cancel]

EXHIBIT A.8 Finding the number of periods using the NPER function in Excel

The mathematical formula for PVA can be derived from the formula for PV and is equal to:

$$PVA_{n,s} = R \frac{1 - \dfrac{1}{(1+r)^n}}{r}$$

where R refers to the periodic payment or withdrawal (commonly called a rent). Calculated values for various combinations of n and r are provided in Exhibit A.9.

The PVA formula can therefore be rewritten as follows:

$$PVA = R(DFA_{n,r})$$

n/r	0.5%	1%	2%	3%	4%	5%	6%	7%	8%	10%	12%
1	0.9950	0.9901	0.9804	0.9709	0.9615	0.9524	0.9434	0.9346	0.9259	0.9091	0.8929
2	1.9851	1.9704	1.9416	1.9135	1.8861	1.8594	1.8334	1.8080	1.7833	1.7355	1.6901
3	2.9702	2.9410	2.8839	2.8286	2.7751	2.7232	2.6730	2.6243	2.5771	2.4869	2.4018
4	3.9505	3.9020	3.8077	3.7171	3.6299	3.5460	3.4651	3.3872	3.3121	3.1699	3.0373
5	4.9259	4.8534	4.7135	4.5797	4.4518	4.3295	4.2124	4.1002	3.9927	3.7908	3.6048
6	5.8964	5.7955	5.6014	5.4172	5.2421	5.0757	4.9173	4.7665	4.6229	4.3553	4.1114
7	6.8621	6.7282	6.4720	6.2303	6.0021	5.7864	5.5824	5.3893	5.2064	4.8684	4.5638
8	7.8230	7.6517	7.3255	7.0197	6.7327	6.4632	6.2098	5.9713	5.7466	5.3349	4.9676
9	8.7791	8.5660	8.1622	7.7861	7.4353	7.1078	6.8017	6.5152	6.2469	5.7590	5.3282
10	9.7304	9.4713	8.9826	8.5302	8.1109	7.7217	7.3601	7.0236	6.7101	6.1446	5.6502
11	10.6770	10.3676	9.7868	9.2526	8.7605	8.3064	7.8869	7.4987	7.1390	6.4951	5.9377
12	11.6189	11.2551	10.5753	9.9540	9.3851	8.8633	8.3838	7.9427	7.5361	6.8137	6.1944
24	22.5629	21.2434	18.9139	16.9355	15.2470	13.7986	12.5504	11.4693	10.5288	8.9847	7.7843
36	32.8710	30.1075	25.4888	21.8323	18.9083	16.5469	14.6210	13.0352	11.7172	9.6765	8.1924
48	42.5803	37.9740	30.6731	25.2667	21.1951	18.0772	15.6500	13.7305	12.1891	9.8969	8.2972

EXHIBIT A.9 Present value of an ordinary annuity

PVA $399 $399 $399 $399 $399 $399 $399 $399 $399 $399 $399 $399 $399 $399 $399 $399 $399 $399 $399 $399 $399 $399 $399 $399

| 0.5% | 0.5% | 0.5% | 0.5% | 0.5% | 0.5% | 0.5% | 0.5% | 0.5% | 0.5% | 0.5% | 0.5% | 0.5% | 0.5% | 0.5% | 0.5% | 0.5% | 0.5% | 0.5% | 0.5% | 0.5% | 0.5% | 0.5% |

0   24 months

As previously discussed, common examples of annuities are mortgages and loans. For example, say you are thinking about buying a new car. Your bank offers to loan you money at a special 6 per cent rate compounded monthly for a 24-month term. If the maximum monthly payment you can afford is $399, how large a car loan can you get? In other words, what is the present value of a $399 annuity paid at the end of each of the next 24 months, assuming an interest rate of 6 per cent compounded monthly? The problem is shown in the time line above:

Mathematically,

$$PVA_{24,0.005} = 399 \frac{1 - \dfrac{1}{(1+0.05)^{24}}}{0.005}$$

Using the DFA table,

$$PVA_{24,.005} = \$399(DFA_{24,.005}) = \$399(22.5629)$$

$$= \$9002.60 \text{ (rounded)}$$

The following steps are common when using a business calculator:

Keys		Display	Description
12	P/YR	12.00	Set periods per year
2×12	N	24.00	Stores number of periods in loan
0	PV	0	Stores the amount left to pay after 2 years
6	I/YR	6	Stores interest rate
399	± PMT	−399.00	Stores desired payment as a negative number
	PV	9,002.58	Calculates the loan you can afford with a $399 per month payment

In Microsoft Excel, the PV function is used to calculate the present value of an annuity, with additional entries for the payment amount (Pmt) and type of annuity (Type). The payment is entered as a negative number, and the annuity type is 0 for ordinary and 1 for an annuity due. The format is therefore PV(Rate, Nper, Pmt, Fv, Type). Entering =PV(.5%,24,−399,0,0) returns a value of $9002.58 (see Exhibit A.10).

The PVA formula can also be used to calculate R, r, and n if the other variables are known. This is most easily accomplished using the DFA table or using a financial calculator. If the car you want to buy costs $20 000 and you can afford a $3000 down payment (your loan balance is $17 000), how much will your 36 monthly payments be, assuming that the bank charges you 6 per cent interest compounded monthly?

Using the DFA table,

$$PVA_{36,.005} = R(DFA_{36,.005})$$

$$\$17\,000 = R(32.871)$$

$$R = \$517.17$$

The following steps are common when using a business calculator:

Keys		Display	Description
12	P/YR	12.00	Set periods per year
3×12	N	36.00	Stores number of periods in loan
0	PV	0	Stores the amount left to pay after 3 years
6	I/YR	6	Stores interest rate
17,000	PV	17,000	Stores amount borrowed
	PMT	−517.17	Calculates the monthly payment

In Microsoft Excel, the calculation is simply = PMT (.005,36, − 17000,0,0) (see Exhibit A.11).

In a similar fashion, assume that a used-car dealer offers you a 'special deal' in which you can borrow $12 000 with low monthly payments of $350 per month for 48 months. What rate of interest are you being charged in this case? Using the DFA table,

$$PVA_{48,.??} = \$350(DFA_{48,.??})$$

$$\$12\,000 = 350(DFA_{48,.??})$$

$$DFA_{48,.??} = 34.2857$$

Looking at the row for an n of 48, we see that a DFA of 34.2857 is about halfway between an r of 1 per cent and r of 2 per cent (closer to 1 per cent), which means that you are being charged an annual rate of almost 18 per cent (1.5% × 12) – not such a good deal after all! Using a business calculator, observe the following:

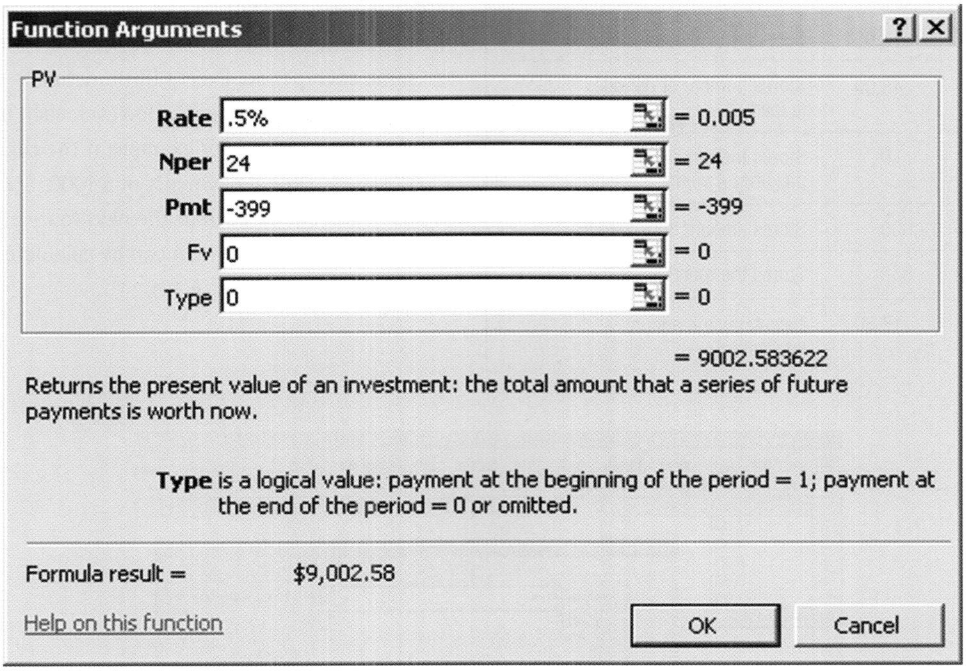

Function Arguments [?][X]

PV

Rate	.5%	📊	= 0.005
Nper	24	📊	= 24
Pmt	-399	📊	= -399
Fv	0	📊	= 0
Type	0	📊	= 0

= 9002.583622

Returns the present value of an investment: the total amount that a series of future payments is worth now.

Type is a logical value: payment at the beginning of the period = 1; payment at the end of the period = 0 or omitted.

Formula result = $9,002.58

Help on this function   [OK]   [Cancel]

EXHIBIT A.10 Finding the present value of an annuity using the PV function in Excel

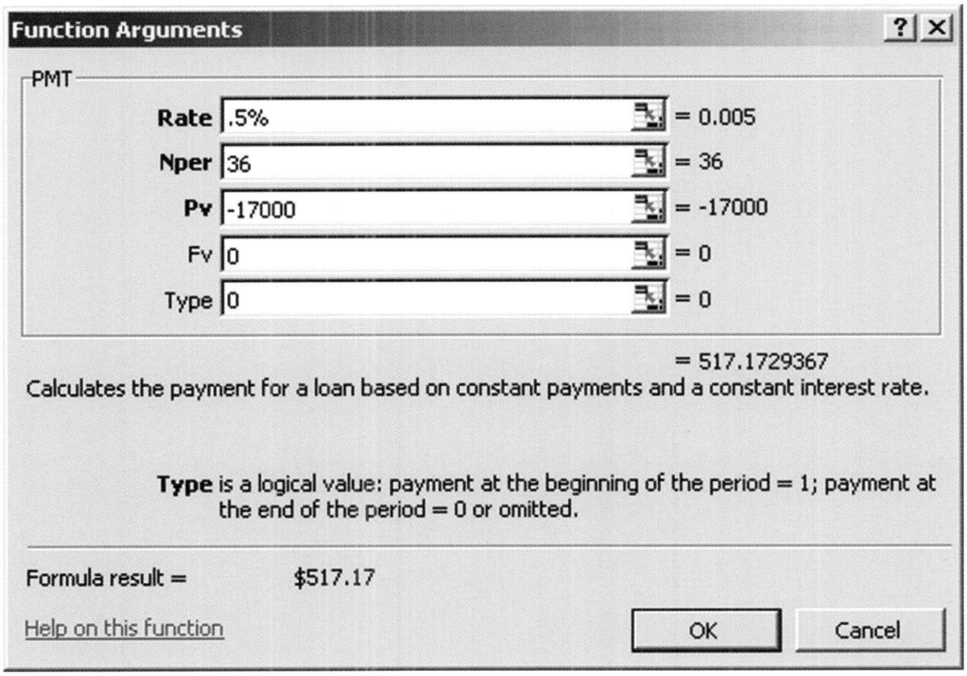

Function Arguments [?][X]

PMT

Rate	.5%	📊	= 0.005
Nper	36	📊	= 36
Pv	-17000	📊	= -17000
Fv	0	📊	= 0
Type	0	📊	= 0

= 517.1729367

Calculates the payment for a loan based on constant payments and a constant interest rate.

Type is a logical value: payment at the beginning of the period = 1; payment at the end of the period = 0 or omitted.

Formula result = $517.17

Help on this function   [OK]   [Cancel]

EXHIBIT A.11 Finding the payment using the PMT function in Excel

Keys	Display	Description
12 [P/YR]	12.00	Set periods per year
4×12 [N]	48.00	Stores number of periods in loan
0 [PV]	0	Stores the amount left to pay after 4 years
12,000 [PV]	12,000	Stores amount borrowed
350 [+/-] [PMT]	−350	Stores the monthly payment
[I/YR]	17.60	Calculates the annual interest rate

In Excel, =RATE(48,−350,12,000,0) generates a monthly rate of 1.4667 per cent and an annual rate of 17.60 per cent. The use of the RATE function requires that the payments are the same each period. Excel's IRR function is more flexible, allowing different payments. However, each payment has to be entered separately. For example, if the car is purchased for $17 000 with annual payments of $4000, $5000, $6000, and $7000 at the end of each of the next four years, the interest rate charged on the car loan can be calculated by using the IRR function (see Exhibit A.12).

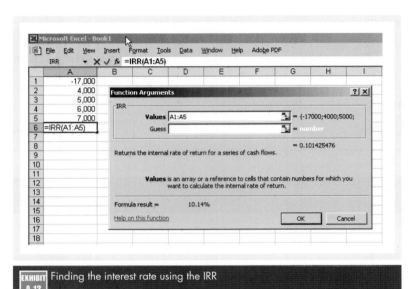

EXHIBIT A.12 Finding the interest rate using the IRR

TEST COMING UP?

NOW WHAT?

ACCT has it all, and you can too. Between the text and online offerings, you have everything at your fingertips to revise and prepare for your test. Make sure you check out all that **ACCT** has to offer:

- Printable flash cards
- Interactive games
- Videos

- Audio downloads
- Case studies
- Chapter review cards

- Online quizzing
- ...and more!

Visit **http://login.cengagebrain.com/** to find the resources you need today!

THE DAILY GRIND[1]

APPENDIX B

Twelve months ago, David opened a coffee shop, The Daily Grind, in Mercy Hospital's former gift shop. David was confident that he had the knowledge to make a success of this new business. He produced a quality product that people needed, had priced the product to be very competitive, and had a great location in a high-traffic area of the hospital.

Material costs

The Daily Grind uses a specialty brand of Kona coffee beans costing $8 per kilo wholesale. Each kilo of coffee beans produces 10 litres of coffee beverage. Coffee is sold in three sizes: a small cup holding 50 ml, a medium cup holding 100 ml, and a large cup holding 200 ml.

The cups needed to serve the coffee cost $.05 for the small cup, $.06 for the medium cup, and $.07 for the large cup. Lids cost $.03 per cup and are the same regardless of cup size. Sleeves cost an additional $.04 per cup. On average, sugar and milk cost $.02 per cup for small cups, $.03 for medium cups, and $.04 for large cups.

Labour costs

The Daily Grind is open 12 hours each day, 7 days a week (365 days per year), and is staffed with three employees during the morning shift (7–11 am), two employees from 11 am until 3 pm, and three employees from 3–7 pm. Labour is a fixed cost, because the employees are paid regardless of whether coffee is sold. David worked 60 hours each week, on average, and paid himself a salary of $30000 during the first year of operations. Fringe benefits for David, including health insurance and payroll taxes, accounted for an additional $10000 of costs for the company. Part-time employees work an average of 24 hours each week and are paid $19 per hour. Payroll taxes and other costs average about $1.00 per hour for part-time employees. As shown in the following table, part-time employees worked from 656 hours to 727 hours each month:

Month	Part-time employee labour hours
January	722 hours
February	656 hours
March	727 hours
April	705 hours
May	727 hours
June	705 hours
July	727 hours
August	727 hours
September	705 hours
October	727 hours
November	705 hours
December	727 hours

Overhead costs

During the first year of operations, the hospital charged rent of $2000 per month. As part of the rental cost, the hospital provided furniture and fixtures for the shop, as well as nightly cleaning services. David leased an espresso machine, refrigerator, coffee grinder, scale, and cash register for $150 per month, total. David paid directly for his utilities (electricity and water). The costs of electricity include the costs of heating and cooling the shop. as well as the cost of running the electric appliances (refrigerator, coffeemaker, etc.).

For the first 12 months of operations, utility expenses were as follows:

Month	Utility expense
January	$ 472
February	$ 510
March	$ 524
April	$ 460
May	$ 440
June	$ 460
July	$ 452
August	$ 430
September	$ 535
October	$ 570
November	$ 580
December	$ 600
Total	$6033

Selling and administrative costs

David incurred $200 a month in accounting fees and spent $500 on various promotional and advertising materials during the year. He also paid $1000 for liability insurance.

Sales revenue

During the first year of operations, David set the shop's prices to be slightly lower than their competitors'. The Daily Grind sells a small cup of coffee for $2.00, a medium cup for $2.50, and a large cup for $3.00. Sales in cups was as follows:

Month	Sales in cups of coffee
January	9 300 cups*
February	9 800
March	10 850
April	9 500
May	9 300
June	9 000
July	8 800
August	8 600
September	11 000
October	11 620
November	12 000
December	12 400

*Coffee sales average 10% small cups (50 ml), 50% medium cups (100 ml), and 40% large cups (200 ml).

Required

1 Calculate the cost of coffee beans per small, medium and large cup.
2 Calculate the cost of cups, lids, sleeves, milk, and sugar per unit for small, medium, and large cups of coffee and in total.
3 Calculate the total labour costs for the year.
4 Prepare an income statement for The Daily Grind for the last year. You can assume that there are no inventories on hand at the end of the year. (All coffee and supplies purchased during the year are consumed.)
5 Determine whether the costs incurred by The Daily Grind are fixed, variable (with respect to number of cups of coffee sold), or mixed.

6 Use regression analysis and the high/low method to calculate the monthly fixed cost and the variable component of the utility expenses incurred by The Daily Grind. Use cups of coffee sold as the independent variable and utility expense as the dependent variable in your regression analysis. After calculating both numbers, round your final answers to two decimal places.
7 Compare the regression results with the high/low results. Which model would you suggest?
8 Calculate the contribution margin earned for each product (round to three decimal places) and the weighted-average contribution margin (round to four decimal places).
9 Assume the sales mix given in the problem. What is The Daily Grind's break-even point in terms of the number of cups of coffee sold during the year?
10 David is contemplating adding a new 300 ml Mega Coffee cup for the coming year and discontinuing sales of the small cup. The new cup, lid, and sleeve cost the same as the 200 ml cup, but milk and sugar is expected to cost $.06 per cup instead of $.04 per cup. The new extra-large cup would be priced at $3.50. David anticipates that the new sales mix would be 50 per cent for the medium cup, 30 per cent for the large cup, and 20 per cent for the new Mega cup. Assume that material, labour, and overhead costs remain the same in the upcoming year. How would this change in sales mix affect the company's break-even point?
11 David would like to increase sales in the second year of operations so that he may raise his salary to $70 000 (not including $15 000 in fringe benefits) while reducing his workload to 40 hours per week with two paid weeks of vacation during the year. Reducing his workload will require increasing the number of hours worked by part-time employees by 1080 hours per year. Assume the introduction of the Mega cup, elimination of the small cup, and the new sales mix as discussed in requirement 10. What level of annual sales would be required in order for David to reach his goal?
12 Write a short memo to David and discuss whether you think he will be able to reach his goal during the second year of operations.

Endnotes

Chapter 1

1 www.cimaglobal.com/Thought-leadership/Research-topics/Development/Improving-decision-making-in-organisations/
2 Milton Friedman, 'The social responsibility of business is to increase its profits', *New York Times Magazine*, 30 September, 1970.
3 Source: http://www.abc.net.au/lateline/business/items/200908/s2655515.htm
4 The APESB Guidelines can be viewed here: www.apesb.org.au/uploads/attachment-7-a-apesb-financial-planning-discussion-paper-aug-08.pdf (page 12).

Chapter 2

1 'Qantas to slash 5,000 jobs, posts $235m half-year loss', by Michael Janda. Published by ABC News, © 2014. http://www.abc.net.au/news/2014-02-27/qantas-profit-result-airline-posts-loss/5287188
2 It should be noted that companies might want to cost other objects in addition to products. For example, a company might want to know the costs of a particular department, division, project, region, or even the costs of servicing a particular customer.
3 Gary Rivlin, 'Who's afraid of China?', *New York Times*, available at www.nytimes.com, 19 December 2004.
4 Ibid.
5 Amrik S. Sohal, (1996), 'Developing a lean production organization: An Australian case study', *International Journal of Operations & Production Management*, Vol. 16 Iss: 2: 91–102.
6 Ibid.

Chapter 6

1 Rhian Silvestro (1999), 'Positioning services along the volume-variety diagonal: The contingencies of service design, control and improvement', *International Journal of Operations & Production Management*, Vol. 19 Iss: 4: 399–421.
2 Ibid.
3 Ibid.
4 www.telstra.com.au/abouttelstra/download/document/tls796-annual-report-2011.pdf.
5 Putting the Service-Profit Chain to Work" by James L. Heskett, Thomas O. Jones, Gary W. Loveman, W. Earl Sasser, Jr., and Leonard A. Schlesinger from *Harvard Business Review*. Published by Harvard Business Publishing, © 2008.
6 Ibid.

Chapter 7

1 Adapted from 'Improving decision making in organizations'. Published by Chartered Institute of Management Accountants, © 2009. www.perthnow.com.au/business/business-old/westpacs-gail-kelly-paid-87m/story-e6frg2qu-1226192893616.

Chapter 8

1 This classification of unit-level, batch-level, product-level and facility-level costs is commonly referred to as Cooper's hierarchy.

Chapter 9

1 Calculating the optimum mix of products to produce given limited resources and demand constraints is addressed in Chapter 10. The optimum mix will result in the highest overall contribution margin and also the highest overall profit for a company.

Chapter 10

1 Although rush orders and orders requiring special handling, packaging, or different manufacturing specifications might be considered 'special orders', these types of decisions are not discussed here.
2 Decisions involving limited resources or constraints often include multiple constraints, such as storage space, machine time, labour hours, and even dollars available to invest. When we have more than one constraining factor, the decision-making process becomes more complicated and is facilitated by the use of computerised linear programming models. A discussion of linear programming is beyond the scope of this text.

Chapter 11

1 Extended present value tables can be found at the end of the Review Cards.
2 The following discussion assumes that readers are already familiar with the basic concepts of discounting and the calculation of present value for single sums and annuities. If not, you should study Appendix A at the end of the book.
3 Hospitals, museums, churches, and a multitude of other organisations are often structured as organisations exempt from income taxes. In order to qualify, they must meet certain requirements as specified by the Australian Taxation Office.
4 When assets are sold during their useful life, it is possible to generate tax-deductible losses as well as taxable gains. When assets are sold at a loss, their after-tax cash flow is more difficult to compute. It consists of the cash received from the sale *plus* the tax savings generated from the deductible loss.
5 Although the equipment would be depreciated over a useful life of five years, tax law generally requires the use of a convention whereby a half year of depreciation is deducted in the year of acquisition (regardless of when the asset is purchased) and a half year's depreciation is deducted in the sixth year. In addition, the tax law currently allows the use of an accelerated method of depreciation for machinery and equipment. The intricacies of tax depreciation rules are beyond the scope of this book.
6 John Graham and Campbell Harvey, 'How do CFOs make capital budgeting and capital structure decisions?' *The Journal of Applied Corporate Finance*, Vol. 15, No. 1: 8–22.

Chapter 12

1 Tim Reason, 'Budgeting in the real world', *CFO Magazine*, www.cfo.com/magazine/, 1 July 2005.
2 Ibid.
3 It would not be unusual for some of the sales to never be collected. If Bob's thinks that some of the accounts receivable are uncollectible, the cash receipts budget should be adjusted accordingly.
4 You will recall that depreciation can have an indirect impact on cash flow through its impact on income taxes. The impact of income tax is taken into account

in the summary cash budget.

5 Anita Dennis, 'Budgeting for curve balls', *Journal of Accountancy*, Vol. 186, No. 3: 89–92.

6 P. Sivabalan, P. Booth, T. Malmi and D.A. Brown (2009), 'An exploratory study of operational reasons to budget', *Accounting and Finance*, Vol. 49: 849–71.

Chapter 13

1 Of course, overhead can be applied using cost drivers other than direct labour. If overhead is applied based on machine hours, AH is simply the actual number of machine hours used and SH is the budgeted number of machine hours allowed for actual production.

Chapter 14

1 In addition to quality improvements, kaizen techniques are used to continually reduce the cost of products and services in target costing.

2 Norihiko Shirouzu, 'Why Toyota wins such high marks on quality surveys', *The Wall Street Journal*, 15 March 2001: A11.

3 Michael R. Ostrega, 'Return on investment through the costs of quality', *Journal of Cost Management*, Summer 1991: 37.

4 'Rewards of quality awards', *Business Week*, 21 September 1998: 26.

5 http://news.toyota.com.au/toyota-australia-announces-recall-on-previous-generation-avalon-camry-v6-and-kluger-models.

Chapter 15

1 'Balancing Act: A Triple Bottom Line Analysis of the Australian Economy, Volume 1', by Barney Foran, Manfred Lenzen and Christopher Dey. Published by The University of Sydney, © 2005 by Commonwealth of Australia.

2 http://thinkinghighways.com/Pages/View-issue/Magazine.aspx?id=450602c8-4c2b-4d7f-971d-f7a2ca2d97ca&issue=83187e8c-a3c5-4566-ad32-95b96ad50248

3 Ibid.

4 Marc J. Epstein and Marie-Josée Roy, 'Sustainability in action: Identifying and measuring the key performance drivers', *Long Range Planning*, Volume 34, Issue 5, October 2001: 585–604.

5 http://www.bhpbilliton.com/home/society/reports/Documents/2014/BHPBillitonSustainabilityReport2014_interactive.pdf, p. 1.

6 BHP Billiton Sustainability Report 2014. www.bhpbilliton.com/home/aboutus/sustainability/reports/Documents/2011/BHPBillitonSustainabilityReport2011_Interactive.pdf, p. 1.

7 Copyright Guardian News & Media Ltd 2012. www.guardian.co.uk/environment/2012/mar/03/bp-settles-gulf-mexico-spill

8 'Three Fitzroy Coal Mines Receive Token Fines', from media release, The Queensland Cabinet and Ministerial Directory. Published by The State of Queensland (Department of the Premier and Cabinet), © 2010.

9 'Australian retailers Rivers, Coles, Target, Kmart linked to Bangladesh factory worker abuse', by Sarah Ferguson. Reproduced by permission of the Australian Broadcasting Corporation and ABC Online. © 2015 ABC. All rights reserved.

Chapter 16

1 http://www.afr.com/f/free/markets/capital/cfo/warning_on_accounting_fraud_as_pressures_NNcDSCaY0DR3cncuGedT0J

2 'Developing ethical business strategies', A CIMA Case Study. Published by Business Case Studies LLP, © 1995-2015.

3 Reproduced with the permission of Accounting Professional & Ethical Standard Board (APSEB), Victoria, Australia.

4 Ibid.

5. Ibid.

6 'Australia a long way behind G20 counterparts on whistleblower protection, says report', by Will Ockenden. Reproduced by permission of the Australian Broadcasting Corporation and ABC Online. © 2015 ABC. All rights reserved.

7 Reproduced with the permission of Accounting Professional & Ethical Standard Board (APSEB), Victoria, Australia.

8 Ibid.

9. Ibid.

10. Ibid.

11. Ibid.

12. Ibid.

13. Ibid.

14. Ibid.

15. Ibid.

16. Ibid.

Appendix A – Time value of money

1 Built-in functions can be accessed in Microsoft Excel by clicking on the Paste function icon, clicking on *financial*, and then scrolling down to the desired function.

2 In logarithmic form, $(1 + r)^6 = 2$ can be rewritten as $\log(1 + r)^6 = \log 2$, or $6{\approx}\log(1 + r) = \log 2$. Therefore, $\log(1 + r) = \log 2 \div 6$, which simplifies to $\log(1 + r) = 0.1155245$. Switching back to the equivalent exponential form, $e0.1155245 = (1 + r)$, $(1 + r) = 1.122462$, and $r = 0.122462$ (12.2462%).

3 Using a business calculator, simply input 1 P/YR, 200 FV, 100 PV, and 12 I/YR and solve for *n*. In logarithmic form, $(1 + 0.12)_n = 2$ can be rewritten as $\log(1 + 0.12)_n = \log 2$, or $n \log 1.12 = \log 2$. Therefore, $n = (\log 2) \div (\log 1.12) = 6.116$.

4 An ordinary annuity is paid or received at the end of each period, whereas an annuity due is paid or received at the beginning of each period. In examples throughout this book, we will assume the annuity is ordinary.

Appendix B – The Daily Grind

1 This comprehensive case includes topics and concepts covered in selected chapters throughout the book. The case also includes a writing requirement. Ideally, it would be assigned after completion of Chapter 6.

Index

Notes

Learning objectives (LO)

LO1 Describe the contemporary view of accounting information systems and describe and give examples of financial and non-financial accounting information.

LO2 Compare and contrast managerial accounting with financial accounting and distinguish between the information needs of external and internal users.

LO3 Recognise the role of relevant factors in decision making.

LO4 Understand sources of ethical issues in business and the importance of maintaining an ethical business environment.

Key concepts

- Accounting information includes both financial and non-financial information used by decision makers.
- Financial accounting information is focused on the information needs of external users, while managerial accounting information is focused on the information needs of internal users.
- Opportunity costs are relevant. Future costs that do not differ among alternatives are not relevant. Sunk costs are not relevant.
- Establishing an ethical business environment encourages employees to act with integrity and conduct business in a fair and just manner.

Concept questions

1 Discuss the relationships among data, information and knowledge.
2 What is the primary purpose of financial accounting and of managerial accounting?
3 Define strategic and operational planning.
4 Briefly describe the role of the finance function within an organisation.
5 Why has the role of the managerial accountant changed in recent years?
6 Define sunk costs and opportunity costs, and discuss their importance in decision making.
7 'Businesses must first do well before they can do good.' Do you agree or disagree with the preceding statement? Why or why not?

Key definitions

Data
Reports such as financial statements, customer lists and inventory records.

Information
Data that have been organised, processed and summarised.

Knowledge
Information that is shared and exploited so that it adds value to an organisation.

Accounting information system (AIS)
A transaction-processing system that captures financial data resulting from accounting transactions within a company.

Financial accounting
The area of accounting primarily concerned with the preparation and use of financial statements by creditors, investors and other users outside the company.

Managerial accounting
The area of accounting primarily concerned with generating financial and non-financial information for use by managers in their decision-making roles within a company.

External users
Shareholders, potential investors, creditors, government taxing agencies, regulators, suppliers, customers and others outside the company.

Internal users
Individual employees, teams, departments, regions, top management and others inside the company – often referred to as managers.

Planning
The development of both the short-term (operational) and long-term (strategic) objectives and goals of an organisation and the identification of the resources needed to achieve them.

Operational planning
The development of short-term objectives and goals (typically, those to be achieved in less than one year).

Strategic planning
Addresses long-term questions of how an organisation positions and distinguishes itself from competitors.

Operating activities
The day-to-day operations of a business.

Controlling activities
The motivation and monitoring of employees and the evaluation of people and other resources used in the operations of the organisation.

Operations and production function
Produces the products or services that an organisation sells to its customers.

Marketing function
Involved with the process of developing, pricing, promoting and distributing goods and services sold to customers.

Finance function
Responsible for managing the financial resources of the organisation.

Human resource function
Concerned with the utilisation of human resources to help an organisation reach its goals.

Decision making
The process of identifying alternative courses of action and selecting an appropriate alternative in a given decision-making situation.

Relevant costs
Those costs that differ among alternatives.

Sunk costs
Costs that have already been incurred.

Opportunity costs
The benefits forgone by choosing one alternative over another.

Ethics programs
Company programs or policies created for the express purpose of establishing and maintaining an ethical business environment.

c1
INTRODUCTION TO
MANAGERIAL ACCOUNTING

Key exhibits

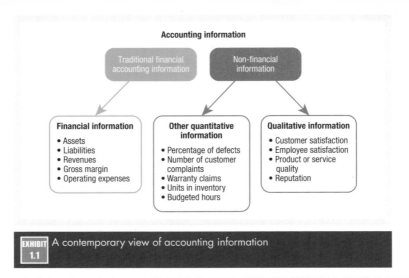

Accounting information

Traditional financial accounting information | Non-financial information

Financial information
- Assets
- Liabilities
- Revenues
- Gross margin
- Operating expenses

Other quantitative information
- Percentage of defects
- Number of customer complaints
- Warranty claims
- Units in inventory
- Budgeted hours

Qualitative information
- Customer satisfaction
- Employee satisfaction
- Product or service quality
- Reputation

EXHIBIT 1.1 A contemporary view of accounting information

	Users	Type of accounting information needed	Source
External	Shareholders and creditors	Sales, gross profit, net income, cash flow, assets and liabilities, earnings per share, etc. Although this information is primarily financial, it may also include non-financial information (units in inventory). This information is often provided in summary form (for the company as a whole) and typically is historical in nature.	Annual reports, financial statements and other available documents
External	Government bodies	Varies by agency but includes taxable income, sales, assets, comparisons of actual expenditures to budgets, etc. This information is usually provided for the company as a whole and is historical in nature. It can include both financial and non-financial information.	Tax returns and other reports
External	Customers and suppliers	Order status, shipping dates, inventory levels, etc. This information must be very detailed and timely to be useful.	Limited-access databases available to specific customers and suppliers
Internal	Marketing, operations and production, finance and human resource managers	Timely and detailed information on sales and expenses, product costs, budget information and measures of performance. Often includes non-financial data (direct labour hours, units to break even, etc.). Accounting information is often needed for segments of an organisation and is more likely future oriented than historical.	Cost reports, budgets and other internal documents

EXHIBIT 1.2 External and internal users of accounting information

Relevant costs	
Future costs that differ among alternatives	Opportunity costs – benefits forgone by choosing one alternative over another
Irrelevant costs	
Future costs that do not differ among alternatives	Sunk costs – costs that have already been incurred

EXHIBIT 1.3 Relevant and irrelevant costs

Key definitions

Manufacturing companies

Companies that purchase raw materials from other companies and transform those raw materials into a finished product, usually with the assistance of labour and other supporting activities, technologies and infrastructure (overheads).

Merchandising companies

Companies that sell products that someone else has manufactured.

Service companies

Companies that do not sell a tangible product as their primary business.

Raw materials inventory

Inventory of materials needed in the production process but not yet moved to the production area. Usually sitting in a warehouse, awaiting transfer into the factory.

Work in process (WIP) inventory

Inventory that is moved out of a warehouse and into a factory – they are in the process of being transformed (in other words, what is left in the factory at the end of the period).

Finished-goods inventory

Inventory of finished product waiting for sale and shipment to customers.

Lean production

A system focused on eliminating waste associated with holding more inventory than required, making more product than is needed, over-processing a product, moving products (and people) further than required and waiting.

Just-in-time (JIT) manufacturing

The philosophy of having raw materials arrive just in time to be used in production and for finished goods inventory to be completed just in time to be shipped to customers.

Manufacturing costs

Costs incurred in the factory or plant to produce a product; typically consists of three elements: direct materials, direct labour and manufacturing overhead.

Direct materials

Materials that can easily and conveniently be traced to the final product.

Direct labour

Labour that can easily and conveniently be traced to particular products.

Manufacturing overhead

Indirect materials and labour and any other expenses related to the production of products but not directly traceable to the specific product.

Learning objectives (LO)

LO1 Describe basic production processes used by manufacturing companies.

LO2 Identify the key characteristics and benefits of lean production and JIT manufacturing.

LO3 Distinguish manufacturing costs from non-manufacturing costs and classify manufacturing costs as direct materials, direct labour or overhead.

LO4 Diagram the flow of costs in manufacturing, merchandising and service companies and calculate the cost of manufacturing or selling goods and services.

LO5 Evaluate the impact of product costs and period costs on a company's income statement and balance sheet.

Key concepts

- Production processes require the combination of raw materials, labour and other items such as electricity and supplies to create finished goods.
- Lean production and JIT provide many benefits, including improved production quality and reduced processing time.
- Manufacturing costs are incurred in the production facility, whereas non-manufacturing costs are incurred elsewhere in the company, such as in the marketing department.
- Costs flow the same way that products flow through a production facility.
- Product costs attach to the product and are expensed only when the product is sold, whereas period costs are expensed in the period in which they are incurred.

Concept questions

1. What is the difference among raw materials inventory, WIP and finished goods inventory?
2. Why are traditional manufacturing systems sometimes called 'push' systems of production whereas JIT systems are called 'pull' systems?
3. Briefly describe a just-in-time manufacturing system.
4. What are some of the advantages of lean production and JIT manufacturing?
5. Describe how some of the principles of lean production might be applied to a bank.
6. Compare the terms *direct cost* and *indirect cost*.
7. Define the three components of manufacturing costs.
8. Define non-manufacturing costs.
9. Briefly describe the flow of costs in a manufacturing company.
10. Are the terms *cost* and *expense* synonymous? Why or why not?
11. Compare product and period costs. Why is the designation important?
12. Why do companies need to determine accurate product costs?

c 2

PRODUCT COSTING: MANUFACTURING PROCESSES, COST TERMINOLOGY AND COST FLOWS

Indirect materials

Materials used in the production of products but not directly traceable to the specific product.

Indirect labour

Labour used in the production of products but not directly traceable to the specific product.

Product costs

Costs that attach to the products as they go through the manufacturing process; also called inventoriable costs. They appear as inventory in the balance sheet and only become expenses when products are sold (as Cost of Goods Sold – COGS).

Non-manufacturing costs

Costs that are not related to the production process are classed as selling and administrative costs. These costs cannot be classed as inventory and must be immediately expensed in the profit and loss statement.

Period costs

Costs that are expensed in the period incurred; attached to the period as opposed to the product.

Actual costing

A product costing system in which actual overhead costs are entered directly into work in process.

Normal costing

A product costing system in which estimated or predetermined overhead rates are used to apply overhead to work in process.

Key exhibits

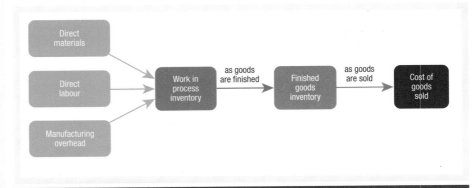

EXHIBIT 2.3 Overview of cost flows in a manufacturing company

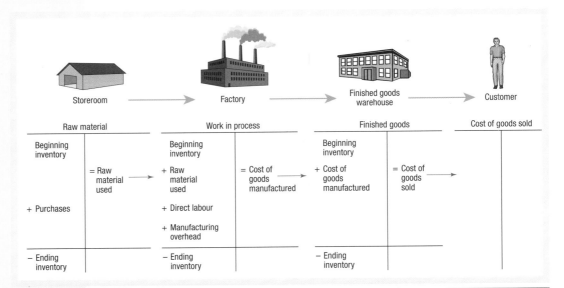

EXHIBIT 2.5 Cost flows in Northern Territory Lights Custom Cabinets

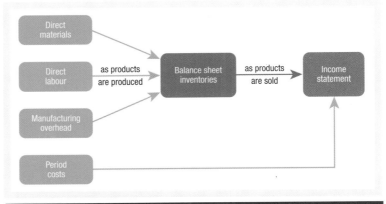

EXHIBIT 2.10 The path to the income statement – product and period costs

review

Key definitions

Cost behaviour
How costs react to changes in production volume or other levels of activity.

Fixed costs
Costs that remain the same in total when production volume increases or decreases but vary per unit.

Variable costs
Costs that stay the same per unit but change in total as production volume increases or decreases.

Relevant range
The normal range of production that can be expected for a particular product and company.

Mixed costs
Costs that include both a fixed and a variable component, making it difficult to predict how the cost changes as production changes – unless the cost is first separated into its fixed and variable components.

Regression analysis
The procedure that uses statistical methods (least squares regression) to fit a cost line (called a regression line) through a number of data points.

Dependent variable
The variable in regression analysis that is dependent on changes in the independent variable.

Independent variable
The variable in regression analysis that drives changes in the dependent variable.

R square (R^2)
A measure of goodness of fit (how well the regression line 'fits' the data).

Absorption (full) costing
A method of costing in which product costs include direct materials, direct labour, and fixed and variable overhead; required for external financial statements and for income tax reporting.

Variable (direct) costing
A method of costing in which product costs include direct materials, direct labour and variable overhead; fixed overhead is treated as a period cost; consistent with a focus on cost behaviour.

Learning objectives (LO)

LO1 Describe the nature and behaviour of fixed and variable costs.

LO2 Define and analyse mixed costs using regression analysis and the high/low method.

LO3 Illustrate the impact of income taxes on costs and decision making.

LO4 Identify the difference between variable costing and absorption costing.

LO5 Identify the impact on the income statement of variable costing and absorption costing.

LO6 Recognise the benefits of using variable costing for decision making.

Key concepts

- Costs behave in predictable ways. Within the relevant range, fixed costs are constant in total and vary per unit, while variable costs vary in total and are constant per unit.
- Mixed costs must be separated into fixed and variable cost components before their behaviour can be understood.
- Many operating costs are tax deductible and most revenues are taxable. Managers must consider the impact of taxes when making decisions.
- The only difference between variable and absorption costing is the treatment of fixed overhead.
- Variable costing is consistent with CVP's focus on differentiating fixed and variable costs and provides useful decision-making information that is often not apparent when using absorption costing.
- Variable costing offers many benefits that focus on managerial performance and cost behaviour.

Concept questions

1. Describe the behaviour of direct material cost in total and per unit as production volume changes.
2. Describe the relevant range and how it relates to cost behaviour.
3. How will fixed costs expressed on a per-unit basis react to a change in the level of activity?
4. Give the equation that best describes the fundamental relationship among total costs (TC), fixed costs (FC) and variable costs per unit (VC). Use TC, FC and VC in formulating your answer.
5. Discuss the meaning of dependent and independent variables in regression analysis.
6. Discuss the meaning of R square in regression analysis. What does an R square of 1.00 mean?
7. Discuss situations in which the high/low method may provide inaccurate estimates of fixed and variable costs.
8. Why are fixed costs not relevant for most short-term decisions?
9. Compare and contrast the terms *relevant costs* and *irrelevant costs* as they pertain to decision making.
10. Discuss the impact of taxes on costs and how that impact affects decision making.
11. If production exceeds sales, which costing method will show higher net income? Why?

12 If sales exceed production, which costing method will show higher net income? Why?

13 How do the two costing methods differ when sales and production are equal? Why?

14 What is the primary difference between absorption costing and variable costing?

15 If a company uses absorption costing to prepare its financial statements, is it possible to increase net income without increasing sales or decreasing expenses? How?

16 How are fixed manufacturing overhead costs moved from one year to another under absorption costing?

17 Under absorption costing, how can net income increase without sales increasing?

18 How are selling and administrative costs treated under variable costing?

Key exhibit

Absorption costing		Variable costing	
Product costs	Period costs	Product costs	Period costs
Direct materials		Direct materials	
Direct labour	Selling, general and administrative costs	Direct labour	Selling, general and administrative costs
Variable overhead		Variable overhead	
Fixed overhead			Fixed overhead

EXHIBIT 3.14 Absorption and variable costing

Key formulas

Key formula 3.1: Variable cost per unit

$$\frac{\text{Change in cost}}{\text{Change in volume}} = \text{Variable cost per unit}$$

Key formula 3.2: After-tax cost

$$\text{After-tax cost} = \text{Pretax cost} \times (1 - \text{tax rate})$$

Key formula 3.3: After-tax benefit

$$\text{After-tax benefit} = \text{Pretax receipts} \times (1 - \text{tax rate})$$

Key formula 3.4: After-tax income

$$\text{After-tax income} = \text{Pretax income} \times (1 - \text{tax rate})$$

review

Key definitions

Job costing
A costing system that accumulates, tracks and assigns costs for each job produced by a company.

Fringe benefits
Payroll costs in addition to the basic hourly wage.

Idle time
Worker time that is not used in the production of the finished product.

Overtime premium
An additional amount added to the basic hourly wage owing to overtime worked by the workers.

Allocation
The process of finding a logical method of assigning overhead costs to the products or services a company produces or provides.

Cost drivers
Factors that cause, or drive, the incurrence of costs.

Cost pools
Groups of overhead costs that are similar; used to simplify the task of assigning costs to products using ABC costing.

Normal costing
A method of costing where predetermined overhead rates are calculated by dividing estimated overhead costs by a 'normal' level of production activity.

Predetermined overhead rates
Used to apply overhead to products; calculated by dividing the estimated overhead for a cost pool by the estimated units of the cost driver.

Overapplied overhead
The amount of applied overhead in excess of actual overhead.

Underapplied overhead
The amount of actual overhead in excess of applied overhead.

Learning objectives (LO)

LO1 Explain how job costing is used to accumulate, track and assign product costs.

LO2 Recognise issues related to the measurement of direct material and direct labour costs in job costing.

LO3 Recognise issues related to the allocation of manufacturing overhead costs to products in job costing.

LO4 Explain the need for using predetermined overhead rates and calculate overhead applied to production in job costing.

LO5 Determine whether overhead has been over- or underapplied and demonstrate the alternative treatments of the over- or underapplied amount in job costing.

Key concepts

- The type of costing system used depends upon the manufacturing process and the nature and availability of cost data.

- Direct material cost includes the cost of the primary materials used in production along with shipping costs and sales taxes. Direct labour cost includes the wages paid to production workers including fringe benefits.

- Overhead cannot be directly tracked to products and services but must instead be allocated using cost drivers.

- In order to provide relevant information for decision making, overhead must often be estimated. Under normal costing, the cost of a product includes the actual amount of direct materials, the actual amount of direct labour and an applied amount of manufacturing overhead.

- Overapplied and underapplied overhead may be allocated to WIP, finished goods and/or costs of goods sold depending upon materiality.

Concept questions

1. Explain the importance of product cost information in the context of management decision making.

2. Briefly describe job costing. Give examples of the types of organisations most likely to use job costing.

3. What two components of product costs must be carefully measured and tracked when a company uses job costing?

4. Describe the basic elements of a job cost sheet.

5. Why is overhead difficult to track and allocate to products in a traditional manufacturing environment?

6. What should managers look for when trying to choose a cost driver for overhead costs?

7. When should a normalised (i.e. predetermined) overhead rate be used?

8. Why would a manager prefer one treatment for overapplied overhead to another?

c4

JOB COSTING AND OVERHEAD COSTING SYSTEMS

Key formulas

Key formula 4.1: Overhead rate

$$\text{Overhead rate} = \frac{\text{Manufacturing overhead}}{\text{Cost driver}}$$

Key formula 4.2: Predetermined overhead rate

$$\frac{\text{Predetermined overhead rate}}{\text{(for a cost pool)}} = \frac{\text{Estimated overhead for the cost pool}}{\text{Estimated units of the cost driver}}$$

Key formula 4.3: Applied overhead

$$\frac{\text{Applied}}{\text{overhead}} = \text{Predetermined overhead rate} \times \text{Actual units of cost driver}$$

review

Key definitions

Job costing
A costing system that accumulates, tracks and assigns costs for each job produced by a company.

Process costing
A costing system that accumulates and tracks costs for each process performed and then assigns those costs equally to each unit produced.

Predetermined overhead rates
Used to apply overhead to products; calculated by dividing the estimated overhead for a cost pool by the estimated units of the cost driver.

Equivalent units
The number of finished units that can be made from the materials, labour and overhead included in partially completed units.

Abnormal spoilage
Defective units discarded from the production process for reasons outside the ordinary course of operations in companies. These costs are usually separately expensed in the profit-and-loss statement.

Normal spoilage
Defective units discarded from the production process for reasons relating to the ordinary course of organisational operations. These costs are usually included as part of WIP inventory cost.

Learning objectives (LO)

LO1 Explain how process costing systems are used to accumulate, track and assign product costs.

LO2 Describe basic process costing and the calculation of equivalent units of production.

LO3 Compare and contrast the weighted average and first-in, first-out (FIFO) methods of process costing and apply each step of the four-step process costing system under both methods.

LO4 Analyse the manner by which spoilage costs are considered in process costing.

LO5 Understand how varying resource types possess different equivalent units in order to better understand costing processes in modern organisations.

Key concepts

- Rather than accumulating the costs for each unit produced and directly tracking and assigning costs to each unique unit, process costing accumulates and tracks costs for each process as products pass through the process and then assigns costs equally to the units that come out of each process.

- The equivalent units of a product is the whole number equivalent of units you completed, as tallied from all complete and incomplete production of goods in a period.

- In the FIFO method, the equivalent units and unit costs for the current period relate only to the work done and the costs incurred in the current period. In contrast, in the weighted average method, the units and costs from the current period are combined with the units and costs from last period in the calculation of equivalent units and unit costs.

- The increasing complexity introduced by automation into manufacturing not only increases the speed and efficiency of production, but also the possibilities for error or spoilage during production runs.

- In many organisations, different resources are consumed at different stages of the production process. While the physical units for all these products may remain the same, the equivalent units for direct materials must be split into different resource types.

Concept questions

1. Explain the importance of product cost information in the context of process costing.

2. Briefly describe process costing. Give an example of the type of organisations most likely to use process costing.

3. What components of product costs must be carefully measured and tracked when a company uses process costing?

4. Define the term *equivalent units of production*.

5. What is spoilage, and how do we differentiate between normal spoilage and abnormal spoilage?

6. Why is the FIFO method preferred for calculating equivalent units and calculating unit costs?

7. Under what circumstances might organisations have direct material costs that possess different equivalent units to conversion costs?

c5

PROCESS COSTING SYSTEMS

Key exhibit

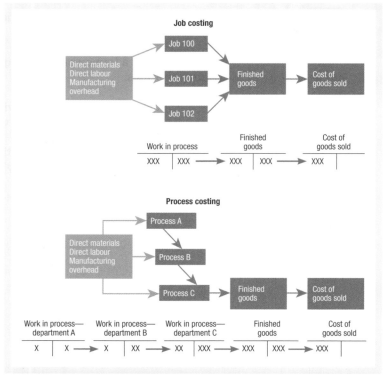

EXHIBIT 5.1 A comparison of cost flows

Key formula

Key formula 5.1: Relationship between beginning units in WIP

Beginning Units + Current units started = Units completed + Ending units

review

Key definitions

Operations costing
A hybrid of job and process costing; used by companies that make products in batches.

Hybrid costing
Methods of costing such as operations costing that involve more than one unique costing model.

Service organisation
An organisation that offers a non-physical, intangible and usually human-sourced skill in order to achieve its objectives.

Mass service
Service organisations that adopt a highly averaged form of costing, offering a generically similar service to all customers.

Professional services
Service organisations that cost each customer uniquely, as they provide a highly customised service.

Service shops
Service organisations that possess the underlying operations of both professional services organisations and mass services organisations.

Service profit chain
A chain emphasising the cause-and–effect model relating attributes of service functions to customer loyalty and profitability.

Learning objectives (LO)

LO1 **Explain operations costing and how it is used to accumulate, track and assign product costs.**

LO2 **Identify a framework for categorising service firms in organisations.**

LO3 **Understand how service activities might contribute to profitability, using a service profit value chain.**

LO4 **Appreciate the link between the service organisation framework and job, process and hybrid costing models.**

LO5 **Recognise the relevance of services and service costs in the retail/merchandising sector.**

Key concepts

- Understanding the role of batch-related output in allowing for job and process costing to aid costing in organisations simultaneously.
- Understanding mass services, service shops and professional services organisational types.
- Appreciating the links between service activities and customer loyalty, and eventually, company profitability.
- Linking mass services, service shops and professional services to process-costing, hybrid-costing and job-costing models respectively.
- Services as an object of costing, including elements of service such as quality in service offerings.

Concept questions

1 Explain the importance of service costing in the context of management decision making in service organisations.
2 What are mass service firms and how does this understanding aid their decision making in organisations from a costing perspective?
3 What are two main components of costs in a service-costing organisation and how might they be measured?
4 Identify a service-shop organisation and describe how it differs from a mass services and professional services organisation.
5 Why is overhead difficult to track in a service environment?
6 How does the knowledge of operations costing help organisations engage in cost control?
7 How might service costing apply in retail organisations? Please cite examples.
8 Give an example of a professional services organisation and discuss the costing system that might align best to this type of organisation.
9 How might the service profit value chain help a mass services firm cost better?

c 6

SERVICE AND OPERATIONS COSTING

Key exhibits

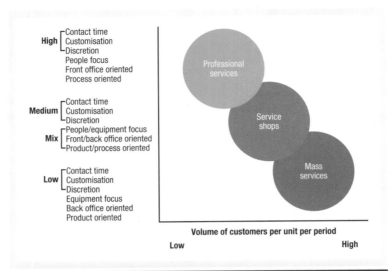

EXHIBIT 6.2 Silvestro (1999) service organisation volume–variety framework

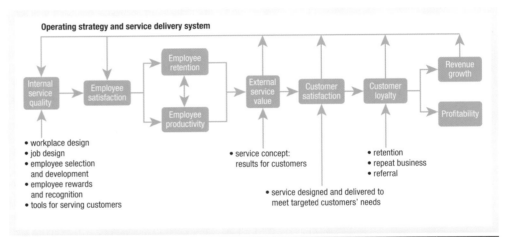

EXHIBIT 6.5 Service-profit value chain (Heskett et al., 2008)

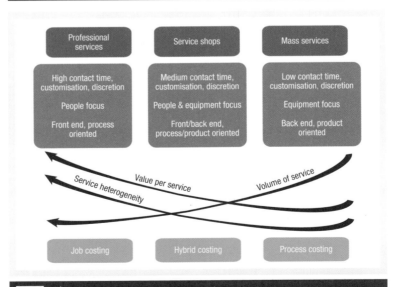

EXHIBIT 6.6 Linking services organisations to costing systems

review

Learning objectives (LO)

LO1 Understand the importance of allocating aggregate costs to individual products/services.

LO2 Understand the difference between direct and indirect departmental overhead costs in assigning overhead costs to departments.

LO3 Appreciate the difference between service and production departments and the three methods for allocating service department overheads to production departments (direct, step-down and reciprocal).

LO4 Understand how production department overheads are allocated to products.

Key definitions

Departmental overhead costing system

An overhead costing system that allows for aggregated overhead costs to be linked to individual products or services, by first allocating them to departments.

Direct departmental overhead costs

Costs that are easily traced to departments.

Indirect departmental overhead costs

Highly aggregated overhead costs that must be shared across departments by identifying cost drivers relating these costs to departments.

Production departments

The departments that actually work on a product and for which cost drivers can be strongly related to products.

Service departments

Departments that are required in order for production to occur, but do not physically conduct production efforts to transform a product or offer a service.

Direct method

A method of allocating service department costs that allocates costs directly to production departments without being allocated to other service departments.

Step-down or sequential method

Recognises that service departments consume resources of other service departments in a one-way direction and allocates those costs to other service departments and then to production departments in a sequential (one-way) fashion.

Reciprocal method

Recognises that service departments mutually consume one another's resources and therefore costs must be allocated between service departments prior to being allocated to production departments.

Key concepts

- The importance of departmental overhead costing for better overall costing, pricing and decision making.
- Link cost pool, cost drivers and cost objects, at a departmental level.
- The nature of linkage between service departments defines the difference between the three methods for service-department reallocation.
- Appreciate the importance of departmental overhead costing for overall product costing.

Concept questions

1 Explain the importance of departmental overhead costing for purposes of decision making in organisations.
2 How is it possible that departmental overhead costs are direct in nature?
3 Under what circumstances is the direct method most appropriate as a departmental overhead costing technique?
4 What is the difference between the step method and the reciprocal method for service-department reallocations?
5 Why might organisations want a separate overhead rate for each producing department?
6 Why do we not simply allocate overhead costs directly to products from service departments?
7 What are the characteristics of a good departmental overhead cost driver?
8 When should a predetermined overhead rate be used?
9 How does the plantwide overhead rate compare to the departmental costing overhead rate?
10 How do we differentiate between direct and indirect departmental overhead costs?

Key exhibits

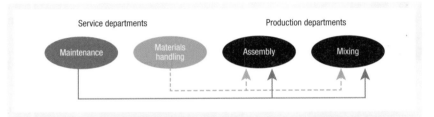

| EXHIBIT 7.2 | Direct method framework |

	Service departments		Production departments	
	Materials handling	Maintenance	Assembly	Mixing
Departmental costs before allocation	$60 000	$50 000	$300 000	$200 000
Handling hours		100	300	200
Maintenance hours	300		4 000	2 000
Direct labour hours			20 000	10 000
Machine hours	150	200	5 000	40 000

| EXHIBIT 7.3 | Service department cost drivers |

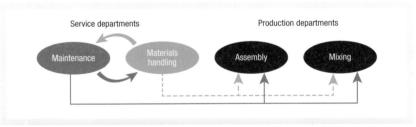

| EXHIBIT 7.7 | Reciprocal method |

Review

Key definitions

Unit-level costs

Costs that are incurred each time a unit is produced.

Batch-level costs

Costs that are incurred each time a batch of goods is produced.

Product-level costs

Costs that are incurred as needed to support the production of each type of product.

Facility-level costs

Costs that are incurred to sustain the overall manufacturing process.

Activity-based costing (ABC)

A system of allocating overhead costs that assumes that activities, not volume of production, cause overhead costs to be incurred.

Activities

Procedures or processes that cause work to be accomplished.

Diverse products

Products that consume resources in different proportions.

Learning objectives (LO)

LO1 Classify overhead costs as unit, batch, product or facility level.

LO2 Describe ABC and recognise typical activities and cost drivers in an ABC system.

LO3 Calculate the cost of a product using ABC and compare traditional volume-based costing to ABC.

LO4 Evaluate the benefits and limitations of ABC systems.

Key concepts

- Activity-based costing allocates costs based on activities that drive overhead rather than simple volume or unit-based measures.

- Unit-level costs are incurred each time a unit is produced. Batch-level costs are incurred each time a batch of goods is produced. Product-level costs are incurred as needed to support the production of each type of product. Facility-level costs simply sustain a facility's general manufacturing process.

- Although there are common activities that drive overhead costs, every organisation should evaluate its activities carefully. Volume-based costing systems often result in overcosting high-volume products and undercosting low-volume products. This cross subsidy is eliminated by the use of ABC.

- ABC systems generally improve the accuracy of cost data, but are often time consuming and expensive to develop.

Concept questions

1. Overhead costs are typically identified as belonging to one of four categories. List and briefly describe each category.
2. Define activity-based costing.
3. Identify and describe the two stages of cost allocation in an activity-based costing system.
4. Discuss the importance of choosing the right cost driver and the potential impact of choosing the wrong cost driver.
5. Why would a company that utilises just-in-time techniques also wish to implement an activity-based costing system?
6. How can activity-based costing techniques be applied to selling and administration activities?
7. What are 'cross subsidies between products' and how can they be controlled?
8. What are some of the benefits of activity-based costing systems?
9. What are some of the downsides of activity-based costing systems?

c8

ACTIVITY-BASED COSTING

Key exhibits

Unit-level costs	Product-level costs
Supplies for factory	Salaries of engineers
Depreciation of factory machinery	Depreciation of engineering equipment
Energy costs for factory machinery	Product development costs (testing)
Repairs and maintenance of factory machinery	Quality control costs
Batch-level costs	**Facility-level costs**
Salaries related to purchasing and receiving	Depreciation of factory building or rent
Salaries related to moving material	Salary of plant manager
Quality control costs	Insurance and taxes on factory building
Depreciation of setup equipment	Employee training

EXHIBIT 8.2 Overhead costs and Cooper's hierarchy

Activity	Level	Typical cost drivers
Repair and maintenance	Unit	Machine hours, labour hours or number of units of factory equipment
Machining of products	Unit	Machine hours
Purchasing	Batch	Number of purchase orders or number of parts
Receiving	Batch	Amount of material or number of receipts
Setting up equipment	Batch	Number of setups
Product testing	Product	Number of change orders, number of tests or hours of testing time
Engineering	Product	Number of engineering hours or number of products
Product design	Product	Number of new or revised products
Quality control	Unit, batch	Number of inspections, hours of inspection, or product number of defective units

EXHIBIT 8.3 Activities and cost drivers

Key definitions

Cost–volume–profit (CVP) analysis

A tool that focuses on the relationship between a company's profits and (1) the selling prices of products or services, (2) the volume of products or services sold, (3) the per unit variable costs, (4) the total fixed costs and (5) the mix of products or services produced.

Gross profit

The difference between sales and cost of goods sold.

Contribution margin per unit (CMU)

The sales price per unit of product less all variable costs to produce and sell the unit of product; used to calculate the change in contribution margin resulting from a change in unit sales.

Contribution margin ratio (CMR)

The contribution margin divided by sales; used to calculate the change in contribution margin resulting from a dollar change in sales.

Break-even point

The level of sales at which contribution margin just covers fixed costs and net profit is equal to zero.

Operating leverage

The contribution margin divided by net profit; used as an indicator of how sensitive net profit is to a change in sales.

Learning objectives (LO)

LO1 Use the contribution margin in its various forms to determine the impact of changes in sales on profit.

LO2 Analyse what-if decisions using CVP analysis.

LO3 Compute a company's break-even point in single- and multi-product environments.

LO4 Analyse target profit before and after the impact of income tax.

LO5 Compute a company's operating leverage and understand its relationship to cost structure.

Key concepts

- The contribution margin income statement is structured to emphasise cost behaviour as opposed to cost function. For every unit (dollar) change in sales, contribution margin will increase or decrease by the contribution margin per unit multiplied by the increase or decrease in sales volume (dollars). The contribution margin per unit and the contribution margin ratio will remain constant as long as sales vary in direct proportion to volume.

- Managers must be careful to consider the implications of choices they make in what-if analyses because of the potential impact decisions may have on production cost or customer demand.

- A thorough understanding of fixed and variable costs is necessary before a manager can calculate and understand a break-even analysis.

- The payment of income taxes is an important variable in target profit and other CVP decisions if managers are to understand the bottom line effect of their decisions.

- A company operating near the break-even point will have a high level of operating leverage, and income will be very sensitive to changes in sales volume.

Concept questions

1. Describe the primary difference between traditional income statements and contribution margin income statements.
2. What happens to the contribution margin when fixed expenses decrease and variable costs per unit remain constant?
3. Define the term *contribution margin*.
4. If the total contribution margin decreases by a given amount, what will be the effect on income?
5. Describe the formula for computing the break-even point in sales dollars and units.
6. How might a company decrease its break-even point?
7. How do income taxes affect CVP computations?
8. As a company nears the break-even point, what happens to its operating leverage?

Key formulas

Key formula 9.2: Contribution margin ratio

$$\text{Contribution margin ratio} = \frac{\text{Contribution margin (in \$)}}{\text{Sales (in \$)}}$$

Key formula 9.3: Break-even point. Break-even (units)

$$\text{Break-even (units)} = \frac{\text{Fixed costs}}{\text{Contribution margin per unit}}$$

Key formula 9.4: Break-even point. Break-even ($)

$$\text{Break-even (\$)} = \frac{\text{Fixed costs}}{\text{Contribution margin ratio}}$$

Key formula 9.5: Break-even point. Break-even (units)

$$\text{Break-even (units)} = \frac{\text{Fixed costs}}{\text{Weighted-average contribution margin per unit}}$$

Key formula 9.6: Target profit analysis. Sales volume (to reach a target profit before tax)

$$\text{Sales volume (to reach a target profit before tax)} = \frac{\text{Fixed costs} + \text{Target profit (before tax)}}{\text{Contribution margin}}$$

Key formula 9.7: Target profit analysis. Sales volume (to reach target profit)

$$\text{Sales volume (to reach a target profit)} = \frac{(\text{Fixed costs} + \text{Target profit})}{\text{Weighted-average contribution margin per unit}}$$

Key formula 9.8: Before-tax profit

$$\text{Before-tax profit} = \frac{\text{After-tax profit}}{(1 - \text{tax rate})}$$

Key formula 9.9: Operating leverage

$$\text{Operating leverage} = \frac{\text{Contribution margin}}{\text{Net income}}$$

review

Key definitions

Special-order decisions

Short-run pricing decisions in which management must decide which sales price is appropriate when customers place orders that are different from those placed in the regular course of business (onetime sale to a foreign customer, etc.).

Make-or-buy decisions

Short-term decisions to outsource labour or to purchase components used in manufacturing from another company rather than to provide services or produce components internally.

Vertical integration

Accomplished when a company is involved in multiple steps of the value chain.

Constraint

A restriction that occurs when the capacity to manufacture a product or to provide a service is limited in some manner.

Resource utilisation decision

A decision requiring an analysis of how best to use a resource that is available in limited supply.

Theory of constraints

A management tool for dealing with constraints; identifies and focuses on bottlenecks in the production process.

Bottlenecks

Production-process steps that limit throughput or the number of finished products that go through the production process.

Learning objectives (LO)

LO1 Analyse the pricing of a special order.

LO2 Analyse a decision involving the outsourcing of labour or making or buying a component.

LO3 Analyse a decision dealing with adding or dropping a product, product line or service.

LO4 Analyse a decision dealing with scarce or limited resources.

LO5 Describe the theory of constraints and explain the importance of identifying bottlenecks in the production process.

LO6 Analyse a decision dealing with selling a product or processing it further.

Key concepts

- The price of a special order must be higher than the additional variable costs plus any opportunity costs incurred in accepting the special order.
- A product should continue to be made internally if the avoidable costs are less than the additional costs that will be incurred by buying or outsourcing.
- A product should be dropped when the fixed costs that are avoided exceed the contribution margin that is lost.
- Resource utilisation decisions hinge on an analysis of the contribution margin earned per unit of the limited resource. The goal is to maximise the contribution margin per unit of the limited resource.
- Bottlenecks must be identified and managed if a business is to be successful in overcoming constraints.
- A product should be processed further if the additional revenue exceeds the additional cost of processing.

Concept questions

1. Production of a special order will increase income when the additional revenue from the special order is greater than what?

2. In considering a special order that will enable a company to make use of presently idle capacity, list the costs that would more than likely be relevant in the decision-making process.

3. What costs are usually relevant in a make-or-buy decision?

4. Name some qualitative factors that would cause a decision maker to favour the buy choice in a make-or-buy decision.

5. What are some of the disadvantages of outsourcing the production of a component part?

6. In deciding whether to manufacture a part or to buy it from an outside supplier, name a cost that would not be relevant to that short-run decision.

7. The decision to drop a product line should be based on what factors?

8. What should be the goal of a manager who is faced with a limited-resource decision?

9. What steps should be taken when dealing with a production bottleneck?

10. What is the general rule of thumb that should be followed when making a decision whether to sell as is or process a particular product further?

c 10

RELEVANT COSTS AND PRODUCT PLANNING DECISIONS

Key exhibits

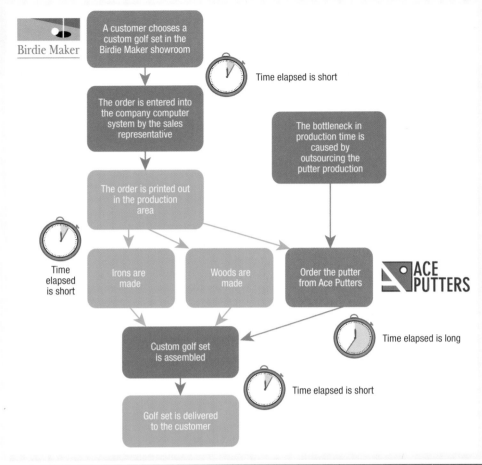

EXHIBIT 10.7 An example of a production bottleneck

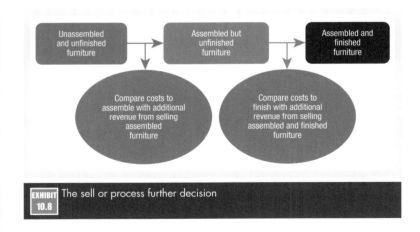

EXHIBIT 10.8 The sell or process further decision

review

Key definitions

Capital investment decisions

Long-term decisions involving the purchase (or lease) of new machinery and equipment and the acquisition or expansion of facilities used in a business.

Time value of money

The concept that a dollar received today is worth more than a dollar received in the future.

Net present value (NPV)

A technique for considering the time value of money whereby the present value of all cash inflows associated with a project is compared with the present value of all cash outflows.

Cost of capital

What the firm would have to pay to borrow (issue bonds) or raise funds through equity (issue stock) in the financial marketplace.

Discount rate

Used as a hurdle rate, or minimum rate of return, in calculations of the time value of money; adjusted to reflect risk and uncertainty.

Internal rate of return (IRR)

The actual yield, or return, earned by an investment.

Screening decisions

Decisions about whether an investment meets a predetermined company standard.

Preference decisions

Decisions that involve choosing between alternatives.

Depreciation tax shield

The tax savings from depreciation.

Payback period

The length of time needed for a long-term project to recapture, or pay back, the initial investment.

Learning objectives (LO)

LO1 Evaluate capital investment decisions using the NPV method.

LO2 Evaluate capital investment decisions using the IRR method.

LO3 Distinguish between screening and preference decisions and use the profitability index to evaluate preference decisions.

LO4 Evaluate the impact of taxes on capital investment decisions.

LO5 Evaluate capital investment decisions using the payback method and discuss the limitations of the method.

Key concepts

- Long-term investment decisions require a consideration of the time value of money. The time value of money is based on the concept that a dollar received today is worth more than a dollar received in the future. If the present value of cash inflows is greater than or equal to the present value of cash outflows (the NPV is greater than or equal to zero), the investment provides a return at least equal to the discount rate (the minimum required rate of return) and the investment is acceptable.

- The internal rate of return (IRR) is the actual yield, or return, earned by an investment.

- The profitability index is a useful tool for making preference decisions because it can be used to compare projects that require investment of different amounts.

- Taxes are a major source of cash outflows for many companies and must be taken into consideration in calculations of the time value of money.

- The payback method can be useful as a quick approximation of the discounted cash flow methods when the cash flows follow similar patterns.

Concept questions

1. Define the term *cost of capital*. How would cost of capital be used in an investment decision?

2. If the net present value of a proposed project is negative, what is the actual rate of return?

3. For the internal rate of return to rank projects the same as net present value, which conditions must exist?

4. Describe the process by which projects are accepted using the internal rate of return.

5. Define profitability index and discuss how it is used in capital investment decisions.

6. Compare screening decisions with preference decisions.

7. Explain the 'depreciation tax shield'. Why should managers consider the tax shield in their decision-making process?

8. Define *payback period*. What are the primary advantages and disadvantages of the method?

c 11

LONG-TERM (CAPITAL INVESTMENT) DECISIONS

Key exhibit

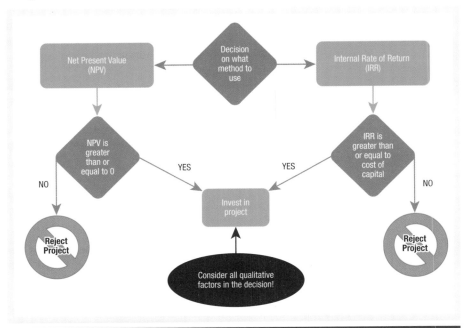

EXHIBIT 11.4 Using NPV and IRR as screening tools

Key formulas

Key formula 11.1: Present value of annuity

$$PVA = R(DFA_{n,r})$$

Key formula 11.2: Payback period

$$\text{Payback period} = \frac{\text{Original investment}}{\text{Net annual cash inflows}}$$

review

Key definitions

Budgets
Plans dealing with the acquisition and use of resources over a specified time period.

Planning
The cornerstone of good management; involves developing objectives and goals for the organisation, as well as the actual preparation of budgets.

Operating
Involves day-to-day decision making by managers, which is often facilitated by budgeting.

Control
Involves ensuring that the objectives and goals developed by the organisation are being attained; often involves a comparison of budgets to actual performance and the use of budgets for performance-evaluation purposes.

Zero-based budgeting
Requires managers to build budgets from the ground up each year.

Participatory budgeting
A budgeting process that starts with departmental managers and flows up through middle management and then to top management. Each new level of management has responsibility for reviewing and negotiating any changes in the proposed budget.

Master budget
Consists of an interrelated set of budgets prepared by a business.

Sales forecast
Combines with the sales budget to form the starting points in the preparation of production budgets for manufacturing companies, purchases budgets for merchandising companies, and labour budgets for service companies.

Sales budget
Used in planning the cash needs for manufacturing, merchandising and service companies.

Operating budgets
Used to plan for the short term (typically one year or less).

Production budget
Used to forecast how many units of product to produce in order to meet the sales projections.

Material purchases budget
Used to project the dollar amount of raw materials purchased for production.

Direct labour budget
Used to project the dollar amount of direct labour cost needed for production.

Manufacturing overhead budget
Used to project the dollar amount of manufacturing overhead needed for production.

Learning objectives (LO)

LO1 Describe the budget development process, behavioural implications of budgeting, advantages of budgeting and the master budget.

LO2 Explain how managers develop a sales forecast and demonstrate the preparation of a sales budget.

LO3 Prepare a production budget and recognise how it relates to the material purchases, direct labour and manufacturing overhead budgets.

LO4 Prepare budgets for material purchases, direct labour, manufacturing overhead, and selling and administrative expenses.

LO5 Explain the importance of budgeting for cash and prepare a cash receipts budget, a cash disbursements budget and a summary cash budget.

LO6 Prepare budgeted income statements and balance sheets and evaluate the importance of budgeted financial statements for decision making.

LO7 Contrast budgeting in a manufacturing company with budgeting in a merchandising company and a service company.

LO8 Differentiate static budgets from flexible budgets.

LO9 Explain and understand the concept of rolling budgets in modern organisations.

Key concepts

- Budgets must start with a top-down strategic plan that guides and integrates the whole company and its individual budgets.
- Budgets are future oriented and make extensive use of estimates and forecasts.
- The sales forecast (budget) is the starting point in the production budget.
- Preparing budgets for material purchases, direct labour, overhead, and selling and administrative expenses is critical because these budgets often require companies to commit to expenditures months in advance.
- Accurate cash flow projections are critical if a company is to pay its employees, suppliers and creditors on a timely basis.
- Preparing budgeted, or pro forma, financial statements allows managers to determine the effects of their budgeting decisions on the company's financial statements.
- A primary focus of budgeting in a service company is on labour (e.g. a time budget).
- Flexible budgets are based on the actual number of units produced rather than on the budgeted units of production.
- Rolling budgets are a series of short-term budgets that are updated periodically in order to help us better manage business uncertainty.

c 12

FIXED AND ROLLING BUDGETS FOR PLANNING AND DECISION MAKING

Cash receipts budget
Used to project the amount of cash expected to be received from sales and cash collections from customers.

Cash disbursements budget
Used to project the amount of cash to be disbursed during the budget period.

Summary cash budget
Consists of three sections: (1) cash flows from operating activities, (2) cash flows from investing activities and (3) cash flows from financing activities; these three sections are the same as those used in the cash flow statement prepared under generally accepted accounting principles (GAAP).

Pro forma financial statements
Budgeted financial statements that are sometimes used for internal planning purposes but more often are used by external users.

Static budgets
Budgets that are set at the beginning of the period and remain constant throughout the budget period.

Flexible budgets
Budgets that take differences in spending owing to volume differences out of the analysis by budgeting for labour (and other costs) based on the actual number of units produced.

Concept questions

1 What are some of the characteristics of a typical budget?

2 Outline, using no amounts, a budget that you might use in managing your personal finances.

3 Why is the sales budget the most important piece of the budgeting process?

4 List and describe some of the major factors and information sources typically used in sales forecasting.

5 What are the essential elements of a production budget?

6 Comment on the following statement: 'The materials, labour and overhead budgets can be prepared before the production budget'.

7 What are several decisions that management can address by using the cash receipts budget?

8 Why is so much emphasis put on cash flow in the budgeting process?

9 Discuss ways that pro forma financial statements might be used both internally and externally.

10 Discuss why financial budgets for merchandising companies are differe from those for manufacturing companies.

11 Discuss the difference between static and flexible budgets.

Key exhibits

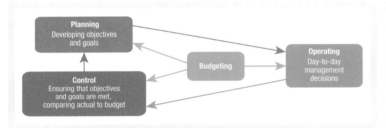

EXHIBIT 12.2 The operating cycle

Key formulas

Key formula 12.1: Required production

Sales forecast (in units)
+ Desired ending inventory of finished goods
= Total budgeted production needs
− Beginning inventory of finished goods
= Required production

Key formula 12.2: Required production

Required production = Budgeted sales + (−) Increase (Decrease) in finished goods inventory

EXHIBIT 12.3 The master budget for a manufacturing company

Key definitions

Control
Involves the motivation and monitoring of employees and the evaluation of people and other resources used in the operations of the organisation.

Variance analysis
Allows managers to see whether sales, production and manufacturing costs are higher or lower than planned and, more importantly, why actual sales, production and costs differ from budget.

Management by exception
The process of taking action only when actual results deviate significantly from planned results.

Standard cost
A budget for a single unit of product or service.

Standard quantity
The budgeted amount of materials, labour or overhead for each product.

Standard price
The budgeted price of the materials, labour or overhead for each unit.

Task analysis
A method of setting standards that also examines the production process in detail to determine what it should cost to produce a product.

Ideal standard
A standard that is attained only when near-perfect conditions are present.

Practical standard
A standard that should be attained under normal, efficient operating conditions.

Flexible budget variance
The difference between the flexible budget operating income and actual operating income.

Sales price variance
The difference between the actual sales price and the flexible budget sales price times the actual sales volume.

Price variance
The difference between the actual price and the standard price times the actual volume purchased.

Usage variance
The difference between the actual quantity and the standard quantity times the standard price.

Budget variance
The difference between the amount of fixed overhead actually incurred and the flexible budget amount; also known as the spending variance.

Volume variance
The difference between the flexible budget amount and the fixed overhead applied to products.

Learning objectives (LO)

Key concepts

- The type of standard (practical or ideal) chosen to evaluate performance can have significant effects on employee morale and behaviour.
- Flexible budgets that are based on standard costs are the centerpiece of effective variance analysis.
- The flexible budget variance is the difference between the flexible budget operating income and the actual operating income.
- The variance analysis model, through the use of both price and usage variances, separates the overall flexible budget into two primary components.
- Purchasing managers are often held responsible for price variances, while production managers are held responsible for usage variances.
- Personnel and production managers are often responsible for direct labour variances.
- The variable overhead efficiency variance does not measure the efficient use of overhead but rather the efficient use of the cost driver, or overhead allocation base, used in the flexible budget.
- The fixed overhead volume variance should not be interpreted as favourable or unfavourable or as a measure of the efficient utilisation of facilities.
- Management by exception is the key to effective variance analysis and involves taking action only when actual and planned results differ significantly.

c 13

MANAGEMENT ACCOUNTING FOR
COST CONTROL AND PERFORMANCE
EVALUATION – FLEXIBLE BUDGETS
AND VARIANCE ANALYSIS

Concept questions

1. Discuss ideal versus practical standards and how they might affect employee behaviour.
2. What is the primary difference between a static budget and a flexible budget?
3. Discuss the value of a flexible budget to management decision making.
4. Which area of management would normally be responsible for sales price variances? Why?
5. How is the standard quantity (SQ) computed in the calculation of the direct material usage variance?
6. What is the focus of a usage variance?
7. What are some possible causes for an unfavourable direct labour efficiency variance?
8. What does a variable overhead efficiency variance tell management?
9. The predetermined fixed overhead application rate is a function of a predetermined 'normal' activity level. If standard hours allowed for good output are equal to this predetermined activity level for a given period, what will the volume variance be?
10. Discuss the advantages and disadvantages of using 'management by exception' techniques.

Key formulas

Key formula 13.1: Sales price variance

Sales price variance = (Actual – Expected sales price) × Actual volume

Key formula 13.2: Price variance

Price variance = Actual quantity (AQ) × [Actual price (AP) – Standard price (SP)]

Key formula 13.3: Usage variance

Usage variance = Standard price (SP) × [Actual quantity (AQ) – Standard quantity (SQ)]

Key formula 13.4: Fixed overhead budget (spending) variance

Fixed overhead budget (spending) variance = Actual fixed overhead – Budgeted fixed overhead

Key formula 13.5: Fixed overhead volume variance

Fixed overhead volume variance = Budgeted fixed overhead – Applied fixed overhead

review

Key definitions

Decentralised organisation

An organisation in which decision-making authority is spread throughout the organisation.

Responsibility accounting

An accounting system that assigns responsibility to a manager for those areas that are under that manager's control.

Cost centre

An organisational segment, or division, in which the manager has control over costs but not over revenue or investment decisions.

Performance report

Provides key financial and non-financial measures of performance for a particular segment.

Revenue centre

An organisational segment, or division, in which the manager has control over revenue but not costs or investment decisions.

Profit centre

An organisational segment, or division, in which the manager has control over both costs and revenue but not investment decisions.

Investment centre

An organisational segment, or division, in which the manager has control over costs, revenue and investment decisions.

Strategic business unit (SBU)

Another term for investment centre.

Segmented profit and loss statements

Reports that calculate profit for each major segment of an organisation in addition to the company as a whole.

Segment costs

All costs attributable to a particular segment of an organisation but only those costs that are actually caused by the segment.

Common costs

Indirect costs that are incurred to benefit more than one segment and cannot be directly traced to a particular segment or allocated in a reasonable manner.

Segment margin

The profit margin of a particular segment of an organisation, typically the best measure of long-term profitability.

Return on investment (ROI)

Measures the rate of return generated by an investment centre's assets.

Margin

For each sales dollar, the percentage that is recognised as net profit.

c 14

DECENTRALISATION AND MODERN PERFORMANCE MANAGEMENT SYSTEMS – THE BALANCED SCORECARD

Learning objectives (LO)

LO1 Describe the structure and management of decentralised organisations and evaluate the benefits and drawbacks of decentralisation.

LO2 Evaluate how responsibility accounting is used to help manage a decentralised organisation.

LO3 Define cost, revenue, profit and investment centres and explain why managers of each must be evaluated differently.

LO4 Compute and interpret segment margin in an organisation.

LO5 Compute, interpret and compare return on investment (ROI) and residual income.

LO6 Describe the balanced scorecard and its key dimensions.

LO7 Define quality costs and explain the trade-offs among prevention costs, appraisal costs, internal failure costs and external failure costs.

LO8 Recognise the importance of using incentives to motivate managers and discuss the advantages and disadvantages of using cash-based, stock-based and other forms of managerial compensation.

Key concepts

- Decentralised organisations must have managers who are competent, experienced, and have the authority required to make decisions.
- The key to effective decision making in a decentralised organisation is responsibility accounting – holding managers responsible for only those things under their control.
- Businesses are often broken into cost, revenue and profit centres as a means to evaluate managers' performance levels.
- Evaluating investment centres requires focusing on the level of investment required in generating a segment's profit.
- Evaluating the performance of investment centre managers is complex and often involves using measures such as ROI and residual income.
- The balanced scorecard approach integrates financial and non-financial performance measures. The balanced scorecard approach requires looking at performance from four different but related perspectives: financial, customer, internal business, and learning and growth.
- The traditional view of quality costs is that total quality costs are minimised at some acceptable level of defects, while the contemporary view is that total quality costs are minimised at a zero defect level.
- In order to motivate managers and ensure goal congruence, the compensation of managers should be linked to performance and based on a combination of short-term and long-term goals.

Concept questions

1 Identify the advantages and disadvantages of decentralisation.
2 What is responsibility accounting, and what is its impact on decision making?
3 Define an investment centre and explain how investment centre managers might be evaluated.
4 Describe segment costs and compare them to common costs.
5 Define residual income and discuss how it compares to ROI.
6 When is ROI a more useful performance measure than residual income?
7 Describe a balanced scorecard and explain how it helps an organisation meet its goals.
8 Discuss what is meant by quality in today's manufacturing environment.
9 Describe the two costs of controlling quality and the two costs of failing to control quality.
10 Why is non-cash compensation important?

Asset turnover

The measure of activity used in the ROI calculation; it measures the sales that are generated for a given level of assets.

Net operating profit

Net profit from operations before interest and taxes.

Operating assets

Typically include cash, accounts receivable, inventory and the property, plant and equipment needed to operate a business.

Balanced scorecard

An approach to performance measurement that uses a set of financial and non-financial measures that relate to the overall strategy of the organisation.

Residual income

The amount of profit earned in excess of a predetermined minimum rate of return on assets.

Productivity

A measure of the relationship between outputs and inputs.

Manufacturing cycle time

The total time a product is in production, which includes process time, inspection time, wait time and move time; cycle time will include both value-added and non-value-added time.

Throughput

The amount of product produced in a given amount of time, such as a day, week or month.

Manufacturing cycle efficiency (MCE)

The value-added time in the production process divided by the throughput, or cycle time.

Quality

Usually defined as meeting or exceeding customers' expectations.

Kaizen

A system of improvement based on a series of gradual and often small improvements.

Hejunka

A system of standardising manufacturing processes to improve efficiency.

Prevention costs

Costs incurred to prevent product failures from occurring, typically related to design and engineering.

Appraisal (detection) costs

Costs incurred to inspect finished products or products in the process of production.

Internal failure costs

Costs incurred once the product is produced and then determined to be defective.

External failure costs

Costs incurred when a defective product is delivered to a customer.

Stock option

The right to buy a share of stock at a set price (called the option price or strike price) at some point in the future.

Restricted stock

A form of management compensation in which employees receive shares of stock with restrictions such as requirements to stay with the company for a set period of time or requirements to meet established performance measures.

Key exhibits

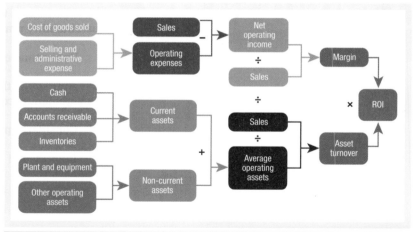

EXHIBIT 14.2 Elements of return on investment (ROI)

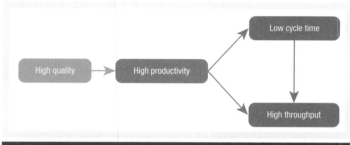

EXHIBIT 14.9 High quality leads to low cycle time and high throughput

Key formulas

Key formula 14.1: Return on investment (ROI)

$$ROI = Margin \times Turnover$$
$$Margin = Net\ operating\ profit + Sales$$
$$Turnover = Sales + Average\ operating\ assets$$
$$ROI = Net\ operating\ income \times Average\ operating\ assets$$
$$ROI = \frac{Net\ operating\ income}{Sales} \times \frac{Sales}{Average\ operating\ assets}$$

or

$$ROI = \frac{Net\ operating\ income}{Average\ operating\ assets}$$

Key formula 14.2: Residual income

$$Residual\ Income = Net\ operating\ profit - (Average\ operating\ assets \times Minimum\ required\ rate\ of\ return)$$

Key formula 14.3: Manufacturing cycle efficiency (MCE)

$$MCE = \frac{Value\text{-}added\ time}{Manufacturing\ cycle\ time}$$

review

Key definitions

Sustainability

The pursuit of endeavours which prolongs the use of or reduces or eliminates resources being consumed in performing transactions to achieve an individual or organisational objective.

Sustainability value chain

A visual depiction identifying key broad categories of activity defining an organisation's activities conducted to deliver value that allows it to attain its objectives.

External costs

Costs that organisations are indirectly responsible for, but which are not captured in their financial statements owing to the entity concept.

Triple bottom line reporting

A form of reporting performance that considers the economic, social and environmental performance of an organisation.

Economic outcomes

The predominantly financial outcomes as captured by accounting values in organisations, affected through the conduct of their operations.

Environmental outcomes

Outcomes relating to the broader environment within which an organisation exists, which it has impacted through its operations.

Social outcomes

Outcomes relating to the broader society within which an organisation exists, which it has impacted through its operations.

Prevention costs

Costs incurred by an organisation to ensure that environmental problems do not arise, or their likelihood of arising is minimised.

Appraisal costs

The costs of monitoring the effects of our operations, in this chapter with respect to our environmental performance.

Internal failure costs

Environmental costs incurred by organisations to address problems that have arisen within an organisation – they include costs to fix technologies, or care for employees owing to environmental incidents that may have occurred.

External failure costs

Environmental costs incurred by organisations to cover the costs or incur fines relating to environmental breaches that have impacted stakeholders outside itself.

Learning objectives (LO)

LO1 Understand the role of management accounting in documenting sustainability practices.

LO2 Understand externalised costs for which organisations are responsible.

LO3 Appreciate the role of sustainability value chains and its link to management accounting.

LO4 Consider triple bottom line reporting and sustainability-related KPIs.

LO5 Identify and understand environmental costs in organisations.

Key concepts

- Accounting as a change agent for organisational practice.
- Organisations being responsible for second and third-order effects of their business conduct.
- Expanding the value chain to consider reuse, recycling.
- Simultaneously understanding social, environmental and economic impacts of organisational operations and their related performance indicators.
- Understanding the nature of prevention, appraisal, internal failure and external failure environmental costs in organisations.

Concept questions

1. How can management accounting add to our understanding of sustainability value chains in organisations.
2. What is the purpose of a triple bottom line report?
3. How do external costs enhance our understanding of an organisation's performance?
4. Briefly describe the role of the four environmental costs in helping organisations better understand their environmental management activities.
5. What is the difference between a social cost and an environmental cost?
6. Do organisations prefer prevention costs to external failure costs? Why?
7. 'Nothing's happening to the environment, as I see it. Why should I bother with environmental cost investments in my organisation?' How do you respond to this question and how might accounting help you in your response?

Key exhibits

Source: Marc J. Epstein and Marie-Josée Roy, 'Sustainability in action: Identifying and measuring the key performance drivers', *Long Range Planning*, Volume 34, Issue 5, October 2001: 585–604.

EXHIBIT 15.1 Drivers of sustainability and financial performance

c 15

ACCOUNTING FOR SUSTAINABILITY – SOCIAL AND ENVIRONMENTAL REPORTING AND MANAGEMENT ACCOUNTING

| | Not achieved | ▶ On track | ◀ Behind schedule | ◆ No change | ▲ Improvement | ▼ Deterioration |

Target*	Performance			Target date
	Result	Trend**	Commentary	
Zero Harm				
Zero fatalities	■	▲	Two fatalities at our controlled operations	Annual
Zero significant environmental incidents and zero significant community incidents	▶	▲	No significant environmental or community incidents reported	Annual
Health				
All operating sites to finalise baseline health exposure assessments on occupational exposure hazards for physical exposures	▶	◆	Finalised FY2010, target met	30 June 2010
15% reduction in potential employee exposures (but for the use of personal protective equipment) over the occupational exposure limit	◀	▲	Total employees† exposed 21,464 (reduction of 7.8% on FY2007 base year)	30 June 2012
30% reduction in the incidence of occupational disease	▶	▲	We are on track to meet the public target with 68 fewer cases than reported in FY2007 (39% reduction)	30 June 2012
Safety				
50% reduction in total recordable injury frequency (TRIF) at sites	◀	▲	The TRIF for FY2011 was 5.0 (32% reduction since FY2007 base year)	30 June 2012
Environment				
Aggregate Group target of 6% reduction in greenhouse gas emissions per unit of production	▶	▲	GHG emissions intensity is 18% lower than FY2006 base year	30 June 2012
Aggregate Group target of a 13% reduction in carbon-based energy per unit of production	▶	▲	Energy intensity is 17% lower than FY2006 base year	30 June 2012
Aggregate Group target of a 10% improvement in the ratio of water recycled/reused to high-quality water consumed	▶	▲	Our water use index is currently tracking at 8% improvement on our FY2007 base year	30 June 2012
Aggregate Group target of a 10% improvement in the land rehabilitation index	◀	◆	There has been a 1% improvement on the FY2007 base year rehabilitation index	30 June 2012
Community				
1% of pre-tax profits to be invested in community programs, including cash, in-kind support and administration, calculated on the average of the previous three years' pre-tax profit	▶	◆	US$195.5 million invested in community programs, including US$30 million deposited into BHP Billiton Sustainable Communities, our UK-based charitable company	Annual

* The baseline year for the target is 1 July 2006 – 30 June 2007, except for Energy Use and Greenhouse Gas Emissions, where it is 1 July 2005 – 30 June 2006.
** Trend compared with previous year.
† Operational assets are the only ones to provide occupational exposure data.

Source: www.bhpbilliton.com/home/aboutus/sustainability/reports/Documents/2011/BHPBillitonSustainability Report2011_Interactive.pdf (p4)

EXHIBIT 15.5 BHP sustainability performance indicators

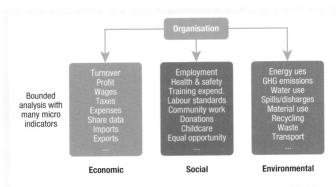

Source: www.cse.csiro.au/publications/2005/balancingact1.pdf (p23)

EXHIBIT 15.6 Triple bottom line elements

review

Learning objectives (LO)

LO1 Defining ethics and understanding the 'grey' in the ethical view of accounting.

LO2 Defining and describing the principles of ethical conduct.

LO3 Defining and describing the threats to ethical conduct.

LO4 Identifying safeguards to the practice of ethics in organisations.

LO5 Understanding an ethical framework for decision making.

Key concepts

- Ethics as a defined body of guiding principles in the accounting profession
- Five key principles (Integrity, Objectivity, Professional Competence and Due Care, Confidentiality, Professional Behaviour)
- Five threats to the principles (Self Interest, Self Review, Advocacy, Familiarity, Intimidation)
- Safeguards in an organisation's work environment, and safeguards created by the profession, regulation or legislation.
- Defining a conflict resolution framework, emphasising an understanding of the facts, key ethical issues involved, principles related to the matter in question, establishment of internal procedures and identifying alternative courses of action.

Concept questions

1 How can ethics inform better management accounting practice?
2 What is the difference between legal conduct and ethical conduct in management accounting?
3 How do organisations reduce the likelihood that unethical conduct might occur?
4 If self interest governs all that we do, why consider it a threat when dealing with ethics in accounting, as per the APES?
5 How can ethics relate to an accountants' ability to uphold the reputation of their profession?
6 To what extent might companies tolerate unethical conduct by certain managers, and is this ultimately positive or negative for the firm concerned?
7 Unethical conduct is necessary in a profitable organisation, so what matters is whether a conduct is legal, not ethical – do you agree or disagree, and why?

Key definitions

Ethics
Taking decisions for moral reasons, with consideration for the wider needs of stakeholders.

Integrity
Requires that accountants are "straightforward and honest in all professional and business relationships". (APES 110 paragraph 100.5 a)

Objectivity
Refers to accountants avoiding "bias, conflict of interest or the undue influence of others to override professional or business judgements". (APES 110 paragraph 110.5 b)

Professional competence and due care
Accountants must "… maintain professional knowledge and skill at the level required to ensure that a client or employer receives competent Professional Services based on current developments in practice, legislation and techniques and act diligently and in accordance with applicable technical and professional standards." (APES 110 paragraph 100.5 c)

Confidentiality
Accountants must respect the private nature of information acquired as a result of professional and business relationships, and not disclose the information to any third parties.

Professional behaviour
An accountant must "… comply with relevant laws and regulations and avoid any action that discredits the profession." (APES 110 paragraph 100.5 e)

Self interest
Placing an individual's personal gain over the corporation or other stakeholder's benefit.

Self review
Occurs when members adjudge their own work, hence tempted to bias in their own evaluation.

Advocacy
As explained in APES 110 paragraph 100.12 c, "the threat that a Member will promote a client's or employer's position to the point that the Member's objectivity is compromised".

Familiarity
Exists when an accountant acts in a way that benefits another individual or institution that is familiar to the accountant.

Intimidation
APES 110 paragraph 100.12 e defines intimidation as "the threat that a Member will be deterred from acting objectively because of actual or perceived pressures, including attempts to exercise undue influence over the Member".

Safeguards
Elements within an organisation's work environment or its profession, legislation, or regulation, that reduce the likelihood of threats manifesting.

Ethical conflict resolution framework
A five-step framework that tackles conflict resolution in the event of an ethical breach in an organisation.

c16
ETHICS AND MANAGEMENT ACCOUNTING

DIMENSION 1 Behaviour that is illegal and unethical	**DIMENSION 2** Behaviour that is illegal yet ethical
DIMENSION 3 Behaviour that is legal yet unethical	**DIMENSION 4** Behaviour that is both legal and ethical

 EXHIBIT 16.1 Four dimensions of ethical behaviour

Present Value of $1 Due in n Periods

$$\text{Factor} = \frac{1}{(1+r)^n}$$

R

Periods	1%	2%	3%	4%	5%	6%	7%	8%	9%	10%	12%	14%	15%	16%	18%	20%	24%
1	0.9901	0.9804	0.9709	0.9615	0.9524	0.9434	0.9346	0.9259	0.9174	0.9091	0.8929	0.8772	0.8696	0.8621	0.8475	0.8333	0.8065
2	0.9803	0.9612	0.9426	0.9426	0.9070	0.8900	0.8734	0.8573	0.8417	0.8264	0.7972	0.7695	0.7561	0.7432	0.7182	0.6944	0.6504
3	0.9706	0.9423	0.9151	0.8890	0.8638	0.8396	0.8163	0.7938	0.7722	0.7513	0.7118	0.6750	0.6575	0.6407	0.6086	0.5787	0.5245
4	0.9610	0.9238	0.8885	0.8548	0.8227	0.7921	0.7629	0.7350	0.7084	0.6830	0.6355	0.5921	0.5718	0.5523	0.5158	0.4823	0.4230
5	0.9515	0.9057	0.8626	0.8219	0.7835	0.7473	0.7130	0.6806	0.6499	0.6209	0.5674	0.5194	0.4972	0.4761	0.43731	0.4019	0.3411
6	0.9420	0.8880	0.8375	0.7903	0.7462	0.7050	0.6663	0.6302	0.5963	0.5645	0.5066	0.4556	0.4323	0.4104	0.3704	0.3349	0.2751
7	0.9327	0.8706	0.8131	0.7599	0.7107	0.6651	0.6227	0.5835	0.5470	0.5132	0.4523	0.3996	0.3759	0.3538	0.3139	0.2791	0.2218
8	0.9235	0.8535	0.7894	0.7307	0.6768	0.6274	0.5820	0.5403	0.5019	0.4665	0.4039	0.3506	0.3269	0.3050	0.2660	0.2326	0.1789
9	0.9143	0.8368	0.7664	0.7026	0.6446	0.5919	0.5439	0.5002	0.4604	0.4241	0.3606	0.3075	0.2843	0.2630	0.2255	0.1938	0.1443
10	0.9053	0.8203	0.7441	0.6756	0.6139	0.5584	0.5083	0.4632	0.4224	0.3855	0.3220	0.2697	0.2472	0.2267	0.1911	0.1615	0.1164
11	0.8963	0.8043	0.7224	0.6496	0.5847	0.5268	0.4751	0.4289	0.3875	0.3505	0.2875	0.2366	0.2149	0.1954	0.1619	0.1346	0.0938
12	0.8874	0.7885	0.7014	0.6246	0.5568	0.4970	0.4440	0.3971	0.3555	0.3186	0.2567	0.2076	0.1869	0.1685	0.1372	0.1122	0.0757
13	0.8787	0.7730	0.6810	0.6006	0.5303	0.4688	0.4150	0.3677	0.3262	0.2897	0.2292	0.1821	0.1625	0.1452	0.1163	0.0935	0.0610
14	0.8700	0.7579	0.6611	0.5775	0.5051	0.4423	0.3878	0.3405	0.2992	0.2633	0.2046	0.1597	0.1413	0.1252	0.0985	0.0779	0.0492
15	0.8613	0.7430	0.6419	0.5553	0.4810	0.4173	0.3624	0.3152	0.2745	0.2394	0.1827	0.1401	0.1229	0.1079	0.0835	0.0649	0.0397
16	0.8528	0.7284	0.6232	0.5339	0.4581	0.3936	0.3387	0.2919	0.2519	0.2176	0.1631	0.1229	0.1069	0.0930	0.0708	0.0541	0.0320
17	0.8444	0.7142	0.6050	0.5134	0.4363	0.3714	0.3166	0.2703	0.2311	0.1978	0.1456	0.1078	0.0929	0.0802	0.0600	0.0451	0.0258
18	0.8360	0.7002	0.5874	0.4936	0.4155	0.3503	0.2959	0.2502	0.2120	0.1799	0.1300	0.0946	0.0808	0.0691	0.0508	0.0376	0.0208
19	0.8277	0.6864	0.5703	0.4746	0.3957	0.3305	0.2765	0.2317	0.1945	0.1635	0.1161	0.0829	0.0703	0.0596	0.0431	0.0313	0.0168
20	0.8195	0.6730	0.5537	0.4564	0.3769	0.3118	0.2584	0.2145	0.1784	0.1486	0.1037	0.0728	0.0611	0.0514	0.0365	0.0261	0.0135
21	0.8114	0.6598	0.5375	0.4388	0.3589	0.2942	0.2415	0.1987	0.1637	0.1351	0.0926	0.0638	0.0531	0.0443	0.0309	0.0217	0.0109
22	0.8034	0.6468	0.5219	0.4220	0.3418	0.2775	0.2257	0.1839	0.1502	0.1228	0.0826	0.0560	0.0462	0.0382	0.0262	0.0181	0.0088
23	0.7954	0.6342	0.5067	0.4057	0.3256	0.2618	0.2109	0.1703	0.1378	0.1117	0.0738	0.0491	0.0402	0.0329	0.0222	0.0151	0.0071
24	0.7876	0.6217	0.4919	0.3901	0.3101	0.2470	0.1971	0.1577	0.1264	0.1015	0.0659	0.0431	0.0349	0.0284	0.0188	0.0126	0.0057
25	0.7798	0.6095	0.4776	0.3751	0.2953	0.2330	0.1842	0.1460	0.1160	0.0923	0.0588	0.0378	0.0304	0.0245	0.0160	0.0105	0.0046
26	0.7720	0.5976	0.4637	0.3607	0.2812	0.2198	0.1722	0.1352	0.1064	0.0839	0.0525	0.0331	0.0264	0.0211	0.0135	0.0087	0.0037
27	0.7644	0.5859	0.4502	0.3468	0.2678	0.2074	0.1609	0.1252	0.0976	0.0763	0.0469	0.0291	0.0230	0.0182	0.0115	0.0073	0.0030
28	0.7568	0.5744	0.4371	0.3335	0.2551	0.1956	0.1504	0.1159	0.0895	0.0693	0.0419	0.0255	0.0200	0.0157	0.0097	0.0061	0.0024
29	0.7493	0.5631	0.4243	0.3207	0.2429	0.1846	0.1406	0.1073	0.0822	0.0630	0.0374	0.0224	0.0174	0.0135	0.0082	0.0051	0.0020
30	0.7419	0.5521	0.4120	0.3083	0.2314	0.1741	0.1314	0.0994	0.0754	0.0573	0.0334	0.0196	0.0151	0.0116	0.0070	0.0042	0.0016

Present Value of an Annuity of $1 per Period

$$\text{Factor} = \dfrac{1 - \dfrac{1}{(1+r)^n}}{r}$$

R

Periods	1%	2%	3%	4%	5%	6%	7%	8%	9%	10%	12%	14%	15%	16%	18%	20%	24%
1	0.9901	0.9804	0.9709	0.9615	0.9524	0.9434	0.9346	0.9259	0.9174	0.9091	0.8929	0.8772	0.8696	0.8621	0.8475	0.8333	0.8065
2	1.9704	1.9416	1.9135	1.8861	1.8594	1.8334	1.8080	1.7833	1.7591	1.7355	1.6901	1.6467	1.6257	1.6052	1.5656	1.5278	1.4568
3	2.9410	2.8839	2.8286	2.7751	2.7232	2.6730	2.6243	2.5771	2.5313	2.4869	2.4018	2.3216	2.2832	2.2459	2.1743	2.1065	1.9813
4	3.9020	3.8077	3.7171	3.6299	3.5460	3.4651	3.3872	3.3121	3.2397	3.1699	3.0373	2.9137	2.8550	2.7982	2.6901	2.5887	2.4043
5	4.8534	4.7135	4.5797	4.4518	4.3295	4.2124	4.1002	3.9927	3.8897	3.7908	3.6048	3.4331	3.3522	3.2743	3.1272	2.9906	2.7454
6	5.7955	5.6014	5.4172	5.2421	5.0757	4.9173	4.7665	4.6229	4.4859	4.3553	4.1114	3.8887	3.7845	3.6847	3.4976	3.3255	3.0205
7	6.7282	6.4720	6.2303	6.0021	5.7864	5.5824	5.3893	5.2064	5.0330	4.8684	4.5638	4.2883	4.1604	4.0386	3.8115	3.6046	3.2423
8	7.6517	7.3255	7.0197	6.7327	6.4632	6.2098	5.9713	5.7466	5.5348	5.3349	4.9676	4.6389	4.4873	4.3436	4.0776	3.8372	3.4212
9	8.5660	8.1622	7.7861	7.4353	7.1078	6.8017	6.5152	6.2469	5.9952	5.7590	5.3282	4.9464	4.7716	4.6065	4.3030	4.0310	3.5655
10	9.4713	8.9826	8.5302	8.1109	7.7217	7.3601	7.0236	6.7101	6.4177	6.1446	5.6502	5.2161	5.0188	4.8332	4.4941	4.1925	3.6819
11	10.3676	9.7868	9.2526	8.7605	8.3064	7.8869	7.4987	7.1390	6.8052	6.4951	5.9377	5.4527	5.2337	5.0286	4.6560	4.3271	3.7757
12	11.2551	10.5753	9.9540	9.3851	8.8633	8.3838	7.9427	7.5361	7.1607	6.8137	6.1944	5.6603	5.4206	5.1971	4.7932	4.4392	3.8514
13	12.1337	11.3484	10.6350	9.9856	9.3936	8.8527	8.3577	7.9038	7.4869	7.1034	6.4235	5.8424	5.5831	5.3423	4.9095	4.5327	3.9124
14	13.0037	12.1062	11.2961	10.5631	9.8986	9.2950	8.7455	8.2442	7.7862	7.3667	6.6283	6.0021	5.7245	5.4675	5.0081	4.6106	3.9616
15	13.8651	12.8493	11.9379	11.1184	10.3797	9.7122	9.1079	8.5595	8.0607	7.6061	6.8109	6.1422	5.8474	5.5755	5.0916	4.6755	4.0013
16	14.7179	13.5777	12.5611	11.6523	10.8378	10.1059	9.4466	8.8514	8.3126	7.8237	6.9740	6.2651	5.9542	5.6685	5.1624	4.7296	4.0333
17	15.5623	14.2919	13.1661	12.1657	11.2741	10.4773	9.7632	9.1216	8.5436	8.0216	7.1196	6.3729	6.0472	5.7487	5.2223	4.7746	4.0591
18	16.3983	14.9920	13.7535	12.6593	11.6896	10.8276	10.0591	9.3719	8.7556	8.2014	7.2497	6.4674	6.1280	5.8178	5.2732	4.8122	4.0799
19	17.2260	15.6785	14.3238	13.1339	12.0853	11.1581	10.3356	9.6036	8.9501	8.3649	7.3658	6.5504	6.1982	5.8775	5.3162	4.8435	4.0967
20	18.0456	16.3514	14.8775	13.5903	12.4622	11.4699	10.5940	9.8181	9.1285	8.5136	7.4694	6.6231	6.2593	5.9288	5.3527	4.8696	4.1103
21	18.8570	17.0112	15.4150	14.0292	12.8212	11.7641	10.8355	10.0168	9.2922	8.6487	7.5620	6.6870	6.3125	5.9731	5.3837	4.8913	4.1212
22	19.6604	17.6580	15.9369	14.4511	13.1630	12.0416	11.0612	10.2007	9.4424	8.7715	7.6446	6.7429	6.3587	6.0113	5.4099	4.9094	4.1300
23	20.4558	18.2922	16.4436	14.8568	13.4886	12.3034	11.2722	10.3711	9.5802	8.8832	7.7184	6.7921	6.3988	6.0422	5.4321	4.9245	4.1371
24	21.2434	18.9139	16.9355	15.2470	13.7986	12.5504	11.4693	10.5288	9.7066	8.9847	7.7843	6.8351	6.4338	6.0726	5.4509	4.9371	4.1428
25	22.0232	19.5235	17.4131	15.6221	14.0939	12.7834	11.6536	10.6748	9.8226	9.0770	7.8431	6.8729	6.4641	6.0971	5.4669	4.9476	4.1474
26	22.7952	20.1210	17.8768	15.9828	14.3752	13.0032	11.8258	10.8100	9.9290	9.1609	7.8957	6.9061	6.4906	6.1182	5.4804	4.9563	4.1511
27	23.5596	20.7069	18.3270	16.3296	14.6430	13.2105	11.9867	10.9352	10.0266	9.2372	7.9426	6.9352	6.5135	6.1364	5.4919	4.9636	4.1542
28	24.3164	21.2813	18.7641	16.6631	14.8981	13.4062	12.1371	11.0511	10.1161	9.3066	7.9844	6.9607	6.5335	6.1520	5.5016	4.9697	4.1566
29	25.0658	21.8444	19.1885	16.9837	15.1411	13.5907	12.2777	11.1584	10.1983	9.3696	8.0218	6.9830	6.5509	6.1656	5.5098	4.9747	4.1585
30	25.8077	22.3965	19.6004	17.2920	15.3725	13.7648	12.4090	11.2578	10.2737	9.4269	8.0552	7.0027	6.5660	6.1772	5.5168	4.9789	4.1601